# The Production of Reality

*Essays and Readings on Social Interaction*

Third Edition

# The Production of Reality

*Essays and Readings on Social Interaction*

## Third Edition

**JODI O'BRIEN**

*Seattle University*

**PETER KOLLOCK**

*University of California, Los Angeles*

**PINE FORGE PRESS**

*Thousand Oaks, California*
*Boston ▪ London ▪ New Delhi*

*Cover art:* "El Milagro," oil on canvas. © Carmen Lomas Garza. Collection of Nicólas and Cristina Hernández, Art Trust, Pasadena, California.

*For information, contact:*

 **Pine Forge Press**
A Sage Publications Company
2455 Teller Road
Thousand Oaks, California 91320
(805) 499-4224
E-mail: order@sagepub.com

**Sage Publications Ltd.**
6 Bonhill Street
London EC2A 4PU
United Kingdom

**Sage Publications India Pvt. Ltd.**
M-32 Market
Greater Kailash I
New Delhi 110 048 India

Printed in the United States of America

This book is printed on acid-free paper.

01  02  03  04  05  06  10  9  8  7  6  5  4  3  2  1

Publisher: *Stephen D. Rutter*
Administrative Assistant: *Kirsten Stoller*
Production Management: *Scratchgravel Publishing Services*
Copy Editor: *Carol Lombardi*
Typesetter: *Scratchgravel Publishing Services*
Indexer: *James Minkin*
Cover Designer: *Michelle Lee*

**Library of Congress Cataloging-in-Publication Data**
O'Brien, Jodi.
     The production of reality: Essays and readings on social interaction
Jodi O'Brien, Peter Kollock.— 3rd ed.
        p.  cm.
     Includes index.
     ISBN 0-8039-6879-5
     1. Social psychology.   I. Kollock, Peter.    II. Title.
HM1033 .O27   2001
302—dc21
                                                  00-012703

*In memory of my grandmothers*
— Jodi

*To Jennifer, listening . . .*
— Peter

## About the Authors

**Jodi O'Brien** is Associate Professor of Sociology at Seattle University. She teaches courses in social psychology, sexuality, inequality, and classical and contemporary theory. She writes and lectures on the cultural politics of transgressive identities and communities. Her other books include *Everyday Inequalities* (Basil Blackwell) and *Social Prisms: Reflections on Everyday Myths and Paradoxes* (Pine Forge Press).

**Peter Kollock** is Associate Professor of Sociology at the University of California, Los Angeles. He teaches courses on markets, cooperation and collective action, and the sociology of cyberspace. He has won teaching awards at UCLA and the University of Washington.

## About the Publisher

Pine Forge Press is a new educational publisher, dedicated to publishing innovative books and software throughout the social sciences. On this and any other of our publications, we welcome your comments and suggestions.

Please call or write us at:

**Pine Forge Press**
A Sage Publications Company
31 St. James Ave., Suite 510
Boston, MA 02116
(617) 753-7512
E-mail: info@pfp.sagepub.com

*Visit our World Wide Web site, your direct link to a multitude of online resources:*

www.pineforge.com

# Brief Contents

# Contents

PART III

# Realizing Symbolic Order through Interaction   187

## NAMING AS AN INTERACTIONAL PROCESS

PART IV

# The Social Construction of Reality

## CONFLICT AND CHANGE IN CULTURAL PRODUCTION

# Epilogue

*It takes insight, courage, and responsibility to engage in mindful production of realities. This mindful engagement is the basis for a meaningful existence.*

# Preface

In our class syllabus for a course in social psychology, we make this statement:

> The main goal of this course is that you understand how we become social creatures and how, through our everyday interactions with one another, we make and re-make ourselves and our social worlds. One important implication of the ideas covered in this course is that if we understand how it is that we participate in the construction of our own realities, then we can take a more active and purposeful approach toward making this the sort of world in which we want to live.

During the production of this book, we were reminded of a scene in *Annie Hall*, wherein Woody Allen (as young man) reports that he is depressed because he has read that the universe is expanding. As the universe expands, it changes shape. Consequently, what we think we know about it changes as well—whatever we think we know today may change tomorrow. Believing that this will eventually mean "the end of everything," young Woody refuses to do his homework: "What's the point?" he sighs.

Indeed, why bother to learn anything if, in fact, everything that we learn now will be invalid later on?

## Why We Bothered

We initially compiled *The Production of Reality* because we wanted to provide our students with a social psychology text that was useful and relevant to their everyday lives. One thing that you will probably learn in your sojourn through higher education, if you haven't already, is that there are many voices, many points of view, and many ways of learning and knowing. Diversity and complexity are hallmarks of life in the new millennium. Our social universe is continually expanding and, as it expands, so too does our stockpile of knowledge. Even more profound is the fact that the more we learn about our social universe, the more it changes shape. How do we make sense of this shifting and complexity? This is one of the most significant questions of the day. Several relatively new fields (for example, cultural studies) have emerged in the past few decades with the aim of studying this particular question. Scholars within established disciplines—such as anthropology, communications,

English, history, philosophy, and even geography—have also taken up this question. The commonality across disciplines of the themes of global expansion, diversity, and complexity is a sign of the importance of this inquiry. It is an exciting time to be a part of this intellectual dialogue.

Sociologists and social psychologists have toiled for more than a century to unearth patterns of human social behavior. As sociologists, we know a great deal about patterns—how to look for them, how to read them, and how to interpret the consequences. In particular, sociologists have a lot to contribute regarding "structured relations of power." *Structured* is the operative word in this phrase. Sociologists and social psychologists know a great deal about "structure" and the ways in which "structure" matters in everyday life. Anyone who wants to make sense of her or his own life needs an understanding of the underlying patterns and material conditions that make up the particular cultural milieu in which he or she lives. Racism, for example, is a persistent problem in U.S. society. The tools for understanding and potentially eradicating racism can be forged through an understanding of *why* and *how* people, even self-professed non-racists, are stuck in a social groove that produces patterns of racism. These "grooves" or "ruts" are what sociologists mean when we talk about "social patterns" and "social structures."

## New Emphases for the Third Edition

In the first edition of *The Production of Reality,* our intent was to ground social psychology in the experiences of our students. In the second edition, we expanded our exploration of the self as a product of interaction and of conflict and contradiction. In this edition, we underscore contemporary questions regarding how people make sense of themselves and others in a social universe that is continually expanding and shifting. How do we account for the theoretical possibility that our worlds are in constant flux and simultaneously identify and analyze what appear to be stable social patterns and structures? This book provides a theoretical framework for making sense of the apparent contradiction between stability and change.

We present a theory of self and society whereby people create their own stability through interactions with one another. People participate in these stabilizing processes as a way of establishing social anchors—anchors of meaning—in constantly changing seas. The experience of "authenticity," "meaning," "value," and "self-worth" are embedded in social relations. Who you are and your ideas of what you think you can do and who you think you can be are shaped by the social relations in which you participate. The "structure" of these social relations, including the meaning that they hold for you, is shaped in turn by your participation. We therefore believe that you will be better equipped to grapple with the timely questions of "What is real?" and "What is good?" by studying the social psychological structure of social relations. In response to the contemporary zeitgeist, we emphasize how people make sense of an expanding, diverse, complex, contradictory world in which there are multiple perspectives about what is true and good—and real.

As in previous editions, we continue to emphasize the dynamics and the process of everyday interaction. This is our contribution to the current dialogue of complexity and diversity. Complexity is a hallmark of a *relevant* social science. It is our goal that readers gain an understanding of this complex, expanding terrain so that they can navigate their own course more clearly.

## The Logic of the Book

This book is organized as a combination of essays and readings. We have written the essays to introduce relevant themes and concepts. The essays constitute the theoretical logic of the book. The readings have been selected to illustrate and elaborate various aspects of the theory of social interaction that is developed in the essays. The readings span several decades and represent many different voices and points of view. Some of the readings are considered sociological classics—material that every well-educated student should be familiar with. Some of the language and examples used by the authors of these older pieces may seem outdated and even offensive. We encourage you to read these selections as a form of social history as well as social theory. In other words, ask yourself what it was that was different about the times in which these authors wrote. Can you be critical and still comprehend why the ideas might have been groundbreaking at the time they were written? The contemporary readings include research studies, narrative essays, and some fiction. It is likely that different readings will resonate for different readers. As you read these diverse selections, consider why it is that certain types of writing and particular themes seem more or less appealing to you. What does your own response as a reader indicate about your social biography?

## Many Questions, Your Own Answers

Our general intent is to immerse you in the puzzles and issues of contemporary social psychology and to provide a framework from which you can begin to construct your own understanding of the social world. Toward this end, we pose many questions and invite you to reflect on them in light of the concepts and theories presented in the book. As you will discover in reading this text, there are no absolute or final answers to the most important human questions. This is because we are constantly creating new ways of understanding ourselves and our social worlds. Through our ability to think and communicate, we are expanding our social universe. The material in this text is intended to provide you with a framework for understanding this creative social-psychological process (as well as for avoiding some of the pitfalls that appear when we fail to recognize our own involvement in the process). We suggest that you approach this material as a set of building blocks that you can assemble and reassemble to construct a framework for making sense of your own life.

If you (unlike Woody) are willing to do your homework, we are confident that your own universe of knowledge will expand in useful and profound ways.

# Acknowledgments

The creation of any product is always a collective enterprise. We acknowledge the roles that many others have played in bringing this book to completion. Our publisher, Steve Rutter, has been singularly supportive in encouraging us to push the boundaries suggested by traditional textbooks currently available in social psychology. We appreciate his confidence in our vision. Sherith Pankratz, associate editor, Ann Makarias and Kirsten Stoller, assistants to the publisher, and the staff of Pine Forge Press have been tremendously helpful in dealing with the myriad details and headaches that accompany such a production. Anne and Greg Draus of Scratchgravel Publishing Services have been a pleasure to work with on the production of the final manuscript. We also appreciate the comprehending tone of our copy editor, Carol Lombardi, and thank her for the Woody Allen reference. We are especially grateful to Judith Howard (University of Washington), who has repeatedly and cheerfully given us the benefit of her keen sociological and editorial eye. We thank David Newman for putting things into perspective during conference pep talks. As always, we are indebted to Ron Obvious simply for being there.

We are tremendously grateful for the honest and constructive comments from the reviewers of this book. For the first edition, these reviewers were: Dick Adams (UCLA), Peter Callero (Western Oregon State College), Jeff Chin (LeMoyne College), Andy Deseran (Louisiana State University), Jennifer Friedman (University of South Florida), John Kinch (San Francisco State University), and Ken Plummer (University of Essex). Reviewers for the second edition were Timothy Anderson (Bentley College), Jeff Breese (St. Mary's College), Ellen Cohn (University of Pittsburgh), Robert E. Emerick (San Diego State University), Rebecca Erickson (University of Akron), Heather Fitz Gibbon (College of Wooster), Tom Gerschick (Illinois State University), Chris Hunter (Grinnell College), Tracy Luff (Viterbo College), Charles Marske (St. Louis University), Bruce Mork (University of Minnesota), Judith Richlin-Klonsky (University of Southern California), Marty Shockey (St. Ambrose University), Ronald Schultz (Queens College), Barbara Smalley (University of North Carolina), Douglas Smith (Pennsylvania State University), Barbara Trepagnier (University of California, Santa Barbara), Sherry Walker (Middle Tennessee State University), and James Zaffiro (University of Minnesota).

Reviewers for the third edition are Monika Ardelt (University of Florida), Ellen Cohn (University of Pittsburgh), Morten G. Ender (United States Military Academy), Timothy Gallagher (Kent State University), David M. Long (Georgia State University), Barbara Trepagnier (Southwest Texas State University), and Ruby Weber (Kent State University).

Our commitment to producing a relevant and useful social psychology text was fostered by our teacher, Fred Campbell, who taught us that the art of teaching is in learning to be purposeful. Our own initiation into social psychology was sparked by diverse mentors. We owe a great deal to Philip Blumstein, Karen Cook, Richard Emerson, Wes Wager, Toshio Yamagishi, and, more recently, Howard Becker, John Delamater, Ed Lawler, Cecilia Ridgeway, Mel Pollner, and Sheldon Stryker. The intersection of their ideas became the launching pad for the development of our own. Much of our thinking as it developed in this book is the result of our conversations and interactions with our students. We thank them for sharing their intellectual passion. We also thank our friends and colleagues who have always been eager to provide us with feedback, share their own visions for this text, or revive us with their inspiring company. They include Kate Bornstein, Wendy Chapkis, Jesse Daniels, John Davis, Jennifer Eichstedt, Tom Gerschick, Steen Halling, Melissa Herbert, Val Jenness, Kevin Krycka, Chuck Lawrence, Kari Lerum, Samm Lindsey, Peter Nardi, Ken Plummer, Mary Romero, Marty Shockey, Pepper Schwartz, France Winddance Twine, Angus Vail, and Linda Van Leuven. Finally, we appreciate the students who write to us about this book, especially Debra Arms, whose comments about the Epilogue have been an inspiration.

## About the Cover Art

Carmen Lomas Garza's painting *El Milagro* (1987) is a depiction of an event that occurred in her youth. There was a rumor going around that the Virgin of Guadalupe had appeared on a water tank in a neighboring rancho. The artist's family visited the rancho and discovered that many people had been there all day praying and trying to make out the image of the Virgin. Some people could see her in the water stains; others did not believe.

We are grateful to Cristina Hernández, who owns the painting and granted permission for its reproduction. Regarding her passion for art, Cristina writes, "Art encompasses the social, economic, racial, gender, intellectual, historical and ideological realities of human existence" (in correspondence with the authors).

*Jodi O'Brien*
*Peter Kollock*

# The Production of Reality

*Essays and Readings on Social Interaction*

Third Edition

# PART I

# Introduction

*A father said to his double-seeing son, "Son, you see two instead of one."*

*"How can that be?" the boy replied. "If that were true, I would see four moons up there in place of two."*

(Idries Shah, *Caravan of Dreams*)

*I have come to see that knowledge contains its own morality, that it begins not in neutrality but in a place of passion within the human soul. Depending on the nature of that passion, our knowledge will follow certain courses and head toward certain ends.*

(Parker Palmer, *To Know as We Are Known*)

# What Is Real?

In rural Central American villages, religious festivals are often a very important part of the local culture. In one case, a documentary film crew was around to record the event. The film shows brightly colored decorations, music, dancing, and a variety of delicious and special foods made for the festival. The special treats are clearly a highlight for everyone, especially the children, who crowd around the stands. In the middle of one crowd of children waiting for a treat is a very large stone bowl. A large stone pillar rises out of the center of the bowl. The pillar seems alive. It is completely covered by shiny black beetles crawling around and over each other. The person in charge takes a tortilla, spreads some sauce on the inside, and grabs a handful of live beetles, quickly folding the tortilla so that the beetles cannot escape. Playfully pushing the beetles back into the tortilla between each bite, a gleeful child eats the burrito with relish. Would you be willing to try a beetle burrito? Is a strip of burnt cow muscle (also known as a steak) inherently any more or less desirable than a beetle burrito? If you had grown up in that village, would you be eating and enjoying beetle burritos? What does your answer have to say about the social and cultural origins of what seems like an almost biological trait—our tastes in food?

In his book *The Te of Piglet* (1992), Benjamin Hoff recounts the following narratives, based on the writings of Chinese Taoist philosophers:

> A man noticed that his axe was missing. Then he saw the neighbor's son pass by. The boy looked like a thief, walked like a thief, behaved like a thief. Later that day, the man found his axe where he had left it the day before. The next time he saw the neighbor's son, the boy looked, walked, and behaved like an honest, ordinary boy.
>
> A man dug a well by the side of the road. For years afterward, grateful travelers talked of the Wonderful Well. But one night, a man fell into it and drowned. After that, people avoided the Dreadful Well. Later it was discovered that the victim was a drunken thief who had left the road to avoid being captured by the night patrol—only to fall into the Justice-Dispensing Well. (p. 172)

What sort of reality do these Chinese tales illustrate? Does the essence of the neighbor boy or the nature of the well change? Or do people's perceptions change? Consider occasions in which your perceptions of someone or something may have been influenced by your own momentary experiences. Is it possible that reality depends on how you look at something? How much does your point of view depend on your own interests?

Consider further: A group of workers from a local factory gathers every night after work to share drinks and conversation. They express dissatisfaction with the conditions of their job and the atrocities committed by the shop manager. One young man recalls a recent incident in which an employee lost her arm to unsafe machinery. "I'm terrified every second of every working hour that the same will happen to me," he admits. A woman complains of sexual harassment from the shop manager and threatens to "give him a piece of my foot in a place that he won't soon forget next time he lays his dirty hands on me." Several of the workers discuss plans for a walkout and, in a final burst of enthusiasm, agree that, at noon on the appointed day, they will step away from their machines and cease to work as a show of protest. The next day, life resumes at the factory. The young man endures his fear in terrified silence and even manages a friendly nod to fellow employees. The woman smiles sweetly when the boss pats her backside and tells her she looks marvelous in blue. At noon a few employees, remembering last night's talk of strike and rebellion, look sheepishly around the plant floor and are relieved to note that no one else has ceased to work. The status quo prevails.

Think about the difference in the late-night and workday activities of these people. What is the source of the disparity between the behaviors in each setting? Are these people being any more or less truthful in either situation? What forces compel people to change their circumstances? What forces constrain this rebellion? When are people likely to think their actions for change might be successful?

One more story. Imagine a small child with a high fever. The child has been bedridden for a few days. At one point the fever is so severe that she begins to hallucinate, seeing monsters in her bedroom. She begins to cry and call out. When her father enters the room, the child is sobbing, saying that monsters are everywhere. Her father comforts her. "There aren't any monsters, dear, it's just a bad dream," he says.

"But I'm not asleep," complains the child. "And I can *see* them!"

The father tries again: "I know you can see them, but they aren't real."

"Then why can I see them?"

"Because you're sick," the father explains. "You have germs."

"What are germs? Where are they?" the little girl asks.

"Well, you can't see germs, but they're real," the father answers with great confidence. Is this a reasonable argument? Should we be surprised if the child believes it? Have you ever seen a germ? Could you identify one? Do you believe they exist? Most of us do, yet for most of us this belief is probably based on what others have told us rather than on direct evidence.

These scenarios have in common a focus on the intersection between social forms of expression and individual perceptions, tastes, and behaviors. In each case, a taken-for-granted body of cultural knowledge influences individual action. The children of Central America consume beetles with gusto while others might look on in horror. Yet we all feel that our tastes are reasonable.

A person's reactions to the world depend on how he or she defines the situation. The definition of the situation can differ from moment to moment, depending on what the person is inclined to see. People also may appear perfectly reasonable in one situation and then appear the opposite in another situation. Indeed, a great deal of human behavior appears unreasonable and illogical if viewed out of context.

Cultural beliefs and practices include rules about what is "real" and what is "not real." These rules are often taken for granted, and we may follow them without necessarily being aware of them. They are not necessarily based on logic or sensory perception. Cultural studies involve figuring out these rules and making them explicit. This book is about how human beings learn and conform to the rules of reality in various situations. These rules enable us to organize and to make sense of our experiences and to share our understanding with others.

When people interact with one another, they do so according to these cultural rules. The result of this interaction is a set of meaningful patterns that we think of as society. It is important to note that these rules are constructed by human beings and that they are meaningful only within a specific social context. In other words, behavior is contextually meaningful. Taken out of context, many behaviors appear contradictory or silly or even immoral (see the essay in Part V, *Wrestling Contradictions in Everyday Life*, for more examples).

How do people know what to expect and what to do in different contexts, especially in situations that may appear contradictory? How do we learn the rules of reality? This ability, to distinguish between contexts and to behave in accordance with social expectations, is a defining feature of humanness and the main subject of this book.

## What Is Humanness?

We are both *Star Trek* fans. We have noted with fascination that the portrayal of certain characters parallels the major currents of thought in social psychology over the past three decades. Consider the contrast between the rational Vulcan, Mr. Spock, of the first *Star Trek* series and the android, Data, featured in *Star Trek: The Next Generation*. Consistent with the dominant cognitive perspective of the 1970s, Spock epitomized the being who operated according to the dictates of pure reason. Unencumbered by emotions (those messy "hot flashes") and cognitive biases, Spock was able to assess his environment and formulate hypotheses with a detachment and accuracy that resembled a computer. Spock was often juxtaposed with Doctor McCoy, who, although a man of science, was frequently amiss in his judgment because of his human biases and social attachments. Some episodes of the early show commented on, and perhaps even lamented, Spock's lack of emotion. However in the end, his unerring rationality always saved the day. The message was clear: Emotion and human quirks, endearing and meaningful as they might seem, get in the way of the human project, which in this case was to explore and chart (and master?) the universe.

*Star Trek: The Next Generation* is just as fixated as was its predecessor on the ideal of a reasoned universal harmony orchestrated by sentient beings. But its claims for the virtue and virility of rationality are more modest. In the new show, Spock has been replaced with a potentially more perfect form of rational life. An android, Data is capable of calculation and theory construction far surpassing the abilities of even the most rational Vulcan. In a fascinating twist, however, *Star Trek: The Next Generation* de-emphasizes Data's rational capabilities in order to play out the theme of humanness as non-rationality. Data is a focus, not because of his amazing cognitive abilities, but because of the limitations his technological nature places on his endeavors to be human.

Data is an amazing piece of machinery. He is stronger than any humanoid, has a life span of unguessed potential, and can assimilate and process any amount of information. He is even programmed to simulate perfectly many of the masters of universal culture. For example, he can play the violin like Isaac Stern, paint like Picasso, and act like Sir Laurence Olivier. Yet despite this technical mastery, he is not human.

Data's existence raises the question What is the nature of humanness? If humanness is not rational, cognitive decision making, as characterized by social psychology in the 1970s, what is the distinctive mark of our species? Spock represented the quest to become more rational, like a computer. Data, who *is* a computer, symbolizes the search for something beyond perfect cognitive activity—an integration of thought, body, and feeling. It's the ideal that shifted, not the definition of humanness: Spock considered humans disorganized and silly. Data thinks they're wonderful. As a scientific culture, we have long admired the computer for its rational, objective, calculating approach to information. A great deal of our industrial technology, cognitive science, and popular mythology focuses on how humans can be more like computers, how we can be more objective and rational. Social psychology has, for many years, separated what are known as "cold" topics (rationality, cognition, and decision making) from "hot" topics (attraction and emotion). Any young scholar who wished to make a mark in the field was admonished to pursue study of the "cold" topics. In recent years, social psychologists have begun to look more closely at those aspects of humanness that are not epitomized by computer technology and to ask what purpose these nonrational human characteristics have in our personal and cultural stories. Our understanding of human behavior has been enriched by studies that focus more holistically on the body, emotions, and cognition.

Among the features that endear Data to other members of the crew are his earnest attempts to be human and his continual failure to hit the mark. In one episode, Data works fervently to understand humor, but the concept is beyond his otherwise "perfect" abilities. In another episode, he explores the question of love and affection and finds that, although he can intellectually comprehend this state of being and is capable of the act of physical sex, he is unable to experience love. To enhance his understanding of humanness, Data attempts to do human things, such as develop hobbies and social attachments. One by one, Data explores various human institutions. His factual knowledge of these institutions would overwhelm even the most advanced student of human culture. But despite this knowledge, the android is incapable of experiencing life as a human being.

This is a different message from that of earlier social psychology. That is, perfect factual knowledge and cognitive ability do not make a human. Humanness is a situated, interactional process. This process is anchored in personal experience and embodied in emotions.

Little by little, Data appears to advance in his comprehension of the human experience—not through his impressive information-processing abilities, but through interactions with human beings. Through exposure to various human institutions—such as love, humor, grief, and betrayal—Data begins to respond to some situations in a particularly humanlike fashion. To the extent that Data is able to experience humanness, it is through his interactions with humans and their endeavors to teach him what otherwise-abstract institutions, like friendship and sorrow, mean. In a word, Data is being socialized into the human community.

Two points are worth noting here. First, Data's various experiences suggest that humanness involves not only a general comprehension of myriad facts and the ability to calculate probable hypotheses, but also an empathic understanding of highly nuanced, situated meaning. We are reminded of Thomas Scheff's 1990 story about a computer directed to translate the sentence "The spirit is willing but the flesh is weak" into Russian. The computer has the necessary glossary and grammar to make this translation. But it translates the phrase as "The vodka is good but the meat is rotten." That is, the computer provides a literal translation, but the translation does not convey the intended meaning of the phrase. The computer is unable to translate the essence of the phrase because it does not have the comprehension of metaphor that humans do.

Second, the extent to which Data begins to comprehend human metaphorical meaning occurs not through his private cognitive calculations but through interactions with his companions. He notes their reactions to his utterances and behaviors and then queries them regarding the reasons for their responses—which are often not what Data would have predicted based on rational calculation alone. In this way, he assembles a litany of human metaphors and expected behaviors that, although not always rational, more closely approximates actual human experience. Thus, the extent to which Data does achieve humanness occurs as the result of social interactions with humans. These interactions provide Data's schooling in the nuanced richness of human life. He learns that the meanings of objects and ideas, despite what his computer archives tell him, are relative to the context. Humans create and re-create meaning in interaction with one another. Reality is not just a codified series of facts and possibilities; it is something produced and reproduced through ongoing human activity.

*Star Trek Voyager,* the most recent show in the ongoing saga, depicts several changes that reflect cultural shifts. One noteworthy change is that the captain of *Voyager* is a woman. Another is the replacement of a Data-like character (an android) with a holographic physician. This new character plays a role similar to Data in that he is nonhuman in body, has perfected cognitive capabilities, but struggles in his attempts to interact *meaningfully* with other members of the crew. What we find interesting is that the doctor's advanced programming (he has many abilities that far surpass those of Data) reflects his creators' increasingly complex understanding of human nature. Frequent references to his programming make the audience aware that the doctor has been created with the ability to comprehend nuance and to respond to human ambiguity. There is no presupposition of rationality. At the same time, his ability to become increasingly "human" (i.e., to engage in meaningful behavior) is a consequence of his *interactions* with the crew. He has perfect encyclopedic knowledge of human history, but the crew members are the ones who teach him how to use this knowledge in meaningful ways. Sometimes we wonder if the writers of the program took social psychology courses similar to the material presented in this book.

## Humanness Is Achieved through Symbolic Interaction

The production of meaningful realities through human interaction is the focus of this book. We intend to demonstrate that human culture is achieved through interactions among individuals who share highly complex, richly nuanced definitions of themselves and the situations in which they participate. We *learn* to be human. And our learning depends on and is achieved through interactions with other humans. The basis for meaningful human behavior is in our capacity for language—not just definitions and grammar, but metaphor.

As illustrated by Data, perfect rationality does not make one human. In some cases, literal, rational calculation may even be a hindrance to meaningful human interaction. Nevertheless, cognitive capabilities are a necessary foundation for the development of humanness and the achievement of culture. To extend the computer analogy, neurological cognitive functions constitute the "hardware" of human existence. But it is the meaningful use of symbols—the "software"—that makes this existence what it is.

This book focuses on everyday interactions and explores the ways in which these interactions constitute the basis of human existence. Our goal is to understand how humans learn to participate in and ultimately to produce and reproduce themselves and their various cultures. We explore a number of questions: What cognitive and emotive capacities are necessary for people to be able to engage in meaningful social interaction? How is social behavior affected by a disruption of these processes? How do interactional dynamics shape our behavior and our sense of who we are and what we can do? How do these processes contribute to the production of culture? How is it possible that, through our own behavior, we may be perpetuating cultural systems to which we may think ourselves opposed (e.g., racism)? Our general aim is to explore the social foundations of mind, self, and culture. Our framework for this exploration is a theoretical perspective known as *symbolic interactionism*. We describe this perspective in detail in the essay "A Perspective for Understanding Self and Social Interaction," which concludes Part I of the book (page 35). For now, we invite you to ponder a bit further on the question What is real? Hopefully by now you realize that the answer depends to some extent on the rules that your culture gives you for determining real/unreal. This includes rules for what is true/false, fact/fiction, right/wrong, and for what counts as "real" knowledge versus superstition or opinion.

Consider two additional examples. You may recall that in 1995, former football player and actor O. J. Simpson was accused of murdering his ex-wife and Ron Goldman, a male companion. After several months of nationally televised trials in criminal court, a jury found him not guilty. Immediately following this verdict, Goldman's family filed a civil suit against Simpson accusing him of wrongful death and demanding several million dollars in damages. This time, a civil court found him guilty and awarded the family the money. What's the truth here? Is Simpson guilty or not guilty? According to the criminal court (wherein the rules are that one must be "proven guilty beyond a reasonable doubt" in order to be convicted of a crime), the case was not adequately made and therefore Simpson is not guilty and is a free man. According to the civil court, an injustice occurred, damages were incurred, and someone should be responsible for those damages. This court determined that it was reasonable to hold Simpson accountable for the damages. The outcome of the two trials is that he is a free man (not guilty) who must pay damages (guilty). One noteworthy feature of this example is that the supposedly contradictory verdicts don't seem to bother people too much. We understand that the different courts are engaged in different activities with different rules of proof. For some observers, money was the common denominator that made sense of this contradiction: Simpson had enough money to buy a good defense in the criminal trial and was perceived, in the civil trial, as having enough money that he should give some to the Goldman family. However you choose to interpret this case, it's clear that, even in such high-profile and supposedly rigorous undertakings such as legal deliberations, there are contradictory rules about what is real, true, and right. Strange as it may seem to an outsider, within a commonly understood context, these contradictory rules make sense.

A second illustration. In many states, when a man beats or kills a male-to-female transgendered person, it is acceptable for the man to enter a plea of "arousal under false pretenses." The logic of this defense plea is that a man may approach someone whom he presumes to be a woman, but later discovers to have the sex characteristics of a physiological male. The shock of this discovery may lead him to react violently toward the person, administering a severe beating or even committing murder. What sort of rules for what is real and what is right are operating in the logic of this defense plea? Is the man heeding the cues of attraction (body/experience) or his cultural training regarding gender and sexuality? The logic of the defense rests on the "fact" that the man is indeed aroused by other person. Apparently he is attracted enough to initiate contact and to pursue amorous relations—at least according to the logic of the defense plea. But when the physiological features don't match the packaging, he flies into a rage. And this rage is, in many cases that come before judges, considered reasonable—a basis that justifies the attack.

This example raises questions about what constitutes "real" gender; "real" feelings of attraction and arousal; and "real" attempts to deceive. It also raises questions about the unspoken rules for who really has rights. In this culture, if someone sells you a product and it doesn't turn out to be what you expected, you have the right to sue, but not to beat up or kill the seller. How are the rules different in the case of this defense plea? What do you make of the information that many judges find this a perfectly acceptable defense plea and usually find the defendant not guilty? Our point with this example is that many people take for granted that this is a reasonable defense plea. Even if the death of another strikes them as unfortunate, their presumption about why the transgendered person was attacked ("He/ She was asking for it") makes sense to them.

## So, What's Real?

According to the symbolic interactionist perspective, "truth" and "reality" are determined by the context in which they are practiced. Does this mean that anything goes? Far from it. Reality may differ across social groups but, within each group, a taken-for-granted system of knowledge establishes boundaries about what is real, true, and right. A central line of inquiry in symbolic interactionism is uncovering what these boundaries consist of and how members of a community produce and reproduce their systems of knowledge through their interactions. For instance, symbolic interactionists have noted that people living in modern, western cultures act as if their reality is based on a "natural" truth (things are the way they are because nature intended them to be that way). Other cultures might have a faith-based reality (things are the way they are because a transcendent god intends them to be that way). These realities include complex, culturally specific rules for how one can know things. Thus, people in one society may believe in the existence of germs that cause illness. They may invest considerable resources to develop the technology necessary to "see" and "control" these germs. In another culture, people may invest similar resources to perfect ceremonies and rituals to "see" and "communicate with" the spirits that control health and well-being.

In place of the question What is real?, we prefer to ask What are some of the beliefs and practices that make up different realities? What are their implications and consequences? What do different perspectives say about the nature of the world and humans' place in it? These questions remind us to scrutinize our own rules of interaction and their implications for self and society, to make the "taken for granted" explicit. One of the major strengths of the symbolic interactionist perspective is that it encourages us to see our own role as authors in the human story and, hopefully, to take responsibility for the scripts we produce and the parts we play.

## Organization of the Book

One general aim of this book is to establish a foundation for understanding symbolic activity based on human thought processes (social cognition) and then to use this foundation to address questions about social order and change. By way of summary, the basic components of this foundation are symbols, the social self, interaction, and social patterns. The materials in this book are organized to present a picture of society as the product of human interactions based on the use of shared social symbols that are incorporated into human conduct through cognitive/emotive processes. Because humans derive cognitive schemas from cultural patterns, these processes reflect a pre-existing social structure. Through our interactions with one another we learn, enact, reproduce, *and* potentially change this structure.

Part I, discussed below, introduces some of these basic components.

In Part II, we focus on how our thoughts and feelings reflect cultural learning and values as well as our distinct and private experiences. For symbolic interactionists, the key to this puzzle is the *symbol*, an abstract representation of something that may or may not exist in a tangible form. For example, *table* is the symbolic representation of a class of objects constructed from hard substances and designed to serve certain purposes. *Guilt* symbolizes a feeling that you are probably familiar with, but it has no actual, physical referent. Complex combinations of symbols used for communication are known as language. Language, according to the general tenets of symbolic interactionism, is the social expression of human thought. Through language, humans are able to incorporate cultural expectations into conscious, reflexive behavior. It is also through language that humans generate, conserve, and alter social structure.

In Part III, we take up the subject of interaction. Humans develop a social self and learn and re-create their culture through interaction.

Social relationships, such as power, are given meaning and come to life when they are acted out by members of a social group. These patterns are discernible in the encounters of everyday life, such as conversations. Basic interaction requires people to project an image of what part they wish to play, what part they want others to play, and how they intend to define the situation. For an interaction to proceed smoothly, the actors must agree on a definition of the situation and perform it together. Even arguments, as we will discuss, hold to a particular definition of the situation ("This is a fight") and follow specific rules of interaction. In addition to defining situations, people negotiate how they will define themselves and others. One of the most significant implications of Part III is that our own self-image, as well as the identities we present to others, is a product of interaction.

The social construction of reality is the focus of Part IV. In this section, we explore the implications of the points raised in Parts II and III for the production and reproduction of social realities. That is, realities are social constructs that exist through shared expectations about how the world is organized. These realities are quite fragile because they depend on the participation of people who are socialized to comprehend and perform patterns and rituals that follow highly structured (but often unrecognized) rules of interaction. Ironically, these implicit rules can be made explicit by violating them and forcing interaction to a confused halt. We present several such "violations" in Part IV as a way of demonstrating how to "see" the rules of interaction. An important question in this section is why certain patterns of reality endure so well, given that they are based on such fragile dynamics.

In Part V, we consider how people grapple with multiple perspectives and contradictions. People have the ability to occupy multiple positions and are able to take on a variety of roles and behaviors. However, many of these positions are contradictory and thus present dilemmas for individuals and groups who seek to establish meaningful patterns of existence. We do not attempt to resolve these contradictions. Rather, we draw your attention to the point that social life is dynamic and complex. Our understanding of who we are and of what is meaningful is forged by wrestling with everyday contradictions.

## Reality as a Collective Hunch

The readings in Part I are intended to whet your appetite for the materials that follow. Together, they illustrate that what we agree is real is often based on the "hunch" that this is what "everybody knows"—*common sense*.

In "Body Rituals among the Nacirema," anthropologist Horace Miner takes an outsider's perspective to demonstrate how behavior can seem odd, and even repulsive, when stripped of insiders' comprehension. Cultural rituals appear alien and unrecognizable when they are no longer alive with the meaning that is infused into them through insiders' eyes. In "The Nature of 'Perspective,'" Joel Charon, who is a sociologist, considers how things appear differently depending on the perspective one holds. Sociologist Earl Babbie extends this line of reasoning to science and the study of human truths in Reading 3 "Truth, Objectivity and Agreement." The piece by Jane Wagner is extracted from her one-woman play (performed by Lily Tomlin), *The Search for Signs of Intelligent Life in the Universe.* The play's narrator, Trudy, a bag lady, provides commentary from the sidelines of contemporary U.S. society. Trudy is an example of someone who has been socialized—she knows what the rules of social conduct are—but has chosen not to play the expected role. Trudy's private culture is simultaneously a product of and a commentary on the general reality she shares with the larger culture.

As you encounter the material in the upcoming pages, we encourage you to refer back to Trudy and to ponder the paradox of how her position simultaneously affirms the existence of a shared symbolic world and points to alternative paths of interaction. Also consider Trudy's experience in taking aliens to see a play. They have difficulty ascertaining just what it is that constitutes art in this culture. After a few moments of observation, the aliens inform Trudy that "the audience is art." She realizes that she forgot to tell them to watch the play, not the audience.

In this book we, too, focus on the audience—or rather on the interactional rules that inform this group of people at this particular moment in time how to be an audience. When we pause to ponder the intricacy of these rules, the coordination that their successful operation requires, and the delicate realities that sustain them, we are inclined to agree with the aliens: The audience is art! Trudy may be correct in her assertion that "reality is a collective hunch." If so, this book is about how we all work together to define and sustain that hunch.

## References

Hoff, B. (1992). *The Te of Piglet.* New York: Penguin.
Palmer, P. (1993). *To know as we are known.* San Francisco: Harper.
Scheff, T. (1990). *Discourse, emotion, and social structure.* Chicago: University of Chicago Press.
Shah, I. (1972). *Caravan of dreams.* Baltimore: Penguin.

# Body Ritual among the Nacirema

## *Horace Miner*

The anthropologist has become so familiar with the diversity of ways in which different peoples behave in similar situations that he is not apt to be surprised by even the most exotic customs. In fact, if all of the logically possible combinations of behavior have not been found somewhere in the world, he is apt to suspect that they must be present in some yet undescribed tribe. This point has, in fact, been expressed with respect to clan organization by Murdock (1949, p. 71). In this light, the magical beliefs and practices of the Nacirema present such unusual aspects that it seems desirable to describe them as an example of the extremes to which human behavior can go.

Professor Linton first brought the ritual of the Nacirema to the attention of anthropologists twenty years ago (1936, p. 326), but the culture of this people is still very poorly understood. They are a North American group living in the territory between the Canadian Cree, the Yaqui and Tarahumara of Mexico, and the Carib and Arawak of the Antilles. Little is known of their origin, although tradition states that they came from the east. According to Nacirema mythology, their nation was originated by a culture hero, Notgnihsaw, who is otherwise known for

two great feats of strength—the throwing of a piece of wampum across the river Pa-To-Mac and the chopping down of a cherry tree in which the Spirit of Truth resided.

Nacirema culture is characterized by a highly developed market economy which has evolved in a rich natural habitat. While much of the people's time is devoted to economic pursuits, a large part of the fruits of these labors and a considerable portion of the day are spent in ritual activity. The focus of this activity is the human body, the appearance and health of which loom as a dominant concern in the ethos of the people. While such a concern is certainly not unusual, its ceremonial aspects and associated philosophy are unique.

The fundamental belief underlying the whole system appears to be that the human body is ugly and that its natural tendency is to debility and disease. Incarcerated in such a body, man's only hope is to avert these characteristics through the use of the powerful influences of ritual and ceremony. Every household has one or more shrines devoted to this purpose. The more powerful individuals in this society have several shrines in their houses and, in fact, the opulence of a house is often referred to in terms of the number of such ritual centers it possesses. Most houses are of wattle and daub construction, but the shrine rooms of the more wealthy are walled with stone. Poorer families imitate the rich by applying pottery plaques to their shrine walls.

"Body Ritual among the Nacirema" by H. Miner, 1956. Reproduced by permission of the American Anthropological Association from *American Anthropologist* 58(3), 503–507, 1956. Not for further reproduction.

While each family has at least one such shrine, the rituals associated with it are not family ceremonies but are private and secret. The rites are normally only discussed with children, and then only during the period when they are being initiated into these mysteries. I was able, however, to establish sufficient rapport with the natives to examine these shrines and to have the rituals described to me.

The focal point of the shrine is a box or chest which is built into the wall. In this chest are kept the many charms and magical potions without which no native believes he could live. These preparations are secured from a variety of specialized practitioners. The most powerful of these are the medicine men, whose assistance must be rewarded with substantial gifts. However, the medicine men do not provide the curative potions for their clients, but decide what the ingredients should be and then write them down in an ancient and secret language. This writing is understood only by the medicine men and by the herbalists who, for another gift, provide the required charm.

The charm is not disposed of after it has served its purpose, but is placed in the charm-box of the household shrine. As these magical materials are specific for certain ills, and the real or imagined maladies of the people are many, the charm-box is usually full to overflowing. The magical packets are so numerous that people forget what their purposes were and fear to use them again. While the natives are very vague on this point, we can only assume that the idea in retaining all the old magical materials is that their presence in the charm-box, before which the body rituals are conducted, will in some way protect the worshipper.

Beneath the charm-box is a small font. Each day every member of the family, in succession, enters the shrine room, bows his head before the charm-box, mingles different sorts of holy water in the font, and proceeds with a brief rite of ablution. The holy waters are secured from the Water Temple of the community, where the priests conduct elaborate ceremonies to make the liquid ritually pure.

In the hierarchy of magical practitioners, and below the medicine men in prestige, are specialists whose designation is best translated "holy-mouth-men." The Nacirema have an almost pathological horror of and fascination with the mouth, the condition of which is believed to have a supernatural influence on all social relationships. Were it not for the rituals of the mouth, they believe that their teeth would fall out, their gums bleed, their jaws shrink, their friends desert them, and their lovers reject them. They also believe that a strong relationship exists between oral and moral characteristics. For example, there is a ritual ablution of the mouth for children which is supposed to improve their moral fiber.

The daily body ritual performed by everyone includes a mouth-rite. Despite the fact that these people are so punctilious about care of the mouth, this rite involves a practice which strikes the uninitiated stranger as revolting. It was reported to me that the ritual consists of inserting a small bundle of hog hairs into the mouth, along with certain magical powders, and then moving the bundle in a highly formalized series of gestures.

In addition to the private mouth-rite, the people seek out a holy-mouth-man once or twice a year. These practitioners have an impressive set of paraphernalia, consisting of a variety of augers, awls, probes, and prods. The use of these objects in the exorcism of the evils of the mouth involves almost unbelievable ritual torture of the client. The holy-mouth-man opens the client's mouth and, using the above-mentioned tools, enlarges any holes which decay may have created in the teeth. Magical materials are put into these holes. If there are no naturally occurring holes in the teeth, large sections of one or more teeth are gouged out so that the supernatural substance can be applied. In the client's view, the purpose of these ministrations is to arrest decay and to draw friends. The extremely sacred and traditional character of the rite is evident in the fact that the natives return to the holy-mouth-man year after year, despite the fact that their teeth continue to decay.

It is to be hoped that, when a thorough study of the Nacirema is made, there will be careful inquiry into the personality structure of these people. One has but to watch the gleam in the eye of a holy-mouth-man, as he jabs an awl into an exposed nerve, to suspect that a certain amount of sadism is involved. If this can be established, a very interesting pattern emerges, for most of the population shows definite masochistic tendencies. It was to these that Professor Linton referred in discussing a distinctive part of the daily body ritual which is performed only by men. This part of the rite involves scraping and lacerating the surface of the face with a sharp instrument. Special women's rites are performed only four times during each lunar month, but what they lack in frequency is made up in barbarity. As part of this ceremony, women bake their heads in small ovens for about an hour. The theoretically interesting point is that what seems to be a preponderantly masochistic people have developed sadistic specialists.

The medicine men have an imposing temple, or *latipso*, in every community of any size. The more elaborate ceremonies required to treat very sick patients can only be performed at this temple. These ceremonies involve not only the thaumaturge but a permanent group of vestal maidens who move sedately about the temple chambers in distinctive costume and headdress.

The *latipso* ceremonies are so harsh that it is phenomenal that a fair proportion of the really sick natives who enter the temple ever recover. Small children whose indoctrination is still incomplete have been known to resist attempts to take them to the temple because "that is where you go to die." Despite this fact, sick adults are not only willing but eager to undergo the protracted ritual purification, if they can afford to do so. No matter how ill the supplicant or how grave the emergency, the guardians of many temples will not admit a client if he cannot give a rich gift to the custodian. Even after one has gained admission and survived the ceremonies, the guardians will not permit the neophyte to leave until he makes still another gift.

The supplicant entering the temple is first stripped of all his or her clothes. In everyday life the Nacirema avoids exposure of his body and its natural functions. Bathing and excretory acts are performed only in the secrecy of the household shrine, where they are ritualized as part of the body-rites. Psychological shock results from the fact that body secrecy is suddenly lost upon entry into the *latipso*. A man, whose own wife has never seen him in an excretory act, suddenly finds himself naked and assisted by a vestal maiden while he performs his natural functions into a sacred vessel. This sort of ceremonial treatment is necessitated by the fact that the excreta are used by a diviner to ascertain the course and nature of the client's sickness. Female clients, on the other hand, find their naked bodies are subjected to the scrutiny, manipulation, and prodding of the medicine men.

Few supplicants in the temple are well enough to do anything but lie on their hard beds. The daily ceremonies, like the rites of the holy-mouth-men, involve discomfort and torture. With ritual precision, the vestals awaken their miserable charges each dawn and roll them about on their beds of pain while performing ablutions, in the formal movements of which the maidens are highly trained. At other times they insert magic wands in the supplicant's mouth or force him to eat substances which are supposed to be healing. From time to time the medicine men come to their clients and jab magically treated needles into their flesh. The fact that these temple ceremonies may not cure, and may even kill the neophyte, in no way decreases the people's faith in the medicine men.

There remains one other kind of practitioner, known as a "listener." This witch-doctor has the power to exorcise the devils that lodge in the heads of people who have been bewitched. The Nacirema believe that parents bewitch their own children. Mothers are particularly suspected of putting a curse on children while teaching them the secret body rituals. The counter-magic of the witch-doctor is unusual in its lack of ritual. The patient simply tells the "listener" all his troubles and fears, beginning with the earliest difficulties he can remember. The memory displayed by the Nacirema in these exorcism sessions is truly remarkable. It is not uncommon for the patient to bemoan the rejection he felt upon being weaned as a babe, and a few individuals even see their troubles going back to the traumatic effects of their own birth.

In conclusion, mention must be made of certain practices which have their base in native esthetics but which depend upon the pervasive aversion to the natural body and its functions. There are ritual fasts to make fat people thin and ceremonial feasts to make thin people fat. Still other rites are used to make women's breasts larger if they are small, and smaller if they are large. General dissatisfaction with breast shape is symbolized in the fact that the ideal form is virtually outside the range of human variation. A few women afflicted with almost inhuman hypermammary development are so idolized that they make a handsome living by simply going from village to village and permitting the natives to stare at them for a fee.

Reference has already been made to the fact that excretory functions are ritualized, routinized, and relegated to secrecy. Natural reproductive functions are similarly distorted. Intercourse is taboo as a topic and scheduled as an act. Efforts are made to avoid pregnancy by the use of magical materials or by limiting intercourse to certain phases of the moon. Conception is actually very infrequent. When pregnant, women dress so as to hide their condition. Parturition takes place in secret, without friends or relatives to assist, and the majority of women do not nurse their infants.

Our review of the ritual life of the Nacirema has certainly shown them to be a magic-ridden people. It is hard to understand how they have managed to exist so long under the burdens which they have imposed upon themselves. But even such exotic customs as these take on real meaning when they are viewed with the insight provided by Malinowski when he wrote (1948, p. 70):

Looking from far and above, from our high places of safety in the developed civilization, it is easy to see all the crudity and irrelevance of magic. But without its power and guidance early man could not have mastered his practical difficulties as he has done, nor could man have advanced to the higher stages of civilization.

## References

Linton, R. (1936). *The study of man*. New York: Appleton-Century.

Malinowski, B. (1948). *Magic, science, and religion*. Glencoe, IL: Free Press.

Murdock, G. P. (1949). *Social structure*. New York: Macmillan.

**2**

# The Nature of "Perspective"

## *Joel Charon*

Teachers and authors throughout my educational career have warned me that truth is very difficult to find indeed. The more I understood, of course, the more I realized they were right. A new dimension to the problem of truth opened up, however, as I was introduced to the concept of *perspective*. Once taken literally, the concept of perspective must lead one to the conclusion that, for human beings, truth about physical reality is impossible in any absolute sense.

Many years ago, I read the following story by A. Averchenko. It underlines the difficulty the human has in knowing what is really happening "out there." I interpreted it as an illustration of bias in perception. I explained to others that here was a good example of how people take a single situation and twist it to meet their needs. Underlying my interpretation of the story was the belief that people tend to be closed-minded, narrow, and less than truthful.

"Men are comic," she said, smiling dreamily. Not knowing whether this indicated praise or blame, I answered noncommittally: "Quite true."

"Really, my husband's a regular Othello. Sometimes I'm sorry I married him." I looked helplessly at her. "Until you explain—" I began.

"Oh, I forgot that you haven't heard. About three weeks ago, I was walking home with my husband through the square. I had a large black

hat on, which suits me awfully well, and my cheeks were quite pink from walking. As we passed under a street light, a pale, dark-haired fellow standing near by glanced at me and suddenly took my husband by his sleeve."

" 'Would you oblige me with a light,' he says. Alexander pulled his arm away, stooped down, and quicker than lightning, banged him on the head with a brick. He fell like a log. Awful!"

"Why, what on earth made your husband get jealous all of a sudden?" She shrugged her shoulders. "I told you men are very comic."

Bidding her farewell, I went out, and at the corner came across her husband.

"Hello, old chap," I said. "They tell me you've been breaking people's heads."

He burst out laughing. "So, you've been talking to my wife. It was jolly lucky that brick came so pat into my hand. Otherwise, just think: I had about fifteen hundred rubles in my pocket, and my wife was wearing her diamond earrings."

"Do you think he wanted to rob you?"

"A man accosts you in a deserted spot, asks for a light and gets hold of your arm. What more do you want?"

Perplexed, I left him and walked on.

"There's no catching you today," I heard a voice from behind.

I looked around and saw a friend I hadn't set eyes upon for three weeks.

"Lord!" I exclaimed. "What on earth has happened to you?"

He smiled faintly and asked in turn: "Do you know whether any lunatics have been at large lately? I was attacked by one three weeks ago. I left the hospital only today."

With sudden interest, I asked: "Three weeks ago? Were you sitting in the square?"

"Yes, I was. The most absurd thing. I was sitting in the square, dying for a smoke. No matches! After ten minutes or so, a gentleman passes with some old hag. He was smoking. I go up to him, touch him on the sleeve and ask in my most polite manner: 'Can you oblige me with a light?' And what do you think? The madman stoops down, picks up something, and the next moment I am lying on the ground with a broken head, unconscious. You probably read about it in the newspapers."

I looked at him and asked earnestly: "Do you really believe you met up with a lunatic?"

"I am sure of it."

Anyhow, afterwards I was eagerly digging in old back numbers of the local paper. At last I found what I was looking for: a short note in the accident column.

UNDER THE INFLUENCE OF DRINK

"Yesterday morning, the keepers of the square found on a bench a young man whose papers show him to be of good family. He had evidently fallen to the ground while in a state of extreme intoxication, and had broken his head on a nearby brick. The distress of the prodigal's parents is indescribable."

The seeker of truth naturally asks, "What really happened?" The police, of course, investigate situations such as this one in order to determine who is *telling the truth*. "Someone must be lying" or "Someone is twisting the truth to fit his or her own needs." It is difficult for most of us to accept the view that all may be telling the "truth." We might see things differently if we imagine that each one of the individuals (including the interviewer) comes to the situation with a different *perspective*, and therefore sees a *different reality*. Although some of these perspectives may be closer to "physical reality" than others, all of them probably capture at least part of that reality, and none of them is able to capture the whole of it. These perspectives are neither omniscient nor all-inclusive.

The story is called "Point of View," and in a sense, a perspective is a point of view, placing observers at various angles in relation to events and influencing them to see these events from these angles. By its very nature, then, a point of view, or perspective, limits what the observer sees by allowing only one side of what is "out there" to be seen.

There is no way that any individual can see all aspects of any situation simultaneously. One must pull out certain stimuli and totally ignore other stimuli. One must also put the stimuli pulled out into a larger context so that what is seen makes sense. That is what perspectives do: They *sensitize* the individual to parts of physical reality, they *desensitize* the individual to other parts, and they help the individual *make sense* of the physical reality to which there is sensitization. Seen in this light, a perspective is absolutely basic to the human being's everyday existence because it is needed to make sense out of what is seen. Yet, because of perspective, the human being cannot encounter physical reality "in the raw," directly, for whatever is seen can only be *part* of the "real situation."

Perspectives are made up of words—it is these words that are used by the observer to make sense out of situations. In a way, the best definition of perspective is a *conceptual framework*, which emphasizes that perspectives are really interrelated sets of words used to order physical reality. The words we use cause us to make assumptions and value judgments about what we are seeing (and not seeing).

Reality, for the individual, depends on the words used to look at situations. If we examine the story by Averchenko in this light, it becomes obvious that the differences between actors' viewpoints depend on the words they used to *see*. The woman uses "Othello," "married," "black hat" ("which suits me"), "pale, dark-haired fellow," all of which reveal that in that situation she was "seeing" according to a perspective associated with a woman concerned with her attractiveness. Her husband, fearful of his money, uses these words: "fifteen hundred rubles," "diamond earrings," "accosts," "deserted," "gets hold of your arm." In both cases, and in other cases too, certain aspects of the situation were pulled out, emphasized, and integrated, according to each person's *perspective*, or conceptual framework. And in each case, the conceptual framework led to various value judgments and assumptions by the actor in the situation.

A college education, in many ways, is an introduction to a variety of perspectives, each telling us something about what is going on around us. Sociology, psychology, history, humanities, art, George Orwell, Machiavelli, Freud, James Joyce, and Malcolm X—each represents a perspective that we might adopt as our own, integrate with others we have or forget entirely after our final exam. Each perspective is a different approach to "reality," and each, therefore, tells us something but cannot include everything.

It seems that the most difficult aspect of "perspective" to grasp is that perspectives cannot capture the whole physical reality. It is probably because we want so desperately to know that what we believe is true that we cannot face the fact that whatever we know must be seen only as a truth gained from a certain *perspective.* We cannot, for example, even agree totally on what a simple object is. One day in the middle of winter, I went outside and picked up something from the ground and brought it to class. I asked, "What is this?" The answers were snow, a snowball, ice crystals, frozen water, something you are showing us to make some point, something little boys use to frighten little girls, the beginning of the world's biggest snowman, molecules, dirty snow, a very interesting shape to draw, the symbol of cold weather. Of course, my response was, "What is this really?" And, of course, the response by them was that it is all of these things, and probably many, many more things. Indeed, whatever that physical reality was is interpreted by people in many ways, depending entirely on the perspective they use to see it. No one of these perspectives could ever claim to have grasped the true essence of that which was brought in from outside. And

even if we might try to claim that all of these perspectives together capture the object completely, we would be missing the point: Perspectives are almost infinite; thus, we can never claim to have found all the possible perspectives on anything.

Human beings are limited by their perspectives; they cannot see outside of their perspectives. Yet perspectives are vitally important: They make it possible for human beings to make sense out of what is "out there."

Perspectives must be judged by individuals according to their usefulness in interpreting situations that arise. Perspectives should not be thought of as true or false (as we might be tempted to do) but as helpful or useless in understanding. We accept or reject various perspectives in our education based on whether or not they make sense to us; that is, Do they help us understand people or situations we encounter? The more useful a perspective is, the more apt we are to regard it as truth, but truths today have a habit of becoming "just *their* opinion" tomorrow, and we find ourselves giving up older perspectives for newer, more useful ones.

### New Perspectives Mean New Realities

Many are familiar with *The Autobiography of Malcolm X.* Malcolm X was an important leader in the Civil Rights movement during the 1960s. He is a good example of an individual whose life situations brought about very definite changes in perspectives and thus opened up whole new worlds for him. With each perspective came a new reality. In seventh grade, for instance, he was elected class president, and in looking back, he reports:

And I was proud: I'm not going to say I wasn't. In fact, by then, I didn't really have much feeling about being a Negro, because I was trying so hard, in every way I could, to be white. . . . I remember one thing that marred this time for me: the movie "Gone with the Wind." When it played in Mason, I was the only Negro in the theater, and when Butterfly McQueen went into her act, I felt like crawling under the rug. (Malcolm X and Haley, 1965:31–32)[1]

Malcolm remembers his perspective changing in school:

It was then that I began to change—inside. I drew away from white people. I came to class, and I answered when called upon. It became a physical strain simply to sit in Mr. Ostrowski's class. Where "nigger" had slipped off my back before, wherever I heard it now, I stopped and looked at whoever said it. And they looked surprised that I did. (p. 37)

Then in New York:

"Man, you can't tell him nothing!" they'd exclaim. And they couldn't. At home in Roxbury, they would see me parading with Sophia, dressed in my wild zoot suits. Then I'd come to work, loud and wild and half-high on liquor or reefers, and I'd stay that way, jamming sandwiches at people until we got to New York. Off the train, I'd go through the Grand Central Station afternoon rush-hour crowd, and many white people simply stopped in their tracks to watch me pass. The drape and the cut of a zoot suit showed to the best advantage if you were tall—and I was over six feet. My conk was fire-red. I was really a clown, but my ignorance made me think I was "sharp." My knob-toed, orange-colored "kick-up" shoes were nothing but Florsheims, the ghetto's Cadillac of shoes in those days. . . . And then, between Small's Paradise, the Braddock Hotel, and other places—as much as my twenty- or twenty-five dollar pay would allow, I drank liquor, smoked marijuana, painted the Big Apple red with increasing numbers of friends, and finally in Mrs. Fisher's rooming house I got a few hours of sleep before the "Yankee Clipper" rolled again. (p. 79)

Malcolm has been seeing the world from the perspective of zoot suits, reefers, conk, Cadillac of shoes, but he is suddenly exposed to a new perspective, which opens up a new world to him:

When Reginald left, he left me rocking with some of the first serious thoughts I had ever had in my life: that the white man was fast losing his power to oppress and exploit the dark world; that the dark world was starting to rise to rule the world again, as it had before; that the white man's world was on the way down, it was on the way out. (p. 162)

Because of this new perspective, Malcolm X becomes sensitive to things in his world he never really saw before. His past takes on a new meaning, and the many situations that took place between blacks and whites in his past are seen differently. He joins the Black Muslims, and he becomes a great leader in that movement. At the height of his activity in that movement, the words he preaches reflect his perspective:

No *sane* black man really wants integration! No *sane* white man really wants integration. No *sane* black man really believes that the white man ever will give the black man anything more than token integration. No! The Honorable Elijah Muhammed teaches that for the black man in America the only solution is complete *separation* from the white man! (p. 248)

And, finally, Malcolm's perspective changes once more, as a result of a pilgrimage he makes to Mecca. As his perspective changes, the world around him becomes transformed:

It was in the Holy World that my attitude was changed, by what I experienced there, and by what I witnessed there, in terms of brotherhood—not just brotherhood toward me, but brotherhood between all men, of all nationalities and complexions, who were there. And now that I am back in America, my attitude here concerning white people has to be governed by what my black brothers and I experience here, and what we witness here—in terms of brotherhood. The *problem* here in America is that we meet such a small minority of individual so-called "good," or "brotherly" white people. . . . (p. 368)

Malcolm X's autobiography is an excellent description of an individual undergoing profound changes in *perspective*. His story is not unique, but what is happening is probably more obvious to us in his story than it would be in many others.

Not only do we all undergo *basic* change in our perspectives many times throughout our lives, but our perspectives change from situation to situation, often many times during the same day. Few of us have one perspective that we can apply to every situation we encounter. Perspectives are situational: In the classroom my perspective is that of teacher/sociologist; in my home it becomes father or husband; on a fishing trip it changes to "seasoned fisherman." Each situation calls forth a different role, which means a different perspective. Some roles we play may have more than one perspective we can use (there are many different *student* perspectives we might draw on depending on the situation we encounter), and some perspectives may apply to more than one role we play (e.g., a Christian may apply his or her perspective as a Christian to a number of roles). Perspectives are a complex matter.

Perspectives are not perceptions but are guides to our perceptions; they influence what we see and how we interpret what we see. They are our "eyeglasses" we put on to see. Figure 1 summarizes the meaning of perspective.

A perspective, then, by its very nature, is a bias; it contains assumptions, value judgments, and ideas; it orders the world; it divides it up in a certain way; and as a result it influences our action in the world. A father and his son see each other from at least two perspectives (one the father's, and the other the son's) and thus define a situation that affects them both (e.g., the use of the car) in two very different ways. Neither is necessarily wrong or in error, although they may certainly disagree. A candidate for president of the United States may see the society as in need of change and promise all kinds of possibilities, but once that person is in office, his or her perspective will change and his or her behavior will be affected. It is not, as may appear to us, that the new president is dishonest, but rather that the definition of the situation has changed because that person now sees the world from the perspective of president, not candidate.

**Is There a "Best" Perspective?**

Are all perspectives equally "good," or can one argue that one perspective is "better" than another? Is, for example, a son's perspective "better" than his father's? Is an artist's perspective "better" than a scientist's?

Whenever any two things (such as perspectives) are compared, there has to be agreement on criteria for comparison. So, for example, Martha is "better" than Marsha if we agree that the criterion is IQ and can agree on how it should be measured. One painting is "better" than another if we use "capturing physical reality" as a criterion for comparison and can agree on how to measure "capturing physical reality."

Some perspectives are therefore "better" than others. All are not equal. To judge which is "better," however, a standard of comparison must be established. Some people, for example, would argue that the best perspective is the one that conforms closest to Holy

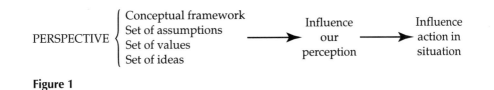

Figure 1

Scripture or the one that comes closest to the "American creed." Thus, atheism is not a good perspective in the first case, and for most of us, a racist perspective is not good in the second case.

Most of us are probably interested in using perspectives that *accurately describe* what is "really" happening in the world around us. Certainly, in the world of scholarship accurate description is one of the most important measurements of a "good perspective." A good perspective gives us insight, clearly describes reality, helps us find the truth. Most scientists, natural and social, make a claim that their perspectives are better than common-sense ones because there is a disciplined control of personal bias. The fruits of science do indeed support the fact that the scientific perspective is superior to the vast majority of perspectives that deal with the natural and social worlds. If given a choice between a scientific perspective and a nonscientific perspective examining exactly the same question, it would be unusual for me to opt for the latter, because it is clear to me that scientific perspectives are usually more reliable than nonscientific ones in accurately answering questions about the natural and social world. It depends a great deal, however, on the nature of the question asked.

Science is far from accurate in answering a number of important questions, and scientists are unable to deal with whole layers of reality that other perspectives deal with. Even in the natural and social worlds that the scientist does examine, there are realities that go unnoticed and are not even looked for, realities too difficult to examine scientifically. To claim that the perspective of science is better than any other because it is more accurate is not a just claim for all questions.

The problem of the "best" perspective is confounded when we try to determine the most accurate scientific perspective. Although scientists share a scientific perspective, they differ in what they focus on in reality, and it would be very difficult to establish criteria for judging which one of the sciences captures reality the best. This could be done, but probably to no good purpose. It is best to understand scientific perspectives as each focusing on a different aspect of the natural and social world, each helping us more clearly understand that aspect. Comparing scientific perspective—indeed, comparing all perspectives—is a difficult task, but it is not impossible if criteria are *carefully* established. . . .

## References

Malcolm X and Alex Haley
1965    *The Autobiography of Malcolm X.* New York: Grove Press. Copyright ©1965 by Alex Haley and Betty Shabazz. Reprinted by permission of Random House, Inc., New York, and the Hutchinson Publishing, Random Century Group Ltd., London.

## Note

1. From *The Autobiography of Malcolm X* by Malcolm X, with the assistance of Alex Haley. Copyright ©1964 by Alex Haley and Malcolm X. Copyright ©1965 by Alex Haley and Betty Shabazz. Reprinted by permission of Random House, Inc., New York, and the Hutchinson Publishing, Random Century Group Ltd., London.

3

# Truth, Objectivity, and Agreement

## Earl Babbie

Science is often portrayed as a search for the truth about reality. That sounds good, but what is *truth*? What is *reality*? Look those words up in a good dictionary, such as the *Oxford English Dictionary*, and you'll find definitions like "the quality of being true" and "the quality of being real." Beyond these basic tautologies are some additional definitions (from the *OED*):

**Truth:**

- Conformity with fact; agreement with reality
- Agreement with a standard or rule; accuracy, correctness
- Genuineness, reality, actual existence
- That which is in accordance with fact
- That which is true, real, or actual; reality

**Reality:**

- The quality of . . . having an actual existence
- Correspondence to fact; truth
- Real existence

Definitions of the words *true* and *real* are similar:

**True:**

- Consistent with fact; agreeing with reality; representing the thing as it is

"Truth, Objectivity, and Agreement," from E. Babbie, *Observing Ourselves* (Prospect Heights, IL: Waveland Press). Reprinted by permission of Waveland Press, Inc., © 1998. All rights reserved.

- Agreeing with a standard, pattern, or rule; exact, accurate, precise, correct, right
- Consistent with, exactly agreeing with
- Conformable to reality; natural
- In accordance with reality

**Real:**

- Having an objective existence; actually existing as a thing
- Actually present or existing as a state or quality of things; having a foundation in fact; actually occurring or happening
- Consisting of actual things

These definitions point to the inherent circularity of language, which is inevitable as long as we use words to define words. In this case, things are true if they're real and real if they're true. The relationship between truth and reality can also be seen in the preponderance of words dealing with agreement: *conformity, accordance, correspondence, consistent with, representing.*

Here's a useful way of seeing the relationship between truth and reality: It is possible to make statements about reality; those that agree with (conform to, are consistent with, represent) reality are true. None of this tells us what truth or reality is, however. It only tells us about their relationship to one another.

Other words in the definitions we've seen may clarify the meanings of truth and reality—words such as *actual*, *existence*, and *fact*.

**Actuality:**
- The state of being actual or real; reality, existing objective fact

**Actual:**
- Existing in act or fact; really acted or acting; carried out; real

**Factual:**
- Pertaining to or concerned with facts; of the nature of fact, actual, real

**Fact:**
- Something that has really occurred or is actually the case
- Truth attested by direct observation or authentic testimony; reality

**Existence:**
- Actuality; reality
- Being; the fact or state of existing

**Exist:**
- To have place in the domain of reality, have objective being

By now, the incestuous circularity of language is getting a little annoying. Consider this abbreviated search for truth:

**Truth** is "That which is real; **reality.**"
**Reality** is "Having an actual **existence.**"
**Existence** is "**Actuality;** reality."
**Actuality** is "Existing objective **fact.**"
**Fact** is "**Truth** attested by direct observation."

In addition to the circularity of these relatively few words defining each other, let's take a cue from the definitions of *exist* and *existence* and add the term *being*.

**Being:**
- Existence
- That which exists or is conceived as existing

**Be:**
- To have or take place in the world of fact; to exist, occur, happen

- To have place in the objective universe or realm of fact, to exist
- To come into existence
- To be the case or the fact

For the most part, these new words simply add to the circularity of definitions that is becoming very familiar in this exercise. . . .

From time to time throughout these definitions, and now in the definition of *be*, the quality of objectivity has appeared as part of the background of a definition. In these cases, *real* does not just have existence, it has "objective existence"; *actuality* is not just a matter of fact but of "objective fact." Now, to *be* is to have a place in the "objective universe." Implicit in these uses is the contrast between objectivity and subjectivity.

**Subjectivity:**
- The quality or condition of viewing things exclusively through the medium of one's own mind or individuality
- The character of existing in the mind only

**Subjective:**
- Relating to the thinking subject, proceeding from or taking place within the subject; having its source in the mind

In stark contrast, *objective* is defined this way:

**Objective:**
- That which is external to the mind

The truth about *truth* eventually comes down to the recognition that we know most of the world through our minds. Moreover, we recognize that our individual minds are not altogether reliable. We have colloquial phrases such as "a figment of your imagination," and we realize that people often "see what they want to see." Simply put, the subjective realm refers to the possibly inaccurate perceptions and thoughts we have through the medium of our minds, yours and mine, whereas the objective realm refers to that which lies outside and is independent of our minds. We often term that objective realm *re-*

*ality,* and term *true* a statement that accurately describes reality.

A couple of snags lie hidden in this construction of objectivity. First, neither you nor I, perceiving reality through our subjective minds, can know whether we perceive it accurately or not. The following scene should make the matter painfully clear.

Imagine that you are sitting in a room that has a small window with a view into another room. A light located in the other room can be turned on or off. Reality in this illustration is simply whether the light is on or off in the other room. Truth is a function of your ability to say accurately whether the light is on or off.

At first impression, nothing could be simpler. I turn the light on in the other room, and you say, "The light is on." I turn it off, and you say, "The light is off." This would be a model of objectivity.

The defect in this model is that your mind and its subjectivity have not been taken into account. But imagine that the small window before you has two shutters. The first shutter has a picture of the other room with the light on, and the second has a picture of the room with the light off. Sometimes the first shutter will close your view of the other room, sometimes the second shutter will, and sometimes there won't be any shutter—but you'll never know.

Now when I ask you whether the light is on in the other room, you will answer based on what you see, but what you see may be the open window or it may be one of the shutters. If you see one of the shutters, the scene you see may correspond with the real condition of the room or it may not.

Relating this illustration to real life, however, you would not be conscious of the possibility that you were looking at a shutter; instead, you would think that what you perceived was reality. You would feel sure that you knew the truth about whether the light was on or off because you saw it with your own eyes. And even if you became aware of the existence of the shutters, you couldn't be sure of reality because you still wouldn't know if what you were seeing was the other room or one of the shutters.

The point of this illustration is that you have no way out. In the normal course of life, you cannot be sure that what you see is really there. But there's a bigger problem than this. Given the subjectivity of your mind, you can't be sure there is *anything* out there at all. In the two-room illustration, maybe there is no window and no other room—only two shutters. Maybe it's all in your mind. How could you ever know?

The answer to both of these dilemmas is the same. If you can't be sure that what your mind tells you is true, you can at least gain some confidence in that regard if you find that my mind has told me the same thing. You say the light is on, and I say the light is on: case closed. Now you may feel doubly sure you know the light is on, not to mention that there's a window, a room, and a light.

Ultimately, our only proof of objectivity is intersubjectivity, and some dictionaries even define *objectivity* that way. When different subjects—with their individual, error-prone subjectivities—report the same thing, we conclude that what they report is objective, existing, actual, factual, real, and true.

Thus, the basis of truth is agreement. Basically, things are true if we agree they are. When Copernicus first said that the earth revolved around the sun, few people agreed; today, most people agree. We say that this view is not only true today but was true when Copernicus first expressed it, and was even true before Copernicus. But we say all that *today* when virtually everyone agrees with the view. Moreover, if all the world's astronomers were to announce a new discovery showing the sun revolved around the earth, we'd soon be saying that Copernicus was wrong and that the sun had always revolved around the earth, even before Copernicus.

When you think about the past history of agreements that were eventually overturned, you won't find much basis for confidence in what you and I now agree to be so. . . . [M]ost of what we "know" today will be thrown out as inaccurate tomorrow.

Where does science figure in all this? What about social science? Don't they offer an exception to this? Aren't they a dependable channel to the truth?

Ultimately, science—social or otherwise—also operates on the basis of agreement: in this case, agreement among fellow scientists. But there are some differences. Scientists recognize that knowledge is continually changing. They know that what they know today may be replaced tomorrow. In fact, the goal of science is to keep changing the truth.

Scientists are aware of the power of subjective biases and are explicitly committed to avoiding them in their research. Social researchers have an advantage in this respect, since bias itself is a subject matter for social science. On the other hand, social researchers have a disadvantage in that their subject matter—religion and politics, for example—is more likely to provoke personal biases than is the subject matter of the natural sciences.

For scientists, observation is a conscious and deliberate activity, whereas it is generally casual and semiconscious for most people in normal life. Thus, you might mistakenly recall that your best friend wore a blue dress yesterday, when it was really green. If you had been recording dress colors as part of a research project, however, you wouldn't have made that mistake.

Moreover, scientists have developed procedures and equipment to aid them in making observations. This also avoids some of the mistakes we make in casual observations. For example, scientists are explicit about the basis for their agreements. Rules of proof are contained within the system of logic prevailing at the time.

More important, perhaps, in the context of this essay, scientists are explicit about the intersubjective nature of truth. Peer review is an established principle: Scientists review each other's work to guard against errors of method or reasoning. Scientific journals perform what is called a gatekeeper function in this regard. Articles submitted for publication are typically circulated among independent reviewers—other scientists knowledgeable in the area covered by the article. Unless the reviewers agree that the article represents a sound and worthwhile contribution to the field, it will not be published.

Scientists are by no means above error, however. Being human, they are susceptible to all the human foibles that afflict nonscientists. Though the scientific enterprise commits them to keeping an open mind with regard to truth, individual scientists can grow attached to particular views. . . .

To understand the nature of science, it is essential to recognize that scientific knowledge at any given time is what scientists agree it is. Because scientific proof is fundamentally based on agreement among scientists, scientific knowledge keeps changing over time. It is probably unavoidable that we see this evolution of scientific knowledge over time as a process through which we get closer and closer to the truth. This view cannot be verified, however. All we can know for sure is that what we know keeps changing.

We can't even bank on views that haven't changed for a long time. Bear in mind, for example, that the idea that the earth was stationary and the sun moved was accepted much longer than our current view has been. Years ago, when I was living in a house on the slopes of a volcano in Hawaii, I took comfort in knowing that the volcano hadn't erupted for 25,000 years and hence probably wouldn't ever erupt again. Then I learned that its previous period of dormancy had been longer than that.

In the case of scientific knowledge, changes are generally occurring faster, not slower, than in the past. . . . [W]hat we learn about social life is often changed by just having the knowledge we've gained. On the whole, then, we'd do better simply to settle for the thrill of discovery than to worry about whether what we've discovered is the ultimate truth or simply a new and currently useful way of viewing things.

**4**

# The Search for Signs of Intelligent Life in the Universe

*Jane Wagner*

Here we are, standing on the corner of
"Walk, Don't Walk."
You look away from me, tryin' not to
    catch my eye,
but you didn't turn fast enough, *did* you?

You don't like my *ra*spy voice, do you?
I got this *ra*spy voice
'cause I have to yell all the time
'cause nobody around here ever
LISTENS to me.

You don't like that I scratch so much: yes,
    and excuse me,
I scratch so much
'cause my neurons are
on *fire*.

And I admit my smile is not at its
    Pepsodent best
'cause I think my
caps must've somehow got
osteo*porosis*.

And if my eyes seem to be twirling
    around like fruit flies—
the better to see you with, my dears!
*Look* at me,
you mammalian-brained LUNKHEADS!

I'm not just talking to myself. I'm talking
    to you, too.
And to you
and you
and you
and you and you and you!

I know what you're thinkin'; you're
    thinkin' I'm crazy.
You think I give a hoot? You people
look at my shopping bags,
call me crazy 'cause I save this junk. What
    should we call the
ones who
*buy* it?

It's my belief we all, at one time or another,
secretly ask ourselves the question,
"Am *I* crazy?"
In my case, the answer came back: A
    resounding
YES!

You're thinkin': How does a person know
    if they're crazy
or not? Well, sometimes you don't know.
    Sometimes you
can go through life suspecting you *are*
but never really knowing for sure.
    Sometimes you know for sure
'cause you got so many people tellin' you
    you're crazy
that it's your word against everyone
    else's.

Another sign is when you see life so clear
     sometimes
you black out.
This is your typical visionary variety
who has flashes of insight
but can't get anyone to listen to 'em
'cause their insights make 'em sound so
     *crazy!*

In my case,
the symptoms are subtle
but unmistakable to the trained eye. For
     instance,
here I am,
standing at the corner of "Walk, Don't
     Walk,"
waiting for these aliens from outer space
     to show up.
I call that crazy, don't you? If I were sane,
I should be waiting for the light like
     everybody else.

They're late
as usual.

You'd think,
as much as they know about time travel,
they could be on time *once* in a while.

I could kick myself.
I told 'em I'd meet 'em on the corner of
     "Walk, Don't Walk"
'round lunchtime.
Do they even know what "lunch" means?
I doubt it.

And "'round." Why did I say "'round"?
     Why wasn't I more
specific? This is so typical of what I do.

Now they're probably stuck somewhere
     in time, wondering
what I meant by
"'round lunchtime." And when they get
     here, they'll be
dying to know what "lunchtime" means.
     And when they
find out it means going to Howard
     Johnson's for fried

clams, I wonder, will they be just a bit let
     down?
I dread having to explain
tartar sauce.

This problem of time just points out
how far apart we really are.
See, our ideas about time and space are
     different
from theirs. When we think of time, we
     tend to think of
clock radios, coffee breaks, afternoon
     naps, leisure time,
halftime activities, parole time, doing
     time, Minute Rice, instant
tea, mid-life crises, that time of the
     month, cocktail hour.
And if I should suddenly
mention *space*—aha! I bet most of you
     thought of your
closets. But when they think of time and
     space, they really think
of
Time and Space.

They asked me once my thoughts on
     infinity and I told 'em
with all I had to think about, infinity was
     not on my list
of things to think about. It could be time
     on an ego trip,
for all I know. After all, when you're
     pressed for time,
infinity may as well
not be there.
They said, to them, infinity is
time-released time.
Frankly, infinity doesn't affect
me personally one way or the other.

You think too long about infinity, you
     could go
stark raving mad.
But I don't ever want to sound negative
     about going crazy.
I don't want to overromanticize it either,
     but frankly,
goin' crazy was the *best* thing ever
     happened to me.

I don't say it's for everybody;
some people couldn't cope.

But for me it came at a time when nothing
     else seemed to be
working. I got the kind of madness
     Socrates talked about,
"A divine release of the soul from the
     yoke of
custom and convention." I refuse to be
     intimidated by
reality anymore.
After all, what is reality anyway? Nothin'
     but a
collective hunch. My space chums think
     reality was once a
primitive method of
crowd control that got out of hand.
In my view, it's absurdity dressed up
in a three-piece business suit.

I made some studies, and
reality is the leading cause of stress
     amongst those in
touch with it. I can take it in small doses,
     but as a lifestyle
I found it too confining.
It was just too needful;
it expected me to be there for it *all* the
     time, and with all
I have to do—
I had to let something go.

Now, since I put reality on a back burner,
     my days are
jam-packed and fun-filled. Like some
     days, I go hang out
around Seventh Avenue; I love to do this
     old joke:
I wait for some music-loving tourist from
     one of the hotels
on Central Park to go up and ask
     someone.
"How do I get to Carnegie Hall?"
Then I run up and yell,
"Practice!"
The expression on people's faces is
     priceless. I never

could've done stuff like that when I was
     in my *right* mind.
I'd be worried people would think I was
     *crazy*.
When I think of the fun I missed,
I try not to be bitter.

See, the human mind is kind of like . . .
a piñata. When it breaks open,
there's a lot of surprises inside. Once you
     get the piñata
perspective, you see that losing your mind
can be a peak experience.

I was not always a bag lady, you know.
I used to be a designer and creative
     consultant. For big
companies!
Who do you think thought up the color
     scheme
for Howard Johnson's?
At the time, nobody was using
orange and aqua
in the same room together.
With fried clams.

Laugh tracks:
*I* gave TV sitcoms the idea for canned
     laughter.
I got the idea, one day I heard voices
and no one was there.

Who do you think had the idea to
     package panty hose
in a plastic goose egg?

One thing I personally don't like about
     panty hose:
When you roll 'em down to the ankles the
     way I like 'em, you
can't walk too good. People seem
     amused, so what's a little
loss of dignity? You got to admit:
It's a look!

The only idea I'm proud of—

my umbrella hat. Protects against
     sunstroke, rain and

muggers. For *some* reason, muggers steer
    clear of people
wearing umbrella hats.

So it should come as no shock . . . I am
    now creative consultant to
these aliens from outer space. They're a
    kinda cosmic
fact-finding committee. Amongst other
    projects, they've been
searching all over for Signs of Intelligent
    Life.

It's a lot trickier than it sounds.

We're collecting all kinds of data
about life here on Earth. We're
    determined to figure out,
once and for all, just what the hell it all
    means.
I write the data on these Post-its and then
    we study it.
Don't worry, before I took the consulting
    job, I gave 'em my whole
psychohistory.

I told 'em what drove *me* crazy was my
    *last* creative consultant
job, with the Ritz Cracker mogul, Mr.
    Nabisco. It was
my job to come up with snack
    inspirations to increase sales.
I got this idea to give Cracker
    Consciousness to the entire
planet.

I said, "Mr. Nabisco, sir! You could be the
    first to sell the
concept of munching to the Third World.
    We got an untapped
market here! These countries got millions
    and millions of
people don't even know where their next
    *meal* is *coming* from.
So the idea of eatin' *between* meals is
    somethin' just never
occurred to 'em!"

I heard myself sayin' *this!*

Must've been when I went off the deep end.
I woke up in the nuthouse. They were
    hookin' me up.
One thing they don't tell you about shock
    treatments, for
months afterwards you got
flyaway hair. And it used to *be* my best
    feature.

See, those shock treatments gave me new
    electrical circuitry
(frankly, I think one of the doctors' hands
    must've been wet).
I started having these time-space
    continuum shifts, I guess
you'd call it. Suddenly, it was like my
    central nervous system
had a patio addition out back.
Not only do I have a linkup to
    extraterrestrial
channels. I also got a hookup with
    humanity as a whole.
Animals and plants, too. I used to talk to
    plants all the time;
then, one day, they started talking back.
    They said,
"Trudy,
shut up!"

I got like this . . .

built-in Betamax in my head. Records
    anything.
It's like somebody's using my brain to
    dial-switch
through humanity. I pick up signals that
    seem to transmit
snatches of people's lives.
My umbrella hat works as a satellite dish.
    I hear this
sizzling sound like white noise. Then I
    know it's
trance time.
That's how I met my space chums. I was
    in one of my trances,
watching a scene from someone's life,
    and I suddenly sense

others were there
watching with me.

Uh-oh.
I see this skinny
punk kid.
Got hair the color of
Froot Loops and she's wearin' a T-shirt
    says "Leave Me Alone."
There's a terrible family squabble going on.
If they're listening to each other,
they're all gonna get their feelings hurt.

I see glitches—
Now I see this dark-haired actress
on a Broadway stage. I know her. I see her
    all the time outside
the Plymouth Theater, Forty-fifth Street . . .

Dial-switch me outta this!
I got enough worries of my own.
These trances are entertaining but
    distracting, especially since
someone *else* has the remote control, and
    if the pause button
should somehow get punched, I could
    have a neurotransmitter
mental meltdown. Causes "lapses of the
    synapses." I forget
things. Never underestimate the power of
    the human mind to
forget. The other day, I forgot where I put
    my house keys—
looked everywhere, then I remembered
I don't have a house. I forget more
    important things, too.
Like the meaning of life.
I forget that.
It'll come to me, though.
Let's just hope when it does,
I'll be in . . .

My space chums say they're learning so
    much about us
since they've begun to time-share my
    trances.
They said to me, "Trudy, the human mind
    is so-o-o strange."

I told 'em, "That's nothin' compared to
    the human genitals."
Next to my trances they love goin'
    through my shopping bags.
Once they found this old box of Cream of
    Wheat. I told 'em, "A
box of cereal." But they saw it as a picture
    of infinity. You know
how on the front is a picture of that guy
    holding up a box of
Cream of Wheat
and on *that* box is a picture of that guy
    holding up a box of
Cream of Wheat
and on *that* box is a picture of that guy
    holding up a box of
Cream of Wheat
and on *that* box is a picture of that guy
    holding up a box of
Cream of Wheat . . .

We think so different.

They find it hard to grasp some things
    that come easy to us,
because they simply don't have our frame
    of reference.
I show 'em this can of Campbell's tomato
    soup.
I say,
"This is soup."
Then I show 'em a picture of Andy
    Warhol's painting
of a can of Campbell's tomato soup.
I say,
"This is art."

"This is soup."

"And this is art."

Then I shuffle the two behind my back.

Now what is this?

No,
*this* is soup
and *this is art!* . . .

Hey, what's this?

"Dear Trudy, thanks for making our stay
    here so jam-packed and
fun-filled. Sorry to abort our mission—it
    is not over,
just temporarily scrapped.

We have orders to go to a higher
    bio-vibrational plane.

Just wanted you to know, the
    neurochemical imprints of our
cardiocortical experiences here on earth
    will remain with us
always, but what we take with us into
    space that we cherish the
most is the 'goose bump' experience."

Did I tell you what happened at the play?
    We were at the back
of the theater, standing there in the dark,
all of a sudden I feel one of 'em tug my
    sleeve,
whispers, "Trudy, look." I said, "Yeah,
    goose bumps. You
definitely
got goose bumps. You really like the play
    that much?" They said
it wasn't the play
gave 'em goose bumps,
it was the audience.

I forgot to tell 'em to watch the play;
    they'd been watching
the *audience*!

Yeah, to see a group of strangers sitting
    together in the dark,
laughing and crying about the same
    things . . . that just knocked
'em out.
They said, "Trudy,
the play was soup . . .
the audience . . .
art."

So they're taking goose bumps
home with 'em.
Goose bumps!
Quite a souvenir.

I like to think of them out there
in the dark, watching us.
Sometimes we'll do something and they'll
    laugh.
Sometimes we'll do something and they'll
    cry.
And maybe one day we'll do something
    so magnificent,
everyone in the universe will get
goose bumps.

# A Perspective for Understanding Self and Social Interaction

Social psychology is the study of the relationship between the individual and the rules and patterns that constitute society. Most sociologists and psychologists agree that human behavior is shaped to some extent by physiological, biological, and neurological properties that are beyond the scope of social psychology. However, social psychologists emphasize that the majority of the activities people engage in and encounter in others on a day-to-day basis constitute *social* behavior—behavior that is both influenced by and expressed through social interaction. Some of the questions that social psychologists ask are How does a person become "socialized"? What are the implications of human socialization for the transmission of culture? How does human action contribute to the production and reproduction of various social institutions?

There is no single answer to these questions. Rather, the answers depend on which group of social psychologists is responding and the context in which their knowledge was developed. Social psychology consists of different theoretical perspectives, each focused on a different version of "reality" regarding human activity and social institutions. This book is written according to a perspective known as *symbolic interactionism*. Although the many approaches to the study of human social behavior have their own strengths and limitations, we find symbolic interactionism to be the most useful perspective for our purposes. In Parts II through V, we will sketch the basic tenets of symbolic interactionism and demonstrate why we think it is a useful approach to the study of the ongoing relationship between the individual and society.

As a point of comparison (and to provide some context for symbolic interactionism as it is developed in this book), this essay will explore some basic themes and perspectives in social psychology. Our lists are not complete, and people with other purposes might offer other themes and perspectives. Nevertheless, our organization of the material represents the intellectual background from which many social psychological theories have developed.

Our discussion is organized around three major themes in the social sciences. If you understand these themes, you will have enough information to place most social psychological perspectives that you may encounter within the historical context from which they were developed. The three major themes addressed are (1) assumptions about human nature and society, (2) how we "know" things (epistemology), and (3) the issue of the (false) separation of the individual and society.

As you read about the themes, pay attention to the contrasts between symbolic interactionism and the other perspectives. It is helpful to imagine that each perspective is similar to a different pair of glasses. Ask yourself, "What do I see through this particular lens?" and "What *don't* I see?" Each perspective contains an untold story as well as the story that it explicitly represents.

## Theme One: Assumptions about Human Nature and Society

All theoretical perspectives are based on assumptions—unquestioned beliefs used as a foundation on which to construct a theory. Every theory must have a starting point, a point at which some central ideas are fixed for the purpose of pursuing the implications of the ideas. Proponents of various perspectives do not necessarily believe that these assumptions are true. They realize that such assumptions allow them to construct and solve puzzles. In order to comprehend and evaluate social theories, we need to know the assumptions on which the theory is based.

In addition, no program of study can pursue every possible line of thought. Therefore, different perspectives scrutinize specific aspects of the social story. Each theory allows us to observe details that might otherwise go unnoticed. Microbiologists, for instance, focus primarily on the cellular structure of the physical body in order to construct theories about how organisms behave; psychologists focus on the internal thoughts and impulses of individuals; sociologists emphasize groups of individuals. Each type of research gives primary emphasis to different units of analysis: cells, individuals, groups.

Researchers sometimes become so focused on their own unit of analysis that they forget it is part of a larger picture. Thus, you will note (even in this book) statements such as "The most interesting aspects of behavior are social." It would be just as easy to say that the most interesting aspects of behavior are biological—although, of course, we personally don't think so. The noteworthy point is that different perspectives give primacy to different aspects of behavior. To effectively evaluate a perspective, we need to be able to mentally locate the primary focus within its larger context—such as the cell within the organ of the body from which it was taken or individual psychology within a social context.

The debate about human nature and its relationship to society centers around two questions: What can be assumed about the human creature in order to build theories of behavior and society? And which aspects of behavior should be the primary focus in the study of the relationship between the individual and society? Social psychologists have addressed these questions from a variety of perspectives. Here we discuss three—utilitarianism, behaviorism, and the cognitive/interpretive perspective—before sketching the basic premises of symbolic interactionism.

## Utilitarianism

Several philosophers in the eighteenth and nineteenth centuries (such as Thomas Hobbes, Jeremy Bentham, John Stuart Mill, and Adam Smith) were interested in new forms of government that would provide peace and order for as many people as possible. These thinkers lived in times characterized by the upheaval and rapid changes forged by the industrial revolution. They were also reacting to social structures in which the many were ruled by a privileged few.

In theorizing about alternative forms of government, these philosophers began with the assumption, based on the writings of Aristotle, that humans have a rational nature. They postulated that the human creature is intelligent and self-interested and is thus motivated to achieve its desires in a pragmatic way. Conflict arises because, in the attempt to satisfy their own desires and pursue scarce resources, people often exploit and injure others.

Hobbes suggested that, because they are reasonable and know what is in their own best interest, people would cooperate with laws that provide order for all. In other words, humans are not dumb brutes who need to be ruled by an intelligent few (as Machiavelli, among others, had argued), but reasonable beings who govern themselves because they desire order. Without laws and order, each person has to be constantly alert to the possibility of attack. Such alertness and defense require a lot of energy and personal resources. Therefore, rational individuals would be willing to give up some degree of freedom, such as the right to harm others, in order to have a government to protect them.

A corresponding assumption of utilitarianism is that a person will pursue the course of action that is most likely to produce the greatest returns for the least cost. Behavior is therefore the result of cost/benefit analysis in the pursuit of desired ends.

From the utilitarian perspective, society consists of two or more individuals exchanging resources that have some value to each. How available a resource is and who holds the resource determine the structure of society. For example, if you own a small forest in an area where there is little wood, others may very well want to exchange something they own for some of your wood. One neighbor may offer you sheep in return for firewood. Another might offer wine in exchange for lumber. If you already have enough sheep of your own, you will probably opt to exchange your wood for wine. When you convert the trees from your forest into lumber, others may approach you to purchase lumber as well. If these exchanges are profitable, you might become a major producer of lumber over time. But to continue exchanging lumber for wine if another neighbor offered you a better deal for your wood would not be rational. The key point is that these exchange relationships are rational; they're based on the law of supply and demand and on rules of trade that promote free exchange.

Utilitarianism is a pillar of modern Western thought. For example, the discipline of economics is based on the utilitarian assumption that humans are rational beings, who calculate risks, costs, and benefits and make decisions accordingly. A major branch of political science is also founded on this tradition. Social psychologists whose research is based on the utilitarian perspective address such questions as how social order is possible among people with competing interests and how people establish power over others to get what they want. This tradition is known as *rational choice theory* in sociology and as *exchange theory* in social psychology.

All these versions of utilitarianism assume that people behave rationally to maximize the attainment of their desires at minimum costs. What their desires are often remains untold, although frequently they are assumed to include some form of material rewards and power. The key point is that these theories assume that individual action is rational. All these versions of utilitarianism also assume that social institutions emerge from rational exchange relationships. In other words, institutions exist and operate as they do because they meet the needs of rational human beings.

The utilitarian tradition does not attempt to explain how humans become rational calculators; it simply assumes that they are. One theoretical implication of utilitarianism is that those individuals who fail to act rationally will not be successful competitors in the exchange market. And because they are not successful, they will not exist as observable cases for a researcher to study. Therefore, theoretically speaking, the perspective needn't be concerned with nonrational actors because such actors, if they did exist, would eventually be weeded out of society. Another implication is that society is very fluid and changes constantly with the redistribution of tangible resources. One noteworthy contribution of utilitarian theory is the idea that we can figure out what people value by looking at what sorts of choices they make. This notion, which economists refer to as "revealed utility," holds that we can only know what a person *really* values when the person has to make a choice. When making a choice, people deliberate, and this process of deliberation reveals their preferences and values. Thus, there are no real values independent of choice-making actions.

The following theoretical perspectives derive from utilitarianism but specifically address questions of individual psychology. Behaviorism, which is closely related to utilitarianism, makes even fewer assumptions about human nature than its theoretical predecessor. The cognitive/interpretive perspective and symbolic interactionism, on the other hand, offer more complex theories of the individual and make different initial assumptions about human nature.

## Behaviorism

Behaviorism is a school of thought generally associated with B. F. Skinner, who assumed behavior to be hedonistic. In other words, humans and other animals seek pleasure and avoid punishment. This logic is similar to utilitarianism, except that it incorporates no assumptions about rational behavior. Organisms, including humans, simply become conditioned by particular stimuli and learn to behave in a manner that produces positive results and avoids negative ones.

Humans are socialized through a process that teaches them that certain actions are accompanied by punishments and certain actions are followed by rewards, or positive reinforcement. For example, if a child is repeatedly spanked for throwing food, the child will learn to associate the conduct with punishment and will avoid this behavior. When the child is rewarded for a behavior, such as successful toilet training, the child will repeat the behavior and thus become socialized to engage in acceptable behavior. In short, a person's behavior is predicted by the person's reinforcement history.

This relationship between the environment and behavior is often referred to as stimulus-response. A stimulus is anything in a person's environment that provokes an action (response). The environment includes internal physiology as well as external forces. Stimuli usually exist in a tangible form, such as food or money, although some researchers also recognize less-tangible stimuli, such as approval or affection.

According to behaviorism, human action can be, and often is, irrational, or "neurotic." Neurotic behavior is the result of conditioned responses to stimuli that may not actually be associated with the outcome but that the actor associates with the desired outcome because of prior conditioning. For example, an animal that has been trained (conditioned) by electric shock not to venture beyond specific boundaries will continue to stay within these boundaries, even when the electric shock is removed. Humans often engage in superstitious behaviors (such as wearing a lucky sweater for exams) in the neurotic belief that certain actions and outcomes are correlated. That is, if a person *perceives* a connection between a particular action and outcome, he or she will persist in the behavior in hopes of producing (or avoiding) the anticipated response.

Behaviorism and its derivative, social learning theory, constitute one building block in most of the predominant social psychology theories. The theories differ, however, with regard to whether a particular stimulus will produce the same response in all subjects. Some behaviorists think that all people desire certain "universal" or "objective" resources and that all avoid certain punishments. Something is said to be "objective" if its effect is independent of the subject's comprehension of it; it is "universal" if it produces the same response in all subjects. The pain of fire, for example, can be considered objective and universal; pain appears to occur in all who come into contact with a flame, regardless of the person's opinion or thoughts about fire.

On the other hand, money, which many assume to be a universal motivator, may have little or no effect on subjects who do not consider it to be important. In other words, the effect of money as a potential stimulus to action depends on a person's *subjective* interpretation of the stimulus. Let's say that a researcher places a subject in a situation where she is predicted to cheat an acquaintance in order to get money. If the subject wants to be seen as a good person more than she wants the money, she may respond in a manner that contradicts the researcher's predictions. Behavior based on subjective perceptions can be predicted only if the researcher knows what the person values, which can be very difficult to ascertain.

Nonetheless, all variants of social psychology assume, in some form, that behavior is based on the desire to gain rewards and avoid punishments. But just what these rewards and punishments are and how the researcher should figure them out is a complex puzzle.

Behaviorism does not offer much of a picture of society. It assumes pre-existing socialized beings, who socialize the next generations through conditioned stimulus-response patterns. (How the first humans became socialized and why they valued certain things are questions that are addressed by evolutionary anthropologists and biologists, among others.) The primary emphasis in behaviorism is on the individual's reinforcement history—in other words, the patterns of learning achieved through the application of particular rewards and punishments. Why, for example, humans in each culture prefer to wear particular types of clothing and why some costumes convey different impressions and are accorded more prestige than others is not a story that can be told from the behaviorist perspective. The story that can be told is how people learn that they must wear clothes if they wish to avoid punishment, such as being spanked or jailed, and that certain clothes bring rewards, such as popularity and dates.

This perspective offers the possibility that one might construct an "ideal" society and train people to behave in a manner that supports its ideals. In *Walden Two* (1976), which was very influential during the 1970s, Skinner illustrates the construction of a utopian society based on "behavioral engineering." His premise is that with the right "reinforcement schedule" (that is, behavioral engineering) people can be taught to engage in socially desirable activities and to avoid socially undesirable actions.

Although we do not offer a full review here, the theories of Freud are a useful point of comparison. In contrast to the behaviorists, Sigmund Freud and his followers argue that behavior is largely the result of *unconscious* desires and impulses that arise in the human psyche. From this perspective, Skinner's utopian society is doomed to failure, because people can never be perfectly socialized. Unconscious desires and impulses, such as sexuality and aggression, counteract the effects of even the most careful behavioral conditioning. Thus, the Freudian perspective sees humans as nonrational and unlikely to act on a reasonable calculation of costs and benefits—quite the opposite of the utilitarian view. Freudians believe that most behavior is an attempt to arrive at some tolerable compromise between the impulses that surge through our unconscious and the desire to live within the boundaries established by our social community.

Freud was one of the first researchers to direct his attention to the human unconscious. In so doing, he unlocked a black box previously ignored by most students of human social behavior. Behaviorists discount the distinction between the conscious and the unconscious. They prefer to focus on the link between an observable stimulus and an observable response. In conversation with a Freudian, a behaviorist might say that unconscious impulses are simply a form of stimulus—in this case, an internal rather than an external stimulus. The important feature for the behaviorist is what happens to a person when he or she acts on impulse. Is the behavior punished and thereby eventually extinguished, or is it rewarded and therefore repeated?

Freud might not have disagreed with this analysis, but he wanted to document what human impulses and drives consist of and how the contradictions inherent in these forces are reconciled through human development. That is, his agenda was to demonstrate that civilization is the product of our attempt to temper and harness our unruly impulses. Social institutions exist to bring some modicum of order where there would otherwise be only the chaos of beasts raping and murdering one another. At the same time, although we may become socialized, we may never fully be reconciled to the "rules" of society.

### The Cognitive/Interpretive Perspective

Another perspective that offers a more complex view of human beings than that assumed by the utilitarians or the behaviorists is the cognitive/interpretive approach. In addition to examining the human psyche, it examines human thought processes, or *cognition.*

Many researchers who agree with the basic proposition of behaviorism—behavior is the result of learning which actions produce pain and which ones produce rewards—also conclude that most forms of stimuli are subjective rather than objective. In other words, the way a person responds to a stimulus depends on how the person *interprets* the stimulus. For example, a person who is hugged will respond differently if the hug is interpreted as an aggressive clinch than if it is thought to be a show of affection. Same stimulus, different subjective interpretations, different responses.

Cognitive social psychologists believe that interpretation—in other words, thought—intervenes between the stimulus and response. The thought processes include paying attention to certain information, storing it, and later recalling it. That is, according to most variants of this perspective, behavior is the result of an individual's selective interpretation of the stimulus. For example, it's not likely that you would drool in anticipation if offered a beetle burrito. But some people, as discussed in the essay "What Is Real?" (page 3), consider a tortilla filled with beetles a delicacy and would respond with enthusiasm. Again, same stimulus, different subjective interpretations, different responses. (We say a great deal more about the process of interpretation in the essay that accompanies Part II.)

Another element of the cognitive/interpretive perspective concerns the question of whether humans are capable of rational thought. In a major research program conducted over the past three decades, two cognitive social psychologists, Daniel Kahnemann and Amos Tversky, have explored this question (Tversky, Kahnemann, & Slovic, 1982). One assumption of rationality is that, if you prefer A to B and B to C, then you should prefer A to C. Kahnemann and Tversky decided to test this assumption, known as *transitivity.* In one experiment, people were asked to select panty hose from a variety of styles and colors. The experiments demonstrated that people who preferred panty hose A to panty hose B and panty hose B to panty hose C did not necessarily prefer A to C. In fact, after having selected A in the choice between A and B and B in the choice between B and C, many participants selected C when given a choice between A and C. In other words, someone who claims to prefer nylon to wool and wool to cotton will presumably prefer nylon to cotton as well. But Kahnemann and Tversky demonstrated that this is not necessarily the case. Many people who preferred nylon to wool and wool to cotton selected cotton in the choice between cotton and nylon.

In another study, a group of researchers observed that even the ability to perform complex mathematical calculations depends on context (Lave, 1988). Women who performed poorly on written math exams were tested on the same skills while grocery shopping. These woman performed very rational calculations while shopping for the best bargains. Conversely, men who performed well on written math tests but whose wives generally did the shopping did not fare well in locating bargains at the grocery store. The same cognitive skill operated differently in different contexts.

Another assumption of rationality that has not held up to experimental scrutiny is decision making based on the laws of probability. Consider this test. A researcher holds 100 cards that contain short biographical statements taken from 30 engineers and 70 lawyers. The following card is selected at random and read: "Bob is in his middle 40s. He enjoys mathematical puzzles, dislikes social gatherings, and likes to build model trains." Is Bob a lawyer or an engineer? Most people guess that he is an engineer. Yet, based on probability, the most rational guess is that he is a lawyer. The tendency to guess Bob's profession based on types of behavior or activities associated with certain professions is a form of stereotyping, which is very different from applying the laws of rational probability.

Social cognition is the manner in which people impose preexisting categories of thought—schemas—on the stimuli in their environment and use these categories to select what to pay attention to, how to interpret the information, and whether to store it in and recall it from memory. In one study of schemas, subjects were shown a film of a woman and a man having a celebration dinner. Half the subjects were told that the woman was a librarian; the others were told that she was a waitress. When asked later to recall details from the film, the subjects recalled information consistent with role schemas: for example, that the librarian wore glasses and mentioned a trip to Europe or that the waitress liked to bowl and drink beer. The subjects not only recalled information consistent with their preestablished stereotypes, but actually made up information that affirmed these schemas as well. For example, subjects reported that the waitress ate a hamburger. Those believing her to be a librarian reported that she ate roast beef. But in the film, she ate neither (Cohen, 1981).

The implication is not that people lie or make things up but rather that perception is influenced by social categories and is a constructive as well as an interpretive process. This perspective also implies that society "exists" in the structure of a person's thoughts.

But if social institutions are individually relative, then how do human groups come to have the shared perceptions and interpretations necessary for communication and the transmission of culture? The cognitive/interpretive perspective theorizes that our social group is the source of our shared schemas. The untold story is how the ideas of "society" get into human minds and influence individual perceptions to begin with. We have placed the term *society* in quotes here to underscore another point regarding the cognitive conception of society—the idea that society is somehow "out there," independent of human actors but able to shape and direct human thought. In addition, because of its emphasis on human thought processes, the cognitive/interpretive perspective has not focused much on actual human behavior. It assumes that thoughts somehow predict behavior. However, without a more developed idea of the relationship between thought and behavior, this perspective cannot easily explain how human actions lead to social patterns.

## Symbolic Interactionism

The foregoing theoretical traditions each have a different view of human nature and focus on different aspects of the relationship between the individual and society. The utilitarian tradition depicts human beings as rational calculators; thus the primary lines of inquiry are the implications of the exchange of goods between rational actors and the effect of these economic exchanges on the structure of society. Behaviorists view the human being as the sum of a history of rewards and punishment. Each person learns to pursue certain lines of action and to avoid others. Social behavior within any particular group is the result of this conditioned learning. Theoretically it should be possible, according to this perspective, to "engineer" different types of social behavior that would result in alternative types of societies. Utilitarians and behaviorists emphasize observable actions and are interested in the effects of these actions on the social environment. In contrast, Freudians and cognitive/interpretivists focus on internal processes. Freudians are interested in how unconscious impulses are dealt with in the process of socializing the human into a healthy adult. Cognitive/interpretivists focus on human thought. For them, a central line of inquiry is how people make sense of the stimuli they encounter, how they perceive and deal with the environment in an organized fashion.

This book presents social psychology from the perspective of symbolic interactionism. This perspective depicts the production of society as an ongoing process of negotiation among social actors. Like the cognitive/interpretive perspective, symbolic interactionism suggests that the potential for society exists in the minds of people who share common expectations about reality. Society is enacted in momentary, situational encounters among humans. In other words, there is no society independent of the human mind and human expressions of culture. The implication, in a strict theoretical sense, is that humans exist as embryonic potential and that anything the mind can conceive is possible. However, symbolic interactionists point out that humans limit these possibilities by creating and maintaining social boundaries that make life orderly and predictable.

Two main points are worth underlining. One is that stable patterns of interaction among human beings can be observed. These patterns, which include relationships of power, affection, exchange, and so forth, give meaning to social existence—they constitute social structure. The second point is that, enduring as these patterns may seem, they are fragile in that they require the constant coordination by and shared understanding from the people involved to maintain them. The tacit compliance of each of the participants is what makes social patterns endure.

Symbolic interactionism shares with utilitarianism the assumption that humans are motivated to make practical use of the things they encounter in their environment (including other people). According to the symbolic interactionist, people may not be necessarily *rational*, but they are *pragmatic*. Humans attempt to mold the environment to their own ends. Symbolic interactionists assume that the ends a person desires and the means he or she employs to achieve these ends are based on socially constructed meanings. Anthropologists—who also study human groups—have long debated whether human interactions should be viewed primarily as an exchange of utilities or as an exchange of socially meaningful symbols. The difference between symbolic interactionists and utilitarians is that the latter focus on the exchange of tangible resources that have some intrinsic utility, whereas the former focus on the exchange of symbolically meaningful items and actions. From the utilitarian perspective, the value of an item used in exchange is in its potential use—for example, as food or currency. Symbolic interactionists would view an item used in exchange in terms of the symbolic gesture it communicates, such as a show of respect, friendship, or solidarity. They consider exchange to be one line of action that occurs within the more general ceremony constituting social life. From the symbolic interactionist perspective, the exchange of utilities would not be possible without the underlying "trust" that exists among those who share the same social expectations.

Unlike utilitarians, symbolic interactionists make no assumptions about rationality, except insofar as rationality constitutes a set of cultural expectations (in modern culture, we are *expected* to be rational). Another significant feature that symbolic interactionism shares with utilitarian theory is the assumption that deliberations—pragmatic choices—*reveal* something about what a person values and how they make sense of their circumstances. For instance, if you are deliberating between reading this text and going to a movie with friends, ask yourself whether your decision to read the text is based on your desire to enhance your knowledge (one type of motivation) or your desire to get a good grade on an exam (an altogether different motivation). You may in fact be influenced by both forms of motivation. The point is that you can probably learn more about yourself by focusing on the sorts of deliberations you make than you can by simply responding to a question such as "Do you value education?" When you deliberate and make pragmatic decisions, you are doing so in accordance with your understanding of a particular context.

This deliberative process also shares common assumptions with behaviorism. When you deliberate, you are considering possible rewards and punishments and weighing the pros and cons. This is actually a cognitive-emotive process, but it reflects your particular "reinforcement history." What do you perceive to be rewarding or punishing? What has occurred to you in the past and what systems of belief do you hold that lead you to these particular assessments?

Symbolic interactionism is similar to behaviorism in emphasizing that human action is motivated by a desire to seek rewards and to avoid punishments. However, symbolic interactionists study the *interactional context;* that is, they study how participants in an interaction negotiate the meaning of the situation to get one another to respond in a desirable way. The emphasis on meaning negotiated through interaction is a more social focus than the individual stimulus-response patterns studied by behaviorists.

Symbolic interactionists acknowledge (in concert with Freudians) that humans are bundles of drives and impulses. Both theories emphasize the manner in which humans learn to observe, comment on, and direct their own impulses. Deliberation can be seen as an internal conversation in which the person is considering whether and how to bring their behavior into line with the expectations of others (a specific reference group).

The symbolic interactionist portrays humans as creatures who are reasonable and pragmatic in the pursuit of rewards and the avoidance of punishment. People learn which behaviors produce which outcomes by observing their own actions and other's reactions. The point to underscore is that symbolic interactionism focuses on subjective interpretations of events that occur in an *interactional* context. The assumption is that, whether we are dealing with someone face to face or having an internal dialogue with an imagined other, most human activity involves evaluating how to respond to others in specific contexts. In this regard, symbolic interaction is the most social of the social psychologies.

The important questions of study from this perspective are what meaning people give to a social context and how they negotiate and enact this meaning through interaction with others. For this reason, symbolic interactionists talk of "performing reality." Society consists of an ongoing, negotiated performance of socially meaningful interactions.

Two points are noteworthy regarding symbolic interactionism in contrast to other social psychological perspectives and the major themes of debate:

1. Symbolic interactionism gives primacy to the social situation over individual psychology. In other words, behavior is assumed to be organized primarily in response to social factors.
2. The focus of study is on observable behavior, but the cause of this behavior is assumed to be nonobservable processes of individual interpretation. In other words, behavior is based on subjective interpretation of the social environment instead of being a direct response to objective stimuli.

## Theme Two: Epistemology

How do we "know" things? How do we discover "truth"? Can the methods of science uncover the "real" truth? In Reading 3 on "truth," Earl Babbie suggests that what we take to be truth is a matter of agreement based on shared rules of what is real. This holds for science as well as for superstitious beliefs. For a long time, scientists believed in a universal "truth" and sought the underlying natural patterns that would reveal this truth. The metaphor that guided their inquiries was that of a watch or clock: They saw the universe as a grand watch ticking merrily away. The scientist's job was to take it apart piece by piece in order to figure out how this amazing machine worked. It's probably no historical accident that this perspective developed alongside the rise of industrial mechanization in the eighteenth and nineteenth centuries.

In the twentieth century, however, physicists, including Werner Heisenberg and Albert Einstein, began to question the possibility of a universal, objective "truth." They observed that different experiments designed to address the same question yielded different results, depending on how the question was asked. For example, when light was hypothesized to be waves, the experiments produced a pattern that suggested it was waves. But when light was hypothesized to be particles, the tests revealed a pattern of particles. Was it possible that light was both wave and particle, both energy and matter, at the same time? Heisenberg concluded that the experimental process itself interacts with reality, that there is no completely objective stance from which to view truth (Biggs & Peat, 1984). That is, scientists shape the outcome to some extent by their interaction with the phenomenon. Einstein summarized: "It is the theory that determines what we can observe."

These observations set the stage for the contemporary debate between those who practice science, with the goal of discovering and verifying truth (sometimes referred to as "positivism"), and those who argue that truth is relative—in the case of science, relative to the theories themselves (constructivism). That is, theories do not reflect "natural" reality. They are a social construction. The philosophy underlying positivism is that natural laws govern the universe and that these laws can be known. The philosophy underlying what came to be known as constructivism is that any order we perceive in nature is the product of our own perspectives for organizing the "facts," or theories. In other words, our theories do not simply verify or refute reality; they actually interact with the observed phenomenon to construct a truth that reflects the original perspective.

### The Symbolic Interactionist View

Symbolic interactionism is a constructivist perspective. According to this perspective, knowledge, including scientific knowledge, is *subjective*, the product of the context within which it was constructed. Humans do not experience the world in its natural state. We do not gather and observe "facts" that interpret themselves; rather, the selection and interpretation of data are based on classification schemes constructed by the observers. No matter how logical and insightful these schemes are, they influence how we make sense of the data and how we arrive at conclusions about "truth."

The case of Copernicus, who was able to convince some of his fellow astronomers in the 1500s that the earth revolved around the sun rather than the other way around, is an example of the relationship between scientific discovery and sociohistorical context. During the time of Copernicus, most people believed that the sun and all other planets known to exist in the heavens circled the earth. This belief was based on mathematical calculations made by Ptolemy in the second century A.D. Several of Copernicus's contemporaries suspected, based on years of charting the movement of the planets, that the earth might actually revolve around the sun. However, the language of the day (the dominant system of thought characterizing the historical epoch) incorporated Ptolemy's scheme of mathematics because it supported the Catholic theology that the earth was the center of the universe and humans the center of all things. Most mathematical calculations, the predominant method for charting the movement of celestial bodies, were based on this theory and in turn supported it.

Copernicus was successful in launching a scientific revolution not because he gathered new empirical evidence that demonstrated conclusively the earth's movement around the sun, but because he developed a mathematical statement that suggested this to be the case. He used the perspective of the time, with a slightly new twist, to advance an alternative theory. The lesson is that existing systems of thought can be used either to affirm or to alter a particular version of scientific truth. The accuracy of a scientific proposition is assessed by the prevailing standards of the time. These standards are also shaped by perspectives. Copernicus was able to reach his colleagues by using the shared language of their knowledge to cast new light on an old question. He met with resistance from the church, however, because his "findings" did not coincide with another, very powerful perspective of the day. A century later, even with the evidence of his telescope to back him up, Galileo was still made to recant similar assertions that the earth revolved around the sun when the church found them to be "incorrect" according to its standards.

A more recent example from paleontology shows how existing classification schemes shape scientific discoveries. In the book *It's a Wonderful Life* (1989), evolutionary biologist, paleontologist, and natural history essayist Stephen Jay Gould tells the story of the Burgess Shale. This limestone quarry, which was formed more than 530 million years ago, supported more life forms than can be found in the oceans today. The Burgess Shale was discovered by modern paleontologists in 1909. According to Gould, its discovery could have changed our entire understanding of biological evolution. However, the first discoverers classified every fossil according to a pre-existing taxonomy, which consisted of only two categories: worms and arthropods. This scheme supported the two dominant perspectives in the study of human evolution: the hierarchical, "ladder of progress" theory (that humans are the ultimate goal/result of evolution) and the "inverted cone" theory (which holds that creatures evolve with increasing diversity and complexity). Gould points out that the first taxonomists were unable to "see" the richness of the Burgess Shale because they were "trapped by history. . . . The familiar iconographies of evolution are all directed toward reinforcing a comfortable view of human inevitability and superiority. The comfortably familiar becomes a prison of thought" (p. 1).

An alternative classification scheme might have enabled paleontologists to see evidence for a different set of theories. For example, a more recent theory, which acknowledges the rich diversity of the species fossilized in the Burgess Shale, does not assume the superiority of human evolution. Instead, its model is an "incredibly prolific bush," in which branches occupied by particular species either break off, branch out, or continue. From this theoretical vantage point, human evolution is an awesome improbability, not an inevitable truth.

So the Burgess Shale fossils were first classified according to theories that assumed the superior nature of the human species, a theme prevalent in the early part of this century. More recently, the fossils have been reclassified, this time according to theories that question assumptions of human superiority. Which perspective is correct? Symbolic interactionists would say that both are "correct" according to the criteria for scientific research holding sway when the classification schemes were developed. The two classifications of the Burgess Shale are consistent with the perspectives of their respective dates of publication.

This story illustrates that "evidence" is inevitably classified and interpreted. The theories that shape the process of classification and interpretation determine the picture of reality that emerges, because these systems of thought provide a lens through which to collect, organize, and interpret the information. The implication then is that scientific knowledge is not a direct representation of the natural world but is based on systems of thought that are culturally and historically bound. Thus, theoretical perspectives generally reflect the prevalent paradigms of thought that characterize a particular culture at a particular time in its history. The following points summarize the symbolic interactionist position regarding the debate over the pursuit of scientific truth:

- Scientific communities create and affirm systems of thought, known as theoretical paradigms, that shape what we can know and how we can know it.

- These theories are socially constructed and reflect the historical context in which they are developed.
- Symbolic interactionism uses *interpretive* methodologies in the behavioral sciences. The researcher attempts to take the perspective of the subject and to interpret the context in which the behavior takes place. Some of the methods used to gather information about human relations include fieldwork, interviews, and participant observation. The point is to seek human truths as they are understood and enacted by the subject.

## Theme Three: The False Separation of the Individual and Society

One of the main tasks of social psychology is to articulate the relationship between society and the individual. The relevant questions are: How does society influence individual action? and How does individual action shape society? One of the dominant assumptions about what human nature is and how to study it is rational individualism. "Rationality" is one shutter on the window of reality (to use Babbie's metaphor) that pervades modern Western thought. Another shutter on the window of reality in our culture is "individualism"— the ideal that individual rights should supersede those of any controlling agency or force; a corollary is the ideal that each individual is responsible for her or his own circumstances.

The twin concepts of rationality and individualism constitute the foundation of legal and political institutions in the United States. Sometimes these concepts also drive research in the social sciences instead of being a subject of inquiry. That is, instead of scrutinizing the extent to which the perspective of rational individualism shapes, and perhaps even obscures, Americans' view of reality, social scientists sometimes make the mistake of assuming that rational individualism *is* reality.

Rational individualism is a pervasive perspective of modern Western culture. Consider how this perspective shapes social science as well as your own world view. Ponder the following questions: Who are you really? Are you a product of your social group, or are you the result of some independent genetic, psychological, or perhaps even spiritual factors? How did you get to be you? Would you be different if your significant associations were another family and other friends than those you now have? What if you had been raised in another culture? How much are you aware of the influence of others in shaping who you are and what you think you can do and be?

---

In 1954, social psychologists Kuhn and McPartland published what they called the "twenty statements test." They asked people to give twenty responses to the question "Who am I?" Most people can do so quickly, without thinking too hard about the question. What Kuhn and McPartland noted was that the answers people gave tended to fall into two categories: social roles (e.g., mother, son, sister, boyfriend, student, politician) or personality expressions (e.g., happy, friendly, helpful, trustworthy, generous). What's interesting about this list is that it reveals that the ways in which people see themselves involve reference to others. You can't be a father without a child to be a father to. Nor can you be "friendly" without someone to be friendly toward and/or someone who has let you know that they consider you to be friendly. Yet, despite the fact that we tend to see ourselves through these social categories and social relations, the prevailing notion in U.S. culture is that the individual is an autonomous island who is (or at least should be) relatively free of social influence.

How does an individual achieve her or his individuality? A survey of popular culture gives the impression that Americans are "endowed" with a spirit of individualism. A pervasive plot in American media concerns the individual pitted against collective forces of evil that threaten to destroy individuality. In film and literature, the individual-as-hero begins to take on shape and definition in the struggle against social forces. The forces themselves are often only a fuzzy background against which the individual can be sharply defined. In many instances, this struggle can be interpreted as the attainment of personal distinction by casting off social chains and rising above one's "background." Indeed, the quest of the U.S. individual may be said to be achieving separation from her or his cultural history. To admit to being a product of social forces is to suggest that one is a cultural sheep. It is preferable to see oneself as having achieved individual distinction through psychological and spiritual struggle. This is the myth of individualism that permeates U.S. culture.

There is evidence that average people act in accordance with this myth. Social psychologists demonstrated some years ago that people are inclined to attribute observed behaviors to individual agency rather than to social or environmental factors. For example, if someone performs poorly on an exam, the cause is likely to be seen as lack of intelligence or lack of studying—that is, as individual ability or choice. The likelihood that poor performance might be due to the exam's cultural bias (a social factor), which might make it difficult for some people to interpret the questions, is often not considered to be a possible explanation. Similarly, if one person is observed hitting another, we are likely to assume that the person is angry or hostile,

myth of individualism

has a short temper, and lacks self-control. We will probably assume that the behavior is connected to certain "personality traits." The possibility that the person was induced to act aggressively through the dynamics of the situation often doesn't enter into our assessment. This tendency to assume individual responsibility over social forces is known as the *fundamental attribution error*. People are more likely to attribute behaviors to individual personality and character traits than to social context.

In recent years, some researchers have suggested that the fundamental attribution error is a U.S. phenomenon (for example, Hewstone, 1983). People in other cultures do not tend to make such individualistic judgments when trying to explain things. This tendency underscores the U.S. cultural attitude that single, individual actions are the primary forces shaping the world. Several observers and critics have also noted that the myth of individualism pervades the U.S. study of social behavior and organizations. The criticism is that individual psychology and development, not environmental factors (particularly social context), are presumed to explain social behavior. European social psychologists criticize their counterparts in the United States for this imbalance between individual psychology and social context.

A popular joke told by sociologists illuminates this imbalance. It goes like this: A person visits a therapist and complains of extreme distress and the inability to function well in his daily tasks. He appears very agitated and disoriented. Therapist A spends several years delving into the client's past, with special emphasis on the person's relationship with his mother. Therapist B administers a battery of psychological tests and conducts in-depth interviews with the client in order to comprehend how he perceives his role vis-à-vis his employer, his wife, and significant private events in his life. This therapy takes several months. Therapist C notices immediately that the patient is presenting serious symptoms of psychological disillusionment, diagnoses the person as schizophrenic, and has him hospitalized. Therapist D asks the client what sorts of things have occurred in his life recently. The distressed man reports that his wife died recently, he was fired from his job a week ago, his kitchen caught fire the previous evening, and his tire blew out driving to the therapist's office. Therapist D informs him that he is suffering from an overload of stressful events and suggests that he take a vacation.

In this scenario, each therapist interprets the situation from the perspective of her or his own training. Therapist A, a Freudian, is inclined to see the man's distress as the result of unresolved psychological impulses and early childhood relations with his parents. Therapist B represents the contemporary cognitive psychologist, who is sympathetic to the man's interpretations of his situation but is overly concerned with cognitive functioning at the expense of social context. Therapist C, a psychiatrist, diagnoses the symptoms that are present in the immediate situation from a medical perspective and disregards their causes. Only Therapist D, trained as a sociologist, is inclined to see the extent to which contextual factors may be responsible for the man's immediate emotional state and behavior.

The utilitarian perspective is represented by each of the therapists as well as the client. In all cases, it is assumed that the man is not behaving as he should. In other words, his ability to reason and to act responsibly are in question. Regardless of the type of treatment prescribed, all therapists agree that he needs treatment to restore his abilities as a rational actor. This unquestioned assumption speaks to the utilitarian underpinnings of Western civilization. Rationality and individualism are the twin pillars of our cultural foundation.

Each of these therapists is a stereotype, of course. But the point is important. Even those who study and treat human behavior often fail to recognize the influence of social context. Psychologists and social psychologists do not necessarily intend to perpetuate individualism. However, they may do so inadvertently when they fail to examine how much the myth of the independent individual pervades their initial assumptions.

One reason for this emphasis on the individual over the social in U.S. social psychology is that these disciplines have themselves been shaped by the cultural context in which they developed. The "cult of individualism," as it is sometimes referred to, represents society as an alien entity that somehow exists independent of human activity. Social forces are something to break away from in order to pursue individual interests. Ironically, the theoretical disciplines that place so much emphasis on human psychology have so separated the individual from society that they cannot explain how human action contributes to the construction of the social world.

The philosophy of individualism implies that social factors shape the individual in ways that hinder or constrain individual freedom. The moral implication is that we must break away from these chains. This line of reasoning assumes that something significant about human social behavior is not social. Herein lies a paradox. If we break away from social chains, we are left with a bundle of passions. A creature that is a bundle of passions cannot assess or direct its own behavior. Such a creature has no potential to become an individual hero, because it cannot take responsibility for its own behavior.

The U.S. legal system distinguishes between those who are capable of understanding the rules of society and those who are deemed incompetent to stand trial because they cannot comprehend the rules. The criminally insane are judged "asocial." The rest of us are judged to be competent players who are capable of governing our behavior in accord with the rules of society. Whether we choose to obey or disobey the law, we make a choice, incorporating general social standards into our decision making. Similarly, in the various ways in which we exercise freedom of choice by breaking away from social norms, we are using these social rules as a standard. Without these social standards, what would be our basis for self-evaluation and action? Social rules provide the structure that enables us to organize our bundle of passions into meaningful behavior, including behavior that we interpret as "breaking away." Without such structure, we would have no basis for aligning our behavior with those around us; we would be cut off from our fellow beings, and free agency would be a moot point.

This philosophy suggests that humans are social creatures, that we use shared social standards to shape and evaluate our own actions. These standards coordinate the activity of creatures who would be otherwise isolated. To pursue the implications of this assumption requires a theory that merges the social and the individual into one. The utilitarian, behaviorist, and cognitive/interpretive perspectives, although each has many merits, all isolate the individual from society and represent society as something apart from us, something that exists "out there." In contrast, the theoretical challenge that underlies this book is how to account for the mutual relationship between individual human actors and society. This theory must be capable of telling us how social standards shape the development of the individual and how, in turn, individual actions contribute to the maintenance or alteration of these standards.

Social standards are relative; they vary from culture to culture. These standards do not exist independent of the social groups who believe in them and act them out. Rationality is not "out there" waiting to bite us on the nose. We are not born with the characteristics of individuality. Paradoxical as it may seem, we develop our "individuality" in the process of being socialized into American culture. Similarly, a Japanese person who develops a sense of "groupness" does so in the process of becoming socialized into her or his culture. Thus, neither individualism nor groupness is more correct or "real" than the other. Which one we are inclined to emphasize depends on our cultural point of view. From the perspective of many Americans, groupness threatens individual freedom. From the perspective of cultures that espouse groupness, however, too much unchecked individual selfishness threatens the long-term interests of everyone in the group.

Our intent here is not to make the case for either individuality or groupness, but to suggest that to understand human social behavior we must focus on the social context of the behavior. Social factors shape our perspective of reality and thereby influence how we act. Even theories of human behavior and society are influenced by general social factors, such as the cultural standards of individuality and rationality. Therefore, to more fully understand the relationship between the individual and society, we must make these cultural standards explicit and attempt to transcend them in our analysis. The point is that individualism is a socially constructed value. It is a set of shared cultural standards by which we as Americans knowingly, or unknowingly, shape our behavior. For instance, regardless of whether you have a "rational reason" for engaging in an enjoyable activity, as a member of a rationalist culture, you must invent such a reason. How often have you not done something pleasurable because you didn't have a good enough rationale? Treating individualism as a social construction enables us to better study the rules we use as social creatures to determine our own behavior.

Ironically, the standard of individual rationality, which presumably gives us the freedom that we so value as Americans, may actually hinder and constrain our behavioral possibilities. To the extent that we assume individualism is a given and necessary aspect of society, we may fail to notice the way in which it limits other possible lines of action.

Unlike the other perspectives, symbolic interactionism recognizes the themes of rationality and individualism as topics of study rather than as assumed states of being or components of a necessary political philosophy. Symbolic interactionism gives theoretical primacy to social situations rather than to the individual. Seen from this perspective, rational individualism is a form of social institution that characterizes Western civilization, particularly contemporary U.S. society. Individualism is therefore a cultural script. This script, which is learned through a process of socialization, tells Americans that the pursuit of individual distinction through rational actions is socially rewarding. In another culture, such pursuits might elicit punishment rather than reward. The point is that people are not inherently rational, nor are they necessarily predisposed to value the individual over the collective; these are culturally specific values.

## Reading Notes for Understanding Symbolic Interactionism

To conclude Part I, we offer the following "reading notes" based on our experience teaching this material. Students of this material sometimes fall into the traps of "psychologism" and "reification" as a consequence of the false separation of individual and social forces.

## Psychologism

Social psychologists who study human cognition note that each of us has a tendency to interpret information in terms of its specific relevance to our own experiences. This information-processing bias is termed *psychologism* (or the self-consensus bias). Psychologism, when coupled with the American ideal of individualism, makes it difficult for students to comprehend theories that pertain to the social group. The tendency is to interpret and evaluate the information offered by these theories in terms of individual psychology and experience: "Does the theoretical perspective match my personal situation?"

Many people view theories that emphasize group knowledge and socialization as antithetical to their own individuality. But this separation of individual and group is based on a false dichotomy. As we discuss throughout this book, there is no possibility of the concept of the "individual" (including individual rights, feelings, and so forth) without the social group.

Remember that you do not have to deny personal experience in order to explore the implications of group knowledge. The question to ask yourself is "How might collective meanings and social interactions shape how I see the world and how I act?" What humans do in interaction with others may or may not be harmonious with their private thoughts. However, and this is the point to emphasize, whether or not people accept or believe in their own public actions, these actions are observable by others and come to be real in their consequences.

## Reification

*Reification* means to treat an abstract concept as if it were real, independent of human activity. For example, people tend to think of "IQ" as a real thing that exists inside our brains and shapes our intelligence. In fact, IQ is simply a score derived from a battery of tests that are not meaningful beyond their direct application. In spite of this, parents and educators often act "as if" IQ is real and make decisions accordingly. Similarly, people sometimes treat sociological concepts—for example, norms—as if they were physical structures that exist somewhere in a state of nature and "do" things to humans. When a concept is reified, or given a life of its own, we tend to forget the extent to which our own beliefs and actions contribute to the construction and perpetuation of the processes described by the concept. Thus students are inclined to write papers in which they make claims such as "Society causes people to be poor."

It's more than a little bit ironic that we tend to think of ourselves as *individuals* who are entirely free of social influence and, at the same time, see many social forces and their consequences for other people as if the forces had a life of their own. This way of thinking reflects a kind of social illiteracy, whereby we fail to see just how firmly entrenched certain social "rules" are and how they shape our personal lives, and at the same time fail to see how our own behavior reflects and contributes to the perpetuation of these social forces. The false separation of the individual and society deters us from a comprehensive and complex understanding of the ways in which we are both products of and producers of society.

Symbolic interactionism offers a way to reconcile the false separation of the individual and society. The perspective teaches us that social reality is the product of coordinated activity among real individuals. The puzzle is how abstract concepts are communicated, shared, and reproduced and how they take on patterns of stability that make them appear "real." The enduring, stable character of social interaction is what we come to know, in a reified way, as "society."

## Conclusion

Symbolic interactionism is conducted at the intersection of individuals and society. From this perspective, it is not possible to make sense of one without incorporating the other. The challenge for symbolic interactionism has been to represent society in a way that avoids reification—in other words, to model social patterns and relationships as the products of ongoing individual activity. At the same time, symbolic interactionism must account for the observation that existing social patterns do influence and constrain individual actions. The ultimate aim of symbolic interactionism, as presented in this book, is to place the individual and society on the same level and to analyze the reciprocal relationships between individual action and social patterns and institutions. Social life is conceived as a dynamic web of reciprocal influences among members of a social group. This web is made up of the interactions of individuals. Individuals spin and respin the web. At the same time, they are influenced by the existing patterns of previously spun strands.

Symbolic interactionism is unique in the study of both psychology and sociology in that it is the only perspective that assumes an active, expressive model of the human actor and treats the individual and the social at the same level of analysis. In gaining an understanding of this perspective, think in terms of process and feedback. This viewpoint is admittedly more complicated than representing social life in terms of simple dichotomies and cause-and-effect reasoning. However, in reality individual existence and social patterns are mutually constitutive—the relationship between the individual and society is reciprocal. Symbolic interactionism offers a rich story about human behavior and its social consequences. We think you will find this story to be instructive and relevant to your personal life and the social world in which you are a participant.

## References

Babbie, E. (1986). *Observing ourselves: Essays in social research.* Belmont, CA: Wadsworth.

Biggs, J., & Peat, D. (1984). *Looking glass universe: The emerging science of wholeness.* New York: Simon & Schuster.

Cohen, C. (1981). Person categories and social perception: Testing some boundaries of the processing effects of prior knowledge. *Journal of Personality and Social Psychology, 40,* 441–452.

Gould, S. J. (1989). *It's a wonderful life: The Burgess Shale and the nature of history.* New York: Norton.

Hewstone, M. (Ed.). (1983). *Attribution theory: Social and functional extensions.* Oxford: Basil Blackwell.

Kuhn, M., & T. McPartland. (1954). An empirical investigation of self-attitude. *American Sociological Review 19,* 68–76.

Lave, J. (1988). *Cognition in practice: Mind, mathematics, and culture in everyday life.* New York: Cambridge University Press.

Skinner, B. F. (1976). *Walden two.* New York: Macmillan.

Tversky, A., Kahnemann, D., & Slovic, P. (Eds.). (1982). *Judgment under uncertainty: Heuristics and biases.* New York: Cambridge University Press.

# PART II

# Humans as Symbolic Creatures

*Human beings act toward things on the basis of the meanings that the things have for them.*

(Herbert Blumer, *Symbolic Interactionism*)

*The limits of my language mean the limits of my world.*

(Ludwig Wittgenstein)

# Shared Meaning as the
# Basis of Humanness

Imagine that you have just been kicked in the knee. How do you respond? Your immediate physical response is probably an upward jerk of the leg. Perhaps a rush of air and a surprised gasp escapes your lips. In a behaviorist's terms, the blow to the knee is considered the stimulus and your direct, physical response is your jerking leg and cry of pain. This physical response to the stimulus of being kicked is the same for most humans.

In addition to this physiological response, you are likely to have additional reactions that are not as predictable. How do you respond to the person who kicked you? You may kick the person in return. You may apologize for being in the way. You may flee. Your response to the person who kicked you depends on how you *interpret* the incident. Do you perceive it to be an act of aggression, an accident, a playful joke? Your interpretation of the incident is in turn based on the situation and the cues you pick up from the person who kicked you. If you are in a crowded space and the kicker smiles apologetically, you are likely to interpret the act as an accident and to respond accordingly. If you have been reading quietly in an empty room and the kicker glares at you menacingly, you are more likely to interpret the kick as an act of aggression than as an accident.

Symbolic interactionists are interested in the process of assigning meaning to actions and in the responses that follow. The meaning that you assign to being kicked determines how you will respond to the kicker and, in turn, how the kicker will respond to you. That is, *how* you perceive the incident will determine how you *feel* about it and your subsequent course of action. This perception will also be the basis for how you store the event in your memory and recall it later.

A jerk of the knee and a cry of pain may be predictable, universal, physical responses. However, there is nothing inherent in the interpretation that can be placed on the event. To symbolic interactionists, the most interesting aspects of human behavior are those that take place when we assign meaning to our own actions or interpret the actions of others. Although it is possible to chart direct stimulus-response patterns in human behavior, symbolic interactionists maintain that these patterns are of limited interest in understanding human behavior and institutions. Most noteworthy behavior involves a process of interpretation between stimulus and response. Thus, the interesting question for the student of human behavior is not what the objective stimulus is (for example, the blow to the knee), but what *meaning* the receiver of the kick assigns to the stimulus (that is, how the blow is perceived). It is the process of assigning meaning that determines how people feel and act.

Symbolic interactionists claim that symbolic activity mediates between stimulus and response. In this essay, we explore the implications of being symbol-using creatures who interpret the world. We also discuss human thought as a process of symbolic gestures achieved through the acquisition of language. From this perspective, social behavior is a manifestation of shared patterns of symbolic meaning.

The philosopher Ernst Cassirer, in Reading 6, "A Clue to the Nature of Man," suggests that "physical reality seems to recede in proportion as man's symbolic activity advances." By this he means that symbol-using creatures do not exist in a direct state of nature. To exist in a state of nature is to be nonconscious, nonreflective, and nonsymbolic. In such a state the organism is propelled directly by the forces of nature, which include internal physiology and the external environment. In contrast, the symbolic creature is able to comprehend, comment on, and organize behavior in accordance with abstract representations that are removed from the state of nature. This does not imply necessarily that humans are "superior" to animals, nor that we do not have an animal form (biologically and physiologically). The point is that most noteworthy human activity is symbolic (abstracted from a direct state of nature). Thus the symbolic interactionist focuses on human behavior and culture *primarily* as expressions of meaningful symbol systems.

A comparison with elephants illustrates this point. When elephants meet, one places its trunk in the mouth of the other. Body temperature and fluids in the mouth indicate whether each elephant is in a state of arousal or aggression or is passive. This encounter triggers the appropriate response—copulating, fighting, fleeing, or traveling together. The elephants, as far as we can tell, do not think about this encounter; they do not interpret the event and assign meaning to it. They simply engage in a series of stimulus-response behaviors with each other in a direct state of nature.

The difference between humans and elephants is that humans do not respond directly to the physical environment. Rather, humans impose symbolic interpretations on experiences and draw conclusions based on these interpretations. It is true that we are attuned to odors and other physiological manifestations of our fellow humans and that we may experience these directly rather than through a process of interpretation. But most of our responses to others are determined by our *interpretation* of various cues. These cues include physiological features, gestures, and accessories and adornments, such as clothing and other symbolically meaningful items.

Those of you who have driven across a border into another country know that it is the duty of border guards to ascertain whether you are bringing merchandise into (or out of) the country in violation of international or national laws. These guards cannot read your mind. Nor can they experience directly whether you are telling the truth when you claim not to be carrying illicit goods. The guards must infer your intentions based on symbolic cues, such as the type of car you are driving, your gender, and the style of your clothes and hair. In other words, the guards guess at your integrity based on their symbolic interpretation of you and the situation. Similarly, the police officer who stops a motorist cannot experience directly whether the accosted driver will be hostile or compliant. The officer must make an inference based on available symbolic cues.

Sociologists are interested in the signs people use to make inferences and the reliability of these signs for predicting the intentions of others. This predictability is not a function of directly reading the "natural" world. Rather, it is the product of the symbolic codes through which we assign meaning to objects. Human behavior is not determined directly from our encounters with the physical world. Our bodies are physical entities that exist in the physical world, but our experience of our own bodies, of other people, and of things in our environment is anchored in the internal conversation that constitutes our conscious thought.

## Symbolic Meaning: It's the Name, Not the Thing

Herbert Blumer is credited with first use of the term *symbolic interactionism* to define the approach to the study of human behavior and society that we have been discussing (Fine, 1990). Blumer, who was a sociologist at the University of California, Berkeley, suggested three basic premises:

- Humans act toward a thing on the basis of the meaning they assign to the thing.
- Meanings are socially derived, which is to say that meaning is not inherent in a state of nature. There is no absolute meaning. Meaning is negotiated through interaction with others.
- The perception and interpretation of social symbols are modified by the individual's own thought processes (Blumer, 1969, p. 2).

## Naming (Assigning Meaning)

When we make sense of a person, space, or occasion, we attach meaning to it. This process is known as *naming*. Naming has three elements: a label, a cognitive-emotive evaluation, and a recommended course of action. The conceptual names we have for persons, spaces, and things include each of these three components. Consider a round, hollow tube made of glass with a single closed end. We can label it a glass. But *glass* is a fairly abstract term, and we might each be imagining a different type of glass. Let's say that we further narrow the meaning of the label by imposing additional classifications—for example, the glass has a stem attached. This description suggests a wine glass, which we may evaluate subjectively as, perhaps, an elegant sort of glass or a decadent sort of glass. Regardless of the specific glass that we each have in mind, we are in agreement as to its general purpose. That is, we know the recommended course of action toward the object that we have labeled a glass: It is a container from which we can drink.

Philosophers, linguists, and cognitive social psychologists agree that to name something is to know it. This process of object identification is central to human perception and appraisal. Humans name things and then respond according to the implications carried by the name. They do not respond to the essence of the thing itself. Thus, we say that human behavior involves not just a response to a stimulus but a process—naming—that mediates between stimulus and response.

Try the following exercise. Work up some saliva in your mouth. How does it feel? Now spit it into a glass. How does it look? Now drink it up. Most of you will probably respond to this last request with some hesitation. Yet we have simply asked you to reabsorb a substance that, in fact, you swallow continually all through the day. Why did you hesitate? Probably because you have an aversion to spit. This aversion is not a direct response to the natural essence of the substance. It is an aversion to the *name*, not the thing. Your reaction is based on a symbolic process whereby you have conceptualized bodily fluids that have left the body as repulsive. The name *spit* implies an evaluative response ("Yuck!") and a course of action (avoidance). You do not respond to the nature of the fluid. Instead, you assign meaning to the fluid and respond to that meaning. Cassirer reminds us of the words of Epictetus: "What disturbs [people] are not things, but their opinions and fancies about things."

## Symbols and Signifying

Emotional and behavioral responses to environmental stimuli are shaped by this naming process. Thus, behavior differs not in response to a particular stimulus but in response to the meaning human actors assign to the stimulus. In Jane Wagner's "The Search for Signs of Intelligent Life in the Universe" (Reading 4 in Part I), Trudy attempts to teach her space chums the difference between a can of Campbell's soup and Andy Warhol's painting of a can of Campbell's soup. One is soup, the other is art. Warhol's rendering of the can of soup is not merely a stand-in image for the soup itself; rather, as "art" it constitutes a class of meaning unto itself. In contemplating the painting, a person doesn't consider whether the actual soup tastes good; rather, the person evaluates the "worth" of the painting based on what he or she knows about art. "Soup" and "art" are both abstract ideas, although each term conjures a different meaning. These different meanings imply different lines of action or responses toward the object. Similarly, the conversation we are now having, in which we are removed from one another's immediate presence, would not be possible if we did not share the abstract ideas of "book," "reading," and a similar symbolic system called "written English."

What are these symbols that we use to assign meaning to our experiences? Symbols are abstract representations. For example, a rectangular piece of cloth with red and white horizontal stripes and a blue square filled with white stars in the upper left-hand corner has significance beyond this physical description—it is a symbol, an abstract representation, of the United States of America.

A flag is a symbol not only of the nation "for which it stands" but also of the social convention of dividing the world into mutually exclusive geo-political units known as "nations." The U.S. flag not only stands for what is considered uniquely American, but also symbolizes a *distinction* from other nations. To be American is also to *not be* Russian, for example. Thus, a symbol defines both what something is and what it is not. The essence of the item you hold in your hands at this moment is tree pulp flattened and pressed into connected sheets with splotches of ink all over them. Most likely you do not think of the item this way, but rather as a book with abstract symbols in the form of written language for you to absorb. It is also likely that you do not consider the book as a source of toilet paper, although its natural essence has properties similar to those contained in toilet paper.

Reading 5, is a short story by Harlem Renaissance artist and writer Langston Hughes. This story illustrates the significance of "naming"—the focus of this section. Hughes's characters are pondering the significance of "Negro blood." Physiologically, there is no difference between white and black blood. This short reading illustrates the point that the difference is symbolic. In this case it is the *idea* of what Negro blood represents that is significant. Hughes's story is an example of a cultural system of meaning.

The study of semiotics and sociolinguistics is the study of the cultural systems of meaning that are conveyed through various symbolic representation. Roland Barthes, for example, has studied food symbolism. All societies have cultural systems that *signify* what foods can be eaten and what foods should be excluded; how certain foods are supposed to be grouped (e.g., breakfast, lunch, dinner, or appetizers, main courses, desserts) and the various rituals of use ("table manners," "picnics," "feasts"). In Reading 4, Trudy's space chums have difficulty comprehending the distinction between "soup" and "art" because they do not share the symbolic understanding whereby an apparently similar physical image is *assigned* to entirely different domains of meaning (food/art). In both examples, the symbolic system *signifies* how things are supposed to be grouped (classified) and how we are supposed to feel about them. Thus:

Naming = Assigning symbolic meaning to things/persons/events

Symbolic meaning = A sign system that conveys messages about how to feel about and respond to the thing/person/event.

In the context of Hughes's story, identifying certain people as having "Negro blood" conveys the symbolic message that black blood is less desirable and more problematic than white blood. This message (the sign) is mutually understood by people who share a cultural system of meaning—in this case, a system of racial prejudice.

## Symbols, Experience, and Culture

Because symbols are abstractions, we can use them to transcend the concrete environment and to have experiences that are not rooted in time and space. Abstraction also allows us to remember, fantasize, plan, and have vicarious experiences. When we imagine something, we formulate an image, a symbolic representation, of something that is not present in the immediate state of nature. Remembering is a similar activity. When we fantasize and make plans, we are manipulating symbolic images. Vicarious experience allows us to learn by observing the actions of others; we need not experience everything ourselves to comprehend what someone else is experiencing. This is a key element in individual survival and in the transmission of culture.

In Reading 7, Joel Charon describes in detail the importance of symbol systems. He demonstrates the theme that, without symbol systems, human experience and culture would not be possible. To comprehend the significance of the human ability to engage in symbolic abstraction, consider how much time you spend in the presence of your intimate friends versus how much time you spend thinking, remembering, fantasizing, and planning about them. Ask yourself if it would be possible for you to experience "love" for someone if you could not imagine (represent conceptually) the person when he or she was not actually physically present.

The final reading in the "Naming" subsection is a selection from case studies written by neurologist Oliver Sacks. In "Yes, Father-Sister," Sacks describes a woman who, because of neurological dissolution associated with language processing, has ceased to have "any 'center' to the mind." She is no longer able to comprehend or express symbolic *meaning*. All social roles are the same for her and can be interchanged at will. Thus, someone in her presence can be "Father," "Sister," or "Doctor" at any given moment. Imagine how disconcerting it would be if one of your parents named you indiscriminately "child," "parent," "lover," "salesclerk." People who are unable to engage in appropriate symbolic activity are islands isolated from meaningful relationships.

## The Source of Symbolic Systems of Meaning: Language

The primary way by which humans exchange symbolic meaning is through language. Language is a system of symbols that allows humans to communicate and share abstract meaning. Language gives humans the capacity to become social creatures—which is to say, the capacity to comprehend and to participate in culture. The purpose of Part II is to demonstrate the importance of language as a set of symbols and to show the relationship between language and thought. We also consider how meaning is transmitted through social interaction.

The basic unit of language is the word. Words are symbols that denote the meaning of something. Words can be conveyed through writing, speech, and sign. The power of words to represent the range of human activity can be seen in the following exercise: Try listing words for as many emotions as you can think of. Then read your list to someone else. Chances are that the person will comprehend the states of being that each word suggests. Now, select an emotion word that is well understood among those who share your language and attempt to communicate this emotion to someone through direct physical contact without the use of words. General emotions such as anger, lust, and fright may possibly be communicated by touch. However, it is likely that the list of emotion words that you generated conveys a much wider range of emotion and greater emotional subtlety than you can communicate effectively without resorting to words. Does this exercise show that there are more emotions than there are ways of expressing them? No. It implies that there are as many emotions as there are words for describing them.

Words assign meaning to our experiences. In many instances a physiological state of arousal is meaningless and may even go unnoticed until the experience has been named. Consider, for example, a young man who, while traveling by plane, experiences a shaky stomach and sweaty palms. He is unable to ascertain whether he is experiencing airsickness or attraction to the woman sitting next to him. Both experiences entail the same physiological responses, but different courses of action are deemed appropriate, depending on whether one labels the experience "nausea" or "love."

Recall that, in Reading 2, Charon quotes from the autobiography of Malcolm X. In this book, Malcolm X tells of a fellow prison inmate who taught him that words are not benign by showing him in a dictionary the different meanings associated with the terms *black* and *white*. Meaning consists not only of isolated words or names but of the additional ideas and experiences associated with particular words. Another instructive exercise is to note words that have parallel definitions in the dictionary but carry very different connotations. *Spinster* and *bachelor* are a case in point. Both are defined simply as the male and female state of being unmarried. But *spinster* raises much less attractive images in the minds of most people than does the term *bachelor.*

## Language and Social Behavior

Language, thought, and social behavior are closely related. We interact with each other by observing ourselves and steering our behavior according to our interpretations of the expectations of others. This process is internal; we *talk* with ourselves about how to name situations, how to name our role in the situation, and how to assign meaning to others in the situation. We determine recipes for action based on the meaning we assign to the situation and experience feelings about the situation depending on how we have defined it. Without language, we would be unable to assign meaning to our own actions or to bring our actions into line with the expectations of our culture. We would be unsocialized.

## Language and Socialization

The social philosopher George Herbert Mead (1934; see Reading 27 in Part III) theorized that language acquisition is an interactional process. The meanings that the child learns to assign to things in the environment, including the self, derive from interactions with significant others. The child does not simply learn to name a spherical object "ball." She learns that a certain activity associated with the ball, such as hurling it across space, meets with particular responses from those around her. She also learns that these responses are either positive or negative and come in the form of reactions toward herself. Thus, she learns that she is the source of the activity that generates the response. She also learns that in certain situations, for example, in an enclosed space, people react more negatively when she hurls the ball than they do when she is on the green stuff called "grass."

The child also learns to distinguish the response of differently named persons in her environment. "Dad" may praise her "athletic ability" when she hurls the ball. "Mom" may attempt to "settle her down." In this way, the child learns to form complex associations among persons, things, and situations. Most importantly, the child learns what stance to adopt in a given setting in relationship to specifically named others and objects. This process of learning "names" and the associated rewards and punishments is the foundation of human socialization.

The readings in this second subsection ("Language and Social Behavior") illustrate the necessity of language in order for human development to occur and for social interaction to proceed normally. In Reading 9, sociologist Kingsley Davis describes the case of a young girl who was subjected to extreme isolation during crucial developmental years. In presenting her case, Davis considers the hypothesis that social intercourse is necessary for the development of language and intellectual activity. In Reading 10, three social psychologists report on some of the social and interactional limitations that occur in people who suffer from neurological disorders that affect their ability for language.

Another case from the files of Oliver Sacks follows in Reading 11. This one, the title story from his book *The Man Who Mistook His Wife for a Hat*, tells of a man who has retained his ability to think in abstractions, but who can no longer relate abstractions to particular situations and practical experience. His conceptual ability is fine; but his common sense is lost. As you read, think about how concepts become infused with experientially based, socially significant meanings. In this case, the man has lost his ability to comprehend the emotive-evaluative components of concepts. He does not experience meaning.

## Language and Thought

As powerful as a single word may be in assigning meaning, the full power of language is in the relationship among words, or the *structure* of language. Words are juxtaposed in such a way as to convey one meaning rather than another. For example, the words *cat, dog,* and *chases* each suggest a particular meaning. The first two are nouns that denote certain types of four-legged mammals, and the third is a verb that names a particular action. Presumably we have a shared understanding of the general class of meaning to which these words refer. Now, consider the alignment of the words "dog chases cat" and "cat chases dog." Does each combination suggest the same events? Try writing other possible combinations of these three words. How many of these combinations make sense to you?

The structure of language, called *syntax*, comprises the rules of grammar. Syntax allows humans to combine words to create strings or clusters of meaning more complex than the meaning suggested by isolated words. The syntax of a language also permits us to convey entirely different meanings by recombining symbols, as in the example of *cat*, *dog*, and *chase*. Another interesting feature of syntax is that humans appear to learn and use the rules of language without necessarily being aware of what these rules are. For example, although most people can give an example of a "yes or no" sentence (for instance, "Is your car red?"), very few could state the formal rules for constructing such a sentence. Nevertheless, people recognize when the rules have been violated. (We will return to this simple but profound point in Part IV in discussing the similarities between language syntax and "social grammar." As with rules of grammar, people are implicitly aware of the rules of interaction and recognize when these rules have been violated, but cannot state explicitly what these rules are.) Thus, the power of language derives from human ability to employ rules to convey meaning without necessarily being aware of the rules. Humans are continually able to represent new meanings, and these novel combinations will be understood by others, provided that the combinations follow accepted syntactical structure.

Linguists refer to the ability to formulate novel but mutually understood statements as the generative property of language. Humans generate their own ideas and codes of meaning; in other words, language and meaning are not predetermined by nature. The extent of this generative ability is profound—it allows small children to formulate novel sentences (rather than just repeating preprogrammed speech) and nuclear physicists to develop abstract and complex theories.

Nonetheless, not all combinations of words are equally meaningful or likely to be generated. What is intriguing is that people can ascertain the difference between "gibberish" and mutually comprehensible strings of words.

The meaning of what is generated is determined by the underlying structure of the language, or the particular "patterns of discourse." Different languages entail distinct patterns of meaning.

These language patterns profoundly influence culture. In short, different languages provide different ways to make sense of ourselves, others, and our circumstances.

During the past few decades, social scientists have debated whether language shapes thought or thought comes before language. Mead theorized that, in the process of learning language, the mind develops and becomes structured in a manner that reflects the individual's culture. Anthropologists, too, have pursued the claim that distinct languages cause people of different cultures to view and think about the world differently. For instance, many anthropologists demonstrate ways in which different cultures divide up "time" and "space" as expressed in their various languages. Some cultures express time in a nonlinear way as compared with Western linear conceptions, for example. Think about what your relationship to time might be if you could refer only to the concepts of "now" and "not now" and had no notion of "past" or "future."

In contrast, linguists such as Noam Chomsky consider language an innate human ability. Chomsky has made a convincing case that the "deep structure" of language is more complex than anyone could "learn" through social contact alone. He argues instead that one feature of the human brain is an inborn "computational modality." That is, humans are "hardwired" to comprehend and generate abstract representations and to piece together complex strings of words that require them to compute various possible lines of meaning and association. This activity is so complex and so unavailable to general consciousness that, according to Chomsky and his supporters, it would be impossible for children to perform the incredible mental gymnastics required to communicate if the brain were not hardwired for language.

One of Chomsky's students, Stephen Pinker, author of the popular book *The Language Instinct*, offers a simple but noteworthy illustration of the computational modality using these three statements:

Ralph is an elephant.

Elephants live in Africa.

Elephants have tusks.

Pinker continues thus:

Our inference-making device [innate computational processor] . . . would deduce "Ralph lives in Africa" and "Ralph has tusks." This sounds fine but isn't. Intelligent you, the reader, knows that the Africa Ralph lives in is the same Africa that all the other elephants live in, but that Ralph's tusks are his own. (1994, p. 79)

Pinker's point is that people make this distinction on the basis of common sense, that there is nothing in the words themselves that conveys this common sense; thus, the meaning is not logically explicit. The fact that people can make the distinction without hesitation is, for Pinker, a demonstration that people "know" things independently of the words used to express them. Thus, the way people think about and structure understanding precedes the language they use to express this understanding. Language itself contains so many ambiguities and oversimplifications that humans must have a larger picture in mind before speaking, otherwise we all would be unable to fill in the blanks and sort through the ambiguities with such unconscious ease.

For Chomsky and Pinker, "mentalese" exists independently of expressed language and consists of (1) innate computational ability and (2) practical, nonlanguage-based experience with the environment. Thus, a specific language is either independent of thought or merely a shorthand expression of "mentalese." It certainly does not structure thought.

### Language: Innate or Socially Produced?

We include a discussion of this debate in this essay because the debate itself is indicative of the split between social scientists who insist that behavior is based on innate biological and physiological properties and those who assert that human behavior is largely determined by social factors.

Which side do we take? As a matter of fact, we think that there is a more useful and accurate (albeit more complex) way to think about human behavior than either of these dichotomous positions. We agree in part with Chomsky—the ability for abstraction and linguistic computation is innate, a fundamental property of humanness. But what is the *source* of the conceptual abstractions that the mental processors are acting on? This puzzle is the untold story in contemporary linguistics and the impetus for the selection of readings in Part II. Let's explore two possibilities: (1) Perhaps humans are all preprogrammed with information as well as the ability to process this information; we're born knowing the actual content of abstract symbols. Or (2) perhaps the meaning of abstractions is something we learn only through experience with the natural world and interaction with others.

Let's return to Ralph the elephant. If humans were preprogrammed with information, infants would be born knowing all there is to know about elephants, Africa, and tusks. Clearly this is a silly speculation. Let's assume, then, that we comprehend the distinction between the sharing of one Africa by many elephants and the possession of tusks by single elephants because we have learned a distinction between being physically located in a space and possessing physical traits. Our ability to generalize these experiential observations and to incorporate them in language is the computational element that Chomsky refers to.

## Language, Thought, and Social Interaction

Our capacity for the abstraction and computation that is necessary to process language may be innate, but the actual content is *learned* through social contact. What Chomsky and colleagues can't tell us, as observers trying to make sense of human behavior, is the *significance* of Ralph in particular and of elephants, tusks, and Africa in general. This significance—people's attitudes, feelings, and behavior toward such strings of words—is determined by the context in which the words appear and the attributes people have learned to associate with these contexts. This is a social process. That is, the human capacity for the abstraction and computation that is necessary to process language may be innate, but the actual content is learned through social contact. Adults use language to teach children not necessarily how to think about, say, elephants/tusks/Africa but what to think about these things—and subsequently, how to respond. People don't need to be taught how to respond physiologically, as, for example, *what* to do physically when kicked in the knee. But the range of possible *social* responses to being kicked that occurs to a person, and her or his understanding of their appropriateness and consequences, are the result of having been taught, through language, what he or she should think about the incident. The name that we each ascribe to an experience acts as a sort of shorthand that shapes our subsequent thoughts about how to respond to the situation. In this way, language, experience, and thought continually interact—they are mutually determining.

A helpful analogy is the relationship between computer hardware and software: Here, the human brain is the hardware and language the software. Humans are born with brain hardware that enables us to engage in complex, computational, abstract, representational thought, but the content—*what* we process—is input by others who provide us with meaningful ideas through the activity of language. In the same way that a fully functional computer cannot operate without being switched on and fed some software, there is considerable evidence that children who are not exposed to language fail to develop normal conceptual abilities.

Oliver Sacks explores this issue in his book about the congenitally deaf, *Seeing Voices* (1989). On the basis of several case studies, Sacks asserts that those born without hearing are endowed with the same intellectual capacity as those who can hear. But in an oral-based culture, the congenitally deaf, in the absence of aural stimulation, fail to develop conceptual thought. The cognitive hardware of the congenitally deaf child may be in perfect working order, but the hearing impairment (deficient perceptual hardware) gets in the way of the necessary start-up. The child's language ability never really gets turned on. For this reason, many deaf children are mistakenly assumed to be developmentally retarded. However, when a congenitally deaf infant is exposed to sign language, the child not only proceeds along a normal course of cognitive development, but actually begins to communicate in sign earlier than hearing infants learn to talk. Some specialists suggest that the ability for communication is switched on before the infant's vocal cords are physically ready for speech. Signing infants don't have to wait for their vocal chords to develop.

Studies of "feral children"—children raised in isolation, who are often assumed to be retarded—suggest similar conclusions. The capacity for abstract thought may be innate but, in order to develop this capacity, the child must be exposed to language-based social interaction. When the child lacks such access, then he or she is effectively denied access to the "switch" (language-based interaction) and the "software" (a specific language) through which conceptual thought develops. The implication is that humans require social stimulation and exposure to abstract symbol systems—language—in order to embark upon the conceptual thought processes that characterize our species.

Thus, human experience is given meaning and is organized through language, and the ability to form complex strings of words and to communicate verbally is innate. But the source of the meaning assigned to the words is social.

## Experience and Conceptualization

In the late 1600s, the philosophers Gottfried Leibnitz and John Locke are said to have exchanged letters in which they debated the following question: Imagine a man who is born blind. How will he learn the difference between the concepts "triangle," "square," and "circle"? Like all children, he can be given blocks to play with. The "platonic solids" consist of blocks that are triangular, cubed, and round. The child could learn to tell the difference through his sense of touch. He could *feel* each one, be told the name and then, whenever someone mentioned the name (e.g., "triangle") he would have an *idea* of what the triangle was. Now here is the question: What would happen if the man were suddenly able to see and the three different blocks were set in front of him? Would he be able to *see* the difference and name them accordingly, or would he still have to *feel* each one? According to Locke, the man would not necessarily be able to *see* the different shapes. His *conceptual* understanding of the shapes would be based in his *experience* of touch. Leibnitz disagreed. He believed that the man would be able to conjecture what each was based on the concept that he held in his head (a concept that was rooted in the experience of touch, not sight).

One of the questions that interests sociolinguists is the relationship between experience, perception, and conceptualization. As Oliver Sacks points out in *The Man Who Mistook His Wife for a Hat*, "seeing" is a matter of conceptualization, not just sensory perception. We use our conceptual knowledge to make sense of what our senses are seeing. More interesting still is the point that *meaningful* concepts resonate with experience. A "glove" is really not the same thing as "a continuous surface unfolded on itself with five outpouchings." The implication is that we learn conceptual meaning *in context*. Socially meaningful concepts reflect specific experiences, experiences that are visceral and imbued with feeling. Thus, when studying how children learn to assign meaning to concrete things in their environment, we have to take into account both the social content and the context of experience.

The Russian linguist and social psychologist Lev Vygotsky wrote extensively on the relationship between language and thought during the 1920s, but his writings have only been available in English since 1960. Writing independently of the North American debate regarding linguistic determinism, Vygotsky, like his fellow Eastern European social scientists, was inclined to see a mutual relationship between individual neurological-cognitive processes and social learning.

According to Vygotsky, children make sense of their environment by grouping things (persons and objects) that seem, through their own experiences, to be connected. The result is "complex thinking," or grouping seemingly related things into "complexes." Concepts generated from the complexes stand in as abstract representations of meaningful relationships between concrete things and experiences. For instance, a child's experiential complex for the family dog might consist of "Ruffy, big, furry, tail, bite." Conceptual thinking replaces the complex when the child learns the general name for the complex—"dog." Initially the child may attempt to interchange the specific name, "Ruffy," with the general name, "dog." She may also experience fear whenever she hears of a "dog" because her complex or cluster includes the experience "bite."

Comprehending a parent's explanation that "the dog will only bite you if you pull its tail" is an illustration of the child's ability to generalize based on abstract thinking. It is also an illustration of the child's ability to learn vicariously through language. The child needn't experiment with pulling the tail of every dog that she encounters to gain an understanding of the conceptual relationship between tail pulling and biting. Rather, she uses the words to formulate a more general idea and to encode both the specific experience and her general interpretation of it in her memory. Thus, she begins to develop a lexicon of experientially based but socially influenced "names" complete with evaluatory and action codes ("Dogs can bite so beware.").

Vygotsky (1961) bridges individual and social cognitive linguistics through his idea of "pseudo-concepts," generalizations like concepts but actually complexes:

> In the experimental setting, the child produces a pseudo-concept every time he surrounds a sample with objects that could just as well have been assembled on the basis of an abstract concept. For instance, when the sample is a yellow triangle and the child picks out all the triangles in the experimental material, he could have been guided by the general idea or concept of a triangle. Experimental analysis shows, however, that in reality the child is guided by concrete, visible likeness and has formed only an associative complex limited to a certain kind of perceptual bond. Although the results are identical, the process by which they are reached is not at all the same as in conceptual thinking.
>
> Pseudo-concepts predominate over all other complexes in the child's thinking for the simple reason that in real life *complexes corresponding to word meanings are not spontaneously developed by the child: The lines along which a complex develops are predetermined by the meaning a given word already has in the language of adults.* . . . . This language, with its stable, permanent meanings, points the way that a child's generalizations will take. The adult cannot pass on to the child his mode of thinking. He merely supplies the ready-made meaning of a word, around which the child forms a complex. . . . The pseudo-concept serves as the connecting link between thinking in complexes and thinking in concepts. Verbal intercourse with adults becomes a powerful factor in the intellectual development of the child. (pp. 67–69)

The point that we derive from Vygotsky is that, in normal cognitive development, children operate at the nexus of practical experience and pre-established concepts. Even as they are forming experience-based groupings of things in their environment, children are learning to use ready-made words that are based on conceptualizations that are already socially established. Thus, both the child's own experiences and social influence, through pre-existing language, play a role in the development of language and cognition. The resulting conceptual knowledge is a combination of experience and social learning. Concrete experiences enable the child to *comprehend* in an embodied, fully feeling way but, without pre-existing language, the child would not be able to transcend the immediate experience and "make sense" of it in a more general way.

## Language, Thought, and Culture

We can discuss language and cognitive structure from one additional angle. Chomsky and others, in their zeal to make the point that humans have an innate capacity for representational computation, have rejected the notion that the particular language of a culture determines the way in which members of the culture classify persons, objects, and events. Anthropologists disagree, as we've already noted, along with scholars working more recently in such areas as discourse theory and cultural studies. We make the case in Part II that language categories do in fact structure the way in which individuals perceive, organize, evaluate, feel about, and respond to their experiences and environments.

Language, as we have already noted, has evaluative and emotive components that make up concepts. Concepts, as Vygotsky details, do not necessarily emerge through direct experience but, rather, are handed down to us through social intercourse with other members of our culture. These concepts shape the way we focus on, categorize, evaluate, respond to, and remember people, objects, and events; in other words, language does structure how we think.

Consider the following string of words: Race is not biologically significant; it is only skin deep. When considered from a chromosomal perspective, this statement may indeed be correct. But is it representative of social reality as you know it? The chromosomes of humans with brown and pink skin may be identical, but the words *black* and *white* carry an entire history of meaning in this country and shape, to a large extent, the way in which Americans are inclined to see, evaluate, and remember others. In short, "race" in the United States is socially significant.

In learning the customs and belief systems of their culture, people learn to classify humans in a variety of ways. They learn that humans can be big, small, short, tall, fat, brown, black, yellow, white, and so forth. And each of these "names" includes emotive-evaluative components and behavioral cues.

Let us stress the point one more time—left to themselves, free of pre-existing cultural influence, children would develop "complexes" that reflect their particular experience with their environment. The meaning that they would attach to words (that is, the abstract concepts and names that emerge from complexes) would thus accurately portray the world as they experienced it. Note that this path of learning leads to a process of stereotyping—if the child is bitten by a big fluffy animal that she later comes to name "dog," she may, through experience, later presume that all such creatures are scary. In other words, her conceptual notion would stand in for "real" experience and would shape her response to such creatures. However, as generations of social scientists have demonstrated, children do not learn in a vacuum. More likely, they begin forming complex associations between named objects, people, and spaces, by asking, "What's that?" The concepts given to them by others contain preconceived associations that reflect shared cultural evaluations. For example, a child who has no direct experience with lions can still learn to identify a picture of one—and, most importantly, will absorb whatever emotive-evaluative-behavioral cues are expressed by the adults explaining what a lion is. Thus, a child can become "scared" by the *thought* of a lion without ever encountering one, because he or she has been taught that lions are "scary."

This process of "naming" has serious implications for the structure of society. For instance, without ever having encountered a Mexican American before, an Anglo American middle-class employer can find himself wondering whether a young "Mexican-looking" job candidate from Texas is likely to be "lazy." The sources of such a stereotype are subtle and many. The employer may not even be aware that he is evaluating the candidate on the basis of a preconceived stereotypical framework. His response is based on a cultural representation that may have no connection to his direct experience or the abilities of the prospective employees.

By studying the way in which names are associated with other emotive-evaluative words, we can learn a great deal about the way in which culture, through language, shapes the thoughts of individuals. The power of language is not simply in words but in the manner in which words can be combined to create clusters of meaning. Reading 12, "Metaphors We Live By" (Lakoff and Johnson), and Reading 13, "The Social Lens" (Zerubavel), describe ways in which specific language forms reflect cultural ideas and how these ideas, in turn, shape how we think and talk. These metaphors and lines of distinction that make up our everyday understanding reflect social divisions, not natural ones.

The process of naming is an act of *categorization*. To categorize is to impose conceptual categories of meaning on things, grouping them in a way that makes them related and gives them order. But categorization also presents problems, which are the subject of Reading 14, "Mindfulness and Mindlessness," by Harvard psychologist Ellen Langer. What she calls mindlessness is characterized by automatic perceptions triggered by a few salient cues. This mode of "shortcut" perception is efficient to the extent that it allows humans to process massive quantities of information quickly and efficiently. The dangers, however, include the omission of other relevant features of the object or person in question and the perpetuation of stereotypes. Langer's thesis is that the names or categories that people use to give meaning to things suggest certain possibilities and omit others. She describes several cases in which seeing something through one category leads to *not* seeing some surprising things.

All languages suggest categorical relationships based on notable symbols. In the absence of specific information, people use these general word-based categories to impose meaning on other people, things, and events and to form judgments that they then rely on to guide their behavior. A border guard, in the absence of any other information, may see a male with a shaved head and five earrings in one ear and infer, based on categorical associations among clusters of symbols, that the person is a punker trying to smuggle drugs into the country. We all have a tendency to make these types of inferences. What is your general image of the border guard? Where did you get this information? Your ability to envision a border guard, even if you have personally never encountered one, is a process of symbolic abstraction. You conjure up the image based on a classification scheme. Chances are that the border guard you imagine is based on a stereotype. This stereotype is most likely male, wearing some type of uniform, and carrying a gun.

In Reading 15, "Changes in Default Words and Images Engendered by Rising Consciousness," Douglas Hofstadter speaks about default assumptions, which are preconceived notions about the likely state of affairs symbolized by words. Default assumptions have a tendency, in Hofstadter's words, to "permeate our mental representations and channel our thoughts." For instance, given the words *cat, dog,* and *chase,* you are likely to think first of a dog chasing a cat.

This line of thought reflects a default assumption that, all else being equal, the dog is more likely to chase the cat than the other way around. Default assumptions are based on prior experience and knowledge of circumstances. They are useful in that people cannot always afford the time it would take to consider every theoretical possibility that confronts them.

Nonetheless, it is possible that default assumptions are wrong. An interesting question is how we might know if we are wrong. Another is whether we change our default assumptions if the facts of the situation prove us wrong. If, for example, the shaved motorist does not have drugs in the car, will the border guard revise her categorical expectations regarding the relationship between male, shaved head, earrings, and drug use? Or will she reaffirm these general expectations with an account to herself of why this particular incident was not as expected? She may decide that the person does, in fact, have drugs in the car; she was simply unable to find them. Thus, the general category shaved head = punker = drugs is confirmed. Furthermore, the category may now be associated with deviousness as well.

Default assumptions are only one type of language-based categorization. Hofstadter is particularly interested in sex-based categorization. To stimulate discussion of sexism as a product of the relationship between language and thought, we have included a satire written by Hofstadter, "A Person Paper on Purity in Language," in which he draws an analogy between sex-based and race-based language differences.

In Reading 16, "Racism in the English Language," Robert Moore considers some of the racial stereotypes and values that are signified in the asymmetries of everyday speech. Reading 17, the final selection in Part II, is a brief excerpt from a novel by New Zealand author Sue Reidy. This is a humorous look at a youthful attempt to make sense of sexuality in a world where adults use euphemistic language.

## Conclusion

Consider another illustration from Stephen Pinker (1994). The following are real headlines he took from various newspapers:

Child's Stool Great for Use in Garden

Stud Tires Out

Stiff Opposition Expected to Casketless Funeral Plan

Drunk Gets Nine Months in Violin Case

Iraqi Head Seeks Arms

Queen Mary Having Bottom Scraped

Columnist Gets Urologist in Trouble with His Peers (p. 79).

Pinker's intent is to show that people's ability to comprehend the double meanings in each of the headlines is indicative of an innate processing ability, a cognitive structure that can handle the complexities and ubiquitous ambiguities of language. We agree that the computational ability required to recognize these double entendres is innate and universal, but we also believe that the content of each—or rather, its double content—and, more significantly, the fact that people find the phrases funny, are due to social processes.

When you have completed the readings in this section, you will be in a position to re-evaluate the relationship between language and thought. We are not concerned with the deep structure of generative grammar, which we agree is probably a universal human feature. Rather, we are interested in the lexicon of meanings available to individuals—the concepts through which they make sense of their experiences, encode these in memory, and feel about and act on them. That is, we are interested in what is said, not said, and how it is said— what names do and don't exist and the evaluative-emotive components of those names. We believe that different languages represent reality differently; that particular languages highlight certain features of life and leave others in the haze of "preconceived" thought. Names/words/concepts reveal certain lines of action and possibilities to individual humans. In this way, although it may be theoretically possible for all humans to generate infinite and similar grammars and lexicons of meanings, it is not probable that members of a given culture will do so. And that which is unnamed is unknown. The idea has been summarized by the mathematician and philosopher Bertrand Russell: "Language serves not only to express thought but to make possible thoughts which could not exist without it."

The assertion that humans process all experience through socially constructed symbol systems has been a source of both caution and enthusiasm. The tension between abstract thought and direct experience is expressed in the following quotation from a brooding poet in *Hyperion*, a science fiction novel:

> Words are the supreme objects. They are minded things. As pure and transcendent as any idea that ever cast a shadow into Plato's dark cave of our perceptions. But they are also pitfalls of deceit and misperception. Words bend our thinking to infinite paths of self-delusion, and the fact that we spend most of our mental lives in brain mansions built of words means that we lack the objectivity necessary to see the terrible distortion of reality which language brings. . . . [Yet] here is the essence of [humankind's] creative genius: not the edifices of civilization nor the bang-flash weapons which can end it, but the *words* which fertilize new concepts. . . . You see, in the beginning was the Word. And the Word was made flesh in the weave of the human universe. Words are the only bullets in truth's bandolier. (Simmons, 1990, pp. 190–191)

To conclude, we emphasize that the process of associating meaning with objects, persons, and events is an ongoing negotiation. In making sense of your world, you negotiate abstract meanings with others (interpersonal negotiation) and you negotiate with yourself to maintain a "fit" between your existing conceptual frameworks and concrete experience (intrapersonal negotiation). This negotiation is done through language; even as you experience "unnamed" thoughts, emotions, and acts, you make sense of them by "fitting" them into the language categories available to you. For instance, if your culture has a category for "lover" that includes the default assumption that the pairing consists of one each of the two sexes and you are paired with someone of the same sex, then you may find yourself without a "name" for this person when conversing with others who want to know about your attachments. Your experience may lead you to search for "alternative names" that stretch the category of "husband/wife" to include those who have same-sex partners. In this way you are generating new concepts reflective of individual experience, but the fact that you have to search for a name for what you do is structured by the existing cultural classifications.

"Meaning" is not simply "out there"; it is something that is created and re-created through everyday interactions. The process reflects the complex interplay between individual experience and social structure. Individuals are constantly working to "fit" their individual thoughts and experiences into a form that can be expressed and shared with others. As you read the articles in this section, ask yourself: How do significant categories of language carve up my world? How do various concepts shape who I think I can be and what I think I can do? What are some of my default assumptions as a result of having absorbed the concepts of my culture? Am I aware that my language reflects a cultural value system?

## References

Barthes, R. (1967/1964). *Elements of semiology*. New York: Hill & Wang.

Blumer, H. (1969). *Symbolic interactionism*. Englewood Cliffs, NJ: Prentice-Hall.

Brown, R. (1986). *Social psychology* (2nd ed.). New York: Free Press.

Charon, J. (1989). *Symbolic interactionism* (3rd ed.). Englewood Cliffs, NJ: Prentice-Hall.

Chomsky, N. (1972). *Language and the mind*. New York: Harcourt Brace Jovanovich.

Fine, G. (1990). Symbolic interactionism in the post-Blumerian age. In G. Ritzer (Ed.), *Frontiers of social theory* (pp. 117–157). New York: Columbia University Press.

Lee, D. (Ed.). (1980). *Wittgenstein's lectures, Cambridge 1930–1932*. Chicago: University of Chicago Press.

Lindesmith, A. R., Strauss, A. L., & Denzin, N. K. (Eds.). (1988). *Social psychology* (6th ed.). Englewood Cliffs, NJ: Prentice-Hall.

Mead, G. H. (1934). *Mind, self and society*. Chicago: University of Chicago Press.

Pinker, S. (1994). *The language instinct: How the mind creates language*. New York: Harper Perennial.

Sacks, O. (1987). *The man who mistook his wife for a hat*. New York: Harper & Row.

Sacks, O. (1989). *Seeing voices*. Berkeley: University of California Press.

Sapir, E. (1921). *Language*. New York: Harcourt, Brace and World.

Simmons, D. (1990). *Hyperion*. New York: Bantam.

Vygotsky, L. S. (1961). *Thought and language*. Cambridge, MA: MIT Press.

# That Powerful Drop

*Langston Hughes*

Leaning on the lamp post in front of the barber shop, Simple was holding up a copy of the *Chicago Defender* and reading about how a man who looks white had just been declared officially colored by an Alabama court.

"It's powerful," he said.

"What?"

"That one drop of Negro blood—because just *one* drop of black blood makes a man colored. *One* drop—you are a Negro! Now, why is that? Why is Negro blood so much more powerful than any other kind of blood in the world? If a man has Irish blood in him, people will say, 'He's *part* Irish.' If he has a little Jewish blood, they'll say, 'He's *half Jewish*.' But if he has just a small bit of colored blood in him, BAM!—'*He's a Negro!*' Not, 'He's *part* Negro.' No, be it ever so little, if that blood is black, '*He's a Negro!*' Now, this is what I do not understand—why our *one* drop is so powerful. Take paint—white will not make black *white*. But black will make white *black*. One drop of black in white paint—and the white ain't white no more! Black is powerful. You can have ninety-nine drops of white blood in your veins down South—but if that other *one* drop is black, shame on you! Even if you look white, you're black. That drop is really powerful. Explain it to me. You're colleged."

"It has no basis in science," I said, "so there's no logical explanation." . . .

6

# A Clue to the Nature of Man: The Symbol

*Ernst Cassirer*

In the human world we find a new characteristic which appears to be the distinctive mark of human life. The functional circle of man is not only quantitatively enlarged; it has also undergone a qualitative change. Man has, as it were, discovered a new method of adapting himself to his environment. Between the receptor system and the effector system, which are to be found in all animal species, we find in man a third link which we may describe as the *symbolic system*. This new acquisition transforms the whole of human life. As compared with the other animals man lives not merely in a broader reality; he lives, so to speak, in a new *dimension* of reality. There is an unmistakable difference between organic reactions and human responses. In the first case a direct and immediate answer is given to an outward stimulus; in the second case the answer is delayed. It is interrupted and retarded by a slow and complicated process of thought. At first sight such a delay may appear to be a very questionable gain. Many philosophers have warned man against this pretended progress. "L'homme qui médite," says Rousseau, "est un animal dépravé": It is not an improvement but a deterioration of human nature to exceed the boundaries of organic life.

Yet there is no remedy against this reversal of the natural order. Man cannot escape from his own achievement. He cannot but adopt the conditions of his own life. No longer in a merely physical universe, man lives in a symbolic universe. Language, myth, art, and religion are parts of this universe. They are the varied threads which weave the symbolic net, the tangled web of human experience. All human progress in thought and experience refines upon and strengthens this net. No longer can man confront reality immediately; he cannot see it, as it were, face to face. Physical reality seems to recede in proportion as man's symbolic activity advances. Instead of dealing with the things themselves man is in a sense constantly conversing with himself. He has so enveloped himself in linguistic forms, in artistic images, in mythical symbols or religious rites that he cannot see or know anything except by the interposition of this artificial medium. His situation is the same in the theoretical as in the practical sphere. Even here man does not live in a world of hard facts, or according to his immediate needs and desires. He lives rather in the midst of imaginary emotions, in hopes and fears, in illusions and disillusions, in his fantasies and dreams. "What disturbs and alarms man," said Epictetus, "are not the things, but his opinions and fancies about the things."

From the point of view at which we have just arrived we may correct and enlarge the classical definition of man. In spite of all the efforts of modern irrationalism this definition of man as an *animal rationale* has not lost its force. Rationality is indeed an inherent feature of all human activities. Mythology itself is not simply a crude mass of superstitions or gross delusions. It is not merely chaotic, for it possesses a systematic or conceptual form.[1] But, on the other hand, it would be impossible to characterize the structure of myth as rational. Language has often been identified with reason, or with the very source of reason. But it is easy to see that this definition fails to cover the whole field. It is a *pars pro toto;* it offers us a part for the whole. For side by side with conceptual language there is an emotional language; side by side with logical or scientific language there is a language of poetic imagination. Primarily language does not express thoughts or ideas, but feelings and affections. And even a religion "within the limits of pure reason" as conceived and worked out by Kant is no more than a mere abstraction. It conveys only the ideal shape, only the shadow, of what a genuine and concrete religious life is. The great thinkers who have defined man as an *animal rationale* were not empiricists, nor did they ever intend to give an empirical account of human nature. By this definition they were expressing rather a fundamental moral imperative. Reason is a very inadequate term with which to comprehend the forms of man's cultural life in all their richness and variety. But all these forms are symbolic forms. Hence, instead of defining man as an *animal rationale*, we should define him as an *animal symbolicum*. By so doing we can designate his specific difference, and we can understand the new way open to man—the way to civilization.

**Note**

1. See E. Cassirer (1922), *Die Begriffsform im mythischen Denken.* Leipzig: B. G. Teubner.

**7**

# The Importance of the Symbol

## *Joel Charon*

Imagine a world without symbols, without language, or without social objects. Our actions would be fixed; we would *respond* to stimuli, not to meaning. We would not problem solve, reflect, imagine, recall the past at all, or teach others anything other than simple responses learned through imitation. We would not be able to depend on culture for our action but would have to rely instead on instinct and/or simple learning. Understanding would cease, worlds outside our immediate physical space would not exist for us, and so much that is abstract—goodness, love, God, freedom, life and death—would not be examined at all and would not exist as a reality for us. Certainly communication with one another would not contain anything like concepts but would be confined to simple "nonmeaningful" gestures.

It is difficult to imagine a world without symbols because the human world is so overwhelmingly symbolic at its very core. Very few cases of non-symbol-using humans appear in history, and the few that do are incomplete studies, making generalizations difficult. Symbol use by the human begins at a very early age, first through understanding others' symbols, then through intentional symbolic expression.

"The Importance of the Symbol," from *Symbolic Interactionism*, 4th ed., by Joel Charon, © 1998. Reprinted by permission of Prentice-Hall, Inc., Upper Saddle River, NJ.

The symbolic interactionist emphasizes that all that humans are can be traced to their symbolic nature. Our world is a symbolic one: We see, we think, we hear, we share, we act symbolically. Symbols are critical for the human precisely because (1) they are *our reality*, (2) they *make our complex group life possible*, and (3) they *make the human being possible*. The purpose of this [essay] will be to explore each of these points in detail in order to show more fully the implications that symbol use has for the human.

### Symbols and Social Reality

The human acts within a world of social objects. That is, we act not toward a world out there but rather toward a world defined by others through symbolic communication. We share with others a definition of the world and its objects. Objects are transformed from physical stimuli responded to automatically into objects socially constructed. Each time we interact with others we come to share a somewhat different view of what we are seeing. We see what is out there in a new light. As we interact we develop a perspective as to what is real and how we are to act toward that reality. This interaction that gives rise to our reality is symbolic—*it is through symbolic interaction with one another that we give the world meaning and develop the reality toward which we act.*

Herbert Blumer (1969) expresses this simple principle in this way: "Meaning . . . arises out of the social interaction that one has with one's fellows" (p. 2).

Whenever there is interaction between persons, there is meaning shared, and this meaning is symbolic in nature as is the reality toward which we act. Humans do not respond to a physical reality but to a symbolic one. *Here lies the first important function of symbols.*

Man operates within an *ideational framework*—that is, a body of ideas of interpretations and analyses, which he has developed, and by means of which his observations of the universe and all that it contains, as well as his reactions to it, become meaningful. He can be said to live in a world of ideas. But it is within and by means of the *linguistic framework* that the ideationally established world exists and operates. Language is the means and mode of man's whole mental existence. (Hertzler, 1965:42)[1]

Kenneth Burke (1966:5) writes that our reality in the world at this split moment is nothing other than what we have learned from a "cluster of symbols about the past combined with whatever things we know mainly through maps, magazines, newspapers, and the like about the present" (p. 5). Whatever we experience *now* is seen through the symbols we use to see, and our ability to tie the present to a bigger picture depends on symbols. Burke concludes:

To meditate on this fact until one sees its full implications is much like peering over the edge of things into an ultimate abyss. And doubtless that's one reason why, though man is typically the symbol-using animal, he clings to a kind of naive verbal realism that refuses to realize the full extent of the role played by symbolicity in his notions of reality. (p. 5)

"A person learns a new language, and as we say, gets a new soul. . . . He becomes in that sense a different individual" (Mead, 1934:283).

## Symbols and Human Social Life

Human social life depends on symbols. *This is the second contribution symbols make to what human beings are.*

It is through symbols that individuals are *socialized*, coming to share the culture of the group and coming to understand their roles in relation to the others. We do not know how to act in society through instinct; we do not learn how to be social simply through imitation or experience. Each individual learns how to act in society through symbols and thus becomes part of society through symbols:

This does not happen by instruction, at least not in the pre-school years; nobody teaches him the principles on which social groups are organized, or their systems of beliefs, nor would he understand it if they tried. It happens indirectly, through the accumulated experience of numerous small events, insignificant in themselves, in which his behavior is guided and controlled, and in the course of which he contracts and develops personal relationships of all kinds. All this takes place through the medium of language. And it is not from the language of the classroom, still less that of courts of law, of moral tracts or of textbooks of sociology, that the child learns about the culture he was born into. The striking fact is that it is the most ordinary everyday uses of language, with parents, brothers and sisters, neighborhood children, in the home, in the street and the park, in the shops and the trains and the buses, that serve to transmit, to the child, the essential qualities of society and the nature of social being. (Halliday, 1978:9)

Recall Tamotsu Shibutani's (1955) "Reference Groups as Perspectives": It is through symbolic communication that we come to share culture, and it is through this communication and resulting culture that social worlds (groups, societies) are able to continue. *Culture, a very important part of every society, is learned through symbols, and it is itself symbolic.* We share ideas, rules, goals, values (all symbolic), and these allow us to continue to interact cooperatively with others.

We seem to grasp almost intuitively the central importance of symbols for our group life. We set up rules (symbolic) to be taught (usually through written or spoken *words*) to newcomers entering an already established group. We assure that the ideas we have developed are somehow shared and that what takes place is fully understood (has the right meaning) to the newcomer. That is true for college-orientation week, where students learn new rules, abbreviations, course names, teacher names, buildings, and requirements for graduation. It is true of the poker club, which must, during breaks in the action, teach the rules, the meanings, the taboos, the appropriate language, the proper betting to the newcomer. Both the college and the poker club know that without some shared reality their very existence may be at stake. And if we look at the group situation from the standpoint of the newcomer, he or she wants to understand the *meanings* attached to all the various acts—to learn immediately the shared reality in order to operate within the group.

*Human society depends on ongoing symbolic communication.* Communication means sharing, and sharing is one very important way that society is held together. Very complex forms of cooperation occur because human beings are able to discuss with one another how to resolve the problems that they face. Indeed, as Ralph Ross (1962) emphasizes, the words *community* and *communication* show an immediate similarity:

They emphasize commonness, togetherness. People gather or live *together* for certain purposes, and they *share* meanings and attitudes; the first presupposes the second, for without communication there is no community. Community depends on shared experience and emotion, the communication enters into and clarifies the sharing. Forms of communication like art and religion and language are themselves shared by a community, and each of them contains and conveys ideas, attitudes, perspectives, and evaluations which are deeply rooted in the history of the community. (pp. 156–57)

But there is much more. Groups have histories, and a long history means a very large corpus of knowledge. *It is by means of symbols that the past is recorded—knowledge and wisdom are not lost but are accumulated.* We can reflect and build on them—each interaction need not start from scratch. What one generation learns does not die when it dies. Joyce O. Hertzler (1965) states that language is "the major vehicle whereby we transmit—that is, impart or send and receive—our factualized experience . . . to others across space and time . . . from one individual, one area, one generation, one era, one cultural group to another" (pp. 50–51). Complex ongoing societies depend heavily on this function of symbols.

In summary, symbols are important to both social reality and social life. Social reality is created in symbolic interaction, and social life depends on symbols for socialization, culture, communication, and cumulation of knowledge (see Figure 1).

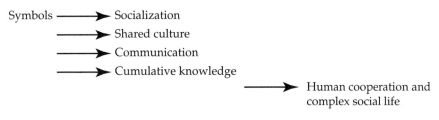

**Figure 1**

## Symbols and the Individual

Reality is symbolic. Society depends on the symbol for its continuation. More than this: The human being comes to act "human" only because he or she takes on symbols. We all may be born with certain prerequisites for acting like others in our species, but it is through the taking on of symbols that we come to act and look human. *Here is the third contribution symbols make.*

It is essential for us to appreciate the central role that the symbol plays for the individual. The symbol, and especially language, transforms the human being from a weak, helpless, unintelligent, simple organism to one whose complexity, flexibility, and intelligence brings about a uniqueness in nature. To gain an understanding of what symbols mean for the individual we will briefly examine nine very basic functions of symbols and/or language.

### Naming, Memorization, Categorizing

Through calling something a name we have identified it, "marked it out," "distinguished" it, and we are able to "store" it for later application. We can recognize similar objects and call them by that name. Naming an object allows us to apply it to another situation without its immediate physical presence. We can identify individual objects that we have never seen before because we have learned their names, that is, what they "are." The name can be stored in memory and can be purposely recalled in a multitude of situations. It might be possible that memory can exist without language (e.g., other animals may be able to recall pictures), but language allows for a much more complex, efficient memory system, one that can be more easily activated, whose parts can be more easily interpreted, transferred, and isolated. As Hertzler (1965) puts it: "the words of language, functioning as categories of experienced reality, not only facilitate more precise analysis, but also aid in the comparison of

one portion of experiential data with other portions" (p. 41).

Related to the naming function, of course, is categorizing. Language is the tool the individual uses to make order out of experience. Language is used to discriminate, to generalize, to make ever so subtle distinctions in one's environment. The world is literally divided up by means of the language we use:

Language has to interpret the whole of our experience, reducing the indefinitely varied phenomena of the world around us, and also of the world inside us, the processes of our own consciousness, to a manageable number of classes of phenomena: types of processes, events and actions, classes of objects, people and institutions, and the like. (Halliday, 1978:21)

### Perception

Language guides us through what our senses experience. It constitutes the individual's *perspectives*, and thus it serves the function of alerting the individual to some parts of the environment and not to others. "A language, once formed, has a self-contained organization somewhat like mathematics, and it previsages possible experience in accordance with accepted formal limitations . . . perception is limited by each language; men put what they perceive into pre-existing linguistic categories" (Shibutani, 1961:122). Symbols are the individual's eyes to the world.

### Thinking

Hertzler calls language "our means of thinking." Thinking can be conceptualized as symbolic interaction with one's self. Thinking is talking to oneself; it is an activity, a constant, ongoing process. Almost every moment, the individual is thinking in this sense—according to Blumer, constantly modifying reality through an "interpretive process." When we act alone we are usually engaged in self-communication; when we are with others we engage in symbolic interaction—we communicate with, we give off meaning to others, but because symbols by their nature are understood by their user, there must be a simultaneous communication with ourselves in all social encounters. To get others to understand us, we must understand ourselves, which demands that we symbolically interact with ourselves as we communicate with others. We are thus constantly engaged in active thinking, often without realizing that we are doing it. Thinking is so central to all we do that it, like language itself, is taken for granted unless pointed out to us.

### Deliberation and Problem Solving

Deliberation is a type of thinking, but it is more "deliberate" and conscious self-communication than the constant, ongoing thinking just described. It occurs most often when a problem is presented, when the situation requires analysis before action. It involves an attempt to consciously manipulate one's situation. The individual views self as an object in the situation, holds back action, analyzes, engages in lengthy discussion with self as action unfolds. In a sense, there is no difference between deliberation and the thinking described in the preceding paragraph, for the difference is really a matter of the degree of consciousness and the degree that one holds back overt action until the situation is fully understood. In fact, it is useful to understand almost all human behavior—but especially social behavior—as involving some deliberation.

Life can be thought of as a multitude of problems confronting the individual, each one calling for handling and solving, and each one demanding at least some deliberation. Each time we interact with someone else, "problems" are presented to us: how to understand the other, how to make ourselves understood, how to influence the other, how to avoid or get to know the other, how to work together or successfully dominate or successfully resist domination. Every time we enter a situation, working through that

situation is a problem that demands decisions on our part. Deliberation means we analyze situations (sometimes very rapidly), interpret the ongoing action (our own and others'), consider alternative plans of action, rehearse our acts before we commit ourselves to overt action, and recall past situations that may be applicable. Problem solving in any situation is an evolving process, so that what we do at any one point can be analyzed at a later point, possibly leading to a new strategy or a new line of action. Deliberation as described here, as well as the ongoing thinking described above, is an integral part of human action and depends fully on the manipulation of *symbols*.

### Transcendence of Space and Time

Problem solving and reflection involve transcending the immediate. Hertzler (1965) states that language

enables men to overcome the limited time-and-space perceptions of the subhuman creatures. It is, in fact, man's means of mentally breaking through the space-time barrier . . . he is also able to inhabit simultaneously the past (through legend, traditions, and formal records), the present and the future (by means of declared ideals, projections, anticipations, plans and programs). (pp. 53–54)

Language allows individuals to understand worlds they have never seen; it allows them to see the future before it occurs and to integrate past, present, and future. For example: I "know" ancient Greece without having been there, and I have a strong notion of what the United States will become in twenty years. I also believe that the United States' unjust treatment of minorities *today* is a result of a painful *history* of racism, and I also see today's policies as having some impact on a more just society *tomorrow*. The individual is guided in social situations by recalling the past, and by looking to the future, immediate and distant. When an individual acts, others outside the immediate situation may be the most important influences, the struggles of societies the individual has never had any contact with may be his or her most important inspiration, and what is going on "in the next room" outside the immediate field of vision and hearing may be perceived to be most influential on the individual's future. Language allows the individual to break out of the present and immediate stimulus environment and adds immeasurably to the factors that influence action.

### Transcendence of One's Own Person

Not only do symbols allow individuals to leave the immediate space-and-time environment, but also symbols allow them to leave their own bodies, to get outside of their selves and imagine the world from the perspectives of others. This very important human quality, which symbolic interactionists refer to as "taking the role of the other," allows us to understand others, to manipulate them, to sympathize with them, to love them. It allows for human beings' understanding of one another's ideas, because the more we are able to see things from the perspective of the people with whom we communicate, the more we are able to truly "see" what other people are saying. It is through language that we come to understand other people, their perspectives, their perceptions, their feelings, and their behavior. This ability to take the role of the other, itself dependent on our symbolic nature, is . . . central to human social life. . . .

### Abstract Reality

Language also allows the human being to imagine and perceive a reality beyond the concrete. Only through language can we establish objects like God, love, freedom, truth, good and evil, afterlife, and a host of other abstract objects that are so much an integral part of our existence. A reality beyond physical reality is open only through words and the manipulation of words into ideas. The concrete world of our senses is transformed by language into a reality not possible to

nonsymbol users. Hertzler (1965) puts it nicely:

> By means of conceptualization, [the human] is able to develop and live in the abstract world of intellectual experience—the world of ethical, aesthetic, evaluational, teleological, spiritual, and supernatural considerations . . . "goodness" as an ethical aspect, or "beauty" as an aesthetic characteristic, are not inherent in the event or the object, they are nonexistent, except in so far as we "perceive" and "conceive" them in terms of words. With language, we can wrestle with such perplexing questions as "truth" and "error," "right" and "wrong," "existential" and "transcendental." Words can stand for such abstractions as electricity, force, justice, time, space, future, deity—ideas which cannot possibly be represented by any visual picture. (p. 55)

Because human beings are symbol users and are able to create an abstract world, human beings can thus imagine goals, ideals, values, and morals that themselves become important motivating factors in human behavior. To die for "my country," to work for "freedom," to try to end "poverty" show a kind of motivation impossible to any except symbol users. This means that the human potential is limited only by human imagination. As long as we believe, for example, that "love" and "goodness" and "equality" are worth working for, we can constantly try to guide our behavior toward those ends. And if we believe that "materialism" or "destruction of others" or "power over others" is important, it becomes a guide to behavior. But symbols by their very nature open up a wide range of behavior possibilities. In a sense, no action is "unnatural" to us, because symbols allow for virtually any possibility.

### Creativity

The symbolic interactionist emphasizes the central importance of language in creating the active rather than passive person. It is through thinking with symbols that each individual is able to create his or her own world beyond the physical, develop highly individual interpretations of reality, and respond uniquely to that reality. Language arises from society, yet it is the tool that the human can use to think about and challenge that society. The key is not so much the symbol as it is *symboling*, the *manipulation of symbols* by active persons, defining and redefining their social situations. Give the child an understanding of certain *words*, and it is impossible to control fully how these words will be combined and recombined. This is the magic of language. To teach "love your country," and to teach "hate other countries," is to create the possibility in students of deciding to hate their country and love other countries. To teach a child what "little" means, what "big" means, what "in a little while" means is to invite from him or her: "No, I'll go to bed in a *big while*." Every sentence is, in a sense, a creative act. To manipulate the words we learn from interaction (society) is to be individual, active, and shaping, not passive and conforming.

### Self-Direction

Language allows the human being to exercise self-direction. Our communication with ourselves is a form of giving orders: Cooperate! Rebel! Listen! Get away! Run! Walk! Turn right! Work harder! Sleep! Think! Any control that we have over ourselves (and the symbolic interactionists claim it is considerable) comes through symbolic interaction with ourselves, through telling ourselves what is going on, what alternatives there are, and what line of action to take. The decision to conform and cooperate as well as the decision to rebel are both a matter of the individual's deciding through symbolic interaction with self what to do.

## Summary

The importance of the symbol for the individual can best be summarized by combining all of these contributions to the individual into a single central point: The human being, because of the symbol, does not re-

spond passively to a reality that imposes itself but actively creates and re-creates the world acted in. Humans name, remember, categorize, perceive, think, deliberate, problem solve, transcend space and time, transcend themselves, create abstractions, create new ideas, and direct themselves—all through the symbol. . . .

There is probably no better summary of the central importance that symbolic interactionists give to symbols than that of S. Morris Eames (1977):

Pragmatic naturalists conceive of humans as a part of nature. Although they share many organic processes with other animals in their life in nature, humans emerge above the animals in certain forms and functions. For instance, humans can construct symbols and languages, they can speak and write, and by these means they can preserve their past experiences, construct new meanings, and entertain goals and ideals. Humans can make plans and by proper selection of the means to the ends carry them through. They can write poetry and novels, compose music and painting, and otherwise engage in aesthetic experiences. They can construct explanatory hypotheses about the world and all that is in it, of electrons, protons, and neutrons, and solar systems far away. They can dream dreams, concoct fantasies, erect heavens above the earth which entice their activities to far-off destinies, and they can imagine hells which stimulate fears of everlasting torture. The emergent functions of symbolic behavior make it possible for humans to transcend parts of their immediate undergoing and experiencing and to know that death and all that it entails is a part of organic life. (pp. 40–41)

Symbols make three contributions to the human being: They are our reality, they form the basis for our social life, and they are central to what it means to be human. . . .

### Note

1. From *A Sociology of Language* by Joyce O. Hertzler. Copyright © 1965 by Random House, Inc. Reprinted by permission of the publisher.

## References

Blumer, Herbert
1969    *Symbolic Interactionism: Perspective and Method*. Englewood, Cliffs, N.J.: Prentice-Hall. Copyright © 1969. Reprinted by permission of Prentice-Hall, Inc.

Burke, Kenneth
1966    *Language as Symbolic Action*. Berkeley: University of California Press.

Cassirer, Ernst
1944    *An Essay on Man*. New Haven: Yale University Press.

Eames, S. Morris
1977    *Pragmatic Naturalism*. Carbondale: Southern Illinois University Press.

Halliday, M. A. K.
1978    *Language as Social Semiotic*. Baltimore: University Park Press.

Hertzler, Joyce O.
1965    *A Sociology of Language*. New York: Random House. Copyright © 1965 by Random House, Inc. Reprinted by permission of Random House, Inc.

Mead, George Herbert
1934    *Mind, Self and Society*. Chicago: University of Chicago Press. Reprinted by permission of The University of Chicago Press. Copyright © 1934 by The University of Chicago. All rights reserved.

Ross, Ralph
1962    *Symbols and Civilization*. San Diego: Harcourt Brace Jovanovich.

Shibutani, Tamotsu
1955    "Reference Groups as Perspectives." *American Journal of Sociology* 60:562–69.

1961    *Society and Personality: An Interactionist Approach to Social Psychology*. Englewood Cliffs, N.J.: Prentice-Hall. Copyright © 1961. Reprinted by permission of Prentice-Hall, Inc.

# Yes, Father-Sister

## *Oliver Sacks*

Mrs. B., a former research chemist, had presented with a rapid personality change, becoming "funny" (facetious, given to wisecracks and puns), impulsive—and "superficial." ("You feel she doesn't care about you," one of her friends said. "She no longer seems to care about anything at all.") At first it was thought that she might be hypomanic, but she turned out to have a cerebral tumor. At craniotomy there was found, not a meningioma as had been hoped, but a huge carcinoma involving the orbitofrontal aspects of both frontal lobes.

When I saw her, she seemed high-spirited, volatile—"a riot" (the nurses called her)—full of quips and cracks, often clever and funny.

"Yes, Father," she said to me on one occasion.

"Yes, Sister," on another.

"Yes, Doctor," on a third.

She seemed to use the terms interchangeably.

"What *am* I?" I asked, stung, after a while.

"I see your face, your beard," she said, "I think of an Archimandrite Priest. I see your white uniform—I think of the Sisters. I see your stethoscope—I think of a doctor."

"You don't look at *all* of me?"

"No, I don't look at all of you."

"Yes, Father-Sister" from *The Man Who Mistook His Wife for a Hat and Other Clinical Tales* (pp. 8–22) by O. Sacks. Copyright © 1970, 1981, 1983, 1984, 1985 by Oliver Sacks. Reprinted by permission of Simon & Schuster.

"You realize the difference between a father, a sister, a doctor?"

"I *know* the difference, but it means nothing to me. Father, sister, doctor—what's the big deal?"

Thereafter, teasingly, she would say: "Yes, father-sister. Yes, sister-doctor," and other combinations.

Testing left-right discrimination was oddly difficult, because she said left or right indifferently (though there was not, in reaction, any confusion of the two, as when there is a lateralizing defect of perception or attention). When I drew her attention to this, she said: "Left/right. Right/left. Why the fuss? What's the difference?"

"*Is* there a difference?" I asked.

"Of course," she said, with a chemist's precision. "You could call them *enantiomorphs* of each other. But they mean nothing to *me*. They're no different for *me*. Hands . . . Doctors . . . Sisters . . . ," she added, seeing my puzzlement. "Don't you understand? They mean nothing—nothing to me. *Nothing means anything* . . . at least to me."

"And . . . this meaning nothing . . . ," I hesitated, afraid to go on, "This meaninglessness . . . does *this* bother you? Does *this* mean anything to you?"

"Nothing at all," she said promptly, with a bright smile, in the tone of one who makes a joke, wins an argument, wins at poker.

Was this denial? Was this a brave show? Was this the "cover" of some unbearable emotion? Her face bore no deeper expression whatever. Her world had been voided of feeling and meaning. Nothing any longer felt "real" (or "unreal"). Everything was now "equivalent" or "equal"—the whole world reduced to a facetious insignificance.

I found this somewhat shocking—her friends and family did too—but she herself, though not without insight, was uncaring, indifferent, even with a sort of funny-dreadful nonchalance or levity.

Mrs. B., though acute and intelligent, was somehow not present—"de-souled"—as a person. I was reminded of William Thompson (and also of Dr. P.). This is the effect of the "equalization" described by Luria. . . .

## Postscript

The sort of facetious indifference and "equalization" shown by this patient is not uncommon—German neurologists call it *Witzelsucht* ("joking disease"), and it was recognized as a fundamental form of nervous "dissolution" by Hughlings Jackson a century ago. It is not uncommon, whereas insight is—and the latter, perhaps mercifully, is lost as the "dissolution" progresses. I see many cases a year with similar phenomenology but the most varied etiologies. Occasionally I am not sure, at first, if the patient is just "being funny," clowning around, or schizophrenic. Thus, almost at random, I find the following in my notes on a patient with cerebral multiple sclerosis, whom I saw (but whose case I could not follow up) in 1981:

She speaks very quickly, impulsively, and (it seems) indifferently . . . so that the important and the trivial, the true and the false, the serious and the joking, are poured out in a rapid, unselective, half-confabulatory stream. . . . She may contradict herself completely within a few seconds . . . will say she loves music, she doesn't, she has a broken hip, she hasn't . . .

I concluded my observation on a note of uncertainty:

How much is cryptannesia-confabulation, how much frontal-lobe indifference-equalization, how much some strange schizophrenic disintegration and shattering-flattening?

Of all forms of "schizophrenia" the "silly-happy," the so-called "hebephrenic," most resembles the organic amnestic and frontal lobe syndromes. They are the most malignant, and the least imaginable—and no one returns from such states to tell us what they were like.

In all these states—"funny" and often ingenious as they appear—the world is taken apart, undermined, reduced to anarchy and chaos. There ceases to be any "center" to the mind, though its formal intellectual powers may be perfectly preserved. The end point of such states is an unfathomable "silliness," an abyss of superficiality, in which all is ungrounded and afloat and comes apart. Luria once spoke of the mind as reduced, in such states, to "mere Brownian movement." I share the sort of horror he clearly felt about them (though this incites, rather than impedes, their accurate description). They make me think, first, of Borges' "Funes," and his remark, "My memory, Sir, is like a garbage-heap," and finally, of the *Dunciad*, the vision of a world reduced to Pure Silliness—Silliness as being the End of the World:

Thy hand, great Anarch, lets the curtain fall;
And Universal Darkness buries All.

# Final Note on a Case of Extreme Isolation

## *Kingsley Davis*

Early in 1940 there appeared . . . an account of a girl called Anna.[1] She had been deprived of normal contact and had received a minimum of human care for almost the whole of her first six years of life. At this time observations were not complete and the report had a tentative character. Now, however, the girl is dead, and with more information available,[2] it is possible to give a fuller and more definitive description of the case from a sociological point of view.

Anna's death, caused by hemorrhagic jaundice, occurred on August 6, 1942. Having been born on March 1 or 6,[3] 1932, she was approximately ten and a half years of age when she died. The previous report covered her development up to the age of almost eight years; the present one recapitulates the earlier period on the basis of new evidence and then covers the last two and a half years of her life.

### Early History

The first few days and weeks of Anna's life were complicated by frequent changes of domicile. It will be recalled that she was an illegitimate child, the second such child born to her mother, and that her grandfather, a widowed farmer in whose house her mother lived, strongly disapproved of this new evidence of the mother's indiscretion. This fact led to the baby's being shifted about.

Two weeks after being born in a nurse's private home, Anna was brought to the family farm, but the grandfather's antagonism was so great that she was shortly taken to the house of one of her mother's friends. At this time a local minister became interested in her and took her to his house with an idea of possible adoption. He decided against adoption, however, when he discovered that she had vaginitis. The infant was then taken to a children's home in the nearest large city. This agency found that at the age of only three weeks she was already in a miserable condition, being "terribly galled and otherwise in very bad shape." It did not regard her as a likely subject for adoption but took her in for a while anyway, hoping to benefit her. After Anna had spent nearly eight weeks in this place, the agency notified her mother to come to get her. The mother responded by sending a man and his wife to the children's home with a view to their adopting Anna, but they made such a poor impression on the agency that permission was refused. Later the mother came herself and took the child out of the home and then gave her to this couple. It was in the home of this pair that a social worker found the girl a short time thereafter. The social worker went to the mother's home and

"Final Note on a Case of Extreme Isolation" by K. Davis, 1947. *American Journal of Sociology, 52,* pp. 432–437. Reprinted by permission of the author.

pleaded with Anna's grandfather to allow the mother to bring the child home. In spite of threats, he refused. The child, by then more than four months old, was next taken to another children's home in a near-by town. A medical examination at this time revealed that she had impetigo, vaginitis, umbilical hernia, and a skin rash.

Anna remained in this second children's home for nearly three weeks, at the end of which time she was transferred to a private foster-home. Since, however, the grandfather would not, and the mother could not, pay for the child's care, she was finally taken back as a last resort to the grandfather's house (at the age of five and a half months). There she remained, kept on the second floor in an attic-like room because her mother hesitated to incur the grandfather's wrath by bringing her downstairs.

The mother, a sturdy woman weighing about 180 pounds, did a man's work on the farm. She engaged in heavy work such as milking cows and tending hogs and had little time for her children. Sometimes she went out at night, in which case Anna was left entirely without attention. Ordinarily, it seems, Anna received only enough care to keep her barely alive. She appears to have been seldom moved from one position to another. Her clothing and bedding were filthy. She apparently had no instruction, no friendly attention.

It is little wonder that, when finally found and removed from the room in the grandfather's house at the age of nearly six years, the child could not talk, walk, or do anything that showed intelligence. She was in an extremely emaciated and undernourished condition, with skeletonlike legs and a bloated abdomen. She had been fed on virtually nothing except cow's milk during the years under her mother's care.

Anna's condition when found, and her subsequent improvement, have been described in the previous report. It now remains to say what happened to her after that.

## Later History

In 1939, nearly two years after being discovered, Anna had progressed, as previously reported, to the point where she could walk, understand simple commands, feed herself, achieve some neatness, remember people, etc. But she still did not speak, and, though she was much more like a normal infant of something over one year of age in mentality, she was far from normal for her age.

On August 30, 1939, she was taken to a private home for retarded children, leaving the county home where she had been for more than a year and a half. In her new setting she made some further progress, but not a great deal. In a report of an examination made November 6 of the same year, the head of the institution pictured the child as follows:

Anna walks about aimlessly, makes periodic rhythmic motions of her hands, and, at intervals, makes guttural and sucking noises. She regards her hands as if she had seen them for the first time. It was impossible to hold her attention for more than a few seconds at a time—not because of distraction due to external stimuli but because of her inability to concentrate. She ignored the task in hand to gaze vacantly about the room. Speech is entirely lacking. Numerous unsuccessful attempts have been made with her in the hope of developing initial sounds. I do not believe that this failure is due to negativism or deafness but that she is not sufficiently developed to accept speech at this time. . . . The prognosis is not favorable. . . .

More than five months later, on April 25, 1940, a clinical psychologist, the late Professor Francis N. Maxfield, examined Anna and reported the following: large for her age; hearing "entirely normal"; vision apparently normal; able to climb stairs; speech in the "babbling stage" and "promise for developing intelligible speech later seems to be good." He said further that "on the Merrill-Palmer scale she made a mental score of 19 months. On the Vineland social maturity scale she made a score of 23 months."[4]

Professor Maxfield very sensibly pointed out that prognosis is difficult in such cases of isolation. "It is very difficult to take scores on tests standardized under average conditions of environment and experience," he wrote, "and interpret them in a case where environment and experience have been so unusual." With this warning he gave it as his opinion at that time that Anna would eventually "attain an adult mental level of six or seven years."[5]

The school for retarded children, on July 1, 1941, reported that Anna had reached 46 inches in height and weighed 60 pounds. She could bounce and catch a ball and was said to conform to group socialization, though as a follower rather than a leader. Toilet habits were firmly established. Food habits were normal, except that she still used a spoon as her sole implement. She could dress herself except for fastening her clothes. Most remarkable of all, she had finally begun to develop speech. She was characterized as being at about the two-year level in this regard. She could call attendants by name and bring in one when she was asked to. She had a few complete sentences to express her wants. The report concluded that there was nothing peculiar about her, except that she was feeble-minded—"probably congenital in type."[6]

A final report from the school made on June 22, 1942, and evidently the last report before the girl's death, pictured only a slight advance over that given above. It said that Anna could follow directions, string beads, identify a few colors, build with blocks, and differentiate between attractive and unattractive pictures. She had a good sense of rhythm and loved a doll. She talked mainly in phrases but would repeat words and try to carry on a conversation. She was clean about clothing. She habitually washed her hands and brushed her teeth. She would try to help other children. She walked well and could run fairly well, though clumsily. Although easily excited, she had a pleasant disposition.

## Interpretation

Such was Anna's condition just before her death. It may seem as if she had not made much progress, but one must remember the condition in which she had been found. One must recall that she had no glimmering of speech, absolutely no ability to walk, no sense of gesture, not the least capacity to feed herself even when the food was put in front of her, and no comprehension of cleanliness. She was so apathetic that it was hard to tell whether or not she could hear. And all this at the age of nearly six years. Compared with this condition, her capacities at the time of her death seem striking indeed, though they do not amount to much more than a two-and-a-half-year mental level. One conclusion therefore seems safe, namely, that her isolation prevented a considerable amount of mental development that was undoubtedly part of her capacity. Just what her original capacity was, of course, is hard to say; but her development after her period of confinement (including the ability to walk and run, to play, dress, fit into a social situation, and, above all, to speak) shows that she had at least this capacity—capacity that never could have been realized in her original condition of isolation.

A further question is this: What would she have been like if she had received a normal upbringing from the moment of birth? A definitive answer would have been impossible in any case, but even an approximate answer is made difficult by her early death. If one assumes, as was tentatively surmised in the previous report, that it is "almost impossible for any child to learn to speak, think, and act like a normal person after a long period of early isolation," it seems likely that Anna might have had a normal or near-normal capacity, genetically speaking. On the other hand, it was pointed out that Anna represented "a marginal case, [because] she was discovered before she had reached six years of age," an age "young enough to allow for some plasticity."[7] While admitting, then, that Anna's isolation may have been the major cause (and was certainly a minor cause) of her lack of rapid mental progress during the four and a half years following her rescue from neglect, it is necessary to entertain the hypothesis that she was congenitally deficient.

In connection with this hypothesis, one suggestive though by no means conclusive circumstance needs consideration, namely, the mentality of Anna's forebears. Information on this subject is easier to obtain, as one might guess, on the mother's than on the father's side. Anna's maternal grandmother, for example, is said to have been college educated and wished to have her children receive a good education, but her husband, Anna's stern grandfather, apparently a shrewd, hard-driving, calculating farmowner, was so penurious that her ambitions in this direction were thwarted. Under the circumstances her daughter (Anna's mother) managed, despite having to do hard work on the farm, to complete the eighth grade in a country school. Even so, however, the daughter was evidently not very smart. "A schoolmate of [Anna's mother] stated that she was retarded in school work; was very gullible at this age; and that her morals even at this time were discussed by other students." Two tests administered to her on March 4, 1938, when she was thirty-two years of age, showed that she was mentally deficient. On the Stanford Revision of the Binet-Simon Scale her performance was equivalent to that of a child of eight years, giving her an I.Q. of 50 and indicating mental deficiency of "middle-grade moron type."[8]

As to the identity of Anna's father, the most persistent theory holds that he was an old man about seventy-four years of age at the time of the girl's birth. If he was the one, there is no indication of mental or other biological deficiency, whatever one may think of his morals. However, someone else may actually have been the father.

To sum up: Anna's heredity is the kind that *might* have given rise to innate mental deficiency, though not necessarily.

## Comparison with Another Case

Perhaps more to the point than speculations about Anna's ancestry would be a case for comparison. If a child could be discovered who had been isolated about the same length of time as Anna but had achieved a much quicker recovery and a greater mental development, it would be a stronger indication that Anna was deficient to start with.

Such a case does exist. It is the case of a girl found at about the same time as Anna and under strikingly similar circumstances. A full description of the details of this case has not been published, but in addition to newspaper reports, an excellent preliminary account by a speech specialist, Dr. Marie K. Mason, who played an important role in the handling of the child, has appeared.[9] Also the late Dr. Francis N. Maxfield, clinical psychologist at Ohio State University, as was Dr. Mason, has written an as yet unpublished but penetrating analysis of the case.[10] Some of his observations have been included in Professor Zingg's book on feral man.[11] The following discussion is drawn mainly from these enlightening materials. The writer, through the kindness of Professors Mason and Maxfield, did have a chance to observe the girl in April, 1940, and to discuss the features of her case with them.

Born apparently one month later than Anna, the girl in question, who has been given the pseudonym Isabelle, was discovered in November, 1938, nine months after the discovery of Anna. At the time she was found she was approximately six and a half years of age. Like Anna, she was an illegitimate child and had been kept in seclusion for that reason. Her mother was a deaf-mute, having become so at the age of two, and it appears that she and Isabelle had spent most of their time together in a dark room shut off from the rest of the mother's family. As a result Isabelle had no chance to develop speech; when she communicated with her mother, it was by means of gestures. Lack of sunshine and inadequacy of diet had caused Isabelle to become rachitic. Her legs in particular were affected; they were so bowed that as she stood erect the soles of her shoes came nearly flat together, and she got about with a skittering gait.[12]

Her behavior toward strangers, especially men, was almost that of a wild animal, manifesting much fear and hostility. In lieu of speech she made only a strange croaking sound. In many ways she acted like an infant. "She was apparently utterly unaware of relationships of any kind. When presented with a ball for the first time, she held it in the palm of her hand, then reached out and stroked my face with it. Such behavior is comparable to that of a child of six months."[13] At first it was even hard to tell whether or not she could hear, so unused were her senses. Many of her actions resembled those of deaf children.

It is small wonder that, once it was established that she could hear, specialists working with her believed her to be feeble-minded. Even on nonverbal tests her performance was so low as to promise little for the future. Her first score on the Stanford-Binet was 19 months, practically at the zero point of the scale. On the Vineland social maturity scale her first score was 39, representing an age level of two and a half years.[14] "The general impression was that she was wholly uneducable and that any attempt to teach her to speak, after so long a period of silence, would meet with failure."[15]

In spite of this interpretation, the individuals in charge of Isabelle launched a systematic and skillful program of training. It seemed hopeless at first. The approach had to be through pantomime and dramatization, suitable to an infant. It required one week of intensive effort before she even made her first attempt at vocalization. Gradually, she began to respond, however, and, after the first

hurdles had at last been overcome, a curious thing happened. She went through the usual stages of learning characteristic of the years from one to six not only in proper succession but far more rapidly than normal. In a little over two months after her first vocalization she was putting sentences together. Nine months after that she could identify words and sentences on the printed page, could write well, could add to ten, and could retell a story after hearing it. Seven months beyond this point she had a vocabulary of 1,500–2,000 words and was asking complicated questions. Starting from an educational level of between one and three years (depending on what aspect one considers), she had reached a normal level by the time she was eight and a half years old. In short, she covered in two years the stages of learning that ordinarily require six.[16] Or, to put it another way, her I.Q. trebled in a year and a half.[17] The speed with which she reached the normal level of mental development seems analogous to the recovery of body weight in a growing child after an illness, the recovery being achieved by an extra fast rate of growth for a period after the illness until normal weight for the given age is again attained.

When the writer saw Isabelle a year and a half after her discovery, she gave him the impression of being a very bright, cheerful, energetic little girl. She spoke well, walked and ran without trouble, and sang with gusto and accuracy. Today she is over fourteen years old and has passed the sixth grade in a public school. Her teachers say that she participates in all school activities as normally as other children. Though older than her classmates, she has fortunately not physically matured too far beyond their level.[18]

Clearly the history of Isabelle's development is different from that of Anna's. In both cases there was an exceedingly low, or rather blank, intellectual level to begin with. In both cases it seemed that the girl might be congenitally feeble-minded. In both a considerably higher level was reached later on. But the Ohio girl achieved a normal mentality within two years, whereas Anna was still marked inadequate at the end of four and a half years. This difference in achievement may suggest that Anna had less initial capacity. But an alternative hypothesis is possible.

One should remember that Anna never received the prolonged and expert attention that Isabelle received. The result of such attention, in the case of the Ohio girl, was to give her speech at an early stage, and her subsequent rapid development seems to have been a consequence of that. "Until Isabelle's speech and language development, she had all the characteristics of a feebleminded child." Had Anna, who, from the standpoint of psychometric tests and early history, closely resembled this girl at the start, been given a mastery of speech at an earlier point by intensive training, her subsequent development might have been much more rapid.[19]

The hypothesis that Anna began with a sharply inferior mental capacity is therefore not established. Even if she were deficient to start with, we have no way of knowing how much so. Under ordinary conditions she might have been a dull normal or, like her mother, a moron. Even after the blight of her isolation, if she had lived to maturity, she might have finally reached virtually the full level of her capacity, whatever it may have been. That her isolation did have a profound effect upon her mentality, there can be no doubt. This is proved by the substantial degree of change during the four and a half years following her rescue.

Consideration of Isabelle's case serves to show, as Anna's case does not clearly show, that isolation up to the age of six, with failure to acquire any form of speech and hence failure to grasp nearly the whole world of cultural meaning, does not preclude the subsequent acquisition of these. Indeed, there seems to be a process of accelerated recovery in which the child goes through the mental stages at a more rapid rate than would be the case in normal development. Just what would be the maximum age at which a person could remain isolated and still retain the capacity for full cultural acquisition is hard to say. Almost certainly it would not be as high as age fifteen; it might possibly be as low as age ten. Undoubtedly various individuals would differ considerably as to the exact age.

Anna's is not an ideal case for showing the effects of extreme isolation, partly because she was possibly deficient to begin with, partly because she did not receive the best training available, and partly because she did not live long enough. Nevertheless, her case is instructive when placed in the record with numerous other cases of extreme isolation. This and the previous article about her are meant to place her in the record. It is to be hoped that other cases will be described in the scientific literature as they are discovered (as unfortunately they will be), for only in these rare cases of extreme isolation is it possible "to observe *concretely separated* two factors in the development of human personality which are always otherwise only analytically separated, the biogenic and the sociogenic factors."[20]

### Notes

1. K. Davis (1940, January), "Extreme social isolation of a child," *American Journal of Sociology*, 45, 554–565.

2. Sincere appreciation is due to the officials in the Department of Welfare, Commonwealth of Pennsylvania, for their kind co-operation in making available the records concerning Anna and discussing the case frankly with the writer. Helen C. Hubbell, Florentine Hackbusch, and Eleanor Meckelnburg were particularly helpful, as was Fanny L. Matchette. Without their aid neither of the reports on Anna could have been written.

3. The records are not clear as to which day.

4. Letter to one of the state officials in charge of the case.

5. Ibid.

6. Progress report of the school.

7. Davis (1940), p. 564.

8. The facts set forth here as to Anna's ancestry are taken chiefly from a report of mental tests administered to Anna's mother by psychologists at a state hospital where she was taken for this purpose after the discovery of Anna's seclusion. This excellent report was not available to the writer when the previous paper on Anna was published.

9. M. K. Mason (1942), "Learning to speak after six and one-half years of silence," *Journal of Speech Disorders, 7,* 295–304.

10. F. N. Maxfield (no date), "What happens when the social environment of a child approaches zero." Unpublished manuscript. The writer is greatly indebted to Mrs. Maxfield and to Professor Horace B. English, a colleague of Professor Maxfield, for the privilege of seeing this manuscript and other materials collected on isolated and feral individuals.

11. J. A. L. Singh & R. M. Zingg (1941), *Wolf-children and feral man.* New York: Harper & Bros., pp. 248–251.

12. Maxfield (no date).

13. Mason (1942), p. 299.

14. Maxfield (no date).

15. Mason (1942), p. 299.

16. Mason (1942), pp. 300–304.

17. Maxfield (no date).

18. Based on a personal letter from Dr. Mason to the writer, May 13, 1946.

19. This point is suggested in a personal letter from Dr. Mason to the writer, October 22, 1946.

20. Singh & Zingg (1941), pp. xxi–xxii, in a foreword by the writer.

# Language and Neurological Disorders

*Alfred Lindesmith, Anselm Strauss, and Norman Denzin*

## Aphasia and Related Neurological Disorders

We have noted how various forms of madness and the uncanny illuminate the complex relationship between the internal environment of people and their speech and language abilities. We shall now briefly discuss aphasia—a language disturbance produced by lesion or disease in the brain—and related neurological disturbances which alter the "normal" relationship between speech, thought, and the internal environment.

Aphasia is often, though not necessarily, brought about by cerebral injury. Aphasic conditions may also be produced under hypnosis or by traumatic experiences. The loss of function associated with aphasia can assume various forms, including the inability to read, write, or name familiar objects.

Consider the following statement from a young Russian soldier who during World War II sustained a severe brain injury which altered his ability to read, think, speak, and write. He is discussing his attempts to write with a pencil (Luria, 1972, pp. 71–72):

I'd forgotten how to use a pencil. I'd twist it back and forth but I just couldn't begin to write. I was shown how to hold it and asked to write something. But when I picked up the pencil all I could

do was draw some crooked lines across the paper and finally moved the pencil across the paper. But looking at the mark I'd made it was impossible to tell where I'd started. It looked something like the scribbling of a child . . .

Often, in the aphasic's world, there is no memory of the past. This means that the patient has difficulty connecting internal, bodily processes with the words that represent those processes. Luria (1972, pp. 87–88) describes the Russian soldier trying to relieve himself. Here are the soldier's words:

After dinner, when the other patients were going to sleep, I suddenly had to relieve myself. To put it plainly, I needed the bedpan. But what a complicated thing it was for me to remember the word and call the nurse. For the life of me I couldn't think of the word *bedpan.* . . . I saw the nurse . . . I yelled . . . calling her *sister,* a word that suddenly entered my mind: "Sister . . . I also . . . need the . . . what's it!"

. . . In the 1890s, Charles Sherrington, a British neurologist, discovered what he called our sixth sense, which he named *proprioception.* By this he referred to our normal ability to know where our bodies are, what position or posture we are in, and so on. We know this subliminally, without looking. Some aphasics appear to lose this proprioceptive sixth sense.

[Oliver] Sacks (1985) had a patient named Christina, who, after routine surgery, developed an acute infection in her nerves which permanently destroyed her proprioceptive nerve fibers. She became, and remains, disembodied. She lacks all instinctive sense of her body, its position, its posture, and its movements. She feels that her body is dead, not-real, not-hers, blind and deaf to itself.

There are a number of different ways to classify aphasia. Head (1926) distinguished four main types: verbal, nominal, syntactic, and semantic aphasia. More recently, in a review of the latest research on aphasia, Wallace (1984, p. 80) suggests that there are two basic types of aphasia. The first involves language disturbances that primarily affect the ability to speak (expressive, or Broca's aphasia), and the second involves the ability to understand language (receptive, or Wernicke's aphasia). Broca was the first to link types of aphasia with areas of the brain. He demonstrated an association between damage in the left hemisphere and aphasia. Patients who suffer brain damage in this area of the brain usually show disturbances in the ability to produce written and spoken language. They often speak slowly and with difficulty. They display poor articulation, improper sentence structure, and omission of small grammatical words and word endings. They may, however, understand written and spoken speech and often have the ability to sing familiar songs.

Wernicke identified another type of aphasia which results in disturbances involving how language is understood (receptive aphasia) as well as in speaking (Wallace, 1984, p. 80). Patients often have fluent and rapid speech, but their utterances are devoid of meaning.

Other types of aphasia have also been identified. Word deafness, for example, refers to a patient's inability to understand spoken language, even though he or she can hear normally, read, and write.

Wernicke proposed a theory of language production which is still held to be valid (Wallace, 1984, p. 80). This theory argues that an underlying utterance originates in Wernicke's area (the temporal lobe of the brain), and then is transferred to Broca's area where a coordinated program for the utterance is produced. This program is then passed to the motor cortex, which "activates the appropriate motor sequences required for the specific utterance" (Wallace, 1984, p. 90).

. . . Jakobson had distinguished those aphasic disorders involving contiguity disorders and those involving similarity disturbances. Jakobson proposed that the two poles of language (syntactical and associative) were revealed in metonymy and metaphor. It is not entirely clear how Jakobson's classification scheme fits with the more recent distinction between expressive and receptive aphasia. However, those theories which explain aphasia in terms of disturbances to specific brain areas are called localization theories (Schutz, 1962, p. 263).

### The Nature of Aphasic Experience

In analyzing the aphasic's experiences, we must maintain a distinction between inner speech and external speech performances (Schutz, 1962, p. 264). Inner speech finds its expression in thought and in the selection of words and word categories which fit the subject's ongoing flow of experience, including how she interprets bodily sensations. External speech performances, or speech acts, locate the inner speech and thought of the subject in a social conversation. In aphasia, this connection between inner thought and outer speech is broken, thought and speech become problematic, and furthermore, words are no longer immediately and directly linked to experience. Clearly those theories of aphasia which explain it in terms of localized injuries to specific areas of the brain speak not to language disturbances per se, but rather to a disturbance in memory. The aphasic loses the ability to deal with concrete, immediate experience. However, localization theories have problems explaining how the same word, spoken by different people in different contexts, is understood as the same word (Schutz, 1962, p. 270).

Merleau-Ponty (1962) has developed this point. The normal mind is able to spontaneously organize its perceptual field and its symbolic structure. It experiences no break or gap between sensation, perception, memory, thought, speech, and action. These accomplishments occur in the lived present. The aphasic is incapable of doing this; for him, the world suddenly becomes strange and problematic. A theory of aphasia which accounts for these disturbances solely in terms of the localization of brain function becomes a mechanistic, physiological account which does not account for how the person engages the world in a continuous process of interaction. Localization theories fall into the dualistic trap of separating mind from body. We can illustrate these points by taking up the introspective reports of aphasics.

### Introspective Reports of Aphasics

Some of the most significant materials on aphasic thought are found in Head's work. The comments of his patients are interesting and provide some insight into their condition. One of them said (1926, p. 256):

"When I think of anything, everything seems to be rolling along. I can't hold it . . . I can see what it is. I seem to see it myself, but I can't put it properly into words like you ought to. I can see what it is myself like. My mind won't stop at any one thing. They keep on rolling. Myself, I imagine when you're talking you're only thinking of what you're talking about. When I'm talking to anybody it seems a lot of things keep going by."

Another patient, attempting to explain the difficulty he had in finding his way about London, said, "You see it's like this: with me it's all in bits. I have to jump like this," marking a thick line between two points with a pencil, "like a man who jumps from one thing to the next. I can see them but I can't express. Really it is that I haven't enough names." (1926, p. 371)

A number of comments by these patients indicate that images and the flow of imagery are profoundly affected by the loss of language that occurs in aphasia. Head always asked his patients to draw pictures, both from a model and from memory. One of the patients who had drawn a jug from a model could not do it from memory. He commented as follows (1926, p. 193):

I was trying to see the glass bottle: the picture seemed to evade me. I knew it was a bottle, and I could describe the drawing. But when it came to seeing it as a picture, I was more or less nonplussed. I often seem to have got the picture, but it seemed to evade me.

When this patient was questioned further it became clear that he experienced images, but that they appeared to be unstable and could not be controlled or evoked at will. He said, "The more I try to make them come the more difficult it is to get in touch with them, as one might say" (1926, p. 193).

Head performed the following test with one of his patients: He rolled bits of paper into wads and had a contest with the patient to see who could toss the improvised balls more accurately into a basket placed some distance away. The aphasic proved more adept than Head. Then a screen was moved in front of the basket so that the basket was not visible, and the contest was repeated. This time Head did far better than the patient; the patient was at a loss as to what to do. He explained his difficulties (1926, p. 208):

When I could see the basket I could follow the line of vision; when it was in the same place . . . I'd seen the basket before you put the screen there; I knew you hadn't changed the position, but in some odd way I didn't feel perfectly confident in my own mind that it was in that position.

. . . [T]hrough the internalized use of language, humans are able to imagine objects and events that are removed in time and space. This point is corroborated in the study of aphasia, for the aphasic's flow of imagery is so disturbed that he or she is unable to visualize objects adequately when they are not in view.

The inability of some aphasics to deal with objects they cannot see or touch is brought out in a curious manner by their inability to strike an imaginary match on an imaginary matchbox, to drive an imaginary nail with a nonexistent hammer, or to demonstrate with an empty glass how one drinks water. These same patients can strike actual matches, drive actual nails, and drink water from a glass when they are thirsty. Goldstein (1940) described these and other inabilities of the aphasic as a regression from an abstract or categorical attitude toward the world to a more concrete attitude.

## Disturbances of Voluntary Activities

Clearly, aphasics appear to have lost a certain flexibility of orientation so that they no longer seem at home in the world. We can put this descriptively by saying that aphasics are not self-starters; they cannot talk effectively to others or to themselves about things that are not actually present. Their inner life is impoverished and simplified, and freedom of thought and action is largely lost. Aphasics are more or less at the mercy of the external stimuli that play upon them.

The aphasic is often able to function normally in simple concrete relations. But when required to act on the basis of long-range goals or abstract principles or merely of remembered events, objects, or persons, as all people constantly are, aphasics tend to fail. This limitation to the concrete present makes impossible much of the voluntary, "creative," kind of human behavior—behavior that seems normal because human beings think about things, events, and people and adapt their behavior to these verbal formulations or interpretations. Aphasics are unable to make these verbal formulations; therefore their responses are piecemeal and unintegrated. Aphasics respond to each concrete situation as such; and when no immediate demand is made upon them, or when excessive demands are made, they tend to lapse into inactivity or anxiety, realizing that there is something wrong with their inner life.

Goldstein has shown how drastically aphasia affected the intimate social relations of one of his patients. The patient, a husband and father, prior to his affliction had been devoted to his family. During his stay at the hospital, however, he appeared to show neither concern nor interest in his absent family and became confused when any attempt was made to call his attention to them. Yet when he was sent home for brief visits, he warmly displayed his former interest and devotion.

Goldstein concluded that this patient's "out of sight, out of mind" attitude toward his wife and family grew directly out of his inability to formulate his relationships to his family when it was physically absent. He could not imagine it adequately, and consequently he could not engage in internalized thinking about it. In short, when his wife and children were not visible to him he was unable to think of them, because he could not produce and manipulate the necessary verbal symbols.

### Failures of Projection

In one of the most significant tests he administered to aphasics, Head required the patient, seated opposite and facing him, to imitate his movements. Head placed his left hand to his right ear, his right hand to his right eye, and so on. Then he repeated the tests while the patient observed and imitated these movements as they were reflected in a mirror.

The patients either had great difficulty with the first part of this test or they found it altogether impossible to imitate Head's movements, whereas they were generally able to imitate the movements correctly when they observed them in a mirror. The reason was not difficult to find: When the doctor and patient sat facing each other the patient could not imitate directly, but had to transpose directions (remembering that his left hand corresponded to the investigator's right hand, and so on). When Head's movements were reflected in the mirror, this action of transposition was unnecessary; all that was required was direct mechanical imitation.

Significantly, this simple but exceedingly effective test demonstrates that the person lacking language cannot project himself or herself into the point of view of another person. Patients are unable to guide actions by imagining them to be in some other position than the one in which they actually are. In a fundamental sense, normal adult social interaction rests upon a person's ability to anticipate and appreciate the actual and possible reactions of other people—in short, to assume the role of another person. The loss of this ability in aphasia (to varying degrees, depending upon the severity of the disorder) thus provides powerful experimental and clinical evidence to support the thesis that language is the basic social and socializing institution.

### Direct and Symbolic Reference

Head made a distinction between what he called "acts of direct reference" and those that require some sort of symbolic formulation between the initiation and the completion of the act. This distinction is roughly equivalent to Goldstein and Scherer's distinction between the "concrete" and the "abstract" (categorical) attitudes (1941). Acts of symbolic reference imply a complex adaptation involving the recognition of signs, logical symbols, or diagrams. Acts of direct reference are organized on a simpler level.

The aphasic generally functions adequately in acts of direct reference but has trouble with acts of symbolic reference. Table 1 provides a few illustrations of the difference between the two classes of acts.

Not all types of behavior listed in the second column are beyond the capacity of all aphasics. There is considerable variation according to the severity of the disorder and the type of aphasia involved. Moreover, aphasics often learn over a period of time to perform some of the more complex acts listed, although usually with difficulty, by resorting to more primitive methods than those used by normal persons. Thus a patient who cannot follow directions in a city may learn a route by sheer repetition and memorization of landmarks. Similarly, he or she may learn to make change properly by repetition and memorization rather than by calculation.

### Unreliability of Introspective Evidence

The data on aphasia indicate that introspective evidence of the role of language must be interpreted cautiously. Just as other functions drop out of consciousness when they become automatic, so may language fade out of the picture when many apparently purely motor and other types of skills of which it is the basis are fully established.

To illustrate our point, we can ask if the game of billiards presupposes language ability. Offhand, there seems to be no possible connection between the propulsion of billiard balls on a green table and the ability to talk. If we ask billiard players about the game, they tell us only that when they aim they make a sort of geometrical calculation and have in their "mind's eye" a kind of geometrical image of the path they wish the cue ball to take, striking first one and then the second of the two other balls involved. It would appear that language plays no part in this activity.

However, such introspective evidence is contradicted by the facts. The aphasic, even though she may have been skillful at billiards prior to the onset of aphasia, usually loses that skill along with language ability, reporting an inability to visualize the three balls simultaneously. The aphasic does not know at what angle to strike the second ball and may even hit it on the wrong side.

Similarly, one would suppose from introspective evidence that the ability to draw a picture of a cow is totally unconnected with language and thus would be unaffected in aphasia. This is not so, as we see from the following example. It was Head's practice to ask his patients to draw pictures of familiar objects from memory. He requested an English army officer, for example, to sketch an

**Table 1**

| Acts of Direct Reference | Acts of Symbolic Reference |
| --- | --- |
| Imitating investigator's movements as reflected in a mirror. | Imitating investigator's movements seated opposite, facing him. |
| Shaving. | Gathering together in advance the necessary articles for shaving. |
| Selecting from a number of objects before him the duplicate of one placed in his hand out of sight. | Selecting from objects placed before him the duplicates of two or more objects placed in his hand out of sight. |
| Tossing ball into a basket that he can see before him. | Tossing a ball into a basket concealed behind a screen. |
| Exact matching of colored skeins of yarn. | Sorting and arranging colored skeins of yarn in a systematic way. |
| Pointing to familiar objects in his room. | Drawing a ground plan of his room that shows the location of familiar objects. |
| Swearing. | Giving the name of the Deity upon command. |
| Recognizing familiar streets and buildings of a city. | Following directions within a familiar city. |
| Repeating, fairly correctly, the numbers up to ten and sometimes beyond that if he is given a start. | Carrying out arithmetical operations, particularly those involving numbers of several digits. |

elephant. Prior to his illness, this officer had spent many years in India and had once shown rather good amateur ability at drawing. Nevertheless, the drawing he produced was exceptionally poor. It lacked some essential parts, such as the trunk and tusks; some of the parts were in wrong relation to one another; and, in general, the whole picture was scarcely recognizable. Later, when the bullet wound that had caused the aphasia had healed and the patient had recovered much of his language ability, he drew upon request a detailed, accurate picture of an elephant.

These two examples point to the conclusion that language may play a vital role in an activity without the individual's introspective awareness of that fact.

### Language Impairment and Thought

We have said a great deal about language and thought . . . , emphasizing that the latter cannot exist without the former. Thought without language is reduced to the level of thinking—if we may call it such—that is characteristic of lower animals. Those who study aphasia sometimes erroneously conceive of thinking and language as two entirely distinct and separate processes. Thinking, speaking to others, and speaking to oneself are inextricably interrelated and dependent processes. Head has compared the aphasic with a man in solitary confinement whose only contact with the outside world is a defective telephone. While this comparison is picturesque, it is incomplete, when the aphasic tries to talk to himself to formulate his own thoughts, he uses the same defective telephone.

Neurologists who study speech-related functions in the brain generally agree with Russell and Espir that in the brain, speech cannot be separate from thought. Luria (1966, p. 34) also comments: "The reorganization of mental activity by means of speech, and the incorporation of the system of speech connections into a large number of processes, hitherto direct in nature, are among the more important factors in the formation of the higher mental functions, whereby man, as distinct from animals, acquires consciousness and volition."

Aphasia and related disorders in their almost bewildering variety of manifestations serve to bring home the enormous complexity of the language function and its interconnections with other processes. Russell and Espir observe that severe aphasia destroys the individual's capacity to enjoy reading a book; he may read slowly, absorb the meaning with difficulty, and lose the train of thought because the previous pages are inadequately remembered. They observe that there are a number of storage systems that he must use in reading: (1) visual patterns acquired much earlier for the recognition of letters and words; (2) the associations that give meaning to the words; and (3) "the capacity to hold something of what he reads for long enough to correlate it with later pages" (1961, p. 105).

These writers observe that intelligence and personality are disorganized in severe aphasia, adding that some of the long-range effects of aphasia are loss of memory, difficulty in concentration, mental fatiguability, irritability, and change of personality. "The scaffolding on which speech is developed," they add, "is built up in relation to hearing, vision, and the sensori-motor skill involved in uttering words." However, this scaffolding "is concerned with much more than speech for it seems to provide a basis for the psychological processes of thinking and learning" (1961, pp. 170–71).

The normal human finds it difficult to imagine how it feels to be an aphasic. There is little in our experience that enables us to project ourselves, as it were, into her position, or to see and experience the impairment of thought that hinges upon her speech difficulties. To better understand, suppose we pretend that we are in a foreign land whose language we know only moderately well. Conversation with others is reduced to simple concrete levels, as considerable facility in the language would be required in order to exchange views on complicated, abstract, or philosophical matters. It is easier to talk—with the aid of gestures—about concrete objects that are present, such as the immediate scene and the weather. If we try to speak of events long past or far in the future, or of objects out of sight, our vocabulary is insufficient. However, if we try to carry on such a slightly involved conversation, the effort is likely to prove exhausting. As an acquaintance of the authors once said:

I went to bed exhausted every night from trying to speak German; particularly when I was with a lot of German people who were engaging in a crossfire of conversation. It was simply exhausting—after a while you felt you wanted to sit down and recuperate. And you felt absolutely frustrated and bottled up; you wonder if you're ever going to think a complex thought again in your life. You can ask for beer and coffee and potatoes, but when you have to discuss a complex feeling or reaction or analyze a political situation, you're simply stalled. You struggle to speak, but you're reduced to the level of your vocabulary.

Suppose that in addition to conversing with others in the foreign language, we also had to converse with ourself (that is, think) using only this same restricted vocabulary. How difficult it would be to carry on internalized conversation that had any semblance of complexity!

### Alzheimer's Disease

It will be instructive to briefly compare aphasia with Alzheimer's disease, which has been called the disease of the century for it is now the "single most devastating illness of old age" (Gubrium, 1986, p. 38). This disease leads to a progressive decline in mental functioning; victims experience forgetfulness, depression, disorientation, confusion, and an inability to plan and organize activities, including simple daily tasks. It is often called the disease that "dims bright minds" (Gubrium, 1986, p. 39). A patient's spouse describes her husband's actions:

I just don't know what to think or feel. It's like he's not even there anymore. . . . He doesn't know me. He thinks I'm a strange woman in the house. He shouts and tries to slap me away from him . . . he makes sounds more like an animal than a person. Do you think he has a mind left? . . . Sometimes I get so upset that I just pound on him and yell at him to come out to me. (Gubrium, 1986, p. 41)

This disease has two victims: the person with the disease and the caregiver. In a particularly insightful interaction analysis, Gubrium (1986, pp. 37–51) has described how caregivers struggle with the meaning of mind and agency in the Alzheimer patient. Especially distressing for the caregiver is the fact that the patient, often a spouse or parent, no longer displays actions which indicate that they know who they are, how they feel, or how they feel toward the caregiver. This leads caregivers to impute a "hidden mind" to the victim, and behind that hidden mind they impute a biographical theory of "agency" which assumes that the victim still loves them and cares for them. The following two accounts (Gubrium, 1986, p. 42) indicate how caregivers struggle to maintain the belief that the victim still has a mind. A man named Jack is discussing his spouse, who he says is just like the living dead:

That's why I'm looking for a nursing home for her. I loved her dearly but she's just not Mary anymore. No matter how hard I try, I can't get myself to believe that she's there anymore. . . . I just know that's not her speaking to me but some knee-jerk reaction. . . .

Another caregiver, Sara, replies:

Well, I know what you've gone through, and I admire your courage, Jack. But you can't be too sure. How do you *really* know that what Mary says at times is not one of those few times she's been able to really reach out to you? You don't really know for sure, do you? . . . I face the same thing day in day out with Richard (her husband). Can I ever finally close him out of my life and say, "Well, it's done. It's over. He's gone"? How do I know that the poor man isn't hidden somewhere, behind all the confusion, trying to reach out and say, "I love you, Sara"? (she weeps)

Gubrium's analysis reveals how the spouses and children of Alzheimer's disease victims impute a theory of minded, intentional, loving conduct to them. Such beliefs keep alive the hope that a "mind is still inside," and that that mind still cares for them. In these ways caregivers indicate how mind is a social, interactional process.

There is no known cure for Alzheimer's disease; however, victims of aphasia can be treated and in many cases there is hope of recovery. These two disorders reveal how disturbances in language ability strip from humans their basic abilities to be feeling, thinking, expressive beings.

## References

Goldstein, K. (1940). *Human nature in light of psychopathology.* Cambridge, MA: Harvard University Press.

Goldstein, K., & Scherer, M. (1941). Abstract and concrete behavior: An experimental study with special tests. *Psychological Monographs, 5,* no. 2.

Gubrium, J. F. (1986). The social preservation of the mind: The Alzheimer's disease experience. *Symbolic Interaction, 9,* 37–51.

Head, H. G. (1926). *Aphasia and kindred disorders of speech.* New York: Macmillan.

Luria, A. R. (1966). *Higher cortical functions in man* (trans. by B. Haigh). New York: Basic Books.

Luria, A. R. (1972). *The man with a shattered world: The history of a brain wound.* New York: Basic Books.

Merleau-Ponty, M. (1962). *The phenomenology of perception.* London: Routledge & Kegan Paul.

Russell, W. R., & Espir, L. E. (1961). *Traumatic aphasia: A study of war wounds of the brain.* New York: Oxford University Press.

Sacks, O. (1985). *The man who mistook his wife for a hat and other clinical tales.* New York: Harper & Row.

Schutz, A. (1962). *Collected papers vol. 1: The problem of social reality.* The Hague: Martinus Nijhoff.

Wallace, P. M. (1984). Aphasia. In R. J. Corsini (Ed.), *Encyclopedia of psychology, vol. 1* (p. 80). New York: Wiley.

11

# The Man Who Mistook His Wife for a Hat

*Oliver Sacks*

Dr. P. was a musician of distinction, well-known for many years as a singer, and then, at the local School of Music, as a teacher. It was here, in relation to his students, that certain strange problems were first observed. Sometimes a student would present himself, and Dr. P. would not recognize him; or, specifically, would not recognize his face. The moment the student spoke, he would be recognized by his voice. Such incidents multiplied, causing embarrassment, perplexity, fear—and, sometimes, comedy. For not only did Dr. P. increasingly fail to see faces, but he saw faces when there were no faces to see: genially, Magoo-like, when in the street he might pat the heads of water hydrants and parking meters, taking these to be the heads of children; he would amiably address carved knobs on the furniture and be astounded when they did not reply. At first these odd mistakes were laughed off as jokes, not least by Dr. P. himself. Had he not always had a quirky sense of humor and been given to Zenlike paradoxes and jests? His musical powers were as dazzling as ever; he did not feel ill—he had never felt better; and the mistakes were so ludicrous—and so ingenious— that they could hardly be serious or betoken anything serious. The notion of there being

"something the matter" did not emerge until some three years later, when diabetes developed. Well aware that diabetes could affect his eyes, Dr. P. consulted an ophthalmologist, who took a careful history and examined his eyes closely. "There's nothing the matter with your eyes," the doctor concluded. "But there is trouble with the visual parts of your brain. You don't need my help, you must see a neurologist." And so, as a result of this referral, Dr. P. came to me.

It was obvious within a few seconds of meeting him that there was no trace of dementia in the ordinary sense. He was a man of great cultivation and charm who talked well and fluently, with imagination and humor. I couldn't think why he had been referred to our clinic.

And yet there *was* something a bit odd. He faced me as he spoke, was oriented toward me, and yet there was something the matter—it was difficult to formulate. He faced me with his *ears*, I came to think, but not with his eyes. These, instead of looking, gazing, at me, "taking me in," in the normal way, made sudden strange fixations—on my nose, on my right ear, down to my chin, up to my right eye—as if noting (even studying) these individual features, but not seeing my whole face, its changing expressions, "me," as a whole. I am not sure that I fully realized this at the time—there was just a teasing strangeness, some failure in the normal interplay of gaze and expression. He saw me, he *scanned* me, and yet. . . .

"What seems to be the matter?" I asked him at length.

"Nothing that I know of," he replied with a smile, "but people seem to think there's something wrong with my eyes."

"But *you* don't recognize any visual problems?"

"No, not directly, but I occasionally make mistakes."

I left the room briefly to talk to his wife. When I came back, Dr. P. was sitting placidly by the window, attentive, listening rather than looking out. "Traffic," he said, "street sounds, distant trains—they make a sort of symphony, do they not? You know Honegger's *Pacific 234*?"

What a lovely man, I thought to myself. How can there be anything seriously the matter? Would he permit me to examine him?

"Yes, of course, Dr. Sacks."

I stilled my disquiet, his perhaps, too, in the soothing routine of a neurological exam—muscle strength, coordination, reflexes, tone. . . . It was while examining his reflexes—a trifle abnormal on the left side—that the first bizarre experience occurred. I had taken off his left shoe and scratched the sole of his foot with a key—a frivolous-seeming but essential test of a reflex—and then, excusing myself to screw my ophthalmoscope together, left him to put on the shoe himself. To my surprise, a minute later, he had not done this.

"Can I help?" I asked.

"Help what? Help whom?"

"Help you put on your shoe."

"Ach," he said, "I had forgotten the shoe," adding, *sotto voce*, "The shoe? The shoe?" He seemed baffled.

"Your shoe," I repeated. "Perhaps you'd put it on."

He continued to look downward, though not at the shoe, with an intense but misplaced concentration. Finally his gaze settled on his foot: "That is my shoe, yes?"

Did I mishear? Did he missee?

"My eyes," he explained, and put a hand to his foot. "*This* is my shoe, no?"

"No, it is not. That is your foot. *There* is your shoe."

"Ah! I thought that was my foot."

Was he joking? Was he mad? Was he blind? If this was one of his "strange mistakes," it was the strangest mistake I had ever come across.

I helped him on with his shoe (his foot), to avoid further complication. Dr. P. himself seemed untroubled, indifferent, maybe amused. I resumed my examination. His visual acuity was good: He had no difficulty seeing a pin on the floor, though sometimes he missed it if it was placed to his left.

He saw all right, but what did he see? I opened out a copy of the *National Geographic Magazine* and asked him to describe some pictures in it.

His responses here were very curious. His eyes would dart from one thing to another, picking up tiny features, individual features, as they had done with my face. A striking brightness, a color, a shape would arrest his attention and elicit comment—but in no case did he get the scene-as-a-whole. He failed to see the whole, seeing only details, which he spotted like blips on a radar screen. He never entered into relation with the picture as a whole—never faced, so to speak, *its* physiognomy. He had no sense whatever of a landscape or scene.

I showed him the cover, an unbroken expanse of Sahara dunes.

"What do you see here?" I asked.

"I see a river," he said. "And a little guesthouse with its terrace on the water. People are dining out on the terrace. I see colored parasols here and there." He was looking, if it was "looking," right off the cover into mid-air and confabulating nonexistent features, as if the absence of features in the actual picture had driven him to imagine the river and the terrace and the colored parasols.

I must have looked aghast, but he seemed to think he had done rather well. There was a hint of a smile on his face. He also appeared to have decided that the examination was over and started to look around for his hat.

He reached out his hand and took hold of his wife's head, tried to lift it off, to put it on. He had apparently mistaken his wife for a hat! His wife looked as if she was used to such things.

I could make no sense of what had occurred in terms of conventional neurology (or neuropsychology). In some ways he seemed perfectly preserved, and in others absolutely, incomprehensibly devastated. How could he, on the one hand, mistake his wife for a hat and, on the other, function, as apparently he still did, as a teacher at the Music School?

I had to think, to see him again—and to see him in his own familiar habitat, at home.

A few days later I called on Dr. P. and his wife at home, with the score of the *Dichterliebe* in my briefcase (I knew he liked Schumann), and a variety of odd objects for the testing of perception. Mrs. P. showed me into a lofty apartment, which recalled fin-de-siècle Berlin. A magnificent old Bösendorfer stood in state in the center of the room, and all around it were music stands, instruments, scores. . . . There were books, there were paintings, but the music was central. Dr. P. came in, a little bowed, and, distracted, advanced with outstretched hand to the grandfather clock, but, hearing my voice, corrected himself, and shook hands with me. We exchanged greetings and chatted a little of current concerts and performances. Diffidently, I asked him if he would sing.

"The *Dichterliebe!*" he exclaimed. "But I can no longer read music. You will play them, yes?"

I said I would try. On that wonderful old piano even my playing sounded right, and Dr. P. was an aged but infinitely mellow Fischer-Dieskau, combining a perfect ear and voice with the most incisive musical intelligence. It was clear that the Music School was not keeping him on out of charity.

Dr. P.'s temporal lobes were obviously intact: He had a wonderful musical cortex. What, I wondered, was going on in his parietal and occipital lobes, especially in those areas where visual processing occurred? I carry the platonic solids in my neurological kit and decided to start with these.

"What is this?" I asked, drawing out the first one.

"A cube, of course."

"Now this?" I asked, brandishing another.

He asked if he might examine it, which he did swiftly and systematically: "A dodecahedron, of course. And don't bother with the others—I'll get the icosahedron, too."

Abstract shapes clearly presented no problems. What about faces? I took out a pack of cards. All of these he identified instantly, including the jacks, queens, kings, and the joker. But these, after all, are stylized designs, and it was impossible to tell whether he saw faces or merely patterns. I decided I would show him a volume of cartoons which I had in my briefcase. Here, again, for the most part, he did well. Churchill's cigar, Schnozzle's nose: as soon as he had picked out a key feature he could identify the face. But cartoons, again, are formal and schematic. It remained to be seen how he would do with real faces, realistically represented.

I turned on the television, keeping the sound off, and found an early Bette Davis film. A love scene was in progress. Dr. P. failed to identify the actress—but this could have been because she had never entered his world. What was more striking was that he failed to identify the expressions on her face or her partner's, though in the course of a single torrid scene these passed from sultry yearning through passion, surprise, disgust, and fury to a melting reconciliation. Dr. P. could make nothing of any of this. He was very unclear as to what was going on, or who was who or even what sex they were. His comments on the scene were positively Martian.

It was just possible that some of his difficulties were associated with the unreality of a celluloid, Hollywood world; and it occurred to me that he might be more successful in identifying faces from his own life. On the walls of the apartment there were photographs of his family, his colleagues, his pupils, himself. I gathered a pile of these together and, with some misgivings, presented them to him. What had been funny, or farcical, in relation to the movie, was tragic in relation to real life. By and large, he recognized nobody: neither his family, nor his colleagues, nor his pupils, nor himself. He recognized a portrait of Einstein because he picked up the characteristic hair and moustache; and the same thing happened with one or two other people. "Ach, Paul!" he said, when shown a portrait of his brother. "That square jaw, those big teeth—I would know Paul anywhere!" But was it Paul he recognized, or one or two of his features, on the basis of which he could make a reasonable guess as to the subject's identity? In the absence of obvious "markers," he was utterly lost. But it was not merely the cognition, the *gnosis*, at fault; there was something radically wrong with the whole way he proceeded. For he approached these faces—even of those near and dear—as if they were abstract puzzles or tests. He did not relate to them, he did not behold. No face was familiar to him, seen as a "thou," being just identified as a set of features, an "it." Thus, there was formal, but no trace of personal gnosis. And with this went his indifference, or blindness, to expression. A face, to us, is a person looking out— we see, as it were, the person through his *persona*, his face. But for Dr. P. there was no *persona* in this sense—no outward *persona*, and no person within.

I had stopped at a florist on my way to his apartment and bought myself an extravagant red rose for my buttonhole. Now I removed this and handed it to him. He took it like a botanist or morphologist given a specimen, not like a person given a flower.

"About six inches in length," he commented. "A convoluted red form with a linear green attachment."

"Yes," I said encouragingly, "and what do you think it is, Dr. P.?"

"Not easy to say." He seemed perplexed. "It lacks the simple symmetry of the platonic solids, although it may have a higher symmetry of its own. . . . I think this could be an inflorescence or flower."

"Could be?" I queried.

"Could be," he confirmed.

"Smell it," I suggested, and he again looked somewhat puzzled, as if I had asked him to smell a higher symmetry. But he complied courteously, and took it to his nose. Now, suddenly, he came to life.

"Beautiful!" he exclaimed. "An early rose. What a heavenly smell!" He started to hum *"Die Rose, die Lillie . . ."* Reality, it seemed, might be conveyed by smell, not by sight.

I tried one final test. It was still a cold day, in early spring, and I had thrown my coat and gloves on the sofa.

"What is this?" I asked, holding up a glove.

"May I examine it?" he asked, and, taking it from me, he proceeded to examine it as he had examined the geometrical shapes.

"A continuous surface," he announced at last, "infolded on itself. It appears to have"— he hesitated—"five outpouchings, if this is the word."

"Yes," I said cautiously. "You have given me a description. Now tell me what it is."

"A container of some sort?"

"Yes," I said, "and what would it contain?"

"It would contain its contents!" said Dr. P., with a laugh. "There are many possibilities. It could be a change purse, for example, for coins of five sizes. It could . . ."

I interrupted the barmy flow. "Does it not look familiar? Do you think it might contain, might fit, a part of your body?"

No light of recognition dawned on his face.*

---

*Later, by accident, he got it on, and exclaimed, "My God, it's a glove!" This was reminiscent of Kurt Goldstein's patient "Lanuti," who could only recognize objects by trying to use them in action.

---

No child would have the power to see and speak of "a continuous surface . . . infolded on itself," but any child, any infant, would immediately know a glove as a glove, see it as familiar, as going with a hand. Dr. P. didn't. He saw nothing as familiar. Visually, he was lost in a world of lifeless abstractions. Indeed, he did not have a real visual world, as he did not have a real visual self. He could speak about things, but did not see them face-to-face. Hughlings Jackson, discussing patients with aphasia and left-hemisphere lesions, says they have lost "abstract" and "propositional" thought—and compares them with dogs (or, rather, he compares dogs to patients with aphasia). Dr. P., on the other hand, functioned precisely as a machine functions. It wasn't merely that he displayed the same indifference to the visual world as a computer but—even more strikingly—he construed the world as a computer construes it, by means of key features and schematic relationships. The scheme might be identified—in an "identi-kit" way—without the reality being grasped at all.

The testing I had done so far told me nothing about Dr. P.'s inner world. Was it possible that his visual memory and imagination were still intact? I asked him to imagine entering one of our local squares from the north side, to walk through it, in imagination or in memory, and tell me the buildings he might pass as he walked. He listed the buildings on his right side, but none of those on his left. I then asked him to imagine entering the square from the south. Again he mentioned only those buildings that were on the right side, although these were the very buildings he had omitted before. Those he had "seen" internally before were not mentioned now; presumably, they were no longer "seen." It was evident that his difficulties with leftness, his visual field deficits, were as much internal as external, bisecting his visual memory and imagination.

What, at a higher level, of his internal visualization? Thinking of the almost hallucinatory intensity with which Tolstoy visualizes and animates his characters, I questioned Dr. P. about *Anna Karenina*. He could remember incidents without difficulty, had an undiminished grasp of the plot, but completely omitted visual characteristics, visual narrative, and scenes. He remembered the words of the characters but not their faces; and though, when asked, he could quote, with his remarkable and almost verbatim memory, the original visual descriptions, these were, it became apparent, quite empty for him and lacked sensorial, imaginal, or emotional reality. Thus, there was an internal agnosia as well.[1]

But this was only the case, it became clear, with certain sorts of visualization. The visualization of faces and scenes, of visual narrative and drama—this was profoundly impaired, almost absent. But the visualization of *schemata* was preserved, perhaps enhanced. Thus, when I engaged him in a game of mental chess, he had no difficulty visualizing the chessboard or the moves—indeed, no difficulty in beating me soundly. . . .

When the examination was over, Mrs. P. called us to the table, where there was coffee and a delicious spread of little cakes. Hungrily, hummingly, Dr. P. started on the cakes. Swiftly, fluently, unthinkingly, melodiously, he pulled the plates toward him and took this and that in a great gurgling stream, an edible song of food, until, suddenly, there came an interruption: a loud, peremptory rat-tat-tat at the door. Startled, taken aback, arrested by the interruption, Dr. P. stopped eating and sat frozen, motionless, at the table, with an indifferent, blind bewilderment on his face. He saw, but no longer saw, the table; no longer perceived it as a table laden with cakes. His wife poured him some coffee: The smell titillated his nose and brought him back to reality. The melody of eating resumed.

How does he do anything? I wondered to myself. What happens when he's dressing, goes to the lavatory, has a bath? I followed his wife into the kitchen and asked her how, for instance, he managed to dress himself.

"It's just like the eating," she explained. "I put his usual clothes out, in all the usual places, and he dresses without difficulty, singing to himself. He does everything singing to himself. But if he is interrupted and loses the thread, he comes to a complete stop, doesn't know his clothes—or his own body. He sings all the time—eating songs, dressing songs, bathing songs, everything. He can't do anything unless he makes it a song."

While we were talking my attention was caught by the pictures on the walls.

"Yes," Mrs. P. said, "he was a gifted painter as well as a singer. The school exhibited his pictures every year."

I strolled past them curiously—they were in chronological order. All his earlier work was naturalistic and realistic, with vivid mood and atmosphere, but finely detailed and concrete. Then, years later, they became less vivid, less concrete, less realistic and naturalistic, but far more abstract, even geometrical and cubist. Finally, in the last paintings, the canvasses became nonsense, or nonsense to me—mere chaotic lines and blotches of paint. I commented on this to Mrs. P.

"Ach, you doctors, you're such Philistines!" she exclaimed. "Can you not see *artistic development*—how he renounced the realism of his earlier years, and advanced into abstract, nonrepresentational art?"

"No, that's not it," I said to myself (but forbore to say it to poor Mrs. P.). He had indeed moved from realism to nonrepresentation to the abstract, yet this was not the artist, but the pathology, advancing—advancing toward a profound visual agnosia, in which all powers of representation and imagery, all sense of the concrete, all sense of reality, were being destroyed. This wall of paintings was a tragic pathological exhibit, which belonged to neurology, not art.

And yet, I wondered, was she not partly right? For there is often a struggle, and sometimes, even more interestingly, a collusion between the powers of pathology and creation. Perhaps, in his cubist period, there

might have been both artistic and pathological development, colluding to engender an original form; for as he lost the concrete, so he might have gained in the abstract, developing a greater sensitivity to all the structural elements of line, boundary, contour—an almost Picasso-like power to see, and equally depict, those abstract organizations embedded in, and normally lost in, the concrete. . . . Though in the final pictures, I feared, there was only chaos and agnosia.

We returned to the great music room, with the Bösendorfer in the center, and Dr. P. humming the last torte.

"Well, Dr. Sacks," he said to me. "You find me an interesting case, I perceive. Can you tell me what you find wrong, make recommendations?"

"I can't tell you what I find wrong," I replied, "but I'll say what I find right. You are a wonderful musician, and music is your life. What I would prescribe, in a case such as yours, is a life which consists entirely of music. Music has been the center, now make it the whole, of your life."

This was four years ago—I never saw him again, but I often wondered about how he apprehended the world, given his strange loss of image, visuality, and the perfect preservation of a great musicality. I think that music, for him, had taken the place of image. He had no body-image, he had body-music: this is why he could move and act as fluently as he did, but came to a total confused stop if the "inner music" stopped. And equally with the outside, the world . . . *

In *The World as Representation and Will*, Schopenhauer speaks of music as "pure will." How fascinated he would have been by Dr. P., a man who had wholly lost the world as representation, but wholly preserved it as music or will.

_____

*Thus, as I learned later from his wife, though he could not recognize his students if they sat still, if they were merely "images," he might suddenly recognize them if they *moved*. "That's Karl," he would cry. "I know his movements, his body-music."

And this, mercifully, held to the end—for despite the gradual advance of his disease (a massive tumor or degenerative process in the visual parts of his brain) Dr. P. lived and taught music to the last days of his life.

## Postscript

How should one interpret Dr. P.'s peculiar inability to interpret, to judge, a glove as a glove? Manifestly, here, he could not make a cognitive judgment, though he was prolific in the production of cognitive hypotheses. A judgment is intuitive, personal, comprehensive, and concrete—we "see" how things stand, in relation to one another and oneself. It was precisely this setting, this relating, that Dr. P. lacked (though his judging, in all other spheres, was prompt and normal). Was this due to lack of visual information, or faulty processing of visual information? (This would be the explanation given by a classical, schematic neurology.) Or was there something amiss in Dr. P.'s attitude, so that he could not relate what he saw to himself?

These explanations, or modes of explanation, are not mutually exclusive—being in different modes they could coexist and both be true. And this is acknowledged, implicitly or explicitly, in classical neurology: implicitly, by Macrae, when he finds the explanation of defective schemata, or defective visual processing and integration, inadequate; explicitly, by Goldstein, when he speaks of "abstract attitude." But abstract attitude, which allows "categorization," also misses the mark with Dr. P.—and, perhaps, with the concept of "judgment" in general. For Dr. P. *had* abstract attitude—indeed, nothing else. And it was precisely this, his absurd abstractness of attitude—absurd because unleavened with anything else—which rendered him incapable of perceiving identity, or particulars, rendered him incapable of judgment.

Neurology and psychology, curiously, though they talk of everything else, almost never talk of "judgment"—and yet it is pre-cisely the downfall of judgment (whether in specific realms, as with Dr. P., or more generally, as in patients with Korsakov's or frontal-lobe syndromes . . . which constitutes the essence of so many neuropsychological disorders. Judgment and identity may be casualties—but neuropsychology never speaks of them.

And yet, whether in a philosophic sense (Kant's sense), or an empirical and evolutionary sense, judgment is the most important faculty we have. An animal, or a man, may get on very well without "abstract attitude" but will speedily perish if deprived of judgment. Judgment must be the *first* faculty of higher life or mind—yet it is ignored, or misinterpreted, by classical (computational) neurology. And if we wonder how such an absurdity can arise, we find it in the assumptions, or the evolution, of neurology itself. For classical neurology (like classical physics) has always been mechanical—from Hughlings Jackson's mechanical analogies to the computer analogies of today.

Of course, the brain *is* a machine and a computer—everything in classical neurology is correct. But our mental processes, which constitute our being and life, are not just abstract and mechanical, but personal, as well—and, as such, involve not just classifying and categorizing, but continual judging and feeling also. If this is missing, we become computer-like, as Dr. P. was. And, by the same token, if we delete feeling and judging, the personal, from the cognitive sciences, we reduce *them* to something as defective as Dr. P.—and we reduce *our* apprehension of the concrete and real.

By a sort of comic and awful analogy, our current cognitive neurology and psychology resemble nothing so much as poor Dr. P.! We need the concrete and real, as he did; and we fail to see this, as he failed to see it. Our cognitive sciences are themselves suffering from an agnosia essentially similar to Dr. P.'s. Dr. P. may therefore serve as a warning and parable—of what happens to a science which eschews the judgmental, the particular, the personal, and becomes entirely abstract and computational.

It was always a matter of great regret to me that, owing to circumstances beyond my control, I was not able to follow his case further, either in the sort of observations and investigations described, or in ascertaining the actual disease pathology.

One always fears that a case is "unique," especially if it has such extraordinary features as those of Dr. P. It was, therefore, with a sense of great interest and delight, not unmixed with relief, that I found, quite by chance—looking through the periodical *Brain* for 1956—a detailed description of an almost comically similar case, similar (indeed identical) neuropsychologically and phenomenologically, though the underlying pathology (an acute head injury) and all personal circumstances were wholly different. The authors speak of their case as "unique in the documented history of this disorder"— and evidently experienced, as I did, amazement at their own findings. The interested reader is referred to the original paper, Macrae and Trolle (1956), of which I here subjoin a brief paraphrase, with quotations from the original.

Their patient was a young man of 32, who, following a severe automobile accident, with unconsciousness for three weeks, ". . . complained, exclusively, of an inability to recognize faces, even those of his wife and children." Not a single face was "familiar" to him, but there were three he could identify; these were workmates: one with an eye-blinking tic, one with a large mole on his cheek, and a third "because he was so tall and thin that no one else was like him." Each of these, Macrae and Trolle bring out, was "recognized solely by the single prominent feature mentioned." In general (like Dr. P.) he recognized familiars only by their voices.

He had difficulty even recognizing himself in a mirror, as Macrae and Trolle describe in detail: "In the early convalescent phase he frequently, especially when shaving, questioned whether the face gazing at him was really his own, and even though he knew it could physically be none other, on several occasions grimaced or stuck out his tongue 'just to make sure.' By carefully studying his face in the mirror he slowly began to recognize it, but 'not in a flash' as in the past—he relied on the hair and facial outline, and on two small moles on his left cheek."

In general he could not recognize objects "at a glance," but would have to seek out, and guess from, one or two features— occasionally his guesses were absurdly wrong. In particular, the authors note, there was difficulty with the *animate*.

On the other hand, simple schematic objects—scissors, watch, key, etc.—presented no difficulties. Macrae and Trolle also note that: "His *topographical memory* was strange: The seeming paradox existed that he could find his way from home to hospital and around the hospital, but yet could not name streets *en route* [unlike Dr. P., he also had some aphasia] or appear to visualize the topography."

It was also evident that visual memories of people, even from long before the accident, were severely impaired—there was memory of conduct, or perhaps a mannerism, but not of visual appearance or face. Similarly, it appeared, when he was questioned closely, that he no longer had visual images in his *dreams*. Thus, as with Dr. P., it was not just visual perception, but visual imagination and memory, the fundamental powers of visual representation, which were essentially damaged in this patient—at least those powers insofar as they pertained to the personal, the familiar, the concrete.

A final, humorous point. Where Dr. P. might mistake his wife for a hat, Macrae's patient, also unable to recognize his wife, needed her to identify herself by a visual *marker*, by ". . . a conspicuous article of clothing, such as a large hat."

## Note

1. I have often wondered about Helen Keller's visual descriptions, whether these, for all their eloquence, are somehow empty as well? Or whether, by the transference of images from the tactile to the visual, or yet more extraordinarily, from the verbal and the metaphorical to the sensorial and the visual, she *did* achieve a power of visual imagery, even though her visual cortex had never been stimulated, directly, by the eyes? But in Dr. P.'s case it is precisely the cortex that was damaged, the organic prerequisite of all pictorial imagery. Interestingly and typically he no longer dreamed pictorially—the "message" of the dream being conveyed in nonvisual terms. . . .

## Reference

Macrae, D. and Trolle, E. (1956). "The Defect of Function in Visual Agnosia." *Brain*, 77: 94–110.

# Metaphors We Live By

## *George Lakoff and Mark Johnson*

. . . The concepts that govern our thought are not just matters of the intellect. They also govern our everyday functioning, down to the most mundane details. Our concepts structure what we perceive, how we get around in the world, and how we relate to other people. Our conceptual system thus plays a central role in defining our everyday realities. If we are right in suggesting that our conceptual system is largely metaphorical, then the way we think, what we experience, and what we do every day is very much a matter of metaphor.

But our conceptual system is not something we are normally aware of. In most of the little things we do every day, we simply think and act more or less automatically along certain lines. Just what these lines are is by no means obvious. One way to find out is by looking at language. Since communication is based on the same conceptual system that we use in thinking and acting, language is an important source of evidence for what that system is like.

Primarily on the basis of linguistic evidence, we have found that most of our ordinary conceptual system is metaphorical in nature. And we have found a way to begin to identify in detail just what the metaphors are that structure how we perceive, how we think, and what we do.

To give some idea of what it could mean for a concept to be metaphorical and for such a concept to structure an everyday activity, let us start with the concept ARGUMENT and the conceptual metaphor ARGUMENT IS WAR. This metaphor is reflected in our everyday language by a wide variety of expressions:

ARGUMENT IS WAR
Your claims are *indefensible.*
He *attacked every weak point* in my argument.
His criticisms were *right on target.*
I *demolished* his argument.
I've never *won* an argument with him.
You disagree? Okay, *shoot!*
If you use that *strategy*, he'll *wipe you out.*
He *shot down* all of my arguments.

It is important to see that we don't just *talk* about arguments in terms of war. We can actually win or lose arguments. We see the person we are arguing with as an opponent. We attack his positions and we defend our own. We gain and lose ground. We plan and use strategies. If we find a position indefensible, we can abandon it and take a new line of attack. Many of the things we *do* in arguing are partially structured by the concept of war. Though there is no physical battle, there is a verbal battle, and the structure of an argument—attack, defense, counterattack, etc.— reflects this. It is in this sense that the ARGUMENT IS WAR metaphor is one that we live by in this culture; it structures the actions we perform in arguing.

Try to imagine a culture where arguments are not viewed in terms of war, where no one wins or loses, where there is no sense of attacking or defending, gaining or losing ground. Imagine a culture where an argument is viewed as a dance, the participants are seen as performers, and the goal is to perform in a balanced and aesthetically pleasing way. In such a culture, people would view arguments differently, experience them differently, carry them out differently, and talk about them differently. But *we* would probably not view them as arguing at all: They would simply be doing something different. It would seem strange even to call what they were doing "arguing." Perhaps the most neutral way of describing this difference between their culture and ours would be to say that we have a discourse form structured in terms of battle and they have one structured in terms of dance.

This is an example of what it means for a metaphorical concept, namely, ARGUMENT IS WAR, to structure (at least in part) what we do and how we understand what we are doing when we argue. *The essence of metaphor is understanding and experiencing one kind of thing in terms of another.* It is not that arguments are a subspecies of war. Arguments and wars are different kinds of things—verbal discourse and armed conflict—and the actions performed are different kinds of actions. But ARGUMENT is partially structured, understood, performed, and talked about in terms of WAR. The concept is metaphorically structured, the activity is metaphorically structured, and, consequently, the language is metaphorically structured.

Moreover, this is the *ordinary* way of having an argument and talking about one. The normal way for us to talk about attacking a position is to use the words "attack a position." Our conventional ways of talking about arguments presuppose a metaphor we are hardly ever conscious of. The metaphor is not merely in the words we use—it is in our very concept of an argument. The language of argument is not poetic, fanciful, or rhetorical; it is literal. We talk about arguments that

way because we conceive of them that way—and we act according to the way we conceive of things. . . .

In each of the examples that follow we give a metaphor and a list of ordinary expressions that are special cases of the metaphor. The English expressions are of two sorts: simple literal expressions and idioms that fit the metaphor and are part of the normal everyday way of talking about the subject.

THEORIES (and ARGUMENTS) ARE BUILDINGS
Is that the *foundation* for your theory? The theory needs more *support*. The argument is *shaky*. We need some more facts or the argument will *fall apart*. We need to *construct* a *strong* argument for that. I haven't figured out yet what the *form* of the argument will be. Here are some more facts to *shore up* the theory. We need to *buttress* the theory with *solid* arguments. The theory will *stand* or *fall* on the *strength* of that argument. The argument *collapsed*. They *exploded* his latest theory. We will show that theory to be without *foundation*. So far we have put together only the *framework* of the theory.

IDEAS ARE FOOD
What he said *left a bad taste in my mouth.* All this paper has in it are *raw facts, half-baked ideas, and warmed-over theories.* There are too many facts here for me to *digest* them all. I just can't *swallow* that claim. That argument *smells fishy.* Let me *stew* over that for a while. Now there's a theory you can really *sink your teeth into.* We need to let that idea *percolate* for a while. That's *food for thought.* He's a *voracious* reader. We don't need to *spoon-feed* our students. He *devoured* the book. Let's let that idea *simmer on the back burner* for a while. This is the *meaty* part of the paper. Let that idea *jell* for a while. That idea has been *fermenting* for years.

With respect to life and death IDEAS ARE ORGANISMS, **either** PEOPLE **or** PLANTS.

IDEAS ARE PEOPLE
The theory of relativity *gave birth to* an enormous number of ideas in physics. He is the

*father* of modern biology. Whose *brainchild* was that? Look at what his ideas have *spawned*. Those ideas *died off* in the Middle Ages. His ideas will *live on* forever. Cognitive psychology is still in its *infancy*. That's an idea that ought to be *resurrected*. Where'd you *dig up* that idea? He *breathed new life into* that idea.

### IDEAS ARE PLANTS

His ideas have finally come to *fruition*. That idea *died on the vine*. That's a *budding* theory. It will take years for that idea to *come to full flower*. He views chemistry as a mere *offshoot* of physics. Mathematics has many *branches*. The *seeds* of his great ideas were *planted* in his youth. She has a *fertile* imagination. Here's an idea that I'd like to *plant* in your mind. He has a *barren* mind.

### IDEAS ARE PRODUCTS

We're really *turning (churning, cranking, grinding) out* new ideas. We've *generated* a lot of ideas this week. He *produces* new ideas at an astounding rate. His *intellectual productivity* has decreased in recent years. We need to *take the rough edges off* that idea, *hone it down, smooth it out*. It's a rough idea; it needs to be *refined*.

### IDEAS ARE COMMODITIES

It's important how you *package* your ideas. He won't *buy* that. That idea just won't *sell*. There is always a *market* for good ideas. That's a *worthless* idea. He's been a source of *valuable* ideas. I wouldn't *give a plugged nickel for* that idea. Your ideas don't have a chance in the *intellectual marketplace*.

### IDEAS ARE RESOURCES

He *ran out of* ideas. Don't *waste* your thoughts on small projects. Let's *pool* our ideas. He's a *resourceful* man. We've *used up* all our ideas. That's a *useless* idea. That idea will *go a long way*.

### IDEAS ARE MONEY

Let me put in my *two cents' worth*. He's *rich* in ideas. That book is a *treasure trove* of ideas. He has a *wealth* of ideas.

### IDEAS ARE CUTTING INSTRUMENTS

That's an *incisive* idea. That *cuts right to the heart of* the matter. That was a *cutting* remark. He's *sharp*. He has a *razor* wit. He has a *keen* mind. She *cut* his argument *to ribbons*.

### IDEAS ARE FASHIONS

That idea went *out of style* years ago. I hear sociobiology *is in* these days. Marxism is currently *fashionable* in western Europe. That idea is *old hat!* That's an *outdated* idea. What are the new *trends* in English criticism? *Old-fashioned* notions have no place in today's society. He keeps *up-to-date* by reading the New York Review of Books. Berkeley is a center of *avant-garde* thought. Semiotics has become quite *chic*. The idea of revolution is no longer *in vogue* in the United States. The transformational grammar *craze* hit the United States in the mid-sixties and has just made it to Europe.

### UNDERSTANDING IS SEEING; IDEAS ARE LIGHT-SOURCES; DISCOURSE IS A LIGHT-MEDIUM

I *see* what you're saying. It *looks* different from my *point of view*. What is your *outlook* on that? I *view* it differently. Now I've got the *whole picture*. Let me *point something out* to you. That's an *insightful* idea. That was a *brilliant* remark. The argument is *clear*. It was a *murky* discussion. Could you *elucidate* your remarks? It's a *transparent* argument. The discussion was *opaque*.

### LOVE IS A PHYSICAL FORCE (ELECTROMAGNETIC, GRAVITATIONAL, etc.)

I could feel the *electricity* between us. There were *sparks*. I was *magnetically drawn* to her. They are uncontrollably *attracted* to each other. They *gravitated* to each other immediately. His whole life *revolves* around her. The *atmosphere* around them is always *charged*. There is incredible *energy* in their relationship. They lost their *momentum*.

### LOVE IS A PATIENT

This is a *sick* relationship. They have a *strong, healthy* marriage. The marriage is *dead*—it can't be *revived*. Their marriage is *on the mend*. We're getting *back on our feet*. Their relationship is *in really good shape*. They've got a *listless* marriage. Their marriage is *on its last legs*. It's a *tired* affair.

## LOVE IS MADNESS

I'm *crazy* about her. She *drives me out of my mind*. He constantly *raves* about her. He's gone *mad* over her. I'm just *wild* about Harry. I'm *insane* about her.

## LOVE IS MAGIC

She *cast her spell* over me. The *magic* is gone. I was *spellbound*. She had me *hypnotized*. He has me *in a trance*. I was *entranced* by him. I'm *charmed* by her. She is *bewitching*.

## LOVE IS WAR

He is known for his many rapid *conquests*. She *fought for* him, but his mistress *won out*. He *fled from* her *advances*. She *pursued* him *relentlessly*. He is slowly *gaining ground* with her. He *won her hand* in marriage. He *overpowered* her. She is *besieged* by suitors. He has to *fend* them *off*. He *enlisted the aid* of her friends. He *made an ally* of her mother. Theirs is a *misalliance* if I've ever seen one.

## WEALTH IS A HIDDEN OBJECT

He's *seeking* his fortune. He's flaunting his *new-found* wealth. He's a *fortune-hunter*. She's a *gold-digger*. He *lost* his fortune. He's *searching for* wealth.

## SIGNIFICANT IS BIG

He's a *big* man in the garment industry. He's a *giant* among writers. That's the *biggest* idea to hit advertising in years. He's *head and shoulders above* everyone in the industry. It was only a *small* crime. That was only a *little* white lie. I was astounded at the *enormity* of the crime. That was one of the *greatest* moments in World Series history. His accomplishments *tower over* those of *lesser* men.

## SEEING IS TOUCHING; EYES ARE LIMBS

I can't *take* my eyes *off* her. He sits with his eyes *glued to* the TV. Her eyes *picked out* every detail of the pattern. Their eyes *met*. She never *moves* her eyes *from* his face. She *ran* her eyes *over* everything in the room. He wants everything *within reach of* his eyes.

## THE EYES ARE CONTAINERS FOR THE EMOTIONS

I could see the fear *in* his eyes. His eyes were *filled* with anger. There was passion *in* her eyes. His eyes *displayed* his compassion. She couldn't *get* the fear *out* of her eyes. Love *showed in* his eyes. Her eyes *welled* with emotion.

## EMOTIONAL EFFECT IS PHYSICAL CONTACT

His mother's death *hit* him *hard*. That idea *bowled me over*. She's a *knockout*. I was *struck* by his sincerity. That really *made an impression* on me. He *made his mark on* the world. I was *touched* by his remark. That *blew me away*.

## PHYSICAL AND EMOTIONAL STATES ARE ENTITIES WITHIN A PERSON

He has a pain *in* his shoulder. Don't *give* me the flu. My cold has *gone from my head to my chest*. His pains *went away*. His depression *returned*. Hot tea and honey will *get rid of* your cough. He could barely *contain* his joy. The smile *left* his face. *Wipe* that sneer *off* your face, private! His fears *keep coming back*. I've got to *shake off* this depression—it keeps *hanging on*. If you've got a cold, drinking lots of tea will *flush it out* of your system. There isn't a *trace* of cowardice *in* him. He hasn't got *an honest bone in his body*.

## VITALITY IS A SUBSTANCE

She's *brimming* with vim and vigor. She's *overflowing* with vitality. He's *devoid* of energy. I don't *have* any energy *left* at the end of the day. I'm *drained*. That *took a lot out of* me.

## LIFE IS A CONTAINER

I've had a *full* life. Life is *empty* for him. There's *not much left* for him *in* life. Her life is *crammed* with activities. *Get the most out of* life. His life *contained* a great deal of sorrow. Live your life *to the fullest*.

## LIFE IS A GAMBLING GAME

I'll *take my chances*. The *odds are against me*. I've got an *ace up my sleeve*. He's *holding all the aces*. It's a *toss-up*. If you *play your cards right*, you can do it. He *won big*. He's a real *loser*. Where is he when the *chips are down*? That's my *ace in the hole*. He's *bluffing*. The president is *playing it close to his vest*. Let's *up the ante*. Maybe we need to *sweeten the pot*. I think we should *stand pat*. That's *the luck of the draw*. Those are *high stakes*.

In this last group of examples we have a collection of what are called "speech formulas," or "fixed-form expressions," or "phrasal lexical items." These function in many ways like single words, and the language has thousands of them. In the examples given, a set of such phrasal lexical items is coherently structured by a single metaphorical concept. Although each of them is an instance of the LIFE IS A GAMBLING GAME metaphor, they are typically used to speak of life, not of gambling situations. They are normal ways of talking about life situations, just as using the word "construct" is a normal way of talking about theories. It is in this sense that we include them in what we have called literal expressions structured by metaphorical concepts. If you say "The odds are against us" or "We'll have to take our chances," you would not be viewed as speaking metaphorically but as using the normal everyday language appropriate to the situation. Nevertheless, your way of talking about, conceiving, and even experiencing your situation would be metaphorically structured. . . .

The most fundamental values in a culture will be coherent with the metaphorical structure of the most fundamental concepts in the culture. As an example, let us consider some cultural values in our society that are coherent with our UP-DOWN spatialization metaphors and whose opposites would not be.

"More is better" is coherent with MORE IS UP and GOOD IS UP.

"Less is better" is not coherent with them.

"Bigger is better" is coherent with MORE IS UP and GOOD IS UP.

"Smaller is better" is not coherent with them.

"The future will be better" is coherent with THE FUTURE IS UP and GOOD IS UP. "The future will be worse" is not.

"There will be more in the future" is coherent with MORE IS UP and THE FUTURE IS UP.

"Your status should be higher in the future" is coherent with HIGH STATUS IS UP and THE FUTURE IS UP.

These are values deeply embedded in our culture. "The future will be better" is a statement of the concept of progress. "There will be more in the future" has as special cases the accumulation of goods and wage inflation. "Your status should be higher in the future" is a statement of careerism. These are coherent with our present spatialization metaphors; their opposites would not be. So it seems that our values are not independent but must form a coherent system with the metaphorical concepts we live by. . . .

### New Meaning

The metaphors we have discussed so far are *conventional* metaphors, that is, metaphors that structure the ordinary conceptual system of our culture, which is reflected in our everyday language. We would now like to turn to metaphors that are outside our conventional conceptual system, metaphors that are imaginative and creative. Such metaphors are capable of giving us a new understanding of our experience. Thus, they can give new meaning to our pasts, to our daily activity, and to what we know and believe.

To see how this is possible, let us consider the new metaphor LOVE IS A COLLABORATIVE WORK OF ART. This is a metaphor that we personally find particularly forceful, insightful, and appropriate, given our experiences as members of our generation and our culture. The reason is that it makes our experiences of love coherent—it makes sense of them. We would like to suggest that new metaphors make sense of our experience in the same way conventional metaphors do: They provide coherent structure, highlighting some things and hiding others.

Like conventional metaphors, new metaphors have entailments, which may include other metaphors and literal statements as well. For example, the entailments of LOVE IS A COLLABORATIVE WORK OF ART arise from our beliefs about, and experiences of, what it means for something to be a collaborative work of art. Our personal views of work and art give rise to at least the following entailments for this metaphor:

Love is work.

Love is active.

Love requires cooperation.

Love requires dedication.

Love requires compromise.

Love requires a discipline.

Love involves shared responsibility.

Love requires patience.

Love requires shared values and goals.

Love demands sacrifice.

Love regularly brings frustration.

Love requires instinctive communication.

Love is an aesthetic experience.

Love is primarily valued for its own sake.

Love involves creativity.

Love requires a shared aesthetic.

Love cannot be achieved by formula.

Love is unique in each instance.

Love is an expression of who you are.

Love creates a reality.

Love reflects how you see the world.

Love requires the greatest honesty.

Love may be transient or permanent.

Love needs funding.

Love yields a shared aesthetic satisfaction from your joint efforts.

Some of these entailments are metaphorical (e.g., "Love is an aesthetic experience"); others are not (e.g., "Love involves shared responsibility"). Each of these entailments may itself have further entailments. The result is a large and coherent network of entailments, which may, on the whole, either fit or not fit our experiences of love. When the network does fit, the experiences form a coherent whole as instances of the metaphor. What we experience with such a metaphor is a kind of reverberation down through the network of entailments that awakens and connects our memories of our past love experiences and serves as a possible guide for future ones.

Let's be more specific about what we mean by "reverberations" in the metaphor LOVE IS A COLLABORATIVE WORK OF ART.

First, the metaphor highlights certain features while suppressing others. For example, the active side of love is brought into the foreground through the notion of WORK both in COLLABORATIVE WORK and in WORK OF ART. This requires the masking of certain aspects of love that are viewed passively. In fact, the emotional aspects of love are almost never viewed as being under the lovers' active control in our conventional conceptual system. Even in the LOVE IS A JOURNEY metaphor, the relationship is viewed as a vehicle that is not in the couple's active control, since it can be *off the tracks,* or *on the rocks,* or *not going anywhere.* In the LOVE IS MADNESS metaphor ("I'm crazy about her," "She's driving me wild"), there is the ultimate lack of control. In the LOVE IS HEALTH metaphor, where the relationship is a patient ("It's a healthy relationship," "It's a sick relationship," "Their relationship is reviving"), the passivity of health in this culture is transferred to love. Thus, in focusing on various aspects of activity (e.g., WORK, CREATION, PURSUING GOALS, BUILDING, HELPING, etc.), the metaphor provides an organization of important love experiences that our conventional conceptual system does not make available.

Second, the metaphor does not merely entail other concepts, like WORK or PURSUING SHARED GOALS, but it entails very specific *aspects* of these concepts. It is not just any work, like working on an automobile assembly line, for instance. It is work that requires that special balance of control and letting-go that is appropriate to artistic creation, since the goal that is pursued is not just any kind of goal but a joint aesthetic goal. And though the metaphor may suppress the out-of-control aspects of the LOVE IS MADNESS metaphor, it highlights another aspect, namely, the sense of almost demonic possession that lies behind our culture's connection between artistic genius and madness.

Third, because the metaphor highlights important love experiences and makes them coherent while it masks other love experiences, the metaphor gives love a new meaning. If those things entailed by the metaphor are for us the most important aspects of our love experiences, then the metaphor can acquire the status of a truth; for many people, love *is* a collaborative work of art. And because it is, the metaphor can have a feedback effect, guiding our future actions in accordance with the metaphor.

Fourth, metaphors can thus be appropriate because they sanction actions, justify inferences, and help us set goals. For example, certain actions, inferences, and goals are dictated by the LOVE IS A COLLABORATIVE WORK OF ART metaphor but not by the LOVE IS MADNESS metaphor. If love is madness, I do not concentrate on what I have to do to maintain it. But if it is work, then it requires activity, and if it is a work of art, it requires a very special *kind* of activity, and if it is collaborative, then it is even further restricted and specified.

Fifth, the meaning a metaphor will have for me will be partly culturally determined and partly tied to my past experiences. The cultural differences can be enormous because each of the concepts in the metaphor under discussion—ART, WORK, COLLABORATION, and LOVE—can vary widely from culture to culture. Thus, LOVE IS A COLLABORATIVE WORK OF ART would mean very different things to a nineteenth-century European Romantic and an Eskimo living in Greenland at the same time. There will also be differences within a culture based on how individuals differ in their views of work and art. LOVE IS A COLLABORATIVE WORK OF ART will mean something very different to two fourteen-year-olds on their first date than to a mature artist couple.

As an example of how the meaning of a metaphor may vary radically within a culture, let us consider some entailments of the metaphor for someone with a view of art very different from our own. Someone who values a work of art not for itself but only as an object for display and someone who thinks that art creates only an illusion, not reality, could see the following as entailments of the metaphor:

Love is an object to be placed on display.

Love exists to be judged and admired by others.

Love creates an illusion.

Love requires hiding the truth.

Because such a person's view of art is different, the metaphor will have a different meaning for him. If his experience of love is pretty much like ours, then the metaphor simply will not fit. In fact, it will be grossly inappropriate. Hence, the same metaphor that gives new meaning to our experiences will not give new meaning to his.

Another example of how a metaphor can create new meaning for us came about by accident. An Iranian student, shortly after his arrival in Berkeley, took a seminar on metaphor from one of us. Among the wondrous things that he found in Berkeley was an expression that he heard over and over and understood as a beautifully sane metaphor. The expression was "the solution of my problems"—which he took to be a large volume of liquid, bubbling and smoking, containing all of your problems, either dissolved or in the form of precipitates, with catalysts constantly dissolving some problems (for the time being) and precipitating out others. He was terribly disillusioned to find that the residents of Berkeley had no such chemical metaphor in mind. And well he might be, for the chemical metaphor is both beautiful and insightful. It gives us a view of problems as things that never disappear utterly and that cannot be solved once and for all. All of your problems are always present, only they may be dissolved and in solution, or they may be in solid form. The best you can hope for is to find a catalyst that will make one problem dissolve without making another one precipitate out. And since you do not have complete control over what goes into the solution, you are constantly finding old and new problems precipitating out and present problems dissolving, partly because of your efforts and partly despite anything you do.

The CHEMICAL metaphor gives us a new view of human problems. It is appropriate to the experience of finding that problems which we once thought were "solved" turn up again and again. The CHEMICAL metaphor says that problems are not the kind of things that can be made to disappear forever. To treat them as things that can be "solved" once and for all is pointless. To live by the CHEMICAL metaphor would be to accept it as a fact that no problem ever disappears forever. Rather than direct your energies toward solving your problems once and for all, you would direct your energies toward finding out what catalysts will dissolve your most pressing problems for the longest time without precipitating out worse ones. The reappearance of a problem is viewed as a natural occurrence rather than a failure on your part to find "the right way to solve it."

To live by the CHEMICAL metaphor would mean that your problems have a different kind of reality for you. A temporary solution would be an accomplishment rather than a failure. Problems would be part of the natural order of things rather than disorders to be "cured." The way you would understand your everyday life and the way you would act in it would be different if you lived by the CHEMICAL metaphor.

We see this as a clear case of the power of metaphor to create a reality rather than simply to give us a way of conceptualizing a preexisting reality. This should not be surprising.

As we saw in the case of the ARGUMENT IS WAR metaphor, there are natural kinds of *activity* (e.g., arguing) that are metaphorical in nature. What the CHEMICAL metaphor reveals is that our current way of dealing with problems is another kind of metaphorical activity. At present most of us deal with problems according to what we might call the PUZZLE metaphor, in which problems are PUZZLES for which, typically, there is a correct solution—and, once solved, they are solved forever. The PROBLEMS ARE PUZZLES metaphor characterizes our present reality. A shift to the CHEMICAL metaphor would characterize a new reality.

But it is by no means an easy matter to change the metaphors we live by. It is one thing to be aware of the possibilities inherent in the CHEMICAL metaphor, but it is a very different and far more difficult thing to live by it. Each of us has, consciously or unconsciously, identified hundreds of problems, and we are constantly at work on solutions for many of them—via the PUZZLE metaphor. So much of our unconscious everyday activity is structured in terms of the PUZZLE metaphor that we could not possibly make a quick or easy change to the CHEMICAL metaphor on the basis of a conscious decision.

Many of our activities (arguing, solving problems, budgeting time, etc.) are metaphorical in nature. The metaphorical concepts that characterize those activities structure our present reality. New metaphors have the power to create a new reality. This can begin to happen when we start to comprehend our experience in terms of a metaphor, and it becomes a deeper reality when we begin to act in terms of it. If a new metaphor enters the conceptual system that we base our actions on, it will alter that conceptual system and the perceptions and actions that the system gives rise to. Much of cultural change arises from the introduction of new metaphorical concepts and the loss of old ones. For example, the Westernization of cultures throughout the world is partly a matter of introducing the TIME IS MONEY metaphor into those cultures.

The idea that metaphors can create realities goes against most traditional views of metaphor. The reason is that metaphor has traditionally been viewed as a matter of mere language rather than primarily as a means of structuring our conceptual system and the kinds of everyday activities we perform. It is reasonable enough to assume that words alone don't change reality. But changes in our conceptual system do change what is real for us and affect how we perceive the world and act upon those perceptions.

The idea that metaphor is just a matter of language and can at best only describe reality stems from the view that what is real is wholly external to, and independent of, how human beings conceptualize the world—as if the study of reality were just the study of the physical world. Such a view of reality—so-called objective reality—leaves out human aspects of reality, in particular the real perceptions, conceptualizations, motivations, and actions that constitute most of what we experience. But the human aspects of reality are most of what matters to us, and these vary from culture to culture, since different cultures have different conceptual systems. Cultures also exist within physical environments, some of them radically different—jungles, deserts, islands, tundra, mountains, cities, etc. In each case there is a physical environment that we interact with, more or less successfully. The conceptual systems of various cultures partly depend on the physical environments they have developed in.

Each culture must provide a more or less successful way of dealing with its environment, both adapting to it and changing it. Moreover, each culture must define a social reality within which people have roles that make sense to them and in terms of which they can function socially. Not surprisingly, the social reality defined by a culture affects its conception of physical reality. What is real for an individual as a member of a culture is a product both of his social reality and of the way in which that shapes his experience of the physical world. Since much of our social reality is understood in metaphorical terms, and since our conception of the physical world is partly metaphorical, metaphor plays a very significant role in determining what is real for us. . . .

## Metaphor, Truth, and Action

In the preceding section we suggested the following:

Metaphors have entailments through which they highlight and make coherent certain aspects of our experience.

A given metaphor may be the only way to highlight and coherently organize exactly those aspects of our experience.

Metaphors may create realities for us, especially social realities. A metaphor may thus be a guide for future action. Such actions will, of course, fit the metaphor. This will, in turn, reinforce the power of the metaphor to make experience coherent. In this sense metaphors can be self-fulfilling prophecies.

For example, faced with the energy crisis, President Carter declared "the moral equivalent of war." The WAR metaphor generated a network of entailments. There was an "enemy," a "threat to national security," which required "setting targets," "reorganizing priorities," "establishing a new chain of command," "plotting new strategy," "gathering intelligence," "marshaling forces," "imposing sanctions," "calling for sacrifices," and on and on. The WAR metaphor highlighted certain realities and hid others. The metaphor was not merely a way of viewing reality; it constituted a license for policy change and political and economic action. The very acceptance of the metaphor provided grounds for certain inferences: there was an external, foreign, hostile enemy (pictured by cartoonists in Arab headdress); energy needed to be given top priorities; the populace would have to make sacrifices; if we didn't meet the threat, we would not survive.

It is important to realize that this was not the only metaphor available.

Carter's WAR metaphor took for granted our current concept of what ENERGY is, and focused on how to get enough of it. On the other hand, Amory Lovins (1977) observed that there are two fundamentally different ways, or PATHS, to supply our energy needs. He characterized these metaphorically as HARD and SOFT. The HARD ENERGY PATH uses energy supplies that are inflexible, nonrenewable, needing military defense and geopolitical control, irreversibly destructive of the environment, and requiring high capital investment, high technology, and highly skilled workers. They include fossil fuels (gas and oil), nuclear power plants, and coal gasification. The SOFT ENERGY PATH uses energy supplies that are flexible, renewable, not needing military defense or geopolitical control, not destructive of the environment, and requiring only low capital investment, low technology, and unskilled labor. They include solar, wind, and hydroelectric power, biomass alcohol, fluidized beds for burning coal or other combustible materials, and a great many other possibilities currently available. Lovins' SOFT ENERGY PATH metaphor highlights the technical, economic, and sociopolitical *structure* of the energy system, which leads him to the conclusion that the "hard" energy paths—coal, oil, and nuclear power—lead to political conflict, economic hardship, and harm to the environment. But Jimmy Carter is more powerful than Amory Lovins. As Charlotte Linde (in conversation) has observed, whether in national politics or in everyday interaction, people in power get to impose their metaphors.

New metaphors, like conventional metaphors, can have the power to define reality. They do this through a coherent network of entailments that highlight some features of reality and hide others. The acceptance of the metaphor, which forces us to focus *only* on those aspects of our experience that it highlights, leads us to view the entailments of the metaphor as being *true*. Such "truths" may be true, of course, only relative to the reality defined by the metaphor. Suppose Carter announces that his administration has won a major energy battle. Is this claim true or false? Even to address oneself to the question requires accepting at least the central parts of the metaphor. If you do not accept the existence of an external enemy, if you think there is no external threat, if you recognize no field of battle, no targets, no clearly defined competing forces, then the issue of objective truth or falsity cannot arise. But if you see reality as defined by the metaphor, that is, if you do see the energy crisis as a war, then you can answer the question relative to whether the metaphorical entailments fit reality. If Carter, by means of strategically employed political and economic sanctions, forced the OPEC nations to cut the price of oil in half, then you would say that he would indeed have won a major battle. If, on the other hand, his strategies had produced only a temporary price freeze, you couldn't be so sure and might be skeptical.

Though questions of truth do arise for new metaphors, the more important questions are those of appropriate action. In most cases, what is at issue is not the truth or falsity of a metaphor but the perceptions and inferences that follow from it and the actions that are sanctioned by it. In all aspects of life, not just in politics or in love, we define our reality in terms of metaphors and then proceed to act on the basis of the metaphors. We draw inferences, set goals, make commitments, and execute plans, all on the basis of how we in part structure our experience, consciously and unconsciously, by means of metaphor. . . .

Metaphors, as we have seen, are conceptual in nature. They are among our principal vehicles for understanding. And they play a central role in the construction of social and political reality. Yet they are typically viewed within philosophy as matters of "mere language," and philosophical discussions of metaphor have not centered on their conceptual nature, their contribution to understanding, or their function in cultural reality. Instead, philosophers have tended to look at metaphors as out-of-the-ordinary imaginative or poetic linguistic expressions, and their discussions have centered on whether these linguistic expressions can be *true*. . . .

We do not believe that there is such a thing as *objective* (absolute and unconditional) *truth*, though it has been a long-standing theme in Western culture that there is. We do believe that there are *truths* but think that the idea of truth need not be tied to the objectivist view. We believe that the idea that there is absolute objective truth is not only mistaken but socially and politically dangerous. As we have seen, truth is always relative to a conceptual system that is defined in large part by metaphor. Most of our metaphors have evolved in our culture over a long period, but many are imposed upon us by people in power—political leaders, religious leaders, business leaders, advertisers, the media, etc. In a culture where the myth of objectivism is very much alive and truth is always absolute truth, the people who get to impose their metaphors on the culture get to define what we consider to be true—absolutely and objectively true. . . .

## An Experientialist Synthesis

What we are offering in the experientalist account of understanding and truth is an alternative which denies that subjectivity and objectivity are our only choices. . . . The reason we have focused so much on metaphor is that it unites reason and imagination. Reason, at the very least, involves categorization, entailment, and inference. Imagination, in one of its many aspects, involves seeing one kind of thing in terms of another kind of thing—what we have called metaphorical thought. Metaphor is thus *imaginative rationality*. Since the categories of our everyday thought are largely metaphorical and our everyday reasoning involves metaphorical entailments and inferences, ordinary rationality is therefore imaginative by its very nature. Given our understanding of poetic metaphor in terms of metaphorical entailments and inferences, we can see that the products of the poetic imagination are, for the same reason, partially rational in nature.

Metaphor is one of our most important tools for trying to comprehend partially what cannot be comprehended totally: our feelings, aesthetic experiences, moral practices, and spiritual awareness. These endeavors of the imagination are not devoid of rationality; since they use metaphor, they employ an imaginative rationality.

An experientialist approach also allows us to bridge the gap between the objectivist and subjectivist myths about impartiality and the possibility of being fair and objective. . . . [T]ruth is relative to understanding, which means that there is no absolute standpoint from which to obtain absolute objective truths about the world. This does not mean that there are no truths; it means only that truth is relative to our conceptual system, which is grounded in, and constantly tested by, our experiences and those of other members of our culture in our daily interactions with other people and with our physical and cultural environments. . . .

## Reference

Lovins, A. (1977). *Soft energy paths.* Cambridge: Ballinger.

13

# The Social Lens

## *Eviatar Zerubavel*

But how could there not be arbitrariness? Nature presents [things] . . . without firmly established divisions. Everything shades off into everything else by imperceptible nuances. And if, on this ocean of objects surrounding us, there should appear a few that seem to break through the surface and to dominate the rest like the crest of a reef, they merely owe this advantage to . . . conventions . . . that have nothing to do with the physical arrangement of beings.[1]

I have thus far drawn a deliberately one-sided picture of reality as an array of insular entities neatly separated from one another by great divides. Such discontinuity, however, is not as inevitable as we normally take it to be. It is a pronouncedly mental scalpel[2] that helps us carve discrete mental slices out of reality: "You get the illusion that [entities] are just there and are being named as they exist. But they can be . . . organized quite differently depending on how the knife moves. . . . It is important to see this knife for what it is and not to be fooled into thinking that [entities] are the way they are just because the knife happened to cut it up that way. It is important to concentrate on the knife itself."[3] The scalpel, of course, is a *social* scalpel. It is society that underlies the way we generate meaningful mental entities.

Reality is not made up of insular chunks unambiguously separated from one another by sharp divides, but, rather, of vague, blurred-edge essences that often "spill over" into one another. It normally presents itself not in black and white, but, rather, in subtle shades of gray, with mental twilight zones as well as intermediate essences connecting entities. Segmenting it into discrete islands of meaning usually rests on some social convention, and most boundaries are, therefore, mere social artifacts. As such, they often vary from one society to another as well as across historical periods within each society. Moreover, the precise location—not to mention the very existence—of such mental partitions is often disputed even within any given society.

## Culture and Classification

There is more than one way to carve discrete chunks out of a given continuum, and different cultures indeed mold out of the same reality quite different archipelagos of meaning. While all cultures, for example, distinguish the edible from the inedible or the young from the old, they usually differ from one another in where they draw the lines between them. The distinction between the sexually accessible and inaccessible is likewise universal (all cultures, for example, have an incest taboo), yet the specific delineation of those who are considered off limits often varies from one culture to another. Surrounding oneself with a bubble of "personal space," too, is a universal practice, yet, in marked contrast to other species, humans exhibit substantial subspecific cultural variations in where they draw its boundaries.[4] (Along similar lines, the precise delineation of one's "personal" circle of intimates also varies from one culture to another.)[5] By the same token, not everyone who is considered "black" in America would necessarily be classified as such in the West Indies or Brazil.

Moreover, cultures often make certain distinctions that other cultures simply do not. Whereas West Germans, for example, perceive Holland and Belgium as two distinct residential regions, Swedes and Italians both tend to regard them as a single undifferentiated whole.[6] Even purely phonic differences that are quite critical in one language are sometimes totally ignored in others, as the same sound range covered by several distinct phonemes in one language may very well be covered by a single phoneme in another. Thus, for example, though they clearly constitute two separate phonemes in both Polish and Romanian, "c" and "q" are fully interchangeable allophones in French.[7] For quite similar reasons, Hebrew speakers usually treat *list* and *least* (or *pull* and *pool*) as homonyms, Spanish speakers often fail to hear the difference between *race* and *raise,* and Koreans may use *rule* and *lure* interchangeably (just as Americans may have trouble distinguishing the French *peur* from *père* or the Spanish *pero* from *perro*).

Languages likewise differ from one another in the way they generate distinct lexical particles,[8] and it is not unusual that a single word in one language would cover the semantic range of several separate words in another. Thus, for example, while there is a single word for both rats and mice in Latin, insects and airplanes in Hopi, and brothers-in-law and grandnephews in the Algonquian language of the Fox, there are separate words for blankets that are folded and spread out, for water in buckets and in lakes, and for dogs that stand and sit in Navajo.[9] Such dif-

ferences have considerable cognitive implications. After all, it is much easier to isolate a distinct mental entity from its surroundings when one has a word to denote it.[10] That explains why the Navajo, who use different verbs to denote the handling of objects with different shapes, indeed tend to classify objects according to shape much more than English speakers.[11] By the same token, lacking the necessary lexical tools for differentiating, it took me, a native speaker of Hebrew, a long time before I could actually notice the mental gaps—so obvious to English speakers—that separate jelly from jam or preserves.

While such cross-cultural variability often leads us to look down on other cultures' classificatory schemas as primitive or "confused," it ought to help us recognize and accept the relative validity of our own. Only their ethnocentric blinders prevent those who claim that "savages" fail to notice obvious mental discontinuities[12] from appreciating the highly sophisticated classificatory skills of these people, who clearly do make distinctions, though rarely among the things that we do.[13]

Classifying presupposes an ability to ignore "trivial" differences among variants of the same mental entity,[14] and what often looks like an inability to differentiate may very well be a deliberate disregard for negligible differences that "make no difference." The Hopi are certainly not blind to the physical dissimilarity of insects and airplanes. Nonetheless, their culture has no significant conceptual distinction that corresponds to such a difference. Along similar lines, when mental distance is a function of the way items are totemically associated with social groups, there is a good reason to ignore differences among items that are regarded as interchangeable manifestations of the same totem.[15] Thus, for the Australian aborigines, who classify the universe by "dividing" it among their various clans, it is far more logical to note the mental affinity between the rosella parrot and the cat, which is associated with the same clan, than its physical resemblance to the cockatoo, which is associated with a different one.[16] Since the "obvious" physical difference between the parrot and the cat is socially irrelevant, it is deliberately ignored. By the same token, while they probably never confuse the parrot with the cockatoo, aborigines may "fail" to differentiate the kangaroo rat from the gum-tree grub or the planet Venus, which are associated with the same clan.

Like these "savages," though we are obviously aware of the differences in taste between milk and sardines or meat and eggs, it makes a lot of sense to ignore them when what concerns us is our calcium intake or cholesterol level. It is likewise more logical to lump shrimps with pigs than with fish if we observe the Jewish dietary laws. To most "savages," however, our ways of classifying must seem as confused as theirs seem to us:

We order the world according to categories that we take for granted simply because they are given. They occupy an epistemological space that is prior to thought, and so they have an extraordinary staying power. When confronted with an alien way of organizing experience, however, we sense the frailty of our own categories. . . . Things hold together only because they can be slotted into a classificatory scheme that remains unquestioned. We classify a Pekinese and a Great Dane together as dogs without hesitating, even though the Pekinese might seem to have more in common with a cat and the Great Dane with a pony.[17]

Thus, though they themselves have only one word for both insects and airplanes, the Hopi must find it odd that English uses a single word to denote water in nature and in containers.[18] They must likewise find it peculiar that it "fails" to differentiate mothers' brothers from fathers' sisters' husbands, maternal from paternal grandfathers, and first from third cousins. Along similar lines, West Indians indeed find it odd that the English perceive all the various shades of dark skin as "black."[19] Most "savages" must also find it bizarre that we keep hamsters and gerbils as pets while ridding our homes of mice.

Any notion of logic is valid only within a particular cultural milieu,[20] and our own classifications are no more logical than those of "savages." We must therefore resist the ethnocentric tendency to regard our own way of classifying reality as the only reasonable way to do it. That entails giving up the idea that some ways of classifying are more correct and "logical" than others[21] and, therefore, also reconsidering the standard tests through which we usually measure intelligence. Thus, for example, "a person, asked in what way wood and alcohol are alike [should not be] given a zero score if he answers: 'Both knock you out' [just] because the examiner prefers logical categories of scientific classification."[22] By the same token, nor should we penalize someone who maintains (as did my daughter, when she was five) that the difference between a bus and an airplane lies in the fact that we need not pay the pilot on boarding a plane.

Ways of classifying reality vary not only across cultures but also across historical periods within the same culture. The last couple of centuries, for example, saw substantial shifts in the location of the lines we draw between the sexes,[23] the "races,"[24] public and private, family and community. Along similar lines, our calendar year did not always begin on January 1,[25] opiates were still legal in America only eighty years ago,[26] and lungs and gills did not become "similar" until comparative anatomists began classifying organisms according to functional rather than morphological features.[27] Even the location of the line separating art from life changes over time—the Romans, for example, would often execute real-life convicts on stage as part of theatrical shows.[28] A few decades ago, Americans were taught to regard the color of one's skin (and Germans the color of one's hair) as most salient for social exclusion. Today they learn to ignore it as socially irrelevant.

In 1792, when Mary Wollstonecraft published her *Vindication of the Rights of Women*, a distinguished Cambridge professor rebutted with a satirical *Vindication of the Rights of Brutes*.[29] Only two centuries ago, the mental gap between the sexes was so wide that women were perceived as "closer" to animals than to men and granting them political rights seemed as ludicrous as extending such rights to beasts. That this sounds so utterly absurd today only comes to show that absurdity is a function of where we draw lines, and that mental distances may change over time. Before the Civil War, when blacks were regarded in the United States as objects rather than persons, granting them civil rights would have legally been just as ludicrous. (In fact, public signs such as Negroes and Dogs Not Allowed suggest that, until quite recently, they were still perceived in the South as "closer" to animals than to whites.[30]) Only a few decades ago, the idea that homosexuals should be regarded as a distinct political minority would have been as absurd as granting such status to music teachers, baseball fans, or vegetarians. Rights have historically been extended to new social categories (prisoners, noncitizens, children, the insane, the preborn) whose legal standing prior to that would have been inconceivable.[31] (By the same token, for many centuries, European criminal courts also prosecuted pigs, rats, bees, and other animals.[32] In 896 Pope Stephen VI put on trial the dead body of his predecessor, and in 1591 a Russian town bell was sentenced to banishment in Siberia, where it was kept in solitary confinement until fully pardoned three hundred years later, for ringing the signal of an insurrection.[33]) The Nazi experiments with Jews and the mentally retarded likewise presupposed (and, in turn, promoted) the idea that the mental partition between true Aryans and such "subhuman" groups was as thick as the one separating person from object. To anyone brought up in such an ideological climate, objecting to experimentation with Jews would have been as absurd as the objection to experimentation with animals seems to many of us today.

The lines we draw vary not only across cultures and historical periods but also within cultures at a given point in history, as one can tell from the joke about the Orthodox Jew from New York who asks a Southerner who is obviously intrigued by his traditional garb and heavy accent, "What's the matter, you've never seen a Yankee before?" At the same time that one needed seven-eighths "white blood" to avoid being considered a "person of color" in Florida, a mere three-quarters would suffice in Nebraska,[34] and in universities that rarely tenure their young faculty, the line normally separating faculty from students may not be as pronounced as the one separating tenured faculty from both students and nontenured faculty. The lines believed by residents of fancy neighborhoods to separate them from those who live in less prestigious neighborhoods nearby are likewise often blurred by the latter.[35] (When I asked the man from whom I bought my house about the nearest train station, he mentioned a station located six minutes away in a fancier neighborhood, yet "forgot" to mention a station located only two minutes away in a much less prestigious one.) Likewise, within the same culture, meat eaters draw the line between what is edible and inedible quite differently than do vegetarians. (Whereas Bertrand Russell would claim that this line ought to be drawn "at the level of the species," vegetarians may not find ordinary meat eaters that different from cannibals.) Similarly, though "*inter*marriage" normally denotes unions between blacks and whites or Jews and Christians, Ashkenazic Jews also use it to refer to marrying Sephardic Jews.

Of course, from the proverbial Martian's standpoint, since we only marry other humans, we are all "boringly endogamous"[36] and any cross-racial or interfaith "intermarriage" is embarrassingly trivial, yet even within the same culture, lines that seem obvious to some groups may be totally ignored by others. Thus, for example, despite their obvious ubiquity to their own members, the boundaries of communes are usually ignored by the state.[37] And the wide mental gaps that nine-year-olds believe separate them from eight-year-olds, or that rat breeders perceive as separating their own "refined" show animals from ordinary rats, are not appreciated by anyone but them. Along similar lines, whereas no radical bookstore would place a book on the women's movement alongside books on beauty or homemaking, bookstores less sensitive to the distinction between feminist and traditional notions of womanhood might well do so.[38] The distinction some current college students make between "stylish radical-chic" and "granola" lesbians is likewise lost on many alumni, "to whom the shadings of lesbian politics are as irrelevant as the difference between Sodom and Gomorrah."[39]

Such diversity also generates discord. As we carve mental entities out of reality, the location as well as the very existence of the lines separating them from one another is quite often disputed.

The prototypical border dispute is a battle over the location of some critical line in actual space, as manifested in disputes ranging from local turf feuds between neighbors or street gangs to full-scale international wars. It is the original on which numerous battles over the location of various partitions in mental space are modeled. Controversies regarding the location of group divisions (the eighteenth-century debate over whether blacks are "closer" to whites or to apes,[40] family fights over who should be invited to a wedding) or moral boundaries (the line separating legal from illegal drugs,[41] the ethical limits of euthanasia) are perfect examples of such border disputes. So are the battles over the fine line between politicians' private and public lives, the definition of work (the distinction between mere "chores" and actual "labor,"[42] the status of housework), and whether phrenology or chiropractic are part of science.[43] Just as disputable is the delineation of frames, as evident from heated arguments between comedians and their audience over whether personal insults are within the limits of the comedy show frame.

Similar in essence are battles over the temporal delineation of historical narratives, such as the debate over the actual beginning of America's involvement in Vietnam (the various versions of which obviously implicate different administrations) or the dispute between Jews and Arabs over the acceptable limits of each side's historical claim to Palestine. The political significance of where we begin and end such narratives is tremendous. Whereas the story of a battle that ends with the evacuation of a settlement will most likely be remembered as a defeat, concluding it with the rebuilding of that settlement several months later allows a nation to define the evacuation as only temporary and preserve the entire event in its collective memory as a heroic symbol.[44] Equally controversial is the temporal delineation of "life." The different medical and legal definitions of the fine line separating life from death,[45] for example, often generate heated battles over the precise point when doctors may turn off life-sustaining respirators. The definition of the precise point when life begins is, likewise, at the heart of the battle over abortion. That point "is not something that is verifiable as a fact. . . . It is a question of labels. Neither side in this . . . debate would ever disagree on the physiological facts. Both sides would agree as to when a heartbeat can first be detected. Both sides would agree as to when brain waves can be first detected. But when you come to try to place the emotional labels . . . that is where people part company."[46] The battle, of course, is over the precise location of the point at which a mere "conceptus" becomes a "fetus" and a pregnant woman's body is transformed from a single into a dual entity. While pro-choicers insist that an abortion involves only the woman's own body, pro-lifers argue that it involves another living being as well. The definition of that critical point has been disputed even within the church, and while some church fathers claimed that ensoulment occurs at conception,[47] leading theologians such as Thomas Aquinas contended that it occurs only forty days (or even eighty, in females) later. If one accepts this view, of course, aborting a still-"inanimate" eleven-week-old female pre-born can hardly be called homicide. As Justice John Paul Stevens recently cautioned the United States Supreme Court, there is no reason why we should protect "the potential life of an embryo that is still seed" any more than that of a sperm or an unfertilized egg.[48] (The rhetorical use of terms like *seed* and *potential*, as well as of others such as *baby*, is obviously of critical moral significance in legal battles over abortion.)[49]

Even when we do not dispute its location, we often still disagree with one another on how impenetrable we expect a given boundary to be. Such disagreement is at the bottom of disputes over the walls of prisons (whether prisoners may take weekend leaves, how often they may be visited, the conditions for paroling them) and nation-states (immigrant quotas, the status of guest workers,[50] the right to travel abroad), battles over the extent to which groups ought to allow their languages to be "contaminated" by foreign words, and family fights over whether children may close the doors to their rooms.[51] Moreover, we often wage battles over the very existence of a given boundary. States, for example, usually ignore boundaries drawn by separatists, while conservatives and liberals fight over the necessity of drawing a line between "X" and "R" rated films and evolutionists and creationists debate the distinction between science and ideology. Along similar lines, animal rights activists defy the "experiment" frame that allows the killing of animals,[52] whereas feminists question the distinction between erotic art and pornography and object to sexism even in fiction or jokes. Governments and dissidents likewise often debate the legitimacy of the frames that distinguish "religious" sermons, "satirical" plays, and "academic" discourse from explicit political protest.

Such battles are basically about whether what may look like several separate entities are indeed just different variants of a single entity. The entire debate over the reunification of East and West Germany or North and South Korea, for example, was basically over whether there should be one or two of each. Such disagreements also led some people to reproach those who found John Poindexter's and Oliver North's reasoning at the Iran-Contra hearings, for example, evocative of the Nuremberg trials, as well as those who compared the secession of Lithuania from the Soviet Union in 1990 to that of South Carolina from the Union in 1860,[53] with "How can you even compare?" The current battle between Israeli liberals and ultranationalists over whether or not to prosecute Jewish vigilantes in the West Bank is, likewise, basically about whether they and others who break the law constitute one moral entity or two separate ones ("lawbreakers" and "overzealous patriots").

Language certainly plays a major role in such disputes. That is why Israel has traditionally refused to recognize Palestinians as a distinct entity and why a seceding East Pakistan immediately renamed itself Bangladesh. When sociology conference organizers debate whether to include a single "Race and Ethnicity" session or two separate ("Race" and "Ethnicity") ones, they are actually fighting over whether or not being black or Oriental is different from being Irish or Italian, and when Czechs and Slovaks debate whether to name their union "Czechoslovakia" or "Czecho-Slovakia,"[54] the separatist overtones of the latter name are quite obvious. The label "*para*psychological" clearly excludes phenomena from the realm of science, whereas the label "nonhuman animals"[55] clearly defies the conventional distinction between human and animal. Moving away from the discrete labels "homosexual" and "heterosexual" to a continuous homosexuality-heterosexuality scale[56] likewise helps rid the gays of their "specialness" stigma, whereas using "Ms." as the counterpart of "Mr." clearly helps feminists downplay the distinction between married ("Mrs.") and unmarried ("Miss") women (which, since it does not apply to men, implies that marriage transforms women more than it does men).

Such labeling politics reveal how attitudes toward (protecting or defying) boundaries and distinctions betray deep sentiments (conservative or progressive) toward the social order in general. Like the heated battles over drugs, censorship, and abortion, they show that not only does the way we cut up the world underlie the way we think, it clearly also touches the deepest emotional as well as moral nerves of the human condition.

## The Color Gray

That the location as well as the very existence of boundaries is often disputed is even more understandable given the pervasive presence of ambiguity in our life. To the rigid mind, the world is a set of discrete entities separated from one another by gaps. Crossing these gaps entails sharp, dramatic breaks. Movement between islands of meaning therefore has a jerky, staccato nature characterized by abrupt transitions. That is why we gain or lose a full hour as we cross time-zone boundaries[57] or experience some shock upon waking up from a daydream.[58] Such experience of reality obviously allows no room for ambiguity. Yet "things," noted Anaxagoras, are rarely "cut off with an axe."[59] In reality, there are no discrete entities literally detached from their surroundings by actual gaps. Nature "refuses to conform to our craving for clear lines of demarcation; she loves twilight zones."[60] Our neat and orderly classifications notwithstanding, the world presents itself not in pure black and white but, rather, in ambiguous shades of gray, with mental twilight zones and intermediate essences. Despite the stubborn efforts of the rigid mind to deny it, at least some element of ambiguity in our life is inevitable.

Differentiating discrete, insular entities from their surrounding environment is certainly not our only mode of perceiving the world. Hearing, taste, and smell, for example, do not allow a sharp delineation of "things" as do touch or vision.[61] Listening to music, for instance, is an entirely different perceptual experience than looking at a map, as sounds, in marked contrast to countries or school districts, cannot be confined within limits. By the same token, it is much easier mentally to detach a camouflaged figure from its surrounding ground than to isolate the distinctive taste of turmeric in a curry. Nor will an olfactory "map" "have the sharp edges of a visual map—it will be fluid . . . literally drifting on the wind, with eddies and intense centers shading off toward ill-defined edges."[62] Our primal "visceral space-sense," in short, is clearly "not about edges, boundaries, outlines."[63] Furthermore, as evident from our use of common contours in drawings,[64] not to mention the critical optical fact that we are almost constantly moving,[65] even what we see are actually blurred-edge essences that visually fade into one another. The fact that it takes congenitally blind persons who gain sight following surgery a long time before they can actually perceive bounded "things"[66] suggests that even visual contours are something we *learn* to see.

The transition from any supposedly discrete "thing" we mentally carve out of ecological continuums (a forest, a mountain, a desert) to its surroundings is more gradual than abrupt and usually involves a zone rather than a sharp line.[67] As we look at coastlines, for example, we see that they actually connect land and water at least as much as they separate them from each other.[68] The absence of clear-cut dividing lines obviously generates ambiguity. When shop interiors and exteriors or sidewalk and street literally interpenetrate one another,[69] our conventional either/or logic is clearly inadequate. . . . Just as ambiguous in the way it actually negotiates inside and outside is the door, the quintessential embodiment of the half-open.[70] Even the notion (on which rests our initial experience of an insular self) that our body is a closed system sharply cut off from everything else is defied by the fact that the air we constantly breathe is part of *both* the self and its environment.[71]

The fact that "framed" experiential realms like art or play are never really totally cut off from their unframed surroundings generates somewhat similar ambiguity. A typical case in point is the ambiguous "slide"[72] we experience as we gradually drift from being wide awake to being sound asleep or out of ordinary reality into the world of make-believe. Moreover, framed events also "spill over" the frames that are supposed to contain them, thereby generating inevitably ambiguous situations.[73] Thus, for example, we sometimes mistake the framed for the unframed, like the hundreds of thousands of panic-stricken listeners who mistook Orson Welles's 1938 radio dramatization of *The War of the Worlds* for a real invasion from Mars. At the same time, however, we sometimes also mistake the unframed for the framed. When comedian Dick Shawn died of a heart attack in the middle of a performance, it took his audience a while before they realized that it was not part of the show,[74] not unlike the spectators at a Halloween costume party who mistook a real murder for a mere gag.[75] Moreover, we cannot always tell parody from plagiarism or clinical from erotic massage, and when Daddy yawns in the middle of reading what Piglet said to Pooh, it may not always be absolutely clear to his child whether it is Daddy or Piglet who is yawning.

Nor are the supposedly discrete temporal blocks we mentally carve out of historical continuums (day and night, childhood and adulthood) really separated from one another by actual gaps. In actuality, they "flow" into each other, essentially connected by borderline ("liminal"[76]) intermediate periods such as twilight and adolescence. As actual mixtures of the essences they connect,[77] such temporal bridges are inevitably ambiguous. That explains why we often feel in limbo when we commute between home and work[78] as well as the ambiguous sense of ownership we experience between the time we sign an agreement to buy a house and the time we actually close the deal. Just as ambiguous are "liminal persons" who are structurally as well as existentially caught in the interstitial cracks betwixt and between several status categories to neither of which they fully belong[79]—newborns who are yet to be circumcised or baptized, students between high school and college, new recruits who are no longer civilians but have yet to be sworn in as full-fledged soldiers, fiancés, presidents-elect, prisoners on parole, and patients in terminal coma.

Just as ambiguous are immigrants, converts, slaves,[80] parvenus, and products of "mixed" marriages. Lying on the proverbial margins of several different social categories, such "marginal" persons[81] are living proof that social life is indeed organized in a web of crosscutting networks rather than confined to insular groups.[82] After all, even a group such as "family" is never fully insular. Not only do we normally transgress its boundaries when we marry; such lines are fuzzy anyway, as they actually entail an entire twilight zone inhabited by borderline individuals whose membership is ambiguous—distant "wakes-and-weddings" relatives, live-in housekeepers, pets we include even in our family photo albums, next-door neighbors, dead members who are psychologically still present.[83] It is not at all clear, for example, whether my third cousin is part of my family and should thus be invited to family reunions and avoided as a sexual partner. (Genetically speaking, of course, we are all cousins to some degree.) The delineation of other clusters of social identity is just as problematic. Thus, for example, despite the rough clustering of white-collar, blue-collar, and agricultural occupations,[84] social classes are about as discrete as families.[85] So are generations, social movements, and subcultures. In fact, even "cultures" and "societies" are not really discrete. Intermarriage has always existed even among Jews[86] and Gypsies, whereas pidgins and creoles attest to the noninsular nature of speech communities. (Even languages like Basque include at least some nonindigenous words.) Color lines are just as fuzzy. Since "races" are never in a state of perfect reproductive isolation, they do not constitute discrete gene pools. As a result, not a single gene that is present in all members of one race and none of another has yet been identified.[87] The differences between the sexes are also just a matter of degree, as even the distributions of purely physiological male and female features are rarely bipolar. While men's voices are usually deeper than women's, and the female body is, on the average, less muscular and hairy than the male's, many women nonetheless do have a deeper voice or a more muscular and hairy body than many men. In fact, even the distinction between human and animal is repeatedly blurred by philosophers and natural scientists who claim that "there are no leaps in nature,"[88] essentially backing Aristotle's notion of a great "chain of being" connecting all classes of living things (as well as living and "lifeless" things[89]) through a continuous gradation of differences rather than sharp-cut divisions.[90] After all, "about 99 percent of our genes are identical to [those of] chimpanzees, so that the remaining 1 percent accounts for all the differences between us. . . . [T]he greater distances by which we stand apart from the gorilla, the orangutan, and the remaining species of living apes and monkeys . . . are only a matter of degree."[91]

In short, instead of well-defined islands unequivocally separated from each other by substantial gaps, the world normally presents itself in the form of blurred-edge essences distinguished from one another only by "insensible gradations."[92] Analytic thinking, therefore, is clearly not the only mode by which we process reality. In fact, even most of the concepts we use to organize our experience are not clear-cut and sharply delineated but, rather, vague[93] and often modified by such "hedges" as "largely," "sort of," "quite," "almost," or "more or less."[94] (Until recently, such an ability to process fuzzy cat-

egories and negotiate subtle nuances actually distinguished our thinking from that of machines.)[95] . . . Membership in categories is basically a matter of degree and the transition from member to nonmember gradual rather than abrupt.[96] We therefore normally process them not in terms of their outlines, but, rather, in terms of their most central, prototypical instances (the "clearest cases"),[97] and as we move away from the latter we get progressively more distant from their core essence through a gradual "fadeout."[98] The fact that the orbits of such mental fields ("light" and "dark," "soft" and "loud," "winter" and "spring") usually overlap[99] obviously makes ambiguity an inevitable presence in our lives.

## The Social Construction of Discontinuity

Breaking up reality into discrete islands of meaning is, thus, an inevitably arbitrary act. The very existence of dividing lines (not to mention their location) is a matter of convention. It is by pure convention, for example, that we regard Danish and Norwegian as two separate languages yet Galician as a mere dialect of Portuguese. It is likewise by sheer convention that we draw a line between heroin and other lethal substances such as alcohol and tobacco (not to mention its own chemical cousins, which we use as painkillers or as controlled substitutes for heroin itself).[100] It is mere convention that similarly leads us to regard cooking or laundering as "service" occupations and fishermen or craftsmen as less skilled than assembly-line workers or parking-lot attendants.[101] Just as arbitrary is the way in which we carve supposedly discrete species out of the continuum of living forms,[102] separate the masculine from the feminine,[103] cut up continuous stretches of land into separate continents (Europe and Asia, North and Central America), or divide the world into time zones.[104] Nor are there any natural divides separating childhood from adulthood, winter from spring, or one day from the next (both my children, indeed, used to refer to the morning before their last afternoon nap as "yesterday"),[105] and if we attribute distinctive qualities to decades ("the Roaring Twenties") or centuries ("nineteenth-century architecture"),[106] it is only because we happen to count by tens. Had we used nine, instead, as the basis of our counting system, we would have undoubtedly discovered the historical significance of 9- , 81- , and 729-year cycles and generated fin-de-siècle and millennary frenzy around the years 1944 and 2187. We probably would also have experienced our midlife crisis at the age of thirty-six!

It is we ourselves who create categories and force reality into supposedly insular compartments.[107] Mental divides as well as the "things" they delineate are pure artifacts that have no basis whatsoever in reality.[108] A category, after all, is "a group of things [yet] things do not present themselves . . . grouped in such a way. . . . [Nor is their resemblance] enough to explain how we are led to group . . . them together in a sort of ideal sphere, enclosed by definite limits."[109] Classification is an artificial process of concept formation rather than of discovering clusters that already exist.[110] Entities such as "vitamins," "politicians," "art," and "crime" certainly do not exist "out there." The way we construct them resembles the way painters and photographers create pictures by mentally isolating supposedly discrete slices of reality from their immediate surroundings.[111] In the real world, there are no divides separating one insular "thing" from another. The "introduction of closure into the real" is a purely mental act.[112]

And yet, while boundaries and mental fields may not exist "out there," neither are they generated solely by our own mind. The discontinuities we experience are neither natural nor universal, yet they are not entirely personal either. We may not all classify reality in a precisely identical manner, yet we certainly do cut it up into rather similar mental chunks with pretty similar outlines.

It is indeed a mind that organizes reality in accordance with a specific logic, yet it is usually a group mind using an unmistakably social logic (and therefore also producing an unmistakably social order).[113] When we cut up the world, we usually do it not as humans or as individuals, but rather as members of societies.

The logic of classification is something we must learn. Socialization involves learning not only society's norms but also its distinctive classificatory schemas. Being socialized or acculturated entails knowing not only how to behave, but also how to perceive reality in a socially appropriate way. An anthropologist who studies another culture, for example, must learn "to see the world as it is constituted for the people themselves, to assimilate their distinctive categories. . . . [H]e may have to abandon the distinction between the natural and the supernatural, relocate the line between life and death, accept a common nature in mankind and animals."[114] Along similar lines, by the time she is three, a child has already internalized the conventional outlines of the category "birthday present" enough to know that, if someone suggests that she bring lima beans as a present, he must be kidding.

Whenever we classify things, we always attend some of their distinctive features[115] in order to note similarities and contrasts among them while ignoring all the rest as irrelevant.[116] The length of a film, for example, or whether it is in color or in black and white is quite irrelevant to the way it is rated. . . . What to stress among what is typically a "plethora of viable alternatives" is largely a social decision,[117] and being socialized entails knowing which features are salient for differentiating items from one another and which ones ought to be ignored as irrelevant.[118] It involves learning, for example, that, whereas adding cheese makes a hamburger a "cheeseburger,"[119] adding lettuce does not make it a "lettuceburger," and that it is the kind of meat and not the condiment that goes with it that gives a sandwich its distinctive identity. It likewise involves learning that the sex of the person for whom they are designed is probably the most distinctive feature of clothes (in department stores men's shirts are more likely to be displayed alongside men's pajamas than alongside women's blouses), and that the way it is spelled may help us locate an eggplant in a dictionary but not in a supermarket. Similarly, we learn that in order to find a book in a bookstore we must attend its substantive focus and the first letters of its author's last name (and ignore, for example, the color of its cover), yet that in order to find it in a book exhibit we must first know who published it. (We also learn that bookstores regard readers' ages as a critical feature of books, thus displaying children's books on dogs alongside children's books on boats rather than alongside general books on dogs.) We likewise learn that, in supermarkets, low-sodium soup is located near the low-sugar pineapple slices ("diet food"), marzipan near the anchovy paste ("gourmet food"), and canned corn near the canned pears (rather than by the fresh or frozen corn). And so we learn that, for the purpose of applying the incest taboo, brotherhood "counts" as a measure of proximity to oneself whereas having the same blood type is irrelevant.[120]

Separating the relevant (figure) from the irrelevant (ground) is not a spontaneous act. Classifying is a normative process, and it is society that leads us to perceive things as similar to or different from one another through unmistakably social *rules of irrelevance*[121] that specify which differences are salient for differentiating entities from one another and which ones are only negligible differences among variants of a single entity. Ignoring differences which "make no difference" involves some social pressure to disregard them. Though we often notice them, we learn to ignore them as irrelevant, just as we inhibit our perception of its ground in order to perceive the figure.[122] Along the same lines, ignoring the stutter or deformity of another is not a spontaneous act but rather a social display of tact.[123] It is rules of irrelevance

that likewise lead judges, professors, and doctors to display "affective neutrality"[124] and acquit innocent defendants, reward good students, and do their best to save patients' lives even when they personally despise them. They also lead bureaucrats who screen applications to exclude applicants' sex or race from their official considerations even if they are personally attentive to it.

The social construction of discontinuity is accomplished largely through language:

> We dissect nature along lines laid down by our native languages. The categories . . . we isolate from the world of phenomena we do not find there because they stare every observer in the face. . . . [T]he world is presented in a kaleidoscopic flux of impressions which has to be organized by our minds—and this means largely by the linguistic systems in our minds. We cut nature up . . . as we do, largely because we are parties to an agreement to organize it in this way—an agreement that . . . is codified in the patterns of our language. . . . [W]e cannot talk at all except by subscribing to the organization and classification of data which the agreement decrees.[125]

Not only does language allow us to detach mental entities from their surroundings and assign them fixed, decontextualized meanings, it also enables us to transform experiential continuums into discontinuous categories ("long" and "short," "hot" and "cold"). As we assign them separate labels, we come to perceive mental essences such as "professionals," "criminals," or "the poor" as if they were indeed discrete.[126] It is language that allows us to carve out of a continuous voice range the discrete categories "alto" and "soprano," distinguish "herbs" (basil, dill) from leaves we would never allow on our table, define vague discomfort in seemingly sharp categories such as "headache" or "nausea," and perceive after-shave lotion as actually different from eau de toilette or cologne. At the same time, it is our ability to assign them a common label that also allows us to lump things together in our mind.[127] Only the concept "classical," for example, makes Ravel's music similar to Vivaldi's, and only the concept "alcoholic" makes wine seem "closer" to vodka than to grape juice.

Since it is the very basis of social reality,[128] we often forget that language rests on mere convention and regard such mental entities, which are our own creation, as if they were real. "The trouble," the Eleatic Stranger reminds young Socrates,

> began at the moment when you [said] that there are two classes of living creature, one of them being mankind, and the other the rest of the animals lumped together. . . . [B]ecause you were able to give the common name "animals" to what was left, namely to all creatures other than man, you thought that these creatures do in actual fact make up one class. . . . [Yet cranes too might] classify the race of cranes as being distinct from all other creatures: the rest they might well lump together, men included, giving them the common appellation of "the beasts." So let us try to be on the watch against mistakes of that kind.[129]

By the same token, as we divide a single continuous process into several conceptual parts ("cause" and "effect,"[130] "life" and "death"[131]), we often commit the fallacy of misplaced concreteness and regard such purely mental constructs as if they were actually separate. We likewise reify the mental divide separating "white-collar" from "manual" labor[132] as well as the purely mental outlines of such entities as races, classes,[133] families, and nations. Like the dwellers of Plato's proverbial cave, we are prisoners of our own minds, mistaking mere social conceptions for actual experiential perceptions.

It is society that helps us carve discrete islands of meaning out of our experience. Only English speakers, for example, can "hear" the gaps between the separate words in "perhapstheyshouldhavetrieditearlier," which everyone else hears as a single chain of sound. Along similar lines, while people who hear jazz for the first time can never understand why a seemingly continuous stretch of music is occasionally interrupted by bursts of applause, jazz connoisseurs can actually "hear" the purely mental divides separating piano, bass, or drum "solos" from mere "accompaniment." Being a member of society entails "seeing" the world through special mental lenses. It is these lenses, which we acquire only through socialization, that allow us to perceive "things." The proverbial Martian cannot see the mental partitions separating Catholics from Protestants, classical from popular music, or the funny from the crude. Like the contours of constellations, we "see" such fine lines only when we learn that we should expect them there. As real as they may feel to us, boundaries are mere figments of our minds. Only the socialized can "see" them. To all cultural outsiders they are totally invisible.

Only through such "glasses" can entities be "seen." As soon as we remove them, boundaries practically disappear and the "things" they delineate fade away. What we then experience is as continuous as is Europe or the Middle East when seen from space or in ancient maps, or our own neighborhood when fog or heavy snow covers curbs and property lines, practically transforming familiar milieus into a visually undifferentiated flux. This is the way reality must appear to the unsocialized—a boundless, unbroken world with no lines. That is the world we would have inhabited were it not for society.

### Notes

1. Denis Diderot, quoted in Darnton, *The Great Cat Massacre*, p. 195.

2. Robert M. Pirsig, *Zen and the Art of Motorcycle Maintenance* (New York: Bantam New Age, 1981 [1974]), p. 66.

3. Ibid.

4. Hall, *The Hidden Dimension*, pp. 131–164.

5. Kurt Lewin, "Some Social-Psychological Differences between the United States and Germany," in *Resolving Social Conflicts* (London: Souvenir, 1973 [1936]), pp. 18–25.

6. Peter Gould and Rodney White, *Mental Maps* (Harmondsworth, England: Penguin, 1974), pp. 182–184.

7. Jakobson, *Six Lectures on Sound and Meaning*, p. 30. See also pp. 28–33, 74–76.

8. Benjamin L. Whorf, "Language, Mind, and Reality," in *Language, Thought, and Reality* (Cambridge: MIT Press, 1956 [1942]), p. 253.

9. Eco, *A Theory of Semiotics*, pp. 76–78; Benjamin L. Whorf, "Science and Linguistics," in *Language, Thought, and Reality*, p. 210; A. R. Radcliffe-Brown, "The Study of Kinship Systems," in *Structure and Function in Primitive Society* (New York: Free Press, 1965 [1941]), p. 73; Gary Witherspoon, *Language and Art in the Navajo Universe* (Ann Arbor: University of Michigan Press, 1977), p. 121.

10. Whorf, "Science and Linguistics"; Whorf, "Language, Mind, and Reality."

11. John B. Carroll and Joseph B. Casagrande, "The Functions of Language Classifications in Behavior," in Eleanor E. Maccoby et al., eds., *Readings in Social Psychology* (New York: Holt, Rinehart and Winston, 1958), pp. 26–31. See also pp. 22–26.

12. See, for example, Lucien Lévy-Bruhl, *How Natives Think* (New York: Washington Square Press, 1966 [1910]).

13. See, for example, Claude Lévi-Strauss, *The Savage Mind* (Chicago: University of Chicago Press, 1966 [1962]).

14. [See E. Zerubavel, *The Fine Line: Making Distinctions in Everyday Life* (New York: Free Press)] on allomorphs, allophones, allokines, allophiles, and allochrones, see notes 97–101 of chapter 1.

15. Durkheim and Mauss, *Primitive Classification*, p. 20.

16. See Durkheim, *The Elementary Forms of the Religious Life*, pp. 167–168.

17. Darnton, *The Great Cat Massacre*, p. 192.

18. See Whorf, "Science and Linguistics," p. 210.

19. Tajfel, *Human Groups and Social Categories*, p. 170.

20. Mannheim, *Ideology and Utopia*, pp. 84–87.

21. See, for example, Bärbel Inhelder and Jean Piaget, *The Early Growth of Logic in the Child* (New York: Humanities Press, 1964), pp. 105, 116–117, 169, 282; Jane Thompson, "The Ability of Children of Different Grade Levels to Generalize on Sorting Tests," *Journal of Psychology* 11 (1941):123.

22. Rudolf Arnheim, *Visual Thinking* (Berkeley: University of California Press, 1969), p. 200.

23. Judith M. Gerson and Kathy Peiss, "Boundaries, Negotiation, Consciousness: Reconceptualizing Gender Relations," *Social Problems* 32 (1985):317–331.

24. Williamson, *New People*; Domínguez, *White by Definition*. See also John K. Chance, *Race and Class in Colonial Oaxaca* (Stanford, Calif.: Stanford University Press, 1978), pp. 94–104, 126–143, 155–159.

25. Reginald L. Poole, "The Beginning of the Year in the Middle Ages," *Proceedings of the British Academy* 10 (1921–1923):113–137. See also Zerubavel, *Patterns of Time in Hospital Life*, p. 8.

26. Stephen J. Gould, "Taxonomy as Politics: The Harm of False Classification," *Dissent*, Winter 1990, p. 74.

27. Foucault, *The Order of Things*, pp. 264–265.

28. Beare, *The Roman Stage*, p. 238.

29. Singer, *Animal Liberation*, p. 1.

30. In the eighteenth century, the governor of Grenada likewise appointed one superintendent for both blacks and mules. See Jordan, *White over Black*, p. 233.

31. Christopher D. Stone, *Should Trees Have Standing?* (Los Altos, Calif.: William Kaufmann, 1974), pp. 6–7.

32. Evans, *The Criminal Prosecution and Capital Punishment of Animals*.

33. Ibid., pp. 198–199, 175. See also p. 172.

34. Stephenson, *Race Distinctions in American Law*, p. 15. See also Williamson, *New People*.

35. Hunter, *Symbolic Communities*, pp. 84, 181.

36. Werner Sollors, *Beyond Ethnicity* (New York: Oxford University Press, 1986), pp. 71–72.

37. Richard Hogan, "The Frontier as Social Control," *Theory and Society* 14 (1985):35–51.

38. Sandra C. Hinson, "How Feminist and Radical Books Are Classified: An Inter-Bookstore Comparison" (unpublished paper, 1986).

39. "Have Gays Taken over Yale?" *Newsweek*, October 12, 1987, p. 96.

40. Jordan, *White over Black*, pp. 217–239, 491–506.

41. Gould, "Taxonomy as Politics."

42. Viviana A. Zelizer, *Pricing the Priceless Child* (New York: Basic Books, 1985), pp. 58, 75, 84.

43. See also Roy Wallis, ed., *On the Margins of Science* (Keele: University of Keele, 1979 [Sociological Review Monograph #27]); Gieryn, "Boundary-Work and the Demarcation of Science from Non-Science."

44. Y. Zerubavel, "The Last Stand," pp. 196–199.

45. M. Martin Halley and William F. Harvey,

"Medical vs. Legal Definitions of Death," *Journal of the American Medical Association* 204 (May 6, 1968):423–425. See also Robert Zussman, *Intensive Care* (Chicago: University of Chicago Press, 1992).

46. The attorney of the Missouri Abortion Clinics, as quoted in the *New York Times,* April 27, 1989, p. B13.

47. See, for example, Tertullian, "On the Soul," in vol. 10 of *The Fathers of the Church* (Washington, D.C.: Catholic University of American Press, 1950) 25:5–9, 27:1–3, 37:2.

48. *New York Times,* April 7, 1989, p. 13.

49. Brenda Danet, "'Baby' or 'Fetus'?: Language and the Construction of Reality in a Manslaughter Trial," *Semiotica* 32 (1980):187–219.

50. Peter G. Brown and Henry Shue, eds., *Boundaries* (Totowa, N.J.: Rowman and Littlefield, 1981), p. 105.

51. Schwartz, "The Social Psychology of Privacy," pp. 748–749.

52. Goffman, *Frame Analysis,* p. 73.

53. George F. Will, "Lithuania and South Carolina," *Newsweek,* January 29, 1990, p. 80.

54. *Newsweek,* April 9, 1990, p. 32.

55. Singer, *Animal Liberation,* pp. 2, 21.

56. Kinsey et al., *Sexual Behavior in the Human Male,* pp. 639–647.

57. See also Eviatar Zerubavel, "The Standardization of Time: A Sociohistorical Perspective," *American Journal of Sociology* 88 (1982):14–15, 19.

58. Schutz, "On Multiple Realities," pp. 231–232. See also Davis, *Smut,* p. 74.

59. Sven-Tage Teodorsson, *Anaxagoras' Theory of Matter* (Goteborg, Sweden: Acta Universitatis Gothoburgensis, 1982), p. 99. See also S. Sambursky, *The Physical World of the Greeks* (New York: Macmillan, 1956), pp. 132–157.

60. Arthur O. Lovejoy, *The Great Chain of Being* (Cambridge: Harvard University Press, 1964 [1936]), p. 56.

61. Tuan, *Segmented Worlds and Self,* pp. 126–128.

62. Richard Schechner, *Environmental Theater* (New York: Hawthorn, 1973), p. 15.

63. Ibid., p. 16.

64. Arnheim, *Art and Visual Perception,* pp. 102–103, 216–220.

65. Merleau-Ponty, *Phenomenology of Perception,* p. 329.

66. M. von Senden, *Space and Sight* (London: Methuen, 1960 [1932]).

67. Fawcett, *Frontiers,* pp. 17–19, 24. See also Guillaume de Greef, *La Structure Générale des Sociétés, vol. 3: Théorie des Frontières et des Classes* (Brussels: Larcier, 1908), p. 273.

68. Ken Wilber, *No Boundary* (Boston: New Science Library, 1981 [1979]), pp. 24–25.

69. See, for example, Tuan, *Segmented Worlds and Self,* p. 130.

70. Gaston Bachelard, *The Poetics of Space* (Boston: Beacon, 1969 [1958]), p. 222. See also Georg Simmel, "Brücke und Tür," in *Brücke und Tür* (Stuttgart: K. F. Koehler, 1957 [1909]), pp. 3–4.

71. Balint, *Thrills and Regressions,* p. 66; Balint, *The Basic Fault,* p. 67.

72. Davis, *Smut,* pp. 45–46.

73. Goffman, *Frame Analysis,* pp. 308–321. See also Gary A. Fine, *Shared Fantasy* (Chicago: University of Chicago Press, 1983), pp. 200–203.

74. Personal communication from Murray Davis.

75. Goffman, *Frame Analysis,* pp. 312–313.

76. Van Gennep, *The Rites of Passage.*

77. In Hebrew, the words for *twilight, evening,* and *mixture* all derive from the same root.

78. Christena Nippert-Eng, "Liminality in Everyday Life: Commuting and the Transition between Home and Work" (paper presented at the annual meeting of the American Sociological Association, Atlanta, August 1988).

79. Turner, "Betwixt and Between"; Victor Turner, *The Ritual Process* (Harmondsworth, England: Penguin, 1974 [1969]).

80. Patterson, *Slavery and Social Death,* pp. 38–39, 46–51.

81. Robert E. Park, "Human Migration and the Marginal Man," *American Journal of Sociology* 33 (1928):881–893; Everett V. Stonequist, *The Marginal Man* (New York: Charles Scribner's Sons, 1937). See also Simmel, "The Stranger."

82. Georg Simmel, "The Web of Group Affiliations," in *Conflict and the Web of Group Affiliations* (New York: Free Press, 1964 [1908]), pp. 127–195.

83. David M. Schneider, "American Kin Terms and Terms for Kinsmen: A Critique of Goodenough's Componential Analysis of Yankee Kinship Terminology," in Stephen A. Tyler, ed., *Cognitive Anthropology* (New York: Holt, Rinehart and Winston, 1969 [1965]), p. 290; Carol B. Stack, *All Our Kin* (New York: Harper & Row, 1974), pp. 62–89; Schneider, *American Kinship,* p. 72; Marc Shell, "The Family Pet," *Representations* 15 (1986): 123;

Constance Perrin, *Belonging in America* (Madison: University of Wisconsin Press, 1988), pp. 26, 107; Gricar, "How Thick Is Blood?" ch. 5.

84. Landecker, "Class Boundaries," pp. 874–875; Blau and Duncan, *The American Occupational Structure*, pp. 59, 65, 78–79, 347.

85. Blau and Duncan, ibid., p. 124.

86. See, for example, Edmund Leach, "The Legitimacy of Solomon: Some Structural Aspects of Old Testament History," *European Journal of Sociology* 7 (1966): 58–101.

87. Stephen J. Gould, "Human Equality Is a Contingent Fact of History," *Natural History* 93 (1984), no. 11:32.

88. Charles Bonnet, quoted in Foucault, *The Order of Things*, p. 147.

89. Aristotle, *The Complete Works* (Princeton: Princeton University Press, 1984): *History of Animals*, book 8, 588b.4–5, 11–13; *Parts of Animals*, book 4, 681.

90. Ibid., *History of Animals*, book 8, 588a.21–588b.3; *Parts of Animals*, book 4, 697a.29–697b.22; John Locke, *An Essay Concerning Human Understanding* (Oxford: Oxford University Press, 1975 [1690]), book 3, chapter 6.12,23; Lovejoy, *The Great Chain of Being;* Joseph Klaits and Barrie Klaits, eds., *Animals and Man in Historical Perspective* (New York: Harper Torchbooks, 1974), pp. 2–4.

91. Wilson, *Biophilia*, p. 130.

92. Henri Bergson, *Matter and Memory* (London: George Allen & Unwin, 1911 [1908]), p. 278.

93. Ludwig Wittgenstein, *Philosophical Investigations* (New York: Macmillan, 1958 [1953]), part I.68–71.

94. George Lakoff, "Hedges: A Study in Meaning Criteria and the Logic of Fuzzy Concepts," *Journal of Philosophical Logic* 2 (1973):458–508; George Lakoff, *Women, Fire, and Dangerous Things* (Chicago: University of Chicago Press, 1987), pp. 122–125.

95. Lotfi A. Zadeh, "A Fuzzy-Set-Theoretic Interpretation of Linguistic Hedges," *Journal of Cybernetics* 2 (1972), no. 3:4.

96. Ibid.; Lotfi A. Zadeh, "Fuzzy Sets," *Information and Control* 8 (1965):339; Eleanor H. Rosch, "On the Internal Structure of Perceptual and Semantic Categories," in Timothy E. Moore, ed., *Cognitive Development and the Acquisition of Language* (New York: Academic Press, 1973), pp. 112, 130; Paul Kay and Chad K. McDaniel, "The Linguistic Significance of the Meanings of Basic Color Terms," *Language* 54 (1978):610–646; Michael E. McCloskey and Sam Glucksberg, "Natural Categories: Well Defined or Fuzzy Sets?" *Memory and Cognition* 6 (1978):462–472; Linda Coleman and Paul Kay, "Prototype Semantics: The English Word *Lie*," *Language* 57 (1981):27; Lakoff, *Women, Fire, and Dangerous Things*, pp. 12, 21, 56, 287–288.

97. Bruner et al., *A Study of Thinking*, p. 64; Rosch, "On the Internal Structure of Perceptual and Semantic Categories," pp. 112, 130; Eleanor H. Rosch, "Human Categorization," in Neil Warren, ed., *Studies in Cross–Cultural Psychology* (London: Academic Press, 1977), vol. 1, pp. 13–14, 25–26; Eleanor H. Rosch, "Principles of Categorization," in Eleanor Rosch and Barbara B. Lloyd, eds., *Cognition and Categorization* (Hillside, N.J.: Lawrence Erlbaum Associates, 1978), pp. 35–36. See also Brent Berlin and Paul Kay, *Basic Color Terms* (Berkeley: University of California Press, 1969), p. 13.

98. Schneider, "American Kin Terms and Terms for Kinsmen," p. 290.

99. William Labov, "The Boundaries of Words and Their Meanings," in Charles-James N. Bailey and Roger W. Shuy, eds., *New Ways of Analyzing Variation in English* (Washington, D.C.: Georgetown University Press, 1973), pp. 340–373; Elaine S. Andersen, "Cups and Glasses: Learning That Boundaries Are Vague," *Journal of Child Language* 2 (1975):79–103; Rodney Needham, "Polythetic Classification: Convergence and Consequences," *Man* 10 (1975):349–369.

100. Gould, "Taxonomy as Politics," p. 74.

101. Harry Braverman, *Labor and Monopoly Capital* (New York: Monthly Review Press, 1974), pp. 360–361, 428–430.

102. Locke, *An Essay Concerning Human Understanding*, book 3, chap. 6.27,30,36,37; Jean–Baptiste Lamarck, *Zoological Philosophy* (New York: Hafner, 1963 [1809]) pp. 20–28; Simpson, *Principles of Animal Taxonomy*, pp. 118–119.

103. Cynthia F. Epstein, *Deceptive Distinctions* (New Haven: Yale University Press, 1988).

104. Zerubavel, "The Standardization of Time," pp. 19–20.

105. See also Zerubavel, *Hidden Rhythms*, pp. 11, 41, 86; Zerubavel, *The Seven-Day Circle*, pp. 11, 139–141.

106. See also Fred Davis, "Decade Labeling: The Play of Collective Memory and Narrative Plot," *Symbolic Interaction* 7 (1984), no. 1:15–24;

Hillel Schwartz, *Century's End* (New York: Doubleday, 1990).

107. Kinsey et al., *Sexual Behavior in the Human Male*, p. 639. See also Bergson, *Matter and Memory*, pp. 239–298.

108. Bergson, ibid., p. 259; Jorge Luis Borges, "The Analytical Language of John Wilkins," in *Other Inquisitions, 1937–1952* (Austin: University of Texas Press 1964 [1952]), p. 104; Edmund Leach, *Culture and Communication* (Cambridge, England: Cambridge University Press, 1976), pp. 33–34.

109. Durkheim and Mauss, *Primitive Classification*, pp. 7–8.

110. Bruner et al., *A Study of Thinking*, p. 232.

111. Arnheim, *The Power of the Center*, p. 42; Ansel Adams, *Camera and Lens* (Hastings-on-Hudson, N.Y.: Morgan & Morgan, 1970), pp. 28–29, 34–37.

112. Wilden, *System and Structure*, p. 204. See also pp. 185, 219.

113. See also Durkheim, *The Elementary Forms of the Religious Life*, pp. 26–33, 479–487.

114. Rodney Needham, "Introduction" to Emile Durkheim and Marcel Mauss, *Primitive Classification* (Chicago: University of Chicago Press, 1973), p. viii.

115. Jakobson, *Six Lectures on Sound and Meaning*, pp. 69–87.

116. Amos Tversky, "Features of Similarity," *Psychological Review* 84 (1977):329.

117. Gould, "Taxonomy as Politics," p. 73.

118. Frake, "The Diagnosis of Disease among the Subanun of Mindanao"; Charles O. Frake, "The Ethnographic Study of Cognitive Systems," in Stephen A. Tyler, ed., *Cognitive Anthropology* (New York: Holt, Rinehart and Winston, 1969 [1962]), pp. 28–41. See also Schutz and Luckmann, *The Structures of the Life-World*, p. 248.

119. Frake, "The Ethnographic Study of Cognitive Systems," p. 36.

120. On how children learn which distinctive features are salient for establishing kinship, see Julie M. Gricar, "Strategies Children Use in the Cognitive Construction of Kinship," *Sociological Studies of Child Development* (forthcoming).

121. Goffman, *Encounters*, pp. 19–26.

122. Bateson, "A Theory of Play and Fantasy," p. 187.

123. See also Goffman, *The Presentation of Self in Everyday Life*, p. 230; Goffman, *Behavior in Public Places*, pp. 83–88.

124. Parsons, *The Social System*, pp. 60, 435, 458–462.

125. Whorf, "Science and Linguistics," pp. 213–214.

126. See also Whorf, "Language, Mind, and Reality," p. 259; Wilber, *No Boundary*, p. 26.

127. See, for example, Locke, *An Essay Concerning Human Understanding*, book 3, chap. 6.39.

128. Emile Durkheim, "The Dualism of Human Nature and Its Social Conditions," in Robert N. Bellah, ed., *On Morality and Society* (Chicago: University of Chicago Press, 1973 [1914]), pp. 151–152, 161–162; George H. Mead, *Mind, Self, and Society* (Chicago: University of Chicago Press, 1934), pp. 46–47; Schutz and Luckmann, *The Structures of the Life-World*, pp. 233–235; Berger and Luckmann, *The Social Construction of Reality*, pp. 37–41, 68–69.

129. Plato, *Statesman* (New Haven: Yale University Press, 1952), 263c–263d.

130. Edward De Bono, *The Mechanism of Mind* (Harmondsworth, England: Penguin, 1971 [1969]), p. 197.

131. Danet, "'Baby' or 'Fetus'?" pp. 187–188. See also Robert S. Morison, "Death: Process or Event?" *Science* 173 (August 20, 1971):694–695.

132. Braverman, *Labor and Monopoly Capital*, pp. 325–326.

133. Bates and Peacock, "Conceptualizing Social Structure," pp. 569–570, 575.

## Bibliography

Aristotle. *The Complete Works*. Princeton: Princeton University Press (Bollingen Series 71. Revised Oxford translation, edited by Jonathan Barnes), 1984.

Arnheim, Rudolf. *Art and Visual Perception*. Berkeley: University of California Press, 1967 (1954).

———. *The Power of the Center*. Berkeley: University of California Press, 1982.

Balint, Michael. *Thrills and Regressions*. New York: International Universities Press, 1959.

———. *The Basic Fault*. London: Tavistock, 1968.

Bates, Frederick L., and Walter G. Peacock. "Conceptualizing Social Structure: The Misuse of Classification in Structural Modeling." *American Sociological Review* 54 (1989):565–577.

Bateson, Gregory. "A Theory of Play and Fantasy." In *Steps to an Ecology of Mind*, pp. 177–193. New York: Ballantine, 1972 (1955).

Beare, William. *The Roman Stage*. 3rd. ed. London: Methuen, 1964.

Berger, Peter L., and Thomas Luckmann. *The Social Construction of Reality*. Garden City, N.Y.: Anchor, 1967.

Bergson, Henri. *Matter and Memory*. London: George Allen & Unwin, 1911 (1908).

Blau, Peter M., and Otis D. Duncan. *The American Occupational Structure*. New York: John Wiley, 1967.

Braverman, Harry. *Labor and Monopoly Capital*. New York: Monthly Review Press, 1974.

Bruner, Jerome S., et al. *A Study of Thinking*. New York: John Wiley, 1956.

Danet, Brenda. "'Baby' or 'Fetus'?: Language and the Construction of Reality in a Manslaughter Trial." *Semiotica* 32 (1980):187–219.

Darnton, Robert. *The Great Cat Massacre and Other Episodes in French Cultural History*. New York: Vintage, 1985.

Davis, Murray S. *Smut*. Chicago: University of Chicago Press, 1983.

Domínguez, Virginia R. *White by Definition*. New Brunswick, N.J.: Rutgers University Press, 1986.

Durkheim, Emile. *The Elementary Forms of the Religious Life*. New York: Free Press, 1965 (1912).

Durkheim, Emile, and Marcel Mauss. *Primitive Classification*. Chicago: University of Chicago Press, 1963 (1903).

Eco, Umberto. *A Theory of Semiotics*. Bloomington: Indiana University Press, 1976.

Evans, E. P. *The Criminal Prosecution and Capital Punishment of Animals*. London: William Heinemann, 1906.

Fawcett, C. B. *Frontiers*. Oxford: Oxford University Press, 1918.

Foucault, Michel. *Madness and Civilization*. New York: Vintage, 1973 (1961).

———. *The Order of Things*. New York: Vintage, 1973 (1966).

Fraiberg, Selma H. *The Magic Years*. New York: Charles Scribner's Sons, 1959.

Frake, Charles O. "The Diagnosis of Disease among the Subanun of Mindanao." *American Anthropologist* 63 (1961):113–132.

———. "The Ethnographic Study of Cognitive Systems." In Stephen A. Tyler, ed., *Cognitive Anthropology*, pp. 28–41. New York: Holt, Rinehart and Winston, 1969 (1962).

Gieryn, Thomas F. "Boundary-Work and the Demarcation of Science from Non-Science: Strains and Interests in Professional Ideologies of Scientists." *American Sociological Review* 48 (1983):781–795.

Goffman, Erving. *The Presentation of Self in Everyday Life*. Garden City, N.Y.: Anchor, 1959.

———. *Encounters*. Indianapolis: Bobbs-Merrill, 1961.

———. *Behavior in Public Places*. New York: Free Press, 1963.

———. *Frame Analysis*. New York: Harper Colophon, 1974.

Gould, Stephen J. "Taxonomy as Politics: The Harm of False Classification." *Dissent* (Winter 1990):73–78.

Gricar, Julie M. "How Thick Is Blood? The Social Construction and Cultural Configuration of Kinship." Ph.D. diss., Columbia University, 1991.

Hall, Edward T. *The Hidden Dimension*. Garden City: Anchor, 1969 (1966).

Hunter, Albert. *Symbolic Communities*. Chicago: University of Chicago Press, 1982 (1974).

Jakobson, Roman. *Six Lectures on Sound and Meaning*. Cambridge: MIT Press, 1978 (1942).

Jordan, Winthrop D. *White over Black*. Chapel Hill: University of North Carolina Press, 1968.

Kinsey, Alfred C., et al. *Sexual Behavior in the Human Male*. Philadelphia: W. B. Saunders, 1948.

Lakoff, George. *Women, Fire, and Dangerous Things*. Chicago: University of Chicago Press, 1987.

Landecker, Werner S. "Class Boundaries." *American Sociological Review* 25 (1960):868–877.

Locke, John. *An Essay Concerning Human Understanding*. Oxford: Oxford University Press, 1975 (1960).

Lovejoy, Arthur O. *The Great Chain of Being*. Cambridge: Harvard University Press, 1964 (1936).

Mannheim, Karl. *Ideology and Utopia*. New York: Harvest, 1936.

Merleau-Ponty, Maurice. "The Child's Relations with Others." In *The Primacy of Perception*, pp. 96–155. Evanston, Ill.: Northwestern University Press, 1964 (1960).

———. *Phenomenology of Perception*. New York: Humanities Press, 1962.

Parsons, Talcott. *The Social System*. New York: Free Press, 1964 (1951).

Patterson, Orlando. *Slavery and Social Death*. Cambridge, England: Cambridge University Press, 1982.

Plato. *Statesman*. Translated by J. B. Skemp. New Haven: Yale University Press, 1952.

Rosch, Eleanor H. "On the Internal Structure of Perceptual and Semantic Categories." In Timothy E. Moore, ed., *Cognitive Development and the Acquisition of Language*, pp. 111–144. New York: Academic Press, 1973.

Schneider, David M. "American Kin Terms and Terms for Kinsmen: A Critique of Goodenough's Componential Analysis of Yankee Kinship Terminology." In Stephen A. Tyler, ed., *Cognitive Anthropology*, pp. 288–311. New York: Holt, Rinehart and Winston, 1969 (1965).

———. *American Kinship*. 2nd ed. Chicago: University of Chicago Press, 1980.

Schutz, Alfred. "On Multiple Realities." *Collected Papers*, vol. 1, pp. 207–259. The Hague: Martinus Nijhoff, 1973 (1945).

Schutz, Alfred, and Thomas Luckmann. *The Structures of the Life-World*. Evanston, Ill.: Northwestern University Press, 1973.

Schwartz, Barry. "The Social Psychology of Privacy." *American Journal of Sociology* 78 (1968): 741–752.

Simmel, Georg. "The Stranger." In *The Sociology of Georg Simmel*, pp. 402–408. (1908).

Simpson, George G. *Principles of Animal Taxonomy*. New York: Columbia University Press, 1961.

Singer, Peter. *Animal Liberation*. New York: Discus, 1977.

Stephenson, Gilbert T. *Race Distinctions in American Law*. New York: D. Appleton, 1910.

Tajfel, Henri. *Human Groups and Social Categories*. Cambridge, England: Cambridge University Press, 1981.

Tertullian. "On the Soul." In *The Fathers of the Church*, vol. 10, pp. 165–309. Washington, D.C.: Catholic University of American Press, 1950.

Tuan, Yi-Fu. *Segmented Worlds and Self*. Minneapolis: University of Minnesota Press, 1982.

Turner, Victor. "Betwixt and Between: The Liminal Period in *Rites de Passage*." In *The Forest of Symbols*, pp. 93–111. Ithaca: Cornell University Press, 1970 (1964).

———. *The Ritual Process*. Harmondsworth, England: Penguin, 1974 (1969).

Van Gennep, Arnold. *The Rites of Passage*. Chicago: University of Chicago Press, 1960 (1908).

Whorf, Benjamin L. "Science and Linguistics." In *Language, Thought, and Reality*, pp. 207–219. Cambridge: MIT Press, 1956 (1940).

———. "Language, Mind, and Reality." In *Language, Thought, and Reality*, pp. 246–270. (1942).

Wilber, Ken. *No Boundary*. Boston: New Science Library, 1981 (1979).

Wilden, Anthony. *System and Structure*. London: Tavistock, 1972.

Williamson, Joel. *New People*. New York: Free Press, 1980.

Wilson, Edward O. *Biophilia*. Cambridge: Harvard University Press, 1984.

Zerubavel, Eviatar. *Patterns of Time in Hospital Life*. Chicago: University of Chicago Press, 1979.

———. *Hidden Rhythms*. Chicago: University of Chicago Press, 1981.

———. "The Standardization of Time: A Sociohistorical Perspective." *American Journal of Sociology* 88 (1982):1–23.

———. *The Seven-Day Circle*. New York: Free Press, 1985.

Zerubavel, Yael. "The Last Stand: On the Transformation of Symbols in Modern Israeli Culture." Ph.D. diss., University of Pennsylvania, 1980.

14

# Mindfulness and Mindlessness

*Ellen Langer*

## Introduction

*I don't like the idea of a unitary subject; I prefer the play of a kaleidoscope: you give it a tap and the little bits of colored glass form a new pattern.*
(Roland Barthes, *The Grain of the Voice*)

One day, at a nursing home in Connecticut, elderly residents were each given a choice of houseplants to care for and were asked to make a number of small decisions about their daily routines. A year and a half later, not only were these people more cheerful, active, and alert than a similar group in the same institution who were not given these choices and responsibilities, but many more of them were still alive. In fact, less than half as many of the decision-making, plant-minding residents had died as had those in the other group. This experiment, with its startling results, began over ten years of research into the powerful effects of what my colleagues and I came to call *mindfulness,* and of its counterpart, the equally powerful but destructive state of *mindlessness.*[1] . . .

Social psychologists usually look for the ways in which behavior depends on context. When mindless, however, people treat information as though it were *context-free*—true regardless of circumstances. For example,

take the statement: Heroin is dangerous. How true is this for a dying individual in intolerable pain?

Once alerted to the dangers of mindlessness and to the possibility of bringing about a more mindful attitude by such deceptively simple measures as those used in the nursing home experiment, I began to see this double-edged phenomenon at work in many different settings. For instance, consider the events that led to the 1985 crash of an Air Florida plane that killed seventy-four passengers. It was a routine flight from Washington, D.C., to Florida with an experienced flight crew. Pilot and copilot were in excellent physical health. Neither was tired, stressed, or under the influence. What went wrong? An extensive examination pointed to the crew's pre-takeoff control checks. As the copilot calls out each control on his list, the pilot makes sure the switches are where he wants them to be. One of these controls is an anti-icer. On this day, the pilot and copilot went over each of the controls as they had always done. They went through their routine and checked "off" when the anti-icer was mentioned. This time, however, the flight was different from their experience. This time they were not flying in the usual warm southern weather. It was icy outside.

As he went through the control checks, one by one as he always did, the pilot appeared to be thinking when he was not.[2] The pre-takeoff routines of pilot and copilot have a lot in common with the tiresome safety demonstrations of flight attendants to experienced, glassy-eyed passengers. When we blindly follow routines or unwittingly carry out senseless orders, we are acting like automatons, with potentially grave consequences for ourselves and others.

## When the Light's On and Nobody's Home

*Out of time we cut "days" and "nights," "summers" and "winters." We say what each part of the sensible continuum is, and all these abstract whats are concepts.*

*The intellectual life of man consists almost wholly in his substitution of a conceptual order for the perceptual order in which his experience originally comes.* (William James, "The World We Live In")

Imagine that it's two o'clock in the morning. Your doorbell rings; you get up, startled, and make your way downstairs. You open the door and see a man standing before you. He wears two diamond rings and a fur coat, and there's a Rolls Royce behind him. He's sorry to wake you at this ridiculous hour, he tells you, but he's in the middle of a scavenger hunt. His ex-wife is in the same contest, which makes it very important to him that he win. He needs a piece of wood about three feet by seven feet. Can you help him? In order to make it worthwhile he'll give you $10,000. You believe him. He's obviously rich. And so you say to yourself, how in the world can I get this piece of wood for him? You think of the lumber yard; you don't know who owns the lumber yard; in fact you're not even sure where the lumber yard is. It would be closed at two o'clock in the morning anyway. You struggle but you can't come up with anything. Reluctantly, you tell him, "Gee, I'm sorry."

The next day, when passing a construction site near a friend's house, you see a piece of wood that's just about the right size, three feet by seven feet—a door. You could have just taken a door off its hinges and given it to him, for $10,000.

Why on earth, you say to yourself, didn't it occur to you to do that? It didn't occur to you because yesterday your door was not a piece of wood. The seven-by-three-foot piece of wood was hidden from you, stuck in the category called "door."

This kind of mindlessness, which usually takes more humdrum forms—"Why didn't I think of Susan? She can unclog sinks"— could be called "entrapment by category." It is one of three definitions that can help us understand the nature of mindlessness. The other two, which we will also explain, are automatic behavior and acting from a single perspective.

### Trapped by Categories

We experience the world by creating categories and making distinctions among them. "This is a Chinese, not a Japanese, vase." "No, he's only a freshman." "The white orchids are endangered." "She's his boss now." In this way, we make a picture of the world, and of ourselves. Without categories the world might seem to escape us. Tibetan Buddhists call this habit of mind "The Lord of Speech":

We adopt sets of categories which serve as ways of managing phenomena. The most fully developed products of this tendency are ideologies, the systems of ideas that rationalize, justify and sanctify our lives. Nationalism, communism, existentialism, Christianity, Buddhism—all provide us with identities, rules of action, and interpretations of how and why things happen as they do.[3]

The creation of new categories, as we will see throughout this book, is a mindful activity. Mindlessness sets in when we rely too rigidly on categories and distinctions created in the past (masculine/feminine, old/young, success/failure). Once distinctions are created, they take on a life of their own. Consider: (1) First there was earth. (2) Then there was land, sea, and sky. (3) Then there were countries. (4) Then there was

Germany. (5) Now there is East Germany versus West Germany. The categories we make gather momentum and are very hard to overthrow. We build our own and our shared realities and then we become victims of them—blind to the fact that they are constructs, ideas.

If we look back at the categories of an earlier age, once firmly established, it is easier to see why new ones might become necessary. The Argentinean writer Jorge Luis Borges quotes from an ancient Chinese encyclopedia in which the animals are classified as "(a) belonging to the Emperor, (b) embalmed, (c) tame, (d) suckling pigs, (e) sirens, (f) stray dogs, (g) included in the present classification, (h) frenzied, (i) innumerable, (j) drawn with a very fine camel brush, (k) et cetera, (l) having just broken the water pitcher, (m) that from a long way off look like flies."[4] To be mindless is to be trapped in a rigid world in which certain creatures always belong to the Emperor, Christianity is always good, certain people are forever untouchable, and doors are only doors.

### Automatic Behavior

Have you ever said "excuse me" to a store mannequin or written a check in January with the previous year's date? When in this mode, we take in and use limited signals from the world around us (the female form, the familiar face of the check) without letting other signals (the motionless pose, a calendar) penetrate as well.

Once, in a small department store, I gave a cashier a new credit card. Noticing that I hadn't signed it, she handed it back to me to sign. Then she took my card, passed it through her machine, handed me the resulting form, and asked me to sign it. I did as I was told. The cashier then held the form next to the newly signed card to see if the signatures matched.

Modern psychology has not paid much attention to how much complicated action may be performed automatically, yet as early as 1896 Leon Solomons and Gertrude Stein looked into this question. (This was *the* Gertrude Stein who, from 1893 to 1898, was a graduate student in experimental psychology at Harvard University, working under William James.) They studied what was then called "double personalities" and which later came to be known as "split personalities," and proposed that the mindless performance of the second personality was essentially similar to that of ordinary people. Ordinary people also engage in a great deal of complex behavior without consciously paying attention to it. Solomons and Stein conducted several experiments in which they were their own subjects, demonstrating that both writing and reading could be done automatically. They succeeded in writing English words while they were otherwise caught up in reading an absorbing story. With much practice, they were even able to take dictation automatically while reading. Afterward, they were completely unable to recall the words they had written but were nevertheless quite certain they had written something. To show that reading could take place automatically, the subject read aloud from a book while a captivating story was read to him or her. Again they found that, after a lot of practice, they could read aloud unhampered while giving full attention to the story being read to them.

Solomons and Stein concluded that a vast number of actions that we think of as intelligent, such as reading and writing, can be done quite automatically: "We have shown a general tendency on the part of normal people, to *act*, without any express desire or conscious volition, in a manner in general accord with the *previous habits* of the person."[5]

An experiment I conducted in 1978 with fellow psychologists Benzion Chanowitz and Arthur Blank explored this kind of mindlessness.[6] Our setting was the Graduate Center at the City University of New York. We approached people using a copying machine and asked whether they would let us copy something then and there. We gave reasons that were either sound or senseless. An identical response to both sound and senseless requests would show that our subjects were not thinking about what was being said. We made one of three requests: "Excuse me, may I use the Xerox machine?"; "Excuse me, may I use the Xerox machine because I want to make copies?"; "Excuse me, may I use the Xerox machine because I'm in a rush?"

The first and second requests are the same in *content*—What else would one do with a copying machine except make copies? Therefore if people were considering what was actually being said, the first two requests should be equally effective. Structurally, however, they are different. The redundant request ("Excuse me, may I use the Xerox machine because I want to make copies?") is more similar to the last one ("Excuse me, may I use the Xerox machine because I'm in a rush?") in that both state the request and give a reason. If people comply with the last two requests in equal numbers, this implies attention to structure rather than conscious attention to content. That, in fact, was just what we found. There was more compliance when a reason was given—whether the reason sounded legitimate or silly. People responded mindlessly to the familiar framework rather than mindfully attending to the content.

Of course, there are limits to this. If someone asked for a very large favor or if the excuse were unusually absurd ("because an elephant is after me"), the individual would be likely to think about what was said. It is not that people don't hear the request the rest of the time; they simply don't think about it actively.

In a similar experiment, we sent an interdepartmental memo around some university offices. The message either requested or demanded the return of the memo to a designated room—and that was all it said.[7] ("Please return this immediately to Room 247," or "This memo is to be returned to Room 247.") Anyone who read such a memo mindfully would ask, "If whoever sent the memo wanted it, why did he or she send it?" and therefore would not return the memo. Half of the memos were designed to look exactly like those usually sent between departments. The other half were made to look in some way different. When the memo looked like those they were used to, 90 percent of the recipients actually returned it. When the memo looked different, 60 percent returned it.

When I was discussing these studies at a university colloquium, a member of the audience told me about a little con game that operated along the same lines. Someone placed an ad in a Los Angeles newspaper that read, "It's not too late to send $1 to _____," and gave the person's own name and address. The reader was promised nothing in return. Many people replied, enclosing a dollar. The person who wrote the ad apparently earned a good sum.

The automatic behavior in evidence in these examples has much in common with habit.[8] Habit, or the tendency to keep on with behavior that has been repeated over time, naturally implies mindlessness. However, as we will see . . . mindless behavior can arise without a long history of repetition, almost instantaneously, in fact.

### Acting from a Single Perspective

So often in our lives, we act as though there were only one set of rules. For instance, in cooking we tend to follow recipes with dutiful precision. We add ingredients as though by official decree. If the recipe calls for a pinch of salt and four pinches fall in, panic strikes, as though the bowl might now explode. Thinking of a recipe only as a rule, we often do not consider how people's tastes vary, or what fun it might be to make up a new dish.

The first experiment I conducted in graduate school explored this problem of the single perspective. It was a pilot study to examine the effectiveness of different requests for help. A fellow investigator stood on a busy sidewalk and told people passing by that she had sprained her knee and needed help. If someone stopped she asked him or her to get an Ace bandage from the nearby drugstore. I stood inside the store and listened while the helpful person gave the request to the pharmacist, who had agreed earlier to say that he was out of Ace bandages. After being told this, not one subject, out of the twenty-five we studied, thought to ask if the pharmacist could recommend something else. People left the drugstore and returned empty-handed to the "victim" and told her the news. We speculated that had she asked for less specific help, she might have received it. But, acting on the single thought that a sprained knee needs an Ace bandage, no one tried to find other kinds of help.

As a little test of how a narrow perspective can dominate our thinking, read the following sentence:

FINAL FOLIOS SEEM TO RESULT FROM YEARS OF DUTIFUL STUDY OF TEXTS ALONG WITH YEARS OF SCIENTIFIC EXPERIENCE.

Now count how many Fs there are, reading only once more through the sentence.

If you find fewer than there actually are (the answer is given in the notes),[9] your counting was probably influenced by the fact that the first two words in the sentence begin with F. In counting, your mind would tend to cling to this clue, or single perspective, and miss some of the Fs hidden within and at the end of words.

Highly specific instructions such as these or the request for an Ace bandage encourage mindlessness. Once we let them in, our minds snap shut like a clam on ice and do not let in new signals.

## Notes

1. E. Langer & J. Rodin (1976), "The effects of enhanced personal responsibility for the aged: A field experiment in an institutional setting," *Journal of Personality and Social Psychology, 34,* 191–198; J. Rodin & E. Langer (1977), "Long-term effects of a control-relevant intervention among the institutionalized aged," *Journal of Personality and Social Psychology, 35,* 897–902.

2. C. Gersick & J. R. Hackman (1990), "Habitual routines in task-performing groups," *Organizational Behavior and Human Decision Processes, 47,* 65–97.

3. C. Trungpa (1973), *Cutting through spiritual materialism,* Boulder & London: Shambhala.

4. T'ai P'ing (978), *Kuang chi* [Extensive records made in the period of peace and prosperity]; cited in J. L. Borges (1967), *Libro de los seres imaginarios,* Buenos Aires: Editorial Kiersa S. A., Fauna China, p. 88.

5. L. Solomons & G. Stein (1896), "Normal motor automation," *Psychological Review, 36,* 492–572.

6. E. Langer, A. Blank, & B. Chanowitz (1978), "The mindlessness of ostensibly thoughtful action: The role of placebic information in interpersonal interaction," *Journal of Personality and Social Psychology, 36,* 635–642.

7. Langer et al. (1978).

8. To understand the more complex relationship between automatic information processing and mindlessness, compare E. Langer (1989), "Minding matters," in L. Berkowitz (Ed.), *Advances in experimental social psychology* (pp. 137–173), New York: Academic Press; and W. Schneider & R. M. Schiffrin (1977), "Controlled and automatic human information processing: I. Detection, search, and attention," *Psychological Review, 84,* 1–66.

9. The correct answer is 8. A similar quiz was printed on the business card of the Copy Service of Miami, Inc.

15

# Changes in Default Words and Images Engendered by Rising Consciousness

*Douglas R. Hofstadter*

A father and his son were driving to a ball game when their car stalled on the railroad tracks. In the distance a train whistle blew a warning. Frantically, the father tried to start the engine, but in his panic, he couldn't turn the key, and the car was hit by the onrushing train. An ambulance sped to the scene and picked them up. On the way to the hospital, the father died. The son was still alive but his condition was very serious, and he needed immediate surgery. The moment they arrived at the hospital, he was wheeled into an emergency operating room, and the surgeon came in, expecting a routine case. However, on seeing the boy, the surgeon blanched and muttered, "I can't operate on this boy—he's my son."

What do you make of this grim riddle? How could it be? Was the surgeon lying or mistaken? No. Did the dead father's soul somehow get reincarnated in the surgeon's body? No. Was the surgeon the boy's true father and the dead man the boy's adopted father? No. What, then, is the explanation? Think it through until you have figured it out on your own—I insist! You'll know when you've got it, don't worry.

Selected excerpts from "Changes in Default Words and Images Engendered by Rising Consciousness" and "A Person Paper on Purity in Language" from *Metamagical Themas* by D. R. Hofstadter. Copyright © 1985 by Basic Books, Inc. Reprinted by permission of Basic Books, a member of Perseus Books, L.L.C.

When I was first asked this riddle, a few years ago, I got the answer within a minute or so. Still, I was ashamed of my performance. I was also disturbed by the average performance of the people in the group I was with—all educated, intelligent people, some men, some women. I was neither the quickest nor the slowest. A couple of them, even after five minutes of scratching their heads, still didn't have the answer! And when they finally hit upon it, their heads hung low.

Whether we light upon the answer quickly or slowly, we all have something to learn from this ingenious riddle. It reveals something very deep about how so-called *default assumptions* permeate our mental representations and channel our thoughts. A default assumption is what holds true in what you might say is the "simplest" or "most natural" or "most likely" possible model of whatever situation is under discussion. In this case, the default assumption is to assign the sex of male to the surgeon. The way things are in our society today, that's the most plausible assumption. But the critical thing about default assumptions—so well revealed by this story—is that they are made automatically, not as a result of consideration and elimination. You didn't explicitly ponder the point and ask yourself, "What is the most plausible sex to assign to the surgeon?" Rather, you let your past experience merely assign a sex for you. Default assumptions are by their nature implicit assumptions. You never were aware of having made any assumption about the surgeon's sex, for if you had been, the riddle would have been easy!

Usually, relying on default assumptions is extremely useful. In fact, it is indispensable in enabling us—or any cognitive machine—to get around in this complex world. We simply can't afford to be constantly distracted by all sorts of theoretically possible but unlikely exceptions to the general rules or models that we have built up by induction from many past experiences. We have to make what amount to shrewd guesses—and we do this with great skill all the time. Our every thought is permeated by myriads of such shrewd guesses—assumptions of normalcy. This strategy seems to work pretty well. For example, we tend to assume that the stores lining the main street of a town we pass through are not just cardboard facades, and for good reason. Probably you're not worried about whether the chair you're sitting on is about to break. Probably the last time you used a salt shaker you didn't consider that it might be filled with sugar. Without much trouble, you could name dozens of assumptions you're making at this very moment—all of which are simply *probably* true, rather than *definitely* true.

This ability to ignore what is very unlikely—*without even considering whether or not to ignore it!*—is part of our evolutionary heritage, coming out of the need to be able to size up a situation quickly but accurately. It is a marvelous and subtle quality of our thought processes; however, once in a while, this marvelous ability leads us astray. And sexist default assumptions are a case in point. . . .

I have continued to ponder these issues with great intensity. And I must say, the more I ponder, the more prickly and confusing the whole matter becomes. I have found appalling unawareness of the problem all around me—in friends, colleagues, students, on radio and television, in magazines, books, films, and so on. The *New York Times* is one of the worst offenders. You can pick it up any day and see prominent women referred to as "chairman" or "congressman." Even more flagrantly obnoxious is when they refer to prominent feminists by titles that feminism repudiates. For example, a long article on Judy Goldsmith (head of NOW, the National Organization for Women [in 1985]) repeatedly referred to her as "Mrs. Goldsmith." The editors' excuse is:

Publications vary in tone, and the titles they affix to names will differ accordingly. The *Times* clings to traditional ones (*Mrs., Miss,* and *Dr.,* for example). As for *Ms.*—that useful business-letter coinage—we reconsider it from time to time; to our ear, it still sounds too contrived for news writing.

As long as they stick with the old terms, they will sound increasingly reactionary and increasingly silly.

Perhaps what bothers me the most is when I hear newscasters on the radio—especially public radio—using blatantly sexist terms when it would be so easy to avoid them. Female announcers are almost uniformly as sexist as male announcers. A typical example is the female newscaster on National Public Radio who spoke of "the employer who pays his employees on a weekly basis" and "the employee who is concerned about his tax return," when both employer and employee were completely hypothetical personages, thus without either gender. Or the male newscaster who described the Pope in Warsaw as "surrounded by throngs of his countrymen." Or the female newscaster who said, "Imagine I'm a worker and I'm on my deathbed and I have no money to support my wife and kids. . . . " Of all people, newscasters should know better.

I attended a lecture in which a famous psychologist uttered the following sentence, *verbatim:* "What the plain man would like, as he comes into an undergraduate psychology course, as a man or a woman, is that he would find out something about emotions." Time and again, I have observed people lecturing in public who, like this psychologist, seem to feel a mild discomfort with generic "he" and generic "man," and who therefore try to compensate, every once in a while, for their constant usage of such terms. After, say, five uses of "he" in describing a hypothetical scientist, they will throw in a meek "he or she" (and perhaps give an embarrassed little chuckle); then, having pacified their guilty conscience, they will go back to "he" and other sexist usages for a while, until the guilt-juices have built up enough again to trigger one more token nonsexist usage.

This is not progress, in my opinion. In fact, in some ways, it is retrograde motion, and damages the cause of nonsexist language. The problem is that these people are simultaneously showing that they recognize that "he" is *not* truly generic and yet continuing to use it as if it were. They are thereby, at one and the same time, increasing other people's recognition of the sham of considering "he" as a generic, and yet reinforcing the old convention of using it anyway. It's a bad bind.

In case anybody needs to be convinced that supposed generics such as "he" and "man" are *not* neutral in people's minds, they should reflect on the following findings. I quote from the chapter called "Who Is Man?" in *Words and Women*, an earlier book by Casey Miller and Kate Swift:

In 1972 two sociologists at Drake University, Joseph Schneider and Sally Hacker, decided to test the hypothesis that *man* is generally understood to embrace *woman*. Some three hundred college students were asked to select from magazines and newspapers a variety of pictures that would appropriately illustrate the different chapters of a sociology textbook being prepared for publication. Half the students were assigned chapter headings like "Social Man," "Industrial Man," and "Political Man." The other half were given different but corresponding headings like "Society," "Industrial Life," and "Political Behavior." Analysis of the pictures selected revealed that in the minds of students of both sexes use of the word *man* evoked, to a statistically significant degree, images of males only—filtering out recognition of women's participation in these major ar-

eas of life—whereas the corresponding headings without *man* evoked images of both males and females. In some instances the differences reached magnitudes of 30 to 40 percent. The authors concluded, "This is rather convincing evidence that when you use the word *man* generically, people do tend to think male, and tend not to think female."

Subsequent experiments along the same lines but involving schoolchildren rather than college students are then described by Miller and Swift. The results are much the same. No matter how generic "man" is claimed to be, there is a residual trace, a subliminal connotation of higher probability of being male than female.

Shortly after this column came out, I hit upon a way of describing one of the problems of sexist language. I call it the *slippery slope of sexism*. The idea is very simple. When a generic term and a "marked" term (i.e., a sex-specific term) coincide, there is a possibility of mental blurring on the part of listeners and even on the part of the speaker. Some of the connotations of the generic will automatically rub off even when the specific is meant, and conversely. The example of "Industrial Man" illustrates one half of this statement, where a trace of male imagery rubs off even when no gender is intended. The reverse is an equally common phenomenon; an example would be when a newscaster speaks of "the four-man crew of next month's space shuttle flight." It may be that all four are actually males, in which case the usage would be precise. Or it may be that there is a woman among them, in which case "man" would be functioning generically (supposedly). But if you're just listening to the news, and you *don't know* whether a woman is among the four, what are you supposed to do?

Some listeners will automatically envision four males, but others, remembering the existence of female astronauts, will leave room in their minds for at least one woman potentially in the crew. Now, the newscaster may know full well that this flight consists of males only. In fact, she may have chosen the phrase "four-man crew" quite deliberately, in order to let you know that no woman is included. For her, "man" may be marked. On the other, she may not have given it a second thought: for her, "man" may be unmarked. But how are you to know? The problem is right there: the slippery slope. Connotations slip back and forth very shiftily, and totally beneath our usual level of awareness—especially (though not exclusively) at the interface between two people whose usages differ.

Let me be a little more precise about the slippery slope. I have chosen a number of salient examples and put them in Figure 1. Each slippery slope involves a little triangle, at the apex of which is a supposed generic, and the bottom two corners of which consist of oppositely marked terms. Along one side of each triangle runs a diagonal line—the dreaded slippery slope itself. Along that line, connotations slosh back and forth freely in the minds of listeners and speakers and readers and writers. And it all happens at a

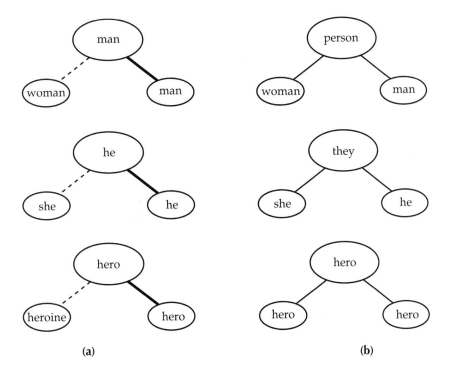

**(a)**  **(b)**

**Figure 1.** The "slippery slope of sexism," illustrated. In each case in (a), a supposed generic (i.e., gender-neutral term) is shown above its two marked particularizations (i.e., gender-specific terms). However, the masculine and generic coincide, which fact is symbolized by the thick heavy line joining them—the slippery slope, along which connotations slosh back and forth, unimpeded. The "most-favored sex" status is thereby accorded the masculine term. In (b), the slippery slopes are replaced by true gender fairness, in which generics are unambiguously generic and marked terms unambiguously marked. Still, it is surprising how often it is totally irrelevant which sex is involved. Do we need—or want—to be able to say such things as, "Her actions were heroic"? Who cares if a hero is male or female, as long as what they did is heroic? The same can be said about actors, sculptors, and a hostess of other terms. The best fix for that kind of slippery slope is simply to drop the marked term, making all three coincide in a felicitously ambisexual ménage à trois.

completely unconscious level, in exactly the same way as a poet's choice of a word subliminally evokes dozens of subtle flavors without anyone's quite understanding how it happens. This wonderful fluid magic of poetry is not quite so wonderful when it imbues one word with all sorts of properties that it should not have.

The essence of the typical slippery slope is this: it establishes a firm "handshake" between the generic and the masculine, in such a way that the feminine term is left out in the cold. The masculine inherits the abstract power of the generic, and the generic inherits the power that comes with specific imagery. Here is an example of the *generic-benefits-from-specific* effect: "Man forging his destiny." Who can resist thinking of some kind of huge mythical brute of a guy hacking his way forward in a jungle or otherwise making progress? Does the image of a woman even come *close* to getting evoked? I seriously doubt it. And now for the converse, consider these gems: "Kennedy was a man for all seasons." "Feynman is the world's smartest man." "Only a man with powerful esthetic intuition could have created the general theory of relativity." "Few men have done more for science than Stephen Hawking." "Leopold and Loeb wanted to test the idea that a perfect crime might be committed by men of sufficient intelligence." Why "man" and "men," here? The answer is: to take advantage of the *specific-benefits-from-generic* effect. The power of the word "man" emanates largely from its close connection with the mythical "ideal man": Man the Thinker, Man the Mover, Man Whose Best Friend Is Dog.

Another way of looking at the slippery-slope effect is to focus on the single isolated corner of the triangle. At first it might seem as if it makes women somehow more distinguished. How nice! But in fact what it does is mark them as *odd*. They are considered nonstandard; the standard case is presumed not to be a woman. In other words, women have to fight their way back into imagery as just-

plain *people*. Here are some examples to make the point.

When I learned French in school, the idea that masculine pronouns covered groups of mixed sex seemed perfectly natural, logical, and unremarkable to me. Much later, that usage came to seem very biased and bizarre to me. However, very recently, I was a bit surprised to catch myself falling into the same trap in different guise. I was perusing a multilingual dictionary, and noticed that instead of the usual *m.* and *f.* to indicate noun genders, they had opted for "+" and "−." Which way, do you suspect? Right! And it seemed just right to me, too—until I realized how dumb I was being.

Heard on the radio news: "A woman motorist is being held after officials observed her to be driving erratically near the White House." Why say "*woman* motorist"? Would you say "man motorist" if it had been a male? Why is gender, and gender alone, such a crucial variable?

Think of the street sign that shows a man in silhouette walking across the street, intended to tell you "Pedestrian Crossing" in sign language. What if it were recognizably a *woman* walking across the street? Since it violates the standard default assumption that people have for people, it would immediately arouse a kind of suspicion: "Hmmm . . . 'Women Crossing'? Is there a nunnery around here?" This would be the reaction not merely of dyed-in-the-wool sexists, but of anyone who grew up in our society, where women are portrayed—not deliberately or consciously, but ubiquitously and subliminally—as "exceptions."

If I write, "In the nineteenth century, the kings of nonsense were Edward Lear and Lewis Carroll," people will with no trouble get the message that those two men were the best of all nonsense writers at that time. But now consider what happens if I write, "The queen of twentieth-century nonsense is Gertrude Stein." The implication is unequivocal: Gertrude Stein is, among *female* writers of nonsense, the best. It leaves completely open her ranking relative to males. She might be way down the list! Now isn't this preposterous? Why is our language so asymmetric? This is hardly chivalry—it is utter condescension.

A remarkable and insidious slippery-slope phenomenon is what has happened recently to formerly all-women's colleges that were paired with formerly all-men's colleges, such as Pembroke and Brown, Radcliffe and Harvard, and so on. As the two merged, the women's school gradually faded out of the picture. Do men now go to Radcliffe or Pembroke or Douglass? Good God, no! But women are proud to go to Harvard and Brown and Rutgers. Sometimes, the women's college keeps some status within the larger unit, but that larger unit is always named after the men's college. In a weird twist on this theme, Stanford University has no sororities at all—but guess what kinds of people it now allows in its fraternities!

Another pernicious slippery slope has arisen quite recently. That is the one involving "gay" as both masculine and generic, and "Lesbian" as feminine. What is problematic here is that some people are very conscious of the problem, and refuse to use "gay" as a generic, replacing it with "gay or Lesbian" or "homosexual." (Thus there are many "Gay and Lesbian Associations.") Other people, however, have eagerly latched onto "gay" as a generic and use it freely that way, referring to "gay people," "gay men," "gay women," "gay rights," and so on. As a consequence, the word "gay" has a much broader flavor to it than does "Lesbian." What does "the San Francisco gay community" conjure up? Now replace "gay" by "Lesbian" and try it again. The former image probably is capable of fitting between that of both sexes and that of men only, while the latter is certainly restricted to women. The point is simply that men are made to seem standard, ordinary, somehow proper; women as special, deviant, excep-

tional. That is the essence of the slippery slope.

Part of the problem in sexism is how deeply ingrained it is. I have noticed a disturbing fact about my observation of language and related phenomena: whenever I encounter a particularly blatant example, I write it down joyfully, and say to friends, "I just heard a *great* example of sexism!" Now, why is it *good* to find a glaring example of something *bad*? Actually, the answer is very simple. You need outrageously clear examples if you want to convince many people that there is a problem worth taking at all seriously.

I was very fortunate to meet the philosopher and feminist Joan Straumanis shortly after my column on sexism appeared. We had a lot to talk over, and particularly enjoyed swapping stories of the sort that make you groan and say, "Isn't that *great?*"—meaning, of course, "How sickening!" Here's one that happened to her. Her husband was in her university office one day, and wanted to make a long-distance phone call. He dialed "0," and a female operator answered. She asked if he was a faculty member. He said no, and she said, "Only faculty members can make calls on these phones." He replied, "My wife is a faculty member. She's in the next room—I'll get her." The operator snapped back, "Oh no—*wives* can't use these phones!"

Another true story that I got from Joan Straumanis, perhaps more provocative and fascinating, is this one. A group of parents arranged a tour of a hospital for a group of twenty children: ten boys and ten girls. At the end of the tour, hospital officials presented each child with a cap: doctors' caps for the boys, nurses' caps for the girls. The parents, outraged at this sexism, went to see the hospital administration. They were promised that in the future, this would be corrected. The next year, a similar tour was arranged, and at the end, the parents came by to pick up their children. What did they find, but the exact same thing—all the boys had on doctors' hats, all the girls had on nurses' hats! Steaming, they stormed up to the director's office and demanded an explanation. The director gently told them, "But it *was* totally different this year: we offered them all *whichever hat they wanted.*"

David Moser, ever an alert observer of the language around him, had tuned into a radio talk show one night, and heard an elderly woman voicing outrage at the mild sentence of two men who had murdered a three-year-old girl. The woman said, "Those two men should get the gas chamber for sure. I think it's terrible what they did! Who knows what that little girl could have grown up to become? Why, she could have been the mother of the next great composer!" The idea that that little girl might have grown up to *be* the next great composer undoubtedly never entered the woman's mind. Still, her remark was not consciously sexist and I find it strangely touching, reminiscent of a quieter era where gender roles were obvious and largely unquestioned, an era when many people felt safe and secure in their socially defined niches. But those times are gone, and we must now move ahead with consciousness raised high.

In one conversation I was in, a man connected with a publisher—let's call it "Freeperson"—said to me, "Aldrich was the liaison between the Freeperson boys and we—er, I mean *us.*" What amused me so much was his instant detection and correction of a *syntactic* error, yet no awareness of his more serious *semantic* error. Isn't that *great?*

I was provoked to write the following piece about a year after the column on sexism came out. It came about this way. One evening I had a very lively conversation at dinner with a group of people who thought of the problem of sexist language as no more than that: dinner-table conversation. Despite all the arguments I put forth, I just couldn't convince them there was anything worth taking seriously there. The next morning I woke up and heard two most interesting pieces of news on the radio: a black Miss America had been picked, and a black man was going to run for president. Both of these violated default assumptions, and it set my mind going along two parallel tracks at once: What if people's default assumptions were violated in all sorts of ways both sexually and racially? And then I started letting the default violations cross all sorts of lines, and pretty soon I was coming up with an image of a totally different society, one in which . . . well, I'll just let you read it.

# A Person Paper on Purity in Language

## William Satire (alias Douglas R. Hofstadter)

It's high time someone blew the whistle on all the silly prattle about revamping our language to suit the purposes of certain political fanatics. You know what I'm talking about— those who accuse speakers of English of what they call "racism." This awkward neologism, constructed by analogy with the well-established term "sexism," does not sit well in the ears, if I may mix my metaphors. But let us grant that in our society there may be injustices here and there in the treatment of either race from time to time, and let us even grant these people their terms "racism" and "racist." How valid, however, are the claims of the self-proclaimed "black libbers," or "negrists"—those who would radically change our language in order to "liberate" us poor dupes from its supposed racist bias?

Most of the clamor, as you certainly know by now, revolves around the age-old usage of the noun "white" and words built from it, such as *chairwhite, mailwhite, repairwhite, clergywhite, middlewhite, Frenchwhite, forewhite, whitepower, whiteslaughter, oneupwhiteship, straw white, whitehandle,* and so on. The negrists claim that using the word "white," either on its own or as a component, to talk about *all* the members of the human species is somehow degrading to blacks and reinforces racism. Therefore the libbers propose that we substitute "person" everywhere where "white" now occurs. Sensitive speakers of our secretary tongue of course find this preposterous. There is great beauty to a phrase such as "All whites are created

equal." Our forebosses who framed the Declaration of Independence well understood the poetry of our language. Think how ugly it would be to say "All persons are created equal," or "All whites and blacks are created equal." Besides, as any schoolwhitey can tell you, such phrases are redundant. In most contexts, it is self-evident when "white" is being used in an inclusive sense, in which case it subsumes members of the darker race just as much as fairskins.

There is nothing denigrating to black people in being subsumed under the rubric "white"—no more than under the rubric "person." After all, white is a mixture of all the colors of the rainbow, including black. Used inclusively, the word "white" has no connotations whatsoever of race. Yet many people are hung up on this point. A prime example is Abraham Moses, one of the more vocal spokeswhites for making such a shift. For years, Niss Moses, authoroon of the well-known negrist tracts *A Handbook of Nonracist Writing* and *Words and Blacks,* has had nothing better to do than go around the country making speeches advocating the downfall of "racist language" that ble objects to. But when you analyze bler objections, you find they all fall apart at the seams. Niss Moses says that words like "chairwhite" suggest to people—most especially impressionable young whiteys and blackeys—that all chairwhites belong to the white race. How absurd! It is quite obvious, for instance, that the chairwhite of the League of Black Voters is going to be a black, not a white. Nobody need think twice about it. As a matter of fact, the suffix "white" is usually not pronounced with a long "i" as in the noun "white," but like "wit," as in the terms *saleswhite, freshwhite, penwhiteship, first basewhite,* and so on. It's just a simple and useful component in building race-neutral words.

But Niss Moses would have you sit up and start hollering "Racism!" In fact, Niss Moses sees evidence of racism under every stone. Ble has written a famous article, in which ble vehemently objects to the immortal and poetic words of the first white on the moon, Captain Nellie Strongarm. If you will recall, whis words were: "One small step for a white, a giant step for whitekind." This noble sentiment is anything but racist; it is simply a celebration of a glorious moment in the history of White.

Another of Niss Moses' shrill objections is to the age-old differentiation of whites from blacks by the third-person pronouns "whe" and "ble." Ble promotes an absurd notion: that what we really need in English is a single pronoun covering *both* races. Numerous suggestions have been made, such as "pe," "tey," and others. These are all repugnant to the nature of the English language, as the average white in the street will testify, even if whe has no linguistic training whatsoever. Then there are advocates of usages such as "whe or ble," "whis or bler," and so forth. This makes for monstrosities such as the sentence "When the next President takes office, whe or ble will have to choose whis or bler cabinet with great care, for whe or ble would not want to offend any minorities." Contrast this with the spare elegance of the normal way of putting it, and there is no question which way we ought to speak. There are, of course, some yapping black libbers who advocate writing "bl/whe" everywhere, which, aside from looking terrible, has no reasonable pronunciation. Shall we say "blooey" all the time when we simply mean "whe"? Who wants to sound like a white with a chronic sneeze?

One of the more hilarious suggestions made by the squawkers for this point of view is to abandon the natural distinction along racial lines, and to replace it with a highly unnatural one along sexual lines. One such suggestion—emanating, no doubt, from the mind of a madwhite—would have us say "he" for male whites (and blacks) and "she" for female whites (and blacks). Can you imagine the outrage with which sensible folk of either sex would greet this "modest proposal"?

Another suggestion is that the plural pronoun "they" be used in place of the inclusive "whe." This would turn the charming proverb "Whe who laughs last, laughs best" into the bizarre concoction "They who laughs last, laughs best." As if anyone in whis right mind could have thought that the original proverb applied only to the white race! No, we don't need a new pronoun to "liberate" our minds. That's the lazy white's way of solving the pseudo-problem of racism. In any case, it's ungrammatical. The pronoun "they" is a plural pronoun, and it grates on the civilized ear to hear it used to denote only one person. Such a usage, if adopted, would merely promote illiteracy and accelerate the already scandalously rapid nosedive of the average intelligence level in our society.

Niss Moses would have us totally revamp the English language to suit bler purposes. If, for instance, we are to substitute "person" for "white," where are we to stop? If we were to follow Niss Moses' ideas to their logical conclusion, we would have to conclude that ble would like to see small blackeys and whiteys playing the game of "Hangperson" and reading the story of "Snow Person and the Seven Dwarfs." And would ble have us rewrite history to say, "Don't shoot until you see the *persons* of their eyes!"? Will pundits and politicians henceforth issue *person* papers? Will we now have egg yolks and egg *persons*? And pledge allegiance to the good old Red, *Person,* and Blue? Will we sing, "I'm dreaming of a *person* Christmas"? Say of a frightened white,

"Whe's *person* as a sheet!"? Lament the increase of *person*-collar crime? Thrill to the chirping of bob*persons* in our gardens? Ask a friend to *person* the table while we go visit the *persons'* room? Come off it, Niss Moses—don't personwash our language!

What conceivable harm is there in such beloved phrases as "No white is an island," "Dog is white's best friend," or "White's inhumanity to white"? Who would revise such classic book titles as Bronob Jacowski's *The Ascent of White* or Eric Steeple Bell's *Whites of Mathematics*? Did the poet who wrote "The best-laid plans of mice and whites gang aft agley" believe that blacks' plans gang *ne'er* agley? Surely not! Such phrases are simply metaphors: Everyone can see beyond that. Whe who interprets them as reinforcing racism must have a perverse desire to feel oppressed.

"Personhandling" the language is a habit that not only Niss Moses but quite a few others have taken up recently. For instance, Nrs. Delilah Buford has urged that we drop the useful distinction between "Niss" and "Nrs." (which, as everybody knows, is pronounced "Nissiz," the reason for which nobody knows!). Bler argument is that there is no need for the public to know whether a black is employed or not. *Need* is, of course, not the point. Ble conveniently sidesteps the fact that there is a *tradition* in our society of calling unemployed blacks "Niss" and employed blacks "Nrs." Most blacks—in fact, the vast majority—prefer it that way. They *want* the world to know what their employment status is, and for good reason. Unemployed blacks want prospective employers to know they are available, without having to ask embarrassing questions. Likewise, employed blacks are proud of having found a job, and wish to let the world know they are employed. This distinction provides a sense of security to all involved, in that everyone knows where ble fits into the scheme of things.

But Nrs. Buford refuses to recognize this simple truth. Instead, ble shiftily turns the argument into one about whites, asking why it is that whites are universally addressed as "Master," without any differentiation between employed and unemployed ones. The answer, of course, is that in America and other Northern societies, we set little store by the employment status of whites. Nrs. Buford can do little to change that reality, for it seems to be tied to innate biological differences between whites and blacks. Many white-years of research, in fact, have gone into trying to understand why it is that employment status matters so much to blacks, yet relatively little to whites. It is true that both races have a longer life expectancy if employed, but of course people often do not act so as to maximize their life expectancy. So far, it remains a mystery. In any case, whites and blacks clearly have different constitutional inclinations, and different goals in life. And so I say, *Vive na différence!*

As for Nrs. Buford's suggestion that both "Niss" and "Nrs." be unified into the single form of address "Ns." (supposed to rhyme with "fizz"), all I have to say is, it is arbitrary and clearly a thousand years ahead of its time. Mind you, this "Ns." is an abbreviation concocted out of thin air: it stands for absolutely nothing. Who ever heard of such toying with language? And while we're on this subject, have you yet run across the recently founded *Ns.* magazine, dedicated to the concerns of the "liberated black"? It's sure to attract the attention of a trendy band of black airheads for a little while, but serious blacks surely will see through its thin veneer of slick, glossy Madison Avenue approaches to life.

Nrs. Buford also finds it insultingly asymmetric that when a black is employed by a white, ble changes bler firmly name to whis firmly name. But what's so bad about that? Every firm's core consists of a boss (whis job is to make sure long-term policies are well charted out) and a secretary (bler job is to keep corporate affairs running smoothly on a day-to-day basis). They are both equally important and vital to the firm's success. No one disputes this. Beyond them there may of course be other firmly members. Now it's quite obvious that all members of a given firm should bear the same firmly name—otherwise, what are you going to call the firm's products? And since it would be nonsense for the boss to change whis name, it falls to the secretary to change bler name. Logic, not racism, dictates this simple convention.

What puzzles me the most is when people cut off their nose to spite their faces. Such is the case with the time-honored colored suffixes "oon" and "roon," found in familiar words such as *ambassadroon*, *stewardoon*, and *sculptroon*. Most blacks find it natural and sensible to add those suffixes onto nouns such as "aviator" or "waiter." A black who flies an airplane may proudly proclaim, "I'm an aviatroon!" But it would sound silly, if not ridiculous, for a black to say of blerself, "I work as a waiter." On the other hand, who could object to my saying that the lively Ticely Cyson is a great actroon, or that the hilarious Quill Bosby is a great comedioon? You guessed it—authoroons such as Niss Mildred Hempsley and Nrs. Charles White, both of whom angrily reject the appellation "authoroon," deep though its roots are in our language. Nrs. White, perhaps one of the finest poetoons of our day, for some reason insists on being known as a "poet." It leads on to wonder, is Nrs. White *ashamed* of being black, perhaps? I should hope not. White needs Black, and Black needs White, and neither race should feel ashamed.

Some extreme negrists object to being treated with politeness and courtesy by whites. For example, they reject the traditional notion of "Negroes first," preferring to open doors for themselves, claiming that having doors opened for them suggest implicitly that society considers them inferior. Well, would they have it the other way? Would these incorrigible grousers prefer to open doors for whites? What do blacks want?

Another unlikely word has recently become a subject of controversy: "blackey." This is, of course, the ordinary term for black children (including teenagers), and by affectionate extension it is often applied to older blacks. Yet, incredible though it seems, many blacks—even teen-age blackeys—now claim to have had their "consciousness raised," and are voguishly skittish about being called "blackeys." Yet it's as old as the hills for blacks employed in the same office to refer to themselves as "the office blackeys." And for their superior to call them "my blackeys" helps make the ambiance more relaxed and comfy for all. It's hardly the mortal insult that libbers claim it to be. Fortunately, most blacks are sensible people and realize that mere words do not demean; they know it's how they are *used* that counts. Most of the time, calling a black—especially an older black—a "blackey" is a thoughtful way of complimenting bler, making bler feel young, fresh, and hirable again. Lord knows, I certainly wouldn't object if someone told me that I looked whiteyish these days!

Many young blackeys go through a stage of wishing they had been born white. Perhaps this is due to popular television shows like *Superwhite* and *Batwhite*, but it doesn't really matter. It is perfectly normal and healthy. Many of our most successful blacks were once tomwhiteys and feel no shame about it. Why should they? Frankly, I think tomwhiteys are often the cutest little blackeys—but that's just my opinion. In any case, Niss Moses (once again) raises a ruckus on this score, asking why we don't have a corresponding word for young whiteys who play blackeys' games and generally manifest a desire to be black. Well, Niss Moses, if this were a common phenomenon, we most assuredly *would* have such a word, but it just happens not to be. Who can say why? But given that tomwhiteys are a dime a dozen, it's nice to have a word for them. The lesson is that White must learn to fit language to reality; White cannot manipulate the world by manipulating mere words. An elementary lesson, to be sure, but for some reason Niss Moses and others of bler ilk resist learning it.

Shifting from the ridiculous to the sublime, let us consider the Holy Bible. The Good Book is of course the source of some of the most beautiful language and profound imagery to be found anywhere. And who is the central character of the Bible? I am sure I need hardly remind you; it is God. As everyone knows, Whe is male and white, and that is an indisputable fact. But have you heard the latest joke promulgated by tasteless negrists? It is said that one of them died and went to Heaven and then returned. What did ble report? "I have seen God, and guess what? Ble's female!" Can anyone say that this is not blasphemy of the highest order? It just goes to show that some people will stoop to any depths in order to shock. I have shared this "joke" with a number of friends of mine (including several blacks, by the way), and, to a white, they have agreed that it sickens them to the core to see Our Lord so shabbily mocked. Some things are just in bad taste, and there are no two ways about it. It is scum like this who are responsible for some of the great problems in our society today, I am sorry to say.

Well, all of this is just another skirmish in the age-old Battle of the Races, I guess, and we shouldn't take it too seriously. I am reminded of words spoken by the great British philosopher Alfred West Malehead in whis commencement address to my *alma secretaria*, the University of North Virginia: "To enrich the language of whites is, certainly, to enlarge the range of their ideas." I agree with this admirable sentiment wholeheartedly. I would merely point out to the overzealous that there are some extravagant notions about language that should be recognized for what they are: cheap attempts to let dogmatic, narrow minds enforce their views on the speakers lucky enough to have inherited the richest, most beautiful and flexible language on earth, a language whose traditions run back through the centuries to such deathless poets as Milton, Shakespeare, Wordsworth, Keats, Walt Whitwhite, and so many others . . . Our language owes an incalculable debt to these whites for their clarity of vision and expression, and if the shallow minds of bandwagon-jumping negrists succeed in destroying this precious heritage for all whites of good will, that will be, without any doubt, a truly female day in the history of Northern White.

## Post Scriptum

Perhaps this piece shocks you. It is meant to. The entire point of it is to use something that we find shocking as leverage to illustrate the fact that something that we usually close our eyes to is also very shocking. The most effective way I know to do so is to develop an extended analogy with something known as shocking and reprehensible. Racism is that thing, in this case. I am happy with this piece, despite—but also because of—its shock value. I think it makes its point better than any factual article could. As a friend of mine said, "It makes you so uncomfortable that you can't ignore it." I admit that rereading it makes even me, the author, uncomfortable!

Numerous friends have warned me that in publishing this piece I am taking a serious risk of earning myself a reputation as a terrible racist. I guess I cannot truly believe that anyone would see this piece that way. To misperceive it this way would be like calling someone a vicious racist for telling other people "The word 'nigger' is extremely offensive." If *allusions* to racism, especially for the purpose of satirizing racism and its cousins, are confused with racism itself, then I think it is time to stop writing.

Some people have asked me if to write this piece, I simply took a genuine William Safire column (appearing weekly in the *New York Times Magazine* under the title "On Language") and "fiddled" with it. That is far from the truth. For years I have collected examples of sexist language, and in order to produce this piece, I dipped into this collection, selected some of the choicest, and ordered them very carefully. "Translating" them into this alternate world was sometimes extremely difficult, and some words took weeks. The hardest terms of all, surprisingly enough, were "Niss," "Nrs.," and "Ns.," even though "Master" came immediately. The piece itself is not based on any particular article by William Safire, but Safire has without doubt been one of the most vocal opponents of nonsexist language reforms, and therefore merits being safired upon.

Interestingly, Master Safire has recently spoken out on sexism in whis column (August 5, 1984). Lamenting the inaccuracy of writing either "Mrs. Ferraro" or "Miss Ferraro" to designate the Democratic vice-presidential candidate whose husband's name is "Zaccaro," whe writes:

It breaks my heart to suggest this, but the time has come for *Ms.* We are no longer faced with a theory, but a condition. It is unacceptable for journalists to dictate to a candidate that she call herself *Miss* or else use her married name; it is equally unacceptable for a candidate to demand that newspapers print a blatant inaccuracy by applying a married honorific to a maiden name.

How disappointing it is when someone finally winds up doing the right thing but for the wrong reasons! In Safire's case, this shift was entirely for journalistic rather than humanistic reasons! It's as if Safire wished that women had never entered the political ring, so that the Grand Old Conventions of English—good enough for our grandfathers—would never have had to be challenged. How heartless of women! How heartbreaking the toll on our beautiful language!

A couple of weeks after I finished this piece, I ran into the book *The Nonsexist Communicator*, by Bobbye Sorrels. In it, there is a satire called "A Tale of Two Sexes," which is very interesting to compare with my "Person Paper." Whereas in mine, I slice the world orthogonally to the way it is actually sliced and then perform a mapping of worlds to establish a disorienting yet powerful new vision of our world, in hers, Ms. Sorrels simply reverses the two halves of our world as it is actually sliced. Her satire is therefore in some ways very much like mine, and in other ways extremely different. It should be read.

I do not know too many publications that discuss sexist language in depth. The finest I have come across are the aforementioned *Handbook of Nonsexist Writing,* by Casey Miller and Kate Swift; *Words and Women,* by the same authors; *Sexist Language: A Modern Philosophical Analysis,* edited by Mary Vetterling-Braggin; *The Nonsexist Communicator,* by Bobbye Sorrels; and a very good journal titled *Women and Language News.* Subscriptions are available at Centenary College of Louisiana, 2911 Centenary Boulevard, Shreveport, Louisiana 71104.

My feeling about nonsexist English is that it is like a foreign language that I am learning. I find that even after years of practice, I still have to translate sometimes from my native language, which is sexist English. I know of no human being who speaks Nonsexist as their native tongue. It will be very interesting to see if such people come to exist. If so, it will have taken a lot of work by a lot of people to reach that point.

One final footnote: My book *Gödel, Escher, Bach,* whose dialogues were the source of my very first trepidations about my own sexism, is now being translated into various languages, and to my delight, the Tortoise, a green-blooded male if ever there was one in English, is becoming *Madame Tortue* in French, *Signorina Tartaruga* in Italian, and so on. Full circle ahead!

**16**

# Racism in the English Language

### Robert B. Moore

## Language and Culture

An integral part of any culture is its language. Language not only develops in conjunction with a society's historical, economic and political evolution; it also reflects that society's attitudes and thinking. Language not only *expresses* ideas and concepts but actually *shapes* thought.[1] If one accepts that our dominant white culture is racist, then one would expect our language—an indispensable transmitter of culture—to be racist as well. Whites, as the dominant group, are not subjected to the same abusive characterization by our language that people of color receive. Aspects of racism in the English language that will be discussed in this essay include terminology, symbolism, politics, ethnocentrism, and context.

Before beginning our analysis of racism in language we would like to quote part of a TV film review which shows the connection between language and culture.[2]

Depending on one's culture, one interacts with time in a very distinct fashion. One example which gives some cross-cultural insights into the concept of time is language. In Spanish, a watch is said to "walk." In English, the watch "runs." In German, the watch "functions." And in French,

"Racism in the English Language" by Robert B. Moore. Reprinted by permission of The Council on Interracial Books for Children, c/o Lawrence Jordan Literary Agency, 250 West 57th Street, Room 1517, New York, NY 10107.

the watch "marches." In the Indian culture of the Southwest, people do not refer to time in this way. The value of the watch is displaced with the value of "what time it's getting to be." Viewing these five cultural perspectives of time, one can see some definite emphasis and values that each culture places on time. For example, a cultural perspective may provide a clue to why the negative stereotype of the slow and lazy Mexican who lives in the "Land of Mañana" exists in the Anglo value system, where time "flies," the watch "runs" and "time is money."

## A Short Play on "Black" and "White" Words

Some may blackly (angrily) accuse me of trying to blacken (defame) the English language, to give it a black eye (a mark of shame) by writing such black words (hostile). They may denigrate (to cast aspersions; to darken) me by accusing me of being blackhearted (malevolent), of having a black outlook (pessimistic, dismal) on life, of being a blackguard (scoundrel)—which would certainly be a black mark (detrimental fact) against me. Some may black-brow (scowl at) me and hope that a black cat crosses in front of me because of this black deed. I may become a black sheep (one who causes shame or embarrassment because of deviation from the accepted standards), who will be blackballed (ostracized) by being placed on a blacklist (list of undesirables) in an attempt to blackmail (to force or coerce into a particular action) me to retract my words. But attempts to blackjack (to compel by threat) me will have a Chinaman's chance of success, for I am not a yellow-bellied Indian-giver of words, who will whitewash (cover up or gloss over vices or crimes) a black lie (harmful, inexcusable). I challenge the purity and innocence (white) of the English language. I don't see things in black and white (entirely bad or entirely good) terms, for I am a white man (marked by upright firmness) if there ever was one. However, it would be a black day when I would not "call a spade a spade," even though some will suggest a white man calling the English language racist is like the pot calling the kettle black. While many may be niggardly (grudging, scanty) in their support, others will be honest and decent—and to them I say, that's very white of you (honest, decent).

The preceding is of course a white lie (not intended to cause harm), meant only to illustrate some examples of racist terminology in the English language.

## Obvious Bigotry

Perhaps the most obvious aspect of racism in language would be terms like "nigger," "spook," "chink," "spic," etc. While these may be facing increasing social disdain, they certainly are not dead. Large numbers of white Americans continue to utilize these terms. "Chink," "gook," and "slant-eyes" were in common usage among U.S. troops in Vietnam. An NBC nightly news broadcast, in February 1972, reported that the basketball team in Pekin, Illinois, was called the "Pekin Chinks" and noted that even though this had been protested by Chinese Americans, the term continued to be used because it was easy, and meant no harm. Spiro Agnew's widely reported "fat Jap" remark and the "little Jap" comment of lawyer John Wilson during the Watergate hearings, are surface indicators of a deep-rooted Archie Bunkerism.

Many white people continue to refer to Black people as "colored," as for instance in a July 30, 1975 *Boston Globe* article on a racist attack by whites on a group of Black people using a public beach in Boston. One white person was quoted as follows:

> We've always welcomed good colored people in South Boston but we will not tolerate radical blacks or Communists. . . . Good colored people are welcome in South Boston, black militants are not.

Many white people may still be unaware of the disdain many African Americans have for the term "colored," but it often appears that whether used intentionally or unintentionally, "colored" people are "good" and "know their place," while "Black" people are perceived as "uppity" and "threatening" to many whites. Similarly, the term "boy" to refer to African American men is now acknowledged to be a demeaning term, though still in common use. Other terms such as "the pot calling the kettle black" and "calling a spade a spade" have negative racial connotations but are still frequently used, as for example when President Ford was quoted in February 1976 saying that even though Daniel Moynihan had left the U.N., the U.S. would continue "calling a spade a spade."

## Color Symbolism

The symbolism of white as positive and black as negative is pervasive in our culture, with the black/white words used in the beginning of this essay only one of many aspects. "Good guys" wear white hats and ride white horses, "bad guys" wear black hats and ride black horses. Angels are white, and devils are black. The definition of *black* includes "without any moral light or goodness, evil, wicked, indicating disgrace, sinful," while that of *white* includes "morally pure, spotless, innocent, free from evil intent."

A children's TV cartoon program, *Captain Scarlet,* is about an organization called Spectrum, whose purpose is to save the world from an evil extraterrestrial force called the

Mysterons. Everyone in Spectrum has a color name—Captain Scarlet, Captain Blue, etc. The one Spectrum agent who has been mysteriously taken over by the Mysterons and works to advance their evil aims is Captain Black. The person who heads Spectrum, the good organization out to defend the world, is Colonel White.

Three of the dictionary definitions of white are "fairness of complexion, purity, innocence." These definitions affect the standards of beauty in our culture, in which whiteness represents the norm. "Blondes have more fun" and "Wouldn't you really rather be a blonde" are sexist in their attitudes toward women generally, but are racist white standards when applied to third world women. A 1971 *Mademoiselle* advertisement pictured a curly-headed, ivory-skinned woman over the caption, "When you go blonde go all the way," and asked: "Isn't this how, in the back of your mind, you always wanted to look? All wide-eyed and silky blonde down to there, and innocent?" Whatever the advertising people meant by this particular woman's innocence, one must remember that "innocent" is one of the definitions of the word white. This standard of beauty when preached to all women is racist. The statement "Isn't this how, in the back of your mind, you always wanted to look?" either ignores third world women or assumes they long to be white.

*Time* magazine in its coverage of the Wimbledon tennis competition between the black Australian Evonne Goolagong and the white American Chris Evert described Ms. Goolagong as "the dusky daughter of an Australian sheepshearer," while Ms. Evert was "a fair young girl from the middle-class groves of Florida." *Dusky* is a synonym of "black" and is defined as "having dark skin; of a dark color; gloomy; dark; swarthy." Its antonyms are "fair" and "blonde." *Fair* is defined in part as "free from blemish, imperfection, or anything that impairs the appearance, quality, or character; pleasing in appearance, attractive; clean; pretty; comely." By defining Evonne Goolagong as "dusky," *Time* technically defined her as the opposite of "pleasing in appearance; attractive; clean; pretty; comely."

The studies of Kenneth B. Clark, Mary Ellen Goodman, Judith Porter and others indicate that this persuasive "rightness of whiteness" in U.S. culture affects children before the age of four, providing white youngsters with a false sense of superiority and encouraging self-hatred among third world youngsters.

### Ethnocentrism or from a White Perspective

Some words and phrases that are commonly used represent particular perspectives and frames of reference, and these often distort the understanding of the reader or listener. David R. Burgest[3] has written about the effect of using the terms "slave" or "master." He argues that the psychological impact of the statement referring to "the master raped his slave" is different from the impact of the same statement substituting the words: "the white captor raped an African woman held in captivity."

Implicit in the English usage of the "master-slave" concept is ownership of the "slave" by the "master," therefore, the "master" is merely abusing his property (slave). In reality, the captives (slave) were African individuals with human worth, right and dignity and the term "slave" denounces that human quality thereby making the mass rape of African women by white captors more acceptable in the minds of people and setting a mental frame of reference for legitimizing the atrocities perpetuated against African people.

The term "slave" connotes a less than human quality and turns the captive person into a thing. For example, two McGraw-Hill Far Eastern Publishers textbooks (1970) stated, "At first it was the slaves who worked the cane and they got only food for it. Now men work cane and get money." Next time you write about slavery or read about it, try transposing all "slaves" into "African people held in captivity," "Black people forced to work for no pay" or "African people stolen from their families and societies." While it is more cumbersome, such phrasing conveys a different meaning. . . .

## Politics and Terminology

"Culturally deprived," "economically disadvantaged" and "underdeveloped" are other terms which mislead and distort our awareness of reality. The application of the term "culturally deprived" and third world children in this society reflects a value judgment. It assumes that the dominant whites are cultured and all others without culture. In fact, third world children generally are bicultural, and many are bilingual, having grown up in their own culture as well as absorbing the dominant culture. In many ways, they are equipped with skills and experiences which white youth have been deprived of, since most white youth develop in a monocultural, monolingual environment. Burgest[5] suggests that the term "culturally deprived" be replaced by "culturally dispossessed," and that the term "economically disadvantaged" be replaced by "economically exploited." Both these terms present a perspective and implication that provide an entirely different frame of reference as to the reality of the third world experience in U.S. society.

Similarly, many nations of the third world are described as "underdeveloped." These less wealthy nations are generally those that suffered under colonialism and neo-colonialism. The "developed" nations are those that exploited their resources and wealth. Therefore, rather than referring to these countries as "underdeveloped," a more appropriate and meaningful designation might be "over exploited." Again, transpose this term next time you read about "underdeveloped nations" and note the different meaning that results.

Terms such as "culturally deprived," "economically disadvantaged" and "under-developed" place the responsibility for their own conditions on those being so described. This is known as "Blaming the Victim."[6] It places responsibility for poverty on the victims of poverty. It removes the blame from those in power who benefit from, and continue to permit, poverty.

Still another example involves the use of "non-white," "minority" or "third world." While people of color are a minority in the U.S., they are part of the vast majority of the world's population, in which white people are a distinct minority. Thus, by utilizing the term minority to describe people of color in the U.S., we can lose sight of the global majority/minority reality—a fact of some importance in the increasing and interconnected struggles of people of color inside and outside the U.S.

To describe people of color as "non-white" is to use whiteness as the standard and norm against which to measure all others. Use of the term "third world" to describe all people of color overcomes the inherent bias of "minority" and "non-white." Moreover, it connects the struggles of third world people in the U.S. with the freedom struggles around the globe.

The term "third world" gained increasing usage after the 1955 Bandung Conference of "non-aligned" nations, which represented a third force outside of the two world superpowers. The "first world" represents the United States, Western Europe and their sphere of influence. The "second world" represents the Soviet Union and its sphere. The "third world" represents, for the most part, nations that were, or are, controlled by the "first world" or West. For the most part, these are nations of Africa, Asia and Latin America.

## "Loaded" Words and Native Americans

Many words lead to a demeaning characterization of groups of people. For instance, Columbus, it is said, "discovered" America. The word *discover* is defined as "to gain sight or knowledge of something previously unseen or unknown; to discover may be to find some existent thing that was previously unknown." Thus, a continent inhabited by millions of human beings cannot be "discovered." For history books to continue this usage represents a Eurocentric (white European) perspective on world history and ignores the existence of, and the perspective of, Native Americans. "Discovery," as used in the Euro-American context, implies the right to take what one finds, ignoring the rights of those who already inhabit or own the "discovered" thing.

Eurocentrism is also apparent in the usage of "victory" and "massacre" to describe the battles between Native Americans and whites. *Victory* is defined in the dictionary as "a success or triumph over an enemy in battle or war; the decisive defeat of an opponent." *Conquest* denotes the "taking over of control by the victor, and the obedience of the conquered." *Massacre* is defined as "the unnecessary, indiscriminate killing of a number of human beings, as in barbarous warfare or persecution, or for revenge or plunder." *Defend* is described as "to ward off attack from; guard against assault or injury; to strive to keep safe by resisting attack."

Eurocentrism turns these definitions around to serve the purpose of distorting history and justifying Euro-American conquest of the Native American homelands. Euro-Americans are not described in history books as invading Native American lands, but rather as defending *their* homes against "Indian" attacks. Since European communities were constantly encroaching on land already occupied, then a more honest interpretation would state that it was the Native Americans who were "warding off," "guarding" and "defending" their homelands.

Native American victories are invariably defined as "massacres," while the indiscriminate killing, extermination and plunder of Native American nations by Euro-Americans is defined as "victory." Distortion of

history by the choice of "loaded" words used to describe historical events is a common racist practice. Rather than portraying Native Americans as human beings in highly defined and complex societies, cultures and civilizations, history books use such adjectives as "savages," "beasts," "primitive," and "backward." Native people are referred to as "squaw," "brave," or "papoose" instead of "woman," "man," or "baby."

Another term that has questionable connotations is *tribe*. The Oxford English Dictionary defines this noun as "a race of people; now applied especially to a primary aggregate of people in a primitive or barbarous condition, under a headman or chief." Morton Fried,[7] discussing "The Myth of Tribe," states that the word "did not become a general term of reference to American Indian society until the nineteenth century. Previously, the words commonly used for Indian populations were 'nation' and 'people.' " Since "tribe" has assumed a connotation of primitiveness or backwardness, it is suggested that the use of "nation" or "people" replace the term whenever possible in referring to Native American peoples.

The term *tribe* invokes even more negative implications when used in reference to American peoples. As Evelyn Jones Rich[8] has noted, the term is "almost always used to refer to third world people and it implies a stage of development which is, in short, a put-down."

## "Loaded" Words and Africans

Conflicts among diverse peoples within African nations are often referred to as "tribal warfare," while conflicts among the diverse peoples within European countries are never described in such terms. If the rivalries between the Ibo and the Hausa and Yoruba in Nigeria are described as "tribal," why not the rivalries between Serbs and Slavs in Yugoslavia, or Scots and English in Great Britain,

Protestants and Catholics in Ireland, or the Basques and the Southern Spaniards in Spain? Conflicts among African peoples in a particular nation have religious, cultural, economic and/or political roots. If we can analyze the roots of conflicts among European peoples in terms other than "tribal warfare," certainly we can do the same with African peoples, including correct reference to the ethnic groups or nations involved. For example, the terms "Kaffirs," "Hottentot" or "Bushmen" are names imposed by white Europeans. The correct names are always those by which a people refer to themselves. (In these instances Xhosa, Khoi-Khoin and San are correct.[9])

The generalized application of "tribal" in reference to Africans—as well as the failure to acknowledge the religious, cultural and social diversity of African peoples—is a decidedly racist dynamic. It is part of the process whereby Euro-Americans justify, or avoid confronting, their oppression of third world peoples. Africa has been particularly insulted by this dynamic, as witness the pervasive "darkest Africa" image. This image, widespread in Western culture, evokes an Africa covered by jungles and inhabited by "uncivilized," "cannibalistic," "pagan," "savage" peoples. This "darkest Africa" image avoids the geographical reality. Less than 20 percent of the African continent is wooded savanna, for example. The image also ignores the history of African cultures and civilizations. Ample evidence suggests this distortion of reality was developed as a convenient rationale for the European and American slave trade. The Western powers, rather than exploiting, were civilizing and christianizing "uncivilized" and "pagan savages" (so the rationalization went). This dynamic also served to justify Western colonialism. From Tarzan movies to racist children's books like *Doctor Dolittle* and *Charlie and the Chocolate Factory,* the image of "savage" Africa and the myth of "the white man's burden" has been perpetuated in Western culture.

A 1972 *Time* magazine editorial lamenting the demise of *Life* magazine, stated that the "lavishness" of *Life*'s enterprises included "organizing safaris into darkest Africa." The same year, the *New York Times'* C. L. Sulzberger wrote that "Africa has a history as dark as the skins of many of its people." Terms such as "darkest Africa," "primitive," "tribe" ("tribal") or "jungle," in reference to Africa, perpetuate myths and are especially inexcusable in such large circulation publications.

Ethnocentrism is similarly reflected in the term "pagan" to describe traditional religions. A February 1973 *Time* magazine article on Uganda stated, "Moslems account for only 500,000 of Uganda's 10 million people. Of the remainder, 5,000,000 are Christians and the rest pagan." *Pagan* is defined as "Heathen, a follower of a polytheistic religion; one that has little or no religion and that is marked by a frank delight in and uninhibited seeking after sensual pleasures and material goods." *Heathen* is defined as "Unenlightened; an unconverted member of a people or nation that does not acknowledge the God of the Bible. A person whose culture or enlightenment is of an inferior grade, especially an irreligious person." Now, the people of Uganda, like almost all Africans, have serious religious beliefs and practices. As used by Westerners, "pagan" connotes something wild, primitive and inferior—another term to watch out for.

The variety of traditional structures that African people live in are their "houses," not "huts." A *hut* is "an often small and temporary dwelling of simple construction." And to describe Africans as "natives" (noun) is derogatory terminology—as in, "the natives are restless." The dictionary definition of *native* includes: "one of a people inhabiting a territorial area at the time of its discovery or becoming familiar to a foreigner; one belonging to a people having a less complex civilization." Therefore, use of "native," like use of "pagan" often implies a value judgement of white superiority.

## Qualifying Adjectives

Words that would normally have positive connotations can have entirely different meanings when used in a racial context. For example, C. L. Sulzberger, the columnist of the *New York Times,* wrote in January 1975, about conservations he had with two people in Namibia. One was the white South African administrator of the country and the other a member of SWAPO, the Namibian liberation movement. The first is described as "Dirk Mudge, who as senior elected member of the administration is a kind of acting Prime Minister. . . ." But the second person is introduced as "Daniel Tijongarero, an intelligent Herero tribesman who is a member of SWAPO. . . ." What need was there for Sulzberger to state that Daniel Tijongarero is "intelligent"? Why not also state that Dirk Mudge was "intelligent"—or do we assume he wasn't?

A similar example from a 1968 *New York Times* article reporting on an address by Lyndon Johnson stated, "The President spoke to the well-dressed Negro officials and their wives." In what similar circumstances can one imagine a reporter finding it necessary to note that an audience of white government officials was "well-dressed?"

Still another word often used in a racist context is "qualified." In the 1960s white Americans often questioned whether Black people were "qualified" to hold public office, a question that was never raised (until too late) about white officials like Wallace, Maddox, Nixon, Agnew, Mitchell, et al. The question of qualifications has been raised even more frequently in recent years as white people question whether Black people are "qualified" to be hired for positions in industry and educational institutions. "We're looking for a qualified Black" has been heard again and again as institutions are confronted with affirmative action goals. Why stipulate that Blacks must be "qualified," when for others it is taken for granted that applicants must be "qualified"?

## Speaking English

Finally, the depiction in movies and children's books of third world people speaking English is often itself racist. Children's books about Puerto Ricans or Chicanos often connect poverty with a failure to speak English or to speak it well, thus blaming the victim and ignoring the racism which affects third world people regardless of their proficiency in English. Asian characters speak a stilted English ("Honorable so and so" or "Confucius say") or have a speech impediment ("rots or ruck," "very solly," "flied lice"). Native American characters speak another variation of stilted English ("Boy not hide. Indian take boy."), repeat certain Hollywood-Indian phrases ("Heap big" and "Many moons") or simply grunt out "Ugh" or "How." The repeated use of these language characterizations functions to make third world people seem less intelligent and less capable than the English-speaking white characters.

## Wrap-Up

A *Saturday Review* editorial[10] on "The Environment of Language" stated that language

. . . has as much to do with the philosophical and political conditioning of a society as geography or climate. . . . people in Western cultures do not realize the extent to which their racial attitudes have been conditioned since early childhood by the power of words to ennoble or condemn, augment or detract, glorify or demean. Negative language infects the subconscious of most Western people from the time they first learn to speak. Prejudice is not merely imparted or superimposed. It is metabolized in the bloodstream of society. What is needed is not so much a change in language as an awareness of the power of words to condition attitudes. If we can at least recognize the underpinnings of prejudice, we may be in a position to deal with the effects.

To recognize the racism in language is an important first step. Consciousness of the influence of language on our perceptions can help to negate much of that influence. But it is not enough to simply become aware of the affects of racism in conditioning attitudes. While we may not be able to change the language, we can definitely change our usage of the language. We can avoid using words that degrade people. We can make a conscious effort to use terminology that reflects a progressive perspective, as opposed to a distorting perspective. It is important for educators to provide students with opportunities to explore racism in language and to increase their awareness of it, as well as learning terminology that is positive and does not perpetuate negative human values.

## Notes

1. Simon Podair, "How Bigotry Builds Through Language," *Negro Digest*, March 1967.

2. Jose Armas, "Antonio and the Mayor: A Cultural Review of the Film," *The Journal of Ethnic Studies*, Fall, 1975.

3. David R. Burgest, "The Racist Use of the English Language," *Black Scholar*, Sept. 1973.

4. Thomas Greenfield, "Race and Passive Voice at Monticello," *Crisis*, April 1975.

5. David R. Burgest, "Racism in Everyday Speech and Social Work Jargon," *Social Work*, July 1973.

6. William Ryan, *Blaming the Victim*, Pantheon Books, 1971.

7. Morton Fried, "The Myth of Tribe," *National History*, April 1975.

8. Evelyn Jones Rich, "Mind Your Language," *Africa Report*, Sept./Oct. 1974.

9. Steve Wolf, "Catalogers in Revolt Against LC's Racist, Sexist Headings," *Bulletin of Interracial Books for Children*, Vol. 6, Nos. 3&4, 1975.

10. "The Environment of Language," *Saturday Review*, April 8, 1967.

Also see:

Roger Bastide, "Color, Racism and Christianity," *Daedalus*, Spring 1967.

Kenneth J. Gergen, "The Significance of Skin Color in Human Relations," *Daedalus*, Spring 1967.

Lloyd Yabura, "Towards a Language of Humanism," *Rhythm*, Summer 1971.

UNESCO, "Recommendations Concerning Terminology in Education on Race Questions," June 1968.

## 17

# The Virgin Martyrs

*Sue Reidy*

*Lucy's eyes were stolen.*
*Joan was burned alive.*
*Agatha lost her breasts.*
*Barbara's father chopped her head off.*
*Agnes had her throat cut.*

### Chatterton 1966

Other children played "Mothers and Fathers," "Cowboys and Indians," or "Cops and Robbers." Catherine and Theresa Flynn played "Martyrs and Suffering Virgins." After school they changed out of their black serge gym frocks and slipped into their saintly roles as Maria, Rose, Anastasia, Agatha, Agnes, Joan, Lucy, or Barbara.

All their heroes were women and most of them had died horribly—their deaths caused, naturally, by men.

• • •

There was glory in dying the noble death of a martyr. It was Test of Faith, then nuns said.

"The martyrs were Saved," said Sister Mary Cecilia. "They live now with God in heaven like one big happy family. *Your heavenly family*, who watch over you."

"I don't want anyone watching over me, I want to be private and think my own thoughts," argued Theresa. She wanted to be like Smoking Nana.

"The Virgin Martyrs," from *The Visitation* by Sue Reidy. Copyright © 1996 by Sue Reidy. Reprinted by permission of Scribner, a division of Simon & Schuster.

"Not a sparrow falls, but . . ." replied her teacher.

St. Agnes refused to worship at the altar of Minerva. She was punished by having her clothes removed in front of a crowd of spectators. She covered up her nakedness by letting down her long hair. Later she was stabbed in the throat. She was twelve years old.

Agnes was their favorite. In their Heroines of God book, dog-eared and worn from constant rereadings, St. Agnes was depicted wearing a long ochre-colored robe and carrying a sacrificial lamb in her arms. Her eyes were raised toward heaven. Her long wavy hair was haloed by soft yellow light. The wound on her white throat was clearly visible.

She was more beautiful than any fairytale princess and braver than Red Riding Hood, Sleeping Beauty, Cinderella, or Snow White, all of whom had waited for someone to save them. Agnes saved herself by choosing to be a martyr. She suffered excruciating pain.

Suffering counted. It guaranteed immediate entry to heaven without first having to endure the flames of Purgatory.

What would it be like to die for someone you couldn't see? The drama and tragedy of the martyred girls fueled their fantasies. Theresa and Catherine always argued over who was to play the part of the beautiful doomed Agnes and who was to be the cruel Roman soldier. The one who was relegated to being the soldier had to whip Agnes and drag her around the back yard where she was scorned and jeered at by the crowd consisting of Francie, Andrew, Tim, and John. Toots lay in his pram snuffling and gurgling while they shrieked around him. Sometimes he projectile-vomited, and this always added an element of unpredictability to the proceedings.

They used cochineal for blood. The old sheets that they used for robes were already splattered with dark mulberry-colored stains from previous games.

They entered easily into the spirit of it. The back yard disappeared and was replaced by dirt streets full of carts and beggars. Bloodthirsty soldiers strode about shouting and brandishing swords. The Flynn children used sharpened tomato stakes until Mrs. Flynn noticed and confiscated them.

"You'd better give up Jesus, or else," hissed Theresa the Roman soldier.

"You can't make me," Catherine replied, clutching at the teddy bear that played the role of Sacrificial Lamb.

"Oh can't I just?" Theresa gave a tug on the rope that was tied around Catherine's foot. She changed voices when she swapped roles, becoming the young man who had fallen in love with Agnes. "Marry me," she pleaded. "I'll save you if you do."

"Never!" cried Catherine, beating her breast. Saints always beat their breasts. It added to the suffering. "I belong to my Savior alone," she said. She eyed Theresa uneasily. Her sister often forgot it was only a game.

"Don't say I didn't warn you," threatened Theresa.

"I'm just an ordinary girl," moaned Catherine. "Have mercy on me."

"Never!" Theresa brandished a broom handle perilously close to Catherine's neck.

Francie ran to save Agnes. She never tired of playing "martas," but often she forgot the plot.

Theresa experimentally poked Catherine in the neck with the broom. Francie attempted to wrestle it from her.

"Francie, stop it will you, Agnes is *supposed* to die." Theresa dragged the broom away from her little sister.

"Let's see if your God will save you now, Agnes," shouted Theresa.

"I want a different ending," begged Francie.

"You're not allowed."

Francie lurched forward and bit Theresa's hand.

Theresa was indignant. "What did you do that for?"

"I got carried away," said Francie.

When they had exhausted the possibilities of Agnes they discovered St. Rose of Lima. Rose wore a hair shirt and she loved to whip herself. She whipped until she bled.

*Whip, whip,* went Theresa with a branch against her blouse. She saw blood splatter everywhere, as it had with Rose of Lima. On the fence. Over the cinerarias, their mother's washing.

"I want to play too," said Catherine, determined not to be left out. It was always Theresa who thought up the most interesting games.

Dead women began to crowd the garden.

The back yard was awash with blood. It became a struggle to reach the house. The younger children swam out to join Theresa and Catherine. They watched their father arrive home from work, climb out of the car and wade through a red soup up to his ankles until he reached the back door.

His black suit was iridescent red.

Catherine was repelled by the gruesome stories of the young virgin martyrs, whereas Theresa relished the descriptions of torment and suffering.

The martyrs had preferred death to relinquishing their virginity. If an unmarried girl lost her virginity, she became a "fallen woman"—a woman who had tumbled from grace. She had dropped out of God's sight and into the devil's lap like a ripe plum.

"How does a girl lose her virginity?" asked Theresa.

"You're too young to know. When you're big girls we'll tell you everything. But not now. Later," promised their mother.

"Later, always later. We want to know now. We *need* to know now."

"What's a Fallen Woman?" they asked Smoking Nana. She was the only person in their lives who could be relied upon always to tell the truth. Already they understood there was Catholic Truth and Non-Catholic Truth and an abyss between them. Their grandmother was a non-Catholic and an atheist.

A disappointed woman, said their mother.

*Godless,* their father said.

*Their* family, they were told, was *God-fearing*. Their parents would have had a *Mixed Marriage* if their mother hadn't become a *Convert* immediately before marrying their father.

Did that mean that once their mother had been Godless, they asked. Or worse, a pagan?

"Certainly not," snapped their father. Their mother had been of a *Different Faith*—Presbyterian—but fortunately for all of them, she had changed her mind and seen the *Light* and been given the Gift of Faith.

Which light? Electric light? Gaslight?

"The light of the One True Faith, of course."

"A fallen woman," said Smoking Nana, "is a Loose Woman. A Fast Woman. A Woman of Easy Virtue. A Woman of Doubtful Reputation. A Scarlet Woman. A Painted Woman. One who is no better than she should be."

"Yes, *yes*," breathed Theresa. Why shouldn't they too become fast, loose, painted, and scarlet? But there was more they could be.

Their grandmother pulled out a thick book containing thousands of tiny words and flipped the pages avidly. She called it a thesaurus. A labyrinth of words they might lose themselves in. So many choices, she told them, it made you dizzy. So many subtly different points of view to take into account.

"Wench," she read out. "Trollop, trull, tart, harlot, whore, strumpet, hooker, scrubber, cocotte, floozy, doxy, moll, temptress, vamp, Jezebel, Delilah. A Bit of Fluff. An odalisque."

Odalisque?

"Female slave," she said, adjusting her glasses and frowning at the page. "Oh dear, in my enthusiasm I seem to have strayed over into kept women and prostitutes. Forget about odalisques, will you, darlings."

"I want to change the world," wished Theresa.

"I want to be someone else," decided Catherine.

"Who?" Theresa idly picked a scab on her knee.

"A nun."

"Don't be stupid."

"A martyr, then. I'll die young and everyone will weep buckets of tears. 'Such a waste,' they'll say."

"It's worth becoming a martyr to be famous. But you can't be one," said Theresa, "because I've already decided that *I'm* going to be the martyr in the family. But you can be the nun if you like."

"What's the point of being famous if you're dead?" retorted Catherine.

Mrs. Flynn covered her ears. "Spare me," she groaned, "this endless drivel. Why can't you go off and become something normal, like nurses, for instance? You can't possibly become martyrs. Don't be so silly," she said, looking up from a crinkled pile of sliced silver beet. "This is New Zealand, not Italy. That sort of thing doesn't go on here."

"Why not?" persisted Theresa.

"Because I said so, that's why."

"You always say that."

"Do I?" Her mother's voice was vague, her attention already elsewhere. She scooped up a curl of fat from the enamel basin beside the stove, melted it in the large aluminum pan and added nine meager mutton chops.

She turned down the heat when they began to spit. Next she picked the eyes from seventeen peeled potatoes with a blunt knife, dropped them into an aluminum pot, covered them with cold water and a teaspoon of salt, put a lid on and set them to boil. Then she picked up a handful of the silver beet.

"If I can't become a martyr, I'll become a film star instead," said Theresa.

Her mother sighed. "Be what you like," she said wearily. "Just so long as you're happy and don't get into any trouble."

. . .

The children were all familiar with the idea of punishment. If they were naughty they were smacked and slapped. But they couldn't understand why anyone would *want* to hurt themselves, or why God might require someone to deliberately cause themselves pain and suffering.

It was almost, thought Theresa, as if the stigmatics gained pleasure from the pain inflicted on them. "Not my will, but thine."

"It sounds like masochism to me," said Smoking Nana when they asked her. She decided she might as well tell them about sadism too while she had their attention.

This was something new for Catherine and Theresa to puzzle over. And, although Smoking Nana couldn't remember exactly how it happened, somehow they moved onto the subjects of sodomy and bestiality as well.

The girls were more confused than ever. No one had fully explained sex to them. Very little of what their grandmother told them made any sense. Their confusion was increased because of the words she used when describing genitals or the sexual act. Words like *willies, fannies, twats, peckers, goolies, John Thomases, intercourse, buns in the oven, up the duff, taking precautions, doing it from the rear end instead of the front.*

The front of what? Whose rear end? It sounded hideous—not something they would ever want to do, or have done to them. And certain words stood out—peculiar words that conjured up disturbing images.

"Scrotum?" they asked. "What's that?"

"A loose bag of skin under the man's John Thomas and it looks like a turkey gizzard," replied Smoking Nana, lighting up another cigarette, her hand shaking slightly. It wasn't her responsibility, it was Moira's. What a tangle she had got herself into.

For once the girls were speechless. The information they had been given so appalled them that they wondered how they would ever be able to bring themselves to marry someone who owned a thing like a turkey gizzard hidden inside his trousers. And was this really connected to a John Thomas with a mind of its own—a feral predatory creature capable of growing to four times its usual size on sighting a naked woman?

"I will never take my clothes off when I marry," vowed Theresa fiercely. "Never, *never.*"

"A very sensible idea," soothed her grandmother, afraid she had gone too far. "Now you mustn't talk to anyone about this," she said, "it's our little secret. Do I have your word on that?" The girls nodded.

. . .

On a Monday night after tea, Mr. Flynn had requested a word with the two eldest girls alone. He followed them to their room and shut the door behind them. He marched over to Catherine's bed, sat down on it and patted the surface of the candlewick spread as an indication for them to be seated.

He smiled. It was not a reassuring smile. They weren't deceived by it—they were in trouble.

"Sit down both of you," he said to them. "It's time we had a little talk."

They sat on the opposite bed. What had they done wrong?

"Each month," said their father, launching immediately into the purpose of his discussion, "your body will produce an egg. Not like a chook's egg. A wee egg that you can't see with the naked eye."

*The naked eye.*

Mr. Flynn crossed his arms and legs as if to hold his body together. He didn't meet their eyes as he spoke, staring fixedly at a point on the wallpaper between them. His voice was hard and raspy like sandpaper.

They didn't took directly at him. They focused instead on the rose pattern which extended in diagonal rows along the walls—anything rather than look at his neck, or his hairiness. A crucifix intersected two entwined rosebuds. A yellowing branch of macrocarpa from Palm Sunday had been tucked behind it. The drooping plastic Christ provided a morsel of comfort while their father rasped out his frightening sentences, each word falling on their ears like a hammer pounding nails into a coffin.

"What are you talking about?" asked Theresa in a tight, angry voice.

"A change is going to take place inside your bodies," he announced in the manner of a prophet predicting doom.

"Each month your egg will ripen and the walls of your uterus will build a lining of spongy tissue loaded with blood. When a woman gets married, the egg or ovum becomes fertilized by her husband and a baby grows."

How revolting, thought Theresa. It would be like being invaded. She wished she were a boy and didn't have to concern herself with eggs or changes. She was impatient for her father to finish and leave the room. The conversation disgusted her.

"Tralaalaaa la la la," she sang inside her head to block out her father's voice. She didn't hear him when he explained that if a girl's egg wasn't fertilized, the walls of the uterus, which had become engorged with blood in preparation for the egg, dissolved and released blood. This was called a *period.*

Catherine understood. Every month, for five days, instead of urinating she would bleed. It wouldn't cause much inconvenience. It didn't sound as if it would hurt. But she usually associated the appearance of blood with pain. How much blood would there be? Would it flow out of her in a rushing torrent or in slow dribbles? What if she couldn't reach the toilet in time? How would she staunch it?

"Tralalalalala," went the voice inside Theresa's head. Inside her stomach, however, she felt a quiver of fear, a queer fluttery feeling. She wanted to stay the way she was.

"Have I made myself clear?" asked their father, still refusing to look at them.

They nodded dumbly, eyes brimming. They wouldn't cry in front of him, it would be too humiliating. They felt debased. Bodies were private. How could he possibly know what sort of mysterious activities went on inside them?

It now seemed that they were to be betrayed by the bodies they had thought they knew so intimately. Inside they were hollow. There was a wound. It was impossible to staunch it. They would bleed, stated their father, for over thirty years before the wound healed and their bodies stopped producing wee ovum seeds.

"Where's Mum?" asked Catherine.

Mr. Flynn coughed and cleared his throat noisily.

"Your mother's not much good at this sort of thing," he said.

She'd be better than you, they thought.

"I don't care," cried Catherine. "I want her to tell me properly." She ran out of the room, almost colliding with her mother, who had been hovering in the hallway dusting the same light switch for the past ten minutes.

". . . Catherine?" she said in a tentative voice and reached out a hand.

Catherine pushed past her without replying. She had an instinctive desire to punish her mother.

"I'm not a good explainer," her mother called after her.

"I don't care," said Catherine coldly. "It doesn't matter."

But it did.

It was true, their mother wasn't very good at explaining. She was only marginally better than their father. Why was it, thought Theresa, that adults so rarely made sense? They always seemed to select the least relevant or the most upsetting details to include in their explanations. These details rarely conveyed the complete picture. The important bits had been forgotten or were deliberately left out.

They could tell that their mother was embarrassed to be discussing such subjects with them. Pubescence, she called it. That was the name of their disease. It wasn't fatal, but it was *lingering*.

"When your monthly arrives, everything will be different," she promised, when she had finally been persuaded to discuss the subject.

How different? Apparently, their bodies, no longer under their control, would undergo bizarre transformations. Hairs would spring up in places that had previously been pale, hidden and private—their genitals, underarms and perhaps even the aureole, the area around their nipples.

Theresa had always believed that breasts appeared on a woman overnight. When she was about twenty—grown-up. She hadn't realized it was a slow process. And that hairs would *gradually* appear.

They had always been taught to refer to their genital area as Gene. But because they had never seen the word actually written down, they had named their vaginas Jean, a friendly name. Jean was a little creature quite separate from themselves who lived "Down There," a place they must never touch because it was a sin. They didn't know why. They had to accept it.

Their father said it was disgusting to touch Jean.

"Don't even think about it," he said.

"But what will happen to us if we do, Daddy?"

"God doesn't like it."

"Why not?"

"Because," he said, "it's filthy. FILTHY. Do you hear me?"

They nodded. Yes. Filthy, a sin. They weren't dirty. They wanted to be good, clean girls.

"Yes, and that's the way you're going to stay—good girls. There'll be no mucking about with yourselves. You must understand that I'm only telling you this for your own good."

"Yes, Dad."

Their father must know what was best. They obeyed him and ignored Jean. They pretended she didn't exist.

• • •

"I want you to keep yourselves clean," said Mr. Flynn.

"And I don't mean hygiene. I'm talking about modesty and purity. Keeping yourself pure for your husbands so they respect you. No man likes second-hand goods. Don't you dare let any Tom, Dick, or Harry slip in through the back door. Do it through the front door, with marriage. I don't want to see either of you end up shacked up with a bloke like some cheap tart who should know better."

"No, Dad."

"It's up to you girls to set the standards, and for the boys to fall into line. If you dress modestly and don't go about looking cheap, you'll attract the right sort of boy."

"Yes, Dad."

"The main point I want to make is that you're not to let any boy touch you down there." He pointed in the general direction of their genital area and their eyes flickered uncomfortably.

"I know what boys are like. They've only got one thing in their filthy minds. I'm warning you. Don't lead them on past the point of no return. Let them boil with lust. That's their problem. Keep your wits about you at all times."

"Why is it us who have to be pure? Why do we have to set the limits?" raged Theresa out of earshot of her father.

"Boys don't have any will-power or self-control," replied Catherine. "You know that. Dad said so."

"Maybe he's wrong," suggested Theresa. "Have you thought about that?"

"How do you know what to do with a man when you finally get married?" asked Theresa.

"Love finds a way," replied their mother gloomily.

Catherine pictured The Way as a dark mysterious cave. It was entered by a monster of a man whose wild uncontrollable thoughts had led him to violent action. Penetration. Ejaculation. A man who didn't care if having his way led to his sperm swimming to the top of the vagina, up into the uterus and over to the Fallopian tubes. And according to her biology book, the bit about human reproduction, it was all to fertilize an unsuspecting little egg that waited patiently above the spongy, blood-lined tunnel of the uterus.

They would have nothing to do with boys. It was safer. Their mother referred darkly to "buns in the oven," of girls being "up the duff." At school the girls knew who was a slut, a slag, a mole. They were the girls who "went all the way." And there were men who didn't use a joey, a Frenchie, a rubber.

It was all very well. But what was a joey—a type of underpants?

They learnt the language, but it didn't mean anything. Naming the parts of the body, describing the act—what did any of it have to do with romance? . . .

# PART III

# Realizing Symbolic Order through Interaction

*All the world's a stage.*
*And all the men and women merely players:*
*They have their exits and their entrances;*
*And one man in his time plays many parts.*

(William Shakespeare, *As You Like It*)

*We are told on good authority, Callicles, that heaven and earth*
*and their respective inhabitants are held together by the bonds*
*of society and love and order and discipline and righteousness,*
*and that is why the universe is an ordered whole or cosmos and*
*not a state of disorder and license.*

(Plato, *Gorgias*)

# Meaning Is Negotiated
# through Interaction

In the early 1950s, during what has come to be known as the "beatnik era," Howard Becker, a young graduate student, spent his evenings playing jazz in Chicago-area nightclubs. Becker noticed that many patrons tried the drug marijuana, but only a few continued to use it. As a budding sociologist, Becker wondered why some people merely "experimented" and others became routine users. He was familiar with the "personality" and "physical" theories of his day, which suggested that those who continued to smoke marijuana were likely to have the sort of personality or physical makeup that inclined them to use drugs. But Becker wasn't satisfied with these theories. They didn't mesh with his observations.

Becker noted that those who continued to use marijuana described it as a "pleasurable" experience; they could rattle off lists of effects that they associated with marijuana, and when they introduced the drug to their friends, they tended to pass on this information. He concluded that those who continued smoking marijuana had "learned" to think of the experience and the effects as enjoyable. He wrote a paper in which he suggested that people learn to "name" experiences and physical responses. This "naming" process shapes a person's reactions to the event—in this case, the smoking of a drug and the corresponding physical reaction. He emphasized that people learn these "names," or responses, through interaction with others. Regardless of how people might feel privately, they get cues from others about how they are expected to feel and behave. They adjust their perceptions and behavior in response. This profoundly "social" explanation for individual behavior—even in response to something as physically based as drug ingestion—altered the course of sociology and gained young Becker a reputation as a formidable social scientist.

In Part II, we developed the theme that humans become social creatures through their ability to formulate conceptual schemas. These conceptual schemas are the basis of the meaning we make out of concrete experiences. That is, we live in a symbolic universe rather than a direct state of nature. We suggested that humans organize their existence into a meaningful reality through symbols and that language is the primary form of symbolic order. One implication of this thesis is that social order exists in the human mind, in the form of meaningful conceptual associations that organize each person's experiences and perceptions. In Part III, we explore the question of how this internal, cognitive order is learned, manifested, and reproduced among groups of people. For a cognitive order to be "social" it must be enacted, or made real—"realized." Realization of a symbolic order is achieved through ongoing interactions in which we each express ourselves to others.

## Naming: An Interactional Process

To engage in meaningful expression, people must translate the thoughts and images in their heads into a form—names—that will be understood by others. The transcription of thought into language is social interaction. If others can be relied upon to use similar names and make similar associations between objects, persons, and events, then the naming process becomes stable. It becomes something that we can take for granted as social "order." The process of naming includes several elements. Ideas and intentions must be *projected* to others. Meaning must be *negotiated*. The ability to successfully project and negotiate intentions is, in part, a function of the *resources* that one has, in the form of interpersonal skills and material goods. The world does not speak for itself. To interact at all, we must learn to *associate* socially significant meanings with objects, persons, and events. Finally, people learn these meanings or names through *interaction*.

As you read Becker's article, Reading 18, "Becoming a Marihuana User," consider the possible range of responses from someone who ingests marijuana but doesn't know what it is. One of the authors (Jodi O'Brien) accidentally inhaled Clorox bleach as a young child. O'Brien recalls, "The physical sensation was similar to the one marijuana produces when it is first inhaled: choking, followed by a burning sensation. I thought I was going to die. I was so convinced of my imminent demise that I wrote a note for my parents to find when they came across my body and didn't know how to explain my death."

Becker asks a pertinent question when considering the relationship between physical stimuli and human response: Why would someone voluntarily seek out and continue an experience that, if evaluated simply as an undefined physical experience, is not likely to be immediately pleasant? Technically, when you first smoke marijuana, you are just as likely to feel like you have inhaled bleach as you are to feel like you have inhaled something that might be a source of pleasure. Becker illustrates the process of interaction and learning that helps us to identify an experience with a particular meaning. One of the key points of his article is that getting high is something that must be *learned in interaction* with other, more experienced users. Becker points out, for example, that it is very common for novices not to feel high the first time they smoke marijuana and for an experienced user to smoke a placebo that smells like marijuana and report feeling high. In other words, smoking marijuana is not a simple physiological response to a psychoactive drug but a socially constructed experience that must be identified or named before people are able to recognize the intended effect. The fact that this article is more than forty-five years old is an important advantage, because it allows us to study a culture in its infancy, before the general public knew much about marijuana and its effects.

Reading 19, "Looks," is a narrative written by a woman who is frequently "misnamed" by strangers trying to guess her ethnicity. Regardless of whether we are aware of it, one of the first things we do in interaction with others is to make assessments regarding gender, ethnicity, class, and age. If something stands out, we may also make quick judgments about sexuality, religion, and able-bodiedness. In other words, we attempt to identify or *name* the person according to these categories. Male or female? Not white? You are probably only aware that you are doing this "naming" or categorizing when you encounter someone you can't classify easily. Did that person have breasts *and* a beard? Once we have classified someone, we think we know something about them and make corresponding decisions about how to treat them. In addition to being a frequent object of people's attempts to classify her, Maeda raises the point that when people can't classify someone, they feel justified in asking for more information and/or challenging the person in ways that might otherwise be considered rude. If you don't appear to fit in with preconceived categories, you are considered strange or "other."

In Reading 20, also on "naming," journalist Peggy Orenstein reports her observations of adolescent interaction in junior high school. In this selection, she discusses the different ways in which boys and girls are taught to think about and express their budding sexuality. She suggests that these differences in adolescent psycho-sexual development (boys are potentially studs, girls are potentially sluts) affect self-esteem profoundly.

## What's Going On? Projecting a Definition of the Situation

In his novel *Tom Sawyer*, Mark Twain (1875/1946) tells this entertaining story. Tom has been given the thankless task of whitewashing a long fence on a weekend afternoon. One of his friends comes by and begins to taunt him:

"Hello, old chap, you got to work, hey?"

Tom wheeled suddenly and said: "Why, it's you, Ben! I warn't noticing."

"Say—I'm going in a-swimming, I am. Don't you wish you could? But of course you'd druther work—wouldn't you? Course you would!"

Tom contemplated the boy a bit, and said: "What do you call work?"

"Why, ain't *that* work?"

Tom resumed his whitewashing, and answered carelessly: "Well, maybe it is, and maybe it ain't. All I know, is, it suits Tom Sawyer."

"Oh come, now, you don't mean to let on that you *like* it?" The brush continued to move.

"Like it? Well, I don't see why I oughtn't to like it. Does a boy get a chance to whitewash a fence every day?"

That put the thing in a new light. Ben stopped nibbling his apple. Tom swept his brush daintily back and forth—stepped back to note the effect—added a touch here and there—criticized the effect again—Ben watching every move and getting more and more interested, more and more absorbed. Presently he said: "Say, Tom, let me whitewash a little." (pp. 18–19)

Soon, boy after boy comes by and begs to exchange food, a toy, or some other treasure for an opportunity to whitewash the fence.

In this story, Tom is an entrepreneur of meaning. Using great skill, he has managed to reframe a presumably unpleasant activity into a rare and desirable opportunity. He has successfully defined the situation in a way that allows him to accomplish his goal (to avoid spending the day whitewashing the fence) and to benefit from it.

The readings in the second section of Part III examine how situations are defined. If an interaction is to proceed successfully, the participants must establish their identities and agree on the sort of situation they find themselves in. The readings point out the work that goes into defining a situation and maintaining a particular definition. They also illustrate that situational definitions are constructed through interaction.

Some people attempt to define a situation in a novel way, as Tom Sawyer did. However, most of us don't project novel definitions of a situation in most circumstances. Rather, we tend to rely on known "scripts" or "plot lines." As discussed in Part II, when we "name" something, we categorize situations and then follow the implied line of response. One sociological perspective uses the imagery and language of the theater to explain the process of interaction among symbolic actors who are attempting to establish and maintain a shared definition of what's going on. According to this perspective, we "frame" the situation (for example, wedding, funeral, trip to the grocery store, classroom, and so forth) and then use the stockpile of cultural information at our disposal to inform us about what to expect and which roles befit ourselves and others in the particular situation.

### Life as Theater

The theater metaphor underlies many of the readings in Part III. Like any metaphor, it is not a complete description of social reality but, in many ways, our interactions with others do seem to resemble a theatrical performance.

The theater metaphor can be seen in the origins of the word *person*, which comes from the Latin *persona*, meaning a mask worn by actors. We behave differently (play different roles) in front of different people (audiences). We pick out clothing (a costume) that is consistent with the image we wish to project. We enlist the help of friends, caterers, decorators (fellow actors and stage crew) to help us successfully "stage" a dinner for a friend, a birthday party for a relative, or a rush party for a sorority or fraternity. And if we need to adjust our clothing or wish to say something unflattering about one of our guests, we are careful to do so out of sight from others (backstage).

The presentation of ourselves to others is known as *dramaturgy*, and the use of the theatrical metaphor for analyzing human interaction is known as the *dramaturgical perspective*. The most noted writer on this perspective is Erving Goffman, who in 1959 published *The Presentation of Self in Everyday Life*. This is still considered the classic treatment of the subject. In Reading 21, Goffman analyzes our everyday "performances." He details the care people take in preparing and presenting their performances—that is, the manner in which people *manage* the impressions others form of them.

Why do people spend so much time and energy thinking about what they should say and how they should look? Some would say that we should simply "be ourselves" and that only those who are deceitful need to worry about managing their image. They would concede that con artists and the insincere have to be concerned about these issues, but what about good, decent people? In fact, however, even saints are concerned with the presentation of self. To tell us to simply "be" ourselves implies that who we are is easily, quickly, and accurately perceived by those with whom we interact. But if we have just met someone or will be interacting with someone for only a short length of time (for example, in a job interview), we certainly can't count on the person to see us as we see ourselves. Dramaturgy can be an issue even when we interact with people who have known us for some time. Who we are may not be obvious to others—most of us do not wear our personal characteristics and convictions tattooed onto our foreheads.

## Private Minds, Public Identities

A simple but profound truth about human interaction is that minds are private. Our thoughts, desires, beliefs, and character cannot be directly perceived and evaluated by others. We are not a race of mind readers, and so we must depend on signs and gestures to comprehend one another. Recall the example of the border guard from the essay in Part II. The guard sizes people up and treats them according to their appearance. Therefore, it is in people's best interest to appear in a way that gets them treated as they wish. In this case, they want to appear "law-abiding."

The fact that minds are private doesn't mean that people are obligated to accurately display their thoughts and desires to others. But it does mean that even the most honest people must be concerned about how they come across to others. Goffman (1959) makes this point in *The Presentation of Self in Everyday Life* (Reading 21):

> Whether an honest performer wishes to convey the truth or whether a dishonest performer wishes to convey a falsehood, both must take care to enliven their performances with appropriate expressions, exclude from their performances expressions that might discredit the impression being fostered, and take care lest the audience impute unintended meanings. (p. 66)

It is crucial to remember that *impression management* is something everyone does in all everyday activities. To one degree or another, we all manage others' impressions of us in interactions. We have to "perform" or "project" our intentions and desires because people can't read our minds.

Because minds are private, people typically behave so as to highlight important facts about themselves that might otherwise go unnoticed. Goffman calls this activity *dramatic realization*. For example, when you are in a job interview, you might describe in great detail a position of responsibility you held in the past. Or if you are in traffic court, you might point out the absence of any past traffic violations to the judge. And although this feature may be true about you, you probably wouldn't bring it up as a way to impress a potential date. Instead you might focus on highlighting your favorite bands or activities. Dramatic realization is an attempt to make traits and characteristics that might otherwise go unnoticed "real" and noticeable. If these traits are not noticed, they don't exist as "real" aspects of the performance. It is up to the individual to bring them into play.

Goffman also makes the point that we often try to present ourselves in a favorable light, a process he calls *idealization*. We might simply accent those aspects about ourselves that are positive (for example, mentioning that you are on the varsity team but not mentioning that you have just lost your job), or we might engage in outright deception (saying you are on the varsity team when you are not).

People also have a general tendency to convey the impression that the role they are currently engaged in is their most important role. For example, when an individual walks into a store to buy an expensive suit, she will be interacting with a "salesperson." The salesperson may also be a spouse, parent, community volunteer, jogger, gardener, and so forth. But if that salesperson is good at the job, he will take part in the interaction as if serving customers is the only (or at least the most important) role in his life at that moment.

Before an interaction can proceed successfully, two actors must agree about the sort of situation they are in and the role each is to play. Is it a friendly chat between acquaintances, a seduction between lovers, a coaching session between subordinate and supervisor? This process is referred to as *identity negotiation*.

People in an interaction each project an identity, and their responses to each other indicate whether they accept the projected identity. For example, if you ask your boss how old she is and she doesn't acknowledge the question, she has chosen not to grant you the identity of "familiar acquaintance." When two people agree on the identities they are both going to play in an interaction, they have arrived at what Goffman refers to as a *working consensus*.

However, *public* agreement on identities need not be an accurate reflection of the actor's *private* beliefs. People often have pleasant chats with co-workers they dislike. There are many possible reasons for doing this—to be polite, to prevent an awkward scene, to ensure good relations in the workplace, or perhaps to stay in the good graces of a person who controls resources that might be needed sometime. Whatever the private reality might be, it is the public, socially agreed upon definition of the situation that will guide the interaction.

Once a public agreement has been reached (whether implicitly or explicitly), it carries the weight of a contract. The working consensus has a moral character to it. Each actor *feels as if* he or she has the right to be treated in a particular way by other actors. The actors also *feel as if* they have an obligation to behave in ways that are consistent with the presented identity. For example, in an interaction between a teacher and a student, the person who is in the role of the teacher expects certain behavior from the person who is the student; these behaviors include being treated respectfully, being treated as a status superior, being treated as an expert in the subject, and so on. At the same time, the person who has claimed the identity of teacher has numerous obligations or duties, such as competently carrying out the teacher's role, being respectful of students, knowing a great deal about the subject, and being able to convey that knowledge to students. The rights and duties associated with an identity that has been publicly accepted must be respected if the small social order of the interaction is to continue. If a math teacher is unable to solve a problem in front of the class or if a student treats the teacher as a younger sibling, the interaction grinds to an uncomfortable halt.

In sum, interaction has two key elements—publicly defining (and presenting) a personal identity and defining what sort of situation the individual is in with others. There are many possible answers to the questions Who am I? Who are you? What's going on? For successful interaction to occur, these definitions must be negotiated by the participants. The participants jockey to claim identities and to define the situation in ways that will help them accomplish their personal goals. Once identities are established, they must be actively maintained.

This process leads people to reproduce taken-for-granted cultural patterns. Because minds are private, we all must dramatize (in other words, signal) the identities we wish to claim and our definition of the situation. To be effective in interactions, we select symbolic representations that we know to be reliable signals of our intentions. This selection of culturally typical or expected symbols is a process of *idealization*. You may not like business suits, for instance, but you will put one on for a job interview because you believe it to be the appropriate costume for presenting the identity of an eager and professional potential employee. When you present yourself with the appropriate costume, props, and mannerisms, you effectively reproduce a set of cultural expectations or *ideals*—one of them being "Businesspeople wear suits." In other words, you will be presenting a symbolic *ideal type* and, through your self-presentation, you will be affirming the ideal type. The implications of idealization for perpetuating social norms are significant. We consider the consequences of "dramatizing the ideal" in both Parts III and IV.

## Who Are We and What Are We Doing Here?

> When an individual enters the presence of others, they commonly seek to acquire information about him [*sic*] or to bring into play information already possessed. They will be interested in his general socio-economic status, his conception of self, his attitude toward them, his competence, his trustworthiness, etc. (Goffman, 1959, p. 1)

The readings in the sections "Projecting the Definition of the Situation" and "Negotiating a Working Consensus" illustrate the active ways in which people strive to present a definition of the role they wish to play in the interactional moment and the definition of the situation as they see it.

In Reading 21, Goffman describes some of the many skills required to bring off a reasonable interactional performance. Because interaction requires the ongoing cooperation of participants, it is vulnerable and can break down. A situation might be defined in an inappropriate way. Or the identities the participants claim might somehow be discredited (as when a math teacher cannot solve a problem in front of the class). In that case, the result is embarrassment.

From a dramaturgical perspective, embarrassment can be defined as a breakdown in a projected identity. It is striking to note how uncomfortable we are made by embarrassment and how hard we work to avoid it. Indeed, embarrassment makes us so uncomfortable that we usually cooperate to prevent or smooth over other people's embarrassing actions, even if they are strangers. We might look away when someone stumbles clumsily, pretend not to hear the fight the couple is having at a nearby table, or readily and eagerly accept other people's explanations for their unacceptable behavior. Engaging in cooperative support of each other's identities to avoid or repair embarrassment is called *tact*. The presence and prevalence of tact is an extraordinary thing. Humans apparently have a very deep commitment to support each other's identities, even the identities of strangers.

True, there are times when someone might react to an embarrassing moment without tact (or even have engineered the moment, if it involves a rival), but these instances stand out because they are exceptions. Practical jokes that make someone look foolish (i.e., discredit someone's "face") would not be funny if they were not a deviation from the usual norm of tact.

The mutual obligation to avoid "scenes" and to be who we claim to be means that whenever a situation or identity is threatened, someone must repair the interaction. When the audience helps in the repair work, they are being tactful—but, of course, the person whose identity is threatened can also work to repair the interaction. Following behavior that threatens an identity, people usually can offer explanations or give an *account* of the actions.

Offering accounts after an inappropriate act does not guarantee that others will accept ("honor") the account. Not every explanation is acceptable. "I had car trouble" might be a reasonable excuse for failing to get to class on time, but not "Voices told me to come late today." And some explanations are acceptable in some situations but not in others. Burning the stew because "I was distracted by a phone call" is acceptable, but the same excuse would certainly not be honored as an explanation for why someone failed to show up for her wedding. What is judged to be an acceptable account varies from situation to situation. It can also vary tremendously from one culture to another.

Goffman emphasizes just how fragile and potentially disruptable interaction routines really are. His intent is not to present people as cynical and calculating so much as it is to draw our attention to the tricky interpersonal gymnastics required of social actors. What is remarkable—and Goffman's respectful awe is apparent in his voluminous writings—is that people somehow do manage to project mutually understood definitions of self and situation, despite all the things that could go wrong.

Brent Staples (author of Reading 22, "Black Men and Public Space") demonstrates one of the dilemmas inherent in identity management—we have to be concerned with dramaturgy regardless of our intentions. In his article, Staples recognizes that a prevalent cultural stereotype casts him, a young black man, in the role of a potentially threatening person. He discusses what is involved in explicitly dramatizing the fact that he intends no harm to anyone.

In Reading 23, Barbara Heyl traces the process of naming or defining an identity and negotiating this identity in interaction in "The Madam as Teacher: The Training of House Prostitutes." She illustrates that identities, like the effects of marijuana, must be defined before they can be experienced or performed in a socially meaningful way. Women do not simply engage in prostitution activities. They must have the activities defined for them and learn how to perform the role before they can "become" prostitutes. This process of learning how to perform an identity extends to all social roles. Once, when we gave a seminar for graduate students about teaching at the college level, we were intrigued to note the similarities between our syllabus and the steps the house madam follows to train her employees.

In "What Does the Service Include?" (Reading 24), Linda Van Leuven writes about the various misperceptions or conflicting expectations that can arise between clients and personal trainers. Trainers learn through experience that they must be quick to establish an initial definition of the situation if they wish to avoid embarrassment later on.

## Negotiating a Working Consensus

The generative quality of social structure is observable in face-to-face encounters. Individuals bring different ideas, goals, and expectations to social encounters. As they strive to achieve a working definition of what is going on, they transcribe their private definitions, as well as their immediate feelings, into a form that they think others will understand and accept. In other words, people manage, despite many differences, to engage in meaningful, sustainable discourses. We all do this through continual negotiation.

The theatrical form most indicative of the generative, negotiated quality of interaction is improvisation. "Theatersports" is a form of entertainment in which the audience calls out a "frame" or "setting"—usually one involving some sort of controversy or misunderstanding—and the actors then improvise their roles within the parameters of the setting. The actors and audience share a general understanding of what the scene or setting consists of, but how it is played out is largely determined by each actor's performance repertoire (that is, each actor's familiarity with how people might react in this situation) and how the other performers respond. If you have participated in Theatersports, you know that the fun is in seeing how diverse actors play off one another when they don't know what the others are likely to do.

Everyday interaction is an ongoing series of such moments. The ability to negotiate working understandings of different situations is the genius of human sociability. The fact that everyday encounters feel more or less like comfortable routines—rather than a madcap scramble of miscues, misunderstandings, and maladies—is a testament to the existence of shared social scripts.

The negotiation process becomes apparent in situations that are less familiar and routine. On those occasions, people are likely to be more aware of the potential gap between the private and projected definitions of various participants.

Reading 25, Joan Emerson's "Behavior in Private Places: Sustaining Definitions of Reality in Gynecological Examinations," graphically illustrates the impression management that must take place when participants have strongly competing definitions of the situation. The patient is likely to feel that the examination is a violation of her body and her dignity, whereas the medical staff tries to establish an air of professional detachment. The doctors and nurses performing this medical procedure must take care to ensure that the situation continues to be defined as a medical examination because the exam includes many sensitive behaviors that could threaten this definition. Although most interactions are not as precarious as this situation, any interaction can end up being redefined in a negative light ("I thought you were being helpful. Now I just think you're being patronizing and manipulative!"). Thus, the concerns and dramaturgical activity that are brought out so clearly in the gynecological examination are relevant to many more ordinary settings.

In Reading 26, "Precarious Situations in a Strip Club," Kari Lerum describes how employees in an erotic dance club work to maintain specific definitions of the situation. In contrast with gynecological exams, in which the intent is to de-sexualize the situation, this study reveals that there are also interaction rules for erotic situations.

## Performing Interaction Rituals

Goffman opens *Presentation of Self* with the following lines from the philosopher George Santayana:

> Masks are arrested expressions and admirable echoes of feelings, at once faithful, discreet, and superlative. Living things in contact with the air acquire a cuticle, and it is not urged against cuticles that they are not hearts; yet some philosophers seem to be angry with images for not being things, and with words for not being feelings. Words and images are like shells, no less integral parts of nature than are the substances they cover, but better addressed to the eye and more open to observation. (p. vi)

Through this quotation, Goffman anticipates readers' reactions to his theory that we "perform" ourselves, our ideals, and our beliefs rather than somehow simply exude them naturally. Some people are inclined to associate "performance" with fakery or trickery. They assume that, behind the stage, there is something "more real."

Goffman and sociologists of his persuasion do not disavow the existence of a physiology, a psyche, and perhaps even a soul that may be independent of social forces, but their theoretical and analytical focus is *social* relations. "Reality" is in the expression of social meaning achieved through interaction. We are, first and foremost, *expressive* creatures. To express ourselves, we must transform individual urges, amorphous images, and fuzzy ideas into communicable form. We do so through interactional speech and gesture. Thus, "reality" consists of shared forms of expression that, as we have noted, take on patterns. Goffman calls these patterns "interaction rituals."

Producing a shared reality requires give and take, concession, and acknowledgment of others. Interaction rituals are enactments of ceremony that reinforce cultural symbols and expectations. The rituals range from simple greeting exchanges (in which people acknowledge the presence of other people) to elaborate ceremonies (such as weddings and funerals). And these interaction rituals have a conservative aspect: Through ritual presentations of the "ideal," people conserve or maintain the status quo.

For Goffman, everyday ceremonies, or rituals, give meaning to our collective existence.

> To the degree that a performance highlights the common official values of the society in which it occurs, we may look upon it as a ceremony—as

an expressive rejuvenation and reaffirmation of the moral values of the community. . . . To stay in one's room away from the place where the party is being given . . . is to stay away from where reality is being performed. The world, in truth, is a wedding. (pp. 35–36)

## From Masks to Selves

One implication of interaction rituals is that they have the potential to become set or routinized. They may become so automatic that people fail to notice the extent to which they themselves engage in these performances. After spending some time at a job or in the company of old friends, people seldom recall the discomfort of the initial interactions—when the job was new or the people were strangers; when they were not sure whether their identity claims would be granted or how to define the situation. Blind dates are a good example of the sticky challenges involved in interaction and identity management.

However, even when interaction rituals performed repeatedly become routine, people still engage in impression management. In the Part II essay, we discussed the work of George Herbert Mead, whose theory suggested that humans learn to treat themselves as objects that have meaning relative to other people and situations, just as they learn to attribute relative meaning to other things in their environment. The ability to treat the self as an object is what makes it possible for us to observe, reflect on, plan, and direct our own behavior. In other words, without the ability to perceive the self as an object, we would be unable to engage in impression management. Mead's article (Reading 27), "The Self, the I, and the Me," explains this view.

One of the things that the self can do is to engage in internal conversation (private thought) and reflect on whether the self's behavior seems "authentic." For example, out of deference and fear of losing your job, you may play the part of a likable clown for your overbearing boss. In private, however, you know that this mask is not the "real" you. The real you is serious and efficient and hates the boss.

As we discussed, notions of how one should present one's self to a boss are based on a set of general expectations that represent the attitudes and values of the culture. These expectations function as the *generalized other* (internalized social expectations) to give people an "ideal script" for acting the proper role in relation to an employer.

The generalized other can be contradictory. For example, in addition to believing you should adopt the mask of a clown, you may also have another set of general expectations that direct you to stand up to the boss. Which set of expectations you act on depends on the specific situation, including who you are interacting with and that person's power to define the situation. Your internal dialogues regarding these contradictions and the way you choose to enact them contribute to the process of self-definition.

An interesting question is the nature of the relationship between the identities that we perform to manage others' impressions of us (our masks) and the *self*, a more stable and enduring understanding of who we are. Identities, as we have seen, vary across situations relative to interaction partners. The self, however, is a more stable construct and serves as the basis of comparison when we reflect on our identity performances and their consequences. Even when we are unable to express our "real" selves in a particular situation, our sense of having a "real" self exists as a touchstone by which we evaluate the authenticity of the identities that we present.

How does an identity become a self? The answer, in part, is in the process of routinization. Identities that we perform repeatedly may become part of our general sense of who we are. On the other hand, some of us perform very routinized identities without ever considering them to be an aspect of our "true self." For example, many people who live and work in Los Angeles, when asked what they do, reply, "I work as a server/delivery person/janitor, but I am really writing a screenplay," or "I am really an actor." The job, even if it is one that they have performed for years, may not be an important aspect of the "real" self, whereas an identity that has yet to be realized may be the core of how they see themselves.

Before reading further, take out a piece of paper and write down twenty responses to the question Who am I? As you read through this section, ponder how each of these aspects of your "real" self came to be.

### The Self as a Product of Interaction

The last group of readings in Part III emphasizes the process of identifying or naming behaviors that we come to see as an aspect of "self." In other words, the self, like other objects, is viewed as a social construction that takes on meaning through interaction—through either internal dialogue or interaction with others.

In much the same way that we each learn to define the meaning of things in our environment, we learn about who we are through observing the responses of others to us, as an object. Charles Horton Cooley, a contemporary of Mead, has suggested the concept of the "looking-glass self," an image of our self based on how we think others see us. These reflected appraisals are the topic of Reading 28, "Looking-Glass Self." Cooley notes that we gain information about ourselves by casting ourselves in the role of an observer, imagining how our actions appear to that person, and then attaching some reaction (such as pride or mortification) to that perceived reaction. According to Cooley and most contemporary social psychologists, "significant others" and "primary groups" have a great deal of potential to shape our possible selves.

In Reading 29, Philip Blumstein focuses on repeated interaction rituals played out with people who are significant to us. "The Production of Selves in Personal Relationships" contains the rudiments of a theory for the development of stable selves through interactions. Blumstein's thesis is that significant others, particularly intimate partners, have the potential to be important contributors to our sense of self, because their reflected appraisals are so valued. For example, in the process of coordinating activities, a couple may name particular identities, such as provider or homemaker. The partners may become attached to, or grow into, these identities through routinization and the reflected appraisals of each other. Blumstein refers to this process as "ossification," meaning that identities have the potential to harden, like bone, into selves.

Under the right circumstances, we begin to think of everyday behaviors as "identities" and then, perhaps, to incorporate these identities into an organized sense of self. The identity masks that we wear to convey information to others have the potential to become part of what we consider our "real" self. This is likely to occur when people whose opinions we value continually reinforce a specific behavior or identity ("I think you have a great sense of fashion"; "I think you are a remarkably kind person"; and so forth). The identity becomes solidified into an aspect of "self" as we incorporate it into our internal dialogue (internalization) and hold it up as a reflection of a personal, ideal sense of being. Consider the implications of this process as you reread your "Who am I?" list. Can you describe the social relations or social processes that occurred over time to give you a sense that you are these roles and possess these characteristics?

Sometimes circumstances arise in which we feel compelled by others to act in a way that we believe to be entirely out of character according to our personal sense of self. In "Shooting an Elephant" (Reading 30), George Orwell describes how the expectations of others drove him to do something—shoot an elephant—he never thought he could actually do. As you read this piece and think about it in light of the Blumstein article (Reading 29), try this writing exercise. Begin a paper with the phrase: "I never thought I would become . . . " Then write about something that you could never see yourself doing (joining a religious cult, becoming a particular type of politician or other social role), and consider the ways in which persons who are significant in your life could actually change your ideals, beliefs, and sense of who you are.

The contrast between imagined selves and the social affirmation of these roles can be extreme for those who have stigmatized identities. In a timely and highly relevant book, *Down on Their Luck*, David Snow and Leon Anderson provide a voice for homeless men and women in the United States. The chapter included here as Reading 31, "Salvaging the Self," is an exploration of the difficulties and strategies of maintaining a self-image while being routinely ignored and denied access to social interactions and social spaces.

In Reading 32 (a chapter from her book *Becoming an Ex*) "Creating the Ex-Role," Helen Rose Fuchs Ebaugh draws on the cases of ex-nuns, ex-professionals, and transsexuals to trace the way in which we adjust to changes in primary identities. We do not simply cease enacting one primary identity and start enacting another with no further thought about the matter. On the contrary, the more we find it necessary to explain the transition to ourselves and to others, the more we can conclude that the abandoned identity has been a significant one in our self-concept.

Interaction is a fluid, intricately coordinated dance that requires actors to participate in meaningful symbolic routines. These interaction rituals serve to define who people are, relative to one another, and what the situation is. The implication is that social life is a production or performance staged by the participants. We have suggested that even the self is a social construction arrived at through processes of meaningful interaction.

By way of conclusion, we invite you to ponder the paradox of the social self. Many Western individuals are uncomfortable with the notion that the self is a social construction. We are all more or less aware that we engage in impression management, but many of us like to think that our "true self" is unchanging and is the product of forces independent of society. Thus, many of us rebel against the "chains of society," thinking that, if only we could break loose from these chains, we would be "free" (Charon, 1989).

Herein lies the paradox: To gain control over our own behavior, we must each develop a self that is capable of observing, reflecting on, and directing that behavior. Without such a self, we are merely passive organisms propelled by the forces of nature. In the process of developing this self, we determine what position to take on our own behavior by observing and by experiencing the reactions of others to our behavior. The implication is that all the behavior we reflect on holds meaning for us only because it has been derived from some form of social interaction. The ability to consider whether we are "free" agents or "controlled" by society is therefore possible only through our ability to engage in internal dialogue regarding the self as an object—which, ironically, is a product of socialization. Free agency is a moot point for the unsocialized being. Such a being cannot reflect on or guide its own behavior and therefore cannot make active choices.

Resolution of this paradox may lie in the recognition that we are all, in Goffman's phrase, "sweet conspirators" in social patterns and interaction rituals. It is more useful to ask ourselves what purpose these patterns and rituals serve, and with what consequences, than to shrug them off as someone else's chains. To ignore our socialization is, according to Goffman, to leave the stage where reality is being performed. The pertinent question for the enlightened social actor is "Just what sort of a performance am I a part of?" Hence the focus on the questions "What is the definition of the situation?" and "What role(s) am I playing?"

## References

Charon, J. (1989). *Symbolic interactionism* (3rd ed.). Englewood Cliffs, NJ: Prentice-Hall.

Goffman, E. (1959). *The presentation of self in everyday life.* Garden City, NY: Doubleday.

Kuhn, M.H., and McPartland ,T.S. (1954). An empirical investigation of self-attitudes. *American Sociological Review* 19:68-76.

Turner, R. (1976). The real self: From institution to impulse. *American Journal of Sociology, 81*, 989–1016.

Twain, M. (1946). *The adventures of Tom Sawyer.* New York: Grosset & Dunlap. (Originally published in 1875)

# Becoming a Marihuana User

*Howard S. Becker*

The use of marihuana is and has been the focus of a good deal of attention on the part of both scientists and laymen. One of the major problems students of the practice have addressed themselves to has been the identification of those individual psychological traits which differentiate marihuana users from nonusers and which are assumed to account for the use of the drug. That approach, common in the study of behavior categorized as deviant, is based on the premise that the presence of a given kind of behavior in an individual can best be explained as the result of some trait which predisposes or motivates him to engage in the behavior.[1]

This study is likewise concerned with accounting for the presence or absence of marihuana use in an individual's behavior. It starts, however, from a different premise: that the presence of a given kind of behavior is the result of a sequence of social experiences during which the person acquires a conception of the meaning of the behavior, and perceptions and judgments of objects and situations, all of which make the activity possible and desirable. Thus, the motivation or disposition to engage in the activity is built up in the course of learning to engage in it and does not antedate this learning process. For such a view it is not necessary to identify those "traits" which "cause" the behavior. Instead, the problem becomes one of describing the set of changes in the person's conception of the activity and of the experience it provides for him.[2]

This paper seeks to describe the sequence of changes in attitude and experience which lead to *the use of marihuana for pleasure*. Marihuana does not produce addiction, as do alcohol and the opiate drugs; there is no withdrawal sickness and no ineradicable craving for the drug.[3] The most frequent pattern of use might be termed "recreational." The drug is used occasionally for the pleasure the user finds in it, a relatively casual kind of behavior in comparison with that connected with the use of addicting drugs. The term "use for pleasure" is meant to emphasize the noncompulsive and casual character of the behavior. It is also meant to eliminate from consideration here those few cases in which marihuana is used for its prestige value only, as a symbol that one is a certain kind of person, with no pleasure at all being derived from its use.

"Becoming a Marihuana User" by H. S. Becker, 1953. Reprinted from *The American Journal of Sociology, 59,* pp. 235–242, by permission of the University of Chicago Press. Copyright © 1953 by the University of Chicago Press.

Read at the meetings of the Midwest Sociological Society in Omaha, Nebraska, April 25, 1953. The research on which this paper is based was done while I was a member of the staff of the Chicago Narcotics Survey, a study done by the Chicago Area Project, Inc., under a grant from the National Institute of Mental Health. My thanks to Solomon Kobrin, Harold Finestone, Henry McKay, and Anselm Strauss, who read and discussed with me earlier versions of this paper.

The analysis presented here is conceived of as demonstrating the greater explanatory usefulness of the kind of theory outlined above as opposed to the predispositional theories now current. This may be seen in two ways: (1) predispositional theories cannot account for that group of users (whose existence is admitted)[4] who do not exhibit the trait or traits considered to cause the behavior and (2) such theories cannot account for the great variability over time of a given individual's behavior with reference to the drug. The same person will at one stage be unable to use the drug for pleasure, at a later stage be able and willing to do so, and still later, again be unable to use it in this way. These changes, difficult to explain from a predispositional or motivational theory, are readily understandable in terms of changes in the individual's conception of the drug as is the existence of "normal" users.

The study attempted to arrive at a general statement of the sequence of changes in individual attitude and experience which have always occurred when the individual has become willing and able to use marihuana for pleasure and which have not occurred or not been permanently maintained when this is not the case. This generalization is stated in universal terms in order that negative cases may be discovered and used to revise the explanatory hypothesis.[5]

Fifty interviews with marihuana users from a variety of social backgrounds and present positions in society constitute the data from which the generalization was constructed and against which it was tested.[6] The interviews focused on the history of the person's experience with the drug, seeking major changes in his attitude toward it and in his actual use of it, and the reasons for these changes. The final generalization is a statement of that sequence of changes in attitude which occurred in every case known to me in which the person came to use marihuana for pleasure. Until a negative case is found, it may be considered as an explanation of all cases of marihuana use for plea-

sure. In addition, changes from use to non-use are shown to be related to similar changes in conception, and in each case it is possible to explain variations in the individual's behavior in these terms.

This paper covers only a portion of the natural history of an individual's use of marihuana,[7] starting with the person having arrived at the point of willingness to try marihuana. He knows that others use it to "get high," but he does not know what this means in concrete terms. He is curious about the experience, ignorant of what it may turn out to be, and afraid that it may be more than he has bargained for. The steps outlined below, if he undergoes them all and maintains the attitudes developed in them, leave him willing and able to use the drug for pleasure when the opportunity presents itself.

I

The novice does not ordinarily get high the first time he smokes marihuana, and several attempts are usually necessary to induce this state. One explanation of this may be that the drug is not smoked "properly," that is, in a way that ensures sufficient dosage to produce real symptoms of intoxication. Most users agree that it cannot be smoked like tobacco if one is to get high:

Take in a lot of air, you know, and . . . I don't know how to describe it, you don't smoke it like a cigarette, you draw in a lot of air and get it deep down in your system and then keep it there. Keep it there as long as you can.

Without the use of some such technique[8] the drug will produce no effects, and the user will be unable to get high:

The trouble with people like that [who are not able to get high] is that they're just not smoking it right, that's all there is to it. Either they're not holding it down long enough, or they're getting too much air and not enough smoke, or the other way around or something like that. A lot of people just don't smoke it right, so naturally nothing's gonna happen.

If nothing happens, it is manifestly impossible for the user to develop a conception of the drug as an object which can be used for pleasure, and use will therefore not continue. The first step in the sequence of events that must occur if the person is to become a user is that he must learn to use the proper smoking technique in order that his use of the drug will produce some effects in terms of which his conception of it can change.

Such a change is, as might be expected, a result of the individual's participation in groups in which marihuana is used. In them the individual learns the proper way to smoke the drug. This may occur through direct teaching:

I was smoking like I did an ordinary cigarette. He said, "No, don't do it like that." He said, "Suck it, you know, draw in and hold it in your lungs till you . . . for a period of time."

I said, "Is there any limit of time to hold it?"

He said, "No, just till you feel that you want to let it out, let it out." So I did that three or four times.

Many new users are ashamed to admit ignorance and, pretending to know already, must learn through the more indirect means of observation and imitation:

I came on like I had turned on [smoked marihuana] many times before, you know. I didn't want to seem like a punk to this cat. See, like I didn't know the first thing about it—how to smoke it, or what was going to happen, or what. I just watched him like a hawk—I didn't take my eyes off him for a second, because I wanted to do everything just as he did it. I watched how he held it, how he smoked it, and everything. Then when he gave it to me I just came on cool, as though I knew exactly what the score was. I held it like he did and took a poke just the way he did.

No person continued marihuana use for pleasure without learning a technique that supplied sufficient dosage for the effects of the drug to appear. Only when this was learned was it possible for a conception of the drug as an object which could be used for pleasure to emerge. Without such a conception marihuana use was considered meaningless and did not continue.

## II

Even after he learns the proper smoking technique, the new user may not get high and thus not form a conception of the drug as something which can be used for pleasure. A remark made by a user suggested the reason for this difficulty in getting high and pointed to the next necessary step on the road to being a user:

I was told during an interview, "As a matter of fact, I've seen a guy who was high out of his mind and didn't know it."

I expressed disbelief: "How can that be, man?"

The interviewee said, "Well, it's pretty strange, I'll grant you that, but I've seen it. This guy got on with me, claiming that he'd never got high, one of those guys, and he got completely stoned. And he kept insisting that he wasn't high. So I had to prove to him that he was."

What does this mean? It suggests that being high consists of two elements: the presence of symptoms caused by marihuana use and the recognition of these symptoms and their connection by the user with his use of the drug. It is not enough, that is, that the effects be present; they alone do not automatically provide the experience of being high. The user must be able to point them out to himself and consciously connect them with his having smoked marihuana before he can have this experience. Otherwise, regardless of the actual effects produced, he considers that the drug has had no effect on him: "I figured it either had no effect on me or other people were exaggerating its effect on them, you know. I thought it was probably psychological, see." Such persons believe that the whole thing is an illusion and that the wish to be high leads the user to deceive himself into believing that something is happening when, in fact, nothing is. They do not continue marihuana use, feeling that "it does nothing" for them.

Typically, however, the novice has faith (developed from his observation of users who do get high) that the drug actually will produce some new experience and continues to experiment with it until it does. His failure to get high worries him, and he is likely to ask more experienced users or provoke comments from them about it. In such conversations he is made aware of specific details of his experience which he may not have noticed or may have noticed but failed to identify as symptoms of being high:

I didn't get high the first time . . . I don't think I held it in long enough. I probably let it out, you know, you're a little afraid. The second time I wasn't sure, and he [smoking companion] told me, like I asked him for some of the symptoms or something, how would I know, you know. . . . So he told me to sit on a stool. I sat on—I think I sat on a bar stool—and he said, "Let your feet hang," and then when I got down my feet were real cold, you know.

And I started feeling it, you know. That was the first time. And then about a week after that, sometime pretty close to it, I really got on. That was the first time I got on a big laughing kick, you know. Then I really knew I was on.

One symptom of being high is an intense hunger. In the next case the novice becomes aware of this and gets high for the first time:

They were just laughing the hell out of me because like I was eating so much. I just scoffed [ate] so much food, and they were just laughing at me, you know. Sometimes I'd be looking at them, you know, wondering why they're laughing, you know, not knowing what I was doing. [Well, did they tell you why they were laughing eventually?] Yeah, yeah, I come back, "Hey, man, what's happening?" Like, you know, like I'd ask, "What's happening?" and all of a sudden I feel weird, you know. "Man, you're on you know. You're on pot [high on marihuana]." I said, "No, am I?" Like I don't know what's happening.

The learning may occur in more indirect ways:

I heard little remarks that were made by other people. Somebody said, "My legs are rubbery," and I can't remember all the remarks that were made because I was very attentively listening for all these cues for what I was supposed to feel like.

The novice, then, eager to have this feeling, picks up from other users some concrete referents of the term "high" and applies these notions to his own experience. The new concepts make it possible for him to locate these symptoms among his own sensations and to point out to himself a "something different" in his experience that he connects with drug use. It is only when he can do this that he is high. In the next case, the contrast between two successive experiences of a user makes clear the crucial importance of the awareness of the symptoms in being high and re-emphasizes the important role of interaction with other users in acquiring the concepts that make this awareness possible:

[Did you get high the first time you turned on?] Yeah, sure. Although, come to think of it, I guess I really didn't. I mean, like that first time it was more or less of a mild drunk. I was happy, I guess, you know what I mean. But I didn't really know I was high, you know what I mean. It was only after the second time I got high that I realized I was high the first time. Then I knew that something different was happening.

[How did you know that?] How did I know? If what happened to me that night would of happened to you, you would've known, believe me. We played the first tune for almost two hours— one tune! Imagine, man! We got on the stand and played this one tune, we started at nine o'clock. When we got finished I looked at my watch, it's a quarter to eleven. Almost two hours on one tune. And it didn't seem like anything. I mean, you know, it does that to you. It's like you have much more time or something. Anyway, when I saw that, man, it was too much. I knew I must really be high or something if anything like that could happen. See, and then they explained to me that that's what it did to you, you had a different sense of time and everything. So I realized that that's what it was. I knew then. Like the first time, I probably felt that way, you know, but I didn't know what's happening.

It is only when the novice becomes able to get high in this sense that he will continue to use marihuana for pleasure. In every case in which use continued, the user had acquired the necessary concepts with which to express to himself the fact that he was experiencing new sensations caused by the drug. That is, for use to continue, it is necessary not only to use the drug so as to produce effects but also to learn to perceive these effects when they occur. In this way marihuana acquires meaning for the user as an object which can be used for pleasure.

With increasing experience the user develops a greater appreciation of the drug's effects; he continues to learn to get high. He examines succeeding experiences closely, looking for new effects, making sure the old ones are still there. Out of this there grows a stable set of categories for experiencing the drug's effects whose presence enables the user to get high with ease.

The ability to perceive the drug's effects must be maintained if use is to continue; if it is lost, marihuana use ceases. Two kinds of evidence support this statement. First, people who become heavy users of alcohol, barbiturates, or opiates do not continue to smoke marihuana, largely because they lose the ability to distinguish between its effects and those of the other drugs.[9] They no longer know whether the marihuana gets them high. Second, in those few cases in which an individual uses marihuana in such quantities that he is always high, he is apt to get this same feeling that the drug has no effect on him, since the essential element of a noticeable difference between feeling high

and feeling normal is missing. In such a situation, use is likely to be given up completely, but temporarily, in order that the user may once again be able to perceive the difference.

## III

One more step is necessary if the user who has now learned to get high is to continue use. He must learn to enjoy the effects he has just learned to experience. Marihuana-produced sensations are not automatically or necessarily pleasurable. The taste for such experience is a socially acquired one, not different in kind from acquired tastes for oysters or dry martinis. The user feels dizzy, thirsty; his scalp tingles; he misjudges time and distances; and so on. Are these things pleasurable? He isn't sure. If he is to continue marihuana use, he must decide that they are. Otherwise, getting high, while a real enough experience, will be an unpleasant one he would rather avoid.

The effects of the drug, when first perceived, may be physically unpleasant or at least ambiguous:

It started taking effect, and I didn't know what was happening, you know, what it was, and I was very sick. I walked around the room, walking around the room trying to get off, you know; it just scared me at first, you know. I wasn't used to that kind of feeling.

In addition, the novice's naive interpretation of what is happening to him may further confuse and frighten him, particularly if he decides, as many do, that he is going insane:

I felt I was insane, you know. Everything people done to me just wigged me. I couldn't hold a conversation, and my mind would be wandering, and I was always thinking, oh, I don't know, weird things, like hearing music different. . . . I get the feeling that I can't talk to anyone. I'll goof completely.

Given these typically frightening and unpleasant first experiences, the beginner will not continue use unless he learns to redefine the sensations as pleasurable:

It was offered to me, and I tried it. I'll tell you one thing. I never did enjoy it at all. I mean it was just nothing that I could enjoy. [Well, did you get high when you turned on?] Oh, yeah, I got definite feelings from it. But I didn't enjoy them. I mean I got plenty of reactions, but they were mostly reactions of fear. [You were frightened?] Yes, I didn't enjoy it. I couldn't seem to relax with it, you know. If you can't relax with a thing, you can't enjoy it, I don't think.

In other cases the first experiences were also definitely unpleasant, but the person did become a marihuana user. This occurred, however, only after a later experience enabled him to redefine the sensations as pleasurable:

[This man's first experience was extremely unpleasant, involving distortion of spatial relationships and sounds, violent thirst, and panic produced by these symptoms.] After the first time I didn't turn on for about, I'd say, ten months to a year. . . . It wasn't a moral thing; it was because I'd gotten so frightened, bein' so high. An' I didn't want to go through that again, I mean, my reaction was, "Well, if this is what they call bein' high, I don't dig [like] it." . . . So I didn't turn on for a year almost, accounta that. . . .

Well, my friends started, an' consequently I started again. But I didn't have any more, I didn't have that same initial reaction, after I started turning on again.

[In interaction with his friends he became able to find pleasure in the effects of the drug and eventually became a regular user.]

In no case will use continue without such a redefinition of the effects as enjoyable.

This redefinition occurs, typically, in interaction with more experienced users who, in a number of ways, teach the novice to find pleasure in this experience which is at first so frightening.[10] They may reassure him as to the temporary character of the unpleasant sensations and minimize their seriousness, at the same time calling attention to the more enjoyable aspects. An experienced user describes how he handles newcomers to marihuana use:

Well, they get pretty high sometimes. The average person isn't ready for that, and it is a little frightening to them sometimes. I mean, they've been high on lush [alcohol], and they get higher that way than they've ever been before, and they don't know what's happening to them. Because they think they're going to keep going up, up, up till they lose their minds or begin doing weird things or something. You have to like reassure them, explain to them that they're not really flipping or anything, that they're gonna be all right. You have to just talk them out of being afraid. Keep talking to them, reassuring, telling them it's all right. And come on with your own story, you know: "The same thing happened to me. You'll get to like that after awhile." Keep coming on like that; pretty soon you talk them out of being scared. And besides they see you doing it and nothing horrible is happening to you, so that gives them more confidence.

The more experienced user may also teach the novice to regulate the amount he smokes more carefully, so as to avoid any severely uncomfortable symptoms while retaining the pleasant ones. Finally, he teaches the new user that he can "get to like it after awhile." He teaches him to regard those ambiguous experiences formerly defined as unpleasant as enjoyable. The older user in the following incident is a person whose tastes have shifted in this way, and his remarks have the effect of helping others to make a similar redefinition:

A new user had her first experience of the effects of marihuana and became frightened and hysterical. She "felt like she was half in and half out of the room" and experienced a number of alarming physical symptoms. One of the more experienced users present said, "She's dragged because she's high like that. I'd give anything to get that high myself. I haven't been that high in years."

In short, what was once frightening and distasteful becomes, after a taste for it is built up, pleasant, desired, and sought after. Enjoyment is introduced by the favorable definition of the experience that one acquires from others. Without this, use will not continue, for marihuana will not be for the user an object he can use for pleasure.

In addition to being a necessary step in becoming a user, this represents an important condition for continued use. It is quite common for experienced users suddenly to have an unpleasant or frightening experience, which they cannot define as pleasurable, either because they have used a larger amount of marihuana than usual or because it turns out to be a higher-quality marihuana than they expected. The user has sensations which go beyond any conception he has of what being high is and is in much the same situation as the novice, uncomfortable and frightened. He may blame it on an overdose and simply be more careful in the future. But he may make this the occasion for a rethinking of his attitude toward the drug and decide that it no longer can give him pleasure. When this occurs and is not followed by a redefinition of the drug as capable of producing pleasure, use will cease.

The likelihood of such a redefinition occurring depends on the degree of the individual's participation with other users. Where this participation is intensive, the individual is quickly talked out of his feeling against marihuana use. In the next case, on the other hand, the experience was very disturbing, and the aftermath of the incident cut the person's participation with other users to almost zero. Use stopped for three years and began again only when a combination of circumstances, important among which was a resumption of ties with users, made possible a redefinition of the nature of the drug:

It was too much, like I only made about four pokes, and I couldn't even get it out of my mouth, I was so high, and I got real flipped. In the basement, you know, I just couldn't stay in there anymore. My heart was pounding real hard, you know, and I was going out of my mind; I thought I was losing my mind completely. So I cut out of this basement, and this other guy, he's out of his mind, told me, "Don't, don't leave me, man. Stay here." And I couldn't.

I walked outside, and it was five below zero, and I thought I was dying, and I had my coat open; I was sweating. I was perspiring. My whole insides were all . . . , and I walked about two blocks away, and I fainted behind a bush. I don't know how long I laid there. I woke up, and I was feeling the worst, I can't describe it at all, so I made it to a bowling alley, man, and I was trying to act normal, I was trying to shoot pool, you know, trying to act real normal, and I couldn't lay and I couldn't stand up and I couldn't sit down, and I went up and laid down where some guys that spot pins lay down, and that didn't help me, and I went down to a doctor's office. I was going to go in there and tell the doctor to put me out of my misery . . . because my heart was pounding so hard, you know. . . . So then all weekend I started flipping, seeing things there and going through hell, you know, all kinds of abnormal things. . . . I just quit for a long time then.

[He went to a doctor who defined the symptoms for him as those of a nervous breakdown caused by "nerves" and "worries." Although he was no longer using marihuana, he had some recurrences of the symptoms which led him to suspect that "it was all his nerves."] So I just stopped worrying, you know; so it was about thirty-six months later I started making it again. I'd just take a few pokes, you know. [He first resumed use in the company of the same user-friend with whom he had been involved in the original incident.]

A person, then, cannot begin to use marihuana for pleasure, or continue its use for pleasure, unless he learns to define its effects as enjoyable, unless it becomes and remains an object which he conceived of as capable of producing pleasure.

## IV

In summary, an individual will be able to use marihuana for pleasure only when he goes through a process of learning to conceive of it as an object which can be used in this way. No one becomes a user without (1) learning to smoke the drug in a way which will produce real effects; (2) learning to recognize the effects and connect them with drug use (learning, in other words, to get high); and (3) learning to enjoy the sensations he perceives. In the course of this process he develops a disposition or motivation to use marihuana which was not and could not have been present when he began use, for it involves and depends on conceptions of the drug which could only grow out of the kind of actual experience detailed above. On completion of this process he is willing and able to use marihuana for pleasure.

He has learned, in short, to answer "Yes" to the question: "Is it fun?" The direction his further use of the drug takes depends on his being able to continue to answer "Yes" to this question and, in addition, on his being able to answer "Yes" to other questions which arise as he becomes aware of the implications of the fact that the society as a whole disapproves of the practice: "Is it expedient?" "Is it moral?" Once he has acquired the ability to get enjoyment out of the drug, use will continue to be possible for him. Considerations of morality and expediency, occasioned by the reactions of society, may interfere and inhibit use, but use continues to be a possibility in terms of his conception of the drug. The act becomes impossible only when the ability to enjoy the experience of being high is lost, through a change in the user's conception of the drug occasioned by certain kinds of experience with it.

In comparing this theory with those which ascribe marihuana use to motives or predispositions rooted deep in individual behavior, the evidence makes it clear that marihuana use for pleasure can occur only when the process described above is undergone and cannot occur without it. This is apparently so without reference to the nature of the individual's personal makeup, or psychic problems. Such theories assume that people have stable modes of response which prede-

termine the way they will act in relation to any particular situation or object and that, when they come in contact with the given object or situation, they act in the way in which their makeup predisposes them.

This analysis of the genesis of marihuana use shows that the individuals who come in contact with a given object may respond to it at first in a great variety of ways. If a stable form of new behavior toward the object is to emerge, a transformation of meanings must occur, in which the person develops a new conception of the nature of the object.[11] This happens in a series of communicative acts in which others point out new aspects of his experience to him, present him with new interpretations of events, and help him achieve a new conceptual organization of his world, without which the new behavior is not possible. Persons who do not achieve the proper kind of conceptualization are unable to engage in the given behavior and turn off in the direction of some other relationship to the object or activity.

This suggests that behavior of any kind might fruitfully be studied developmentally, in terms of changes in meanings and concepts, their organization and reorganization, and the way they channel behavior, making some acts possible while excluding others.

## Notes

1. See, as examples of this approach, the following: E. Marcovitz & H. J. Meyers (1944, December), "The marihuana addict in the army," *War Medicine, 6*, 382–391; H. S. Gaskill (1945, September), "Marihuana, an intoxicant," *American Journal of Psychiatry, 102*, 202–204; S. Charen & L. Perelman (1946, March), "Personality studies of marihuana addicts," *American Journal of Psychiatry, 102*, 674–682.

2. This approach stems from George Herbert Mead's (1934) discussion of objects in *Mind, self, and society*, Chicago: University of Chicago Press, pp. 277–280.

3. Cf. R. Adams (1942, November), "Marihuana," *Bulletin of the New York Academy of Medicine, 18*, 705–730.

4. Cf. L. Kolb (1938, July), "Marihuana," *Federal Probation, 2,* 22–25; and W. Bromberg (1939, July 1), "Marihuana: A psychiatric study," *Journal of the American Medical Association, 113,* 11.

5. The method used is that described in A. R. Lindesmith (1947), *Opiate addiction,* Bloomington, IN: Principia, chap. i. I would like also to acknowledge the important role Lindesmith's work played in shaping my thinking about the genesis of marihuana use.

6. Most of the interviews were done by the author. I am grateful to Solomon Kobrin and Harold Finestone for allowing me to make use of interviews done by them.

7. I hope to discuss elsewhere other stages in this natural history.

8. A pharmacologist notes that this ritual is in fact an extremely efficient way of getting the drug into the blood stream. R. P. Walton (1938), *Marihuana: America's new drug problem,* Philadelphia: J. B. Lippincott, p. 48.

9. "Smokers have repeatedly stated that the consumption of whiskey while smoking negates the potency of the drug. They find it very difficult to get 'high' while drinking whiskey and because of that smokers will not drink while using the 'weed.'" Cf. New York City Mayor's Committee on Marihuana (1944), *The marihuana problem in the city of New York,* Lancaster, PA: Jacques Cattel, p. 13.

10. Charen & Perelman (1946), p. 679.

11. Cf. A. Strauss (1952, June), "The development and transformation of monetary meanings in the child," *American Sociological Review, 17,* 275–286.

**19**

# Looks

### *Karen Allman Maeda*

I can't keep track of how I look. I know that sounds odd, but that's how it is. I don't know if it was moving here from Arizona, or knowing more people of Asian descent, or knowing more queers, or how much I weigh, or what I'm wearing. I just know that I look different.

A few years ago, I even changed my name. Karen Allman just didn't seem to fit me anymore. Maybe you know the drill—you meet someone and you can see them scrutinizing your face for some clue as to why your name doesn't fit what they think you are. Whatever that is. They just know that there's . . . "something wrong here . . . let's see . . . oriental, Polynesian, Hawaiian, Mexican . . . uhhhh excuse me, but what are you?" What are you?

Of course, with that name, Karen Allman, when I meet someone who actually is from Japan, they often exclaim, "It can't be!! Are you sure?? I don't think so!" Oh right, I think. I'd be confused about where my own mother is from? I didn't say I was adopted. Actually if they aren't busily claiming that I look "white" then they helpfully let me know that they'd been sure all along that I was Korean . . . wasn't I really Korean? Something other than Japanese anyway.

Karen Allman Maeda is a writer and performance artist. This reading, "Looks," is taken from a text that she performed in Seattle in 1998. Reprinted with permission from the author.

Don't all Americans think that Korea, Japan, and China are really all the same place?

I was 30 when I first met a Korean-American. Her father's white, too. Her mother grew up in Japan, but she really is Korean. When my friend goes out shopping she always gets called sir, even when she's wearing a dress and lipstick. She doesn't fit into that image of a petite Asian woman—she's a loud, deep-voiced, broad-shouldered, working-class gal from the Midwest. Once she pulled an attacker off of a bus driver in a bus going 50 miles an hour on an I-5 onramp during rush hour. The witnesses said a guy did it, but her husband had been sitting there in shock the whole time. Later someone, a white woman friend, told her she shouldn't have gotten involved. She could have gotten hurt. I guess that's why she gets called sir and not ma'am. I wonder what I would have done. No one has ever called me sir.

It's not bad when people assume that, because of how I look, and because I know how to say "Tlingit" and say Indian "indin" like Indian people I know say those words, I'm maybe some kind of indin too. Maybe Athabascan because I look like this guy John's cousin back home or maybe Tlingit because they're from here and they have that sort of Asian look—or maybe Asians have that sort of Tlingit look. Or maybe I'm standing in front of a whole display of books by Native Americans and I seem to know what I'm talking about. I'm passionate when I'm talking about these books and I have a sense of humor. Or maybe I'm wearing that necklace I got at the Two Spirit gathering or those earrings I got at a pow wow or from a friend. I check to see what I'm wearing. Looong hair, understated. Yeah, I could be Indian maybe, but I'm not.

I've occasionally been mistaken for Black in parts of the country where identifying yourself as a "person of color" really does mean you're saying you're Black. Since it's widely if painfully accepted in the community that people of African descent come in every hue with every hair texture, it seems perfectly plausible. I have to say, "I don't think I'm Black but I could be." White people do lie about that, and half of my people are white. Some Black people who think I'm Indian are friendly until they find out I'm really Asian (or something). I don't know if that's because they're embarrassed that they made a mistake or if they just like Indians better. I'm not Indian.

One time this traveling man passing down my alley delivered this whole long flirty speech in Spanish. This used to happen to me a lot in Arizona and, feeling nostalgic, I smiled at him. "Sorry, but I don't speak Spanish," I called. No, I'm not Mexican. Yes, I'm sure. His parting comment was delivered in English: "Well you don't have to lie about it. It's nothing to be ashamed of, being Mexican. You should be proud!" I thought about the people I've known who've worked so hard to erase any trace of a non-standard American accent, smoothed out any edges from their facial features, plucked their hair, whitened up their skins, added eyelid folds. . . . Nothing to be ashamed of.

"Look here," I was telling my lover recently, "I have one eye that's Japanese and one eye that's not. Look closely." I can tell that she doesn't want to look. "Your two eyes look the same. Beautiful," she says. I don't believe her.

Look, I tell her, I KNOW one eye looks more Japanese than the other because when I used to wear eye makeup it was such a pain. Funny thing is, I can't remember which one

was which anymore. I keep looking in the mirror, but I still can't tell.

Sometimes I get that certain, slow smile from a white man while we wait on the sidewalk for the traffic light to change. That knowing smile is accompanied by a faraway look in the eye and followed with a hand shake that's just a little too friendly and goes on just a little too long. Then: "When I was in 'Nam . . ." or maybe it was Korea or Japan or . . .

I think, "You must be mistaken."

If it's an Asian-American man, maybe he moves away from me, sneering: Uh huh. Some white guy, maybe in 'Nam or Korea or Japan or maybe in my hometown. "Hey," I want to say, "it wasn't my idea!"

"You remind those men of their pain," an Asian-American woman once told me. "White men get so many of the Asian-American women, especially the Japanese ones. It's a matter of pride. Who are they going to date?" I remember that she's been dateless herself awhile. Why does this sound to me like a turf war for Asian woman booty, just dressed up? Hey, I date women too. Does that make me the competition? Doubly traitorous? What if Asian women date each other? I think of the Asian-American lesbians I see with white women. Would they look twice at me?

Actually, I do try to understand, especially when I remember my mother once telling me, "Don't marry a Japanese man!" I know she had her reasons. She didn't want to become a farm wife and get stuck in some Japanese hicktown. I knew that trying to explain or to argue is fruitless. I didn't even know any Japanese men near my age at the time.

After I came out to her, I wondered if she regretted having said that. One time, we were at the mall and I was reaching out to touch an organic cotton, terrycloth bath robe. "That's a man's robe! Do you want to be a man now?" she shrieked. "No! No! I just. . . ." Somehow this was a much bigger deal than someone having mistaken me for Mexican or

Korean. Later I thought about how that exact same robe, priced at maybe 40 percent more, was probably hanging in the Women's Lingerie department of the same store. What if someone hung that robe in the wrong place and my mother bought it?

I never particularly minded that word "queer," really. I've had a harder time getting used to dyke, fag, lesbo even lesbian. . . . Queer . . . now there's a word that really describes how I feel. I'm used to having my athletically inclined, het women friends mistaken for lesbian while I walk by, invisible, because I don't "look" like a dyke and they do. But then, they're white. Sound familiar? What are you?

Norma Field (1993) has written that biracials, including Amerasians like herself and like me, are "nothing if not the embodiment of sex itself." We are walking evidence of someone having had sex. Our existence is often the consequence of war. We are the flesh and blood evidence of sexual domination, and we are also the resistance of that domination. I believe that I am as much a product of an imperialist war and a country's occupation as of my parents' love for each other. Do people see this contradiction when I pass them, or do they try to imagine that sexual combination/domination? Do they think I am queer? What about me is queer?

Being multiracial and being queer are alike in that, like it or not, unless one is passing, one's sexuality is always on display, ripe for the projection of someone else's sexual anxieties, racial anxieties, hopes, fears, dreams, anger, and pain. Paradoxically, because my own queerness (in the lesbian sense) is often invisible, it's my own parents' interracial, heterosexual union that makes me seem queer. It's no wonder that I am. Queer.

### Reference

Norma Field (1993). *In the Realm of the Dying Emperor.* New York: Vintage.

**20**

# Fear of Falling: Sluts

*Peggy Orenstein*

There is only one label worse than "school-girl" at Weston, and that's her inverse, the fallen girl, or in student parlance, the slut. A "slut" is not merely a girl who "does it," but any girl who—through her clothes, her makeup, her hairstyle, or her speech—seems as if she *might*. Girls may protest the prudish connotations of "schoolgirl," but they fear the prurience of "slut": in order to find the middle ground between the two, a place from which they can function safely and with approval, girls have to monitor both their expressions of intelligence and their budding sexual desire. They must keep vigilant watch, over each other and over themselves.

### The Danger of Desire

On a warm day, Evie DiLeo and I buy a couple of Cokes after school and walk to a park near downtown Weston. Evie is wearing a loose red T-shirt with a clavicle-high neck, blue-jean shorts, and broken-down huaraches. Her dark hair is in a ponytail, and when she smiles, she displays a mouthful of braces with rubber bands that match her

shirt. She'd like to wear sexier clothes, Evie tells me, regarding her current outfit with disapproval, but she had to battle her mother just to get to wear lipstick, and even then, she was the last among her friends to be allowed.

Evie is a fast-talking, matter-of-fact young woman, the daughter of a lawyer mother and a computer programmer father who have been divorced for eight years. Like Lindsay, she is enrolled in Weston's gifted program. Evie has a thoughtful, analytical gaze, and from our first meeting was unusually forthcoming in her observations. She rarely pauses before answering my questions, and follows every assertion with a deepening "because" clause. Sometimes she's so eager to get her opinions out that she doesn't wait to understand my question. Once, she told me she thought girls had an advantage: Since more was expected of boys, they had to play by the rules, while girls could be more creative. Yes, I said, but boys still end up ahead. She nodded her head emphatically, said "Yeah," and then went on for a sentence or two before pausing and saying, "What do you mean by that?"

Although she frequently declares herself "a feminist" and "independent," Evie's self-confidence is held in check by the rules she is learning about female sexuality. She is keenly conscious of which girls at Weston are sluts, and she readily points them out to her friends and to me. Sometimes she does so casually, saying, "She's kind of a slut," when I mention a particular girl I've been interviewing. Other times, she has grabbed my arm and pointed sluts out to me. I wonder, as the year progresses, whether her point isn't so much to help me distinguish the characteristics that comprise "slut" as to reassure herself of the safe distance between her and them.

Evie tells me she was in love with a boy named Bradley Davis all through sixth and seventh grade. When she described Bradley, it took a moment for me to place him. Bradley is not a boy an adult would take much notice of: average height, average grades, average looks. But Evie says she would've done anything to secure Bradley's affection and that, apparently, was what he hoped: Starting in sixth grade, in math class, Bradley began asking Evie if she would have sex with him.

"At first I wanted to say 'yes,'" she admits. "I wanted to do it—I didn't know what it would feel like. It was sort of like a mystery, something that I wanted to know about. But then I thought, 'My dad would kill me,' so I just said 'no.' 'No, Bradley!' and he'd say, 'Why not?' I'd just say, 'No!'"

When Evie refused to relent, Bradley shut her out. He ignored her for the remainder of sixth grade and the first semester of seventh, although her own feelings remained strong. "He didn't talk to me, he didn't want to be around me, he didn't need me," she says bitterly. So when she regained Bradley's affections in the spring of seventh grade, and he propositioned her again, she knew the price of saying "no." This time, she says, "I said 'yes.' I was ready to do it. I was convinced I'd made a mistake and it would be all right this time. And I was just curious. I mean, why not?"

In truth, Evie didn't exactly say "yes" to Bradley; when he asked her over the phone if she would "have sex" with him she was silent, and both of them interpreted her silence as consent. "It was like I said 'yes,' because I didn't say 'no,'" she explains now. Bradley began to make plans: a date, a time, a place. But as the moment grew near, Evie began to worry: what if she had sex with Bradley and then became a slut?

Evie begins to pick nervously at the grass where we sit.

"After I said 'yes,'" she says, "I started having these dreams about this friend of mine. She started having sex in sixth grade. This guy told her he loved her so she'd have sex with him, then he dropped her. Then he did the same thing again, and she'd run to him every time. Now she's in a special school for troublemakers.

"I had thought girls like that were bad and terrible and they didn't give it a second thought," she continues. "But now I feel like I understand what she was going through. I think you're more pulled into it. It's not like you just decide to have sex: It's like you don't have a choice. You're so emotionally torn, you just say, 'Do it, get it over with, nothing will happen.' But socially, mentally, physically, something does happen. You change. Even your hairstyle changes. That girl, she'd had her hair back and pinned up and a happy face. Then suddenly it was down and across her face, over her eye. She started dressing in tight clothes, a tank top pulled down so it's low in front and high in back—one of those cropped tops. She'd lay on the grass on her belly and put her chin on her hand so the guys could see her breasts. It was dramatic: her whole opinion of herself changed, and everyone else's opinion of her changed, too. The guy told all of the other guys and some of the girls knew. So everyone thought she was a slut and she thought so, too. *Her* life changed, but the guy, he's still in school. He's popular. It didn't damage his image, just hers. And he just forgot about her, used her until she left. In my dreams, that's what happens to me."

Just before their agreed-upon date, Bradley telephoned Evie to confirm their plans; this time, she made her feelings clear. "I said, 'No, Bradley.' And he said, 'No to what?' I said, 'No to *everything*.' He said his dad was coming and he hung up. Now he ignores me again."

Evie looks down at the ground when she finishes her story. Although the incident is over, it still haunts her. "I feel scummy," she says, softly, fluffing the grass with her fingers. "Even though I didn't actually do it, I feel like a total slut inside. I feel like a slut for considering it. It damaged my personality and my opinion of myself. And if people knew, nothing would happen to him, but it would damage the way *I* was treated. That transformation that happened to my friend would happen to me. Not the clothes—my parents wouldn't let me even look at a crop top—but inside. Inside, my attitude would change.

"I wish I could just forget it," she says, rolling over on her back. "It makes me feel so bad about myself. I'm ashamed of myself. I wish I could wipe the glass clean. Like if I had Windex for my soul."

Evie's story is typical of Weston girls' encounters with sex. It is the story of male aggression and female defense; it is the story of innuendo serving as consent; of a fixation, much too young, on intercourse as the fulcrum of sex; and it is a story, most of all, of shame. Evie's shame, articulated several times in our conversation, comes not from actually having sex, but from *thinking* about it: from admitting desire. At thirteen, just as she is awakening to her own sexuality, she has learned she must suppress it immediately; she has learned, in fact, to convert it into feelings of disgust, and to make girls who express sexuality into untouchables—"sluts." Evie knows that desire is dangerous: a girl who explores it, like the girl in her cautionary dream, forfeits respect, integrity, and intelligence. "I don't know why," Evie says during one conversation, "but usually the slut girls aren't very smart."

Sexual entitlement—a sense of autonomy over one's body and desires—is an essential component of a healthy adult self. Even Sigmund Freud, before yielding to the conventions of his time, once recognized the importance of voicing female desire. More recently, Germaine Greer wrote that women's freedom is contingent on a positive definition of female sexuality. But the harsh either-or dichotomy imposed by "slut" precludes self-determination. Just as, at adolescence, girls learn to disconnect from their "bad" feelings, they must also disengage from their "bad" bodies. Quite suddenly, as Simone de Beauvoir has written, "it seems to [a girl] that she has been doubled; instead of coinciding exactly with herself, she now begins to exist *outside*." Evie's own mother, Margaret, has advocated the duality—for her daughter's own good—during what Evie calls "the sex talk." "Your body wants one thing and your mind says another and you'll always feel that way," Margaret told her. It is the girl, she warned, who is "in the driver's seat and she has to make the decisions and it's difficult because your body is telling you, 'Yes, yes, yes, yes, yes, yes, yes! I want to do this, it feels wonderful.' " But the conventional assumption, one that Evie believes, is that a boy cannot be expected to stop, so a girl must listen to her "mind" and say no.

It is difficult to consider allowing girls to unleash their sexuality. Like Evie's mother, many parents and educators believe that we protect our daughters by exacerbating their vulnerability, by instilling them with what we know are the perils of sex: the fears of victimization, of pregnancy, of disease. Those fears are, of course, all too real, but so is desire, and we do not teach girls that. We do not, as a culture, give girls clues as to how to navigate between the two toward a healthy, joyous eroticism, to what Audre Lorde has called "the *yes* within ourselves." Instead we consciously infuse girls with a sense of shame.

Boys have far fewer constraints. At Weston, girls may be "sluts," but boys are "players." Girls are "whores"; boys are "studs." Sex "ruins" girls; it enhances boys. In their youth, they may be snips and snails and puppy dogs' tails, but by adolescence, boys learn that they are "made of" nothing but desire, that, as Naomi Wolf has written, their "sexuality simply *is*": a natural force that girls don't possess. Girls are, in fact, supposed to provide the moral inertia that (temporarily) slows that force. Just as in the classroom, just as in the family, girls' sexual behavior is seen as containable; boys' as inevitable. The Weston girls themselves participate in this dynamic, shunning sexually active girls, but excusing male behavior by saying, "Boys only think with their dicks." But what would ensue if we whispered the truth to girls, if we admitted that their desire could be as powerful as boys'?

In her groundbreaking work on girls' sexuality, psychologist Deborah Tolman points out that encouraging girls to disengage from their appetites not only does them a disservice but is an ineffective strategy for lowering the rates of teen pregnancy and transmission of disease. Banishing sexual feelings dissuades girls from considering the numerous ways *other* than intercourse in which they might explore their desire, ways that might be more appropriate, more fun, and certainly less risky to their health. Evie, for instance, does not suggest to Bradley that, at the age of twelve, they might want to try kissing or even touching before proceeding to intercourse; in the good girl/bad girl construct, sex to Evie means only one thing, "going all the way," and only a slut does it. What's more, Tolman notes that, although negative attitudes toward sexuality rarely deter sexual activity, they do discourage contraceptive use: Responsible preparation for intercourse requires an active admission of desire, something girls have little incentive to make. In fact, if a girl fears that by saying "yes" she may subsequently become a pariah, consent itself becomes a murky issue. Evie, for instance, believes she said "yes" to Bradley, when, in fact, not a word was uttered. Absent a language of female desire, boys like Bradley learn that they may interpret silence and passivity (perhaps even "no") as consent. Sometimes it is; sometimes they intuit incorrectly, and sex becomes coercion or straight-out rape. Yet as long as girls feel they cannot say "yes," boys will continue—unwittingly and willfully—to misconstrue "no." As Tolman says, "I'm uncomfortable with this, but I know in my heart of hearts that 'no' cannot always mean 'no.' How can 'no' always mean 'no' if you're not allowed to say 'yes'?"

## Sex Education: Don't Ask, Don't Tell

Desire and the dynamics of power embedded in it are rarely broached in sex education curricula, especially as it pertains to girls. Educator Michelle Fine has written that boys' desire is included in classrooms, intrinsic to the biological lessons of erections, ejaculation, and wet dreams. Girls' pleasure, however, is evaded, and their sexuality is discussed primarily through the veil of reproduction: the onset of menstruation, the identification of ovaries and the uterus. Desire, as it relates to girls, is reduced in most classrooms to one element: whether to say "yes" or "no"—not even to themselves, but to boys. By emphasizing refusal and ignoring desire, Fine argues, schools contribute to the repression of girls' sexual selves. The "official" version of sexuality that is taught, she says, becomes a discourse "based on the male in search of desire and the female in search of protection."

At Weston Middle School, as in many schools, the community dictates what children may or may not learn in sex education classes. Principal Andrea Murray estimates that 25 percent of the students at Weston are already sexually active. And if "sexually active" is measured solely by engaging in intercourse, that's probably about right: The average age of sexual initiation dropped steadily in the 1980s, and some studies have found that up to 53 percent of middle and junior high school students have had sexual intercourse at least once. If national statistics hold, one out of five of those sexually active girls at Weston will become pregnant before she graduates high school. Yet the sex education curriculum endorsed by the community forbids a discussion of contraception until tenth grade, precisely because of the fear that contraceptive knowledge will promote desire.

Maureen Webster, a young, maternal woman with a throaty voice, teaches the middle school's sex education course, which students take as seventh graders. During the course, she may not mention birth control in class—she is even prohibited from informing her students that condoms are a source of protection against HIV, lest the information in some way sanction homosexuality (activity which, free from the possibility of procreation, is necessarily based on desire).

"It's got to change," she tells me when I visit her classroom one day. "But right now some parents think that if you talk about contraception you're giving the kids a license." Ms. Webster says that if a student specifically asks about condoms, or some other taboo topic, she may answer the question, saying, for instance, "a condom is a sheath that fits over the penis," without revealing its purpose or in any way detailing its proper use. Essentially, though, if Weston's students want to know how to prevent unwanted pregnancy or sexually transmitted diseases, she says, "they have to find it out elsewhere." Ms. Webster says that the Weston community even bridles at her clinical explanation of masturbation, an activity that provides plenty of entertainment without the side effects of either pregnancy or disease. "I try to answer as correctly as I can," she says, "but I know that the parents are concerned. So when some boy asks, 'How do girls masturbate?' I'll say, 'Just as boys can fondle their private areas, likewise a girl can,' and leave it at that."

The curriculum Ms. Webster uses includes a month's worth of lessons, but since the course falls within a larger, quarter-long health class, and time is limited, she usually condenses it into a week or two, which is still somewhat longer than most sex education classes. That leaves one class period each for male and female anatomy and one class period devoted to a lecture on how sexually transmitted diseases are spread (but not how they can be prevented). Given both communal and temporal constraints, a useful discussion of sexual desire—or any talk of sexual

activity that isn't grounded in "consequences"—would be unthinkable. Yet although issues of sexual entitlement are never overtly addressed in Ms. Webster's class, when the bell rings, the power dynamics of "slut" and "stud" are firmly in place.

Ms. Webster had invited me to visit on the fourth day of the sex education unit. The students have already zipped through male and female anatomy, which included a lecture on the female reproductive system but—because there wasn't time for the more comprehensive film Ms. Webster had planned to show—no identification of the clitoris or even the labia. Today, Ms. Webster is trying to illustrate the effect of sleeping with multiple partners on disease transmission. She has passed out a photocopied work sheet which summarizes the symptoms of eight STDs and now stands at the front of the room.

"We'll use a woman," she says, drawing the Greek symbol for woman on the blackboard. "Let's say she is infected, but she hasn't really noticed yet, so she has sex with three men."

Ms. Webster draws three symbols for man on the board, and as she does, a heavy-set boy in a Chicago Bulls cap stagewhispers, "What a slut," and the class titters.

"Okay," says Ms. Webster, who doesn't hear the comment. "Now the first guy has three sexual encounters in six months." She turns to draw three more women's signs, her back to the class, and several of the boys point at themselves proudly, striking exaggerated macho poses.

"The second guy was very active, he had intercourse with five women." As she turns to the diagram again, two boys stand and take bows.

"Now the third guy was smart—he didn't sleep with *anyone*." She draws a happy face and the boys point at each other derisively, mouthing, "You! You!"

During the entire diagramming process, the girls in the class remain silent.

This drama is played out without the teacher's noticing. She goes on to explain the remaining diseases, allotting several minutes to each and ten minutes to AIDS. When the bell rings, the students shove the handout into their backpacks. I doubt whether, in this short time, they've truly learned the risks of disease; but they certainly have been reminded of the rules of desire.

## Objects of Desire

In late October, four sections of Weston's eighth-grade social studies classes are learning about the creation of history by making their own time capsules. Each student contributes a one-page description of an object that she or he thinks will best represent contemporary culture to people in the year 3000. Some of the essays are on neutral topics (since it's almost Halloween, Lindsay, for instance, writes about candy); others describe the scourges of our era, such as AIDS, violence, and drugs. Overwhelmingly, though, the boys in each class have chosen computers, CD players, VCRs, guns, and sports equipment to epitomize the twentieth century. The girls, meanwhile, have chosen clothing, hair-care products, and makeup. One girl even details which colors of which brands are appropriate for specific skin types: "Now for an example, I will tell you what colors will look good on a person such as me, fair complected," she writes, listing products for eyes, cheeks, and lips.

Whether their chosen objects are beneficial or destructive to society, in their essays boys are engaged by action: technology, sports, weapons, musical instruments. The girls take a more passive stance. Their message to the people of the future is that appearance supersedes all else. The symbols of the culture that are the most valuable to them are those that assist in the quest to please others: the objects that will help girls themselves become perfect objects. In the language of the hidden curriculum, the time capsule essays show that, as much as girls repress desire, they embrace desirability. From an early age, girls learn to stand outside of themselves, to disconnect and evaluate themselves as others might. As they mature, then, the question they begin to ask themselves is not whether they *desire* (a notion they quickly suppress) but whether or not someone would desire *them*. The idea, as articulated in the time capsules, is to look sexy, but say "no"; to be feminine, but not sexual; to attract boys' desire, but never to respond to one's own.

When being desirable supplants desiring, sexual activity takes on a frightening dimension: It becomes an attempt to confirm one's self-worth, one's lovability, through someone else. This confused motive only intensifies the conundrum of the "slut": She earns her peers' contempt by engaging in the very activity she believes will bolster her self-respect. It may also, in part, explain why girls who have sex as young teenagers regret their decision at twice the rate of boys, and why, although sexually active girls have lower self-esteem than their nonactive counterparts, boys show no such difference.

Girls emphasize being lovable when they lose faith in their competence. Yet according to *Shortchanging Girls, Shortchanging America*, girls' evaluation of their overall abilities drops sharply in adolescence: The young women surveyed were about half as likely as boys to cite their talents as "the thing I like most about myself," while they were twice as likely as boys to cite an aspect of their appearance. The biggest exception, again, comes among girls who continue to enjoy math and science. Without that fundamental faith in her ability, desirability becomes the central component of a girl's self-image; and the more she invests in her desirability, the more vulnerable she becomes to sexual manipulation.

## Midnight Confessions

It turns out that Evie isn't the only one with a Bradley Davis story. In mid-October, Amy,

Evie, their chum Becca, and a newer friend, Jennifer, attend a slumber party at another girl's house. In the middle of the night, after the prank phone calls, the pizza, the popcorn, and the séances, the girls dim the lights and their talk turns intimate and confessional. Evie confides the secret she's been carrying about her encounters with Bradley, and her friends do not condemn her as she feared. Instead, Amy and Jennifer—who have both had long-term crushes on Bradley—admit that he has approached them too.

After a rehearsal of a school play, Amy says, Bradley came into the area where she was changing. He approached her from behind and slid one hand languorously up her leg, lifting the hem of her slip. Then, he began to slide his other hand under her shirt toward her breast. "I didn't know what to do," she tells me later, "I just stood there. I couldn't even say anything. I didn't want him to do it, but it's like I couldn't talk. Finally I told him to go away and he did, and he didn't speak to me for the rest of the year. And he said that if I told anyone what he'd done, he'd ruin my reputation."

Jennifer is a small, nearly silent girl, the daughter of a Caucasian father and a Chinese American mother who are in the throes of a bitter divorce. Her hair is light brown and falls across one eye like a veil. She says that Bradley calls her when everyone else turns him down. Although she knows she shouldn't, she goes to his house and, as she puts it, lets him "do things to me," which she doesn't enjoy much but thinks will keep his affection. Once, she says, "he put his hand up my shirt, and I said 'no,' but he kept doing it and I was too afraid to stop him because I liked him so much and I wanted him to like me. I thought it would make him like me more if I let him."

Evie and Amy have been "best friends" since sixth grade, but because both have been attracted to Bradley, there has been an undercurrent of jealousy in their relationship. They occasionally spread gossip about each other,

or pass cruel notes; more than once during the year they refuse to speak to one another because of conflicts over boys. But that night, their disclosures brought them closer together. They hugged and cried when they finished their tales, and they hugged Jennifer, too, because, as Amy later said, "we all felt so used." They swore to one another that they were through with Bradley, and vowed to engage in a sort of conspiracy of silence: They will neither confront Bradley nor tell anyone else (even other girls whom he's pursuing) about their experiences with him. The fear of the fallen girl is so strong that every time I ask the girls, individually or together, why they don't challenge Bradley, they react violently: They can't, they say, because, even though they refused him, *their* reputations, not his, are in jeopardy. "The thing is, we don't have control," Evie explains. "He could just say we were asking for it or that we wanted it. Then everyone will think we're sluts."

The girls aren't just guarding their reputations. Secretly, they're also hedging their bets: Since, to varying degrees, male approval determines their self-esteem, none of them is willing to destroy the possibility of a future relationship with Bradley. Later, when we're alone, Amy adds, "I don't know. I still like him." She holds her thumb and forefinger apart, indicating that her feelings are still there, a little bit. "He's really nice when you know him; he's got a cute personality. I can't help it, I still sort of love him."

A few days after her friends' slumber party confessions, Evie and I walk to the park again. The days are beginning to shorten, and it's almost dusk as we settle in to talk. A beat-up brown Camaro pulls up to the curb, some thirty feet away, and continues along at a crawl. The two young men inside, half hidden in shadows, laugh loudly, but we don't turn. Then one yells, "Fucking cunts!" and the car peels out.

"Gross," Evie says, staring blankly after them.

Evie informs me that, since the slumber party, she has made a decision: She is going to remain a virgin until marriage. Sex and what she calls "guys' hormones" are just too volatile, too much "can happen." Yet even with that brave thought, Evie cannot fully insulate herself against desire. Immediately after making her announcement, she adds, "Bradley asked me to have sex with him again. This time I left it at a maybe. I don't know why, I feel ashamed of it. I kept the most control I have so far, but eventually"— she lowers her voice in a husky imitation of Bradley's—"he got into my head and I just said what he wanted me to say." She pauses, and her voice returns to its customary timbre. "He just starts talking, I can't explain it, and your face starts getting hot and you just don't think about what you're saying anymore. My hands start shaking . . . it really bugs me, but I can't stop it. It's not like you're even thinking you should say 'no'; you just automatically say 'yes.' "

# The Presentation of Self in Everyday Life: Selections

*Erving Goffman*

## Introduction

I mean this report to serve as a sort of handbook detailing one sociological perspective from which social life can be studied, especially the kind of social life that is organized within the physical confines of a building or plant. A set of features will be described which together form a framework that can be applied to any concrete social establishment, be it domestic, industrial, or commercial.

The perspective employed in this report is that of the theatrical performance; the principles derived are dramaturgical ones. I shall consider the way in which the individual in ordinary work situations presents himself and his activity to others, the ways in which he guides and controls the impression they form of him, and the kinds of things he may and may not do while sustaining his performance before them. In using this model I will attempt not to make light of its obvious inadequacies. The stage presents things that are make-believe; presumably life presents things that are real and sometimes not well rehearsed. More important, perhaps, on the stage one player presents himself in the guise of a character to characters projected by other

players; the audience constitutes a third party to the interaction—one that is essential and yet, if the stage performance were real, one that would not be there. In real life, the three parties are compressed into two; the part one individual plays is tailored to the parts played by the others present, and yet these others also constitute the audience. Still other inadequacies in this model will be considered later.

The illustrative materials used in this study are of mixed status: some are taken from respectable researches where qualified generalizations are given concerning reliably recorded regularities; some are taken from informal memoirs written by colorful people; many fall in between. In addition, frequent use is made of a study of my own of a Shetland Island crofting (subsistence farming) community.[1] The justification for this approach (as I take to be the justification for Simmel's also) is that the illustrations together fit into a coherent framework that ties together bits of experience the reader has already had and provides the student with a guide worth testing in case-studies of institutional social life. . . .

. . .

When an individual enters the presence of others, they commonly seek to acquire information about him or to bring into play information about him already possessed. They will be interested in his general socio-economic status his conception of self, his attitude toward them, his competence, his trustworthiness, etc. Although some of this information seems to be sought almost as an end in itself, there are usually quite practical reasons for acquiring it. Information about the individual helps to define the situation, enabling others to know in advance what he will expect of them and what they may expect of him. Informed in these ways, the others will know how best to act in order to call forth a desired response from him.

For those present, many sources of information become accessible and many carriers (or "sign-vehicles") become available for conveying this information. If unacquainted with the individual, observers can glean clues from his conduct and appearance which allow them to apply their previous experience with individuals roughly similar to the one before them or, more important, to apply untested stereotypes to him. They can also assume from past experience that only individuals of a particular kind are likely to be found in a given social setting. They can rely on what the individual says about himself or on documentary evidence he provides as to who and what he is. If they know, or know of, the individual by virtue of experience prior to the interaction, they can rely on assumptions as to the persistence and generality of psychological traits as a means of predicting his present and future behavior.

However, during the period in which the individual is in the immediate presence of the others, few events may occur which directly provide the others with the conclusive information they will need if they are to direct wisely their own activity. Many crucial facts lie beyond the time and place of interaction or be concealed within it. For example, the "true" or "real" attitudes, beliefs, and emotions of the individual can be ascertained only indirectly, through his avowals or through what appears to be involuntary expressive behavior. Similarly, if the individual offers the others a product or service, they will often find that during the interaction there will be no time and place immediately available for eating the pudding that the proof can be found in. They will be forced to accept some events as conventional or natural signs of something not directly available to the senses. In Ichheiser's terms,[2] the individual will have to act so that he intentionally or unintentionally *expresses* himself, and the others will in turn have to be *impressed* in some way by him.

The expressiveness of the individual (and therefore his capacity to give impressions) appears to involve two radically different kinds of sign activity: the expression that he *gives*, and the expression that he *gives off*. The first involves verbal symbols or their substitutes which he uses admittedly and solely to convey the information that he and the others are known to attach to these symbols. This is communication in the traditional and narrow sense. The second involves a wide range of action that others can treat as symptomatic of the actor, the expectation being that the action was performed for reasons other than the information conveyed in this way. As we shall have to see, this distinction has an only initial validity. The individual does of course intentionally convey misinformation by means of both of these types of communication, the first involving deceit, the second feigning.

Taking communication in both its narrow and broad sense, one finds that when the individual is in the immediate presence of others, his activity will have a promissory character. The others are likely to find that they must accept the individual on faith, offering him a just return while he is present before them in exchange for something whose true value will not be established until after he has left their presence. (Of course, the others also live by inference in their dealings with the physical world, but it is only in the world of social interaction that the objects about which they make inferences will purposely facilitate and hinder this inferential process.) The security that they justifiably feel in making inferences about the individual will vary, of course, depending on such factors as the amount of information they already possess about him, but no amount of such past evidence can entirely obviate the necessity of acting on the basis of inferences. As William I. Thomas suggested:

It is also highly important for us to realize that we do not as a matter of fact lead our lives, make our decisions, and reach our goals in everyday life either statistically or scientifically. We live by inference. I am, let us say, your guest. You do not know, you cannot determine scientifically, that I will not steal your money or your spoons. But inferentially I will not and inferentially you have me as a guest.[3]

Let us now turn from the others to the point of view of the individual who presents himself before them. He may wish them to think highly of him, or to think that he thinks highly of them, or to perceive how in fact he feels toward them, or to obtain no clear-cut impression; he may wish to ensure sufficient harmony so that the interaction can be sustained, or to defraud, get rid of, confuse, mislead, antagonize, or insult them. Regardless of the particular objective which the individual has in mind and of his motive for having this objective, it will be in his interests to control the conduct of the others, especially their responsive treatment of him.[4] This control is achieved largely by influencing the definition of the situation which the others come to formulate, and he can influence this definition by expressing himself in such a way as to give them the kind of impression that will lead them to act voluntarily in accordance with his own plan. Thus, when an individual appears in the presence of others, there will usually be some reason for him to mobilize his activity so that it will convey an impression to others which it is in his interests to convey. Since a girl's dormitory mates will glean evidence of her popularity from the calls she receives on the phone, we can suspect that some girls will arrange for calls to be made, and Willard Waller's finding can be anticipated:

It has been reported by many observers that a girl who is called to the telephone in the dormitories will often allow herself to be called several times, in order to give all the other girls ample opportunity to hear her paged.[5]

Of the two lands of communication—expressions given and expressions given off—this report will be primarily concerned with the latter, with the more theatrical and contextual kind, the nonverbal, presumably unintentional kind, whether this communication be purposely engineered or not. As an example of what we must try to examine, I would like to cite at length a novelistic incident in which Preedy, a vacationing Englishman, makes his first appearance on the beach of his summer hotel in Spain:

But in any case he took care to avoid catching anyone's eye. First of all, he had to make it clear to those potential companions of his holiday that they were of no concern to him whatsoever. He stared through them, round them, over them— eyes lost in space. The beach might have been empty. If by chance a ball was thrown his way, he looked surprised; then let a smile of amusement lighten his face (Kindly Preedy), looked round dazed to see that there *were* people on the beach, tossed it back with a smile to himself and not a smile *at* the people, and then resumed carelessly his nonchalant survey of space.

But it was time to institute a little parade, the parade of the Ideal Preedy. By devious handlings he gave any who wanted to look a chance to see the title of his book—a Spanish translation of Homer, classic thus, but not daring, cosmopolitan too—and then gathered together his beach-wrap and bag into a neat sand-resistant pile (Methodical and Sensible Preedy), rose slowly to stretch at ease his huge frame (Big-Cat Preedy), and tossed aside his sandals (Carefree Preedy, after all).

The marriage of Preedy and the sea! There were alternative rituals. The first involved the stroll that turns into a run and a dive straight into the water, thereafter smoothing into a strong splashless crawl towards the horizon. But of course not really to the horizon. Quite suddenly he would turn on to his back and thrash great white splashes with his legs, somehow thus showing that he could have swum further had he wanted to, and then would stand up a quarter out of water for all to see who it was.

The alternative course was simpler, it avoided the cold-water shock and it avoided the risk of appearing too high-spirited. The point was to appear to be so used to the sea, the Mediterranean, and this particular beach, that one might as well be in the sea as out of it. It involved a slow stroll down and into the edge of the water—not even noticing his toes were wet, land and water all the same to *him!*—with his eyes up at the sky gravely surveying portents, invisible to others, of the weather (Local Fisherman Preedy).[6]

The novelist means us to see that Preedy is improperly concerned with the extensive impressions he feels his sheer bodily action is giving off to those around him. We can malign Preedy further by assuming that he has acted merely in order to give a particular impression, that this is a false impression, and that the others present receive either no impression at all, or, worse still, the impression that Preedy is affectedly trying to cause them to receive this particular impression. But the important point for us here is that the kind of impression Preedy thinks he is making is in fact the kind of impression that others correctly and incorrectly glean from someone in their midst.

I have said that when an individual appears before others his actions will influence the definition of the situation which they come to have. Sometimes the individual will act in a thoroughly calculating manner, expressing himself in a given way solely in order to give the kind of impression to others that is likely to evoke from them a specific response he is concerned to obtain. Sometimes the individual will be calculating in his activity but be relatively unaware that this is the case. Sometimes he will intentionally and consciously express himself in a particular way, but chiefly because the tradition of his group or social status require this kind of expression and not because of any particular response (other than vague acceptance or approval) that is likely to be evoked from those impressed by the expression. Sometimes the

traditions of an individual's role will lead him to give a well-designed impression of a particular kind and yet he may be neither consciously nor unconsciously disposed to create such an impression. The others, in their turn, may be suitably impressed by the individual's efforts to convey something, or may misunderstand the situation and come to conclusions that are warranted neither by the individual's intent nor by the facts. In any case, in so far as the others act *as if* the individual had conveyed a particular impression, we may take a functional or pragmatic view and say that the individual has "effectively" projected a given definition of the situation and "effectively" fostered the understanding that a given state of affairs obtains.

There is one aspect of the others' response that bears special comment here. Knowing that the individual is likely to present himself in a light that is favorable to him, the others may divide what they witness into two parts; a part that is relatively easy for the individual to manipulate at will, being chiefly his verbal assertions, and a part in regard to which he seems to have little concern or control, being chiefly derived from the expressions he gives off. The others may then use what are considered to be the ungovernable aspects of his expressive behavior as a check upon the validity of what is conveyed by the governable aspects. In this a fundamental asymmetry is demonstrated in the communication process, the individual presumably being aware of only one stream of his communication, the witnesses of this stream and one other. For example, in Shetland Isle one crofter wife, in serving native dishes to a visitor from the mainland of Britain, would listen with a polite smile to his polite claims of liking what he was eating; at the same time she would take note of the rapidity with which the visitor lifted his fork or spoon to his mouth, the eagerness with which he passed food into his mouth, and the gusto expressed in chewing the food, using these signs as a check on the stated feelings of the eater. The same woman, in order to discover what one acquaintance (A) "actually" thought of another acquaintance (B), would wait until B was in the presence of A but engaged in conversation with still another person (C). She would then covertly examine the facial expressions of A as he regarded B in conversation with C. Not being in conversation with B, and not being directly observed by him, A would sometimes relax usual constraints and tactful deceptions, and freely express what he was "actually" feeling about B. This Shetlander, in short, would observe the unobserved observer.

Now given the fact that others are likely to check up on the more controllable aspects of behavior by means of the less controllable, one can expect that sometimes the individual will try to exploit this very possibility, guiding the impression he makes through behavior felt to be reliably informing.[7] For example, in gaining admission to a tight social circle, the participant observer may not only wear an accepting look while listening to an informant, but may also be careful to wear the same look when observing the informant talking to others; observers of the observer will then not as easily discover where he actually stands. A specific illustration may be cited from Shetland Isle. When a neighbor dropped in to have a cup of tea, he would ordinarily wear at least a hint of an expectant warm smile as he passed through the door into the cottage. Since lack of physical obstructions outside the cottage and lack of light within it usually made it possible to observe the visitor unobserved as he approached the house, Islanders sometimes took pleasure in watching the visitor drop whatever expression he was manifesting and replace it with a sociable one just before reaching the door. However, some visitors, in appreciating that this examination was occurring, would blindly adopt a social face a long distance from the house, thus ensuring the projection of a constant image.

This kind of control upon the part of the individual reinstates the symmetry of the

communication process, and sets the stage for a kind of information game—a potentially infinite cycle of concealment, discovery, false revelation, and rediscovery. It should be added that since the others are likely to be relatively unsuspicious of the presumably unguided aspect of the individual's conduct, he can gain much by controlling it. The others of course may sense that the individual is manipulating the presumably spontaneous aspects of his behavior, and seek in this very act of manipulation some shading of conduct that the individual has not managed to control. This again provides a check upon the individual's behavior, this time his presumably uncalculated behavior, thus reestablishing the asymmetry of the communication process. . . .

When we allow that the individual projects a definition of the situation when he appears before others, we must also see that the others, however passive their role may seem to be, will themselves effectively project a definition of the situation by virtue of their response to the individual and by virtue of any lines of action they initiate to him. Ordinarily the definitions of the situation projected by the several different participants are sufficiently attuned to one another so that open contradiction will not occur. I do not mean that there will be the kind of consensus that arises when each individual present candidly expresses what he really feels and honestly agrees with the expressed feelings of the others present. This kind of harmony is an optimistic ideal and in any case not necessary for the smooth working of society. Rather, each participant is expected to suppress his immediate heartfelt feelings, conveying a view of the situation which he feels the others will be able to find at least temporarily acceptable. The maintenance of this surface of agreement, this veneer of consensus, is facilitated by each participant concealing his own wants behind statements which assert values to which everyone present feels obliged to give lip service. Further, there is usually a kind of division of definitional labor. Each participant is allowed to establish the tentative official ruling regarding matters which are vital to him but not immediately important to others, e.g., the rationalizations and justifications by which he accounts for his past activity. In exchange for this courtesy he remains silent or noncommittal on matters important to others but not immediately important to him. We have then a kind of interactional *modus vivendi*. Together the participants contribute to a single over-all definition of the situation which involves not so much a real agreement as to what exists but rather a real agreement as to whose claims concerning what issues will be temporarily honored. Real agreement will also exist concerning the desirability of avoiding an open conflict of definitions of the situation.[8] I will refer to this level of agreement as a "working consensus." It is to be understood that the working consensus established in one interaction setting will be quite different in content from the working consensus established in a different type of setting. Thus, between two friends at lunch, a reciprocal show of affection, respect, and concern for the other is maintained. In service occupations, on the other hand, the specialist often maintains an image of disinterested involvement in the problem of the client, while the client responds with a show of respect for the competence and integrity of the specialist. Regardless of such differences in content however, the general form of these working arrangements is the same. . . .

In everyday life, of course, there is a clear understanding that first impressions are important. Thus, the work adjustment of those in service occupations will often hinge upon a capacity to seize and hold the initiative in the service relation, a capacity that will require subtle aggressiveness on the part of the server when he is of lower socio-economic status than his client. W. F. Whyte suggests the waitress as an example:

> The first point that stands out is that the waitress who bears up under pressure does not sim-

ply respond to her customers. She acts with some skill to control their behavior. The first question to ask when we look at the customer relationship is, "Does the waitress get the jump on the customer, or does the customer get the jump on the waitress?" The skilled waitress realizes the crucial nature of this question. . . .

> The skilled waitress tackles the customer with confidence and without hesitation. For example, she may find that a new customer has seated himself before she could clear off the dirty dishes and change the cloth. He is now leaning on the table studying the menu. She greets him, says, "May I change the cover, please?" and, without waiting for an answer, takes his menu away from him so that he moves back from the table, and she goes about her work. The relationship is handled politely but firmly, and there is never any question as to who is in charge.[9]

When the interaction that is initiated by "first impressions" is itself merely the initial interaction in an extended series of interactions involving the same participants, we speak of "getting off on the right foot" and feel that it is crucial that we do so. Thus, one learns that some teachers take the following view:

> You can't ever let them get the upper hand on you or you're through. So I start out tough. The first day I get a new class in, I let them know who's boss . . . you've got to start off tough, then you can ease up as you go along. If you start out easy-going, when you try to get tough, they'll just look at you and laugh.[10]

Similarly, attendants in mental institutions may feel that if the new patient is sharply put in his place the first day on the ward and made to see who is boss, much future difficulty will be prevented.[11]

Given the fact that the individual effectively projects a definition of the situation when he enters the presence of others, we can assume that events may occur within the interaction which contradict, discredit, or otherwise throw doubt upon this projection. When these disruptive events occur, the interaction itself may come to a confused and embarrassed halt. Some of the assumptions upon which the responses of the participants had been predicated become untenable, and the participants find themselves lodged in an interaction for which the situation has been wrongly defined and is now no longer defined. At such moments the individual whose presentation has been discredited may feel ashamed while the others present may feel hostile, and all the participants may come to feel ill at ease, nonplussed, out of countenance, embarrassed, experiencing the kind of anomy that is generated when the minute social system of face-to-face interaction breaks down. . . .

We find that preventive practices are constantly employed to avoid these embarrassments and that corrective practices are constantly employed to compensate for discrediting occurrences that have not been successfully avoided. When the individual employs these strategies and tactics to protect his own projections, we may refer to them as "defensive practices"; when a participant employs them to save the definition of the situation projected by another, we speak of "protective practices" or "tact." Together, defensive and protective practices comprise the techniques employed to safeguard the impression fostered by an individual during his presence before others. It should be added that while we may be ready to see that no fostered impression would survive if defensive practices were not employed, we are less ready perhaps to see that few impressions could survive if those who received the impression did not exert tact in their reception of it.

In addition to the fact that precautions are taken to prevent disruption of projected definitions, we may also note that an intense interest in these disruptions comes to play a significant role in the social life of the group. Practical jokes and social games are played in which embarrassments which are to be taken unseriously are purposely engineered.[12] Fantasies are created in which devastating exposures occur. Anecdotes from the past—real, embroidered, or fictitious— are told and retold, detailing disruptions which occurred, almost occurred, or occurred and were admirably resolved. There seems to be no grouping which does not have a ready supply of these games, reveries, and cautionary tales, to be used as a source of humor, a catharsis for anxieties, and a sanction for inducing individuals to be modest in their claims and reasonable in their projected expectations. The individual may tell himself through dreams of getting into impossible positions. Families tell of the time a guest got his dates mixed and arrived when neither the house nor anyone in it was ready for him. Journalists tell of times when an all-too-meaningful misprint occurred, and the papers assumption of objectivity or decorum was humorously discredited. Public servants tell of times a client ridiculously misunderstood form instructions, giving answers which implied an unanticipated and bizarre definition of the situation.[13] Seamen, whose home away from home is rigorously he-man, tell stories of coming back home and inadvertently asking mother to "pass the fucking butter."[14] Diplomats tell of the time a near-sighted queen asked a republican ambassador about the health of his king.[15]

To summarize, then, I assume that when an individual appears before others he will have many motives for trying to control the impression they receive of the situation. This report is concerned with some of the common techniques that persons employ to sustain such impressions and with some of the common contingencies associated with the employment of these techniques. The specific content of any activity presented by the individual participant, or the role it plays in the interdependent activities of an ongoing social system, will not be at issue; I shall be concerned only with the participant's dramaturgical problems of presenting the activity before others. The issues dealt with by stagecraft and stage management are sometimes trivial but they are quite general; they seem to occur everywhere in social life, providing a clear-cut dimension for formal sociological analysis.

It will be convenient to end this introduction with some definitions that are implied in what has gone before and required for what is to follow. For the purpose of this report, interaction (that is, face-to-face interaction) may be roughly defined as the reciprocal influence of individuals upon one another's actions when in one another's immediate physical presence. *An* interaction may be defined as all the interaction which occurs throughout any one occasion when a given set of individuals are in one another's continuous presence; the term "an encounter" would do as well. A "performance" may be defined as all the activity of a given participant on a given occasion which serves to influence in any way any of the other participants. Taking a particular participant and his performance as a basic point of reference, we may refer to those who contribute the other performances as the audience, observers, or co-participants. The pre-established pattern of action which is unfolded during a performance and which may be presented or played *through* on other occasions may be called a "part" or "routine."[16] These situational terms can easily be related to conventional structural ones. When an individual or performer plays the same part to the same audience on different occasions, a social relationship is likely to arise. Defining social role as the enactment of rights and duties attached to a given status, we can say that a social role will involve one or more parts and that each of these different parts may be presented by the performer on a series of occasions to the same kinds of audience or to an audience of the same persons. . . .

## Performances

### Front

I [use] the term "performance" to refer to all the activity of an individual which occurs during a period marked by his continuous presence before a particular set of observers and which has some influence on the observers. It will be convenient to label as "front" that part of the individual's performance which regularly functions in a general and fixed fashion to define the situation for those who observe the performance. Front, then, is the expressive equipment of a standard kind intentionally or unwittingly employed by the individual during his performance. For preliminary purposes, it will be convenient to distinguish and label what seem to be the standard parts of front.

First, there is the "setting," involving furniture, décor, physical layout, and other background items which supply the scenery and stage props for the spate of human action played out before, within, or upon it. A setting tends to stay put, geographically speaking, so that those who would use a particular setting as part of their performance cannot begin their act until they have brought themselves to the appropriate place and must terminate their performance when they leave it. It is only in exceptional circumstances that the setting follows along with the performers; we see this in the funeral cortège, the civic parade, and the dreamlike processions that kings and queens are made of. In the main, these exceptions seem to offer some kind of extra protection for performers who are, or who have momentarily become, highly sacred. . . .

It is sometimes convenient to divide the stimuli which make up personal front into "appearance" and "manner," according to the function performed by the information that these stimuli convey. "Appearance" may be taken to refer to those stimuli *which* function at the time to tell us of the performer's social statuses. These stimuli also tell us of the individual's temporary ritual state, that is, whether he is engaging in formal social activity, work, or informal recreation, whether or not he is celebrating a new phase in the season cycle or in his life-cycle. "Manner" may be taken to refer to those stimuli which function at the time to warn us of the interaction role the performer will expect to play in the oncoming situation. Thus a haughty, aggressive manner may give the impression that the performer expects to be the one who will initiate the verbal interaction and direct its course. A meek, apologetic manner may give the impression that the performer expects to follow the lead of others, or at least that he can be led to do so. . . .

### Dramatic Realization

While in the presence of others, the individual typically infuses his activity with signs which dramatically highlight and portray confirmatory facts that might otherwise remain unapparent or obscure. For if the individual's activity is to become significant to others, he must mobilize his activity so that it will express *during the interaction* what he wishes to convey. In fact, the performer may be required not only to express his claimed capacities during the interaction but also to do so during a split second in the interaction. Thus, if a baseball umpire is to give the impression that he is sure of his judgment, he must forgo the moment of thought which might make him sure of his judgment; he must give an instantaneous decision so that the audience will be sure that he is sure of his judgment.[17] . . .

Similarly, the proprietor of a service establishment may find it difficult to dramatize what is actually being done for clients because the clients cannot "see" the overhead costs of the service rendered them. Undertakers must therefore charge a great deal for their highly visible product—a coffin that has been transformed into a casket—because many of the other costs of conducting a funeral are ones that cannot be readily dramatized.[18] Merchants, too, find that they must charge high prices for things that look intrinsically inexpensive in order to compensate the establishment for expensive things like insurance, slack periods, etc., that never appear before the customers' eyes. . . .

### Idealization

. . . I want to consider here another important aspect of this socialization process—the tendency for performers to offer their observers an impression that is idealized in several different ways.

The notion that a performance presents an idealized view of the situation is, of course, quite common. Cooley's view may be taken as an illustration:

> If we never tried to seem a little better than we are, how could we improve or "train ourselves from the outside inward?" And the same impulse to show the world a better or idealized aspect of ourselves finds an organized expression in the various professions and classes, each of which has to some extent a cant or pose, which its members assume unconsciously, for the most part, but which has the effect of a conspiracy to work upon the credulity of the rest of the world. There is a cant not only of theology and of philanthropy, but also of law, medicine, teaching, even of science—perhaps especially of science, just now, since the more a particular kind of merit is recognized and admired, the more it is likely to be assumed by the unworthy.[19]

Thus, when the individual presents himself before others, his performance will tend to incorporate and exemplify the officially accredited values of the society, more so, in fact, than does his behavior as a whole.

To the degree that a performance highlights the common official values of the society in which it occurs, we may look upon it, in the manner of Durkheim and Radcliffe-Brown, as a ceremony—as an expressive rejuvenation and reaffirmation of the moral values of the community. Furthermore, insofar as the expressive bias of performances comes to be accepted as reality, then that which is accepted at the moment as reality will have some of the characteristics of a celebration. To stay in one's room away from the place where the party is given, or away from where the practitioner attends his client, is to stay away from where reality is being performed. The world, in truth, is a wedding.

One of the richest sources of data on the presentation of idealized performances is the literature on social mobility. In most societies there seems to be a major or general system of stratification, and in most stratified societies there is an idealization of the higher strata and some aspiration on the part of those in low places to move to higher ones. (One must be careful to appreciate that this involves not merely a desire for a prestigeful place but also a desire for a place close to the sacred center of the common values of the society.) Commonly we find that upward mobility involves the presentation of proper performances and that efforts to move upward and efforts to keep from moving downward are expressed in terms of sacrifices made for the maintenance of front. Once the proper sign-equipment has been obtained and familiarity gained in the management of it, then this equipment can be used to embellish and illumine one's daily performances with a favorable social style.

Perhaps the most important piece of sign-equipment associated with social class consists of the status symbols through which material wealth is expressed. American society is similar to others in this regard but seems to have been singled out as an extreme example of wealth-oriented class structure—perhaps because in America the license to employ symbols of wealth and financial capacity to do so are so widely distributed. . . .

### [Negative Idealization]

In fact, however, many classes of persons have had many different reasons for exercising systematic modesty and for underplaying any expressions of wealth, capacity, spiritual strength, or self-respect.

The ignorant, shiftless, happy-go-lucky manner which Negroes in the Southern states sometimes felt obliged to affect during interaction with whites illustrates how a performance can play up ideal values which accord to the performer a lower position than he covertly accepts for himself. . . .

American college girls did, and no doubt do, play down their intelligence, skills, and determinativeness when in the presence of datable boys, thereby manifesting a profound psychic discipline in spite of their international reputation for flightiness.[20] These performers are reported to allow their boy friends to explain things to them tediously that they already know; they conceal proficiency in mathematics from their less able consorts; they lose ping-pong games just before the ending:

"One of the nicest techniques is to spell long words incorrectly once in a while. My boy friend seems to get a great kick out of it and writes back, 'Honey, you certainly don't know how to spell.'"[21]

Through all of this the natural superiority of the male is demonstrated, and the weaker role of the female affirmed. . . .

### Mystification

I have suggested ways in which the performance of an individual accentuates certain matters and conceals others. If we see perception as a form of contact and communion, then control over what is perceived is control over contact that is made, and the limitation and regulation of what is shown is a limitation and regulation of contact. There is a relation here between informational terms and ritual ones. Failure to regulate the information acquired by the audience involves possible disruption of the projected definition of the situation; failure to regulate contact involves possible ritual contamination of the performer.

It is a widely held notion that restrictions placed upon contact, the maintenance of social distance, provide a way in which awe can be generated and sustained in the audience—a way, as Kenneth Burke has said, in which the audience can be held in a state of mystification in regard to the performer. Cooley's statement may serve as an illustration:

How far it is possible for a man to work upon others through a false idea of himself depends upon a variety of circumstances. As already pointed out, the man himself may be a mere incident with no definite relation to the idea of him, the latter being a separate product of the imagination. This can hardly be except where there is no immediate contact between leader and follower, and partly explains why authority, especially if it covers intrinsic personal weakness, has always a tendency to surround itself with forms and artificial mystery, whose object is to prevent familiar contact and so give the imagination a chance to idealize. . . . The discipline of armies and navies, for instance, very distinctly recognizes the necessity of those forms which separate superior from inferior, and so help to establish an unscrutinized ascendancy in the former. In the same way manners, as Professor Ross remarks in his work on Social Control, are largely used by men of the world as a means of self-concealment, and this self-concealment serves, among other purposes, that of preserving a sort of ascendancy over the unsophisticated.[22]

Ponsonby, in giving advice to the King of Norway, gives voice to the same theory:

One night King Haakon told me of his difficulties in face of the republican leanings of the opposition and how careful in consequence he had to be in all he did and said. He intended, he said, to go as much as possible among the people and thought it would be popular if, instead of going in a motor car, he and Queen Maud were to use the tramways.

I told him frankly that I thought this would be a great mistake as familiarity bred contempt. As a naval officer he would know that the captain of a ship never had his meals with the other officers but remained quite aloof. This was, of course, to stop any familiarity with them. I told him that he must get up on a pedestal and remain there. He could then step off occasionally and no harm would be done. The people didn't want a King with whom they could hob-nob but something nebulous like the Delphic oracle. The Monarchy was really the creation of each individual's brain. Every man liked to think what he would do, if he was King. People invested the Monarch with every conceivable virtue and talent. They were bound therefore to be disappointed if they saw

him going about like an ordinary man in the street.[23]

The logical extreme implied in this kind of theory, whether it is in fact correct or not, is to prohibit the audience from looking at the performer at all, and at times when celestial qualities and powers have been claimed by a performer, this logical conclusion seems to have been put into effect.

Of course, in the matter of keeping social distance, the audience itself will often cooperate by acting in a respectful fashion, in awed regard for the sacred integrity imputed to the performer. As Simmel suggests:

To act upon the second of these decisions corresponds to the feeling (which also operates elsewhere) that an ideal sphere lies around every human being. Although differing in size in various directions and differing according to the person with whom one entertains relations, this sphere cannot be penetrated, unless the personality value of the individual is thereby destroyed. A sphere of this sort is placed around man by his "honor." Language very poignantly designates an insult to one's honor as "coming too close": the radius of this sphere marks, as it were, the distance whose trespassing by another person insults one's honor.[24]

Durkheim makes a similar point:

The human personality is a sacred thing; one does not violate it nor infringe its bounds, while at the same time the greatest good is in communion with others.[25]

It must be made quite clear, in contradiction to the implications of Cooley's remarks, that awe and distance are felt toward performers of equal and inferior status as well as (albeit not as much) toward performers of superordinate status.

Whatever their function for the audience, these inhibitions of the audience allow the performer some elbow room in building up an impression of his own choice and allow him to function, for his own good or the audience's, as a protection or a threat that close inspection would destroy.

I would like, finally, to add that the matters which the audience leave alone because of their awe of the performer are likely to be the matters about which he would feel shame were a disclosure to occur. As Riezler has suggested, we have, then, a basic social coin, with awe on one side and shame on the other.[26] The audience senses secret mysteries and powers behind the performance, and the performer senses that his chief secrets are petty ones. As countless folk tales and initiation rites show, often the real secret behind the mystery is that there really is no mystery; the real problem is to prevent the audience from learning this too.

### Reality and Contrivance

In our own Anglo-American culture there seems to be two common-sense models according to which we formulate our conceptions of behavior: the real, sincere, or honest performance; and the false one that thorough fabricators assemble for us, whether meant to be taken unseriously, as in the work of stage actors, or seriously, as in the work of confidence men. We tend to see real performances as something not purposely put together at all, being an unintentional product of the individual's unselfconscious response to the facts in his situation. And contrived performances we tend to see as something painstakingly pasted together, one false item on another, since there is no reality to which the items of behavior could be a direct response. It will be necessary to see now that these dichotomous conceptions are by way of being the ideology of honest performers, providing strength to the show they put on, but a poor analysis of it.

First, let it be said that there are many individuals who sincerely believe that the definition of the situation they habitually project is the real reality. In this report I do not mean to question their proportion in the population but rather the structural relation of their sincerity to the performances they offer. If a performance is to come off, the witnesses by and large must be able to believe that the performers are sincere. This is the structural place of sincerity in the drama of events. Performers may be sincere—or be insincere but sincerely convinced of their own sincerity—but this kind of affection for one's part is not necessary for its convincing performance. There are not many French cooks who are really Russian spies, and perhaps there are not many women who play the part of wife to one man and mistress to another but these duplicities do occur, often being sustained successfully for long periods of time. This suggests that while persons usually are what they appear to be, such appearances could still have been managed. There is, then, a statistical relation between appearances and reality, not an intrinsic or necessary one. In fact, given the unanticipated threats that play upon a performance, and given the need (later to be discussed) to maintain solidarity with one's fellow performers and some distance from the witnesses, we find that a rigid incapacity to depart from one's inward view of reality may at times endanger one's performance. Some performances are carried off successfully with complete dishonesty, others with complete honesty; but for performances in general neither of these extremes is essential and neither, perhaps, is dramaturgically advisable.

The implication here is that an honest, sincere, serious performance is less firmly connected with the solid world than one might first assume. And this implication will be strengthened if we look again at the distance usually placed between quite honest performances and quite contrived ones. In this connection take, for example, the remarkable phenomenon of stage acting. It does take deep skill, long training, and psychological capacity to become a good stage actor. But this fact should not blind us to another one: that almost anyone can quickly learn a script well enough to give a charitable audience some sense of realness in what is being contrived before them. And it seems this is so because ordinary social intercourse is itself put together as a scene is put together, by the exchange of dramatically inflated actions, counteractions, and terminating replies. Scripts even in the hands of unpracticed players can come to life because life itself is a dramatically enacted thing. All the world is not, of course, a stage, but the crucial ways in which it isn't are not easy to specify. . . .

When the individual does move into a new position in society and obtains a new part to perform, he is not likely to be told in full detail how to conduct himself, nor will the facts of his new situation press sufficiently on him from the start to determine his conduct without his further giving thought to it. Ordinarily he will be given only a few cues, hints, and stage directions, and it will be assumed that he already has in his repertoire a large number of bits and pieces of performances that will be required in the new setting. The individual will already have a fair idea of what modesty, deference, or righteous indignation looks like, and can make a pass at playing these bits when necessary. He may even be able to play out the part of a hypnotic subject[27] or commit a "compulsive" crime[28] on the basis of models for these activities that he is already familiar with.

A theatrical performance or a staged confidence game requires a thorough scripting of the spoken content of the routine; but the vast part involving "expression given off" is often determined by meager stage directions. It is expected that the performer of illusions will already know a good deal about how to manage his voice, his face, and his body, although he—as well as any person who directs him—may find it difficult indeed to provide a detailed verbal statement of this kind of knowledge. And in this, of course, we approach the situation of the straightforward man in the street. Socialization may not so much involve a learning of the many specific details of a single concrete part—often there could not be enough time or energy for this. What does seem to be required of the individual is that he learn enough pieces of expression to be able to "fill in" and manage, more or less, any part that he is likely to be given. The legitimate performances of everyday life are not "acted" or "put on" in the sense that the performer knows in advance just what he is going to do, and does this solely because of the effect it is likely to have. The expressions it is felt he is giving off will be especially "inaccessible" to him.[29] But as in the case of less legitimate performers, the incapacity of the ordinary individual to formulate in advance the movements of his eyes and body does not mean that he will not express himself through these devices in a way that is dramatized and pre-formed in his repertoire of actions. In short, we all act better than we know how.

When we watch a television wrestler gouge, foul, and snarl at his opponent we are quite ready to see that, in spite of the dust, he is, and knows he is, merely playing at being the "heavy," and that in another match he may be given the other role, that of clean-cut wrestler, and perform this with equal verve and proficiency. We seem less ready to see, however, that while such details as the number and character of the falls may be fixed beforehand, the details of the expressions and movements used do not come from a script but from command of an idiom, a command that is exercised from moment to moment with little calculation or forethought. . . .

## Conclusion

### The Framework

A social establishment is any place surrounded by fixed barriers to perception in which a particular kind of activity regularly takes place. I have suggested that any social establishment may be studied profitably from the point of view of impression management. Within the walls of a social establishment we find a team of performers who cooperate to present to an audience a given definition of the situation. This will include the conception of own team and of audience and assumptions concerning the ethos that is to be maintained by rules of politeness and decorum. We often find a division into back region, where the performance of a routine is prepared, and front region, where the performance is presented. Access to these regions is controlled in order to prevent the audience from seeing backstage and to prevent outsiders from coming into a performance that is not addressed to them. Among members of the team we find that familiarity prevails, solidarity is likely to develop, and that secrets that could give the show away are shared and kept. A tacit agreement is maintained between performers and audience to act as if a given degree of opposition and of accord existed between them. Typically, but not always, agreement is stressed and opposition is underplayed. The resulting working consensus tends to be contradicted by the attitude toward the audience which the performers express in the absence of the audience and by carefully controlled communication out of character conveyed by the performers while the audience is present. We find that discrepant roles develop: Some of the individuals who are apparently teammates, or audience, or outsiders acquire information about the performance and relations to the team which are not apparent and which complicate the problem of putting on a show. Sometimes disruptions occur through unmeant gestures, faux pas, and scenes, thus discrediting or contradicting the definition of the situation that is being maintained. The mythology of the team will dwell upon these disruptive events. We find that performers, audience, and outsiders all utilize techniques for saving the show, whether by avoiding likely disruptions or by correcting for unavoided ones, or by making it possible for others to do so. To ensure that these techniques will be employed, the team will tend to select members who are loyal, disciplined, and circumspect, and to select an audience that is tactful.

These features and elements, then, comprise the framework I claim to be characteristic of much social interaction as it occurs in natural settings in our Anglo-American society. This framework is formal and abstract in the sense that it can be applied to any social establishment; it is not, however, merely a static classification. The framework bears upon dynamic issues created by the motivation to sustain a definition of the situation that has been projected before others. . . .

### Personality-Interaction-Society

In recent years there have been elaborate attempts to bring into one framework the concepts and findings derived from three different areas of inquiry: the individual personality, social interaction, and society. I would like to suggest here a simple addition to these inter-disciplinary attempts.

When an individual appears before others, he knowingly and unwittingly projects a definition of the situation, of which a conception of himself is an important part. When an event occurs which is expressively incompatible with this fostered impression, significant consequences are simultaneously felt in three levels of social reality, each of which involves a different point of reference and a different order of fact.

First, the social interaction, treated here as a dialogue between two teams may come to an embarrassed and confused halt; the situation may cease to be defined. Previous positions may become no longer tenable, and participants may find themselves without a charted course of action. The participants typically sense a false note in the situation and come to feel awkward, flustered, and, literally, out of countenance. In other words, the minute social system created and sustained by orderly social interaction becomes disorganized. These are the consequences that the disruption has from the point of view of social interaction.

Secondly, in addition to these disorganizing consequences for action at the moment, performance disruptions may have consequences of a more far-reaching kind. Audiences tend to accept the self projected by the individual performer during any current performance as a responsible representative of his colleague-grouping, of his team, and of his social establishment. Audiences also accept the individual's particular performance as evidence of his capacity to perform the routine and even as evidence of his capacity to perform any routine. In a sense these larger social units—teams, establishments, etc.—become committed every time the individual performs his routine; with each performance the legitimacy of these units will tend to be tested anew and their permanent reputation put at stake. This kind of commitment is especially strong during some performances. Thus, when a surgeon and his nurse both turn from the operating table and the anesthetized patient accidentally rolls off the table to his death, not only is the operation disrupted in an embarrassing way, but the reputation of the doctor, as a doctor and as a man, and also the reputation of the hospital may be weakened. These are the consequences that disruptions may have from the point of view of social structure.

Finally, we often find that the individual may deeply involve his ego in his identification with a particular part, establishment, and group, and in his self-conception as someone who does not disrupt social interaction or let down the social units which depend upon that interaction. When a disruption occurs, then, we may find that the self-conceptions around which his personality has been built may become discredited. These are consequences that disruptions may have from the point of view of individual personality.

Performance disruptions, then, have consequences at three levels of abstraction: personality, interaction, and social structure. While the likelihood of disruption will vary widely from interaction to interaction, and while the social importance of likely disruptions will vary from interaction to interaction, still it seems that there is no interaction in which the participants do not take an appreciable chance, of being slightly embar-

rassed or a slight chance of being deeply humiliated. Life may not be much of a gamble, but interaction is. Further, insofar as individuals make efforts to avoid disruptions or to correct for ones not avoided, these efforts, too, will have simultaneous consequences at the three levels. Here, then, we have one simple way of articulating three levels of abstraction and three perspectives from which social life has been studied.

### Staging and the Self

The general notion that we make a presentation of ourselves to others is hardly novel; what ought to be stressed in conclusion is that the very structure of the self can be seen in terms of how we arrange for such performances in our Anglo-American society.

In this report, the individual was divided by implication into two basic parts: he was viewed as a *performer*, a harried fabricator of impressions involved in the all-too-human task of staging a performance; he was viewed as a *character*, a figure, typically a fine one, whose spirit, strength, and other sterling qualities the performance was designed to evoke. The attributes of a performer and the attributes of a character are of a different order, quite basically so, yet both sets have their meaning in terms of the show that must go on.

First, character. In our society the character one performs and one's self are somewhat equated, and this self-as-character is usually seen as something housed within the body of its possessor, especially the upper parts thereof, being a nodule, somehow, in the psychobiology of personality. I suggest that this view is an implied part of what we are all trying to present, but provides, just because of this, a bad analysis of the presentation. In this report the performed self was seen as some kind of image, usually creditable, which the individual on stage and in character effectively attempts to induce others to hold in regard to him. While this image is entertained *concerning* the individual, so that a self is imputed to him, this self itself does not derive from its possessor, but from the whole scene of his action, being generated by that attribute of local events which renders them interpretable by witnesses. A correctly staged and performed scene leads the audience to impute a self to a performed character, but this imputation—this self—is a *product* of a scene that comes off, and is not a *cause* of it. The self, then, as a performed character, is not an organic thing that has a specific location, whose fundamental fate is to be born, to mature, and to die; it is a dramatic effect arising diffusely from a scene that is presented, and the characteristic issue, the crucial concern, is whether it will be credited or discredited.

In analyzing the self then we are drawn from its possessor, from the person who will profit or lose most by it, for he and his body merely provide the peg on which something of collaborative manufacture will be hung for a time. And the means for producing and maintaining selves do not reside inside the peg; in fact these means are often bolted down in social establishments. There will be a back region with its tools for shaping the body, and a front region with its fixed props. There will be a team of persons whose activity on stage in conjunction with available props will constitute the scene from which the performed character's self will emerge, and another team, the audience, whose interpretive activity will be necessary for this emergence. The self is a product of all of these arrangements, and in all of its parts bears the marks of this genesis.

The whole machinery of self-production is cumbersome, of course, and sometimes breaks down, exposing its separate components: back region control; team collusion; audience tact; and so forth. But, well oiled, impressions will flow from it fast enough to put us in the grips of one of our types of reality—the performance will come off and the firm self accorded each performed character will appear to emanate intrinsically from its performer.

Let us turn now from the individual as character performed to the individual as performer. He has a capacity to learn, this being exercised in the task of training for a part. He is given to having fantasies and dreams, some that pleasurably unfold a triumphant performance, others full of anxiety and dread that nervously deal with vital discreditings in a public front region. He often manifests a gregarious desire for teammates and audiences, a tactful considerateness for their concerns; and he has a capacity for deeply felt shame, leading him to minimize the chances he takes of exposure.

These attributes of the individual *qua* performer are not merely a depicted effect of particular performances; they are psychobiological in nature, and yet they seem to arise out of intimate interaction with the contingencies of staging performances.

And now a final comment. In developing the conceptual framework employed in this report, some language of the stage was used. I spoke of performers and audiences; of routines and parts; of performances coming off or falling flat; of cues, stage settings, and backstage; of dramaturgical needs, dramaturgical skills, and dramaturgical strategies. Now it should be admitted that this attempt to press a mere analogy so far was in part a rhetoric and a maneuver.

The claim that all the world's a stage is sufficiently commonplace for readers to be familiar with its limitations and tolerant of its presentation, knowing that at any time they will easily be able to demonstrate to themselves that it is not to be taken too seriously. An action staged in a theater is a relatively contrived illusion and an admitted one; unlike ordinary life, nothing real or actual can happen to the performed characters—although at another level of course something real and actual can happen to the reputation of performers *qua* professionals whose everyday job is to put on theatrical performances.

And so here the language and mask of the stage will be dropped. Scaffolds, after all, are to build other things with, and should be erected with an eye to taking them down.

This report is not concerned with aspects of theater that creep into everyday life. It is concerned with the structure of social encounters—the structure of those entities in social life that come into being whenever persons enter one another's immediate physical presence. The key factor in this structure is the maintenance of a single definition of the situation, this definition having to be expressed, and this expression sustained in the face of a multitude of potential disruptions.

A character staged in a theater is not in some ways real, nor does it have the same kind of real consequences as does the thoroughly contrived character performed by a confidence man; but the *successful* staging of either of these types of false figures involves use of *real* techniques—the same techniques by which everyday persons sustain their real social situations. Those who conduct face to face interaction on a theater's stage must meet the key requirement of real situations; they must expressively sustain a definition of the situation: but this they do in circumstances that have facilitated their developing an apt terminology for the interactional tasks that all of us share.

## Notes

1. Reported in pad in E. Goffman, "Communication Conduct in an Island Community" (unpublished Ph.D. dissertation, Department of Sociology, University of Chicago, 1953). The community hereafter will be called "Shetland Isle."

2. Gustav Ichheiser, "Misunderstandings in Human Relations," Supplement to *The American Journal of Sociology*, LV (September, 1949), pp. 6–7.

3. Quoted in E. H. Volkart, editor, *Social Behavior and Personality*, Contributions of W. I. Thomas to Theory and Social Research (New York: Social Science Research Council, 1951), p. 9.

4. Here I owe much to an unpublished paper by Tom Burns of the University of Edinburgh. He presents the argument that in all interaction a basic underlying theme is the desire of each participant to guide and control the responses made by the others present. A similar argument has been advanced by Jay Haley in a recent unpublished paper, but in regard to a special kind of control, that having to do with defining the nature of the relationship of those involved in the interaction.

5. Willard Waller, "The Rating and Dating Complex," *American Sociological Review*, II, p. 730.

6. William Sansom, *A Contest of Ladies* (London: Hogarth, 1956), pp. 230–32.

7. The widely read and rather sound writings of Stephen Potter are concerned in part with signs that can be engineered to give a shrewd observer the apparently incidental cues he needs to discover concealed virtues the gamesman does not in fact possess.

8. An interaction can be purposely set up as a time and place for voicing differences in opinion. But in such cases participants *must* be careful to agree not to disagree on the proper tone of voice, vocabulary, and degree of seriousness in which all arguments are to be phrased, and upon the mutual respect which disagreeing participants must carefully continue *to* express toward one another. This debaters' or academic definition of the situation may also be invoked suddenly and judiciously as a way of translating a serious conflict of views into one that can be handled within a framework acceptable to all present.

9. W. F. Whyte, "When Workers and Customers Meet," Chap. VII, *Industry and Society*, ed. W. F. Whyte (New York: McGraw-Hill 1946), pp. 132–33.

10. Teacher interview quoted by Howard S. Becker, "Social Class Variations in the Teacher-Pupil Relationship," *Journal of Educational Sociology*, XXV, p. 459.

11. Harold Taxel, "Authority Structure in a Mental Hospital Ward" (unpublished Master's thesis, Department of Sociology, University of Chicago, 1953).

12. Goffman, *op. cit.*, pp. 319–27.

13. Peter Blau, "Dynamics of Bureaucracy" (Ph.D. dissertation, Department of Sociology, Columbia University, forthcoming, University of Chicago Press), pp. 127–29.

14. Walter M. Beattie, Jr., "The Merchant Seaman" (unpublished M.A. Report, Department of Sociology, University of Chicago, 1950), p. 35.

15. Sir Frederick Ponsonby, *Recollections of Three Reigns* (New York: Dutton, 1952), p. 46.

16. For comments on the importance of distinguishing between a routine *of* interaction and *any* particular instance when this routine *is* played

through, see John van Neumann and Oskar Morgenstern, *The Theory of Games and Economic Behaviour* (2nd ed.) (Princeton: Princeton University Press, 1947), p. 49.

17. See Babe Pinelli, as told to Joe King, *Mr. Ump* (Philadelphia: Westminister Press, 1953), p. 75.

18. Material on the burial business used throughout this report is taken from Robert W. Habenstein, "The American Funeral Director" (unpublished Ph.D. dissertation, Department of Sociology, University of Chicago, 1954). I owe much to Mr. Habenstein's analysis of a funeral as a performance.

19. Charles H. Cooley, *Human Nature and the Social Order* (New York: Scribner's, 1922), pp. 352–53.

20. Mirra Komarovsky, "Cultural Contradictions and Sex Roles," *American Journal of Sociology,* LII, pp. 186–88.

21. *Ibid.,* p. 187.

22. Cooley, *op. cit.,* p. 351.

23. Ponsonby, *op. cit.,* p. 277.

24. *The Sociology of Georg Simmel,* trans. and ed. Kurt H. Wolff (Glencoe, Ill.: The Free Press, 1950), p. 321.

25. Emile Durkheim, *Sociology and Philosophy,* trans. D. F. Pocock (London: Cohen & West, 1953), p. 37.

26. Kurt Riezler, "Comment on the Social Psychology of Shame," *American Journal of Sociology,* XLVIII, p. 462 ff.

27. This view of hypnosis is neatly presented by T. R. Sarbin, "Contributions to Role-Taking Theory. I: Hypnotic Behavior," *Psychological Review,* 57, pp. 255–70.

28. See D. R. Cressey, "The Differential Association Theory and Compulsive Crimes," *Journal of Criminal Law, Criminology and Police Science,* 45, pp. 29–40.

29. This concept derives from T. R. Sarbin, "Role Theory," in Gardner Lindzey, *Handbook of Social Psychology* (Cambridge: Addison-Wesley, 1954), Vol. 1, pp. 235–36.

**22**

# Black Men and Public Space

## *Brent Staples*

My first victim was a woman—white, well dressed, probably in her early twenties. I came upon her late one evening on a deserted street in Hyde Park, a relatively affluent neighborhood in an otherwise mean, impoverished section of Chicago. As I swung onto the avenue behind her, there seemed to be a discreet, uninflammatory distance between us. Not so. She cast back a worried glance. To her, the youngish black man—a broad six feet two inches with a beard and billowing hair, both hands shoved into the pockets of a bulky military jacket—seemed menacingly close. After a few more quick glimpses, she picked up her pace and was soon running in earnest. Within seconds she disappeared into a cross street.

That was more than a decade ago. I was twenty-two years old, a graduate student newly arrived at the University of Chicago. It was in the echo of that terrified woman's footfalls that I first began to know the unwieldy inheritance I'd come into—the ability to alter public space in ugly ways. It was clear that she thought herself the quarry of a mugger, a rapist, or worse. Suffering a bout of insomnia, however, I was stalking sleep, not defenseless wayfarers. As a softy who is

"Black Men and Public Space" by B. Staples from *Life Studies* (pp. 29–32), edited by D. Cavitch, 1992. Boston: Bedford Books. Reprinted by permission of the author. Brent Staples writes editorials for *The New York Times* and is the author of the memoir *Parallel Time: Growing Up in Black and White*.

scarcely able to take a knife to a raw chicken—let alone hold one to a person's throat—I was surprised, embarrassed, and dismayed all at once. Her flight made me feel like an accomplice in tyranny. It also made it clear that I was indistinguishable from the muggers who occasionally seeped into the area from the surrounding ghetto. That first encounter, and those that followed, signified that a vast, unnerving gulf lay between nighttime pedestrians—particularly women—and me. And I soon gathered that being perceived as dangerous is a hazard in itself. I only needed to turn a corner into a dicey situation, or crowd some frightened, armed person in a foyer somewhere, or make an errant move after being pulled over by a policeman. Where fear and weapons meet—and they often do in urban America—there is always the possibility of death.

In that first year, my first away from my hometown, I was to become thoroughly familiar with the language of fear. At dark, shadowy intersections, I could cross in front of a car stopped at a traffic light and elicit the *thunk, thunk, thunk, thunk* of the driver—black, white, male, or female—hammering down the door locks. On less traveled streets after dark, I grew accustomed to but never comfortable with people crossing to the other side of the street rather than pass me. Then there were the standard unpleasantries with policemen, doormen, bouncers, cabdrivers, and others whose business it is to screen out troublesome individuals *before* there is any nastiness.

I moved to New York nearly two years ago and I have remained an avid night walker. In central Manhattan, the near-constant crowd cover minimizes tense one-on-one street encounters. Elsewhere—in SoHo, for example, where sidewalks are narrow and tightly spaced buildings shut out the sky—things can get very taut indeed.

After dark, on the warrenlike streets of Brooklyn where I live, I often see women who fear the worst from me. They seem to have set their faces on neutral, and with their purse straps strung across their chests bandolier-style, they forge ahead as though bracing themselves against being tackled. I understand, of course, that the danger they perceive is not a hallucination. Women are particularly vulnerable to street violence, and young black males are drastically over-represented among the perpetrators of that violence. Yet these truths are no solace against the kind of alienation that comes of being ever the suspect, a fearsome entity with whom pedestrians avoid making eye contact.

It is not altogether clear to me how I reached the ripe old age of twenty-two without being conscious of the lethality nighttime pedestrians attributed to me. Perhaps it was because in Chester, Pennsylvania, the small, angry industrial town where I came of age in the 1960s, I was scarcely noticeable against a backdrop of gang warfare, street knifings, and murders. I grew up one of the good boys, had perhaps a half-dozen fistfights. In retrospect, my shyness of combat has clear sources.

As a boy, I saw countless tough guys locked away; I have since buried several, too. They were babies, really—a teenage cousin, a brother of twenty-two, a childhood friend in his mid-twenties—all gone down in episodes of bravado played out in the streets. I came to doubt the virtues of intimidation early on. I chose, perhaps unconsciously, to remain a shadow—timid, but a survivor.

The fearsomeness mistakenly attributed to me in public places often has a perilous flavor. The most frightening of these confusions occurred in the late 1970s and early 1980s, when I worked as a journalist in Chicago. One day, rushing into the office of a magazine I was writing for with a deadline story in hand, I was mistaken for a burglar. The office manager called security and, with an ad hoc posse, pursued me through the labyrinthine halls, nearly to my editor's door. I had no way of proving who I was. I could only move briskly toward the company of someone who knew me.

Another time I was on assignment for a local paper and killing time before an interview. I entered a jewelry store on the city's affluent Near North Side. The proprietor excused herself and returned with an enormous red Doberman Pinscher straining at the end of a leash. She stood, the dog extended toward me, silent to my questions, her eyes bulging nearly out of her head. I took a cursory look around, nodded, and bade her good night.

Relatively speaking, however, I never fared as badly as another black male journalist. He went to nearby Waukegan, Illinois, a couple of summers ago to work on a story about a murderer who was born there. Mistaking the reporter for the killer, police officers hauled him from his car at gunpoint and but for his press credentials would probably have tried to book him. Such episodes are not uncommon. Black men trade tales like this all the time.

Over the years, I learned to smother the rage I felt at so often being taken for a criminal. Not to do so would surely have led to madness. I now take precautions to make myself less threatening. I move about with care, particularly late in the evening. I give a wide berth to nervous people on subway platforms during the wee hours, particularly when I have exchanged business clothes for jeans. If I happen to be entering a building behind some people who appear skittish, I may walk by, letting them clear the lobby before I return, so as not to seem to be following them. I have been calm and extremely congenial on those rare occasions when I've been pulled over by the police.

And on late-evening constitutionals I employ what has proved to be an excellent tension-reducing measure: I whistle melodies from Beethoven and Vivaldi and the more popular classical composers. Even steely New Yorkers hunching toward nighttime destinations seem to relax, and occasionally they even join in the tune. Virtually everybody seems to sense that a mugger wouldn't be warbling bright, sunny selections from Vivaldi's *Four Seasons*. It is my equivalent of the cowbell that hikers wear when they know they are in bear country.

**23**

# The Madam as Teacher:
# The Training of House Prostitutes

*Barbara Sherman Heyl*

### Ann's Turn-out Establishment

A professional prostitute, whether she works as a streetwalker, house prostitute, or call girl, can usually pick out one person in her past who "turned her out," that is, who taught her the basic techniques and rules of the prostitute's occupation. For women who begin working at the house level, that person may be a pimp, another "working girl," or a madam. Most madams and managers of prostitution establishments, however, prefer not to take on novice prostitutes, and they may even have a specific policy against hiring turn-outs (see Erwin, 1960, pp. 204–205; and Lewis, 1942, p. 22). The turn-out's inexperience may cost the madam clients and money; to train the novice, on the other hand, costs her time and energy. Most madams and managers simply do not want the additional burden.

It was precisely the madam's typical disdain for turn-outs that led to the emergence of the house discussed in this paper—a house specifically devoted to training new prostitutes. The madam of this operation,

"The Madam as Teacher: The Training of House Prostitutes" by B. S. Heyl, 1977. *Social Problems, 24*, no. 5 (June), pp. 545–555. Also found in *The Madam as Entrepreneur* by B. S. Heyl, 1979 (New Brunswick, NJ: Transaction Books). Copyright © 1977 by the Society for the Study of Social Problems. Reprinted by permission.

whom we shall call Ann, is forty-one years old and has been in the prostitution world twenty-three years, working primarily at the house level. Ann knew that pimps who manage women at this level have difficulty placing novices in houses. After operating several houses staffed by professional prostitutes, she decided to run a school for turn-outs partly as a strategy for acquiring a continually changing staff of young women for her house. Pimps are the active recruiters of new prostitutes, and Ann found that, upon demonstrating that she could transform the pimps' new, square women into trained prostitutes easily placed in professional houses, pimps would help keep her business staffed. Ann's house is a small operation in a middle-sized, industrial city (population 300,000), with a limited clientele of primarily working-class men retained as customers for ten to fifteen years and offered low rates to maintain their patronage.

Although Ann insists that every turn-out is different, her group of novices is remarkably homogeneous in some ways. Ann has turned out approximately twenty women a year over the six years while she has operated a training school. Except for one Chicano, one black, and one American Indian, the women were all white. They ranged in age from eighteen to twenty-seven. Until three years ago, all the women she hired had pimps. Since then, more women are independent (so-called "outlaws"), although many come to Ann sponsored by a pimp. That is, in return for being placed with Ann, the turn-out gives the pimp a percentage of her earnings for a specific length of time. At present eighty percent of the turn-outs come to Ann without a long-term commitment to a pimp. The turn-outs stay at Ann's on the average of two to three months. This is the same average length of time Bryan (1965, p. 289) finds for the apprenticeship in his call-girl study. Ann seldom has more than two or three women in training at any one time. Most turn-outs live at the house, often just a large apartment near the older business section of the city.

### The Content of the Training

The data for the following analysis are of three kinds. First, tape recordings from actual training sessions with fourteen novices helped specify the structure and content of the training provided. Second, lengthy interviews with three of the novices and multiple interviews with Ann were conducted to obtain data on the training during the novice's first few days at the house before the first group training sessions were conducted and recorded by Ann. And third, visits to the house on ten occasions and observations of Ann's interaction with the novices during teaching periods extended the data on training techniques used and the relationship between madam and novice. In addition, weekly contact with Ann over a four-year period allowed repeated review of current problems and strategies in training turn-outs.

The content analysis of the taped training sessions produced three major topics of discussion and revealed the relative amount of time Ann devoted to each. The first two most frequently discussed topics can be categorized under Bryan's dimension of interpersonal skills; they were devoted to teaching situational strategies for managing clients. The third topic resembles Bryan's value dimension (1965, pp. 291–292).

The first topic stressed physical skills and strategies. Included in this category were instruction on how to perform certain sexual acts and specification of their prices, discussion of particular clients, and instruction in techniques for dealing with certain categories of clients, such as "older men" or "kinky" tricks. This topic of physical skills also included discussion of, and Ann's demonstration of, positions designed to provide the woman maximum comfort and protection from the man during different sexual acts. Defense tactics, such as ways to get out of a sexual position and out of the bedroom quickly, were practiced by the novices. Much time was devoted to analyzing past encounters with particular clients. Bryan finds similar discussions of individual tricks among novice call girls and their trainers (1965, p. 293). In the case of Ann's turn-outs these discussions were often initiated by a novice's complaint or question about a certain client and his requests or behavior in the bedroom. The novice always received tips and advice from Ann and the other women present on how to manage that type of bedroom encounter. Such sharing of tactics allow the turn-out to learn what Gagnon and Simon call "patterns of client management" (1973, p. 231).

The second most frequently discussed topic could be labeled client management-verbal skills. Ann's primary concern was teaching what she calls "hustling." "Hustling" is similar to what Bryan terms a "sales pitch" for call girls (1965, p. 292), but in the house setting it takes place in the bedroom while the client is deciding how much to spend and what sexual acts he wishes performed. "Hustling" is designed to encourage the client to spend more than the minimum rate. The prominence on the teaching tapes of instruction in this verbal skill shows its importance in Ann's training of novices.

On one of the tapes Ann uses her own turning-out experience to explain to two novices (both with pimps) why she always teaches hustling skills as an integral part of working in a house.

### Ann as a Turn-out

*Ann:* Of course, I can remember a time when I didn't know that I was supposed to hustle. So that's why I understand that it's difficult to *learn* to hustle. When I turned out it was $2 a throw. They came in. They gave me their $2. They got a hell of a fuck. And that was it. Then one Saturday night I turned *forty-four* tricks! And Penny [the madam] used to put the number of tricks at the top of the page and the amount of money at the bottom of the page— she used these big ledger books. Lloyd [Ann's pimp] came in at six o'clock and he looked at that book and he just *knew* I had made all kinds of money. Would you believe I had turned forty-two $2 tricks and two $3 tricks— because two of 'em got generous and gave me an extra buck! [Laughs] I got my ass whipped. And I was so tired—I thought I was going to die—I was 15 years old. And I got my ass whipped for it. [Ann imitates an angry Lloyd:] "Don't you know you're supposed to ask for more money?!" No, I didn't. Nobody told me that. All they told me was it was $2. So that is learning it the *hard* way. I'm trying to help you learn it the *easy* way, if there is an easy way to do it.

In the same session Ann asks one of the turn-outs (Linda, age eighteen) to practice her hustling rap.

### Learning the Hustling Rap

*Ann:* I'm going to be a trick. You've checked me. I want you to carry it from there. [Ann begins role-playing: she plays the client; Linda, the hustler.]

*Linda:* [mechanically] What kind of party would you like to have?

*Ann:* That had all the enthusiasm of a wet noodle. I really wouldn't *want* any party with that because you evidently don't want to give me one.

*Linda:* What kind of party would you *like* to have?

*Ann:* I usually take a half and half.

*Linda:* Uh, the money?

*Ann:* What money?

*Linda:* The money you're supposed to have! [loudly] 'Cause you ain't getting it for free!

*Ann:* [upset] Linda, if you *ever,* ever say that in my joint . . . Because that's fine for street hustling. In street hustling, you're going to *have* to hard-hustle those guys or they're not going to come up with anything. Because they're going to *try* and get it for free. But when they walk in here, they *know* they're not going to get it for free to begin with. So try another tack—just a little more friendly, not quite so hard-nosed. [Returning to role-playing:] I just take a half and half.

*Linda:* How about fifteen [dollars]?

*Ann:* You're leading into the money too fast. Try: "What are you going to spend?" or "How much money are you going to spend?" or something like that.

*Linda:* How much would you like to spend?

*Ann:* No! Not "like." 'Cause they don't *like* to spend anything.

*Linda:* How much *would* you like to spend?

*Ann:* Make it a very definitive, positive statement: "How much are you going to spend?"

Ann considers teaching hustling skills her most difficult and important task. In spite of her lengthy discussion on the tapes of the rules and techniques for dealings with the customer sexually, Ann states that it may take only a few minutes to "show a girl how to turn a trick." A substantially longer period is required, however, to teach her to hustle. To be adept at hustling, the woman must be mentally alert and sensitive to the client's response to what she is saying and doing and be able to act on those perceptions of his reactions. The hustler must maintain a steady patter of verbal coaxing, during which her tone of voice maybe more important than her actual words.

In Ann's framework, then, hustling is a form of verbal sexual aggression. Referring to the problems in teaching novices to hustle, Ann notes that "taking the aggressive part is something women are not used to doing, particularly young women." No doubt, hustling is difficult to teach partly because the woman must learn to discuss sexual acts, whereas in her previous experience, sexual behavior and preferences had been negotiated nonverbally (see Gagnon & Simon, 1973, p. 228). Ann feels that to be effective, each woman's "hustling rap" must be her own—one that comes naturally and will strike the clients as sincere. All of that takes practice. But Ann is aware that the difficulty in learning to hustle stems more from the fact that it involves inappropriate sex-role behavior. Bryan concludes that it is precisely this aspect of soliciting men on the telephone that causes the greatest distress to the novice call girl (1965, p. 293). Thus, the call girl's income is affected by how much business she can bring in by her calls, that is, by how well she can learn to be socially aggressive on the telephone. The income of the house prostitute, in turn, depends heavily on her hustling skills in the bedroom. Ann's task, then, is to train the novice, who has recently come from a culture where young women are not expected to be sexually aggressive, to assume that role with a persuasive naturalness.

Following the first two major topics—client management through physical and verbal skills—the teaching of "racket" (prostitution world) values was the third-ranking topic of training and discussion on the teaching tapes. Bryan notes that the major value taught to call girls is "that of maximizing gains and minimizing effort, even if this requires transgressions of either a legal or moral nature" (1965, p. 291). In her training, however, Ann avoids communicating the notion that the novices may exploit the customers in any way they can. For example, stealing or cheating clients is grounds for dismissal from the house. Ann cannot afford the reputation among her tricks that they risk being robbed when they visit her. Moreover, being honest with clients is extolled as a virtue. Thus, Ann urges the novices to tell the trick if she is nervous or unsure, to let him know she is new to the business. This is in direct contradiction to the advice pimps usually give their new women to hide their inexperience from the trick. Ann asserts that honesty in this case usually means that the client will be more tolerant of mistakes in sexual technique, be less likely to interpret hesitancy as coldness, and be generally more helpful and sympathetic. Putting her "basic principle" in the form of a simple directive,

Ann declares: "Please the trick, but at the same time get as much money for pleasing him as you possibly can." Ann does not consider hustling to be client exploitation. It is simply the attempt to sell the customer the product with the highest profit margin. That is, she would defend hustling in terms familiar to the businessman or sales manager.

That Ann teaches hustling as a value is revealed in the following discussion between Ann and Sandy—a former hustler and longtime friend of Ann. Sandy, who married a former trick and still lives in town, has come over to the house to help instruct several novices in the hustling business.

### Whores, Prostitutes, and Hustlers

*Ann:* [To the turn-outs:] Don't get up-tight that you're hesitating or you're fumbling, within the first week or even the first five years. Because it takes that long to become a good hustler. I mean you can be a whore in one night. There's nothing to that. The first time you take money you're a whore.

*Sandy:* This girl in Midtown [a small, Midwestern city] informed me—I had been working there awhile—that I was a "whore" and she was a "prostitute." And I said: "Now what the hell does that mean?" Well, the difference was that a prostitute could pick her customer and a whore had to take anybody. I said: "Well honey, I want to tell you something. I'm neither one." She said: "Well, you *work.*" I said: "I know, but I'm a *hustler.* I make *money* for what I do."

*Ann:* And this is what I turn out—or try to turn out—hustlers. Not prostitutes. Not whores. But hustlers.

For Ann and Sandy the hustler deserves high status in the prostitution business because she has mastered a specific set of skills that, even with many repeat clients, earn her premiums above the going rate for sexual acts.

In the ideological training of call girls Bryan finds that "values such as fairness with other working girls, or fidelity to a pimp, may occasionally be taught" (1965, pp. 291–292); the teaching tapes revealed Ann's affirmation of both these virtues. When a pimp brings a woman to Ann, she supports his control over the woman. For example, if during her stay at the house, the novice breaks any of the basic rules—by using drugs, holding back money (from either Ann or the pimp), lying, or seeing another man—Ann will report the infractions to the woman's pimp. Ann notes: "If I don't do that and the pimp finds out, he knows I'm not training her right, and he won't bring his future ladies to me for training." Ann knows she is dependent on the pimps to help supply her with turn-outs. Bryan, likewise, finds a willingness among call girls' trainers to defer to the pimps' wishes during the apprenticeship period (1965, p. 290).

Teaching fairness to other prostitutes is particularly relevant to the madam who daily faces the problem of maintaining peace among competing women at work under one roof. If two streetwalkers or two call girls find they cannot get along, they need not work near one another. But if a woman leaves a house because of personal conflicts, the madam loses a source of income. To minimize potential negative feelings among novices, Ann stresses mutual support, prohibits "criticizing another girl," and denigrates the "prima donna"—the prostitute who flaunts her financial success before the other women.

In still another strategy to encourage fair treatment of one's colleagues in the establishment, Ann emphasizes a set of rules prohibiting "dirty hustling"—behavior engaged in by one prostitute that would undercut the business of other women in the house. Tabooed under the label of "dirty hustling" are the following: appearing in the line-up partially unclothed; performing certain disapproved sexual positions, such as anal intercourse; and allowing approved sexual extras without charging additional fees. The norms governing acceptable behavior vary from house to house and region to region, and Ann warns the turn-outs to ask about such rules when they begin work in a new establishment. The woman who breaks the work

norms in a house, either knowingly or unknowingly, will draw the anger of the other women and can be fired by a madam eager to restore peace and order in the house.

Other topics considered on the tapes—in addition to physical skills, "hustling," and work values—were instruction on personal hygiene and grooming, role-playing of conversational skills with tricks on topics not related to sex or hustling ("living room talk"), house rules not related to hustling (such as punctuality, no perfume, no drugs), and guidelines for what to do during an arrest. There were specific suggestions on how to handle personal criticism, questions, and insults from clients. In addition, the discussions on the tapes provided the novices with many general strategies for becoming "professionals" at their work, for example, the importance of personal style, enthusiasm ("the customer is always right"), and sense of humor. In some ways these guidelines resemble a beginning course in salesmanship. But they also provide clues, particularly in combination with the topics on handling client insults and the emphasis on hustling, on how the house prostitute learns to manage a stable and limited clientele and cope psychologically with the repetition of the clients and the sheer tedium of the physical work (Hughes, 1971, pp. 342–345).

### Training House Prostitutes—A Process of Professional Socialization

Observing how Ann trains turn-outs is a study in techniques to facilitate identity change (see also Davis, 1971; Heyl, 1974, chap. 2). Ann uses a variety of persuasive strategies to help give the turn-outs a new occupational identity as a "professional." One strategy is to rely heavily on the new values taught the novice to isolate her from her previous life style and acquaintances. Bryan finds that "The value structure [taught to novice call girls] serves, in general, to create in-group solidarity and to alienate the girl from 'square' society" (1965, p. 292). Whereas alienation from conventional society may be an indirect effect of values taught to call girls, in Ann's training of house prostitutes the expectation that the novice will immerse herself in the prostitution world ("racket life") is made dramatically explicit.

In the following transcription from one of the teaching tapes, the participants are Ann (age thirty-six at the time the tape was made), Bonnie (an experienced turn-out, age twenty-five), and Kristy (a new turn-out, age eighteen). Kristy has recently linked up with a pimp for the first time and volunteers to Ann and Bonnie her difficulty in adjusting to the racket rule of minimal contact with the square world—a rule her pimp is enforcing by not allowing Kristy to meet and talk with her old friends. Ann (A) and Bonnie (B) have listened to Kristy's (K) complaints and are making suggestions. (The notation "B-K" indicates that Bonnie is addressing Kristy.)

### Kristy's Isolation from the Square World

*B-K:* What you gotta do is sit down and talk to him and weed out your friends and find the ones he thinks are suitable companions for you—in your new type of life.

*K-B:* None of them.

*A-K:* What about *his* friends?

*K-A:* I haven't met very many of his friends. I don't like any of 'em so far.

*A-K:* You are making the same mistake that makes me so goddamned irritated with square broads! You're taking a man and trying to train *him,* instead of letting the man train you.

*K-A:* What?! I'm not trying to train him, I'm just . . .

*A-K:* All right, you're trying to force him to accept your friends.

*K-A:* I don't care whether he accepts them or not. I just can't go around not talking to anybody.

*A-K:* "Anybody" is your old man! He is your world. And the people he says you can talk to are the people that are your world. But what you're trying to do is force your square world on a racket guy. It's like oil and water. There's just no way a square and a racket person can get together. That's why when you turn out

you've got to change your mind completely from square to racket. And you're still trying to hang with squares. You can't do it.

Strauss' (1969) concept of "coaching" illuminates a more subtle technique Ann employs as she helps the novice along, step by step, from "square" to "racket" values and life style. She observes carefully how the novice progresses, elicits responses from her about what she is experiencing, and then interprets those responses for her. In the following excerpt from one of the teaching tapes, Ann prepares two novices for feelings of depression over their newly made decisions to become prostitutes.

### Turn-out Blues

*Ann:* And while I'm on the subject—depression. You know they've got a word for it when you have a baby—it's called "postpartum blues." Now, I call it "turn-out blues." Every girl that ever turns out has 'em. And, depending on the girl, it comes about the third or fourth day. You'll go into a depression for no apparent reason. You'll wake up one morning and you'll say: "Why in the hell am I doing this? Why am I here? I wanna go home!" And I can't do a thing to help you. The only thing I can do is leave you alone and hope that you'll fight the battle yourself. But knowing that it will come, and knowing that everybody else goes through it too, does help. Just pray it's a busy night! So if you get blue and you get down, remember: "turn-out blues"—everybody gets it. Here's when you'll decide whether you're going to stay or you're gonna quit.

Ann's description of "turn-out blues" is a good example of Strauss' account (1969, pp. 111–112) of how coaches will use prophecy to increase their persuasive power over their novices. In the case of "turn-out blues," the novice, if she becomes depressed about her decision to enter prostitution, will recall Ann's prediction that this would happen and that it happens to all turn-outs. This recollection may or may not end the woman's misgivings about her decision, but it will surely enhance the turn-out's impression of Ann's competence. Ann's use of her past experience to make such predictions is a form of positive leverage; it increases the probability that what she says will be respected and followed in the future.

In Bryan's study the call girls reported that their training was more a matter of observation than direct instruction from their trainer (1965, p. 294). Ann, on the other hand, relies on a variety of teaching techniques, including lecturing and discussion involving other turn-outs who are further along in the training process and can reinforce Ann's views. Ann even brings in guest speakers, such as Sandy, the former hustler, who participates in the discussion with the novices in the role of the experienced resource person. "Learning the Hustling Rap," above, offers an example of role-playing—another teaching technique Ann frequently employs to help the turn-outs develop verbal skills. Ann may have to rely on more varied teaching approaches than the call-girl trainer because: (1) Ann herself is not working, thus her novices have fewer opportunities to watch their trainer interact with clients than do the call-girl novices; and (2) Ann's livelihood depends more directly on the success of her teaching efforts than does that of the call-girl trainer. Ann feels that if a woman under her direction does not "turn out well," not only will the woman earn less money while she is at her house (affecting Ann's own income), but Ann could also lose clients and future turn-outs from her teaching "failure."

The dissolution of the training relationship marks the end of the course. Bryan claims that the sharp break between trainer and trainee shows that the training process itself is largely unrelated to the acquisition of a skill. But one would scarcely have expected the trainee to report "that the final disruption of the apprenticeship was the result of the completion of adequate training" (1965, p. 296). Such establishments do not offer diplomas and terminal degrees. The present study, too, indicates that abrupt breaks in the training relationship are quite common. But what is significant is that the break is precipitated by personal conflicts exacerbated by both the narrowing of the skill gap between trainer and trainee and the consequent increase in the novice's confidence that she can make it on her own. Thus, skill acquisition counts in such an equation, not in a formal sense ("completion of adequate training"), but rather insofar as it works to break down the earlier bonds of dependence between trainer and trainee.

## References

Bryan, J. H. (1965, Winter). Apprenticeships in prostitution. *Social Problems, 12*, 287–297.

Bryan, J. H. (1966, Spring). Occupational ideologies and individual attitudes of call girls. *Social Problems, 13*, 441–450.

Davis, N. J. (1971). The prostitute: Developing a deviant identity. In J. M. Henslin (Ed.), *Studies in the sociology of sex.* New York: Appleton-Century-Crofts.

Erwin, C. (1960). *The orderly disorderly house.* Garden City, NY: Doubleday.

Gagnon, J. H., & Simon, W. (1973). *Sexual conduct: The social sources of human sexuality.* Chicago: Aldine.

Heyl, B. S. (1974, Spring). The madam as entrepreneur. *Sociological Symposium, 11*, 61–82.

Hughes, E. C. (1971). Work and self. In *The sociological eye: Selected papers* (pp. 338–347). Chicago: Aldine-Atherton.

Lewis, G. A. (1942). *Call house madam: The story of the career of Beverly Davis.* San Francisco: Martin Tudordale.

Strauss, A. L. (1969). *Mirrors and masks: The search for identity.* San Francisco: Sociology Press.

24

# What Does the Service Include?

*Linda Van Leuven*

Imagine walking into your favorite coffee place and ordering a double-tall latte. The person behind the counter asks how you've been, and mentions that they haven't seen you for awhile. You chat for a bit, then as they hand you your change, they ask if you'd like to "go out sometime."

When you interact with someone, how do you know who you are to each other? Do you both have the same understanding of what is going on, and of the goal of your encounter? What are the terms and parameters of your relating? Might this change over time?

People continuously interpret each other's actions in order to clarify and make claims about the direction and scope of their involvement. Having an awareness of this process of interpretation, however, might depend on the situation. For example, being approached by a stranger on the street can raise suspicions and create uncertainty regarding their intentions. Do they need directions? the time? or are they going to mug you? Often, such overt attempts to "figure it out" occur because there is no clear context for the contact. But what happens when two people have a reason to meet, such as in a service encounter—seeing a doctor, ordering food at McDonald's, buying a pair of chinos at The Gap?

This paper, "What Does the Service Include?" is based on research that the author is conducting for her dissertation. Linda Van Leuven is a graduate student at the University of California, Los Angeles.

In service situations, people who might otherwise be "strangers" to each other step into seemingly pre-fashioned relational relevance: They become doctor/patient, worker/customer, dispatcher/caller. However, even people in service encounters must determine their relational relevance. Although the roles often appear defined, and the purpose of the encounter clear, these participants must continuously negotiate their relational status. . . .

That people can have concurrent, multiple identities and engage in more than one activity in a given situation has been investigated to some degree. For example, as Goffman (1961) notes, surgeons can move between two seemingly competing activities during an operation, such as asking for a scalpel and making a personal joke or comment to an attending nurse/doctor. Invoking personal talk during a surgical procedure might seem in direct conflict with maintaining the definition of the event as surgery—and hence a serious affair—and of the people involved as professionals. Ironically, acknowledging other relational characteristics (e.g., friend, golf buddy) can actually assist the performance by taking an edge off tension in the situation. That a surgical procedure can support such relational variance among participants is perhaps aided by the fact that the person receiving the service, the patient, is unconscious.

However, even when participants in an encounter are aware of the possible range of their relevant identities, they might not acknowledge or play them out. Some situations, such as gynecological exams, are precarious endeavors precisely because either the doctor or the patient might have multiple interpretations of what it means to view and touch genitalia. Therefore both participants usually work to achieve a medical definition of the situation, suppressing possible sexual counter-themes. The gynecological encounter therefore is structured with certain conventions that enable both doctor and patient to mute any ambiguities.[1] For example, contact between doctor and patient is often divided into distinct stages that reflect differing relational relevance: pre-patient, patient, post-patient (Henslin and Biggs, 1971). Only in the pre-patient and post-patient phases is the whole person acknowledged and talk of a personal or social nature exchanged; in the patient stage, however, talk is limited to medical aspects, and emphasis is placed on medical terms. Thus, compartmentalizing the contact allows both parties to recognize the personal and professional dimensions of their relationship, but only during specific times. . . .

In this paper, I explore personal training relationships as one type of service encounter that involves extended and personalized contact. I look at how participants establish their relational roles as trainer and client, and once "in" these roles, how they use these positions to maneuver to other activities and identities, some of which may be more acceptable than others. My reflections are based on observing trainer/client sessions and extensive interviews with both parties. In these situations of personal training, who people are to each other is an ongoing negotiation from the first contact and every time they meet.

## What's Included in the Service?

So how do people get into personal training relationships? In the simplest sense, some folks answer ads for trainers, or find trainers

at their local gym, or have a friend who has a trainer. But finding a trainer is often just the beginning. In this section, I outline two aspects of the process of establishing a training relationship: defining the situation as "training," and also screening for an orientation to training as "work."

### Defining the Situation as "Training"

Ostensibly, "personal training" involves a "trainer" working out the body of a "client." One might assume that this definition of training is a shared understanding and that folks who are interested in personal training are indeed concerned with issues of fitness and working out. However, just what people are interested in "working out" might be debatable.

There are a variety of reasons why people say they train: Some are related to health and wellness (feeling good, injury rehabilitation, weight loss), others are more aesthetic or appearance oriented (bikini season, movie role), still others involve a client's need for motivation and discipline ("I just can't work out on my own"). Whereas these might seem like obvious reasons people would seek out the help of a trainer, the list does not end here. Trainers report that those expressing a desire to train often have other interests. Some are looking for friendship and someone to talk to. As Gia says, "Most people hire a trainer, they *think* for one reason, and it ends up I'm their psychiatrist, I'm their friend—they'd just rather stand and talk." Another trainer likened the service to "Rent-a-friend." Alternatively, some folks look to training for excitement, an escape from their life, or a possible sexual liaison. Aware of these diverse agendas, trainers pre-screen their would-be clients to establish that training is actually what they seek.

So how do trainers know what the client is interested in? Body language and "vibes" are two key factors trainers report they use in distinguishing which type of contact the prospective client desires. Bill, a muscular former Marine sergeant, pays particular attention to "vibes" and how folks use their eyes when they approach him to "train":

I can tell when someone's agenda is something other than training right away . . . it's kind of a sixth sense. It's the way they look at you, . . . you can tell by the glare in the eye, that lustful glare. They're not really making eye contact with you, or you've seen them even weeks before they've approached you and they've just been staring you up and down with the eyes. Even when they do approach you, they're studying your body, [but] they're not looking so much at your muscles as they are at your basket.

A "basket" refers to a male's groin area. Thus, looking at a trainer's basket is a definite giveaway that more is sought from the relationship than fitness training.

However, some initial contacts are made by phone, which limits the visual cues; therefore, one trainer, Donald, arranges an in-person interview with prospective clients outside the gym, so he can get a better feel for the person, sit down, and discuss training goals. One might think a discussion of training goals would secure the definition of the situation as training. However, sometimes the discussion of training goals clarifies just what a prospective client is interested in. Donald states:

Well I had this one guy who's a hairdresser, and I was asking him what he wanted to do. [He says,] "Well, I want to build my chest my arms and my legs need some help," and I say, "Well we can definitely work on that." He says, "So what can you do for my legs? Can you get them as thick and as silky as yours?" I said, "I wouldn't say that my legs are s-silky. I said I could *work* on trying to get them as thick as mine are but you know I can only do so much—you have to do your part." And he said, "Well what is that?" I say, "That is when I tell you something to do, you have to concentrate on what you're doing." Then he said to me, "Well you know, working out with you it'd be hard to concentrate." Then I said, "Maybe you don't need me as a trainer."

Here, this potential client uses a discussion of training goals to introduce his alternative interest: an attraction to Donald. Even after this comment about silky legs, Donald tries to keep the fitness focus by suggesting the client's responsibility for workout success. But the would-be client takes Donald's talk of concentration in training to make his intentions perfectly clear. It is at this point that Donald closes the door on their working together. Whereas Donald may not like it when people use his offer of personal training as a pick-up attempt, he understands it. He later states, "But in a way people have to use whatever avenue they can to get whatever they want." Service relationships offer people the opportunity to have contact with persons they typically might not have the chance to be around.

For the most part, it is the trainers who need to scan prospective clients for intentions, but in some circumstances, clients might also need to secure the definition of the situation as "training." In this next excerpt, Steve describes his first phone contact with one particular woman who sought training:

The whole phone conversation was, "I had to fire my last trainer because he fell in love with me, and I'm serious about my training, I'm serious about this." She asked me if I was gay, she asked me if I had a girlfriend, she asked me if I was married—and I'm lookin' at the phone like this must be a sixty year old ugly lady who has no concept about what's goin' on. I said, "No I'm not gay." She said, "Well maybe you should be, you know that way. . . ." I'm like, this lady must be wacked. I went to her house and this lady was literally a Playboy [Play]mate, she had the body of that, yes, and we became the best friends, just by establishing that little conversation on the phone. She knew what she wanted, and I knew what I wanted. . . . I wanted a client and she wanted a trainer. And when I met her, I could easily see that that coulda went a different direction if she didn't set up the parameters first.

This woman's history of dealing with an amorous trainer prompts her extensive probing of Steve's background and her explicit detailing of what she is looking for: a trainer.

It is a good thing she does this, for without the pre-setting of parameters, Steve admits his own desire might have been to move the training relationship into more personal realms.

In addition to defining the situation as training—and not dating—trainers also pre-screen for serious approaches to training as "work." Training involves close and intimate contact with the client and includes emotional labor (Hoschchild, 1983). For instance, one trainer notes, "They come in with low self-esteem about whatever it is that makes them angry and they dump it on you, so their bad day becomes your bad day." By finding clients who want to work, trainers aim to eliminate these problematic people.

In initial phone contacts, trainers interview for serious attitudes. For example, Chandra is on the lookout for anyone who is already trying to yank her around:

I *immediately* want to find out how serious they are, because it's a lot to take on. . . . A lot of times people will want to start talking about their personal issues or their life before they've even met me, and it's not on their time. You know, this is a free consultation basically over the phone. So they might start to talk about, "Oh things have just been really crazy at work, and um, I'd like to come at three but I know at three I have a hair appointment. Now what about Saturday? Saturday I could come in the morning, now would you . . . ," and they want to see how much they can get outta me. They want to see how much I'm going to bend over for them, and how far they can push me. So I'm really feeling for that because that is a sign early on that they're really not in it to do the work. They're in it for some other reason: either to say that they have a trainer, to think that if they have a trainer for a month that their body's gonna change . . . like they had plastic surgery or something. And so, [I'm looking for] are they genuine?

Too much personal talk, too soon, and difficulty in scheduling alert Chandra that this person does not share her understanding that training is work and takes effort. Without this shared understanding, Chandra will not take on the prospective client.

In sum, establishing a training relationship is often a complex social process. For many trainers and clients, this process entails defining the situation as training and then screening for similar, and serious, understandings of what training entails: work. These initial contacts are key because in them participants set the terms of the relationship and what activities both trainer and client might anticipate.

### Negotiating Relational Boundaries through Talk

Those who have "passed the test" get to be client and trainer; but this is not where the story ends. Rather, the seemingly established roles allow both parties latitude to expand their relational identities: either by adjusting the activities that can be included within the service time, or by extending their contact to out-of-work events.[2] Since many trainers motivate their clients through friendly talk, they continue to have to negotiate the boundaries of that friendliness. Clients also engage in this on-going defining of the relationship.

People talk about a lot of things while training. There is talk about the body and the workout; there is social talk about current events, stocks, movies, etc., and then there is personal talk, which includes the most intimate details of one's private life.

Talk about the body is common, and references to glutes, quads, and delts clearly reference the training relationship. However, trainers often make other comments about the appearance of their client that are more personal in nature. In the following fieldnote, Chandra's client, Max, is getting ready to do incline dumbbell presses:

Max raises the weights to chest level, and Chandra puts her hands underneath his arms as support. He is in position. She says to him, "I love your hair slicked back. OK ready?" Max begins the exercise as she counts out his reps.

Now exactly what does Max's hair have to do with his incline dumbbell presses? Probably little. But by casually commenting on his hair, Chandra not only recognizes Max's social self, but positions herself as someone who can make such statements; in addition to being aware of his workout form, she can appreciate Max as an attractive person.

Clients often share the personal details of their lives with their trainers. These details range from the mundane to the most intimate—from what they ate last night, to what they dreamt last night, to whom they slept with last night. This variety of personal talk has implications for their relationship, as one trainer notes:

We talk about everything. A lot of times I feel like a therapist cuz people just pour their guts out. We discuss their problems, and once in a while I do the same, I bounce ideas off them, but mostly I let them talk about what's bothering them. . . . [It's] mostly work and relationships.

In many situations, trainers are referred to as "therapists" or "friends." And what do good therapists or friends do? They listen and sometimes give feedback or advice. Giving feedback is also an integral part of being a good trainer, such as correcting a client's form. But responding to a client's tale of woe with supportive counsel can create trouble, as Gia notes:

[Once], a woman was telling me about her husband, about how he controls the money, [and] doesn't let her do things. I told her her worth, and what I felt she should do. Well of course they're always gonna, it's like the wife-beater, the wife sticks up for the husband. And I lost a few [clients] that way.

Gia's seemingly natural response of positive support and offer of advice goes awry. Why? Because she misreads her client's talk of problems as a serious request for her help. As Jefferson and Lee (1981) suggest, people who talk of troubles, or even directly request advice, are not always seeking answers, but rather are simply looking for empathy. Discerning what a client is after in these situations is difficult, particularly if one occupies a service position through which one routinely gives supportive feedback.

In sum, trainers and clients often talk about a range of topics during a training session, many of which have little to do with "training." Whereas making comments on appearance and giving supportive feedback are all aspects of what trainers do as "trainers," when extended into more personal realms, these comments represent claims of intimacy between participants. This intimate talk may or may not be tolerated within the relationship.

### Negotiating Relational Power through Activities

But talk is not the only emergent feature of negotiating a training relationship; another aspect open to constant negotiation is "Who's the boss?" So, who decides what is included in the workout session? The trainer or the client? Negotiating power in a training relationship might include who leads the workout, which equipment is used, or what they do for that day. What gets included in the service often reflects how trainers and clients make claims based on their relational power.

Practices that are considered standard in training, such as touching and counting reps, are also subject to negotiation. One would think that the trainer has the authority to decide these matters, nevertheless, in some instances the trainer defers to the client. In the following, Chandra tells how one problematic client dictates training fundamentals:

I've come close to firing [this client] a number of times. He has a lot of issues about certain things in the way that I touch him or handle him. There are certain ways that if I touch him it triggers something and he's like, "Don't touch me like that." And I've always apologized and I honor all of those issues. One thing that was a very important thing for me to learn [was] that he did not want me to count. And I count with every other client. Counting is part of what a trainer does! And I can't count with him. So he has gotten a little bit peeved when I accidentally start counting. He looks at me and gives me this eye, and it's really sort of evil and angry—he's a very angry man. And that's part of what my job is, to deal with his anger, and it's a lot.

Touching and counting are part of what trainers do, but not with this client. Whereas trainers often have to negotiate how they touch clients for obvious interpersonal reasons, haggling over counting seems extreme. Chandra tolerates this client's behavior because she understands managing his anger as part of her job. However, she also reserves the right to "fire" him if she can't cope. So although the client might have won this round, Chandra reminds herself that the situation is not completely out of her control.

Clients routinely make claims on the trainer's attention. Whereas most clients expect trainers to be focused upon them and not wander off to talk to others, some clients demand a particular type of attention. In this next excerpt, Gia tells how one male client requests a certain brand of exclusivity:

[He] says to me, "You know do me a favor, you are mine for the hour, OK? I'm the only man that exists in this gym for an hour." I'm like, "OK:ay?" I call him King. "OK King." Even though I'm joking, he's serious. He's dead serious. You know what, it's like so no big deal to me cuz I make a lot of money off him a year. I mean he pays me a lot of money. So I'll do it.

It is not uncommon for clients to express ownership of the trainer, such as "You are mine for the hour." However, what is unique is this client's gendered spin: "I'm the only man that exists in this gym . . ."; here, this person wants to be seen as more than just a client, he wants to be seen as a man. Gia uses humor to deal with his demands and pokes fun at his exalted sense of self by calling him "King." Ultimately, she accepts the terms of this relationship because he pays her enough, thus making it appear to be her choice.

In addition to attempts to control the behaviors of trainers—their touching, counting, focus of attention—some clients want to add certain activities to their workout. Sometimes these acts are interpreted as an affront to the goals of training and the trainer's reputation. Bill details his encounter with a client who wanted to eat while working out:

I dealt with her about six months, then I came in one day and she, just for the spite of it—I had her on the treadmill—and she was eating bagels. She brought in a bag of bagels from Noah's Deli and started eating bagels in front of me, and it was almost like, "Fuck you, I'm doing this." And I basically said, "No, you know what, not fuck me, fuck you," because my philosophy is that I can get someone else to fill that fifty dollar slot and this reflects, it really is a reflection on your image as a trainer if someone's like scarfing down bagels and looking like a cow after six months with you. It just doesn't look good on your record.

Bill understands his client's eating during exercise as open disregard for his authority and position. What he won't stand for is the public challenge to his reputation, because it reflects negatively on his status of being a good trainer.

When the workout is done outside the scrutiny of others, however, trainers often allow clients to include activities that seem to contradict the ideals of health and fitness. Jan describes one particular time she and her client use the training time to go for a friendly drink:

I have one woman that I see three times a week and she dictates what she wants to do. I go to her house. When we started we used to do floor exercises and now we just walk for an hour . . . we just walk around. Last week I went to her house and she comes downstairs and she has a bag over her shoulder, a purse. So I said, "You have your bag, you don't need this." She said, "No. This is gonna be the workout today. We're walking over to Vita [a restaurant], we're gonna have a martini and we're walking home." I went, "Fine. Thanks." So we did and it was the best workout ever. We stayed there for about half an hour and talked, and I really really like her, she's a terrific woman. I like the whole family. She [paid for the martini]. I said, "I didn't bring any money." She said, "No no *no* this is on me." She had two drinks and I had one. But she works hard.

Here, Jan characterizes this session as "the best workout ever" and explains why this type of workout occurred: The client dictates what's included in the sessions. Therefore, going for a martini is not a problem for Jan, it's a good time; she gets a free drink, some talk, and gets paid for the session. Jan further rationalizes her deference to the client's wishes, and subsequent alcohol consumption, by stating, "But she works hard."

In sum, trainers and clients assert their relational power by either making overt claims on what activities get included during training or by more subtly rationalizing why they put up with such behavior. Relatedly, what's allowed in the session also reflects participants' understandings of their relational identities. Is someone your trainer and also your drinking buddy? Being in a "training relationship" allows both parties some latitude to expand, or make claims on, their relational boundaries. However, attempts to redefine the relationship which reflect negatively, and publicly, on the reputation of the trainer as a "good trainer" are not tolerated.

## Making Relational Claims: Sexualizing the Encounter

Because training sessions involve levels of physical and emotional closeness, they are often interpreted by participants as perfect for introducing sexualized elements. Sexualizing a training encounter presents a special type of negotiation, in part, because of the precariousness of the contact, but also because the sexual is typically considered taboo or restricted to intimate relations. Thus, sexualizing a training session "makes certain claims about the nature of the relationship between participants, such that 'I can say this sort of thing to you'" (Van Leuven, 1998:92). In addition to making claims on the relationship, sexualizing might be done for specific

reasons: to expand what is included in the service, or to make moves toward out-of-gym erotic contacts. Either way, it is up to participants to set the boundaries of what is acceptable in their relationship.

Sometimes clients manage to get into a "training" relationship, only to quickly reveal that their interests lie in other areas. Bill recalls how one client demonstrates his desires, rather pointedly:

I was training one guy at the Fitness Club where they pretty much let their clientele walk around in jockstraps if they like, and I had a client come out [to train] with an erection with a jock strap on. I made him go back and put clothes on. I continued with the workout, I went and did the hour's time, after the hour's time I told him if he wanted to continue to train he'd have to take a more serious attitude, that I'm not that kind of trainer, that's not what I'm offering in my training regime. And it was understood. Obviously he wasn't getting what he wanted and that training/client relationship didn't last.

Whereas many clients might wear jockstraps during training, they are not typically worn as outer garments. That this client also sports an erection with his jockstrap suggests his choice of attire signifies more than a Madonna-inspired sense of fashion. But Bill makes it clear he's "not that kind of a trainer," which puts an end to their contact.

Sometimes clients use the fundamentals of training—touching and commenting on the body—to make moves that are interpreted by trainers as crossing relational boundaries. In the following, Donald discusses the strategy of one male client and his own ingenious response:

It [sex innuendo] had come up several times with one client. He would say things like, "My chest is really swelling, do you want to touch it?" [I said], "No, I can look at your chest and see that it's getting bigger. It's getting bigger because of the effort that you're putting forth," and he says, "Well look at my arms they're really bulging." I said, "Because you're really working hard on them and I think that's great! and I'm glad that you've noticed that and I'm glad that you brought it to my attention." So that's how I do it. I make it a compliment that this is what's happening and something we've both had to do with this. Then I cut it short right there. . . . bring it back to working out and bring it back from something personal into something professional.

Here, Donald beats this client at his own game. Whereas the client uses "gym talk" to suggest a move into closer personal contact, Donald uses the same talk, here invoking a training framework for the muscle growth, "It's getting bigger because of the effort you're putting forth." With this he puts both himself and the client firmly back in their training roles. As he says, he turns it into a compliment and gets out quickly.

Relatedly, in situations where a client is continually making passes, trainers develop pat responses that again use invoking a "training role" to set the boundaries. Stan explains what he does with one male client:

Jack is a piece of work . . . he has made so many passes at me, so many. That's one person I've had to fend off for the entire year I've know him. . . . Whenever he makes a sexual innuendo I have this phrase, I say, "Health care professional, Jack, Don't cross the line." [For example], if I've got a boy problem I'll be talking and he'll say, "Well you need to come see me . . . I'll put that bubble butt—I'll help you. . . ." [I say] "Jack, health care professional!" then he clams up. He knows when he's crossed the line.

Here, Stan uses humor to deflect recurrent open passes by his client, Jack. Despite the fact that Stan enjoys personal talk about relationships, he does not tolerate Jack's offer to help which implies a sexual encounter with *him*. Stan reminds Jack that he's a "health care professional," drawing a firm boundary which Jack recognizes at least for the moment.

In contrast, sometimes both client and trainer enjoy the sexual banter and play, such that they incorporate it into a running gag to be shared with others as a statement of their relationship. The following interaction oc-

curred the first time I observed Anne work out with her trainer Todd:

Anne and her trainer Todd walk over to the hamstring curl machine. Anne reaches out, pulls at the snaps on the sides of Todd's Adidas workout pants, and says, "I love unsnapping these pants." Todd pulls back and in a playful tone says, "Will you get outta there!" He then adds, "She would undress me if she could." Anne says that she can't help it, adding, "Todd, you're just such a piece of meat." They both laugh. Later, Todd is stretching Anne, and they are talking about the short shorts he sometimes wears when he trains her. Anne says she likes that particular outfit because she can see up his shorts. They both laugh.

For this training duo, sexualized allusions run throughout their contact, providing great sources of amusement for both. These allusions are clearly maintained as ongoing "jokes." Most interesting is that references to unsnapping pants, undressing the trainer, and revealing outfits are mutually constructed, with both parties taking turns and adding to the sexualized talk. This co-construction signifies a level of agreement between these two regarding what is allowed in their contact.

At other times, sex is joked about, but against the backdrop of a real possible encounter. Jan explains how she handled her trainer, Sam, who has a reputation for his sexual exploits with clients:

Oh I think he [the trainer] made it clear if I were up for it [we'd have sex]. But I also made it extremely clear, I said, "There's no way on the face of this earth that anything's gonna happen between the two of us." And we would joke about it, and then I'd tell him if he gave me like a year's worth of free sessions I'd give him a blow job or something like that, because I knew that money was much more important to him than even sex. I knew I was safe, and he would just [say], "No way!" [I'd say], "Don't say I'm not there for ya babe, but these are the terms of the deal."

Jan draws a firm boundary that there will be no physical sexual liaison with Sam. After doing so, however, Jan feels free to engage in sex talk with him. In fact, she even goes so far as to set the terms of a possible encounter: a blow job in exchange for training sessions. This offer is calculated, however, and based on her awareness of Sam's own boundaries and priorities: No real threat exists—not because Sam wouldn't have sex with her—but because she knows money is more important to him than sex.

Sexualizing is situational, and what is acceptable in one relationship might not be in another. In the next example, Jan advises her trainer, Sam, that his explicit sexual behaviors might not be appreciated by his other female clients:

He told me was he was quite graphic to some women. He would fondle them in the stretching situation, or he would go up to them and tell them exactly what he would do [to them]. He's done this to me too—and tell 'em very very graphically what he would do to them in a certain position they were in in the exercise machine. And I would laugh, but it wasn't funny. I told him, I said, "You can do this with me because I find it funny, but you cannot do this with anybody else. You just can't. It's disgusting! . . . He didn't care. He just liked to intimidate women I think that way.

Jan draws a clear distinction between what's acceptable in her relationship with Sam, and what might be unacceptable in his relationships with other clients. But in relating this story, Jan presents competing interpretations of Sam's behavior. By her own report, Jan *treated* Sam's graphic overtures as "funny" and something that he could do to her in their contact. However, she also makes it clear to me that she did not *experience* his behaviors as always amusing: "And I would laugh, but it wasn't funny." Perhaps this contrast between how she treated, and how she experienced the sexualization is due to hindsight; or maybe Jan was conflicted about Sam's behavior. Ultimately, her intuition that others would find his behavior offensive turned out to be accurate: After putting the moves on a lesbian client, who then threatened to sue, Sam was kicked out of the gym.

In ongoing training relations, clients and trainers use the scheduled contact and standards of training—such as talk and touch—to make moves into other activities either to be contained within the hour's time, or to possibly move to outside gym contact. In many of these instances, trainers and clients report drawing firm lines as to what is acceptable training behavior. Sometimes this is done through humor and invoking a training identity ("Health care professional, Jack"), or making a client put on clothes. But even telling a trainer "There's no way anything's ever gonna happen between us" does not mean that sexual jokes cannot be exchanged, and deals offered ("I'd give him a blow job . . ."). Interestingly, even the most overt sexualizing doesn't always signal the end of the training contact, but rather can be incorporated and managed as an aspect of the relationship.

## Conclusion

People often enter situations with multiple understandings of what is going on. To what degree these understandings disrupt the encounter often depends on when they are revealed. For example, expressing different ideas of what personal training involves is not tolerated during the initial contact. In fact, some demonstration of a seriousness in fitness training has to be displayed by both parties. However, once a "training" relationship begins, trainers and clients appear more resilient and tolerant of ambiguity or move to expand what is included in their relationships; so tolerant that even what seems like blatant boundary crossings do not necessarily signal the end of the relationship.

Negotiating relational boundaries often comes down to what trainers and clients are willing to include in the service: Personal talk? Getting advice? Sometimes what is included or excluded reflects participants' claims on relational power: Can a trainer count for her client? Look at other patrons? Why can some training relationships support martinis and not bagels? It all depends upon the specific trainer and client and how they understand their relational boundaries. In some instances, moving into personal realms or including non-training activities is unproblematic for trainers and clients; but not always.

Likewise, whether or not the training relationship could be sexualized, and to what extent, depends upon several factors: when the sexualized move is made; who makes the move; and what type of move s/he is making? Maybe, as one trainer states, allowing clients to make sexualized moves might all come down to "Are you interested in them?" Ultimately, however, trainers are much more tolerant of sustaining erotic illusions with clients who aren't perceived as "threatening" on a sexual level. But what is considered threatening is also a negotiation, and situationally specific. In addition, although participants tolerate sexualized elements, it does not mean that they might not also be conflicted about them. For this reason, the dynamics of what gets perceived as "unwanted" sexualization is complex. Thus, investigations of "sexual harassment" must take into account considerations of how specific participants have negotiated their relational boundaries. For what is appropriate in one moment between individuals might not be tolerated on another occasion.

Service contacts that are ongoing, that involve sociability, physical closeness, and touching, present certain issues for participants that are not found in one-shot encounters such as ordering food at McDonald's. In contrast, these ongoing contacts routinely provide opportunities for participants to expand the dimensions of their relational relevance. However, in this expansion, it is not always easy to pinpoint what is going on between them; is it all just included in "training?" Further, these type of encounters present challenges to researchers interested in studying relational relevance. That researchers might have difficulty in determining clear-cut relational boundaries perhaps mirrors some of the problems faced by participants in these situations: having to determine what is going on, and who these people are to each other is an ever evolving, and often elusive, thing.

## Notes

1. Most notable of these conventions is that the exam takes place in a doctor's office and not in the backseat of a car.

2. The myriad ways that trainers/clients extend their relationship to include out-of-work contact and socializing is explored in the paper "Is This Included in the Service? Negotiating Relevant Identities and Relational Boundaries in Personal Training"; forthcoming.

## References

Emerson, Joan P. (1970). "Behavior in Private Places: Sustaining Definitions of Reality in Gynecological Examinations" in *Recent Sociology*, no. 2, ed. by P. Dreitsel. New York: Macmillan, pp. 74–97.

Goffman, Erving. (1961). *Encounters*. New York: The Bobbs-Merrill Company.

Henslin, James M., and Mae A. Biggs. (1971). "Dramaturgical Desexualization: The Sociology of the Vaginal Examination," in James M. Henslin (ed.), *Studies in the Sociology of Sex*. New York: Appleton-Century-Crofts.

Hochschild, Arlie. (1983). *The Managed Heart*. Berkeley: University of California Press.

Jefferson, Gail, and John R. E. Lee. (1981). "The Rejection of Advice: Managing the Problematic Convergence of a 'Troubles-Telling' and a 'Service Encounter.'" *Journal of Pragmatics 5*. North-Holland Publishing Company, pp. 399–422.

Leidner, Robyn. (1993). *Fast Food, Fast Talk*. Berkeley: University of California Press.

Van Leuven, Linda. (1998). "'I Need a Screw': Workplace Sexualization as an Interactional Achievement," in J. O'Brien and J. Howard (eds.), *Everyday Inequalities: Critical Inquiries*. London: Blackwell Publishers, pp. 73–96.

Whalen, M., and D. Zimmerman. (1987). "Sequential and Institutional Contexts in Calls for Help," *Social Psychological Quarterly* 50(2): pp. 172–185.

Zimmerman, D. (1992). "The Interactional Organization of Calls for Emergency Assistance." In P. Drew and J. Heritage (eds.), *Talk at Work*. Cambridge: Cambridge University Press, pp. 418–469.

# Behavior in Private Places: Sustaining Definitions of Reality in Gynecological Examinations

*Joan P. Emerson*

## Introduction

In *The Social Construction of Reality*, Berger and Luckmann discuss how people construct social order and yet construe the reality of everyday life to exist independently of themselves.[1] Berger and Luckmann's work succeeds in synthesizing some existing answers with new insights. Many sociologists have pointed to the importance of social consensus in what people believe; if everyone else seems to believe in something, a person tends to accept the common belief without question. Other sociologists have discussed the concept of legitimacy, an acknowledgment that what exists has the right to exist, and delineated various lines of argument

"Behavior in Private Places: Sustaining Definitions of Reality in Gynecological Examinations" by J. P. Emerson from *Recent Sociology* (pp. 74–97), edited by P. Dreitsel, 1970. New York: Macmillan. Reprinted by permission of the author.

    Arlene K. Daniels has applied her talent for editing and organizing to several drafts of this paper. Robert M. Emerson, Roger Pritchard, and Thomas J. Scheff have also commented on the material. The investigation was supported in part by a predoctoral fellowship from the National Institute of Mental Health (Fellowship Number MPM-18,239) and by Behavioral Sciences Training Grant MH-8104 from the National Institute of Mental Health, as well as General Research Support Grant I-SOI-FR-05441 from the National Institutes of Health, U.S. Department of Health, Education, and Welfare, to the School of Public Health, University of California, Berkeley.

which can be taken to justify a state of affairs. Berger and Luckmann emphasize three additional processes that provide persons with evidence that things have an objective existence apart from themselves. Perhaps most important is the experience that reality seems to be out there before we arrive on the scene. This notion is fostered by the nature of language, which contains an all-inclusive scheme of categories, is shared by a community, and must be learned laboriously by each new member. Further, definitions of reality are continuously validated by apparently trivial features of the social scene, such as details of the setting, persons' appearance and demeanor, and "inconsequential" talk. Finally, each part of a systematic world view serves as evidence for all the other parts, so that reality is solidified by a process of intervalidation of supposedly independent events.

Because Berger and Luckmann's contribution is theoretical, their units of analysis are abstract processes. But they take those processes to be grounded in social encounters. Thus, Berger and Luckmann's theory provides a framework for making sense of social interaction. In this paper observations of a concrete situation will be interpreted to show how reality is embodied in routines and reaffirmed in social interaction.

Situations differ in how much effort it takes to sustain the current definition of the situation. Some situations are relatively stable; others are precarious.[2] Stability depends on the likelihood of three types of disconforming events. Intrusions on the scene may threaten definitions of reality, as when people smell smoke in a theater or when a third person joins a couple and calls one member by a name the second member does not recognize. Participants may deliberately decline to validate the current reality, like Quakers who refused to take off their hats to the king. Sometimes participants are unable to produce the gestures which would validate the current reality. Perhaps a person is ignorant of the relevant vocabulary of gestures. Or a person, understanding how he should behave, may have limited social skills so that he cannot carry off the performance he would like to. For those who insist on "sincerity," a performance becomes especially taxing if they lack conviction about the trueness of the reality they are attempting to project.

A reality can hardly seem self-evident if a person is simultaneously aware of a counter-reality. Berger and Luckmann write as though definitions of reality were internally congruent. However, the ordinary reality may contain not only a dominant definition, but in addition counterthemes opposing or qualifying the dominant definition. Thus, several contradictory definitions must be sustained at the same time. Because each element tends to challenge the other elements, such composite definitions of reality are inherently precarious even if the probability of disconfirming events is low.

A situation where the definition of reality is relatively precarious has advantages for the analysis proposed here, for processes of sustaining reality should be more obvious where that reality is problematic. The situation chosen, the gynecological examination,[3] is precarious for both reasons discussed above. First, it is an excellent example of multiple contradictory definitions of reality, as described in the next section. Second,

while intrusive and deliberate threats are not important, there is a substantial threat from participants' incapacity to perform.

Dramaturgical abilities are taxed in gynecological examinations because the less convincing reality internalized by secondary socialization is unusually discrepant with rival perspectives taken for granted in primary socialization.[4] Gynecological examinations share similar problems of reality-maintenance with any medical procedure, but the issues are more prominent because the site of the medical task is a woman's genitals. Because touching usually connotes personal intimacy, persons may have to work at accepting the physician's privileged access to the patient's genitals.[5] Participants are not entirely convinced that modesty is out of place. Since a woman's genitals are commonly accessible only in a sexual context, sexual connotations come readily to mind. Although most people realize that sexual responses are inappropriate, they may be unable to dismiss the sexual reaction privately and it may interfere with the conviction with which they undertake their impersonal performance. The structure of a gynecological examination highlights the very features which the participants are supposed to disattend. So the more attentive the participants are to the social situation, the more the unmentionable is forced on their attention.

The next section will characterize the complex composition of the definition of reality routinely sustained in gynecological examinations. Then some of the routine arrangements and interactional maneuvers which embody and express this definition will be described. A later section will discuss threats to the definition which arise in the course of the encounter. Measures that serve to neutralize the threats and reaffirm the definition will be analyzed. The concluding section will turn to the theoretical issues of precariousness, multiple contradictory definitions of reality, and implicit communication.

## The Medical Definition and Its Counterthemes

Sometimes people are in each other's presence in what they take to be a "gynecological examination." What happens in a gynecological examination is part of the common stock of knowledge. Most people know that a gynecological examination is when a doctor examines a woman's genitals in a medical setting. Women who have undergone this experience know that the examination takes place in a special examining room where the patient lies with her buttocks down to the edge of the table and her feet in stirrups, that usually a nurse is present as a chaperone, that the actual examining lasts only a few minutes, and so forth. Besides knowing what equipment to provide for the doctor, the nurse has in mind a typology of responses patients have to this situation, and a typology of doctors' styles of performance. The doctor has technical knowledge about the examining procedures, what observations may be taken to indicate ways of getting patients to relax, and so on.

Immersed in the medical world where the scene constitutes a routine, the staff assume the responsibility for a credible performance. The staff take part in gynecological examinations many times a day, while the patient is a fleeting visitor. More deeply convinced of the reality themselves, the staff are willing to convince skeptical patients. The physician guides the patient through the precarious scene in a contained manner: taking the initiative, controlling the encounter, keeping the patient in line, defining the situation by his reaction, and giving cues that "this is done" and "other people go through this all the time."

Not only must people continue to believe that "this is a gynecological examination," but also that "this is a gynecological examination going right." The major definition to be sustained for this purpose is "this is a medical situation" (not a party, sexual as-sault, psychological experiment, or anything else). If it is a medical situation, then it follows that "no one is embarrassed"[6] and "no one is thinking in sexual terms."[7] Anyone who indicates the contrary must be swayed by some nonmedical definition.

The medical definition calls for a matter-of-fact stance. One of the most striking observations about a gynecological examination is the marked implication underlying the staff's demeanor toward the patient: "Of course, you take this as matter-of-factly as we do." The staff implicitly contend: "In the medical world the pelvic area is like any other part of the body; its private and sexual connotations are left behind when you enter the hospital." The staff want it understood that their gazes take in only medically pertinent facts, so they are not concerned with an aesthetic inspection of a patient's body. Their nonchalant pose attempts to put a gynecological examination in the same light as an internal examination of the ear.

Another implication of the medical definition is that the patient is a technical object to the staff. It is as if the staff work on an assembly line for repairing bodies; similar body parts continually roll by and the staff have a particular job to do on them. The staff are concerned with the typical features of the body part and its pathology rather than with the unique features used to define a person's identity. The staff disattend the connection between a part of the body and some intangible self that is supposed to inhabit the body.

The scene is credible precisely because the staff act as if they have every right to do what they are doing. Any hint of doubt from the staff would compromise the medical definition. Since the patient's nonchalance merely serves to validate the staff's right, it may be dispensed with or without the same threat. Furthermore, the staff claim to be merely agents of the medical system, which is intent on providing good health care to patients. This medical system imposes procedures and standards which the staff are merely following in this particular instance. That is, what the staff do derives from external coercion—"We have to do it this way"—rather than from personal choices which they would be free to revise in order to accommodate the patient.

The medical definition grants the staff the right to carry out their task. If not for the medical definition the staff's routine activities could be defined as unconscionable assaults on the dignity of individuals. The topics of talk, particularly inquiries about bodily functioning, sexual experience, and death of relatives might be taken as offenses against propriety. As for exposure and manipulation of the patient's body, it would be a shocking and degrading invasion of privacy were the patient not defined as a technical object. The infliction of pain would be mere cruelty. The medical definition justifies the request that a presumably competent adult give up most of his autonomy to persons often subordinate in age, sex, and social class. The patient needs the medical definition to minimize the threat to his dignity; the staff need it in order to inveigle the patient into cooperating.

Yet definitions that appear to contradict the medical definition are routinely expressed in the course of gynecological examinations. Some gestures acknowledge the pelvic area as special; other gestures acknowledge the patient as a person. These counterdefinitions are as essential to the encounter as the medical definition. We have already discussed how an actor's lack of conviction may interfere with his performance. Implicit acknowledgments of the special meaning of the pelvic area help those players hampered by lack of conviction to perform adequately. If a player's sense of "how things really are" is implicitly acknowledged, he often finds it easier to adhere outwardly to a contrary definition.

A physician may gain a patient's cooperation by acknowledging her as a person. The physician wants the patient to acknowledge the medical definition, cooperate with the procedures of the examination, and acknowl-edge his professional competence. The physician is in a position to bargain with the patient in order to obtain this cooperation. He can offer her attention and acknowledgment as a person. At times he does so.

Although defining a person as a technical object is necessary in order for medical activities to proceed, it constitutes an indignity in itself. This indignity can be canceled or at least qualified by simultaneously acknowledging the patient as a person.

The medical world contains special activities and special perspectives. Yet the inhabitants of the medical world travel back and forth to the general community where modesty, death, and other medically relevant matters are regarded quite differently. It is not so easy to dismiss general community meanings for the time one finds oneself in a medical setting. The counterthemes that the pelvic area is special and that patients are persons provide an opportunity to show deference to general community meanings at the same time that one is disregarding them.

Sustaining the reality of a gynecological examination does not mean sustaining the medical definition, then. What is to be sustained is a shifting balance between medical definition and counterthemes.[8] Too much emphasis on the medical definition alone would undermine the reality, as would a flamboyant manifestation of the counterthemes apart from the medical definition. The next three sections will suggest how this balance is achieved.

### Sustaining the Reality

The appropriate balance between medical definition and counterthemes has to be created anew at every moment. However, some routinized procedures and demeanor are available to participants in gynecological examinations. Persons recognize that if certain limits are exceeded, the situation would be irremediably shattered. Some arrangements have been found useful because they simultaneously express medical definition and countertheme. Routine ways of meeting the task requirements and also dealing with "normal trouble" are available. This section will describe how themes and counterthemes are embodied in routinized procedures and demeanor.

The pervasiveness of the medical definition is expressed by indicators that the scene is enacted under medical auspices.[9] The action is located in "medical space" (hospital or doctor's office). Features of the setting such as divisions of space, decor, and equipment are constant reminders that it is indeed "medical space." Even background details such as the loudspeaker calling, "Dr. Morris. Dr. Armand Morris" serve as evidence for medical reality (suppose the loudspeaker were to announce instead, "Five minutes until post time"). The staff wear medical uniforms, don medical gloves, use medical instruments. The exclusion of lay persons, particularly visitors of the patient who may be accustomed to the patient's nudity at home, helps to preclude confusion between the contact of medicine and the contact of intimacy.[10]

Some routine practices simultaneously acknowledge the medical definition and qualify it by making special provision for the pelvic area. For instance, rituals of respect express dignity for the patient. The patient's body is draped so as to expose only that part which is to receive the technical attention of the doctor. The presence of a nurse acting as "chaperone" cancels any residual suggestiveness of male and female alone in a room.[11]

Medical talk stands for and continually expresses allegiance to the medical definition. Yet certain features of medical talk acknowledge a nonmedical delicacy. Despite the fact that persons present on a gynecological ward must attend to many topics connected with the pelvic area and various bodily functions, these topics are generally not discussed. Strict conventions dictate what unmentionables are to be acknowledged under what circumstances. However,

persons are exceptionally free to refer to the genitals and related matters on the obstetrics-gynecology service. If technical matters in regard to the pelvic area come up, they are to be discussed nonchalantly.

The special language found in staff-patient contacts contributes to depersonalization and desexualization of the encounter. Scientific-sounding medical terms facilitate such communication. Substituting dictionary terms for everyday words adds formality. The definite article replaces the pronoun adjective in reference to body parts, so that for example, the doctor refers to "the vagina" and never "your vagina." Instructions to the patient in the course of the examination are couched in language which bypasses sexual imagery; the vulgar connotation of "spread your legs" is generally metamorphosed into the innocuous "let your knees fall apart."

While among themselves the staff generally use explicit technical terms, explicit terminology is often avoided in staff-patient contacts.[12] The reference to the pelvic area may be merely understood, as when a patient says: "I feel so uncomfortable there right now" or "They didn't go near to this area, so why did they have to shave it?" In speaking with patients the staff frequently uses euphemisms. A doctor asks: "When did you first notice difficulty down below?" and a nurse inquires: "Did you wash between your legs?" Persons characteristically refer to pelvic examinations euphemistically in staff-patient encounters. "The doctors want to take a peek at you," a nurse tells a patient. Or "Dr. Ryan wants to see you in the examining room."

In one pelvic examination there was a striking contrast between the language of staff and patient. The patient was graphic; she used action words connoting physical contact to refer to the examination procedure: feeling, poking, touching, and punching. Yet she never located this action in regard to her body, always omitting to state where the physical contact occurred. The staff used impersonal medical language and euphemisms: "I'm going to examine you"; "I'm just cleaning out some blood clots"; "He's just trying to fix you up a bit."

Sometimes the staff introduce explicit terminology to clarify a patient's remark. A patient tells the doctor, "It's bleeding now" and the doctor answers, "You? From the vagina?" Such a response indicates the appropriate vocabulary, the degree of freedom permitted in technically oriented conversation, and the proper detachment. Yet the common avoidance of explicit terminology in staff-patient contacts suggests that despite all the precautions to assure that the medical definition prevails, many patients remain somewhat embarrassed by the whole subject. To avoid provoking this embarrassment, euphemisms and understood references are used when possible.

Highly specific requirements for everybody's behavior during a gynecological examination curtail the leeway for the introduction of discordant notes. Routine technical procedures organize the event from beginning to end, indicating what action each person should take at each moment. Verbal exchanges are also constrained by the technical task, in that the doctor uses routine phrases of direction and reassurance to the patient. There is little margin for ad-libbing during a gynecological examination.

The specifications for demeanor are elaborate. Foremost is that both staff and patient should be nonchalant about what is happening. According to the staff, the exemplary patient should be "in play": showing she is attentive to the situation by her bodily tautness, facial expression, direction of glance, tone of voice, tempo of speech and bodily movements, timing and appropriateness of responses. The patient's voice should be controlled, mildly pleasant, self-confident, and impersonal. Her facial expression should be attentive and neutral, leaning toward the mildly pleasant and friendly side, as if she were talking to the doctor in his office, fully dressed and seated in a chair. The patient is to have an attentive glance upward, at the ceiling or at other persons in the room, eyes open, not dreamy or "away," but ready at a second's notice to revert to the doctor's face for a specific verbal exchange. Except for such a verbal exchange, however, the patient is supposed to avoid looking into the doctor's eyes during the actual examination because direct eye contact between the two at this time is provocative. Her role calls for passivity and self-effacement. The patient should show willingness to relinquish control to the doctor. She should refrain from speaking at length and from making inquiries which would require the doctor to reply at length. So as not to point up her undignified position, she should not project her personality profusely. The self must be eclipsed in order to sustain the definition that the doctor is working on a technical object and not a person.

The physician's demeanor is highly stylized. He intersperses his examination with remarks to the patient in a soothing tone of voice: "Now relax as much as you can"; "I'll be as gentle as I can"; "Is that tender right there?" Most of the phrases with which he encourages the patient to relax are routine even though his delivery may suggest a unique relationship. He demonstrates that he is the detached professional and the patient demonstrates that it never enters her mind that he could be anything except detached. Since intimacy can be introduced into instrumental physical contact by a "loving" demeanor (lingering, caressing motions and contact beyond what the task requires), a doctor must take special pains to ensure that his demeanor remains a brisk, no-nonsense show of efficiency.[13]

Once I witnessed a gynecological examination of a forty-year-old woman who played the charming and scatterbrained Southern belle. The attending physician stood near the patient's head and carried on a flippant conversation with her while a resident and medical student actually performed the examination. The patient completely ignored the examination, except for brief answers to the examining doctor's inquiries. Under these somewhat trying circumstances she attempted to carry off a gay, attractive pose and the attending physician cooperated with her by making a series of bantering remarks.

Most physicians are not so lucky as to have a colleague conversing in cocktail-hour style with the patient while they are probing her vagina. Ordinarily the physician must play both parts at once, treating the patient as an object with his hands while simultaneously acknowledging her as a person with his voice. In this incident, where two physicians simultaneously deal with the patient in two distinct ways, the dual approach to the patient usually maintained by the examining physician becomes more obvious.[14]

The doctor needs to communicate with the patient as a person for technical reasons. Should he want to know when the patient feels pain in the course of examination or information about other medical matters, he must address her as a person. Also the doctor may want to instruct the patient on how to facilitate the examination. The most reiterated instruction refers to relaxation. Most patients are not sufficiently relaxed when the doctor is ready to begin. He then reverts to a primitive level of communication and treats the patient almost like a young child. He speaks in a soft, soothing voice, probably calling the patient by her first name, and it is not so much the words as his manner which is significant. This caressing voice is routinely used by hospital staff members to patients in critical situations, as when the patient is overtly frightened or disoriented. By using it here the doctor heightens his interpersonal relation with the patient, trying to reassure her as a person in order to get her to relax.

Moreover even during a gynecological examination, failing to acknowledge another as a person is an insult. It is insulting to be entirely instrumental about instrumental contacts. Some acknowledgment of the intimate connotations of touching must occur. Therefore, a measure of "loving" demeanor

is subtly injected. A doctor cannot employ the full gamut of loving insinuations that a lover might infuse into instrumental touching. So he indirectly implies a hint of intimacy which is intended to counter the insult and make the procedure acceptable to the woman. The doctor conveys this loving demeanor not by lingering or superfluous contact, but by radiating concern in his general manner, offering extra assistance, and occasionally by sacrificing the task requirements to "gentleness."

In short, the doctor must convey an optimal combination of impersonality and hints of intimacy that simultaneously avoid the insult of sexual familiarity and the insult of unacknowledged identity. The doctor must manage this even though the behavior emanating from each definition is contradictory. If the doctor can achieve this feat, it will contribute to keeping the patient in line. In the next section, we will see how the patient may threaten this precarious balance.

## Precariousness in Gynecological Examinations

Threats to the reality of a gynecological examination may occur if the balance of opposing definitions is not maintained as described above. Reality in gynecological examinations is challenged mainly by patients. Occasionally a medical student, who might be considerably more of a novice than an experienced patient, seemed uncomfortable in the scene.[15] Experienced staff members were rarely observed to undermine the reality.

Certain threatening events which could occur in any staff-patient encounter bring an added dimension of precariousness to a gynecological examination because the medical aegis screens so much more audacity at that time. In general, staff expect patients to remain poised and in play like a friendly office receptionist; any show of emotion except in a controlled fashion is objectionable. Patients should not focus on identities of themselves or the staff outside those relevant to the medical exchange. Intractable patients may complain about the pain, discomfort, and indignities of submitting to medical treatment and care. Patients may go so far as to show they are reluctant to comply with the staff. Even if they are complying, they may indirectly challenge the expert status of the staff, as by "asking too many questions."

Failure to maintain a poised performance is a possible threat in any social situation. Subtle failures of tone are common, as when a performer seems to lack assurance. Performers may fumble for their lines: hesitate, begin a line again, or correct themselves. A show of embarrassment, such as blushing, has special relevance in gynecological examinations. On rare occasions when a person shows signs of sexual response, he or she really has something to blush about. A more subtle threat is an indication that the actor is putting an effort into the task of maintaining nonchalant demeanor; if it requires such an effort, perhaps it is not a "natural" response.

Such effort may be indicated, for example, in regard to the direction of glance. Most situations have a common visual focus of attention, but in a gynecological examination the logical focus, the patient's internal organs, is not accessible; and none of the alternatives, such as staring at the patient's face, locking glances with others, or looking out the window are feasible. The unavailability of an acceptable place to rest the eyes is more evident when the presence of several medical students creates a "crowd" atmosphere in the small cubicle. The lack of a visual focus of attention and the necessity to shift the eyes from object to object requires the participants to remain vaguely aware of their directions of glance. Normally the resting place of the eyes is a background matter automatically managed without conscious attention. Attentiveness to this background detail is a constant reminder of how awkward the situation is.

Certain lapses in patients' demeanor are so common as hardly to be threatening.

When patients express pain it can be overlooked if the patient is giving other signs of trying to behave well, because it can be taken that the patient is temporarily overwhelmed by a physiological state. The demonstrated presence of pain recalls the illness framework and counters sexual connotations. Crying can be accredited to pain and dismissed in a similar way. Withdrawing attention from the scene, so that one is not ready with an immediate comeback when called upon, is also relatively innocuous because it is close to the required passive but in play demeanor.

Some threats derive from the patient's ignorance of how to strike an acceptable balance between medical and nonmedical definitions, despite her willingness to do so. In two areas in particular, patients stumble over the subtleties of what is expected: physical decorum (proprieties of sights, sounds, and smells of the body) and modesty. While the staff is largely concerned with behavioral decorum and not about lapses in physical decorum, patients are more concerned about the latter, whether due to their medical condition or the procedure. Patients sometimes even let behavioral decorum lapse in order to express their concern about unappealing conditions of their bodies, particularly discharges and odors. This concern is a vestige of a nonmedical definition of the situation, for an attractive body is relevant only in a personal situation and not in a medical one.

Some patients fail to know when to display their private parts unashamedly to others and when to conceal them like anyone else. A patient may make an " inappropriate" show of modesty, thus not granting the staff the right to view what medical personnel have the right to view and others do not. But if patients act as though they literally accept the medical definition this also constitutes a threat. If a patient insists on acting as if the exposure of her breasts, buttocks, and pelvic area are no different from exposure of her arm or leg, she is "immodest." The medical definition is supposed to be in force only as necessary to facilitate specific medical tasks. If a patient becomes nonchalant enough to allow herself to remain uncovered for much longer than is technically necessary she becomes a threat. This also holds for verbal remarks about personal matters. Patients who misinterpret the license by exceeding its limits unwittingly challenge the definition of reality.[16]

### Neutralizing Threatening Events

Most gynecological examinations proceed smoothly and the definition of reality is sustained without conscious attention.[17] Sometimes subtle threats to the definition arise, and occasionally staff and patient struggle covertly over the definition throughout the encounters.[18] The staff take more preventive measures where they anticipate the most trouble: young, unmarried girls; persons known to be temporarily upset; and persons with reputations as uncooperative. In such cases the doctor may explain the technical details of the procedure more carefully and offer direct reassurance. Perhaps he will take extra time to establish personal rapport, as by medically related inquiries ("How are you feeling?" "Do you have as much pain today?"), personal inquiries ("Where do you live?"), addressing the patient by her first name, expressing direct sympathy, praising the patient for her behavior in this difficult situation, speaking in a caressing voice, and affectionate gestures. Doctors also attempt to reinforce rapport as a response to threatening events.

The foremost technique in neutralizing threatening events is to sustain a nonchalant demeanor even if the patient is blushing with embarrassment, blanching from fear, or moaning in pain. The patient's inappropriate gestures may be ignored as the staff convey, "We're waiting until you are ready to play along." Working to bring the scene off, the staff may claim that this is routine, or happens to patients in general; invoke the "for your own good" clause; counterclaim that

something is less important than the patient indicates; assert that the unpleasant medical procedure is almost over; and contend that the staff do not like to cause pain or trouble to patients (as by saying, "I'm sorry" when they appear to be causing pain). The staff may verbally contradict a patient, give an evasive answer to a question, or try to distract the patient. By giving a technical explanation or rephrasing in the appropriate hospital language something the patient has referred to in a nonmedical way, the staff member reinstates the medical definition.

Redefinition is another tactic available to the staff. Signs of embarrassment and sexual arousal in patients may be redefined as "fear of pain." Sometimes sexual arousal will be labeled "ticklishness." After one examination the doctor thanked the patient, presumably for her cooperation, thus typifying the patient's behavior as cooperative and so omitting a series of uncooperative acts which he had previously acknowledged.

Humor may be used to discount the line the patient is taking. At the same time, humor provides a safety valve for all parties whereby the sexual connotations and general concern about gynecological examinations may be expressed by indirection. Without taking the responsibility that a serious form of the message would entail, the participants may communicate with each other about the events at hand. They may discount the derogatory implications of what would be an invasion of privacy in another setting by dismissing the procedure with a laugh. If a person can joke on a topic, he demonstrates to others that he possesses a laudatory degree of detachment.

For example, in one encounter a patient vehemently protests, "Oh, Dr. Raleigh, what are you doing?" Dr. Raleigh, exaggerating his southern accent, answers, "Nothin'." His levity conveys: "However much you may dislike this, we have to go on with it for your own good. Since you know that perfectly well, your protest could not be calling for a serious answer." Dr. Raleigh also plays the seducer claiming innocence, thus obliquely referring to the sexual connotations of where his hand is at the moment. In another incident Dr. Ryan is attempting to remove some gauze which has been placed in the vagina to stop the bleeding. He flippantly announces that the remaining piece of gauze has disappeared inside the patient. After a thorough search Dr. Ryan holds up a piece of gauze on the instrument triumphantly: "Well, here it is. Do you want to take it home and put it in your scrapbook?" By this remark Dr. Ryan ridicules the degree of involvement in one's own medical condition which would induce a patient to save this kind of memento. Later in the same examination Dr. Ryan announces he will do a rectal examination and the (elderly) patient protests, "Oh, honey, don't bother." Dr. Ryan assures her jokingly, "It's no bother, really." The indirect message of all three jokes is that one should take gynecological procedures casually. Yet simultaneously an undercurrent of each joke acknowledges a perspective contrary to the medical definition.

While in most encounters the nurse remains quietly in the background, she comes forward to deal actively with the patient if the definition of reality is threatened. In fact, one of the main functions of her presence is to provide a team member for the doctor in those occasional instances where the patient threatens to get out of line. Team members can create a more convincing reality than one person alone. Doctor and nurse may collude against an uncooperative patient, as by giving each other significant looks. If things reach the point of staff collusion, however, it may mean that only by excluding the patient can the definition of reality be reaffirmed. A more drastic form of solidifying the definition by excluding recalcitrant participants is to cast the patient into the role of an "emotionally disturbed person." Whatever an "emotionally disturbed person" may think or do does not count against the reality the rest of us acknowledge.

Perhaps the major safeguard of reality is that challenge is channeled outside the examination. Comments about the unpleasantness of the procedure and unaesthetic features of the patient's body occur mainly between women, two patients or a nurse and a patient. Such comments are most frequent while the patient gets ready for the examination and waits for the doctor or after the doctor leaves. The patient may establish a momentary "fellow-woman aura" as she quietly voices her distaste for the procedure to the nurse. "What we women have to go through" the patient may say. Or, "I wish all gynecologists were women." Why? "They understand because they've been through it themselves." The patient's confiding manner implies: "I have no right to say this, or even feel it, and yet I do." This phenomenon suggests that patients actually have strong negative reactions to gynecological examinations which belie their acquiescence in the actual situation. Yet patients' doubts are expressed in an innocuous way which does not undermine the definition of reality when it is most needed.

To construct the scene convincingly, participants constantly monitor their own behavior and that of others. The tremendous work of producing the scene is contained in subtle maneuvers in regard to details which may appear inconsequential to the layman. Since awareness may interfere with a convincing performance, the participants may have an investment in being as unselfconscious as possible. But the sociologist is free to recognize the significance of "inconsequential details" in constructing reality.

## Conclusion

In a gynecological examination the reality sustained is not the medical definition alone, but a dissonance of themes and counterthemes. What is done to acknowledge one theme undermines the others. No theme can be taken for granted because its opposite is always in mind. That is why the reality of a gynecological examination can never be routinized, but always remains precarious.

The gynecological examination should not be dismissed as an anomaly. The phenomenon is revealed more clearly in this case because it is an extreme example. But the gynecological examination merely exaggerates the internally contradictory nature of definitions of reality found in most situations. Many situations where the dominant definition is occupational or technical have a secondary theme of sociality which must be implicitly acknowledged (as in buttering up the secretary, small talk with sales clerks, or the undertaker's show of concern for the bereaved family). In "business entertaining" and conventions of professional associations a composite definition of work and pleasure is sustained. Under many circumstances a composite definition of action as both deviant and unproblematic prevails. For example, while Donald Ball stresses the claim of respectability in his description of an abortion clinic, his material illustrates the interplay of the dominant theme of respectability and a countertheme wherein the illicitness of the situation is acknowledged.[19] Internally inconsistent definitions also are sustained in many settings on who persons are and what their relation is to each other.

Sustaining a sense of the solidness of a reality composed of multiple contradictory definitions takes unremitting effort. The required balance among the various definitions fluctuates from moment to moment. The appropriate balance depends on what the participants are trying to do at that moment. As soon as one matter is dealt with, something else comes into focus, calling for a different balance. Sometimes even before one issue is completed, another may impose itself as taking priority. Further, each balance contains the seeds of its own demise, in that a temporary emphasis on one theme may disturb the long-run balance unless subsequent emphasis on the countertheme negates it. Because the most effective balance depends on many unpredictable factors, it is difficult to routinize the balance into formulas that prescribe a specific balance for given conditions. Routinization is also impractical because the particular forms by which the themes are expressed are opportunistic. That is, persons seize opportunities for expression according to what would be a suitable move at each unique moment of an encounter. Therefore, a person constantly must attend to how to express the balance of themes via the currently available means.

Multiple contradictory realities are expressed on various levels of explicitness and implicitness. Sustaining a sense of solidness of reality depends on the right balance of explicit and implicit expressions of each theme through a series of points in time. The most effective gestures express a multitude of themes on different levels. The advantages of multiple themes in the same gesture are simultaneous qualification of one theme by another, hedging (the gesture lacks one definite meaning), and economy of gestures.

Rational choices of explicit and implicit levels would take the following into account. The explicit level carries the most weight, unless countered by deliberate effort. Things made explicit are hard to dismiss or discount compared to what is left implicit. In fact, if the solidification of explication is judged to be nonreversible, use of the explicit level may not be worth the risk. On the other hand, when participants sense that the implicit level is greatly in use, their whole edifice of belief may become shaken. "I sense that a lot is going on underneath" makes a person wonder about the reality he is accepting. There must be a lot he does not know, some of which might be evidence which would undermine what he currently accepts.

The invalidation of one theme by the concurrent expression of its countertheme must be avoided by various maneuvers. The guiding principle is that participants must prevent a definition that a contradiction exists between theme and countertheme from emerging. Certain measures routinely contribute to this purpose. Persons must try to hedge on both theme and countertheme by expressing them tentatively rather than definitely and simultaneously alluding to and discounting each theme. Theme and countertheme should not be presented simultaneously or contiguously on the explicit level unless it is possible to discount their contradictory features. Finally, each actor must work to keep the implicit level out of awareness for the other participants.

The technique of constructing reality depends on good judgment about when to make things explicit and when to leave them implicit, how to use the implicit level to reinforce and qualify the explicit level, distributing themes among explicit and implicit levels at any one moment, and seizing opportunities to embody messages. To pursue further these tentative suggestions on how important explicit and implicit levels are for sustaining reality, implicit levels of communication must be explored more systematically.

## Notes

1. P. Berger & T. Luckmann (1966), *The social construction of reality*, Garden City, NY: Doubleday.

2. The precarious nature of social interaction is discussed throughout the work of Erving Goffman.

3. The data in this article are based on observations of approximately 75 gynecological examinations conducted by male physicians on an obstetrics-gynecology ward and some observations from a medical ward for comparison. For a full account of this study, see J. P. Emerson (1963), "Social functions of humor in a hospital setting," unpublished doctoral dissertation, University of California at Berkeley. For a sociological discussion of a similar setting, see W. P. Rosengren & S. DeVault (1963), "The sociology of time and space in an obstetrical hospital," in E. Freidson (Ed.), *The hospital in modern society* (pp. 266–292), New York: Free Press of Glencoe.

4. "It takes severe biographical shocks to disintegrate the massive reality internalized in early childhood; much less to destroy the realities internalized later. Beyond this, it is relatively easy to set aside the reality of the secondary internalizations." Berger & Luckmann (1966), p. 142.

5. As stated by Lief and Fox: "The amounts and occasions of bodily contact are carefully regulated in all societies, and very much so in ours. Thus, the kind of access to the body of the patient that a physician in our society has is a uniquely privileged one. Even in the course of a so-called routine physical examination, the physician is permitted to handle the patient's body in ways otherwise permitted only to special intimates, and in the case of procedures such as rectal and vaginal examinations in ways normally not even permitted to a sexual partner." H. I. Lief & R. C. Fox (1963), "Training for 'detached concern' in medical students," in H. I. Lief et al. (Eds.), *The psychological basis of medical practice*, New York: Harper & Row, p. 32. As Edward Hall remarks, North Americans have an inarticulated convention that discourages touching except in moments of intimacy. E. T. Hall (1959), *The silent language*, Garden City, NY: Doubleday, p. 149.

6. For comments on embarrassment in the doctor-patient relation, see M. Balint (1957), *The doctor, his patient, and the illness*, New York: International Universities Press, p. 57.

7. Physicians are aware of the possibility that their routine technical behavior may be interpreted as sexual by the patient. The following quotation states a view held by some physicians: "It is not unusual for a suspicious hysterical woman with fantasies of being seduced to misinterpret an ordinary movement in the physical examination as an amorous advance." E. Weiss & O. S. English (1949), *Psychosomatic medicine*, Philadelphia: W. B. Saunders; quoted in M. Hollender (1958), *The psychology of medical practice*, Philadelphia: W. B. Saunders, p. 22. An extreme case suggests that pelvic examinations are not without their hazards for physicians, particularly during training: "A third-year student who had prided himself on his excellent adjustment to the stresses of medical school developed acute anxiety when about to perform, for the first time, a pelvic examination on a gynecological patient. Prominent in his fantasies were memories of a punishing father who would unquestionably forbid any such explicitly sexual behavior." S. Bojar (1961), "Psychi-

atric problems of medical students," in G. B. Glaine, Jr., et al. (Eds.), *Emotional problems of the student,* Garden City, NY: Doubleday, p. 248.

8. Many other claims and assumptions are being negotiated or sustained in addition to this basic definition of the situation. Efforts in regard to some of these other claims and assumptions have important consequences for the fate of the basic definition. That is, in the actual situation any one gesture usually has relevance for a number of realities, so that the fates of the various realities are intertwined with each other. For example, each participant is putting forth a version of himself which he wants validated. A doctor's jockeying about claims about competence may reinforce the medical definition and so may a patient's interest in appearing poised. But a patient's ambition to "understand what is really happening" may lead to undermining of the medical definition. Understanding that sustaining the basic definition of the situation is intertwined with numerous other projects, however, we will proceed to focus on that reality alone.

9. Compare Donald Ball's account of how the medical definition is conveyed in an abortion clinic, where it serves to counter the definition of the situation as deviant. D. W. Ball (1967, Winter), "An abortion clinic ethnography," *Social Problems, 14,* 293–301.

10. Glaser and Strauss discuss the hospital prohibition against examinations and exposure of the body in the presence of intimates of the patient. B. Glaser & A. Strauss (1965), *Awareness of dying,* Chicago: Aldine, p. 162.

11. Sudnow reports that at the county hospital he studied, male physicians routinely did pelvic examinations without nurses being present, except in the emergency ward. D. Sudnow (1967), *Passing on: The social organization of dying,* Englewood Cliffs, NJ: Prentice-Hall, p. 78.

12. The following quotation suggests that euphemisms and understood references may be used because the staff often has the choice of using "lewd words" or not being understood. "Our popular vocabulary for describing sexual behavior has been compounded of about equal parts of euphemism and obscenity, and popular attitude and sentiment have followed the same duality. Among both his male and female subjects, the interviewers found many who knew only the lewd words for features of their own anatomy and physiology." N. N. Foote (1955), "Sex as play," in J. Himelhock & S. F. Fava, *Sexual behavior in American society,* New York: Norton, p. 239.

13. The doctor's demeanor typically varies with his experience. In his early contacts with patients the young medical student may use an extreme degree of impersonality generated by his own discomfort in his role. By the time he has become accustomed to doctor-patient encounters, the fourth-year student and intern may use a newcomer's gentleness, treating the scene almost as an intimate situation by relying on elements of the "loving" demeanor previously learned in nonprofessional situations. By the time he is a resident and focusing primarily on the technical details of the medical task, the physician may be substituting a competent impersonality, although he never reverts to the extreme impersonality of the very beginning. The senior doctor, having mastered not only the technical details but an attitude of detached concern as well, reintroduces a mild gentleness, without the involved intimacy of the intern.

14. The management of closeness and detachment in professional-client relations is discussed in C. Kadushin (1962, March), "Social distance between client and professional," *American Journal of Sociology, 67,* 517–531. Wilensky and Lebeaux discuss how intimacy with strangers in the social worker-client relation is handled by accenting the technical aspects of the situation, limiting the relationship to the task at hand, and observing the norms of emotional neutrality, impartiality, and altruistic service. H. L. Wilensky & C. N. Lebeaux (1958), *Industrial society and social welfare,* New York: Russell Sage Foundation, pp. 299–303.

15. For a discussion of the socialization of medical students toward a generally detached attitude, see Lief & Fox (1963), pp. 12–35. See also M. J. Daniels (1960, November), "Affect and its control in the medical intern," *American Journal of Sociology, 66,* 259–267.

16. The following incident illustrates how a patient may exceed the limits. Mrs. Lane, a young married woman, was considered by the physicians a "seductive patient," although her technique was subtle and her behavior never improper. After examining Mrs. Lane, an intern privately called my attention to a point in the examination when he was pressing on the patient's ovaries and she remarked to the nurse: "I have this pain in intercourse until my insides are about to come out." The intern told me that Mrs. Lane

said that to the nurse, but she wanted him to hear. He didn't want to know that, he said; it wasn't necessary for her to say that. The intern evidently felt that Mrs. Lane's remark had exceeded the bounds of decorum. A specific medical necessity makes the imparting of private information acceptable, the doctor's reaction suggests, and not merely the definition of the situation as medical.

17. There is reason to think that those patients who would have most difficulty in maintaining their poise generally avoid the situation altogether. Evidence that some uncool women avoid pelvic examinations is found in respondents' remarks quoted by Rainwater: "I have thought of going to a clinic for a diaphragm, but I'm real backward about doing that. I don't even go to the doctor to be examined when I'm pregnant. I never go until about a month before I have the baby." "I tell you frankly, I'd like a diaphragm but I'm just too embarrassed to go get one." L. Rainwater (1960), *And the poor get children,* Chicago: Quadrangle, pp. 10, 31.

18. An example of such a struggle is analyzed in J. P. Emerson (1970), "Nothing unusual is happening," in T. Shibutani (Ed.), *Human nature and collective behavior. Papers in honor of Herbert Blumer,* Englewood Cliffs, NJ: Prentice-Hall.

19. Donald Ball (1967).

26

# "Precarious Situations" in a Strip Club: Exotic Dancers and the Problem of Reality Maintenance

## Kari Lerum

In her classic article, "Behavior in Private Places: Sustaining Definitions of Reality in Gynecological Examinations" (1970), Joan Emerson uses the example of a gynecological exam to demonstrate how social order can prevail even when a social situation is rife with contradictions. In this article, I use Emerson's work as a reference point for another contradictory social situation: a contemporary strip club. The point of this comparison is to examine some similarities and differences in how "reality" is created, threatened, and maintained in each setting, and to gain insight into how specific social conditions impact the process of reality maintenance.

### Defining Reality in a Precarious Situation

Emerson explains that the process of undergoing a gynecological exam can bring about two diametrically opposed messages: (1) the gynecological exam is *sexual and/or intimate* because it involves the (female) patient's

genitals being touched by a (male) physician, and (2) the gynecological exam is merely a *routine, scientific procedure*; therefore the exam is completely free of sexual or emotional meaning. Such contradictory messages create what Emerson calls "the problem of reality maintenance"; a problem that is particularly acute for the people most invested in maintaining a certain understanding of reality. In Emerson's case, those people are the gynecologists—since they (as well as most medical experts) base their professional legitimacy upon behaving in a scientific, professional manner, they have tremendous incentive to project an objective, detached image, while extinguishing any threats to this image.

For gynecologists, a contradictory image takes root when their client considers the following question: "Is this *truly* just a professional routine, or is it a sexual and/or intimate act?" Interestingly, in my research of the commercial sex industry, including field work as a waitress in a strip club,[1] I have seen the reverse question arise among clients of sex workers; that is, "Is this *truly* a sexual and/or intimate act, or is it just a professional routine?" In both cases these questions cast doubt on the definition of reality projected by the worker, thus jeopardizing their control over clients.

This paper, "'Precarious Situations' in a Strip Club: Exotic Dancers and the Problem of Reality Maintenance," by Kari Lerum, is based on research for the author's dissertation, titled *Doing the Dirty Work: Emotion Work, Professionalism, and Sexuality in a Customer Service Context*. University of Washington, 2000.

It is within these questioning moments, suspended between contradictory definitions of what is "really" going on, that Emerson sees a "precarious situation." The situation is precarious because the pendulum of meaning could easily swing either way; if it swings in favor of the worker's definition, the worker succeeds in performing her or his transaction with professional and personal integrity intact. If, however, the pendulum swings in favor of any contradictory definition, the routine is disrupted and the worker's grip on the situation is loosened.

To some extent, this problem is embedded everywhere; all social situations contain symbols or messages that people may interpret in numerous ways. However, this only becomes a problem when new perceptions of reality conflict with institutionalized ones. If people perceive an institution to have meaning contradictory to its "purpose," people are left with no established pattern, or guide, for behavior. Lacking any clear definition of what is "really" going on, the situation becomes one of confusion; people may get nervous and perplexed, and their behavior becomes unpredictable.

This is an unsettling possibility for anyone engaged in an activity requiring the full cooperation of others such as performing a gynecological exam or performing a private "lap dance"[2] at a strip club. While at first glance these two actions may seem to have little in common—the first being an unpleasant but necessary medical procedure performed on a woman for "her own good"; the second being an unnecessary act performed primarily on men simply because it "feels good"—workers in both situations face strikingly similar problems of reality maintenance.

In both cases, the medical worker and the sex worker perform actions that their clients may interpret in contradictory ways. Due to the precarious situation that this brings, a considerable amount of effort on the part of workers is needed to ensure client coopera-tion. Initially, the desired definitions of reality appear as opposites—medical workers want their actions understood as *standardized* and *non-intimate* while sex workers want their actions understood as *intimate* and *non-standardized*. However, in both cases workers also occasionally find it useful to intentionally project contradictory messages, or counterthemes. For example, the gynecologist occasionally includes a few personal (non-standardized) touches to keep the patient from feeling humiliated and dehumanized; the sex worker occasionally reminds the customer of his customer (standardized) role as a way to squelch any expectations that their relationship will carry on outside of work boundaries. As a result, skillful workers in both fields alternate between themes of standardized professionalism and personalized intimacy as it suits their immediate needs.

The point of these maneuvers is to get clients to succumb to the worker's definition of reality, thus allowing the worker to complete a successful transaction. However, since both transactions involve objects or behaviors with deeply symbolic meanings (for the gynecological exam, exposure to genitals = sexual intimacy; for the lap dance, sexual intimacy = a "real" relationship), convincing people to think otherwise is not an easy task. Reality maintenance in these circumstances requires considerable skill and collective effort; it is a process that works best when it is invisible to the client. As Emerson (1970) writes, successful reality maintenance creates the feeling that "reality seems to be out there before we arrive on the scene."

Due to the symbolic and contradictory meanings found in both gynecological exams and lap dancing, many of the ways that the medical worker's definition of reality is maintained in a gynecological exam also work toward maintaining the sex worker's definition of reality in a strip club. However, a number of structural and interactional factors make the process of reality maintenance in the strip club more precarious.

## Factors That Exacerbate Precarious Situations

Perhaps the most important factor that impacts the management of a precarious situation is that of institutional legitimacy. Unlike the gynecological business, whose legitimacy is protected by massive institutions like the American Medical Association and the U.S. government, the social and legal legitimacy of exotic dancing is far shakier and subject to regional, state, and local variation.

This lack of institutional legitimacy in many strip club settings leads to a number of related problems, including the likelihood of intrusive troublemakers. Namely, a strip club's projection of reality is subject to constant and serious threat from troublemakers such as police officers, jealous lovers, and misguided customers (imagine a jealous husband or a police officer busting up a gynecological exam). All of these intrusions interfere with normal business, sometimes requiring workers to halt operations.

In addition to serious troublemakers, clients in strip clubs are generally less predictable and cooperative than clients in gynecological exams. In part, this lack of customer predictability is due to the nature of the business: One-on-one interactions with customers require the worker to individually tailor her approach. However, workers who provide other intimate, individually tailored services (such as hair styling, massage, counseling, or even gynecological exams) do not generally face uncooperative customers, so it is clear that the problem again stems from a lack of social legitimacy. In other words, customers might simply not see the worker as "legitimate"; thus an internalized sense of respect for the worker is lacking.

Additionally, the stigmatized work of selling and performing exotic dances may pose unique emotional requirements. As opposed to working within an arena built on emotional detachment (such as medicine), sex work requires the simultaneous *encouragement* of and *containment* of highly charged emotions. This, in addition to managing the stigma of sex work, may require more emotional labor for the sex practitioner in both managing her own and her customers' emotions. This in turn may make the process of reality maintenance more precarious.

Finally, the gendered, service-oriented nature of female erotic dancing might give customers the idea that control and power is in their hands rather than in the workers'. Since the broader culture still deems men more legitimately powerful than women, women in many occupations face problems of establishing interactional legitimacy. This combined with a culture of customer service (where the customer is allegedly "always right"), makes for a situation where worker control is not guaranteed.

In sum, with a lack of institutional, social, and interactional legitimacy, erotic dancers (and sex workers in general) cannot take their control for granted. Not only is their work itself often precarious legally, but on an interactional level, control over the definition of the situation must be continuously negotiated. Thus, in these settings, workers are more challenged in maintaining their definition of the situation.

## Maintaining Reality in a Strip Club

Despite differences in legitimacy, in both the gynecological examining room and the strip club, a successful reality maintenance campaign involves a practiced performance using several techniques. These techniques fall into two steps of reality maintenance: (1) *setting the mood* (setting and maintaining an overall message or atmosphere), and (2) *enforcing the rules* (enacting and enforcing that message with individual clients). When both levels of reality maintenance are employed, the likelihood of client cooperation increases.

### Setting the Mood

The creation of an overall "mood" or atmosphere is accomplished through the use of several techniques, images, and props, all of which work in concert. In gynecological exams, an atmosphere of *objectivity*, *rationality*, and *standardization* is projected by normalizing and routinizing the exam, donning medical uniforms, and downplaying any emotional content. In the strip club where I worked (referred to here as "Club X"), an atmosphere of *excitement*, *intrigue*, and *exclusivity* was accomplished by heightening clients' emotions, making them believe that the experience was fun, sexy, exclusive, and slightly taboo, although also legitimate and professional. In both settings, workers intentionally influence the content and tone of clients' emotions. In one setting, the worker maintains control by making sure the client does not blush; in another setting, the worker maintains control by making sure the client *does*.

At Club X, the goal of making clients both emotionally "charged up" *and* compliant to workers' wishes was first accomplished by routinizing and standardizing the club's "mood." This was achieved by manipulating the appearance, language, and behavior of staff members, the images projected, the music and lighting, and the DJ's announcements.

On a typical night at Club X, the DJ had the greatest immediate influence over the mood; thus this person's routine was key for reality maintenance. The DJ was responsible for controlling the television channel (linked to five TV monitors in the club), as well as the light level of the club and, of course, the music. Each DJ had their unique style (one favored loud music, another kept the light level low), but all DJs had to ultimately comply with the company CEO's standards—the club could not be "too" dark, "too" loud, and the music had to stay fairly upbeat.

The DJ was also the official "voice" of the club; his or her words and tone influenced the mood and acted as a vocal tour guide for customers, encouraging them to see the experience from the club's point of view. One such viewpoint was that the experience was exciting and fun, similar to a sporting event. This message was made most explicit once

an hour, when the DJ announced that it was time for the "Texas Teaser." All the dancers (sometimes numbering over thirty) gathered on the front stage, smiling, posing, and flirting with the customers on the floor, while the DJ goaded the crowd:

Just *look* at all those gorgeous ladies! Guys, what do you say?! Take your hands out of your pockets and show some appreciation! On the count of three I want you to all shout as loud as you can, and the guy who makes the most noise will get a *free pass* to the club!! One . . . Two . . .Threeeee!!!! [The crowd goes wild, some young men standing on their seats, yelling, and pumping their arms in the air.]

These exuberant displays of concentrated emotion might have resulted in a loss of control for the workers, but interestingly, it rarely did. Rather, customers seemed to clearly understand that this game was not serious and that the workers controlled the rules. This understanding was reinforced immediately after the contest—the dancers would descend from the stage, flood the floor, and choose a customer for a "free" dance (while the DJ explained that they must buy a second dance). Since not every customer could get chosen for this free dance, and since the choosing process was up to the dancer, in a matter of moments the customers' demeanor shifted from noisy swaggering to humble anticipation (or dread). If a customer was overlooked this would sometimes turn to embarrassment; as one young man said to me, laughing and pointing to his friend, "Look at him, he was sitting there waiting on the couch, but no one wanted to give him a dance!"

In addition to the vulnerability that comes with waiting to be chosen, customers were also put in their place by the DJ, who routinely teased them by questioning both their heterosexual virility ("What are ya, a bunch of wussies?! What's wrong with you, don't ya like naked chicks?!") and their manners ("Didn't your mother teach you any manners?! Show some appreciation and buy a dance. And buy that lady a drink while you're at it.").

During all this excitement and teasing, an implicit message of professionalism and customer service was also projected by workers. One way this was demonstrated was in the standardized dress of staff members. Just as medical professionals and staff wear specific and unique clothing to both distinguish themselves from their patients and to project a certain (detached) message, the dancers and staff of Club X also used clothing as a method of intentional reality maintenance. One obvious use of this method was found in the rule that all staff members—including waitresses, doormen, bartenders, DJs, floor managers, and the parking lot attendant— wear the same uniform: a white tuxedo shirt, black slacks, and black shoes. The one variation in this uniform was that male staff members (essentially, everyone except the waitresses) were additionally required to wear a bow tie. As a fellow waitress explained to me, this dress code was established because "some of the waitresses were wearing really short skirts . . . but they [the management] wanted us to look classier."

This "professional" and sexually deemphasized dress code for staff members also created a distinct contrast to the dancers—all of whom wore costumes meant to symbolize and create a sexually alluring image. None of the dancers wore identical outfits, and these outfits often changed by the night (and sometimes two or three times on the same night), but most of them fell within a narrow range of variability, ranging from short tight dresses to lingerie and g-string panties. These differences between the dancers' and staff members' costumes are not unlike the costume differences found within medical staff ranks where each variation symbolizes a difference in the person's status and role. However, in the strip club setting, costume variety between dancers and staff members also served to simultaneously portray a seemingly contradictory mixture of messages.

Another mood-shaping tool in Club X were the TV monitors. When I first began working at this club, every night brought a variety of soundless video images. Many of these images were of male sporting events, but sometimes the DJ would decide to watch the news, cartoons, or the Nature channel. Scrolling across these images were club advertisements such as "Welcome to Club X!," "$5 table dances; $12 couch dances, and $20 VIP dances!" and "If you've been overcharged, contact a manager." While these messages seemed congruent with images of football, race cars, and wrestling, the image of Dan Rather discussing Middle East politics made for a comically ironic fit. Eventually, these contradictory video messages stirred higher management to create new rules about acceptable video images. At one employee meeting, the general manager of Club X was particularly upset about the showing of cartoons, inspiring him to instigate a "no cartoon" rule.

Absolutely no cartoons! That drives me crazy! No more cartoons! You wanna know why? Cuz cartoons make you think of kids. When I see cartoons, I think of my kids. It makes me miss my kids, I wish I could see them more often. So if you've got some pervert in here, spending three, four hundred dollars, and he sees cartoons up on the TV, he's going to think of his kids, feel like shit, and he's going to leave. So no more cartoons!

In other words, the point of these televised images was to encourage a specific mood as well as to sustain customers' attention by keeping them entranced and undistracted by their external emotional ties.[3]

The language of the staff also shaped the club's mood. Just as the use of clinical terms in a gynecological office creates an atmosphere of emotional and sexual detachment, the language at Club X was used to create an atmosphere that was sexually exciting as well as professional and polite. The DJ would routinely describe a dancer as a "beautiful showgirl" or a "hottie," but the language in this club was generally not sexually explicit. Rather, body parts were euphemized or avoided altogether. As a result, the club could be distinguished as a "gentlemen's club" rather than as "pornographic" or "raunchy."

The language of waitresses and doormen also served to create an atmosphere of exclusivity and politeness to both customers and dancers. Club X advertised that it gave *every* customer "VIP" treatment, and staff members were instructed to treat dancers with old-fashioned respect (at least in front of customers). For instance, when a dancer was found sitting with a customer, waitresses were trained to formally ask the customer, "Would you like to buy the lady a drink?" As Emerson puts it, such scripted language serves to "embody intentional themes." In other words, by routinizing worker behavior, specific messages can be reliably portrayed to customers. Thus, by consistently referring to dancers as "ladies," the message was sent that—although this was a place where one could get rowdy and receive good service—this was a place where one had to be polite to dancers.

In both the gynecological examining room and in the strip club, the work routine also includes similar specialized work areas—a table in the examining room; a couch in the strip club. Both also have "chaperones" (either a floor manager or a nurse) whose presence serves to discourage deviations from the intended reality.

Although the DJ was a heavyweight in creating the initial "mood," Club X's reality relied on the cooperation of all employees. Management was aware of this need for cooperation, judging by the messages staff members received such as a sign in the breakroom which read: "T.E.A.M.—together everyone achieves more." Here the point of working together was to create a reality that was "respectable," service-oriented, and profitable. This emphasis on professional customer service is evident from the following quote from the general manager of Club X:

Our competitors turned up the music, turned down the lights, and let the hand jobs fly . . . but that's not the kind of operation I'm running here . . . we need to stress service and entertainment. . . . When people go to a restaurant, they don't go there for the service, but it is what brings them back. So when customers come in, take care of them . . . be friendly, say, "Hey how's it going? If you see a girl you'd like, just let me know, and I'll get her for you." You know, take care of them.

From the worker's point of view, the ideal result of all these images, routines, and props is to prevent situations from becoming precarious—to barrage the client with consistent implicit (and sometimes explicit) messages, asserting that "this is how it's done here," and hoping for client cooperation.

### Enforcing the Rules

Once the mood is set, a secondary process of enforcement is sometimes necessary. In both Emerson's observations of the gynecological exam and my own at Club X, rule enforcement was typically accomplished by simply instructing uninitiated clients (as well as coworkers) about their expected roles. In both settings, workers expect obedience and passivity from clients. And just as the physician guides the patient through the precarious scene by taking the initiative, controlling the encounter, and carefully monitoring the patient's reactions, so does the exotic dancer.

At Club X, once a dancer got a customer to agree to a dance, she was responsible for guiding the client into his or her proper role. While some role expectations were basic and mandatory (e.g., "no touching" and "keep your hands by your sides"), other role expectations were subtler—requiring the dancer to strategically combine her messages.

For instance, when an ambivalent customer conceded to a dance, dancers often found it useful to interact with the customer in a way that made him (or her) feel special and "really" cared for, yet also aware that the feeling came with a price. After getting paid, a dancer sometimes gave her customer a friendly hug and kiss on the cheek, reinforcing the message that she really did care about him. With younger male customers (who were notoriously "cheap" and who might have been embarrassed about paying for a temporary girlfriend), dancers would frequently walk with them hand-in-hand, leading them to the cash machine, but looking like high school kids going steady. With such shy, young, "cheap," emotionally sensitive, or uninitiated customers, subtle emotional management was often required.

For the hostile or uncooperative customer, rule enforcement relied upon the threat of physical force from male employee "chaperones." The primary chaperone at Club X was the floor manager, but all employees (especially male employees) were expected to jump in if trouble started. This club also had an informal enforcement team, composed of a few men who were allegedly not employees, but who were frequent visitors and known as "friends of the club." As one veteran waitress explained to me, these "friends" "watch out for the girls and pitch in if they're needed."

Fortunately, the majority of customers accepted the reality of Club X and played along with the expected rules: that is, they applauded the dancers on stage, stood up and yelled when the DJ told them to do so, accepted all "free" dances, sat passively while a private dance was performed on them, and then graciously paid the previously negotiated price (mostly ranging from ten to forty dollars, with the average being twenty dollars a dance). However, some customers remained mystified or shy observers, some were arrogantly skeptical of the rules, and others became aggressive or hostile.

In one case, Nicki[4] had just finished two lap dances and had successfully collected her fee, but as she turned to leave the customer reached his hand up inside of her underwear and squeezed her buttock. Nicki became very upset and immediately told Aaron, who was working as the doorman. As Aaron later told me the story, he "told the guy to get the fuck out of here" before he "beat the shit out of him." The threat worked, and the deviant customer departed.

Other, perhaps even more troublesome intruders were jealous lovers of dancers, delusional customers who refused to accept that they could not have a "real" relationship with their favorite dancer, as well as customers who were simply belligerent and looking for a fight. Due to the highly explosive nature of these situations, staff members had to stay alert and immediately call for help if needed—even if this involved asking for help from another set of troublesome intruders, the police.

Despite their role as potential protectors, the most precarious situations often arose with the entrance of the police. Since this club was in a suburban area where strip clubs were a highly contentious political issue, police officers occasionally stopped by to make their presence known and to monitor the club's activities. When this happened, Club X's reality was severely interrupted. Word would quickly spread throughout the club that the police were there. If there was enough lead time, special red lights would flash behind the bar to warn workers that the police were coming. The manager would then put on a friendly face, greet the officers at the door, and give them a tour of the facility. While business appeared to continue, with waitresses serving drinks, the music continuing, and the DJ introducing each dancer as she appeared on stage, the money exchange would essentially halt; dancers would quit performing lap dances and sit quietly next to their customers or with each other. Sometimes, if a dancer was not notified quickly enough of the threat, she would get caught in the middle of an illegal lap dance[5] and be ticketed. The heart of the entire business (lap dances) would not resume until the departure of the police.

Although far less frequent, precarious situations also rose from the actions of dancers. Often coming from dancers who had previously worked in more sexually lenient clubs, their deviations came in the form of intimacy transgressions—in other words, they went "too far" with their customers. In my six months of work at Club X, there were several cases of dancers who were chastised and sanctioned by other dancers for such transgressions.

For example, Tasha, a dancer at Club X who routinely grabbed at men's genitals through their trousers, was overwhelmingly disliked by the other dancers and staff. As one waitress told me, "You know who I really don't like? Tasha. She's really not classy; that's when I hate working here, when it feels like a whorehouse." It probably was no coincidence that Tasha did not last long as a Club X dancer; without the respect of the other dancers and staff members, negotiation of precarious situations becomes far more difficult.

In some cases, the initiation of a new dancer or the sanctioning of an established dancer simply involved a cold shoulder. But many times the punishment of inappropriate behavior was more direct. In one case, Janessa—a dancer with experience at several other clubs around the United States—was surrounded by several dancers in the dressing room and scolded for putting her crotch in a customer's face. Janessa left her shift early, crying.

In another case, a veteran Club X dancer lashed out at a newer dancer who she felt had gone "too far." The verbal explosion (below) was witnessed by several other dancers and staff:

I'm fucking old school! Remember how much shit you gave me when I started working here?! [directed at another veteran dancer, who nods her head.] That Regina girl's letting people grab her and shit and only charging twelve dollars! If she wants to do that she should put her ass on the street!! I'm fucking old school. She needs to be taught.

The newer dancer also took a verbal shot or two, but the veteran had publicly and definitively made her point. The manager then quickly intervened, taking both dancers into her office for a private "consultation."

If a manager directly witnessed an intimacy transgression, the dancer would risk harsher penalties. Officially, each dancer was allowed two warnings about such behavior, and on the third offense they would get "termed" (i.e., their independent business contract with the club would be terminated). In one case, a new dancer, Cyndi, performed stage shows that were more sexually graphic than the norm (which other dancers described as "gross"). She was also observed on a number of occasions physically groping the genitals of her customers (through their clothing)—which is against both the club's rules and the state's laws. In her short time at the club, Cyndi had already received two warnings. I observed Cyndi's third offense: She was on a female customer's lap, fondling her breast, and kissing her on the lips. It was the kissing more than anything that shocked the rest of the dancers and staff, since kissing in these circumstances was seen as outrageously intimate. The floor manager was notified and Cyndi was immediately termed.

In all of these examples, it is clear that when a dancer heightened her sexual intimacy with customers, the club's (as well as the dancers') definition of reality was threatened. These actions made the club more at risk of legal sanctions, increased customers' expectations (which subsequently created more competition between dancers), and threatened the "high class" aim of Club X. In an atmosphere where workers were greatly invested in distancing themselves from prostitutes, most dancers and staff members were personally offended by such behavior.

## Conclusions

Comparing Emerson's observations on gynecological exams with my own observations of

Club X leads to a number of insights about reality maintenance. One is simply that the process of creating and maintaining reality in both situations is strikingly similar. However, by examining the contrasting points of each case, one also finds that different settings create the need for different techniques. The most relevant contrasts are the *level of institutionalized legitimacy* and the *required amount of client management*. It seems that the higher the social legitimacy of an industry, and the lower the need to constantly monitor and manage one's customers, the lower the threat of a precarious situation. In such a situation, the worker's power is assured and automatic client compliance is likely. In contrast, lower social legitimacy combined with a "high maintenance" customer results in a more precarious situation that needs constant monitoring, manipulation, and rule enforcement.

While rule enforcement at Club X occasionally required the threat of physical force, the vast majority of this enforcement was enacted through the skillful manipulation of messages. Emerson claims that if one pays better attention to the interplay between implicit and explicit messages, then a richer understanding of reality maintenance will emerge. Unlike gynecological exams, contradictory *explicit* messages are the key to reality maintenance at Club X. In other words, in order for the sex workers in this context to "pull it off," a simultaneous explicit expression of both professionalism and intimacy was not only possible, but necessary to maintain control.

In sum, strip clubs and gynecological exam rooms are both infused with contradictory messages, which can result in precarious definitions of the situation. In a sense, both are getting away with highly "intimate" acts in a commercial setting. However, Club X is doing so with a lack of social and legal legitimacy, making it more dependent on the efforts of individual workers to create a reality where business can be done.

## Notes

1. As part of my dissertation research, during 1998–1999 I spent six months working as a strip club waitress.

2. In contrast to a stage dance, where dancers perform for the entire audience and sometimes collect tips, lap dances are performed for the enjoyment of one customer and must be individually paid for. For most exotic dancers, the lap dance is the primary source of income.

3. Interestingly, pornography was rarely shown at Club X. During my six months of work, I only saw it shown twice. On both occasions, dancers complained loudly, calling these images lewd and disgusting.

4. All names have been changed.

5. Strip clubs within this police jurisdiction are subject to a "four-foot" rule; that is, erotic dances performed closer than four feet away from the patron are against the law. The problem is, it is virtually impossible for a dancer to make any money unless she dances closer than four feet.

## Reference

Emerson, J. P. (1970). "Behavior in Private Places: Sustaining Definitions of Reality in Gynecological Examinations." In P. Dreitsel (ed.), *Recent Sociology* (pp. 74–97). New York: Macmillan.

# The Self, the I, and the Me

*George Herbert Mead*

We can distinguish very definitely between the self and the body. The body can be there and can operate in a very intelligent fashion without there being a self involved in the experience. The self has the characteristic that it is an object to itself, and that characteristic distinguishes it from other objects and from the body. It is perfectly true that the eye can see the foot, but it does not see the body as a whole. We cannot see our backs; we can feel certain portions of them, if we are agile, but we cannot get an experience of our whole body. There are, of course, experiences which are somewhat vague and difficult of location, but the bodily experiences are for us organized about a self. The foot and hand belong to the self. We can see our feet, especially if we look at them from the wrong end of an opera glass, as strange things which we have difficulty in recognizing as our own. The parts of the body are quite distinguishable from the self. We can lose parts of the body without any serious invasion of the self. The mere ability to experience different parts of the body is not different from the experience of a table. The table presents a different feel from what the hand does when one hand feels another, but it is an experience of something with which we come defi-

nitely into contact. The body does not experience itself as a whole, in the sense in which the self in some way enters into the experience of the self.

It is the characteristic of the self as an object to itself that I want to bring out. This characteristic is represented in the word "self," which is a reflexive, and indicates that which can be both subject and object. This type of object is essentially different from other objects, and in the past it has been distinguished as conscious, a term which indicates an experience with, an experience of, one's self. It was assumed that consciousness in some way carried this capacity of being an object to itself. In giving a behavioristic statement of consciousness we have to look for some sort of experience in which the physical organism can become an object to itself.

When one is running to get away from someone who is chasing him, he is entirely occupied in this action, and his experience may be swallowed up in the objects about him, so that he has, at the time being, no consciousness of self at all. We must be, of course, very completely occupied to have that take place, but we can, I think, recognize that sort of a possible experience in which the self does not enter. We can, perhaps, get some light on that situation through those experiences in which in very intense action there appears in the experience of the individual, back of this intense action, memories, and anticipations. Tolstoi as an officer in the war gives an account of having pictures of his past experience in the midst of his most intense action. There are also the pictures that flash into a person's mind when he is drowning. In such instances there is a contrast between an experience that is absolutely wound up in outside activity in which the self as an object does not enter, and an activity of memory and imagination in which the self is the principal object. The self is then entirely distinguishable from an organism that is surrounded by things and acts with reference to things, including parts of its own body. These latter may be objects like other objects, but they are just objects out there in the field, and they do not involve a self that is an object to the organism. This is, I think, frequently overlooked. It is that fact which makes our anthropomorphic reconstructions of animal life so fallacious. How can an individual get outside himself (experientially) in such a way as to become an object to himself? This is the essential psychological problem of selfhood or of self-consciousness; and its solution is to be found by referring to the process of social conduct or activity in which the given person or individual is implicated. The apparatus of reason would not be complete unless it swept itself into its own analysis of the field of experience; or unless the individual brought himself into the same experiential field as that of the other individual selves in relation to whom he acts in any given social situation. Reason cannot become impersonal unless it takes an objective, non-affective attitude toward itself; otherwise we have just consciousness, not *self*-consciousness. And it is necessary to rational conduct that the individual should thus take an objective, impersonal attitude toward himself, that he should become an object to himself. For the individual organism is obviously an essential and important fact or constituent element of the empirical situation in which it acts; and without taking objective account of itself as such, it cannot act intelligently, or rationally.

The individual experiences himself as such, not directly, but only indirectly, from the particular standpoints of other individual members of the same social group, or from the generalized standpoint of the social group as a whole to which he belongs. For he enters his own experience as a self or individual, not directly or immediately, not by becoming a subject to himself, but only in so far as he first becomes an object to himself just as other individuals are objects to him or in his experience; and he becomes an object to himself only by taking the attitudes of other individuals toward himself within a social environment or context of experience and behavior in which both he and they are involved.

The importance of what we term "communication" lies in the fact that it provides a form of behavior in which the organism or the individual may become an object to himself. It is that sort of communication which we have been discussing—not communication in the sense of the cluck of the hen to the chickens, or the bark of a wolf to the pack, or the lowing of a cow, but communication in the sense of significant symbols, communication which is directed not only to others but also to the individual himself. So far as that type of communication is a part of behavior it at least introduces a self. Of course, one may hear without listening; one may see things that he does not realize; do things that he is not really aware of. But it is where one does respond to that which he addresses to another and where that response of his own becomes a part of his conduct, where he not only hears himself but responds to himself, talks and replies to himself as truly as the other person replies to him, that we have behavior in which the individuals become objects to themselves.

Such a self is not, I would say, primarily the physiological organism. The physiological organism is essential to it, but we are at least able to think of a self without it. Persons who believe in immortality, or believe in ghosts, or in the possibility of the self leaving the body, assume a self which is quite distinguishable from the body. How successfully they can hold these conceptions is an open question, but we do, as a fact, separate the self and the organism. It is fair to say that the beginning of the self as an object, so far as we can see, is to be found in the experiences of people that lead to the conception of a "double." Primitive people assume that there is a double, located presumably in the diaphragm, that leaves the body temporarily in sleep and completely in death. It can be enticed out of the body of one's enemy and perhaps killed. It is represented in infancy by the imaginary playmates which children set up, and through which they come to control their experiences in their play.

The self, as that which can be an object to itself, is essentially a social structure, and it arises in social experience. After a self has arisen, it in a certain sense provides for itself its social experiences, and so we can conceive of an absolutely solitary self. But it is impossible to conceive of a self arising outside of social experience. When it has arisen we can think of a person in solitary confinement for the rest of his life, but who still has himself as a companion, and is able to think and to converse with himself as he had communicated with others. That process to which I have just referred, of responding to one's self as another responds to it, taking part in one's own conversation with others, being aware of what one is saying and using that awareness of what one is saying to determine what one is going to say thereafter—that is a process with which we are all familiar. We are continually following up our own address to other persons by an understanding of what we are saying, and using that understanding in the direction of our continued speech. We are finding out what we are going to say, what we are going to do, by saying and doing, and in the process we are continually controlling the process itself. In the conversation of gestures what we say calls out a certain response in another and that in turn changes our own action, so that we shift from what we started to do because of the reply the other makes. The conversation of ges-

tures is the beginning of communication. The individual comes to carry on a conversation of gestures with himself. He says something, and that calls out a certain reply in himself which makes him change what he was going to say. One starts to say something, we will presume an unpleasant something, but when he starts to say it he realizes it is cruel. The effect on himself of what he is saying checks him; there is here a conversation of gestures between the individual and himself. We mean by significant speech that the action is one that affects the individual himself, and that the effect upon the individual himself is part of the intelligent carrying-out of the conversation with others. Now we, so to speak, amputate that social phase and dispense with it for the time being, so that one is talking to one's self as one would talk to another person.

This process of abstraction cannot be carried on indefinitely. One inevitably seeks an audience, has to pour himself out to somebody. In reflective intelligence one thinks to act, and to act solely so that this action remains a part of a social process. Thinking becomes preparatory to social action. The very process of thinking is, of course, simply an inner conversation that goes on, but it is a conversation of gestures which in its completion implies the expression of that which one thinks to an audience. One separates the significance of what he is saying to others from the actual speech and gets it ready before saying it. He thinks it out, and perhaps writes it in the form of a book; but it is still a part of social intercourse in which one is addressing other persons and at the same time addressing one's self, and in which one controls the address to other persons by the response made to one's own gesture. That the person should be responding to himself is necessary to the self, and it is this sort of social conduct which provides behavior within which that self appears. I know of no other form of behavior than the linguistic in which the individual is an object to himself, and, so far as I can see, the individual is not a self in the reflexive sense unless he is an object to himself. It is this fact that gives a critical importance to communication, since this is a type of behavior in which the individual does so respond to himself.

We realize in everyday conduct and experience that an individual does not mean a great deal of what he is doing and saying. We frequently say that such an individual is not himself. We come away from an interview with a realization that we have left out important things, that there are parts of the self that did not get into what was said. What determines the amount of the self that gets into communication is the social experience itself. Of course, a good deal of the self does not need to get expression. We carry on a whole series of different relationships to different people. We are one thing to one man and another thing to another. There are parts of the self which exist only for the self in relationship to itself. We divide ourselves up in all sorts of different selves with reference to our acquaintances. We discuss politics with one and religion with another. There are all sorts of different selves answering to all sorts of different social reactions. It is the social process itself that is responsible for the appearance of the self; it is not there as a self apart from this type of experience.

A multiple personality is in a certain sense normal, as I have just pointed out. There is usually an organization of the whole self with reference to the community to which we belong, and the situation in which we find ourselves. What the society is, whether we are living with people of the present, people of our own imaginations, people of the past, varies, of course, with different individuals. Normally, within the sort of community as a whole to which we belong, there is a unified self, but that may be broken up. To a person who is somewhat unstable nervously and in whom there is a line of cleavage, certain activities become impossible, and that set of activities may separate and evolve another self. Two separate "me's" and "I's," two different selves, result, and

that is the condition under which there is a tendency to break up the personality. There is an account of a professor of education who disappeared, was lost to the community, and later turned up in a logging camp in the West. He freed himself of his occupation and turned to the woods where he felt, if you like, more at home. The pathological side of it was the forgetting, the leaving out of the rest of the self. This result involved getting rid of certain bodily memories which would identify the individual to himself. We often recognize the lines of cleavage that run through us. We would be glad to forget certain things, get rid of things the self is bound up with in past experiences. What we have here is a situation in which there can be different selves, and it is dependent upon the set of social reactions that is involved as to which self we are going to be. If we can forget everything involved in one set of activities, obviously we relinquish that part of the self. Take a person who is unstable, get him occupied by speech, and at the same time get his eye on something you are writing so that he is carrying on two separate lines of communication, and if you go about it in the right way you can get those two currents going so that they do not run into each other. You can get two entirely different sets of activities going on. You can bring about in that way the dissociation of a person's self. It is a process of setting up two sorts of communication which separate the behavior of the individual. For one individual it is this thing said and heard, and for the other individual there exists only that which he sees written. You must, of course, keep one experience out of the field of the other. Dissociations are apt to take place when an event leads to emotional upheavals. That which is separated goes on in its own way.

The unity and structure of the complete self reflects the unity and structure of the social process as a whole; and each of the elementary selves of which it is composed reflects the unity and structure of one of the various aspects of that process in which the individual is implicated. In other words, the various elementary selves which constitute, or are organized into, a complete self are the various aspects of the structure of that complete self answering to the various aspects of the structure of the social process as a whole; the structure of the complete self is thus a reflection of the complete social process. The organization and unification of a social group is identical with the organization and unification of any one of the selves arising within the social process in which that group is engaged, or which it is carrying on.

The phenomenon of dissociation of personality is caused by a breaking up of the complete, unitary self into the component selves of which it is composed, and which respectively correspond to different aspects of the social process in which the person is involved, and within which his complete or unitary self has arisen; these aspects being the different social groups to which he belongs within that process. . . .

Rational society, of course, is not limited to any specific set of individuals. Any person who is rational can become a part of it. The attitude of the community toward our own response is imported into ourselves in terms of the meaning of what we are doing. This occurs in its widest extent in universal discourse, in the reply which the rational world makes to our remark. The meaning is as universal as the community; it is necessarily involved in the rational character of that community; it is the response that the world made up out of rational beings inevitably makes to our own statement. We both get the object and ourselves into experience in terms of such a process; the other appears in our own experience insofar as we do take such an organized and generalized attitude.

If one meets a person on the street whom he fails to recognize, one's reaction toward him is that toward any other who is a member of the same community. He is the other, the organized, generalized other, if you like. One takes his attitude over against one's

self. If he turns in one direction one is to go in another direction. One has his response as an attitude within himself. It is having that attitude within himself that makes it possible for one to be a self. That involves something beyond the mere turning to the right, as we say, instinctively, without self-consciousness. To have self-consciousness one must have the attitude of the other in one's own organism as controlling the thing that he is going to do. What appears in the immediate experience of one's self in taking that attitude is what we term the "me." It is that self which is able to maintain itself in the community, that is recognized in the community insofar as it recognizes the others. Such is the phase of the self which I have referred to as that of the "me."

Over against the "me" is the "I." The individual not only has rights, but he has duties; he is not only a citizen, a member of the community, but he is one who reacts to this community and in his reaction to it, as we have seen in the conversation of gestures, changes it. The "I" is the response of the individual to the attitude of the community as this appears in his own experience. His response to that organized attitude in turn changes it. As we have pointed out, this is a change which is not present in his own experience until after it takes place. The "I" appears in our experience in memory. It is only after we have acted that we know what we have done; it is only after we have spoken that we know what we have said. The adjustment to that organized world which is present in our own nature is one that represents the "me" and is constantly there. But if the response to it is a response which is of the nature of the conversation of gestures, if it creates a situation which is in some sense novel, if one puts up his side of the case, asserts himself over against others and insists that they take a different attitude toward himself, then there is something important occurring that is not previously present in experience.

28

# Looking-Glass Self

## *Charles Horton Cooley*

The social origin of [self] comes by the pathway of intercourse with other persons. There is no sense of "I" . . . without its correlative sense of you, or he, or they. . . . In a very large and interesting class of cases the social reference takes the form of a somewhat definite imagination of how one's self—that is any idea he appropriates—appears in a particular mind, and the kind of self-feeling one has is determined by the attitude . . . attributed to that other mind. A social self of this sort might be called the reflected or looking-glass self:

Each to each a looking-glass
Reflects the other that doth pass.

As we see our face, figure, and dress in the glass, and are interested in them because they are ours, and pleased or otherwise with them according as they do or do not answer to what we should like them to be; so in imagination we perceive in another's mind some thought of our appearance, manners, aims, deeds, character, friends, and so on, and are variously affected by it.

A self-idea of this sort seems to have three principal elements: the imagination of our appearance to the other person; the imagination of his judgment of that appearance, and some sort of self-feeling, such as pride or

mortification. The comparison with a looking-glass hardly suggests the second element, the imagined judgment, which is quite essential. The thing that moves us to pride or shame is not the mere mechanical reflection of ourselves, but an imputed sentiment, the imagined effect of this reflection upon another's mind. This is evident from the fact that the character and weight of that other, in whose mind we see ourselves, makes all the difference with our feeling. We are ashamed to seem evasive in the presence of a straightforward man, cowardly in the presence of a brave one, gross in the eyes of a refined one, and so on. We always imagine, and in imagining share, the judgments of the other mind. A man will boast to one person of an action—say some sharp transaction in trade—which he would be ashamed to own to another.

The process by which self-feeling of the looking-glass sort develops in children may be followed without much difficulty. Studying the movements of others as closely as they do they soon see a connection between their own acts and changes in those movements; that is, they perceive their own influence or power over persons. The child appropriates the visible actions of his parent or nurse, over which he finds he has some control, in quite the same way as he appropriates one of his own members or a plaything, and he will try to do things with this new possession, just as he will with his hand or his rattle. A girl six months old will attempt in the most evident and deliberate manner to attract attention to herself, to set going by her actions some of those movements of other persons that she has appropriated. She has tasted the joy of being a cause, of exerting social power, and wishes more of it. She will tug at her mother's skirts, wriggle, gurgle, stretch out her arms, etc., all the time watching for the hoped-for effect. These performances often give the child, even at this age, an appearance of what is called affectation, that is, she seems to be unduly preoccupied with what other people think of her. Affectation, at any age, exists when the passion to influence others seems to overbalance the established character and give it an obvious twist or pose. It is instructive to find that even Darwin was, in his childhood, capable of departing from truth for the sake of making an impression. "For instance," he says in his autobiography, "I once gathered much valuable fruit from my father's trees and hid it in the shrubbery and then ran in breathless haste to spread the news that I had discovered a hoard of stolen fruit."[1]

The young performer soon learns to be different things to different people, showing that he begins to apprehend personality and to foresee its operation. If the mother or nurse is more tender than just, she will almost certainly be "worked" by systematic weeping. It is a matter of common observation that children often behave worse with their mother than with other and less sympathetic people. Of the new persons that a child sees, it is evident that some make a strong impression and awaken a desire to interest and please them, while others are indifferent or repugnant. Sometimes the reason can be perceived or guessed, sometimes not; but the fact of selective interest, admiration, prestige, is obvious before the end of the second year. By that time a child already cares much for the reflection of himself upon one personality and little for that upon another. Moreover he soon claims intimate and tractable persons as *mine*, classes them among his other possessions, and maintains his ownership

against all comers. M., at three years of age, vigorously resented R.'s claim upon their mother. The latter was "*my* mamma," whenever the point was raised.

Strong joy and grief depend upon the treatment this rudimentary social self receives. In the case of M. I noticed as early as the fourth month a "hurt" way of crying which seemed to indicate a sense of personal slight. It was quite different from the cry of pain or that of anger, but seemed about the same as the cry of fright. The slightest tone of reproof would produce it. On the other hand, if people took notice and laughed and encouraged, she was hilarious. At about fifteen months old she had become "a perfect little actress," seeming to live largely in imaginations of her effect upon other people. She constantly and obviously laid traps for attention, and looked abashed or wept at any signs of disapproval or indifference. At times it would seem as if she could not get over these repulses, but would cry long in a grieved way, refusing to be comforted. If she hit upon any little trick that made people laugh she would be sure to repeat it, laughing loudly and affectedly in imitation. She had quite a repertory of these small performances, which she would display to a sympathetic audience, or even try upon strangers. I have seen her at sixteen months, when R. refused to give her the scissors, sit down and make-believe cry, putting up her under lip and snuffling, meanwhile looking up now and then to see what effect she was producing.

In such phenomena we have plainly enough, it seems to me, the germ of personal ambition of every sort. Imagination cooperating with instinctive self-feeling has already created a social "I," and this has become a principal object of interest and endeavor.

Progress from this point is chiefly in the way of a greater definiteness, fullness, and inwardness in the imagination of the other's state of mind. A little child thinks of and tries to elicit certain visible or audible phenomena, and does not go back of them; but what a grown-up person desires to produce in others is an internal, invisible condition which his own richer experience enables him to imagine, and of which expression is only the sign. Even adults, however, make no separation between what other people think and the visible expression of that thought. They imagine the whole thing at once, and their idea differs from that of a child chiefly in the comparative richness and complexity of the elements that accompany and interpret the visible or audible sign. There is also a progress from the naive to the subtle in socially self-assertive action. A child obviously and simply, at first, does things for effect. Later there is an endeavor to suppress the appearance of doing so; affection, indifference, contempt, etc., are simulated to hide the real wish to affect the self-image. It is perceived that an obvious seeking after good opinion is weak and disagreeable.

## Note

1. Darwin, F. (1959). *Life and letters of Charles Darwin.* New York: Basic Books, p. 27.

**29**

# The Production of Selves
# in Personal Relationships

## *Philip Blumstein*

## Introduction

Innumerable words have been written and uttered on the fundamental relationship between the person and society, many of them inspiring discussion of the *social* nature of the self. As Rosenberg (1981) summarizes,

Social factors play a major role in . . . formation [of the self]. . . . [It] arises out of social experience and interaction; it both incorporates and is influenced by the individual's location in the social structure; it is formed within institutional systems . . . ; it is constructed from the materials of the culture, and it is affected by immediate social and environmental contexts. (p. 593)

The significance of this simple point cannot be overstated: It has been one of sociology's guiding principles for many years, it has been offered as an epiphany to generations of undergraduates, and it has inspired countless research studies. Nevertheless, the concrete social processes captured in the simple but elegant notion of the social creation of the self remain, after all these years, only

"The Production of Selves in Personal Relationships" by P. Blumstein from *The Self-Society Dynamic* (pp. 305–322), edited by J. Howard and P. Callero, 1991. New York: Cambridge University Press. Reprinted with the permission of Cambridge University Press and Judith A. Howard, Personal Representative, Estate of Philip Blumstein.

vaguely understood. The picture is incomplete. Surely social interaction generates selves, but the question that continues to deserve our attention is *how*.

From the early work of Cooley (1902), it has been a commonplace to locate much of the development of self in *primary groups*, by which is generally meant families and similar intimate relationships. This classical theme is the point of departure for this [paper], in which I address the question of how selves are created, maintained, and changed by virtue of the structure of intimate relationships and the nature of interaction that occurs in them.

## Self and Identity

The terms *self* and *identity* have been used in a dizzying diversity of ways, and no definitional synthesis will be attempted here. My approach here is largely dramaturgical, relying on the numerous discussions of self and identity that followed the 1959 publication of Goffman's *The Presentation of Self in Everyday Life* (e.g., Messinger, Sampson, & Towne, 1962; Weinstein & Deutschberger, 1963; McCall & Simmons, 1966; Gergen, 1968; Blumstein, 1975). In my usage, *self* is a personal intrapsychic structure and is only knowable by the person to whom it belongs.

In this view the self can be part of the mechanics that motivate the actor's behavior (McCall & Simmons, 1966; Blumstein, 1975; Rosenberg, 1981; Swann, 1987). In contrast, I will use the term *identity* as a shorthand for *situational* or *situated identity* (Weinstein & Deutschberger, 1963; Alexander & Wiley, 1981), referring to the *face* that is publicly displayed, perhaps quite fleeting, in interaction. In this usage, identity is Goffman's *presented self* and, as such, it requires no private commitment on the part of actor or audience to its being a valid reflection of the "true" self.

Numerous attempts have been made to characterize the relationship between identity and self (McCall & Simmons, 1966; Gergen, 1968; Blumstein, 1975; Swann & Read, 1981; Wiley & Alexander, 1987). First, it is necessary to consider the relationship between self and behavior. Although the various approaches to this question differ in detail, a common theme can be identified: The self finds expression in behavior, even if that expression may be mediated in complex ways. The actor's behavior, according to the most general model, invokes a response in alter. Out of that response ego receives information with implications for his or her self, information that ultimately may modify that self. The self, it is posited, has enormous motivation consequences for interactive behavior, and all interactive behavior, it is further posited, can be analyzed in terms of the situated identities being presented. Perhaps the best articulated version of the view that self produces identity is found in McCall and Simmons's (1966) discussion of individuals' ubiquitous motive to seek *role-support*, which they define as "a set of reactions and performances by others the expressive implications of which tend to confirm one's detailed and imaginative view of himself. . . . Role-support is centrally the implied confirmation of the specific *content* of one's idealized and idiosyncratic imaginations of self" (p. 73). Since people are universally motivated to seek role-support for cherished aspects of the self, they tend to present (enact) identities

consistent with that self in order to maximize the likelihood of receiving that role-support.

I have no quarrel with this view of the relationship between self and identity. However, in this [paper] I wish to explore a different causal ordering, one less commonly considered, that is, that identity affects self. Going back to the work of Bem (1972), numerous social psychologists have argued that actors perceive their own behavior (whatever its sources), and in the process they make attributions to the self. If one translates this into a dramaturgical framework, instead of *behavior* one may speak of the *identities* people project. Individuals observe the identities they project, and in some circumstances they may attribute this enactment to a true expression of the self. In spite of any constraints the self may place on the identities presented (Blumstein, 1975), these enacted behaviors may frequently have nothing to do with any sincere underlying dimensions of self.

A central assertion of this [paper] is that if identities are projected frequently enough, they eventually produce modifications in the self. In searching for a term to capture this process whereby repeated enactment of identities produce selves, I have chosen the concept of *ossification*. Whereas the work of people on self-attribution has dealt with the intrapsychic process whereby one's own behavior is observed and inferences are made about it, I focus more on the interpersonal aspects of how and why identities ossify into selves.

The process of ossification is very slow and gradual, and consequently is not easy to study with our conventional research methods. It is the process that we infer has occurred when we awaken one morning to discover we are not the same person we were twenty years earlier. Or more commonly when we encounter a person from our past and are reminded by the interaction of how much our self has drifted over the years. Surely the meanderings of our social environment are responsible for the drift, but I would argue that it is particularly in our intimate relationships that the ossification process takes place. To say that the self is subject to drift does not contradict the idea of ossification. Indeed the two concepts may be seen as constituting two ends of a continuum. Drift occurs as a function of changes in the individual's interpersonal environment. Ossification has as a necessary condition continuity in the interpersonal environment, and accelerates during those periods of continuity. Ossification means that we enact identities with great frequency and we *become* the person whom we have enacted.

Why, in so much writing about the self has the idea of ossification (or some equivalent) not been prominent? The answer lies in a shortcoming of dramaturgical analysis, that is, its inattention to the development of durable social structures. Microsociology seems recently to have undergone a shift away from an exclusive focus on interaction to a greater recognition of ongoing relationships. When the model, especially in Goffman's work, was built on unanchored, situationally bounded, evanescent exchanges between near strangers, the implications for self of the identity presented seemed trivial. But so much of social life occurs in relationships that, even if not always intense, have histories and futures, and for that reason the identities that are enacted in intimate relationships should have important implications for the self.

## Couple Identity Work

There is a form of seemingly insignificant talk heard frequently from husbands, wives, and from partners in other kinds of intimate marriagelike relationships. Possibly it is occasionally heard in the speech of close friends. Here are three simulated examples:

My husband can't be allowed into the kitchen. He wouldn't know how to boil water. He would ruin it and make a mess in the process.

We are different about dirt. I hate it and clean it up the minute it appears. She waits until it begins to accumulate and then goes after it with a vengeance. We are both very clean, just different about it.

We are not like other couples. They are all interested in showing what they earn and what they can buy, but we prefer to content ourselves with a more spiritual approach to life.

This form of verbal behavior, *couple identity work,* is often heard when one interviews couples, as well as in the spontaneous speech of ordinary people. It is frequently directed to persons outside the relationship, but I believe it also arises when intimates are alone talking together about themselves and about their relationship. As is clear from the examples, these are not ponderous discussions of "the relationship," but instead rather mundane characterizations of who the two partners are, frequently with a tone of who they are vis-à-vis one another.

I have called this process couple *identity* work; what does it have to do with the *self?* Although there is certainly identity work going on in the examples, it has already been acknowledged that situated identities and selves are not the same. However, one of the important ways in which personal relationships differ from simple Goffmanesque interaction is that in the former situated identities are potentially much more apt to have long-lasting implications for the self. Again, this is the process I have called ossification.

One might argue that these couples are only announcing the truth about themselves and their partners. Indeed this is a compelling observation because who will be more keenly aware of the dispositions of another than his or her spouse or partner? The very nature of intimacy implies that two people have developed a profound awareness of who the other is. It is, however, the publicness of the display, the apparent felt necessity of locating oneself, one's partner, and the relatedness of the two in some kind of conceptual space that suggests that the relationship engenders or demands reality creation work that is separate and apart from the simple reporting on a preexisting reality (cf. Goffman, 1971, on tie-signs). In these interactions couples are displaying a reality they have created, while at the same time they are allowing us to witness a sample of the processes through which this reality was created over the months and years.

## Motivation

A husband may learn for the first time that he cannot cook as his wife describes his culinary failures to a group of assembled friends. If he hears such commentary with sufficient frequency, both in front of guests and in solitary conversation with his wife, one may expect that he will come to incorporate culinary incompetence into his self. Moreover, if no circumstances arise to propel him into the kitchen, he will have no opportunity to challenge that aspect of self. This example is particularly useful because it leads to speculations about motivation: What goals or purposes would a wife be likely to achieve by fostering the reality that her husband is incompetent in the kitchen? What goals or purposes does a husband achieve in passively acceding to that definition of the situation? One can ask a further set of questions, more on the level of social structure, such as, What is it about the institution of marriage that led to this bit of reality creation in which, ultimately, both spouses have colluded? Moreover, in what ways did this minute exercise in reality creation contribute to the reproduction of the marital institution?

A fundamental concept in dramaturgical analysis is *interpersonal control* (Weinstein, 1969). It links the motivational states of purposive actors to the self-presentational strategies they employ. It draws attention to the connection between hedonistic actors and processes of reality presentation and reality negotiation. A focus on interpersonal control lends motivational enrichment to the drama-turgical model, with the simple principle that actors' purposes (desires, goals) can best be served by the identities they choose to enact and the identities into which they are able to cast their interaction partner(s) (Weinstein & Deutschberger, 1963, 1964; Weinstein, 1969). If one accepts that frequently enacted identities eventually may ossify into selves, then the implication of interpersonal control as a motivational concept is that selves grow out of motivational states (both ego's and alter's—the opposite of the usual position on causality).

In close relationships, just as in Goffman's disconnected focused gatherings, it must be acknowledged that ego takes active, though perhaps not conscious, involvement in shaping alter's identity, and his or her motivation may frequently be purely selfish. Ego may best pursue his or her desired outcomes in interaction and/or relationship by shaping the distribution of identities (both ego's and alter's) that are incorporated into the working consensus. But intimate relationships are significantly different from the interactions that Goffman analyzed. Among intimates, who have durable relationships with anticipatable futures, it is generally much more efficient to shape the underlying self of alter, such that by simply *being* that self, alter will assume a situated identity congruent with ego's goals. The less efficient alternative would be for ego to try to manipulate alter's situational identity afresh in each encounter. For example, once a husband has incorporated as a part of his self a sense of ineptitude in the kitchen, then his wife need never again altercast him in that light because his sense of self keeps him from entering her mysterious domain.

So far, little has been said about the content of actors' motivational systems. Aside from the everyday motivations—scratch my neck, take the children off my hands, do not drink too much in front of my parents—I would posit one central motivation in close relationships: the desire to keep alter committed to the relationship, and equally or more committed than oneself. The first part of this motivation involves the creation of solidarity through interdependence; the second involves the potential creation of hierarchy, that is, a partner who is either equal or inferior in terms of power and status. Both can be achieved if one finds ways to encourage alter's dependency (Emerson, 1962). But alter's dependency is encouraged at the same time that he or she is encouraged to perform services that increase his or her worth and consequently ego's own dependency (Emerson, 1972).

### Definitions of Reality

The process of identity negotiations should be viewed as ubiquitous because there are identity implications (hence potential self-implications) in even the most insignificant nuances of communication. For example, in a study of the division of labor in conversation, Kollock, Blumstein, and Schwartz (1985) showed that interruptions (violations of turn-taking norms) appear to be the right of the powerful. It is reasonable to argue a related phenomenon, that is, that actors infer from how much they successfully achieve interruption, or how often they are successfully interrupted, what their power or status is in an encounter. Some evidence indirectly supports this assertion: In an experimental study Robinson and Reis (1988) found that people who interrupt are more likely than those who do not to be perceived as more masculine and less feminine. Based on the research of Kollock et al. (1985), it could be argued that the dimensions being measured by Robinson and Reis as perceived masculinity and perceived femininity are really perceived hierarchy in the relationship between the speakers. If research subjects make such judgments about third parties who interrupt, it seems very reasonable that ordinary people make similar judgments about the interruptions that occur in their own ongoing relationships. To be interrupted at alter's will

is to learn the worth of one's contribution, and if this pattern is experienced repeatedly, it should affect the self in significant ways, even if alter is not intentionally trying to altercast ego into a subordinate position by his or her interruptions.

Another example of this logic comes from a study of influence tactics used by couples (Howard, Blumstein, & Schwartz, 1986) that found the weaker partner tends to use indirection to get his or her way. By extension, one might expect that by using indirection, one *becomes* a certain kind of person in the shared definition of reality, and that eventually this is incorporated into the self. Additionally, Goody (1978) has argued very convincingly that the simple act of asking a question is, for the lowly, one of the few legitimate avenues for inducing a high-status other into conversation. How one is required to enter a conversation, with head raised or bowed, sets a situational identity, and if this scenario occurs repeatedly, it eventually shapes the self.

Situations of open conflict have particular capacity for creating realities that may force modifications in the self. Frequently in the opening rounds of conflict in intimate relationships one partner offers a definition of the situation, usually a narrative containing complaints easily translatable into assertions about both situational identities and about dispositions, that is, selves, of the actors (see Turner, 1970, for an analysis of conflict between intimates). Information expressed in conflict situations has the patina of deep veracity because the extreme emotions are believed to undermine the expressive control necessary for strategic interaction. The other partner may find the asserted characterizations of self that emerge during intense conflict enormously discontinuous with respect to the self held dear, and must come to grips with what may be a persuasive but unsettling definition offered by a person who has been granted unparalleled permission to define situations. Alter may also have a counterdefinition to offer, one that may neutralize the self-implications of ego's statements. Nevertheless, alter has learned a possibly new way of framing the self, and even if ego recants his or her asserted truth, that truth, once uttered, continues to exist as a potential resource in the production of self for alter.

An intimate dyad has two fundamental properties when it comes to defining reality: (1) By being intimate, each partner grants the other enormous authority to shape the collective reality of the pair, and (2) by being a dyad, there may often be little in the way of third-party adjudication as to whose definition of reality—definition of selves—bears resemblance to some reality above or beyond the couple (a reality that actors take to be objective). This is why members of couples in conflict feel a need to discuss their problems with third parties, in order to bring the weight of validation to bear on one or the other of the potentially compelling realities. And, of course, central to the realities being crafted are the selves of both parties.

This brings us back to dependency. Even in a structure as simple as a dyad, the process of reality construction can be very complex. Two of the many factors that enter into the process are *power* and *competence*. For the relationship to be close, both partners are highly dependent on one another and therefore both are very powerful. Nevertheless, in most cases one is likely to be even more powerful than the other, reflecting differences in resources and alternatives (Emerson, 1962). The generally more powerful partner, one might expect, will not only have greater capacity to get his or her way, but also in more subtle ways to control the definition of the situation, and by extension, the selves expressed within that definition (Scheff, 1968).

Not all forms of power are the same, and indeed one should expect that power that reflects one partner's particular expertise will be especially useful in defining relevant realities. For example, modern women have been granted the right of expertise over the subject of love (Cancian, 1985), and as a consequence, one would expect women in het-erosexual relationships to have legitimacy in defining their partner's competence at such qualities as expressiveness, tenderness, and the like. This does not mean that these women are either generally more powerful or generally more capable of shaping the collective definition of the situation.

Interpersonal competence is an aggregation of skills that allow one actor to prevail over another in defining the situation, that is, in assuring that the working consensus captures a reality that supports his or her goals and desires. It includes such qualities as role-taking ability and the possession of a large and unfettered repertoire of lines of actions (Weinstein, 1969). Competent actors will generally be more successful at shaping their partner's identity *and* their partner's self, even without being relatively more powerful. Indeed the less powerful partner is more likely to resort to interpersonal tactics of indirection (Howard et al., 1986), and one form of indirection may be the subtle yet constant efforts to change alter's self so that he or she will behave more cooperatively. Following this line of argument, one encounters an interesting paradox: The more powerful partner is in a better position to change alter's definition of himself or herself, yet the less powerful partner has a greater desire to change alter's self because he or she does not have as many alternative means to change alter's behavior.

Another aspect of reality work in relationships is worth noting: In the everyday negotiation of reality, there is a norm of passive acceptance such that if the costs are small to endorsing alter's definition of the situation, then people will permit that definition to prevail. Given this premise, dramaturgically astute actors can gradually create a definition of the relationship and the selves of its members that will take enormous effort, and possibly engender hostility and conflict, if alter wishes to amend it. Collective meanings may accrue that one partner feels unable to modify, even though he or she neither believes in them nor feels strategically safe by accepting their implications. This is why such culturally significant relationships as marriage have developed rich elaboration around defining the relationship in an inescapable way. For example, ego's proposal of marriage is a last chance, however fraught with risk of momentary unpleasantness and discomfort, for alter to say that the inadvertent accretion of meaning that may have occurred cannot be sustained.

## Roles and Relationships

The motivational states of the actors are not the only place to look for sources of the reality-creating processes in intimate relationships whereby selves are likely to be produced. Other places include the social structure and the structure of intimacy.

There is evidence in the work of social psychologists that roles shape selves (e.g., Huntington, 1957; Kadushin, 1969; Turner, 1978). The role structure of heterosexual marriage, in particular, has clear self-producing properties. Marital roles set important markers that are widely used to define traits or dispositions of role incumbents. The *provider* role, the *homemaker* roles, the *parent* role, the *lover* role, and so on, all have highly elaborated cultural standards that can be used to measure one's own and one's partner's adequacy as a person, as a man, as a woman, and so on. I will not attempt it here, but I think it would be a fruitful enterprise to analyze some of the subtleties in the content of marital roles with respect to the potential for self-implications. For example, what are the implications for the self to live under the conception that one's house can never be too clean, that one can never earn too much money, or that the delinquency of one's children reflects upon the quality of their home life?

Intimate relationships are at the same time *role relationships* and *personal relationships* (Blumstein & Kollock, 1988). As role relationships they provide common cultural scripts for their enactment, and these scripts, I have argued, shape selves. As personal relationships they have a set of internal processes, growing from the structure of intimacy, that also shape selves. Unlike roles, which are scripted particularly for each type of relationships, these internal processes have more to do with the structure of intimacy per se.

I would posit two dynamics in intimate relationships, particularly those that involve the complex coordination problems of living together—the *centripetal* and *centrifugal*. They are akin to the dual and contradictory needs for security/inclusion and autonomy/freedom. The former leads to projections of similarity or sameness; the latter to projections of difference or uniqueness (Maslach, 1974; Snyder & Fromkin, 1980). Projections of difference are very risky because they easily and inadvertently (perhaps inevitably) shade off into hierarchy.

In order to predict when these two dynamics will occur, one must consider both the motivational states of the actors and the constraints of social structure. What can ego accomplish by being similar to or the same as his or her partner? What can ego accomplish by being different? better? How does the relationship function when there is a shared reality of sameness? If there is a shared reality of difference?

## Differentiation

Differentiation is one of the internal processes inherent to close relationships. Some differentiation comes with the role structure, as in the case of traditional heterosexual marriage, although the institution of marriage seems to be losing some of its role rigidity. However, this does not mean that as the cultural and structural sources of difference wither, spouses will not create differences, perhaps smaller, more subtle, more idiosyncratic, and personally less repugnant, but differences nevertheless.

There are several connections between forces of differentiation and self-production processes—the contrast effect, the division of labor, and the avoidance of competition. The first, and most evident is the *contrast effect*. Inevitably, as two people become intimately acquainted with one another, they simply will note that they react differently to a situation. The question is how such a simple set of personal observations may enter the interpersonal realm, and from there be elaborated upon to the point where they have potency in the production of selves.

The situation occurs frequently when there are serious potential coordination problems that are being exacerbated by the perceived difference. A good example is in the realm of sexuality, where small differences in sexual appetite or preferred sexual scripts can become highly elaborated under some circumstances. The coordination problems help to heighten each partner's awareness of his or her own dispositions, and this awareness in itself can transform a disposition into a feature of self. But at another level, the couple may need to achieve a shared conceptualization to account for enduring imperfection or compromises in their solutions to the problems of sexual coordination. The consequence is that the dispositional differences are magnified, abstracted, reified, and typified. Through this process, the small differences become a more real feature of the individuals' selves.

Much of our thinking about intimacy derives from a heterosexual marital or dating context. Here a wealth of cultural resources is available for the creation of differences, and it is interesting to wonder whether this availability increases or decreases the potential impact on selves. Returning to the example of sexual coordination, one might wonder what occurs when a wife has a ready cultural basis for understanding the difference between her sexual appetite and that of her husband (i.e., Men are more sexual than women). What are the consequences for her self? In structuring an answer to this ques-

tion, it might prove fruitful to contrast the wife's situation to that of a partner in a lesbian couple where a similar asymmetry of initiating and declining sex is present. In this case, it is much more difficult to find relevant cultural materials for contextualizing the observed differences between the two partners. Without an obvious categorical basis of observed differences, then any differences are likely to be treated as idiosyncratic (cf. Jones, Davis, & Gergen, 1961). The questions, then, become: In which kind of couple—two sexes or one—are the problematics of sexual coordination more likely to become part of the shared consciousness and rhetoric? In which kind of couple is that shared definition going to lead to a creation of a reality of dispositional difference? In which kind of couple will the creation of a reality of difference become ossified in the selves of the actors? Given the cultural belief that women have less sexual appetite than men, it would seem that the wife in our example would have as a central feature of her self her female sex, but that the *typical* aspects associated with her sex would in general not feature centrally in her self. The lesbian in our example does not have any category membership to account for her comparatively low sexual appetite and so her uniqueness (relative to her partner) would make sexual appetite a more salient dimension of self-organization. Indeed she may carry her typification of self as a person low in sexual appetite into a subsequent relationship where the facts might cast her self-perception in doubt.

The second force of differentiation is the tendency for all forms of social organization to create a *division of labor* even when there is none preassigned. In my research I have observed that struggle as some couples might to avoid differentiation in household tasks and other instrumental activities, they face a monumental uphill battle. The antagonism to a division of labor seems to have two sources: (1) a fear that it will resemble the traditional patriarchal divisions of heterosexual marriage with their attendant inequality, and

(2) a desire to perform tasks together in order to maximize the amount of shared couple time. Couples report, however, that the pressures of efficiency, differences in aptitude, and different tastes all conspire to push them into a division of labor even when they fervently wish to avoid one.

The third process has some parallels to the creation of a division of labor. It involves the *avoidance of competition*. Inspiration for focusing the discussion of competition avoidance comes from the work on self-evaluation maintenance processes described by Tesser (1988). Couples face the problem of competitiveness whenever their selves are constructed such that the realms in which competence is salient are the same for both of them. This means that rather than identifying with the other's success, each may feel diminished by it. The powerful bonds of identification (Turner, 1970) are inhibited by the evils of social comparison processes (Festinger, 1954; Suls & Miller, 1977). According to Tesser's model, there are two dynamic processes: *reflection processes*, which involve what has been called identification by others, such that the successful performance of a person with whom we are close reflects favorably on us (see Cialdini & Richardson, 1980), and *comparison processes*, which involve the sense of diminished worth of our own performance in comparison to the superior performance of the other. Turner (1970) has argued persuasively that bonds based on identification are salutary for intimate relationships, and by implication, the competitiveness that can grow out of comparison processes is detrimental.

The traditional differentiation of gender and its institutionalization in marital roles provided a significant buffer against competitiveness between spouses. However, as these institutions have changed, as men's and women's lives have become more similar and the distinction between their realms (private versus public) has withered, couples have clearly developed an increased potential for competition. Although many couples are probably crippled or brought to dissolution by that competition, I believe I have observed among couples I have interviewed that many others find ways of moving away from the conditions that lead to competitiveness.

Based on my impressionistic observation, I would suggest that couples whose similarity in skills, talents, and performances makes them vulnerable to competition rather than identification work collectively to create rich elaborations on tiny differences. Initially this is an act of reality construction, and eventually an act of self-production. By focusing and elaborating on small and apparent differences, they eventually *become* different. The couple who early in their relationship develop a shared hobby of cooking discovers that one is slightly better at desserts and the other slightly better at salads. Years later they may be discovered to have one salad-maker and one pastry chef, with each taking pride in the other's "unique" talent. Of course, the system is self-perpetuating, that is, the more each partner comes to define herself or himself as different from the other, the more that partner will come to behave differently and thereby be validated in the reflection from others in that self-definition. There is not a lot of strong evidence on the consequences of such differentiation for couples, but one study suggests that when couples can agree on which partner has greater knowledge in various domains, they also express greater satisfaction with their relationship (Wegner, 1986).

**Sameness**

The creation of differentness, both symbolic and real, must have limits in order for close relationships to survive. Indeed, it might be hypothesized that relationships can only create differences to the extent that their solidarity or bondedness (Turner, 1970) is secure. Indeed, similarity abounds. Homogamy among married couples is one of the most durable empirical facts in the social sciences (Buss,

1984, 1985; Buss & Barnes, 1986), and there is also recent evidence for homogamy in same-sex couples (Kurdek & Schmitt, 1987; Howard, Blumstein, & Schwartz, 1989) as well as in friendship choice (Verbrugge, 1977; Duck & Craig, 1978; Kandel, 1978; Feld, 1982). The usual discussion of homogamy is based on assumptions of similarity of stable values, opinions, social statuses, and personality traits, all qualities the partners bring to the relationship. Without denying the validity of the literature on homogamy, I would suggest that homogamy in the "softer" areas, that is, values, opinions, *perceived* dispositions, may be something that couples *achieve* together once in the relationship. They accomplish the achievement through interpersonal processes of reality construction layered with supporting self-modifications.

Some examples of the social construction of sameness come from my study in collaboration with Pepper Schwartz on four types of couples: married couples, heterosexual cohabitors, lesbian couples, and gay male couples (Blumstein & Schwartz, 1983). One of the lesbian couples was striking in this regard. When they arrived for their interview they wore the same hairstyle and virtually identical clothes. During the interview one partner exemplified couple identity work directed at sameness:

I could honestly believe in reincarnation. We think so much alike and we have so much in common and we do these dumb things like get the same clothes on. We buy the same things. We bought each other the same valentine at different stores at different times. . . . We go out and buy the same groceries, not having discussed what we wanted ahead of time. . . . We'll shop at the same place and drift into each other. We drive up nose to nose in the same parking lots at the same moments. (p. 454)

There is little to be gained in treating these coincidences as either valid facts or as hallucinations. Rather one can look at these *stories* (which in the interview did not seem to be told for the first time), and the narrative

they formed. One can understand how this narrative allows the couple to key into deep cultural themes of *love as merger,* and thereby multiply the symbolic solidarity and perfect taken-for-grantedness of the *happily ever after scenario* for their relationship. One can also understand how by the telling of these stories by both women (or when one woman tells them in the other's presence and the latter does not balk or object), each is saying something, either actively or passively, about her self and about the self of her partner. And if one is cynical about it, one can imagine each woman awaking in the morning and subconsciously choosing what clothing to wear in order to enhance the likelihood of confirming that they have "discovered" the uniquely perfect match in partners. I would suggest that she would choose that dress, not because she is consciously taking the role of her partner, but rather because she has come to see herself as "the kind of person who looks good in and likes wearing pastel colors." The motive is to construct togetherness through coincidence; the product is a pair of selves that will allow that motive to succeed.

Another example (Blumstein & Schwartz, 1983) comes from a partner in a gay male relationship, who said:

We go to the opera and I know that at the first intermission he will have a strong opinion one way or the other. Sometimes I have a gut level reaction to the opera, but generally I fall somewhere in the middle. The opera is somewhere between pretty good and quite bad, and I'm really not sure how I feel. But I do know that I feel a need to have an opinion to express at the intermission. And I realized the other night as I sit there, I'm getting anxious about what my opinion will be. So I asked myself why I was anxious about having an opinion, and I realized that when we both spontaneously love something, or we both spontaneously hate something, I feel this great, euphoric sense of rapport, of we-ness, that we are well matched and are therefore a "natural," "meant-to-be" couple. And when we disagree, or see the same thing very differently, I feel distant and alienated from him. It's like the spell has been broken. So as I sit in the opera wondering what my opinion is, I am really hoping that I will wind up with the opinion that will allow us to blend into one sweep of unanimity and be overwhelmed with that warm glow of coupleness.

This couple may not be typical; many couples feel free to disagree over heartfelt issues without any constraint to create a mystical couple reality, and do not experience their relationship as diminished by the agreement to disagree. They have learned that they agree on enough basic matters that a few displays of uniqueness are not distressing. Indeed such displays may be salutary in precisely the ways described in our discussion of differentiation processes. Examples such as this are probably most common in the early phases of relationships, where the participants may be eager to give assistance to whatever emerging similarities they may be discovering in one another. They feel genuine in the exaggerated sameness they project, but as I have argued, the projection of a self has the grave potential for the becoming of a self.

### Anchors against Drift

A fundamental fact about close relationships is that their attractiveness emerges from their predictability (Kelly, 1955; Bateson, 1972; Kelley & Thibaut, 1978). Costs associated with learning new scripts with each new person one meets are reduced, role taking is simplified, coordination problems are minimized. How do couples accomplish this predictability? It is more than simply learning the other; rather it is by imposing a set of constraints on selves such that partners actually *become* more predictable. I would posit a fundamental overarching obligation in close relationships: to live up to the dispositional qualities that have become part of the working consensus (Athay & Darley, 1981; Swann, 1984). That is why personal relationships are inherently conservative: because an actor is constrained today to be the same person he or she was yesterday. Because of the constraints

on actors to exhibit stable dispositional traits, close relationships can depart rather markedly from cultural scripts as the two participants create and maintain their own private culture.

Many people might object to this view of the conservative effects of intimate relationships. They would see close relationships as vehicles of personal growth and change (Cancian, 1987; Aron & Aron, 1989). They would argue that the extreme interdependence found in close relationships would provide a safe haven for the partners to explore alternative definitions of self. Although this logic is very persuasive, it ignores the fact that the selves of the partners are finely interwoven. One partner cannot express a self if there is no complementary self with which to resonate. One cannot enact incompetent dependency unless one's partner plays effective authority. To the extent that each partner has cathected the elements of his or her self, then that person is deeply invested in the complementary aspects of the self of the other. Certainly relationships can sometimes survive significant and abrupt changes in one of the selves. But it is indeed a matter of survival, because newly adopted selves create new demands on the other to give role-support, demands that cannot always be met, even with the best of intentions.

### References

Alexander, C. N., Jr., & Wiley, M. (1981). Situated activity and identity formation. In M. Rosenberg & R. H. Turner (Eds.), *Social psychology: Sociological perspectives* (pp. 269–289). New York: Basic Books.

Aron, A., & Aron, E. (1989). *New research on the self-expansion model*. Paper presented at the Nags Head Conference on Interaction Process and Analysis, Nags Head, NC.

Athay, M., & Darley, J. M. (1981). Toward an interaction centered theory of personality. In N. Cantor & J. F. Kihlstrom (Eds.), *Personality, cognition, and social interaction* (pp. 281–308). Hillsdale, NJ: Lawrence Erlbaum.

Bateson, G. (1972). *Steps to an ecology of mind*. New York: Ballantine.

Bem, D. J. (1972). Self-perception theory. In L. Berkowitz (Ed.), *Advances in experimental social psychology* (Vol. 6, pp. 1–62). New York: Academic Press.

Blumstein, P. (1975). Identity bargaining and self-conception. *Social Forces, 53*, 476–485.

Blumstein, P., & Kollock, P. (1988). Personal relationships. *Annual Review of Sociology, 14*, 467–490.

Blumstein, P., & Schwartz, P. (1983). *American couples: Money, work, and sex*. New York: William Morrow.

Buss, D. M. (1984). Toward a psychology of person-environment (PE) correlations: The role of spouse selection. *Journal of Personality and Social Psychology, 47*, 361–377.

Buss, D. M. (1985). Human mate selection. *American Scientist, 73*, 47–51.

Buss, D. M., & Barnes, M. (1986). Preferences in human mate selection. *Journal of Personality and Social Psychology, 50*, 559–570.

Cancian, F. (1985). Gender politics: Love and power in the private and public spheres. In A. S. Rossi (Ed.), *Gender and the life course* (pp. 253–264). New York: Aldine.

Cancian, F. (1987). *Love in America: Gender and self-development*. New York: Cambridge University Press.

Cialdini, R. B., & Richardson, K. D. (1980). Two indirect tactics of image management: Basking and blasting. *Journal of Personality and Social Psychology, 39*, 406–415.

Cooley, C. H. (1902). *Human nature and the social order*. New York: Scribner.

Duck, S. W., & Craig, R. G. (1978). Personality similarity and the development of friendship. *British Journal of Social and Clinical Psychology, 17*, 237–242.

Emerson, R. M. (1962). Power-dependence relations. *American Sociological Review, 27*, 31–41.

Emerson, R. M. (1972). Exchange theory, part II: Exchange relations and networks. In J. Berger, M. Zelditch, & B. Anderson (Eds.), *Sociological theories in progress* (Vol. 2, pp. 58–87). Boston: Houghton Mifflin.

Feld, S. L. (1982). Social structural determinants of similarity among associates. *American Sociological Review, 47*, 797–801.

Festinger, L. (1954). A theory of social comparison processes. *Human Relations, 7*, 117–140.

Gergen, K. J. (1968). Personal consistency and the presentation of self. In C. Gordon & K. J. Gergen (Eds.), *The self in social interaction* (pp. 299–308). New York: John Wiley.

Goffman, E. (1959). *The presentation of self in everyday life*. New York: Doubleday.

Goffman, E. (1971). *Relations in public: Microstudies of the public order*. New York: Basic Books.

Goody, E. N. (1978). Toward a theory of questions. In E. N. Goody (Ed.), *Questions and politeness: Strategies in social interaction* (pp. 17–43). London: Cambridge University Press.

Howard, J. A., Blumstein, P., & Schwartz, P. (1986). Sex, power, and influence tactics in intimate relationships. *Journal of Personality and Social Psychology, 51*, 102–109.

Howard, J. A., Blumstein, P., & Schwartz, P. (1989). *Homogamy in intimate relationships: Why birds of a feather flock together*. Paper presented at the annual meeting of the American Sociological Association, San Francisco.

Huntington, M. J. (1957). The development of a professional self image. In R. K. Merton, G. G. Reeder, & P. Kendall (Eds.), *The student physician* (pp. 179–187). Cambridge: Harvard University Press.

Jones, E. E., Davis, K. E., & Gergen, K. J. (1961). Role playing variations and their informational value for person perception. *Journal of Abnormal and Social Psychology, 63*, 302–310.

Kadushin, C. (1969). The professional self-concept of music students. *American Journal of Sociology, 75*, 389–404.

Kandel, D. B. (1978). Homophily, selection and socialization in adolescent friendships. *American Journal of Sociology, 84*, 427–436.

Kelley, H. H., & Thibaut, J. W. (1978). *Interpersonal relations: A theory of interdependence*. New York: John Wiley.

Kelly, G. A. (1955). *The psychology of personal constructs*. New York: Norton.

Kollock, P., Blumstein, P., & Schwartz, P. (1985). Sex and power in interaction: Conversational privileges and duties. *American Sociological Review, 50*, 34–46.

Kurdek, L., & Schmitt, J. P. (1987). Partner homogamy in married, heterosexual cohabiting, gay, and lesbian couples. *Journal of Sex Research, 23*, 212–232.

Maslach, C. (1974). Social and personal bases of individuation. *Journal of Personality and Social Psychology, 29*, 411–425.

McCall, G. J., & Simmons, J. L. (1966). *Identities and interactions*. New York: Free Press.

Messinger, S. L., with H. Sampson & R. D. Towne. (1962). Life as theatre: Some notes on the dramaturgical approach to social reality. *Sociometry, 25*, 98–110.

Robinson, L. F., & Reis, H. T. (1988). *The effects of interruption, gender, and leadership position in interpersonal perceptions*. Paper presented at the International Conference on Personal Relationships. Vancouver, Canada.

Rosenberg, M. (1981). The self-concept: Social product and social force. In M. Rosenberg & R. H. Turner (Eds.), *Social psychology: Sociological perspectives* (pp. 593–624). New York: Basic Books.

Scheff, T. J. (1968). Negotiating reality: Notes on power in the assessment of responsibility. *Social Problems, 16*, 3–17.

Snyder, C. R., & Fromkin, H. L. (1980). *Uniqueness: The human pursuit of difference*. New York: Plenum.

Suls, J. M., & Miller, R. L. (Eds.). (1977). *Social comparison processes: Theoretical and empirical perspectives*. Washington, DC: Hemisphere.

Swann, W. B., Jr. (1984). Quest for accuracy in person perception: A matter of pragmatics. *Psychological Review, 91*, 457–477.

Swann, W. B., Jr. (1987). Identity negotiation: Where two roads meet. *Journal of Personality and Social Psychology, 53*, 1038–1051.

Swann, W. B., Jr., & Read, S. J. (1981). Self-verification processes: How we sustain our self-conceptions. *Journal of Experimental Social Psychology, 17*, 351–372.

Tesser, A. (1988). Toward a self-evaluation maintenance model of social behavior. In L. Berkowitz (Ed.), *Advances in experimental social psychology* (Vol. 21, pp. 181–227). San Diego: Academic Press.

Turner, R. (1970). *Family interaction*. New York: John Wiley.

Turner, R. (1978). The role and the person. *American Journal of Sociology, 84*, 1–23.

Verbrugge, L. M. (1977). The structure of adult friendship choices. *Social Forces, 56*, 576–597.

Wegner, D. M. (1986). Transactive memory: A contemporary analysis of the group mind. In B. Mullen & G. R. Goethals (Eds.), *Theories of group behavior* (pp. 185–208). New York: Springer-Verlag.

Weinstein, E. A. (1969). The development of interpersonal competence. In D. A. Goslin (Ed.), *Handbook of socialization theory and research* (pp. 753–775). Chicago: Rand McNally.

Weinstein, E. A., & Deutschberger, P. (1963). Some dimensions of altercasting. *Sociometry, 26*, 454–466.

Weinstein, E. A., & Deutschberger, P. (1964). Tasks, bargains, and identities in social interaction. *Social Forces, 42*, 451–456.

Wiley, M. G., & Alexander, C. N. (1987). From situated activity to self-attribution: The impact of social structural schemata. In K. Yardley & T. Honess (Eds.), *Self and identity: Psychosocial perspectives* (pp. 105–117). Chichester, UK: John Wiley.

30

# Shooting an Elephant

*George Orwell*

In Moulmein, in lower Burma, I was hated by large numbers of people—the only time in my life that I have been important enough for this to happen to me. I was sub-divisional police officer of the town, and in an aimless, petty kind of way anti-European feeling was very bitter. No one had the guts to raise a riot, but if a European woman went through the bazaars alone somebody would probably spit betel juice over her dress. As a police officer I was an obvious target and was baited whenever it seemed safe to do so. When a nimble Burman tripped me up on the football field and the referee (another Burman) looked the other way, the crowd yelled with hideous laughter. This happened more than once. In the end the sneering yellow faces of young men that met me everywhere, the insults hooted after me when I was at a safe distance, got badly on my nerves. The young Buddhist priests were the worst of all. There were several thousand of them in the town and none of them seemed to have anything to do except stand on street corners and jeer at Europeans.

All this was perplexing and upsetting. For all the time I had already made up my

mind that imperialism was an evil thing and the sooner I chucked up my job and got out of it the better. Theoretically—and secretly, of course—I was all for the Burmese and all against their oppressors, the British. As for the job I was doing, I hated it more bitterly than I can perhaps make clear. In a job like that you see the dirty work of Empire at close quarters. The wretched prisoners huddling in the stinking cages of the lock-ups, the gray, cowed faces of the long-term convicts, the scarred buttocks of the men who had been flogged with bamboos—all these oppressed me with an intolerable sense of guilt. But I could get nothing into perspective. I was young and ill educated and I had had to think out my problems in the utter silence that is imposed on every Englishman in the East. I did not even know that the British Empire is dying, still less did I know that it is a great deal better than the younger empires that are going to supplant it. All I knew was that I was stuck between my hatred of the empire I served and my rage against the evil-spirited little beasts who tried to make my job impossible. With one part of my mind I thought of the British Raj as an unbreakable tyranny, as something clamped down, in *saecula saeculorum*, upon the will of prostrate peoples; with another part I thought that the greatest joy in the world would be to drive a bayonet into a Buddhist priest's guts. Feelings like these are the normal by-products of imperialism; ask any Anglo-Indian official, if you can catch him off duty.

One day something happened which in a roundabout way was enlightening. It was a tiny incident in itself, but it gave me a better glimpse than I had had before of the real nature of imperialism—the real motives for which despotic governments act. Early one morning the sub-inspector at a police station the other end of the town rang me up on the phone and said that an elephant was ravaging the bazaar. Would I please come and do something about it? I did not know what I could do, but I wanted to see what was happening and I got on to a pony and started out. I took my rifle, an old .44 Winchester and much too small to kill an elephant, but I thought the noise might be useful *in terrorem*. Various Burmans stopped me on the way and told me about the elephant's doing. It was not, of course, a wild elephant, but a tame one which had gone "must." It had been chained up, as tame elephants always are when their attack of "must" is due, but on the previous night it had broken its chain and escaped. Its mahout, the only person who could manage it when it was in that state, had set out in pursuit, but had taken the wrong direction and was now twelve hours' journey away, and in the morning the elephant had suddenly reappeared in the town. The Burmese population had no weapons and were quite helpless against it. It had already destroyed somebody's bamboo hut, killed a cow and raided some fruit-stalls and devoured the stock; also it had met the municipal rubbish van and, when the driver jumped out and took to his heels, turned the van over and inflicted violences upon it.

The Burmese sub-inspector and some Indian constables were waiting for me in the quarter where the elephant had been seen. It was a very poor quarter, a labyrinth of squalid bamboo huts, thatched with palm-leaf, winding all over a steep hillside. I remember that it was a cloudy, stuffy morning at the beginning of the rains. We began questioning the people as to where the elephant had gone and, as usual, failed to get any definite information. That is invariably the case in the East; a story always sounds clear enough at a distance, but the nearer you get to the scene of events the vaguer it becomes. Some of the people said that the elephant had gone in one direction, some said that he had gone in another, some professed not even to have heard of any elephant. I had almost made up my mind that the whole story was a pack of lies, when we heard yells a little distance away. There was a loud, scandalized cry of "Go away, child! Go away this instant!" and an old woman with a switch in her hand came round the corner of a hut, violently shooing away a crowd of naked children. Some more women followed, clicking their tongues and exclaiming; evidently there was something that the children ought not to have seen. I rounded the hut and saw a man's dead body sprawling in the mud. He was an Indian, a black Dravidian coolie, almost naked, and he could not have been dead many minutes. The people said that the elephant had come suddenly upon him round the corner of the hut, caught him with its trunk, put its foot on his back and ground him into the earth. This was the rainy season and the ground was soft, and his face had scored a trench a foot deep and a couple of yards long. He was lying on his belly with arms crucified and head sharply twisted to one side. His face was coated with mud, the eyes wide open, the teeth bared and grinning with an expression of unendurable agony. (Never tell me, by the way, that the dead look peaceful. Most of the corpses I have seen looked devilish.) The friction of the great beast's foot had stripped the skin from his back as neatly as one skins a rabbit. As soon as I saw the dead man I sent an orderly to a friend's house nearby to borrow an elephant rifle. I had already sent back the pony, not wanting it to go mad with fright and throw me if it smelt the elephant.

The orderly came back in a few minutes with a rifle and five cartridges, and meanwhile some Burmans had arrived and told us that the elephant was in the paddy fields below, only a few hundred yards away. As I started forward practically the whole population of the quarter flocked out of the houses and followed me. They had seen the rifle and were all shouting excitedly that I was going to shoot the elephant. They had not shown much interest in the elephant when he was merely ravaging their homes, but it was different now that he was going to be shot. It was a bit of fun to them, as it would be to an English crowd; besides they wanted the meat. It made me vaguely uneasy. I had no intention of shooting the elephant—I had merely sent for the rifle to defend myself if necessary—and it is always unnerving to have a crowd following you. I marched down the hill, looking and feeling a fool, with the rifle over my shoulder and an ever-growing army of people jostling at my heels. At the bottom, when you got away from the huts, there was a metalled road and beyond that a miry waste of paddy fields a thousand yards across, not yet ploughed but soggy from the first rains and dotted with coarse grass. The elephant was standing eight yards from the road, his left side toward us. He took not the slightest notice of the crowd's approach. He was tearing up branches of grass, beating them against his knees to clean them, and stuffing them into his mouth.

I had halted on the road. As soon as I saw the elephant I knew with perfect certainty that I ought not to shoot him. It is a serious matter to shoot a working elephant—it is comparable to destroying a huge and costly piece of machinery—and obviously one ought not to do it if it can possibly be avoided. And at that distance, peacefully eating, the elephant looked no more dangerous than a cow. I thought then and I think now that his attack of "must" was already passing off; in which case he would merely wander harmlessly about until the mahout came back and caught him. Moreover, I did not in the least want to shoot him. I decided that I would watch him for a little while to make

sure that he did not turn savage again, and then go home.

But at that moment I glanced round at the crowd that had followed me. It was an immense crowd, two thousand at the least and growing every minute. It blocked the road for a long distance on either side. I looked at the sea of yellow faces above the garish clothes—faces all happy and excited over this bit of fun, all certain that the elephant was going to be shot. They were watching me as they would watch a conjurer about to perform a trick. They did not like me, but with the magical rifle in my hands I was momentarily worth watching. And suddenly I realized that I should have to shoot the elephant after all. The people expected it of me and I had got to do it; I could feel their two thousand wills pressing me forward, irresistibly. And it was at this moment, as I stood there with the rifle in my hands, that I first grasped the hollowness, the futility of the white man's dominion in the East. Here was I, the white man with his gun, standing in front of the unarmed native crowd—seemingly the leading actor of the piece; but in reality I was only an absurd puppet pushed to and fro by the will of those yellow faces behind. I perceived in this moment that when the white man turns tyrant it is his own freedom that he destroys. He becomes a sort of hollow, posing dummy, the conventionalized figure of a sahib. For it is the condition of his rule that he shall spend his life in trying to impress the "natives," and so in every crisis he has got to do what the "natives" expect of him. He wears a mask, and his face grows to fit it. I had got to shoot the elephant. I had committed myself to doing it when I sent for the rifle. A sahib has got to act like a sahib; he has got to appear resolute, to know his own mind and do definite things. To come all that way, rifle in hand, with two thousand people marching at my heels, and then to trail feebly away, having done nothing—no, that was impossible. The crowd would laugh at me. And my whole life, every white man's life in the East, was one long struggle not to be laughed at.

But I did not want to shoot the elephant. I watched him beating his bunch of grass against his knees with that preoccupied grandmotherly air that elephants have. It seemed to me that it would be murder to shoot him. At that age I was not squeamish about killing animals, but I had never shot an elephant and never wanted to. (Somehow it always seems worse to kill a *large* animal.) Besides, there was the beast's owner to be considered. Alive, the elephant was worth at least a hundred pounds; dead, he would only be worth the value of his tusks, five pounds, possibly. But I had got to act quickly. I turned to some experienced-looking Burmans who had been there when he arrived, and asked them how the elephant had been behaving. They all said the same thing: he took no notice of you if you left him alone, but he might charge if you went too close to him.

It was perfectly clear to me what I ought to do. I ought to walk up to within, say, twenty-five yards of the elephant and test his behavior. If he charged, I could shoot; if he took no notice of me, it would be safe to leave him until the mahout came back. But also I knew that I was going to do no such thing. I was a poor shot with a rifle and the ground was soft mud into which one would sink at every step. If the elephant charged and I missed him, I should have about as much chance as a toad under a steam-roller. But even then I was not thinking particularly of my own skin, only of the watchful yellow faces behind. For at that moment, with the crowd watching me, I was not afraid in the ordinary sense, as I would have been if I had been alone. A white man mustn't be frightened in front of "natives"; and so, in general, he isn't frightened. The sole thought in my mind was that if anything went wrong those two thousand Burmans would see me pursued, caught, trampled on, and reduced to a grinning corpse like that Indian up the hill. And if that happened it was quite probable that some of them would laugh. That would

never do. There was only one alternative. I shoved the cartridges into the magazine and lay down on the road to get a better aim.

The crowd grew very still, and a deep, low, happy sigh, as of people who see the theater curtain go up at last, breathed from innumerable throats. They were going to have their bit of fun after all. The rifle was a beautiful German thing with cross-hair sights. I did not then know that in shooting an elephant one should shoot to cut an imaginary bar running from ear-hole to ear-hole. I ought, therefore, as the elephant was sideways on, to have aimed straight at his ear-hole; actually I aimed several inches in front of this, thinking the brain would be further forward.

When I pulled the trigger I did not hear the bang or feel the kick—one never does when a shot goes home—but I heard the devilish roar of glee that went up from the crowd. In that instant, in too short a time, one would have thought, even for the bullet to get there, a mysterious, terrible change had come over the elephant. He neither stirred nor fell, but every line of his body altered. He looked suddenly, stricken, shrunken, immensely old, as though the frightful impact of the bullet had paralyzed him without knocking him down. At last, after what seemed a long time—it might have been five seconds, I dare say—he sagged flabbily to his knees. His mouth slobbered. An enormous senility seemed to have settled upon him. One could have imagined him thousands of years old. I fired again into the same spot. At the second shot he did not collapse but climbed with desperate slowness to his feet and stood weakly upright, with legs sagging and head drooping. I fired a third time. That was the shot that did for him. You could see the agony of it jolt his whole body and knock the last remnant of strength from his legs. But in falling he seemed for a moment to rise, for as his hind legs collapsed beneath him he seemed to tower upward like a huge rock toppling, his trunk reaching skyward like a tree. He trumpeted, for the first and only time. And then down he came, his belly toward me, with a crash that seemed to shake the ground even where I lay.

I got up. The Burmans were already racing past me across the mud. It was obvious that the elephant would never rise again, but he was not dead. He was breathing very rhythmically with long rattling gasps, his great mound of a side painfully rising and failing. His mouth was wide open—I could see far down into caverns of pale pink throat. I waited a long time for him to die, but his breathing did not weaken. Finally I fired my two remaining shots into the spot where I thought his heart must be. The thick blood welled out of him like red velvet, but still he did not die. His body did not even jerk when the shots hit him, the tortured breathing continued without a pause. He was dying, very slowly and in great agony, but in some world remote from me where not even a bullet could damage him further. I felt that I had got to put an end to that dreadful noise. It seemed dreadful to see the great beast lying there, powerless to move and yet powerless to die, and not even to be able to finish him. I sent back for my small rifle and poured shot after shot into his heart and down his throat. They seemed to make no impression. The tortured gasps continued as steadily as the ticking of a clock.

In the end I could not stand it any longer and went away. I heard later that it took him half an hour to die. Burmans were bringing dahs and baskets even before I left, and I was told they had stripped his body almost to the bones by the afternoon.

Afterward, of course, there were endless discussions about the shooting of the elephant. The owner was furious, but he was only an Indian and could do nothing. Besides, legally I had done the right thing, for a mad elephant has to be killed, like a mad dog, if its owner fails to control it. Among the Europeans opinion was divided. The older men said I was right, the younger men said it was a damn shame to shoot an elephant for killing a coolie, because an elephant was worth more than any damn Coringhee coolie. And afterward I was very glad that the coolie had been killed; it put me legally in the right and it gave me a sufficient pretext for shooting the elephant. I often wondered whether any of the others grasped that I had done it solely to avoid looking a fool.

# Salvaging the Self

## David Snow and Leon Anderson

To be homeless in America is not only to have fallen to the bottom of the status system; it is also to be confronted with gnawing doubts about self-worth and the meaning of existence. Such vexing concerns are not just the psychic fallout of having descended onto the streets, but are also stoked by encounters with the domiciled that constantly remind the homeless of where they stand in relation to others.

One such encounter occurred early in the course of our fieldwork. It was late afternoon, and the homeless were congregating in front of the Sally [the Salvation Army building] for dinner. A school bus approached that was packed with Anglo junior high school students being bused from an eastside barrio school to their upper-middle- and upper-class homes in the city's northwest neighborhoods. As the bus rolled by, a fusillade of coins came flying out the windows, as the students made obscene gestures and shouted, "Get a job." Some of the homeless gestured back, some scrambled for the scattered coins—mostly pennies, others angrily threw the coins at the bus, and a few seemed oblivious to the encounter. For the passing junior high schoolers, the exchange was harmless

fun, a way to work off the restless energy built up in school; but for the homeless it was a stark reminder of their stigmatized status and of the extent to which they are the objects of negative attention.

Initially, we did not give much thought to this encounter. We were more interested in other issues and were neither fully aware of the frequency of such occurrences nor appreciative of their psychological consequences. We quickly came to learn, however, that this was hardly an isolated incident. The buses passed by the Sally every weekday afternoon during the school year; other domiciled citizens occasionally found pleasure in driving by and similarly hurling insults at the homeless and pennies at their feet; and . . . the hippie tramps and other homeless in the university area were derisively called "Drag worms," the police often harassed the homeless, and a number of neighborhoods took turns vilifying and derogating them.

Not all encounters with the domiciled are so stridently and intentionally demeaning, of course, but they are no less piercingly stigmatizing. One Saturday morning, for instance, as we walked with Willie Hastings and Ron Whitaker along a downtown street, a woman with a station wagon full of children drove by. As they passed, several of the children pointed at us and shouted, "Hey, Mama, look at the street people!" Ron responded angrily:

"Mama, look at the street people!" You know, it pisses me off the way fucking thieves steal shit and they can still hold their heads high 'cause they got money. Sure, they have to go to prison sometimes, but when they're out, nobody looks down on them. But I wouldn't steal from nobody, and look how those kids stare at us!

The pain of being objects of curiosity and negative attention is experienced fairly regularly by the homeless, but they suffer just as frequently from what has been called "attention deprivation." In *The Pursuit of Attention*, Charles Derber commented that "members of the subordinate classes are regarded as less worthy of attention in relations with members of dominant classes and so are subjected to subtle yet systematic face-to-face deprivation." For no one is Derber's observation more true than for the homeless, who are routinely ignored or avoided by the domiciled. . . . Pedestrians frequently avert their eyes when passing the homeless on the sidewalk, and they often hasten their pace and increase the distance between themselves and the homeless when they sense they may be targeted by a panhandler. Pedestrians sometimes go so far as to cross the street in order to avoid anticipated interaction with the homeless. Because of the fear and anxiety presumably engendered in the domiciled by actual or threatened contact with the homeless, efforts are often made at the community level . . . to regulate and segregate the homeless both spatially and institutionally. Although these avoidance rituals and segregative measures are not as overtly demeaning as the more active and immediate kinds of negative attention the homeless receive, they can be equally stigmatizing, for they also cast the homeless as objects of contamination. This, too, constitutes an assault upon the self, albeit a more subtle and perhaps more insidious one.

Occurring alongside the negative attention and attention deprivation the homeless experience are an array of gestures and acts that are frequently altruistic and clearly indicative of goodwill. People do on occasion give to panhandlers and beggars out of sincere concern rather than merely to get them off their backs. Domiciled citizens sometimes even provide assistance without being asked. One evening, for instance, we found Pat Manchester sitting on a bench near the university eating pizza. "Man, I was just sitting here," he told us, "and this dude walked up and gave me half a pizza and two dollar bills." Several of the students who worked at restaurants in the university area occasionally brought leftovers to Rhyming Mike and other hippie tramps. Other community members occasionally took street people to their home for a shower, dinner, and a good night's sleep. Even Jorge Herrera, who was nearly incoherent, appeared never to wash or bathe, and was covered with rashes and open sores, was the recipient of such assistance. Twice during our field research he appeared on the streets after a brief absence in clean clothes, shaved, and with a new haircut. When we asked about the changes in his appearance, he told us that someone had taken him home, cleaned him up, and let him spend the night. These kinds of unorganized, sporadic gestures of goodwill clearly facilitate the survival of some of the homeless, but the numbers they touch in comparison to those in need are minuscule. Nor do they occur in sufficient quantity or consistently enough to neutralize the stigmatizing and demeaning consequences of not only being on the streets but being objects of negative attention or little attention at all.

In addition to those who make sporadic gestures of goodwill, thousands of domiciled citizens devote occasional time and energy to serving the homeless in an organized fashion in churches, soup kitchens, and shelters. Angels House kitchen was staffed in part by such volunteers, and their support was essential to the operation of the kitchen. Yet the relationship between these well-meaning volunteers and the homeless is highly structured and sanitized. The volunteers typically prepare sandwiches and other foods in a separate area from the homeless or encounter them only across the divide of a serving counter that underscores the distance between the servers and the served. Thus, however sincere and helpful the efforts of domiciled volunteers, the structure of their encounters with the homeless often underscores the immense status differences and thereby reminds the homeless again of where they stand in relation to others.

Gestures of goodwill toward the homeless and the kinds of attention they receive are not constant over time. Instead, they tend to follow an annual cycle, with sympathetic interest increasing with the first cold snap in the fall and reaching its zenith during the Christmas holiday season. . . . Based on a frequency count of newspaper stories on the homeless across the country, the figure reveals a dramatic increase in the number of stories as the Thanksgiving/Christmas holiday season approaches. Moreover, once Christmas passes, coverage declines precipitously. This same pattern was seen in Austin in the activities both of the media and of many community residents. At times this expression of holiday concern reached almost comical dimensions. One Thanksgiving Day, for instance, the homeless were inundated with food. In the morning several domiciled citizens came to the Labor Corner to hand out sandwiches, and a few gave away whole turkeys, assuming they would be devoured on the spot. The Assembly of God Church served a large meal around noon, and the Salvation Army served its traditional Thanksgiving meal in midafternoon. At one point in the early afternoon the Sally officials appeared to be worried that only a few people would show up for the meal. Newspaper and television reporters lingered around the Sally much of the afternoon, taking pictures and interviewing both officials and street people for stories that would be aired that evening or would appear in the morning newspaper.

After Christmas, charitable interest in the homeless declined dramatically. The public span of sympathy seemed to have run its course. Thus, except for a two- to three-month period, the homeless tend to be recipients only of negative attention, ignored altogether, or dealt with in a segregated and sanitized fashion that underscores their stigmatized status.

The task the homeless face of salvaging the self is not easy, especially since wherever they turn they are reminded that they are at the very bottom of the status system. As Sonny McCallister lamented shortly after he became homeless, "The hardest thing's been getting used to the way people look down on street people. It's real hard to feel good about yourself when almost everyone you see is looking down on you." Tom Fisk, who had been on the streets longer, agreed. But he said that he had become more calloused over time:

I used to let it bother me when people stared at me while I was trying to sleep on the roof of my car or change clothes out of my trunk, but I don't let it get to me anymore. I mean, they don't know who I am, so what gives them the right to judge me? I know I'm okay.

But there was equivocation and uncertainty in his voice. Moreover, even if he no longer felt the stares and comments of others, he still had to make sense of the distance between himself and them.

How, then, do the homeless deal with the negative attention they receive or the indifference they encounter as they struggle to survive materially? How do they salvage their selves? And to what extent do the webs of meaning they spin and the personal identities they construct vary with patterns of adaptation? We address these questions . . . by considering two kinds of meaning: existential and identity-oriented. The former term refers to the kinds of accounts the homeless invoke in order to make sense of their plight; the latter refers to the kinds of meaning they attach to self in interactions with others.

## Making Sense of the Plight of Homelessness

. . . How do the homeless carve out a sense of meaning in the seemingly insane and meaningless situation in which they find themselves? Are they able to make sense of their plight in a fashion that helps to salvage the self?

Some are able to do so and others are not. Many of the homeless invoke causal accounts of their situation that infuse it with meaning and rescue the self. . . .

### Invoking Causal Accounts

By causal accounts we refer to the reasons people give to render understandable their behavior or the situations in which they find themselves. Such accounts are essentially commonsense attributions that are invoked in order to explain some problematic action or situation. Whether such accounts seem reasonable to an observer is irrelevant; what is at issue is their meaningfulness to the actor.

These explanatory accounts are seldom new constructions. Rather, they are likely to be variants of folk understandings or aphorisms that are invoked from time to time by many citizens and thus constitute part of a larger cultural vocabulary. This view of causal accounts accords with the contention that culture can best be thought of as a repertoire or " 'tool kit' of symbols, stories, rituals, and world views which people use in varying configurations to solve different kinds of problems" (Swidler, 1986: 273). These stories, symbols, or accounts are not pulled out of that cultural tool kit at random, however. Instead, the appropriation and articulation process is driven by some pressing problem or imperative. In the case of the homeless, that predicament is the existential need to infuse their situation with a sense of meaning that helps to salvage the self. In the service of that imperative, three folk adages or accounts surfaced rather widely and frequently among the homeless in Austin in their conversations with us and each other. One says,

"I'm down on my luck." Another reminds us, "What goes around, comes around." And the third says, "I've paid my dues."

*"I'm down on my luck."* The term *luck,* which most citizens invoke from time to time to account for unanticipated happenings in their lives, is generally reserved for events that influence the individual's life but are thought to be beyond his or her control. To assert that "I'm down on my luck," then, is to attribute my plight to misfortune, to chance. For the homeless, such an attribution not only helps to make sense of their situation, but it does so in a manner that is psychologically functional in two ways: It exempts the homeless from responsibility for their plight, and it leaves open the possibility of a better future.

Exemption from personal responsibility was a consistent theme in the causal accounts we overheard. As Willie Hastings asserted aggressively in discussing with Ron Whitaker and us the negative attention heaped on all of us just a few minutes earlier by the children in the passing car:

Shit, it ain't my fault I'm on the streets. I didn't choose to become homeless. I just had a lot of bad luck. And that ain't my fault. Hell, who knows? Those kids and their old lady might get unlucky and wake up on the streets someday. It can happen to anyone, you know!

Ron chipped in:

Yeah, a lot of people think we're lazy, that we don't give a shit, that this is what we want. But that sure in hell ain't so—at least not for me. It wasn't my fault I lost my job in Denver. If I'd been working down the street, maybe I'd still be there. I was just at the wrong place at the wrong time. Like Willie said, some people just ain't got no luck!

Sonny McCallister, Tom Fisk, Tony Jones, Tanner Sutton, and Hoyt Page would all have agreed, in large part because their recently dislocated or straddler status makes them take street life less for granted than the out-

---

*The Self as a Product of Interaction* **317**

siders do and therefore prompts them to try to explain their situation. But why invoke luck? Why not fix the blame for their plight on more direct, tangible factors, such as family discord, low wages, or being laid off? Not only are such biographic and structural factors clearly operative in their lives, . . . but reference to them can also exempt people from personal responsibility for their plight. After all, it was not Tony Jones's fault that he lost his job as a security guard at a Chicago steel mill when the plant cut back. Yet, although he referred to this event as the one that triggered his descent onto the streets, he still maintained that he was primarily the victim of "bad luck" rather than less mysterious structural forces that clearly intruded into his life. Apparently, he felt that had he chanced to work at a different job or in a different factory, his fate would have been different.

The same logic is evident in Hoyt's efforts to make sense of his situation. His biography is strewn with a host of factors not of his own doing, such as having been orphaned and not having received proper attention for a learning disorder, which could have been woven into a responsibility-free account for being homeless. Yet, he too often said that he was simply "down on my luck."

This tendency to cling to the luck factor in lieu of structural or biographic accounts of homelessness does not stem from ignorance about these other factors or from false consciousness regarding their causal influence. . . . The homeless often name structural and biographic factors when discussing the reasons for their homelessness. But the bad-luck account more readily allows for the possibility of a better day down the road. The victim of bad luck can become the recipient of good luck. "Luck changes," as we were frequently reminded. So, too, do structural trends and biographic experiences, but perhaps not so readily or positively from the standpoint of the homeless. Luck is also more fickle and mysterious, and its effects are supposedly distributed more randomly across the social order than are the effects of most structural

trends. For good reason, then, some of the homeless cling to the luck factor.

Yet, the lives of most homeless are devoid of much good fortune, as is clear from the biographies of virtually all of our key informants. Why, then, do some of the homeless talk as if good luck is about to come their way? The answer resides in two other frequently invoked causal accounts that are intertwined with the luck factor: "What goes around, comes around," and "I've paid my dues."

*"What goes around, comes around."* . . . [I]nsofar as there is a moral code affecting interpersonal relations on the streets, it is manifested in the phrase, "What goes around, comes around." But the relevance of this phrase is not confined solely to the interpersonal domain. It is also brought into service with respect to the issue of meaning in general and the luck factor in particular.

Regarding the former, the contention that "what goes around, comes around" suggests a cyclical rather than linear conception of the process by which events unfold. This circularity implies, among other things, a transposition of opposites at some point in the life course. Biblical examples of such transpositions abound, as in the New Testament declarations that "The last shall be first and the first last" and "The meek shall inherit the earth." Although few homeless harbor realistic thoughts of such dramatic transpositions, many do assume that things will get better because "what goes around, comes around."

This logic also holds for luck. Thus, if a person has been down on his or her luck, it follows that the person's luck is subject to change. Hoyt, among others, talked as though he believed this proposition. "Look," he told us one evening over dinner and a few beers at a local steak house:

I've been down on my luck for so damn long, it's got to change. . . . Like I said before, I believe what goes around, comes around, so I'm due a run of good luck, don't you think?

We nodded in agreement, but not without wondering how strongly Hoyt and others actually believed in the presumed link between luck and the cyclical principle of "what goes around, comes around." Whatever the answer, there is certainly good reason for harboring such a belief, for it introduces a ray of hope into a dismal situation and thereby infuses it with meaning of the kind that helps keep the self afloat.

*"I've paid my dues."* This linkage is buttressed further by the third frequently articulated causal account: "I've paid my dues." To invoke this saying is to assert, as Marilyn Fisch often did in her more sober moments, that "I deserve better" after "what I've been through" or "what I've done." The phrase implies that if there are preconditions for a run of good luck, then those conditions have been met. Thus, Gypsy Bill told us one afternoon that he felt his luck was about to change as he was fantasizing about coming into some money. "You may think I'm crazy," he said, "but it's this feeling I've got. Besides, I deserve it 'cause I've paid my dues." A street acquaintance of Gypsy's, a man who fancied himself as "a great blues harmonica player," broke in:

Yeah, man, I know what you mean. I was playing the blues on Bleeker Street once when Jeff Beck comes by and tells me I'm the best blues harmonica player he's ever heard. "Where do you live?" he asks me. And I tell him, "Here on this sidewalk, and I sleep in the subways." And he asks me, "What do you want from me?" And I tell him, "Nothing, man. A handshake." And he reaches into his pocket and pulls out a hundred-dollar bill and gives it to me 'cause I had it coming! I know the blues, man. I live them. I sleep on the fucking street, paying my dues. That's why no one plays the blues like me!

He then pointed to the knapsack on his back and asked if we knew what was in it. We shook our heads, and he said, "My jeans, man. I fucking pissed in 'em last night, I was so drunk. That's what I'm saying: I know the blues, man! I've paid my dues."

So a streak of good luck, however fleeting, or anticipation of such a streak, albeit a more sustained one, is rationalized in terms of the hardships endured. The more a person has suffered, the greater the dues that have been paid and the more, therefore, a run of good luck is deserved. Perhaps this is why some of those with the longest stretches of time on the streets, namely, outsiders, were heard to assert more often than others that "I've paid my dues." As Shotgun explained in one of his moments of sobriety, "I been on the streets for about fifteen years. . . . I've rode the boxcars and slept out in the wintertime. That's how you pay your dues." Yet, many outsiders do not often invoke this phrase. The reason, we suspect, is that they have been down on their luck for so long that their current fate seems impervious to change and they have therefore resigned themselves to life on the streets. Those who assert that they've paid their dues, however, invoke the phrase in service of the luck factor and the corollary principle of what goes around, comes around. And for good reason. Together, these accounts both exempt the homeless from responsibility for their plight and hold the door ajar for a change in luck. . . .

### Constructing Identity-Oriented Meaning

However the homeless deal with the issue of existential meaning, . . . they are still confronted with establishing who they are in the course of interaction with others, for interaction between two or more individuals minimally requires that they be situated or placed as social objects. In other words, situationally specific identities must be established. Such identities can be established in two ways: They can be attributed or imputed by others, or they can be claimed or asserted by the actor. The former can be thought of as social or role identities in that they are imputations based primarily on information gleaned from the appearance or behavior of others and from the time and location of their action, as when children in a passing car look out the window and yell,

"Hey Mama, look at the street people!" or when junior high school students yell out the windows of their school bus to the homeless lining up for dinner in front of the Sally, "Get a job, you bums!" In each case, the homeless in question have been situated as social objects and thus assigned social identities.

When individuals claim or assert an identity, by contrast, they attribute meaning to themselves. Such self-attributions can be thought of as personal identities rather than social identities, in that they are self-designations brought into play or avowed during the course of actual or anticipated interaction with others. Personal identities may be consistent with imputed social identities, as when Shotgun claims to be "a tramp," or inconsistent, as when Tony Jones yells back to the passing junior high schoolers, "Fuck you, I ain't no lazy bum!" The presented personal identities of individuals who are frequent objects of negative attention or attention deprivation, as are the homeless, can be especially revealing, because they offer a glimpse of how those people deal interactionally with their pariah-like status and the demeaning social identities into which they are frequently cast. Personal identities thus provide further insight into the ways the homeless attempt to salvage the self.

What, then, are the personal identities that the homeless construct and negotiate when in interaction with others? Are they merely a reflection of the highly stereotypic and stigmatized identities attributed to them, or do they reflect a more positive sense of self or at least an attempt to carve out and sustain a less demeaning self-conception?

The construction of personal identity typically involves a number of complementary activities: (a) procurement and arrangement of physical settings and props; (b) cosmetic face work or the arrangement of personal appearance; (c) selective association with other individuals and groups; and (d) verbal construction and assertion of personal identity. Although some of the homeless engage in conscious manipulation of props and appearance—for example, Pushcart, with his fully loaded shopping cart, and Shotgun, who fancies himself a con artist—most do not resort to such measures. Instead, the primary means by which the homeless announce their personal identities is verbal. They engage, in other words, in a good bit of identity talk. This is understandable, since the homeless seldom have the financial or social resources to pursue the other identity construction activities. Additionally, since the structure of their daily routines ensures that they spend a great deal of time waiting here and there, they have ample opportunity to converse with each other.

Sprinkled throughout these conversations with each other, as well as those with agency personnel and, occasionally, with the domiciled, are numerous examples of identity talk. Inspection of the instances of the identity talk to which we were privy yielded three generic patterns: (1) distancing; (2) embracement; and (3) fictive storytelling. Each pattern was found to contain several subtypes that tend to vary in use according to whether the speaker is recently dislocated, a straddler, or an outsider. We elaborate in turn each of the generic patterns, their varieties, and how they vary in use among the different types of homeless.

### Distancing

When individuals have to enact roles, associate with others, or utilize institutions that imply social identities inconsistent with their actual or desired self-conceptions, they often attempt to distance themselves from those roles, associations, or institutions. A substantial proportion of the identity talk we recorded was consciously focused on distancing from other homeless individuals, from street and occupational roles, and from the caretaker agencies servicing the homeless. . . .

*Associational distancing.* Since a claim to a particular self is partly contingent on the imputed social identities of the person's associates, one way people can substantiate that claim when their associates are negatively evaluated is to distance themselves from those associates. This distancing technique manifested itself in two ways among the homeless: disassociation from the homeless as a general social category, and disassociation from specific groupings of homeless individuals.

Categoric associational distancing was particularly evident among the recently dislocated. Illustrative is Tony Jones's comment in response to our initial query about life on the streets:

I'm not like the other guys who hang out down at the Sally. If you want to know about street people, I can tell you about them; but you can't really learn about street people from studying me, because I'm different.

Such categorical distancing also occurred among those individuals who saw themselves as on the verge of getting off the street. After securing two jobs in the hope of raising enough money to rent an apartment, Ron Whitaker indicated, for example, that he was different from other street people. "They've gotten used to living on the streets and they're satisfied with it, but not me!" he told us. "Next to my salvation, getting off the streets is the most important thing in my life." This variety of categorical distancing was particularly pronounced among homeless individuals who had taken jobs at the Sally and thus had one foot off the streets. These individuals were frequently criticized by other homeless for their condescending attitude. As Marilyn put it, "As soon as these guys get inside, they're better than the rest of us. They've been out on the streets for years, and as soon as they're inside they forget it."

Among the outsiders, who had been on the streets for some time and who appeared firmly rooted in that life-style, there were few examples of categorical distancing. Instead, these individuals frequently distinguished themselves from other groups of homeless. This form of associational distancing was most conspicuous among those, such as the hippie tramps and redneck bums, who were not regular social-service or shelter users and who saw themselves as especially independent and resourceful. These individuals not only wasted little time in pointing out that they were "not like those Sally users," but were also given to derogating the more institutionally dependent. Indeed, although they are among the furthest removed from a middle-class life-style, they sound at times much like middle-class citizens berating welfare recipients. As Marilyn explained, "A lot of these people staying at the Sally, they're reruns. Every day they're wanting something. People get tired of giving. All you hear is gimme, gimme. And we transients are getting sick of it."

*Role distancing.* Role distancing, the second form of distancing employed by the homeless, involves a self-conscious attempt to foster the impression of a lack of commitment or attachment to a particular role in order to deny the self implied. Thus, when individuals find themselves cast into roles in which the social identities implied are inconsistent with desired or actual self-conceptions, role distancing is likely to occur. Since the homeless routinely find themselves being cast into or enacting low-status, negatively evaluated roles, it should not be surprising that many of them attempt to disassociate themselves from those roles.

As did associational distancing, role distancing manifested itself in two ways: distancing from the general role of street person, and distancing from specific occupational roles. The former, which is also a type of categorical distancing, was particularly evident among the recently dislocated. It was not uncommon for these individuals to state explicitly that they should "not be mistaken as a typical street person." Role distancing of the less categoric and more situationally specific type was most evident among those who performed day labor, such as painters' helpers, hod carriers, warehouse and van unloaders, and those in unskilled service occupations such as dishwashing and janitorial work. As we saw earlier, the majority of the homeless we encountered would avail themselves of such job opportunities, but they seldom did so enthusiastically, since the jobs offered low status and low wages. This was especially true of the straddlers and some of the outsiders, who frequently reminded others of their disdain for such jobs and of the belief that they deserved better, as exemplified by the remarks of a drunk young man who had worked the previous day as a painter's helper: "I made $36.00 off the Labor Corner, but it was just nigger work. I'm twenty-four years old, man. I deserve better than that."

Similar distancing laments were frequently voiced over the disparity between job demands and wages. We were conversing with a small gathering of homeless men on a Sunday afternoon, for example, when one of them revealed that earlier in the day he had turned down a job to carry shingles up a ladder for $4.00 an hour because he found it demeaning to "do that hard a work for that low a pay." Since day-labor jobs seldom last for more than six hours, perhaps not much is lost monetarily in forgoing such jobs in comparison to what can be gained in pride. But even when the ratio of dollars to pride appears to make rejection costly, as in the case of permanent jobs, dissatisfaction with the low status of menial jobs may prod some homeless individuals to engage in the ultimate form of role distancing by quitting currently held jobs. As Ron Whitaker recounted the day after he quit in the middle of his shift as a dishwasher at a local restaurant:

My boss told me, "You can't walk out on me." And I told her, "Fuck you, just watch me. I'm gonna walk out of here right now." And I did. "You can't walk out on me," she said. I said, "Fuck you, I'm gone."

The forgoing illustrations suggest that the social identities lodged in available work roles are frequently inconsistent with the desired or idealized self-conceptions of some of the homeless. Consequently, "bitching about," "turning down," and even "blowing off" such work may function as a means of social-identity disavowal, on the one hand, and personal-identity assertion on the other. Such techniques provide a way of saying, "Hey, I have some pride. I'm in control. I'm my own person." This is especially the case among those individuals for whom such work is no longer just a stopgap measure but an apparently permanent feature of their lives.

*Institutional distancing.* An equally prevalent distancing technique involved the derogation of the caretaker agencies that attended to the needs of the homeless. The agency that was the most frequent object of these harangues was the Sally. Many of the homeless who used it described it as a greedy corporation run by inhumane personnel more interested in lining their own pockets than in serving the needy. Willie Hastings claimed, for example, that "the major is money-hungry and feeds people the cheapest way he can. He never talks to people except to gripe at them." He then added that the "Sally is supposed to be a Christian organization, but it doesn't have a Christian spirit. It looks down on people. . . . The Salvation Army is a national business that is more worried about making money than helping people." Ron Whitaker concurred, noting on another occasion that the "Sally here doesn't nearly do as much as it could for people. The people who work there take bags of groceries and put them in their cars. People donate to the Sally, and then the workers there cream off the best." Another straddler told us after he had spent several nights at the winter shelter, "If you spend a week here, you'll see how come people lose hope. You're treated just like an animal."

Because the Salvation Army is the only local facility that provides free shelter, breakfast, and dinner, attention is understandably focused on it. But that the Sally would be frequently derogated by the people whose survival it facilitates may appear puzzling at first glance, especially given its highly accommodative orientation. The answer lies in part in the organization and dissemination of its services. Clients are processed in an impersonal, highly structured assembly line–like fashion. The result is a leveling of individual differences and a decline in personal autonomy. Bitching and complaining about such settings create psychic distance from the self implied and secure a modicum of personal autonomy. This variety of distancing, though observable among all of the homeless, was most prevalent among the straddlers and outsiders. Since these individuals have used street agencies over a longer period of time, their self-concepts are more deeply implicated in them, thus necessitating distancing from those institutions and the self implied. Criticizing the Sally, then, provides some users with a means of dealing with the implications of their dependency on it. It is, in short, a way of presenting and sustaining a somewhat contrary personal identity.

Thus far we have elaborated how some of the homeless distance themselves from other homeless individuals, from general and specific roles, and from the institutions that deal with them. Such distancing behavior and talk represent attempts to salvage a measure of self-worth. In the process, of course, the homeless are asserting more favorable personal identities. Not all homeless individuals engage in similar distancing behavior and talk, however. . . . [C]ategorical distancing tends to be concentrated among the recently dislocated. Among those who are more firmly entrenched in street life, distancing tends to be confined to distinguishing themselves from specific groups of homeless, such as novices and the institutionally dependent, from specific occupational roles, or from the institutions with which they have occasional contact.

### Embracement

Embracement connotes a person's verbal and expressive confirmation of acceptance of and attachment to the social identity associated with a general or specific role, a set of social relationships, or a particular ideology. So defined, embracement implies that social identity is congruent with personal identity. Thus, embracement involves the avowal of implied social identities rather than their disavowal, as in the case of distancing. . . .

*Role embracement.* The most conspicuous kind of embracement encountered was categoric role embracement, which typically manifested itself by the avowal and acceptance of street-role identities such as tramp and bum. Occasionally we would encounter an individual who would immediately announce that he or she was a tramp or a bum. A case in point is provided by our initial encounter with Shotgun, when he proudly told us that he was "the tramp who was on the front page of yesterday's newspaper." In that and subsequent conversations his talk was peppered with references to himself as a tramp. He said, for example, that he had appeared on a television show in St. Louis as a tramp and that he "tramped" his way across the country, and he revealed several "cons" that "tramps use to survive on the road."

Shotgun and others like him identified themselves as traditional "brethren of the road" tramps. A number of other individuals identified themselves as "hippie tramps." When confronted by a passing group of young punk-rockers, for instance, Gimpy Dan and several other hippie tramps voiced agreement with the remark one made that "these kids will change but we'll stay the same." As if to buttress this claim, they went on to talk about "Rainbow," the previously mentioned annual gathering of old hippies which functions in part as a kind of identity-reaffirmation ritual. For these street people, there was little doubt about who they were;

they not only saw themselves as hippie tramps, but they embraced that identity both verbally and expressively.

This sort of embracement also surfaced on occasion with skid row–like bums, as was evidenced by Gypsy Bill's repeated references to himself as a bum. As a corollary of such categoric role embracement, most individuals who identified themselves as tramps or bums adopted nicknames congruent with these roles, such as Shotgun, Boxcar Billie, Gypsy Bill, and Pushcart. Such street names thus symbolize a break with their domiciled past and suggest, as well, a fairly thorough-going embracement of life on the streets.

Role-specific embracement was also encountered occasionally, as when Gypsy would refer to himself as an "expert dumpster diver." Many street people occasionally engage in this survival activity, but relatively few pridefully identify with it. Other role-specific survival activities embraced included panhandling, small-time drug-dealing, and performing, such as playing a musical instrument or singing on a street corner for money. "Rhyming Mike," . . . made his money by composing short poems for spare change from passersby, and routinely referred to himself as a street poet. For some homeless individuals, then, the street roles and routines they enact function as sources of positive identity and self-worth.

*Associational embracement.* A second variety of embracement entails reference to oneself as a friend or as an individual who takes his or her social relationships seriously. Gypsy provides a case in point. On one occasion he told us that he had several friends who either refused or quit jobs at the Sally because they "weren't allowed to associate with other guys on the streets who were their friends." Such a policy struck him as immoral. "They expect you to forget who your friends are and where you came from when you go to work there," he told us angrily. "They asked me to work there once and I told them, 'No way.' I'm a bum and I know who my friends

are." Self-identification as a person who willingly shares limited resources, such as cigarettes and alcohol, also occurred frequently, particularly among self-avowed tramps and bums.

Associational embracement was also sometimes expressed in claims of protecting buddies. . . . JJ and Indio repeatedly said they "looked out for each other." When Indio was telling about having been assaulted and robbed while walking through an alley, JJ said, almost apologetically, "It wouldn't have happened if I was with you. I wouldn't have let them get away with that." Similar claims were made to one of us, as when two straddlers said one evening after an ambiguous encounter with a clique of half a dozen other street people, "If it wasn't for us, they'd have had your ass."

Although protective behaviors that entailed risk were seldom observed, protective claims, and particularly promises, were heard frequently. Whatever the relationship between such claims and action, they not only illustrate adherence to the moral code of "what goes around, comes around," but they also express the claimant's desire to be identified as a trustworthy friend.

*Ideological embracement.* The third variety of embracement entails adherence to an ideology or an alternative reality and the avowal of a personal identity that is cognitively congruent with that ideology. Banjo, for example, routinely identifies himself as a Christian. He painted on his banjo case "Wealth Means Nothing Without God," and his talk is sprinkled with references to his Christian beliefs. He can often be found giving testimony about "the power and grace of Jesus" to other homeless around the Sally, and he witnesses regularly at the Central Assembly of God Church. Moreover, he frequently points out that his religious beliefs transcend his situation on the streets. As he told us once, "It would have to be a bigger purpose than just money to get me off the streets, like a religious mission."

A source of identity as powerful as religion, but less common, is the occult and related alternative realities. Since traditional occupational roles are not readily available to the homeless as a basis for identity, and since few street people have the material resources that can be used for construction of positive personal identities, it is little wonder that some of them find in alternative realities a locus for a positive identity. As we noted earlier, Tanner Sutton identifies himself as a "spirit guide" who can see into the future, prophesying, for instance, that "humans will be transformed into another life form."

Like mainstream religious traditions and occult realities, conversionist, restorative ideologies such as that associated with Alcoholics Anonymous provide an identity for some homeless people who are willing to accept AA's doctrines and adhere to its program. Interestingly, AA's successes seldom remain on the streets. Consequently, those street people who have previously associated with AA seldom use it as a basis for identity assertion. Nonetheless, it does constitute a potentially salient identity peg.

We have seen how the personal identities of the homeless may be derived from embracement of the social identities associated with certain stereotypic street roles, such as the tramp and the bum; with role-specific survival activities, such as dumpster-diving; with certain social relationships, such as friend and protector; or with certain religious and occult ideologies or alternative realities. We have also noted that the use of embracement tends to vary across the different types of homeless. . . . [C]ategoric embracement in particular and embracement talk in general occur most frequently among outsiders and rarely among the recently dislocated.

### Fictive Storytelling

A third form of identity talk engaged in by the homeless is fictive storytelling about past, present, or future experiences and accomplishments. We characterize as fictive stories that range from minor exaggerations of experience to full-fledged fabrications. We observed two types of fictive storytelling: embellishment of the past and present, and fantasizing about the future. Slightly more than a third of the identity statements we recorded fell into one of these two categories.

*Embellishment.* By *embellishment* we refer to the exaggeration of past *or* present experiences with fanciful and fictitious particulars so as to assert a positive personal identity. Embellishment involves enlargement of the truth, an overstatement of what transpired or is unfolding. Embellished stories, then, are only partly fictional.

Examples of embellishment for identity construction abound among the homeless. Although a wide array of events and experiences, ranging from the accomplishments of offspring to sexual and drinking exploits and predatory activities, were embellished, such storytelling was most commonly associated with past and current occupational and financial themes. The typical story of financial embellishment entailed an exaggerated claim regarding past or current wages. A case in point is provided by a forty-year-old homeless man who spent much of his time hanging around a bar boasting about having been offered a job as a Harley-Davidson mechanic for $18.50 per hour, although at the same time he constantly begged for cigarettes and spare change for beer.

Equally illustrative of such embellishment was an encounter we overheard between Marilyn, who was passing out discarded burritos, and a homeless man in his early twenties. After this fellow had taken several burritos, he chided Marilyn for being "drunk." She yelled back angrily, "I'm a Sheetrock taper and I make 14 bucks an hour. What the fuck do you make?" In addition to putting the young man in his place, Marilyn thus announced to him and to others overhearing the encounter her desired identity as a person who earns a good wage and must therefore be treated respectfully. Subsequent interaction with her revealed that she worked only sporadically, and then most often for not much more than minimum wage. There was, then, a considerable gap between claims and reality.

Disjunctures between identity assertions and reality appear to be quite common and were readily discernible on occasion, as in the case of a forty-five-year-old straddler from Pittsburgh who had been on the streets for a year and who was given to substantial embellishment of his former military experiences. On several occasions he was overheard telling about "patrolling the Alaskan/Russian border in Alaskan Siberia" and his encounters with Russian guards who traded him vodka for coffee. Since there is no border between Alaska and Siberia, it is obvious that this tale is outlandish. Nonetheless, such tales, however embellished, can be construed as attempts to communicate specifics about the person and the person's sense of self. Additionally, they focus a ray of positive attention on the storyteller and thereby enable him or her to garner momentarily a valued resource that is typically in short supply on the streets.

*Fantasizing.* The second type of fictive storytelling among the homeless is verbal fantasizing, which involves the articulation of fabrications about the speaker's future. Such fabrications place the narrator in positively framed situations that seem far removed from, if at all connected to, his or her past and present. These fabrications are almost always benign, usually have a Walter Mitty/pipe dream quality to them, and vary from fanciful reveries involving little self-deception to fantastic stories in which the narrator appears to be taken in by his or her constructions.

Regardless of the degree of self-deception, the verbal fantasies we heard were generally organized around one or more of four themes: self-employment, money, material possessions, and women. Fanciful constructions concerning self-employment usually involved business schemes. On several occa-

sions, for example, Tony Jones told us and others about his plans to set up a little shop near the university to sell leather hats and silver work imported from New York. In an even more expansive vein, two straddlers who had befriended each other seemed to be scheming constantly about how they were going to start one lucrative business after another. Once we overheard them talking about "going into business" for themselves, "either roofing houses or rebuilding classic cars and selling them." A few days later, they were observed trying to find a third party to bankroll one of these business ventures, and they even asked us if we "could come up with some cash."

An equally prominent source of fanciful identity construction is the fantasy of becoming rich. Some of the homeless just daydreamed about what they would do if they had a million dollars. Pat Manchester, for instance, assured us that if he "won a million dollars in a lottery," he was mature enough that he "wouldn't blow it." Others made bold claims about future riches without offering any details. And still others confidently spun fairly detailed stories about being extravagant familial providers in the future, as Tom Fisk did when he returned to town after a futile effort to establish himself in a city closer to his girlfriend. Despite his continuing financial setbacks, he assured us, "I'm going to get my fiancée a new pet monkey, even if it costs a thousand dollars. And I'm going to get her two parrots too, just to show her how much I love her."

Fanciful identity assertions were also constructed around material possessions and sexual encounters with women. These two identity pegs were clearly illustrated one evening among several homeless men along the city's major nightlife strip. During the course of making numerous overtures to passing women, two of the fellows jointly fantasized about how they would attract these women in the future. "Man, these chicks are going to be all over us when we come back into town with our new suits and

Corvettes," one exclaimed. The other added, "We'll have to get some cocaine too. Cocaine will get you women every time." This episode and fantasy occurred early in the second month of our fieldwork, and we quickly came to learn that such fantasizing was fairly commonplace and that it was typically occasioned by "woman-watching," which exemplifies one of the ways in which homeless men are both deprived of attention and respond to that deprivation.

One place homeless men would often watch women was along a jogging trail in one of the city's parks adjacent to the river. Here on warm afternoons they would drink beer and call out to women who jogged or walked along the trail or came to the park to sun themselves. Most of the women moved nervously by, ignoring the overtures of the men. But some responded with a smile, a wave, or even a quick "Hi!" Starved for female attention, the homeless men are quick to fantasize, attributing great significance to the slightest response. One Saturday afternoon, for example, as we were sitting by the jogging trail drinking beer with Pat Manchester and Ron Whitaker, we noticed several groups of young women who had laid out blankets on the grassy strip that borders the trail. Pat and Ron were especially interested in the women who were wearing shorts and halter tops. Pat called out for them to take their tops off. It was not clear that they heard him, but he insisted, "They really want it. I can tell they do." He suggested we go over with him to "see what we can get," but he was unwilling to go by himself. Instead, he constructed a fantasy in which the young women were very interested in him. Occasionally the women glanced toward us with apprehension, and Pat always acted as though it was a sign of interest. "If I go over there and they want to wrap me up in that blanket and fuck me," he said, "man, I'm going for it." Nonetheless, he continued to sit and fantasize, unwilling to acknowledge openly the obdurate reality staring him in the face.

Although respectable work, financial wealth, material possessions, and women are intimately interconnected in actuality, only one or two of the themes were typically highlighted in the stories we heard. Occasionally, however, we encountered a particularly accomplished storyteller who wove together all four themes in a grand scenario. Such was the case with the straddler from Pittsburgh who told the following tale over a meal of bean stew and stale bread at the Sally, and repeated it after lights-outs as he lay on the concrete floor of the winter warehouse: "Tomorrow morning I'm going to get my money and say, 'Fuck this shit.' I'm going to catch a plane to Pittsburgh and tomorrow night I'll take a hot bath, have a dinner of linguine and red wine in my own restaurant, and have a woman hanging on my arm." When encountered on the street the next evening, he attempted to explain his continued presence on the streets by saying, "I've been informed that all my money is tied up in a legal battle back in Pittsburgh," an apparently fanciful amplification of the original fabrication.

. . . [E]mbellishment occurred among all the homeless but was most pronounced among the straddlers and outsiders. Fantasizing, on the other hand, occurred most frequently among those who still had one foot anchored in the world they came from and who could still envision a future, and it occurred least often among those individuals who appeared acclimated to street life and who tended to embrace one or more street identities. For these individuals, especially those who have been on the streets for some time, the future is apparently too remote to provide a solid anchor for identity-oriented fictions that are of this world. It is not surprising, then, that it is also these individuals who exhibit the greatest tendency to drift into alternative realities, as did a thirty-three-year-old black female who claimed to be "the Interracial Princess," a status allegedly bestowed on her by "a famous astrologer from New York."

We have elaborated three generic patterns of talk through which the homeless construct and avow personal identities. We have seen that each pattern of this identity talk—distancing, embracement, and fictive story-telling—contains several varieties, and that their frequency of use varies among the types of homeless. Categoric role and associational distancing and the construction of fanciful identities occur most frequently among the recently dislocated, for example; whereas categoric embracement and embellishment tend to manifest themselves most frequently among the outsiders. Overall, then, many of the homeless are active agents in the construction and negotiation of identities as they interact with others. They do not, in other words, passively accept the social identities their appearance sometimes exudes or into which they are cast. This is not to suggest that the homeless do not sometimes view themselves in terms of the more negative, stereotypical identities frequently imputed to them. One afternoon, for example, we encountered Gypsy stretched out on a mattress in the back of his old car. Drunk and downhearted, he muttered glumly:

I've just about given up on life. I can't get any work and all my friends do is keep me drunk. Crazy, just crazy—that's all I am. Don't have any desire to do anything for myself. This car is all I've got, and even it won't work. It's not even worth trying. I'm nothing but an asshole and a bum anymore.

But on other occasions, as we have seen, Gypsy was not only more cheerful but even managed to cull shreds of self-respect and dignity from his pariah-like existence. Moreover, we found that self-deprecating lamentations like Gypsy's were relatively rare compared to the avowal of positive personal identities. This should not be particularly surprising, since every human needs to be an object of value and since the homeless have little to supply that sense of value other than their own identity-construction efforts.

## Summary

All animals are confronted with the challenge of material subsistence, but only humans are saddled with the vexing question of its meaning. We must not only sustain ourselves physically to survive, but we are also impelled to make sense of our mode of subsistence, to place it in some meaningful context, to develop an account of our situation that does not destroy our sense of self-worth. Otherwise, the will to persist falters and interest in tomorrow wanes. The biblical prophets understood this well when they told us that "man does not live by bread alone." The homeless appear to understand this existential dilemma, too, at least experientially; for while they struggle to subsist materially, they confront the meaning of their predicament and its implications for the self. These concerns weigh particularly heavily on the recently dislocated, but they gnaw at the other homeless as well—sometimes when they drift off at night, sometimes when they are jarred from sleep by their own dreams or the cries of others, and often throughout the day when their encounters with other homeless and with the domiciled remind them in myriad subtle and not-so-subtle ways of their descent into the lowest reaches of the social system and of their resultant stigmatized status.

In this [article] we have explored the ways the homeless deal with their plight, both existentially and interactionally, by attempting to construct and maintain a sense of meaning and self-worth that helps them stay afloat. Not all of the homeless succeed, of course. The selves of some have been so brutalized that they are abandoned in favor of alcohol, drugs, or out-of-this-world fantasies. And many would probably not score high on a questionnaire evaluating self-esteem. But the issue for us has not been how well the homeless fare in comparison to others on measures of self-esteem, but that they do, in fact, attempt to salvage the self, and that this struggle is an ongoing feature of the experience of living on the streets.

The homeless we studied are not the only individuals who have fallen or been pushed through the cracks of society who nevertheless try to carve a modicum of meaning and personal significance out of what must seem to those perched higher in the social order as an anomic void. Other examples of such salvaging work have been found in mental hospitals, concentration camps, and among black street-corner men. In these and presumably in other such cases of marginality, the attempt to carve out and maintain a sense of meaning and self-worth seems especially critical for survival because it is the one thread that enables those situated at the bottom to salvage their humanity. It follows, then, that it is not out of disinterest that some people find it difficult to salvage their respective selves, but that it results instead from the scarcity of material and social resources at their disposal. That many of the homeless are indeed able to make some culturally meaningful sense of their situation and secure a measure of self-worth testifies to their psychological resourcefulness and resolve, and to the resilience of the human spirit.

Considering these observations, it is puzzling why most research on the homeless has focused almost solely on their demographics and disabilities, to the exclusion of their inner lives. Perhaps it is because many social scientists have long assumed that the issues of meaning and self-worth are irrelevant, or at least of secondary importance, in the face of pressing physiological survival needs. This assumption is firmly rooted in Abraham Maslow's well-known hierarchy of needs, which holds that the satisfaction of physiological and safety needs is a necessary condition for the emergence and gratification of higher-level needs such as the need for self-esteem or for a positive personal identity. This thesis has become almost a cliché in spite of the fact that relevant research is scanty and ambiguous at best. Our finding that concern with both existential and identity-oriented meaning can be readily gleaned from the talk of homeless street people, clearly some of the most destitute in terms of physiological and safety needs, provides an empirical counterpoint to this popular assumption. Moreover, our observations suggest that the salience of such cognitive concerns is not necessarily contingent on the prior satisfaction of physiological survival requisites. Instead, such needs appear to coexist, even at the most rudimentary levels of human existence. The homeless we came to know clearly evidence such concerns.

## Reference

Swidler, Ann. 1986. "Culture in Action: Symbols and Strategies." *American Sociological Review* 51: 273–286.

32

# Creating the Ex-Role

*Helen Rose Fuchs Ebaugh*

... The ex-role constitutes a unique sociological phenomenon in that the expectations, norms, and identity associated with it do not so much consist in what one is currently doing but rather stem from expectations, social obligations, and norms related to one's previous role. In a very real sense, the process of becoming an ex involves tension between one's past, present, and future. One's previous role identification has to be taken into account and incorporated into a future identity. To be an ex is different from never having been a member of a particular group or role-set. Nonmembers do not carry with them the "hangover identity" of a previous role and therefore do not face the challenge of incorporating a previous role identity into a current self-concept.

. . . A person who is establishing him- or herself in a new identity is engrossed in a number of social and psychological processes which are often painful and undetermined by role models. At the same time that the individual is going through this self-transformation, people in society are expecting certain role behaviors based on a previous identity. The essential dilemma involved in the ex-role is the incongruity and tension that exists between self-definition and social expectations.

"Creating the Ex-Role" from *Becoming an Ex: The Process of Role Exit* (pp. 149–180) by H. R. Fuchs, 1988. Chicago: University of Chicago Press. Copyright © 1988 by University of Chicago.

The individual going through the exit process is trying to shake off and deemphasize the previous identity. An important moment in the exit process occurs when one's friends, family, and co-workers begin to think of one as other than an ex. . . . "In . . . commonsense terms, the woman is no longer ex-wife or divorcée primarily, but first of all co-worker, date or bride" (Goode, 1956: 9).

While many variations existed among our interviewees with regard to disidentifying with a previous role and entering a new one, six areas stood out as issues with which the vast majority of interviewees struggled in becoming exes: presentation of self after the exit, social reactions, intimacies, shifting friendships, relating to group members and other exes, and role residual. . . .

### Presentation of Self: Cuing Behavior

Once an individual has disengaged from a role and is beginning the process of entering a new role, he or she begins to emit cues that such a change has taken place. Like actors on a stage, exiters signal to audiences that they expect to be treated and reacted to differently than in the past. These presentations of self, or cues, are like masks that indicate a specific role change. Outward cues indicate to others inward identity and help others place the individual within the structure of a new social role with all of its normative expectations, values, and social interests.

The dramaturgical model, which views social life as actors on a stage, is emphasized and accentuated by Goffman's analysis of role behavior as the way we present ourselves to one another (Goffman 1959a). He stresses the role of impression management and social interaction and argues that people shape situations so as to convey symbolic meaning that will work to their benefit. He sees social situations as dramas in which people are actors who use "props" and "scenery" in creating impressions.

For most exiters that I interviewed, this presentation of self to others was a major factor in the adjustment process. Much time and attention was devoted to giving the kinds of cues that would portray a changed role identity. A dramatic example occurred in the case of ex-nuns who had left religious orders in the 1960s and early 1970s, for whom physical expressions of a change in identity were paramount. Clothes, for example, were a critical issue for most ex-nuns. While these nuns had been in modern habit for a short time, the habit was usually not the latest fashion. There was considerable anxiety and attention given to ways of dressing as a single woman in society as well as to hairstyles and makeup. As the identity of the ex-nun shifted in the direction of a new role, the shift was reflected in changes in appearance. When dating and relating as a laywoman became a central concern, clothes became one way of demonstrating a successful presentation of self. Many ex-nuns began reading fashion magazines or going to stores to see what was available. It was common immediately after leaving the convent to choose basic classic styles, such as a basic suit or simple skirt and blouse. To move from the clothes of even the modern nun to sexy bathing suits and low-cut dresses frequently took time for the ex-nun and indicated changes in her self-image. As ex-nuns came to define themselves more and more in terms of new roles, clothing styles tended to express these changes in self-perception.

One ex-nun who left in the early 1970s learned a very painful lesson in terms of the presentation of self. As she described,

After I left I wore miniskirts and enjoyed showing my legs and getting male attention. I felt lost, everything was new. I met a man in a bar and was dancing and bumping and grinding with him and wearing a miniskirt. We went to the bar to have a drink and he started coming on to me. I got frightened and told him I was an ex-nun. He didn't believe me until I produced pictures. He then took me home, made me change into a longer skirt, and explained to me how men would interpret certain things and I feel he taught me a lot because I was so naive I didn't understand how people perceived things. I still say prayers for him.

Length of hair was frequently an indication that a nun was in the process of transition. When a nun began to let her hair grow and became concerned about its management this often signaled that she was in the process of leaving the convent. The ex-nun faced the task of learning how to wear her hair in such fashion that it did not signal her ex-nun status. For years nuns wore their hair cropped short underneath their coifs and bonnets. On leaving, these nuns usually let their hair grow and began to wear it stylishly in order not to signal the fact that they were ex-nuns.

In the traditional system of religious life, mannerisms and physical expressions were highly regulated. Nuns frequently received instructions in how to walk, how to speak softly and articulately, and even how to raise and lower their eyes in a way appropriate to religious women. Several nuns in the early sample had received instructions in "religious walk." After internalizing these physical mannerisms for years, ex-nuns were forced to relearn ways of carrying their bodies so that they would not be identified as "nunnish." Ex-nuns, therefore, had to relearn the whole world of feminine gestures in order not to be labeled as ex-nuns and in order to make their way in the world of single women.

In the early and mid-1970s, habits such as smoking were frequently taken up by ex-nuns. Smoking was absolutely forbidden in the traditional convent system; therefore, to take up smoking on leaving often became symbolic to the individual of a drastic change in behavior. In the early 1970s, it was still fashionable for professional women to be smokers. Many ex-nuns therefore took up smoking as a sign in making the transition to the world of single women and as a way of indicating a new social status.

For the ex-nuns who exited in the 1980s, the issue of the presentation of self by means of external cues was less dramatic since they had been wearing modern clothes, using makeup, and wearing more fashionable hairstyles while still nuns. Strangely enough, however, the issue of making the transition to an ex-status was in some ways more difficult for the recent leavers precisely because there was less dramatic change in external cues. There was less external manifestation of a role change, and fewer cues were available to indicate to significant others that a change had taken place.

In no instance is the presentation of self on the part of role exiters more dramatic than in the case of transsexuals. Learning not only to dress as a member of the opposite sex but how to wear makeup, walk, talk, and use gestures is a critical issue for transsexuals after sex-change surgery. Much time, attention, and effort is given to learning the ways of presenting oneself differently from the gender identity in which one was socialized as a child. To complicate the situation, men who have become women are often large-boned and have masculine characteristics which they are eager to compensate for and overcome in terms of gestures and mannerisms. The opposite is also true for women who become men and are faced with learning masculine gestures and mannerisms. To fully "pass" in society as a member of the opposite sex, however, it is important that the individual be able to cue correct gender identity.

It is on this basis that others respond to the individual.

For divorced people who were returning to the single life, presentations of self also took on great importance. . . . [D]ivorced people reported that external manifestation of their role change was a big issue for them upon exiting. Most invested in some kind of new wardrobe after the divorce, not only for a psychological lift but, more importantly for them, as a way of cuing to others that they were no longer married. Two women had breast augmentations and one woman had cosmetic surgery. In all three cases, the individuals said that this was something they had wanted to do for a long while and that they had decided that now, as they were beginning a new life, was the opportune time. Weight loss as a way of improving one's appearance was also a common technique after divorce. Taking off one's wedding ring or beginning to wear it on the opposite hand also had great symbolic importance as a way of cuing availability. As one woman said, "At first I felt naked when I took off my wedding ring; however, immediately men began to react differently to me when they didn't see a wedding ring on my left hand. I began to like their reactions." Another divorcée commented: "I went out and bought a new wardrobe. When I was married I took care of everybody else first. Now I take care of myself first. The children are taken care of too, but I definitely make sure I have nice clothes."

A mother who had given up custody of her children reported that she was eager to let people know that she was no longer married or in a mother role. Therefore, she took up smoking, drank heavily, and led a very active social life, except when her children were around when she again reverted to her old life-style so as not to give them the message that she no longer cared. However, the minute they left, she again took on the stance of a single woman available for a social life with men.

The ex-alcoholics were also concerned with presenting a different image to society once they felt they had really stopped drinking. The majority reported that they began to dress better, bought new clothes, began taking care of their hair, and began weight control and exercises in order both to improve their health and to present an image to society as one who had now decided to go straight. Many of them were reacting to the image of alcoholics as down and out bums or derelicts who did not care for themselves. They were eager to replace that image with one more acceptable to society and to themselves. An ex-alcoholic commented, "I was sloppy and wore the same outfit all the time. When I sobered up I bought new clothes. I have more care with my appearance now. I cut my hair, I am more polite and considerate, and try to conduct myself as an adult." Even the doctors who gave up medicine reported that they changed their presentations of self, usually by dressing less formally, giving up leather shoes and suits as everyday attire, and learning to be less formal and controlling.

Cuing to others that one has made a role change is a major area of concern for most role exiters. Mechanisms for the presentation of a "new self" range from changes in dress and mannerisms to taking up new habits as an indication that one has made a major role change. The major impact of the presentation of a new self is that other people pick up the cues and respond to them.

## Social Reactions

One of the most important dynamics in being an ex and moving into an ex-role are the social reactions of other people. As an ex presents cues and indications that he or she is no longer in the role previously associated with him or her, people begin to react to the individual differently than before the exit. In many instances, however, ex-statuses are more salient to other people than current roles. For some ex-roles society has linguistic designations, such as divorcé, widow, alumnus. In other cases, however, the person is simply known as an "ex," (ex-physician, ex-nun, ex-alcoholic, ex-con). Those ex-roles that are more common and are more widely experienced in society carry less stigma and are more institutionalized in terms of expected behaviors. Those ex-roles that are less well defined institutionally tend to be what Glaser and Strauss call "emergent passages," that is, statuses which are created, discovered, and shaped by the parties as they go along (Glaser and Strauss 1971). In emergent passages there are few guidelines, precedents, or models to facilitate transfer between roles. Likewise, social reactions to such ex-roles are less well defined.

There are two types of role exits. First, there are those that are socially desirable, that is, role changes that society approves of such as the exit from alcoholic to ex-alcoholic, from convict to ex-convict, from prostitute to ex-prostitute. In these instances, society approves of the role change and tends to evaluate the individual more highly in his or her current status than in the previous one. However, in these instances, role residual, or the "hangover identity" from a previous status, often impacts current expectations and evaluations. Second, there are exits which are considered socially undesirable. These range from that of the transsexual to that of the ex-physician and also include such exits as those of the divorced person, mother without custody, and ex-nun. In each of these instances there is social stigma associated with the role change and often elements of status degradation (Garfinkel 1956).

In the case of socially desirable exits, while society lauds the exit itself, there is stigma attached to the role previously held by the individual (see Goffman 1963). Ex-convicts, for example, face the social stigma and labeling associated with having previously been in prison. There are numerous accounts of ex-cons who cannot find employment because of their previous records. The ex-con is in a continuous dilemma because not to admit the previous identity can be prosecuted as fraud; however, to admit a previous felony jeopardizes his or her chances at current employment.

A car mechanic in our study who had served three years in the penitentiary reported that customers who knew about his record didn't want him to work on their cars because they didn't trust him. Likewise, another mechanic at a radiator shop who was an ex-con reported that customers veered away from him and tried to keep their distance. Friends of his brother were also wary of his previous record and were reluctant to be seen with him in public. The man reported that any time he was in a group he attempted to stay out in the open because if the group were caught in illegal activities he would be the first person to be held suspect.

Ex-alcoholics also report that people who know about their previous alcoholic condition are often uncomfortable with them and do not understand that alcoholism is a disease and not a moral depravity. It is common for ex-alcoholics to associate primarily with other ex-alcoholics in order to avoid both the social reactions to their previous alcoholism as well as the temptations which society might offer in terms of a drinking environment. As one ex-alcoholic expressed it, "People often consider me a leper, a morally depraved individual, rather than someone with a disease. If they find out that I'm an ex-alcoholic, they often avoid me as if I would contaminate them." In addition to actually experiencing negative reactions, some ex-alcoholics were afraid of how people might react if they discovered their previous alcoholism. As one ex-alcoholic woman told us,

Yeah, I felt rejected and once again it's my own perceptions. For a long time I was guarded about divulging the fact that I was a member of Alcoholics Anonymous and that I was alcoholic. In dealing with that openly with others I would not talk about it. I think what I have uncovered for me is that somehow there was a reservation in back of my mind that it was not a disease, but that it was a moral issue and that other people would be looking at me as if I were some kind of leper or some kind of weakling. I felt a necessity for a long time to kind of live in an AA ghetto.

. . . Of the socially undesirable role changes, that is, those which society stigmatizes in varying degrees, probably the most stigmatized and socially unacceptable at this point in time is that of the transsexual. The general social reaction to sex-change surgery for most people is still horror, shock, and disapproval of tampering with "God-given identity." Every transsexual interviewed struggled with negative social reactions on the part of various people to the sex change. In every instance some family member rejected the individual because of it. In only one case were parents accepting of the individual's decision. In the remaining cases, family, including parents, rejected the individual because of the decision to undergo sex-change surgery. Interestingly enough, parents became more accepting over time in all but one of the latter cases. Children were afraid to be accepting because of what their friends and others would think of them having a mother or father who used to be a person of the opposite sex. In the case of one woman who used to be a man, three of her four children ostracized her because of their fear of what their mother's reputation might do to their own.

Almost as stigmatized as transsexuals are the mothers who have given up custody of their children. Our society views these individuals as "weirdos" who are "totally irresponsible," "depraved and immoral," or "crazy." Undoubtedly the most difficult experiences that mothers without custody have to face are the negative social reactions of friends and acquaintances. This negative societal reaction often makes it difficult for the individual to gain a positive self-concept after having given up custody. One mother who had given up custody of her children commented about the reactions of others:

It's kind of like people go *"oh"* when they find out. Like they're thinking, well, you know, "you're a bad mother." In fact, I had an incident around the corner from my house the other day. A lady was out there and she said, "Well, where's your little boy?" I said, "He's not here, he lives with his daddy." She said, "Oh," and then went on to something else like she was very uncomfortable with the idea. They don't want to discuss it, they don't want to probe it. Most of them say, "Oh," and then they just drop the subject, bury it someplace, will not discuss it. That's how ninety-five percent of the people react.

Another mother who had given up custody responded, "They think something must be wrong with you. They either think that you don't want the child or they think that the courts took them away from you and nobody bothers to ask why."

Most of the divorced people we interviewed also felt that society still considers divorce a stigmatized status and continues to value marriage over the single life in society. For these individuals, to be divorced carries more social stigma than having never been married. They felt divorce connotes failure, irresponsibility, and a threat to the basic social system.

Ex-nuns, especially in the 1960s and 1970s but even today in the 1980s, experience negative social reactions. Even if the ex-nun is partially successful in deemphasizing her past identity in terms of her own self-image, she is frequently confronted by other people who remind her that she is an ex. People expect different things of the ex-nun. For Catholics, being an ex-nun usually means having certain religious qualities and values. To see her in lay clothes with makeup and feminine mannerisms and frequently in the company of a man is often shocking. For non-Catholics, the realization that a woman is an ex-nun frequently arouses bizarre ideas, or at least great curiosity about her former life. It is common for an ex-nun meeting non-Catholics who realize her status as an ex-nun to be barraged with questions about what her previous life was like. It is difficult for these ex-nuns to try to disengage from that previous status in the face of such attention and curiosity about who they used to be.

In the area of social reactions, there is little difference among ex-nuns between the early and the later leavers. It is as difficult for the later exiters to deal with the reactions of other people as it was for those who left earlier. Ex-nuns from both samples go through a series of stages in dealing with the issue of revealing their ex-status to others. Initially, while the individual is very sensitive to her recent identity, it is common to want to make sure that people know immediately whom she used to be. Then comes a period of wanting to hide that previous identity in an effort to deal with the new status herself. In time, ex-nuns seem to take their ex-status more naturally and allow it to come up in conversation only if it seems appropriate. As one ex-nun said, "Initially after I left I would blurt out right away the fact that I used to be a nun in the hopes that such initial disclosure would prevent future embarrassments. Then I moved to a stage where I switched completely and didn't reveal my ex-identity at all. Finally, I am now at a point where I take being an ex-nun as part of my life and my past. It is simply someone I used to be that has become incorporated in who I now am."

The ex-physicians also experienced varying social reactions. Some colleagues and social acquaintances admired the doctor for being able to make such a role change. Others, however, thought the ex-physician crazy to give up a privileged role in society. Most people tended to consider the ex-physician still part of the medical role and often continued to call him or her doctor even after he or she had left the role. It is as though it is "once a doctor, always a doctor" in society's image of the physician.

The combination of an exiter's presentation of self after a role exit and society's reaction to that exit makes the adaptation process either more difficult or easier for the individual. The kinds of feelings and coping mechanisms that exiters experience in the weeks and months after making the exit are highly dependent on how significant others react to the exit.

Related to the reactions of other people toward a role exiter is the process of labeling, that is, attaching names to categories of people that become self-fulfilling prophecies. Labeling theory was developed by sociologists interested in processes of social deviance (Kitsuse 1962; Lemert 1951, 1967; Scheff 1966; Schur 1971; Liska 1981). These theorists argue that society labels deviance and associates stereotypical behavior with these labels. In response, people so labeled tend to be true to that label. For example, a child who is labeled a troublemaker by a teacher is prone to make trouble because that's what people expect. Labels often become self-fulfilling prophecies whereby individuals live up to the expectations of the label. Likewise, drug addicts who are often labeled by nonaddicts as "bums" or "degenerates" find it difficult to have a positive self-regard in the face of such labels (Ray 1964).

Over the years there are labels that have been applied to various types of role exits. "Ex-convict," for example, conjures up images of dishonesty, nonreliability, aggressiveness, and danger. When a person is labeled an ex-convict, therefore, these stereotypes become associated with the given individual. As several ex-convicts explained, they faced the dilemma when filling out formal applications of whether or not to label themselves ex-convicts because of their fear of what effect these stereotypes would have. Employers are wary of trusting an ex-con. Many welfare agencies and social service agencies treat ex-convicts differently from other people eligible for assistance. It is as though the ex-convict gives up basic social rights and the right to be respected as an individual human being.

The term "mother without custody" has become a label in our society indicating irresponsibility, hard-heartedness, selfishness, and a lack of maternal instincts. The general stereotype of a mother without custody seems to be someone who doesn't care about her children and puts herself before them. Women who struggle with intense feelings of guilt after giving up custody struggle to regain self-confidence and self-esteem. One of the prohibitive factors is the constant labeling process that they face in society.

"Ex-nun" connotes images of naïveté, inexperience, innocence, noninvolvement in worldly affairs, modesty, and a sweet, caring personality. As an ex-nun struggles to learn the ways of the world, she is constantly challenged by the stereotypes associated with being an ex-nun. As she struggles to be accepted as an ordinary woman in society, she constantly has to disprove the label society gives her. In many instances the ex-nun goes overboard in trying to prove the label inaccurate in her regard. About half of the ex-nuns interviewed admitted that they went wild in regard to clothes, makeup, and behavior in order to prove that the stereotype of ex-nun was inaccurate in their particular cases. As one ex-nun expressed it, "When I left I went crazy in regard to clothes and makeup and how I acted. I didn't want people to label me as an ex-nun so I wanted to make sure I didn't fit the usual stereotype. Another ex-nun I was living with wanted to have sex immediately and was running around and picking up men. We moved from Cleveland so that no one would know we were ex-nuns and we would be treated as plain ordinary women."

Transsexuals also face the difficulty of living with a label. The general reaction in society toward transsexuals is still one not only of curiosity but of disapproval. Many people label transsexuals as unstable, crazy, mixed up, and immoral for trying to change nature. To be labeled a transsexual, therefore, carries these connotations. It is one of the difficulties that all of the transsexuals in our study constantly faced. Several of them commented that they struggled continually against the labels placed on them.

## Intimacies

For three of the groups I interviewed, a primary area of social adjustment had to do with sexuality and intimate relationships. For most ex-nuns it had been five to twenty years since they had dated. Most nuns enter the convent either during or directly after high school. High school dating, especially in the 1950s and 1960s, was very different from the situation in which nuns found themselves after exiting the convent. The rules of the game had changed. As one interviewee put it, "Gee, men have become aggressive and permissive since I last dealt with them. To accept a dinner date almost inevitably meant sexual favors in return." Another said, "When I dated twenty years ago it was considered inappropriate for a man to expect a prolonged good night kiss at the door. Now men are offended if they are not invited into your apartment after a night out."

While nuns had been associating with men in educational and social situations prior to leaving, and while some had begun dating before they actually left, a major area of adjustment for them was learning to handle dating situations. This was true for both the early and the recent leavers. While recent ex-nuns had had more associations with men prior to exiting, the prescriptions of their religious roles influenced the nature of those relationships. Being a nun signaled sexual nonavailability. Ex-nuns, particularly those interested in marriage, realized that it was important to be successful in the area of relating to men. Ex-nuns reported feeling very insecure about sexual scripts, that is, what was expected of them in relating to a man in social life (Gagnon and Simon 1973). Part of sexual scripts involves cues which were strange to these ex-nuns since cues had changed over the years. Many ex-nuns reported misinterpreting cues, and frequently ex-nuns found themselves in embarrassing situations in which the man interpreted cues very differently from the way they had intended. For example, ex-nuns said they learned quickly that accepting an invitation to a date's apartment after going out to dinner or the theater indicated to him that she was interested in sexual involvement.

In the traditional system of religious life, "particular friendships" were forbidden. There were numerous structural mechanisms to discourage close personal relationships among nuns, such as drawing numbers to determine with whom a nun would walk or converse. This exercise reduced the probability that individual nuns would get too attached to one another. While fear of lesbian relationships may have been the covert rationale for forbidding particular friendships, the stated rationale was to encourage universal love among nuns for each other. Many ex-nuns wanted to develop close personal relationships with both males and females, but only gradually were the majority of them able to develop close friendships with lay people. In fact, the development of such friendships indicated successful adjustment to an identity other than that of ex-nun.

For the recent sample of leavers, issues of clothing, makeup, and hairstyles were significantly less traumatic than for the earlier sample since nuns in the renewed orders had more freedom to choose individual styles. In fact, most of the interviewees reported very little change necessary in physical appearance. It was in the area of intimacy and sexuality that the recent sample of ex-nuns found most difficulty. While they had been relating to men in many contexts before leaving, identity as a nun proscribed sexual behavior. On leaving, these ex-nuns reported difficulty in learning to relate to men in an available fashion. Most of them were eager to explore their sexuality and yet had to learn both the cues and the behavior appropriate to greater freedom in this area. As one ex-nun who left recently said, "I desperately wanted to date but I was not used to being available to men sexually. The freedom to respond emotionally was new. I didn't have it before since vows didn't allow that freedom. Now I had permission. I could go places and do things freely; however, I had to learn how to cue to men that I was available and interested and then I had a lot to learn about behavior with men once I was asked out. It was very scary at first. It was hard to make myself initiate relationships but I desperately wanted them."

Most ex-nuns soon discovered that eligible men had been previously married, at least men in their own age cohort. They then had to decide how they felt about dating a divorcé, or in some cases a married man who had not yet divorced. In some cases dating a divorcé also meant coming to know his children. Serious dating relationships brought forth the possibility of being a stepparent. In some instances, then, during the first year or so after leaving the order ex-nuns faced not only the issue of negotiating male-female relationships but also the possibility of becoming both wife and stepparent simultaneously.

One of the big issues for an ex-nun in a dating situation was whether to reveal to her date that she used to be a nun. Usually, people who are beginning to date discuss their pasts, where they were born, where they went to school, where they have been the past year. For the ex-nun, the question was always, Should I tell him or shouldn't I? To tell frequently caused embarrassment. Once a man realized that his date had been a nun, his reactions frequently depended on his own knowledge and experiences concerning nuns. Frequently, it was difficult for an ex-nun to explain where she had been and what she had done the past year without reference to her former identity. Most of the nuns we interviewed mentioned this dilemma as central when they began dating.

Another group that was especially concerned about dating in the adjustment process were divorced people. As with ex-nuns, it had been years since most of them were part of the dating game and they were scared and nervous. Eleven of the fifteen interviewees said dating was the hardest adjustment. They felt "awkward," "scared,"

"strange," "like a teenager again," "clumsy." In some instances they felt compelled to tell their dates immediately that they were divorced, as if to get that out front right away to see if it were important. Others were very hesitant to tell their dates they were divorced for fear he or she would not want to date them. The majority of interviewees felt that it was still a stigma to be divorced and that society still didn't consider divorce normal and acceptable. Several said the dating game had changed since they were last involved in it: Women were more forward and aggressive; there was a freer attitude toward sex and more openness in discussing feelings. Several women were afraid that men wouldn't want to date them because of their children. They soon realized, however, that "everyone was in the same boat." As in the case of ex-nuns, people who were leaving marriages in which they had been a good number of years faced a world of new sexual stress in which the cues had changed. Like the ex-nuns, they had to relearn cues appropriate to the dating game.

For the transsexuals who had recently undergone sex-change surgery, dating and the area of sexual intimacy was also a critical area of adjustment. As one transsexual put it, "I could hardly wait to have sex after surgery. I knew it was going to be an interesting experience. All of a sudden I didn't have a penis to stand in the way of sexual pleasure. I did have sex with a friend of mine who worked with me. I didn't get too much from the first time. It felt good but I had no orgasm. In subsequent sex I did have orgasms. It is not easy to do. Sex, however, is more normal than it used to be."

All of the transsexuals we interviewed were both excited and scared anticipating their first sexual experience after surgery. It seemed to be a predominant concern in their first weeks after sex-change surgery. After all, these individuals had in most instances been having sex with people of the same sex before surgery, ostensibly a homosexual situation. After surgery, they were entering a heterosexual world. An interesting question posed by several of the transsexuals was whether sex previous to surgery had in effect been homosexual. Although they had sex with same-sex partners, they had heterosexual feelings. Most transsexuals had been involved in a gay life before surgery. In some instances transsexuals wanted to move out of the gay life and into a straight life after surgery. However, many of their close friends and acquaintances were part of the gay world. Most transsexuals that we interviewed continued some association with their gay friends even after sex-change surgery. As one transsexual said, "I don't see how you can get away completely from the gay life. I wouldn't want to cut away completely. These are my friends, people I've run around with. Even though I may not have sex with them, I have an understanding of them that most people in society don't. I want to have some gay friends and if I marry someday I want my husband to know there will be gay people in our lives. You can't run to straight people when you're in trouble and tell them your whole past history. They'll throw you out. Gays will understand better, especially friends."

Like the ex-nuns, the transsexuals were also faced with the dilemma of whether to reveal their past gender identity to dates and new acquaintances. Most of the transsexuals we interviewed did share their pasts with people they dated. In only one instance did a male-to-female transsexual ask me not to call her home because her fiancé did not know of her past. She intended to wait until after her wedding to tell him for fear of his reaction.

Reactions to knowledge of a partner's sex-change surgery varied and tended to determine the future of the relationship. In some instances, partners were horrified and eager to end the relationship. In other cases, partners were stunned, intrigued, and challenged to continue the relationship, fre-

quently out of curiosity. In no instance did a transsexual report that a partner accepted the gender change as "normal." Rather, dealing with the knowledge of sex-change surgery became a major issue in each heterosexual relationship mentioned by interviewees.

The ways in which people labeled exiters and their reactions to knowledge of an individual's past identity was a major area of adjustment for interviewees. Related to this fact was the constant necessity of deciding whether or not to reveal their pasts. In addition to the impact of social reactions upon postexit adjustment, exiters also experienced shifts in their friendship networks.

## Shifting Friendship Networks

The adjustment associated with role exiting also involves changes in the individual's friendship groups. Very rarely do exiters experience a role exit without some changes in the people they value and with whom they associate as friends. The most dramatic instance is probably the ex-alcoholics who tended to shift from other drinking alcoholics as friends to nondrinking alcoholics, often other members of Alcoholics Anonymous or some other self-support group. The majority of the alcoholics I interviewed indicated that prior to their rehabilitation they had associated primarily with people who were also alcoholics. One of the reasons for this is that in such friendship situations they didn't feel different or deviant; rather they were behaving as their friends behaved. Also, by having other alcoholic friends they were not challenged to change their behavior. However, at the point at which an alcoholic stopped drinking and became an ex-alcoholic, many considered it mandatory to stop associating with other alcoholics and to make friends with people who would discourage drinking. In the majority of cases, nondrinking alcoholics shifted friendship patterns to fellow members of self-help groups who understood their problem and also understood the necessity of supporting each other and not drinking. As a nondrinking alcoholic put it, "I was glad I was part of AA, that I belonged. At least I felt like I belonged. It felt good to be there. It was safe; therefore, I was inclined to associate with other AA members who knew my problem and would encourage me in nondrinking. In fact, I gave up all my old alcoholic friends and began to establish friends in the group."

Divorced people likewise tended to shift friendship patterns dramatically after divorce. (Vaughn [1986] found the same pattern for those uncoupling from intimate relationships.) They tended to be involved less with couples, especially those whom both they and their spouses knew previously, and to become closer friends with other single and divorced people. Almost every interviewee commented on being invited less frequently to couples affairs, such as dinners and parties, because of the awkwardness of being alone. Equally as common was being invited to every affair where someone needed an "extra" to complete a party. As one person said, "There is no room for uncouples. All invitations say Mr. and Mrs. and now there is no Mrs." It was also common for shifts to occur among friends of both husband and wife. It was as if former friends felt they had to take sides and wanted to avoid awkward conversations and situations. As one man explained, "Mutual friends were uncomfortable around me and avoided certain subjects."

After divorce, many people renewed friendships with old classmates whom their spouses didn't know well, people with whom they felt on common ground. Several people also became close to friends who were also divorced. Not only did they have more interests in common with these single friends but their life situations and social life were more in harmony. Nights and weekends were not tied up with family. One woman said she was no longer invited to friends' get-togethers because they felt funny with her around. She didn't invite people over because she didn't know what to do with the males.

## Relating to Group Members and Other Exes

One characteristic unique to the ex-role is the fact that an ex once shared a role identity with other people, many of whom are still part of the previous role. Equally as important is the fact that usually there is a cohort or aggregate of other exes who have left the previous group. Therefore, exes are faced with the challenge of relating both to former group members as well as other exes. This is sociologically different from being a nonmember of a group. Nonmembers have never belonged in the role and, therefore, have not established in-group relationships with others in that role. People who have never been part of the previous group also do not share the common characteristics of being an ex of that particular group.

In the case of ex-nuns, many who left in the late 1960s and early 1970s felt hostile or angry about their years in the convent. Many of them felt they had wasted years that might have been devoted to marriage and a family. Some of them left at an age which prohibited having children, and in many instances the age factor also mitigated against entering certain professions. Among these nuns who were early leavers there was frequently little interest in maintaining a relationship with the former order; rather the desire was to start a new, independent life. At the same time, exiting was frequently considered a threat to those who remained in the order. In fact, in pre-Vatican II orders a member who was exiting was whisked away in the middle of the night so that other members of the group had no involvement with her. Nuns would wake up the next morning and realize that someone was missing from morning prayers or breakfast. It was usually indirectly that they realized the person was a defector. No correspondence or personal contact with ex-members was allowed. Even though ex-members were not publicly ridiculed, silence on the part of superiors often indicated disapproval. There was often little attempt on the part of the order to maintain relationships with those who left; rather, it was as though the former member were cut off from association with the group. No doubt, exiting was a threat to those who remained in the order.

In contemporary orders the situation has changed dramatically. The recent leavers all felt a close relationship both to the order in general and to individual members in particular and desired to continue some relationships with these people. However, the majority of them indicated that the quality of relationships with former members did change once they left. For many of them this was a sad experience. As one recent ex-nun put it,

The hardest thing about leaving was to tell the other Sisters that I was close to. Especially those who didn't realize it was coming. There was a sense of loss on both parts. They lost part of the community they were committed to and I did, too. I lost community and they lost a person from the group. Especially now that median ages are increasing, to lose a young member is a tough thing. I still have many friends in the order and want to continue my relationship with them; however, for the most part these relationships changed once I left. It was difficult for me to deal with the fact that it had to be so.

Unlike the earlier leavers, therefore, recent ex-nuns on the whole want to maintain contact with the group. Simultaneously, contemporary orders are making attempts to maintain contact with former members. In the more open, modern system the philosophy of orders is that former members are who they are because of association with the group and, likewise, that the group has benefited from the contributions of former members. Many orders have established ex-member associations and invite ex-members to meetings, conventions, and social activities sponsored by the order.

A major difference between exiters in the previous system and those now exiting concerns the relationships that exist between ex-members themselves. In the previous system there were cohorts of exiters—nuns tended to leave in groups or at least in temporal proximity. Frequently, ex-nuns lived together in the first months after exiting as a way of maximizing financial resources as well as for mutual support. It was common in the 1970s to find two, three, or four ex-nuns living together. In many orders it was also common for ex-nuns to maintain an informal network among themselves and to socialize together. Finding ex-nuns to interview in the 1970s was a simple process because of the informal network that existed among leavers from a particular order. Today the exiting rate from orders has slowed down and nuns are no longer leaving in cohorts. It is therefore more common to find ex-nuns living alone in apartments. Networks among ex-nuns are also less common today. In the previous system, it was as though ex-nuns came together as a cohesive group ostracized by the former group. Theirs was frequently a "we against them" attitude. Today, such an attitude is no longer necessary since orders themselves are more open and positive toward ex-members. It is more common today, therefore, to find ex-members associating with former group members than with other exes. Ex-members today tend to be organized more formally by the orders themselves rather than through informal friendship networks.

Among the transsexual sample, there is much intellectual awareness of having previously been part of a social group of other transsexuals; however, the tendency is for transsexuals to move away emotionally from other transsexuals after sex-change surgery. The desire to become "normal" in society makes them reluctant to associate either with transsexuals who have not yet gone through the surgery or with other postsurgery transsexuals. As far as I am aware, there are no transsexual self-help groups organized for people who have been through the surgery.

In the past several years, self-help groups for mothers without custody of children have mushroomed in the United States. Increasing numbers of mothers without custody are joining together in an attempt to share problems and deal with feelings associated with this ex-role. The majority of interviewees in our sample belonged to such a self-help group and found it extremely helpful in adjusting to the ex-role. There is great camaraderie among women who have given up custody of their children and many of the interviewees commented on the therapeutic support such groups offer.

The entire basis of Alcoholics Anonymous is the mutual support that nondrinking alcoholics can give each other, and especially newcomers to the group. The philosophy of the group is to develop strong emotional ties among nondrinking alcoholics and to encourage the lack of association between members and drinking alcoholics. All of the nondrinking alcoholics I interviewed were fearful of maintaining association with previous group members, that is, drinking alcoholics.

Most of the exiters interviewed commented on having had to learn to deal with both members of the group they left and also other exes from the group. The nature of the kinds of relationships that were established depended on the type of group that was exited and also on the degree of "hangover identity" that a person maintained after the exit.

## Role Residual

In the process of role exiting some individuals are better able to shake off their identification with a previous role than other individuals. . . . We can think about role residual as "hangover identity," that is, as aspects of self-identity that remain with an individual from a prior role even after exiting. . . .

Analysis of occupational role exits shows that individuals exiting professional and semiprofessional roles tend to have more role residual than individuals exiting nonprofessional roles (see Phillips 1984). In the process of becoming a professional, changes occur in the self-identity of a person to the extent that identity and role expectations merge. As individuals internalize a professional role, they define themselves in terms of role expectations. The professionals in our study experienced more role residual than the semiprofessionals. The nonprofessional exiters had the least amount of role residual. Exceptions to the above findings, however, occurred in the cases of nonprofessional exiters who occupied highly visible roles in society, such as ex-opera singer, ex-astronauts, and ex-professional athlete. In all of these instances, role residual was as strong as it was for the professional exiters. One explanation for this finding has to do with the social visibility involved in these particular roles. Roles that are highly visible in society and which involve social support and social acceptability tend to be roles that are very difficult to exit from in a complete fashion. One reason is that the public keeps reminding the individual of exiting. As one ex-professional athlete in our sample put it,

I think the first thing that happened to me when I left was that I kind of became shy. A little introverted because I didn't have my Samson hair real long. It had been cut short. I think one of the hardest things an athlete has that reaches that level is that so much of his life is made up of what he has done on Sunday and what people want to make you. It becomes a part of your life without your realizing it and once you realize that you don't have that to rely on anymore it gets kind of scary. People are always asking if you're going to go back and try out with the USFL. They want you to do it because they know you and they want you to be out there. So, they don't let go of it and you're always saying, no, no. And of course all that input you get all the time keeps working on your mind. It's like, well, maybe I should. As much as you try to consciously deal with it and work the things out yourself, then as soon as you do that you turn the corner and a guy says, "Hey, are you gonna try out next year"?

. . . The high idealism a professional generally carries into his or her role may also help in explaining why professionals experience role residual more often than semiprofessionals or nonprofessionals. Often an individual is attracted to the professional role at an early age and plans to enter a particular career for an extended period of time prior to beginning the training process. During this time, high expectations are formed and one becomes very idealistic concerning the role. For instance, one ex-surgeon who entered the medical field because his grandfather had been a doctor said, "I never thought of being anything else." Another former doctor had been practicing medicine for thirty years and had gone into practice because "It was always something I wanted to do. Medicine always intrigued me." He found his role very rewarding but was disappointed when patients became hostile when he could not cure them. Thinking there had to be more to life, he suddenly became responsible for managing some family money and decided after two years to leave medicine. He had no regret in leaving but constantly had the idea that at some point in time he might open an office by himself and see patients on a part-time basis.

Even though he is no longer actively practicing medicine, he said that he still always answers the phone, "This is Dr. ——" rather than "This is Mr. ——." He said, "I feel like a doctor. I still have my diploma." His sister once introduced him as an ex-doctor, and he told her, "They didn't take my diploma away. I still have my degree." He explained that at the present time "I feel I am not contributing too much to society. One thing about medicine, even if you are paid well, when you're practicing full-time, you feel you're performing a service that people

need. Just managing my money is a kind of selfish thing to do. I think I am wasting my time. I ought to do something." Although the doctor had become disillusioned with several facets of the doctor role, he never regretted entering the medical field and never lost identification with his former role. As he said, "If I were eighteen years old, I would go to medical school again. I would be a doctor again."

All but one of the ex-physicians interviewed maintained affiliations with professional medical associations and still attended medical meetings. All of them still used their title "doctor" in specific circumstances. An interesting issue is when ex-physicians use the title "doctor" and when they use the title "mister." Most of them use "doctor" when speaking with other medical professionals or when the title will gain them entry into a particular social or business situation. At times when they want to deemphasize their previous role and be simply a business associate or a social acquaintance they use the title "mister."

Since all of the role exits included in this study deal with roles central to identity, there was some role residual present in almost all cases. Individuals were not only aware of a previous role but carried that awareness into aspects of their current role expectations and self-identity. It is safe to say that the more personal involvement and commitment an individual had in a former role, that is, the more self-identity was equated with role definitions, the more role residual tended to manifest itself after the exit. Time in a previous role was not as important as the amount of training and preparation for the role and the centrality of the role to a person's identity. Ex-professionals and ex-nuns manifested substantial role residual due in part to the extensive training involved for both roles and the identification of the person with the role. In the case of transsexuals there was almost constant role residual in that having experienced a sex change seemed to be a central part of the identity of all of the transsexuals interviewed. Likewise, ex-alcoholics were constantly aware of the fact that they are alcoholics, although now nondrinking alcoholics. Central to the identity of the ex-alcoholics was the idea that they are alcoholics, have been drinking alcoholics, and cannot allow themselves to fall back into that pattern. . . .

Another way in which role residual lingers after a person leaves a given role is in the form of dreams. Approximately one-fifth of our interviewees indicated that they have recurrent dreams about still being part of the former role. In several cases, the dreams were painful nightmares centering around the struggle to make a decision whether to leave the role. As a former nun said, "About once a month I dream that I am still a nun and am agonizing over the decision to leave or not. Sometimes my husband and children are waiting for me to come home and I want to go home to them but have to struggle to make a firm decision to leave the convent. I think the dream shows what a painful decision it was to leave." All of those who said they have such dreams indicated that they never regretted leaving the former role. Dreams, therefore, do not appear to be related to ambivalent feelings about the decision but rather to deep-seated memories of the anguish involved in the decision-making process.

## Summary

Being an ex is a unique role experience because identity as an ex rests not on one's current role but on who one was in the past. As exes struggle to disidentify with a previous role, others with whom they associate take their previous identities into account and frequently relate to them in terms of who they used to be. There are six major areas of adjustment that role exiters face as they begin to create a new identity as an ex: ways of presenting themselves and their ex-status; learning to deal with social reactions to their ex-status, including stereotypes associated with the labeling process; negotiating and establishing intimate relationships; shifting networks of friends; relating to members who are still part of the former group as well as fellow exes; and learning to deal with role residual that lingers after the exit. Successful adjustment to an ex-status required interviewees to find successful solutions to each of these challenges. To the extent that they were able to do so, exiters felt successful in having made a smooth transition in the role-exit process.

## References

Davis, Fred. 1979. *Yearning for Yesterday: A Sociology of Nostalgia*. New York: The Free Press.

Gagnon, J., and William Simon. 1973. *Sexual Conduct: The Social Sources of Human Sexuality*. Chicago: Aldine.

Garfinkel, Harold. 1956. Conditions of Successful Degradation Ceremonies. *American Journal of Sociology* 61: 420–424.

Glaser, Barney G., and Anselm L. Strauss. 1971. *Status Passage: A Formal Theory*. New York: Aldine-Atherton.

Goffman, Erving. 1959a. *The Presentation of Self in Everyday Life*. Garden City, N.Y.: Doubleday.

———. 1959b. *Encounters: Two Studies in the Sociology of Interaction*. Indianapolis: Bobbs-Merrill.

———. 1963. *Stigma: Notes on the Management of Spoiled Identity*. Englewood Cliffs, N.J.: Prentice-Hall.

Goode, William J. 1956. *After Divorce*. New York: The Free Press.

Kitsuse, John I. 1962. Societal Reactions to Deviant Behavior: Problems of Theory and Method. *Social Problems* 9: 247–256.

Lemert, Edwin. 1951. *Social Pathology*. New York: McGraw-Hill.

———. 1967. The Concept of Secondary Deviance. In Lemert, ed., *Human Deviance, Social Problems and Social Control*, pp. 40–64. Englewood Cliffs, N.J.: Prentice-Hall.

Liska, Allen E. 1981. *Perspectives on Deviance*. Englewood Cliffs, N.J.: Prentice-Hall.

Phillips, Deena J. 1984. *Role Residual and the Role Exit Process*. M.A. thesis, University of Houston.

Ray, Marsh B. 1964. The Cycle of Abstinence and Relapse Among Heroin Addicts. In Howard S. Becker, ed., *The Other Side: Perspectives on Deviance*, pp. 163–177. New York: The Free Press.

Scheff, Thomas J. 1966. *Being Mentally Ill: A Sociological Theory*. Chicago: Aldine.

Schur, Edwin. 1971. *Labeling Deviant Behavior: Its Sociological Implications*. New York: Harper and Row.

Turner, Ralph H. 1978. The Role and the Person. *American Journal of Sociology* 84: 1–23.

Vaughn, Diana. 1986. *Uncoupling: Turning Points in Intimate Relationships*. New York: Oxford University Press.

# PART IV

# The Social Construction of Reality

*If [people] define situations as real, they are real in their consequences.*

(W. I. Thomas and Dorothy Thomas, *The Child in America*)

*[People] make their own history, but they do not make it just as they please; they do not make it under circumstances chosen by themselves, but under circumstances directly encountered, given and transmitted from the past. The tradition of all the dead generations weighs like a nightmare on the brain of the living.*

(Karl Marx, *The 18th Brumaire of Louis Bonaparte*)

# Building and Breaching Reality

In 1986, one of the authors (Peter Kollock) spent the summer in the Caribbean, sailing a boat with five other people from island to island and eventually sailing across the Gulf of Mexico to deliver the boat to Galveston. Kollock recalls:

> A number of times, my companions and I sailed long stretches of ocean over several days, never seeing land. During these long passages, everyone on the boat hallucinated at one time or another.
>
> We were in good health, of sound mind. None of us was on medications or taking drugs or drinking alcohol. Yet each of us experienced very vivid hallucinations several times. The hallucinations often occurred when we were alone at night at the tiller. Almost everyone reported having long conversations with people (sometimes crewmates, sometimes friends back in the United States) who were not really there. Seeing colored lights and hearing voices were also common occurrences. These hallucinations were not fleeting, fuzzy things. Some of them seemed as real as the book you are now holding.
>
> We were not bothered by the hallucinations and, after a time, recognized them "for what they were." At times I simply sat back and looked at the hallucination with the same detached interest as a person examining an artifact in a museum, saying to myself, "Here I go again."
>
> Hallucinations are nothing new in the world of long-distance sailing, and as well-socialized members of the Western world, we had at our disposal an entire litany of "facts" for explaining why we were hallucinating and why the objects we saw and voices we heard were not real. These explanations included sleep deprivation (our rotating schedules meant we rarely got more than a few hours sleep), sensory deprivation, poor nutrition, mild dehydration, mild heat exhaustion (in 110-degree weather it's difficult to eat properly or drink enough water). In other words, we flatly denied the evidence of our eyes and used "common sense" to explain away what we saw.
>
> At one point, the boat was sailing near Haiti, and I wondered what might have happened if we had stopped in that country to pick up another crew member. If that person had been a member of the Haitian traditional religion known as vodoun, her or his common sense would include such obvious and taken-for-granted facts as the knowledge that people can communicate with spirits and see visions. Overhearing me and my crewmates explaining away our visions, this Haitian sailor might have looked on us with a mixture of confusion and pity. We were experiencing vivid images of great power, and yet we refused to acknowledge that the images were real. We experienced visions repeatedly,

we all experienced them, and the visions had common themes. We knew we were not intoxicated when we saw them, and yet we denied their existence out of hand. "What unreasonable, illogical people," the Haitian might conclude.

## Common Sense

The repository for our most basic knowledge of "reality"—as defined by "the language of the day" in a particular culture—we call *common sense*. Common sense is a set of shared cultural rules for making sense of the world. These rules are so well established and taken for granted that they often require no justification. To the question "How did you know that?" or "Why did you do that?" one can reply simply, "It's just common sense." These rules are the bedrock of cultural knowledge; they seem obviously true.

One of the most powerful ways of demonstrating that reality is a social construction is to show the limitations and arbitrariness of common sense, either by pointing out inconsistencies or by contrasting one culture's common sense to another's, as in Kollock's story about the hallucinations.

The quotation from Karl Marx at the beginning of this part suggests that people make their own history, but that they do so within the confines of the circumstances they encounter. When he spoke of "circumstances encountered from the past," Marx had in mind the economic conditions—the "mode of production"—that shaped the existence of a group of people. In this section, we explore the broader social circumstances that form the basis of the economic and political life of a group. These circumstances consist of the systems of belief that groups of people use to structure their shared reality.

As contradictory as it may seem at first, we also agree with the dictum of the sociologist W. I. Thomas: What people define as real will be real in its consequences. He implies that anything we can imagine has the potential to become reality. In theory this may be true. In practice, however, the definitions that people use to organize and direct their own lives are generally based on, in Marx's terms, "the traditions of the dead generations." As we discussed in Part II, language-based knowledge systems shape our perceptions. Hence, although all definitions of a situation may be possible, we actually work within a system of beliefs inherited from our social ancestors. To the extent that our "common sense" limits certain lines of action and affirms arbitrary "truths," it can be said that these traditions "weigh like a nightmare" on our existence. In acting out these traditions of thought uncritically, we both create and re-create the circumstances of the past.

The social construction of reality—the title of this part—is perhaps the most central and profound topic treated in this book. The phrase deserves careful attention. Note first the claim that reality is a *construction*. This idea in itself can seem counterintuitive or even nonsensical. Surely reality is simply the objective world that exists "out there," the subject of study of our sciences. But the alternative claim is that reality is malleable. Different groups or different cultures or different historical epochs may hold completely different (even diametrically opposed) beliefs about what is "real," what is "obviously true," what is "good," and what is "desired." The second noteworthy element in the title is that reality is a *social* construction. That is, the subjective realities that are created and maintained are the product, not of isolated individuals, but of relationships, communities, groups, institutions, and entire cultures.

The readings that follow demonstrate that "reality" can be an amazingly malleable thing. But are there limits to how reality might be constructed? In other words, is any definition of reality, no matter how outlandish, possible? A separate but related question is whether all realities are equally probable. Is any definition of the situation as likely as any other to emerge? Or are there constraints that limit which definitions might be viable? If so, what is the nature of these constraints?

Another significant question is, Who's doing the defining? Are certain people, or groups of people, more or less able to define things in a particular way? Questions such as these raise the issue of power. Power, in a symbolic interactionist sense, is the ability to define a situation in a particular way and to have others act in accordance with this definition. Reality may be a social construction, but we are not all equal participants in this construction. What are the sources of this power and how might it be used, abused, or resisted? These issues are explored in the sections that follow.

## A Theory of Reality

The first reading in this section is "Five Features of Reality," by Hugh Mehan and Houston Wood. It serves both as an introduction to this section and as a framework for organizing many of the readings in Part IV. It is a chapter from a book about ethnomethodology, a tradition in sociology that explores the folk methods people use ("ethno methods") to construct a sense of reality. Realities, in this sense, consist of a system of taken-for-granted beliefs and assumptions shared by a group of people. These realities structure existence. Five key features of reality are discussed in this reading: Reality is reflexive, coherent, interactional, fragile, and permeable.

## Reflexive

Realities are *reflexive*. In other words, realities contain self-sealing beliefs—unquestioned beliefs that cannot be proven wrong. For example, if you place your pencil on your desk while you go for a snack and cannot find the pencil when you return, you will assume that you somehow misplaced it. If it reappears where you left it, you will assume that you just overlooked it the first time. In this culture, people hold an unquestioned belief regarding the immobility of "inanimate" objects, so it's unlikely that you would entertain the notion that your pencil left by itself and then returned. That possibility is precluded by your unquestioned assumptions about reality.

Here's another illustration. Do you watch the five-day weather forecast? A newcomer to our culture might assume that one needed to watch the forecast only every five days: Presumably a five-day forecast will give useful weather information for the next five days. Right? "No!" you exclaim. "You need to watch it every day." The newcomer looks at you, puzzled. "Because the forecast changes," you continue. Now the newcomer is really confused. Why watch a "forecast" if you already know it will not be accurate? Think about this: You watch weather forecasts because you want to know what the weather will be, but you also recognize that the predictions are often inaccurate. So you watch the forecast again to see how it has changed. Does the frequent inaccuracy of the predictions make you doubt the "reality" that we can forecast the weather? No. Instead of questioning the validity of forecasting the weather, you probably explain away the inaccuracies as human error or the inadequacy of present meteorological technology. What you are not likely to do is question the taken-for-granted assumption that there is a pattern to nature, and that, with the right theories and technology, we can know this pattern and make predictions based on it. In other words, you are not likely to assume that the weather is actually random. An unquestioned belief of modern Western thought is that there is order in nature. The cultural enterprise of predicting weather is based on this assumption.

Keep this belief in mind as you read Mehan and Wood's example of the Azande's use of an oracle to make important decisions. Unquestioned beliefs are often more easily noticed when examining a culture different from our own. In many cases, others' beliefs are described as superstitious or magical. However, Mehan and Wood demonstrate that any culture, including ours, is filled with unquestioned beliefs. The idea that we rely on assumptions seems to undermine our treasured image of ourselves as lay scientists, testing our ideas against the evidence of the world and revising our beliefs when they are contradicted. What Mehan and Wood conclude is that "all people are equally superstitious." People continue to hold certain unquestioned beliefs in the face of contradictory evidence.

### Coherent

A second feature of realities is that they have an order and structure to them; realities are *coherent*. Even realities that seem nonsensical and anarchical to outsiders reveal their own order and logic on careful examination.

### Interactional

Mehan and Wood's third feature is that realities are *interactional*. Realities are created, maintained, and changed through interaction with other people. In other words, realities are social constructions. People do not create realities in isolation.

### Fragile

The fourth feature of reality draws from the third. Because realities are based on ongoing interactions, they are subject to performance breakdowns (recall the discussion in Part III). Thus, realities are *fragile*. Any reality can be disrupted or "breached," often by a seemingly trivial act. Examples of breaching reality range from standing in an elevator facing the people inside instead of the door, to ending a conversation with "hello" instead of "good-bye."

### Permeable

The fifth feature is that realities are *permeable*. It is possible to move out of one reality into another. If the conditions are right, one can even move into a radically different reality. For example, soldiers move between a reality in which they are trained to kill other humans into another where they are expected to respect human life: In one reality they are expected to kill; in the other reality killing is defined as murder.

Each of the following readings highlights one or more of the key features of realities. Reading 34, "A Conception of and Experiments with 'Trust' as a Condition of Concerted Stable Actions," is an excerpt from an article by Harold Garfinkel, the founder of ethnomethodology. He achieved great fame and notoriety with the breaching experiments he and his students conducted at UCLA in the 1960s. Breaching entails making the underlying structure of reality explicit by acting in a manner inconsistent with the taken-for-granted rules of interaction that maintain the reality. When reality is breached, interaction often comes to a confused halt. Garfinkel's reading describes a variety of breaching experiments as well as people's reactions to these experiments.

In our classes, we ask students to design and perform their own breaching experiments. One example is volunteering to pay more than the posted price for an item. Another is shopping from others' carts in a grocery store. The taken-for-granted routine is that once you have placed an item in your cart, it belongs to you. The students who performed this "breach" matter-of-factly took items from the carts of others. When questioned, they responded simply that the item in the cart had been more convenient to reach than the one on the shelf. When assumptions are breached, people look for a "reasonable" explanation—something that reaffirms the underlying assumptions. "Oh, I'm sorry, I thought that was my cart" is an example of a reasonable explanation for taking something from someone else's cart. But to act as if there is nothing wrong with doing so confuses the other person and makes her or him question, just for a moment, the reality of the situation.

In another breaching experiment, a student cheerfully asked a McDonald's clerk for a Whopper, a menu item at rival Burger King. Rather than say, "We don't carry that," the McDonald's clerk asked the student to repeat the order. When the request for a Whopper was repeated, the clerk looked around to see if fellow employees had heard this "bizarre" request. In other words, he searched for interactional corroboration of his reality that "everyone knows" McDonald's menu and anyone who doesn't is obviously weird. Something as simple as a sideways glance and raised eyebrows from a co-worker can indicate that one's reality is intact and that the momentary experience is merely an aberration that can be ignored. In this case, however, the students were particularly tenacious in testing reactions to breaching. After the first person breached the fast food order routine, another classmate stepped up and ordered a slice of pizza, which, of course, McDonald's restaurants don't serve.

Reading 35 also demonstrates many of the features of reality. "The Social Construction of Unreality: A Case Study of a Family's Attribution of Competence to a Severely Retarded Child" is a provocative account of the skills and strategies used by a family to maintain a reality in the face of what seems to be massive evidence contradicting their beliefs. The family insists that the youngest child—diagnosed as severely retarded—is capable of complex and sophisticated interaction. To maintain this reality, the family engages in such techniques as "framing" an interaction so that almost anything the child does can be interpreted as meaningful, and physically leading the child through some action ("puppeteering") and then interpreting the action as the result of autonomous decisions on the child's part.

The reading concludes with an interesting commentary by David Reiss, who suggests that the features characterizing this family also characterize radical scientific groups. He cautions against making too close a connection, but the commentary suggests how close madness and creativity might be. As you read this article, also ask yourself what unquestioned beliefs the authors, Melvin Pollner and Lynn McDonald-Wikler, hold about their own reality.

## Believing Makes It So—Self-Fulfilling Prophecies

The readings in this section illustrate another feature of reality—beliefs are sometimes self-fulfilling. In Reading 36, "Self-Fulfilling Prophecies," Paul Watzlawick asserts that "a self-fulfilling prophecy is an assumption or prediction that, purely as a result of having been made, causes the expected or predicted event to occur and thus confirms its own 'accuracy.'" Watzlawick discusses self-fulfilling prophecies in a variety of settings, ranging from public events (for example, a predicted gas shortage that led thousands of motorists to rush out and fill their tanks to the top, thus creating the shortage) to interpersonal relationships and medical ailments.

Self-fulfilling prophecies illustrate an important point made throughout this book: Often what is important is not what is factually correct, but rather what is defined as real. People's actions are based on their *definitions* of what is real. That is, we respond not to the direct event but to our interpretation of it. An important message in Watzlawick's article is that, by becoming aware of self-fulfilling prophecies, we will be better able to recognize and resist potentially damaging outcomes. Paradoxically, a crucial step in becoming more free is to become more aware of the constraints we face as social actors and the manner in which certain definitions of the situation either enable or inhibit possible lines of action.

Socially held beliefs about the characteristics of groups of people—in other words, stereotypes—often result in self-fulfilling outcomes. One illustration of this process can be seen in Reading 37 by Mark Snyder ("When Belief Creates Reality: The Self-Fulfilling Impact of First Impressions on Social Interaction"). In this reading, Snyder reports on experimental work that he and his colleagues conducted to demonstrate that the stereotypes about attractive versus unattractive people can be self-fulfilling. On the basis of the stereotype that attractive individuals are more friendly and likable, people may actually behave in ways that encourage such individuals to respond in a friendly and likable manner. The reverse is also true.

Consider the implications for the self-fulfilling potential of other stereotypes. In Reading 38, "Pygmalion in the Classroom," Robert Rosenthal and Lenore Jacobson report on their famous study of the effects of preconceived beliefs about intelligence on the performance of schoolchildren. Rosenthal and Jacobson told elementary school teachers that they had administered a test indicating that a number of the students in the teachers' classes were likely to show significant academic improvement over the course of the year. In fact, the researchers had simply picked a group of students randomly. However, by the end of the year students who were expected by their teachers to improve had indeed improved (as measured by a standard IQ test). This remarkable study demonstrates that expecting superior performance, especially in younger children, can actually create that superior performance. This outcome occurs because the teachers behave toward the children according to how they have defined them. In so doing, they elicit the expected response. However, there is also a troubling side to this process. If students who were not expected to "bloom" did in fact improve over the year, teachers were more likely to rate such students as less well adjusted and less interesting. The self-fulfilling aspect of expectations is double-edged. They may benefit those people about whom we have positive beliefs and oppress those about whom we have negative beliefs.

David Rosenhan, in Reading 39, "On Being Sane in Insane Places," describes another very famous and controversial study. He began with a simple question: Can the sane be reliably distinguished from the insane? By sending sane people into psychiatric hospitals, he discovered that the answer to this question seems to be no. Psychiatric staff expect patients to be insane, so they interpret the behavior of any person presumed to be a patient, even the behavior of "normal" researchers, as insane. Like the other readings, this one illustrates several of the different features of reality. The self-sealing nature of beliefs, the interactional nature of reality, and the self-fulfilling nature of psychiatric diagnoses are all demonstrated here.

## Caveat Regarding Breaching Experiments

Occasionally students using previous editions of this text have raised the concern that breaching experiments are a violation of social trust. This concern indicates an excellent insight regarding the theories of Goffman and Garfinkel—both are saying that social order (interaction routines) are based on trust. We *trust* one another to know the routines and to follow them through. In this way, we are able to carry on interactions with one another without the fear of being hurt or violated. As the authors of this text, we cannot speak directly for

Goffman or Garfinkel. This is our own response to students and instructors who have concerns about the breaching experiments. Recall that one of the lessons in Part II is the extent to which we all participate in acts of categorization (stereotyping) that we may not be aware of. Much of our behavior is "mindless." Similarly, many of our interaction rituals are mindless and also taken for granted. Our own position is that we would never advocate the senseless disruption of another person's routine or status quo just for the sake of doing it. However, breaching experiments, handled with care and sensitivity, can be a way to raise consciousness and to invite others to think critically about their own participation in mindless routines. We honestly believe that persons are not truly free to defend or change their patterns of behavior unless they are aware of these patterns. Thus, we opt to engage in forms of social interaction that serve to highlight these patterns (breaching). Keep in mind that there are many forms of breaching that do not have to involve someone else directly. Just thinking up the experiments can be a great exercise in consciousness-raising. If you do decide to implicate others, consider situations in which the others are also likely to be able to learn something useful from the encounter. Breaching is not the equivalent of being mean or cruel. Our own experience with breaching is that, once people settle down and recover from the breach, they are often eager to discuss the experiment.

The important feature is that persons performing these experiments take the time to debrief their subjects and to engage with them in a discussion of what occurred. This can be a significant occasion in which to practice "interpersonal ethics"—i.e., to use the situation to gain greater understanding among all parties involved. Remember the point is to define and make explicit routines that reflect taken-for-granted assumptions about reality—not to hurt someone or make them needlessly uncomfortable. The best breaching experiments are those in which the person doing them is able to recognize her or his own participation in a taken-for-granted status quo.

## The Social Construction of the Status Quo

This set of readings highlights some of the processes of cultural production. Some cultural institutions are better established than others—that is, a large percentage of the population is likely to take them for granted as a source of authority for certain aspects of social organization. These institutions and practices constitute a cultural status quo. How are these institutional beliefs and practices enacted and maintained over time? This is the question we look at in this section. The theory of reality as a social construction can be used to address this question. As you read this material, another useful question to ask about these "dominant" cultural institutions is what alternatives might exist and how the situation might be defined and approached differently if others were in charge of the cultural definition of the situation.

One of the most well-established and least-questioned institutions in this country is the medical profession. Medicine is one of the relatively undisputed sources of authority regarding what constitutes "acceptable" behavior. Those who exhibit unusual or inappropriate behaviors are often referred for medical treatment. Both the cause and treatment of these behaviors are part of the body of organized knowledge that constitutes medicine. One feature of this form of knowledge is that certain types of actions and feelings are considered "natural." Deviations from the "natural" patterns are considered "pathological."

In Reading 40, "The Discovery of Hyperkinesis: Notes on the Medicalization of Deviant Behavior," Peter Conrad explores the emergence of a medical name (hyperkinesis) for hyperactivity in children—behavior that is considered distracting and "out of control" in everyday interactions. He uses the term *medicalization* to mean "defining behavior as a medical problem or illness and mandating or licensing the medical profession to provide some type of treatment for it." Our culture has a pervasive tendency to define everything from depression to alcoholism as a physiological disease. Hyperkinesis is particularly interesting because it exhibits none of the usual physiological correlates of disease (for example, fever, bacteria, viruses, changes in blood chemistry), and the symptomatic behaviors—rebelliousness, frustration, excitability—seem to have as much to do with social protest as with organic disease.

Conrad and his colleagues have written extensively on the medicalization of deviant behaviors. For example, all cultures have people who are "mad"—that is, people who violate behavioral boundaries accepted by the great majority of the group. Beliefs about what these people should be called, who should deal with them, and how they should be handled differ remarkably, however. Certain cultures see their "mad" as divinely inspired. In these cultures, madness is attributed to spiritual possession rather than natural pathology. For example, the word "schizophrenia" is derived from a Hebrew term that means "prophet." People who were so filled with the presence of God that they could not harness themselves to the chains of worldly conduct were labeled schizophrenic—they had transcended society.

In our own culture, one social-psychological alternative to the medical model of madness and other forms of asocial conduct is based on the theory that those people who are unusually bright and creative experience an overload of contradictions when they try to meet standard expectations for behavior. These people are thought to be responding to a very complex and contradictory set of "generalized others," reacting rapidly to strong creative passions and urges. This complex creativity is manifest as a resistance to socialization. And those who have the necessary interpersonal skills and material resources may avoid medical labeling and may become significant contributors in areas such as the arts. Because of their contributions, their "inappropriate" behavior is sometimes labeled "eccentric" rather than "mentally ill."

If you are interested in exploring this topic more, you might begin with some of the writings of one of the framers of this alternative perspective, Thomas Szasz. In a 1971 article, Szasz describes an extreme, even horrific, example of the medicalization of a deviant behavior. This historical case, reported in a prestigious medical journal in 1851, concerned a disease manifest among slaves. The primary symptom of the ominous-sounding disorder called "drapetomania" was running away from plantations!

Despite the increasing cultural awareness of the limitations and misapplications of the medical model of deviance, many medical practitioners continue to treat "conditions" such as transgendered expressions, homosexuality, and "female emotion" as symptoms of pathology. There are still respected scientists who use the medical model to claim that certain people may be more inclined to "social pathology" than others based on racial ethnicity. Medicine is a powerful and influential cultural institution that has done much to improve our quality of life, but it also warrants careful scrutiny. Be aware of its limitations and untold stories.

In contrast to the well-established medical profession, many cultural organizations are fledgling institutions. They must be explicitly concerned with maintaining boundaries because of the many pressures that threaten to undermine them. One such case is reported in Reading 41, "The Nudist Management of Respectability," by Martin Weinberg. Nudist camps face the task of establishing the situational definition that "nudity and sexuality are unrelated [and] that there is nothing shameful about the human body." These ideas are contrary to the socialization of many people. Nudists have the challenge of constructing and maintaining this fragile reality against the backdrop of the larger cultural definition that public nudity is unacceptable and immoral. The "permeability" of realities is evident in the manner in which members are able to move, with apparent fluidity, between weekend activities as nudists and weekday activities in a "clothed" society.

The interesting point of conflict is the strategies that nudists must design and adhere to while in their camps to project the definition that their enterprise is nonsexual. Many behaviors that would go unnoticed in a clothed environment, such as casually referring to the body or looking directly at someone, are rigidly prohibited among nudists. Nudists forgo much personal freedom of expression in order to convey the collective impression that they are nonsexual. "Nudists are prudists," Weinberg observes, because they must work so hard to disassociate themselves from sexuality. This article thus reveals a paradox regarding groups and cultural production—the more fragile the group's boundaries, the less deviance it can tolerate. Alternative or radical groups, contrary to common belief, are often more rigid than mainstream groups in their governance of member behavior.

We have said that realities are constructed and maintained through interaction. Erving Goffman speaks of "dramatizing the ideal," of people employing the "ideals" suggested by their particular cultural reality in shaping their interactions with others. In acting out these ideals, people affirm and re-create them. Such behavior may help maintain realities that foster our dissatisfaction or oppression. Through our participation in various interaction rituals, we actually reinforce the status quo. This is a particularly noteworthy process regarding the perpetuation of social hierarchies. Scholars who study social power emphasize these points:

First, it is difficult or impossible to rule solely through raw force or oppression. In order for people "in charge" to rule over others, those "beneath" them must willingly comply to some extent. This compliance is accomplished through the performance of "legitimacy rituals" that establish and maintain the authority of those in power. Whether or not a person accepts the officials' authority in her or his private mind, participation in legitimacy rituals contributes to the construction of the status quo. The existing power structure is "realized" through the performance. The proverb "When the great lord passes, the wise peasant bows deeply and silently farts" says that the cultural relationship of dominance is (re)affirmed in the gesture of the bow while the peasant's sense of self as outside this oppression is also affirmed, by the private gesture of the fart. It is the public gesture that contributes to the production of the status quo, even as the private gesture reconciles contradiction and conflict within the self.

Any social system, be it oppressive or humane, requires the cooperation of both the powerful and the weak. Both play a role in defining reality; both encounter limits. Some constraints arise from culture and tradition, which provide the precedents and the symbolic material that make some definitions so easy and others nearly impossible.

Other constraints are the result of having or lacking tangible resources. Regardless of how you define a situation, if you are at the wrong end of a gun you can be hurt. But guns alone make for a very fragile social order.

In Reading 42, sociologist Cecilia Ridgeway describes a theory that she has developed to explain the perpetuation of gender inequality in employment. Despite many formal institutional changes in the past three decades that have made it unlawful to discriminate against women in employment, women still lag significantly behind men in promotions and raises. Ridgeway explains this lag as a manifestation of a particular status quo in which both men and women *perceive* women as being less competent than men in certain employment situations. According to prevailing cultural scripts and stereotypes, women just aren't as effective as men. This interactional explanation is an important contribution to understanding how gender inequality is perpetuated even when people intend to be fair.

In this society, many aspects of social power are revealed in courts of law. The way a court defines, presents, and decides a case sends a powerful message regarding what sorts of people and activities are legitimate, what is not acceptable, and what will be tolerated or ignored. Several studies indicate, for instance, that when courts excuse acts of discrimination and abuse against particular groups, people feel more free to act out their hatred for those groups. Presumably, persons who are inclined to engage in hate crimes refrain from acting out their hate when doing so is deemed illegal. But if they observe that their expressions of hate are likely to be ignored by cultural and legal authorities, they may feel that violent expressions of hate are permissible and (implicitly) legitimate.

In a related discussion of the negotiation of cultural definitions of reality, Kim Lane Scheppele, professor of both law and sociology, considers how "truth" is determined in a court of law. In "Practices of Truth-Finding in a Court of Law" (Reading 43), she follows the way in which stories are told, revised, and then re-revised. All court reports are "narratives," she states, and narratives are always undergoing revision—this is a fact of stories; they are continuously revised. But some types of narrative are given more legitimacy than others. In the minds of the jury, narratives that have obviously been revised are often deemed "less true" than those that appear to be constant over time. She considers several cases of narratives of "harassment." She notes that juries tend to doubt the credibility of someone who claims past harassment if she or he did not make the same claim at the time when the incident took place.

# Stories We Live By

Writer and philosopher Antonin Artaud once remarked that humans are beasts with stories on their backs. Interactional routines and the coherent realities through which these routines take on meaning can be analyzed as stories. We use these stories to organize and give meaning to our lives. Stories have an organizational logic to them. They are contextual realities that provide the scripts for defining the situation and the identities appropriate to the situation. The question we are often asked by our students is what is the connection between the "performance scripts" described in Part III and the "stories" or "realities" that we describe here. We think of scripts as possible lines of action that can take place within a particular type of story. Types of stories are referred to as "genre." For instance, you are probably familiar with the differences between the horror genre and the romance genre. There are many different scripts that can be written within the parameters of the horror genre, but you recognize each of them as a manifestation of the particular genre because it has familiar characters and plots and storylines.

Similarly, social realities can be recognized in the ways in which people share expectations about the storyline, the types of characters, and associated behaviors and feelings. These storylines or realities are often taken for granted until someone steps out of character or violates expected routines. These breaches cause us to reflect on the expected story in ways that end up either changing the routine or reinforcing it. One of the most common (but also most taken-for-granted) realities or stories in contemporary U.S. culture comes in the form of a "romance genre." According to this story, our main life-quest is to find our "true mate," form a union together, produce biological offspring, and live happily ever after. Even persons who have chosen not to pursue this quest are implicated in the story to the extent that they are constantly asked by others to justify or make sense of their non-participation. This story is so prevalent that we tend to think it is "natural" for all humans to want to do this, even though the emergence of (heterosexual) romantic love as a basis for family organization is a relatively recent historical development.

Part IV explores the way in which people collectively participate in writing, rewriting, and performing various cultural stories. If you view human behavior as a form of living through story, it may be easier to comprehend how and why people disregard or reinterpret contradictory evidence and behave in a way that results in self-fulfilling prophecies. It can be said that we attend to stimuli that resonate with the situational story and that we interpret incongruent stimuli in a way that maintains the storyline. In this way, realities become self-sealing. Either we find some way to incorporate our experiences into mutually understood stories, or we disregard the experiences as much as possible.

In the novel *Generation X*, Douglas Coupland (1991) writes about a group of young people who are caught between historical moments. The stories of the previous generation don't quite jibe with life as they experience it. But they haven't yet fully conceptualized alternative stories for organizing their own experiences. Throughout the book, the friends produce a reality together by telling stories to one another. Coupland's protagonist, Andy, ponders this process:

> Claire breaks the silence by saying that it's not healthy to live life as a succession of isolated cool little moments. "Either our lives become stories, or there's just no way to get through them." I agree. Dag agrees. We know this is why the three of us left our lives behind and came to the desert—to tell stories and make our own lives worthwhile tales in the process. (p. 13)

Notice that, even in the process of searching for alternatives, these characters are part of a story. The story in this case is one of feeling outside the mainstream. Searching for oneself in a place far removed from day-to-day realities, such as the desert, is a well-worn story in Western culture. Because realities are coherent and self-reflexive, the alternatives that we create tend to be variations on existing stories. Even as we are driven to find new names and create new meanings for ourselves and our experiences, we are bound by existing forms of reality.

Notice also that this reality—that of being apart from the mainstream and searching for new stories—is shared among this group of friends. Through interaction, they come to realize and reaffirm the stories that they live. Eventually, these stories have a self-fulfilling tendency. By defining themselves as "outsiders" and subsequently removing themselves from many of the activities that constitute a mainstream life, Coupland's characters do in fact become marginal members of society. They no longer aspire to the goals held by members of the previous generation who have similar educational and economic backgrounds. It is important to note that, in eschewing one reality, the characters do not simply step into a void; rather, they often painstakingly create an alternative reality for themselves through a re-enactment of stories.

Stories are a useful epistemology through which to understand how collective life comes to have recognizable patterns. Realities, like stories, do not exist unless people tell them to themselves and to others. Some realities, like some stories, are more comprehensible to the group than are others. Certain stories, and ways of telling them, are considered more or less acceptable. As you ponder the material in this part of the book, ask yourself what storyline underlies each of the different realities described: What sort of meaning is attached to persons, situations, and events in each of these stories? Who has the power to write and rewrite stories? How conscious are you of the stories that constitute your realities? The concept of stories illustrates how realities continue and how they change.

## References

Berger, P., & Luckmann, T. (1966). *The social construction of reality*. Garden City, NY: Doubleday.

Coupland, D. (1991). *Generation X*. New York: St. Martin's Press.

Marx, K. (1963). *The 18th Brumaire of Louis Bonaparte*. New York: International Publishing Company.

Pollner, M., & Goode, D. (1990). Ethnomethodology and person-centering practices. *Person-Centered Review, 5*(2), 213–220.

Szasz, T. (1971). "The sane slave: An historical note on medical diagnosis as justificatory rhetoric." *American Journal of Psychotherapy, 25*, 228–239.

Thomas, W. I., & Thomas, D. (1928). *The child in America*. New York: Knopf.

Watzlawick, P. (Ed.). (1984). *The invented reality*. New York: Norton.

# Five Features of Reality

## Hugh Mehan and Houston Wood

### Reality as a Reflexive Activity

When the Azande of Africa are faced with important decisions, decisions about where to build their houses, or whom to marry, or whether the sick will live, for example, they consult an oracle. They prepare for these consultations by following a strictly prescribed ritual. First, a substance is gathered from the bark of a certain type of tree. Then this substance is prepared in a special way during a seancelike ceremony. The Azande then pose the question in a form that permits a simple yes or no answer, and feed the substance to a small chicken. The Azande decide beforehand whether the death of the chicken will signal an affirmative or negative response, and so they always receive an unequivocal answer to their questions.

For monumental decisions, the Azande add a second step. They feed the substance to a second chicken, asking the same question but reversing the import of the chicken's death. If in the first consultation sparing the chicken's life meant the oracle had said yes, in the second reading the oracle must now kill the chicken to once more reply in the affirmative and be consistent with its first response.

Our Western scientific knowledge tells us that the tree bark used by the Azande contains a poisonous substance that kills some chickens. The Azande have no knowledge of the tree's poisonous qualities. They do not believe the tree plays a part in the oracular ceremony. The ritual that comes between the gathering of the bark and the administration of the substance to a fowl transforms the tree into an oracle. The bark is but a vessel for the oracle to enter. As the ritual is completed the oracle takes possession of the substance. The fact that it was once a part of a tree is irrelevant. Chickens then live or die, not because of the properties of the tree, but because the oracle "hears like a person and settles cases like a king" (Evans-Pritchard, 1937, p. 321).

The Westerner sees insuperable difficulties in maintaining such beliefs when the oracle contradicts itself. Knowing the oracle's bark is "really" poison, we wonder what happens when, for example, the first and second administration of the oracle produces first a positive and then a negative answer. Or, suppose someone else consults the oracle about the same question, and contradictory answers occur? What if the oracle is contradicted by later events? The house site approved by the oracle, for example, may promptly be flooded; or the wife the oracle selected may die or be a shrew. How is it possible for the Azande to continue to believe in oracles in the face of so many evident contradictions to his faith?

What I have called contradictions are not contradictions for the Azande. They are only contradictions because these events are being viewed from the reality of Western science. Westerners look at oracular practices to determine if in fact there is an oracle. The Azande *know* that an oracle exists. That is their beginning premise. All that subsequently happens they experience from that beginning assumption.

The Azande belief in oracles is much like the mathematician's belief in certain axioms. Gasking (1955) has described such unquestioned and unquestionable axioms as *incorrigible propositions*:

An incorrigible proposition is one which you would never admit to be false whatever happens: it therefore does not tell you what happens. . . . The truth of an incorrigible proposition . . . is compatible with any and every conceivable state of affairs. (For example: whatever is your experience on counting, it is still true that 7 + 5 = 12.) (p. 432)

The incorrigible faith in the oracle is "compatible with any and every conceivable state of affairs." It is not so much a faith about a fact in the world as a faith in the facticity of the world itself. It is the same as the faith many of us have that 7 + 5 always equals 12. (cf. Polanyi, 1958, pp. 190–193, 257–261).

Just as Gasking suggests we explain away empirical experiences that deny this mathematical truth, the Azande too have available to them what Evans-Pritchard (1937) calls "secondary elaborations of belief" (p. 330). They explain the failure of the oracle by retaining the unquestioned absolute reality of oracles. When events occurred that revealed the inadequacy of the mystical faith in oracles, Evans-Pritchard tried to make the Azande understand these failures as he did. They only laughed, or met his arguments:

sometimes by point-blank assertions, sometimes by one of the evasive secondary elaborations of belief . . . sometimes by polite pity, but always by an entanglement of linguistic obstacles, for one

cannot well express in its language objections not formulated by a culture. (p. 319)

Evans-Pritchard goes on to write:

Let the reader consider any argument that would utterly demolish all Zande claims for the power of the oracle. If it were translated into Zande modes of thought it would serve to support their entire structure of belief. For their mystical notions are eminently coherent, being interrelated by a network of logical ties, and are so ordered that they never too crudely contradict sensory experience, but, instead, experience seems to justify them. *The Zande is immersed in a sea of mystical notions, and if he speaks about his poison oracle he must speak in a mystical idiom* [italics added]. (pp. 319–320)

Seeming contradictions are explained away by saying such things as a taboo must have been breached, or that sorcerers, witches, ghosts, or gods must have intervened. These "mystical" notions reaffirm the reality of a world in which oracles are a basic feature. Failures do not challenge the oracle. They are elaborated in such a way that they provide evidence for the constant success of oracles. Beginning with the incorrigible belief in oracles, all events *reflexively* become evidence for that belief.[1]

The mathematician, as Gasking suggests, uses a similar process:

But it does lay it down, so to speak, that if on counting 7 + 5 you do get 11, you are to describe what has happened in some such way as this: Either "I have made a mistake in my counting" or "Someone has played a practical joke and abstracted one of the objects when I was not looking" or "Two of the objects have coalesced" or "One of the objects has disappeared," etc. (Gasking, 1955; quoted in Pollner, 1973, pp. 15–16)

Consider the analogous case of a Western scientist using chloroform to asphyxiate butterflies. The incorrigible idiom called chemistry tells the scientist, among other things, that substances have certain constant properties. Chloroform of a certain volume and mix is capable of killing butterflies. One evening the scientist administers the chloroform as usual, and is dismayed to see the animal continue to flutter about.

Here is a contradiction of the scientist's reality, just as oracle use sometimes produces contradictions. Like the Azande, scientists have many secondary elaborations of belief they can bring to bear on such occurrences, short of rejecting the Western causal belief. Instead of rejecting chemistry they can explain the poison's failure by such things as "faulty manufacturing," "mislabeling," "sabotage," or "practical joke." Whatever the conclusion, it would continue to reaffirm the causal premise of science. This reaffirmation reflexively supports the reality that produced the poison's unexpected failure in the first place.

The use of contradictions to reaffirm incorrigible propositions can be observed in other branches of science. In the Ptolemaic system of astronomy, the sun was seen as a planet of the earth. When astronomers looked at the sun, they saw it as an orb circling the earth. When the Copernican system arose as an alternative to this view, it offered little new empirical data. Instead, it described the old "facts" in a different way. A shift of vision was required for people to see the sun as a star, not a planet of the earth.

Seeing the sun as a star and seeing it as a planet circling the earth are merely alternatives. There is no a priori warrant for believing that either empirical determination is necessarily superior to the other.

How is a choice between equally compelling empirical determinations made? The convert to the Copernican system could have said: "I used to see a planet, but now I see a star" (cf. Kuhn, 1970, p. 115). But to talk that way is to allow the belief that an object can be both a star and a planet at the same time. Such a belief is not allowed in Western science. So, instead, the Copernican concludes that the sun was a star all along. By so concluding, the astronomer exhibits an incorrigible proposition of Western thought, the *object constancy assumption*.[2] This is the belief that objects remain the same over time, across viewings from different positions and people. When presented with seemingly contradictory empirical determinations, the convert to Copernicanism does not consider that the sun changes through time. Instead he says: "I once took the sun to be a planet, but I was mistaken." The "discovery" of the sun as a star does not challenge the object constancy belief any more than an oracular "failure" challenges the ultimate reality of Azande belief.

The reaffirmation of incorrigible propositions is not limited to mystical and scientific ways of knowing. This reflexive work operates in commonsense reasoning as well. Each time you search for an object you knew was "right there" the same reflexive process is operating. Say, for example, you find a missing pen in a place you know you searched before. Although the evidence indicates that the pen was first absent and then present, that conclusion is not reached. To do so would challenge the incorrigibility of the object constancy belief. Instead, secondary elaborations—"I must have overlooked it," "I must not have looked there"—are invoked to retain the integrity of the object constancy proposition.

Without an object constancy assumption, there would be no problems about alternative determinations. But, with this assumption as an incorrigible proposition, the person faced with alternative seeings must choose one and only one as real. In choosing one, the other is automatically revealed as false. The falsehood of the rejected alternative may be explained in various ways. It may be due to a defective sensory apparatus, or a cognitive bias, or idiosyncratic psychological dynamics. We explain the inconstancy of the experienced object by saying that inconstancy is a product of the experiencing, not a feature of the object itself.[3]

Once an alternative seeing is explained away, the accepted explanation provides evidence for the object constancy assumption that made the explanation necessary in the first place. By demanding that we dismiss one of two equally valid empirical determinations, the object constancy assumption leads to a body of work that validates that assumption. The work then justifies itself afterward, in the world it has created. This self-preservative reflexive process is common to oracular, scientific, and common-sense reasoning.

So far I have approached the reflexive feature of realities as if it were a form of reasoning. But reflexivity is not only a facet of reasoning. It is a recurrent fact of everyday social life. For example, *talk itself is reflexive* (cf. Garfinkel, 1967; Cicourel, 1973). An utterance not only delivers some particular information, it also creates a world in which information itself can appear.

Zimmerman (1973, p. 25) provides a means for understanding the reflexivity of talk at the level of a single word. He presents three identical shapes:

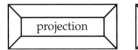 

The first and third differ from the second: They each contain single words. These words interact with the box in which they appear so as to change the nature of that box. In so doing, they reflexively illumine themselves. For example, the word "projection," appearing in some other setting, would not mean what it does here. For me it means that I am to see the back panel and the word "projection" as illustrative of a projection. The word "projection" does not merely appear in the scene reporting on that scene. It creates the scene in which it appears as a reasonable object.

Similarly, the word "indentation" not only takes its meaning from the context in which it appears, it reflexively creates that very context. It creates a reality in which it may stand as a part of that reality.

These examples only hint at the reflexivity of talk. . . . Actual conversations are more complex than single words. The social context in which talk occurs, while analogous to one of these static boxes, is enormously ambiguous and potentially infinitely referential. Nonetheless, conversation operates like the printed "projection" and "indentation." An analysis of greetings can be used to show how talk partially constitutes the context and then comes to be seen as independent of it.[4]

To say "hello" both creates and sustains a world in which persons acknowledge . . . (1) [that] they sometimes can see one another; [and] (2) a world in which it is possible for persons to signal to each other, and (3) expect to be signaled back to, by (4) some others but not all of them. This is a partial and only illustrative list of some of the things a greeting accomplishes. Without the superstitious use of greetings, no world in which greetings are possible "objects" would arise. A greeting creates "room" for itself. But once such verbal behaviors are regularly done, a world is built up that can take their use for granted (cf. Sacks, Schegloff, & Jefferson, 1974).

When we say "hello" and the other replies with the expected counter greeting, the reflexive work of our initial utterance is masked. If the other scowls and walks on, then we are reminded that we were attempting to create a scene of greetings and that we failed. Rather than treat this as evidence that greetings are not "real," however, the rejected greeter ordinarily turns it into an occasion for affirming the reality of greetings. He formulates "secondary elaborations" of belief about greetings. He says, "He didn't hear me," "She is not feeling well," "It doesn't matter anyway."

Reflexivity provides grounds for absolute faith in the validity of knowledge. The Azande takes the truth of the oracle for granted, the scientist assumes the facticity of science, the layman accepts the tenets of common sense. The incorrigible propositions of a reality serve as criteria to judge other ways of knowing. Using his absolute faith in the oracle, the Azande dismisses Evans-Pritchard's Western science contradictions. Evans-Pritchard, steeped in the efficacy of science, dismissed the oracle as superstitious. An absolute faith in the incorrigibility of one's own knowledge enables believers to repel contrary evidence. This suggests that all people are equally superstitious.

## Reality as a Coherent Body of Knowledge

The phenomenon of reflexivity is a feature of every reality. It interacts with the coherence, interactional, fragility, and permeability features I describe in the rest of this chapter. These five features are incorrigible propositions of the reality of ethnomethodology. They appear as facts of the external world due to the ethnomethodologist's unquestioned assumption that they constitute the world. In other words, these features themselves exhibit reflexivity.

This reflexive loop constitutes the interior structure of ethnomethodology. This will become clearer as I describe the second feature of realities, their exhibition of a coherent body of knowledge. To illustrate this feature I will extrapolate from the work of Zimmerman and Wieder (n.d.), who investigated the life of a number of self-named "freaks," frequent drug users within America's counterculture. Both freaks and their academic ethnographers (e.g., Reich, 1970; Roszack, 1969) describe freaks as radical opponents of the straight culture from which they sprang. As Zimmerman and Wieder (n.d.) write:

From the standpoint of the "straight" members of society, freaks are deliberately irrational. . . .They disavow an interest in efficiency, making long-range plans, and concerns about costs of property (etc.) which are valued by the straight members of American society and are understood by them as indicators of rationality. (p. 103)

On first appearance, here is a reality that seems anarchical. Nonetheless, Zimmerman and Wieder found that:

when it comes to those activities most highly valued by freaks, such as taking drugs, making love, and other "cheap thrills," there is an elaborately developed body of lore. Freaks and others use that knowledge of taking drugs, making love, etc., reasonably, deliberately, planfully, projecting various consequences, predicting outcomes, conceiving of the possibilities of action in more or less clear and distinct ways, and choosing between two or more means of reaching the same end. (pp. 102–103)

The most vivid illustration that freaks use a coherent body of knowledge comes from Zimmerman's and Wieder's discoveries about the place of drugs in the everyday freak life. At first glance such drug use appears irrational. Yet, among freaks, taking drugs "is something as ordinary and unremarkable as their parents regard taking or offering a cup of coffee" (p. 57). Freak behavior is not a function of the freaks' ignorance of chemical and medical "facts" about drugs. The freaks studied knew chemical and medical facts well. They organized these facts into a different, yet coherent corpus of knowledge.

One of the team's research assistants, Peter Suczek, was able to systematize the freaks' knowledge of drugs into a taxonomic schemata (see Table 1).

What the freak calls "dope," the chemist calls "psychotropic drugs." Within the family of dope, freaks distinguish "mind-expanding" and "body" dope. Freaks further subdivide each of these species. In addition, freaks share a common body of knowledge informing them of the practicalities surrounding the use of each type of dope. All knowledge of dope use is grounded in the incorrigible proposition that dope is to be used. One must, of course, know how to use it.

Zimmerman and Wieder (n.d.) found the following knowledge about "psychedelic mind-expanding dope" to be common among freaks:

The folk pharmacology of psychedelic drugs may be characterized as a method whereby drug users

**Table 1**

The Folk Pharmacology for Dope

| Types of Dope | Subcategories |
| --- | --- |
| Mind-expanding dope | (Untitled) |
| | "grass" (marijuana) |
| | "hash" (hashish) |
| | "LSD" or "acid" |
| | (lysergic acid) |
| | Psychedelics |
| | mescaline |
| | synthetic |
| | organic |
| | natural, peyote |
| | psilocybin |
| | synthetic |
| | organic |
| | natural, mushrooms |
| | "DMT" |
| | miscellaneous |
| | (e.g., Angel's Dust) |
| Body dope | "speed" (amphetamines) |
| | "downers" (barbiturates) |
| | "tranks" (tranquilizers) |
| | "coke" (cocaine) |
| | "shit" (heroin) |

Zimmerman and Wieder (n.d.), p. 107.

rationally assess choices among kinds of drugs, choices among instances of the same kind of drug, the choice to ingest or not, the time of the act of ingestion relative to the state of one's physiology and relative to the state of one's psyche, the timing relative to social and practical demands, the appropriateness of the setting for having a psychedelic experience, the size of the dose, and the effectiveness and risk of mixing drugs. (p. 118)

Freaks share similar knowledge for the rest of the taxonomy. Being a freak means living within the auspices of such knowledge and using it according to a plan, as the chemist uses his. Both the freaks' and the scientists' realities are concerned with "the facts." Though the facts differ, each reality reflexively proves its facts as absolute.

Consider how the freak assembles the knowledge he uses. He is not loath to borrow from the discoveries of science. But before accepting what the scientist says, he first tests scientific "facts" against the auspices of his own incorrigible propositions. He does not use the scientists' findings to determine the danger of the drug, but rather to indicate the particular dosage, setting, etc., under which a drug is to be taken.

Scientific drug researchers frequently attend to the experiences of freaks in a comparable way. They incorporate the facts that freaks report about dope into their coherent idiom. The two then are like independent teams of investigators working on the same phenomenon with different purposes. They are like artists and botanists who share a common interest in the vegetable kingdom, but who employ different incorrigibles.

The freak's knowledge, like all knowledge, is sustained through reflexive interactional work. For example, the knowledge contained in the drug taxonomy (Table 1) sometimes "fails," that is, it produces not a "high" but a "bummer." The incorrigible propositions of freak pharmacology are not then questioned. Instead, these propositions are invoked to explain the bummer's occurrence. "For example," Zimmerman and Wieder (n.d.) write:

A "bad trip" may be explained in such terms as the following: it was a bad time and place to drop; my head wasn't ready for it; or it was bad acid or mescaline, meaning that it was cut with something impure or that it was some other drug altogether. (p. 118)

The reflexive use of the freak taxonomy recalls my previous discussion of the Azande. When the oracle seemed to contradict itself, the contradiction became but one more occasion for proving the oracular way of knowing. The reality of oracles is appealed to in explaining the failure of the oracle, just as the reality of freak pharmacology is used to explain a bad trip. It would be as futile for a chemist to explain the bad trip scientifically to a freak as it was for Evans-Pritchard to try to convince the Azande that failures of the oracle demonstrated their unreality.

The coherence of knowledge is a reflexive consequence of the researcher's attention. Zimmerman and Wieder, in the best social science tradition, employed many methods to construct the freak's taxonomy. Freaks were interviewed by sociology graduate students and by their peers. These interviewers provided accounts of their own drug experiences as well. Additional freaks not acquainted with the purposes of the research were paid to keep personal diaries of their day-to-day experiences. Zimmerman and Wieder used a portion of this massive data to construct the freak taxonomy, then tested its validity against further portions of the data.

Such systematizations are always the researcher's construction (Wallace, 1972). To claim that any reality, including the researcher's own, exhibits a coherent body of knowledge is but to claim that coherence can be found *upon analysis*. The coherence located in a reality is found there by the ethnomethodologist's interactional work. The coherence feature, like all features of realities, operates as an incorrigible proposition, reflexively sustained.

Consider the analogous work of linguists (e.g., Chomsky, 1965). Within language-using communities, linguists discover the "rules of grammar." Although the linguist empirically establishes these grammatical rules, speaker-hearers of that language cannot list them. Rules can be located in their talk, upon analysis, but language users cannot describe them.

Similarly, freaks could not supply the taxonomy Zimmerman and Wieder claim they "really" know. It was found upon analysis. It is an imposition of the researcher's logic upon the freak's logic.

Castañeda's (1968, 1971) attempts to explain the reality of Yaqui sorcery further illustrates the reflexity of analysis. In his initial report, *The Teachings of Don Juan*, Castañeda (1968) begins with a detailed ethnography of his experiences of his encounter with a Yaqui sorcerer, Don Juan. In this reality it is common for time to stop, for men to turn into animals and animals into men, for animals and men to converse with one another, and for great distances to be covered while the body remains still.

In the final section of his report, Castañeda systematizes his experiences with the sorcerer. He presents a coherent body of knowledge undergirding Don Juan's teachings. Thus Castañeda, like Zimmerman and Wieder, organizes a "nonordinary" reality into a coherent system of knowledge.

In a second book Castañeda (1971) describes Don Juan's reaction to his systematization of a peyote session, a "mitote." Castañeda told Don Juan he had discovered that mitotes are a "result of a subtle and complex system of cueing." He writes:

It took me close to two hours to read and explain to Don Juan the scheme I had constructed. I ended by begging him to tell me in his own words what were the exact procedures for reaching agreement.

When I had finished he frowned. I thought he must have found my explanation challenging; he appeared to be involved in deep deliberation. After a reasonable silence I asked him what he thought about my idea.

My question made him suddenly turn his frown into a smile and then into roaring laughter. I tried to laugh too and asked nervously what was so funny.

"You're deranged!" he exclaimed. "Why should anyone be bothered with cueing at such an important time as a mitote? Do you think one ever fools around with Mescalito?"

I thought for a moment that he was being evasive; he was not really answering my question.

"Why should anyone cue?" Don Juan asked stubbornly. "You have been in mitotes. You should know that no one told you how to feel, or what to do; no one except Mescalito himself."

I insisted that such an explanation was not possible and begged him again to tell me how the agreement was reached.

"I know why you have come," Don Juan said in a mysterious tone. "I can't help you in your endeavor because there is no system of cueing."

"But how can all those persons agree about Mescalito's presence?"

"They agree because they *see*," Don Juan said dramatically, and then added casually, "Why don't you attend another mitote and see for yourself?" (pp. 37–38)

Don Juan finds Castañeda's account ridiculous. This rejection is not evidence that Castañeda's attempt at systematization is incorrect. It indicates that the investigator reflexively organizes the realities he investigates. All realities may *upon analysis* exhibit a coherent system of knowledge, but knowledge of this coherence is not necessarily part of the awareness of its members.

Features emerging "upon analysis" is a particular instance of reflexivity. These features exist only within the reflexive work of those researchers who make them exist. This does not deny their reality. There is no need to pursue the chimera of a presuppositionless inquiry. Because all realities are ultimately superstitious the reflexive location of reflexivity is not a problem within ethnomethodological studies. Rather, it provides them with their most intriguing phenomenon.

My discussion of these first two features of realities also shows that any one feature is separate from the other only upon analysis. In my description of reflexivity, I was forced to assume the existence of a coherent body of knowledge. Similarly, in the present discussion I could not speak about the existence of coherent systems of knowledge without introducing the caveat of "upon analysis," an implicit reference to reflexivity. This situation will continue as I discuss the remaining three features. Though I attempt to keep them separate from one another, I will only be partially successful, since the five are inextricably intertwined. Nevertheless, I will continue to talk of them as five separate features, not as one. I acknowledge that this talk is more heuristic than literal—it provides a ladder with five steps that may be climbed and then thrown away (cf. Wittgenstein, 1921/1961).

## Reality as Interactional Activity

Realities are also dependent upon ceaseless social interactional work. Wood's study of a mental hospital illustrates the reality of this reality work. He discovered that psychiatric attendants shared a body of knowledge. Wood's (1968) analysis of the attendants' interaction with the patients uncovered labels like: "baby," "child," "epileptic," "mean old man," "alcoholic," "lost soul," "good patient," "depressive," "sociopath," and "nigger" (p. 36). Though borrowed from psychiatry, these terms constitute a corpus of knowledge which reflects the attendants' own practical nursing concerns. These terms can be arranged in a systematic taxonomy (see Table 2). Each is shown to differ from the others according to four parameters of nursing problems.

Wood's study explored how the attendants used this taxonomy to construct meanings for the mental patients' behavior. One explanation of label use is called a "matching procedure." The matching model of labeling patient behavior is essentially a psychological theory. It treats behavior as a private, internal state, not influenced by social dimensions. The matching model assumes the patients' behavior has obvious features. Trained personnel monitor and automatically apply the appropriate label to patients' behavior.

Wood presents five case histories that show that labels are not applied by a simple matching process. They are molded in the day-to-day interaction of the attendants with one another and with the patients. The labeling of patients is a social activity, not a psychological one.

Wood (1968, pp. 51–91) describes the labeling history of patient Jimmy Lee Jackson. Over the course of his three-month hospitalization, Jackson held the same official psychiatric label, that of "psychoneurotic reaction, depressive type." However, the ward attendants saw Jackson within the web of their own practical circumstances. For them, at

**Table 2**

The Meaning of the Labels

| Psychiatric Attendant Label | *Nursing Trouble* | | | | |
| --- | --- | --- | --- | --- | --- |
| | *Work* | *Cleanliness* | *Supervisory* | *Miscellaneous* | *Frequency × 60* |
| Mean old man | yes | yes | yes | yes | 2 |
| Baby | yes | yes | yes | — | 20 |
| Child | yes | yes | — | yes | 4 |
| Nigger | yes | — | yes | yes | 1 |
| Epileptic | — | yes | — | yes | 4 |
| Sociopath | yes | — | — | yes | 3 |
| Depressive | — | — | — | yes | 2 |
| Alcoholic | — | — | yes | — | 8 |
| Lost soul | yes | — | — | — | 12 |
| Good patient | — | — | — | — | 6 |

Wood (1968), p. 45.

one time he was a "nigger," at another a "depressive," and at yet another a "sociopath." These seeings reflected a deep change in the meaning Jackson had for the attendants. When he was seen as a "nigger," for example, it meant that the attendants considered he was "lazy, and . . . without morals or scruples and . . . that the patient is cunning and will attempt to ingratiate himself with the attendants in order to get attention and 'use' them for his own ends" (p. 52). When Jackson became a depressive type, all these negative attributes were withdrawn. The change in attribution, Wood shows, cannot be explained by a matching procedure. The attendants' social interactional work produced the change, independent of Jackson's behavior. This suggests that realities are fundamentally interactional activities.

One evening Jackson was suffering from a toothache. Unable to secure medical attention, he ran his arm through a window pane in one of the ward's locked doors. He suffered a severe laceration of his forearm which required stitches. When the attendants who were on duty during this episode returned to work the following afternoon, they discovered that the preceding morning shift had decided that Jackson had attempted suicide. Jackson was no longer presented to them as a nigger. The morning shift found that persons who had not even witnessed the event had given it a meaning they themselves had never considered. Nevertheless, the evening shift accepted the validity of this label change.

The label change indexed a far larger change. Jackson's past history on the ward was reinterpreted. He now was accorded different treatment by attendants on all shifts. He was listened to sympathetically, given whatever he requested, and no longer exhorted to do more ward work. All the attendants came to believe that he had always been a depressive and that they had always seen him as such.

A few weeks later Jackson became yet another person, a "sociopath." The attendants no longer accepted that he was capable of a suicide attempt. The new label was once again applied retrospectively. Not only was Jackson believed to be incapable of committing suicide now, he was thought to have always been incapable of it. The attendants agreed that the window-breaking incident had been a "fake" or "con,"—just the sort of thing a sociopath would do. Attendants who had praised Jackson as a hard worker when he was labeled a depressive now pointed to this same work as proof he was a "conniver." Requests for attention and medicine that had been promptly fulfilled for the depressive Jackson were now ignored for the sociopath Jackson, or used as occasions to attack him verbally.

Yet, as Wood describes Jackson, he remained constant despite these changes in attendant behavior. He did the same amount of work and sought the same amount of attention and medicine whether he was labeled a nigger or a depressive or a sociopath. What Jackson was at any time was determined by the reality work of the attendants.

In the final pages of his study, Wood (1968) further illustrates the power of interactional work to create an external world:

The evening that he [Jackson] cut his arm, I, like the PAs [psychiatric attendants], was overcome by the blood and did not reflect on its "larger" meaning concerning his proper label. The next day, when I heard all of the morning shift PAs refer to his action as a suicide attempt, I too labeled Jackson a "depressive" and the cut arm as a suicide attempt. When the label changed in future weeks I was working as a PA on the ward up to 12 hours a day. It was only two months later when I had left the ward, as I reviewed my notes and my memory, that I recognized the "peculiar" label changes that had occurred. While I was on the ward, it had not seemed strange to think that cutting an arm in a window was a serious attempt to kill oneself. Only as an "outsider" did I come to think that Jackson had "really" stayed the same through his three label changes. (pp. 137–138)

As Wood says, Jackson could never have a meaning apart from *some* social context. Meanings unfold only within an unending sequence of practical actions.[5]

The *matching* theory of label use assumes a correspondence theory of signs (cf. Garfinkel, 1952, pp. 91ff.; Wieder, 1970). This theory of signs has three analytically sepa-

rate elements: ideas that exist in the head, signs that appear in symbolic representations, and objects and events that appear in the world. Meaning is the relation among these elements. Signs can stand on behalf of the ideas in the head or refer to objects in the world. This theory of signs implies that signs stand in a point-by-point relation to thoughts in one's mind or objects in the world. Meanings are stable across time and space. They are not dependent upon the concrete participants or upon the specific scenes in which they appear.

Wood's study indicates that labels are not applied in accordance with correspondence principles. Instead, labels are *indexical expressions*. Meanings are situationally determined. They are dependent upon the concrete context in which they appear. The participants' interactional activity structured the indexical meaning of the labels used on the ward. The relationship of the participants to the object, the setting in which events occur, and the circumstances surrounding a definition determine the meaning of labels and of objects.

The interactional feature indicates that realities do not possess symbols, like so many tools in a box. A reality and its signs are "mutually determinative" (Wieder, 1973, p. 216). Alone, neither expresses sense. Intertwining through the course of indexical interaction, they form a life.

## The Fragility of Realities

Every reality depends upon (1) ceaseless reflexive use of (2) a body of knowledge in (3) interaction. Every reality is also fragile. Suppression of the activities that the first three features describe disrupts the reality. Every reality is equally capable of dissolution. The presence of this fragility feature of realities has been demonstrated by studies called "incongruity procedures" or "breaching experiments."

In one of the simplest of these, Garfinkel used 67 students as "experimenters." These students engaged a total of 253 "subjects" in a game of tick-tack-toe. When the figure necessary for the game was drawn, the experimenters requested the subject to make the first move. After the subject made his mark, the experimenter took his turn. Rather than simply marking another cell, the experimenter erased the subject's mark and moved it to another cell. Continuing as if this were expected behavior, the experimenter then placed his own mark in one of the now empty cells. The experimenters reported that their action produced extreme bewilderment and confusion in the subjects. The reality of the game, which before the experimenter's move seemed stable and external, suddenly fell apart. For a moment the subjects exhibited an "amnesia for social structure" (Garfinkel, 1963, p. 189).

This fragility feature is even more evident in everyday life, where the rules are not explicit. People interact without listing the rules of conduct. Continued reference is made to this knowledge nonetheless. This referencing is not ordinarily available as long as the reality work continues normally. When the reality is disrupted, the interactional activity structuring the reality becomes visible. This is what occurred in the tick-tack-toe game. A usually unnoticed feature of the game is a "rule" prohibiting erasing an opponent's mark. When this unspoken "rule" is broken, it makes its first public appearance. If we were aware of the fragility of our realities, they would not seem real.

Thus Garfinkel (1963) found that when the "incongruity-inducing procedures" developed in games

were applied in "real life" situations, it was unnerving to find the seemingly endless variety of events that lent themselves to the production of really nasty surprises. These events ranged from . . . standing very, very close to a person while otherwise maintaining an innocuous conversation, to others . . . like saying "hello" at the termination of a conversation. . . . Both procedures elicited anxiety, indignation, strong feelings on the part of the experimenter and subject alike of hu-miliation and regret, demands by the subjects for explanations, and so on. (p. 198)

Another of the procedures Garfinkel developed was to send student experimenters into stores and restaurants where they were told to "mistake" customers for salespersons and waiters. . . . [See pp. 384–385, Case 4, for details of one such experiment.]

The breaching experiments were subsequently refined, such that:

The person [subject] could not turn the situation into a play, a joke, an experiment, a deception, and the like . . . ; that he have insufficient time to work through a redefinition of his real circumstances; and that he be deprived of consensual support for an alternative definition of social reality. (Garfinkel, 1964; in 1967, p. 58)

This meant that subjects were not allowed to reflexively turn the disruption into a revalidation of their realities. The incorrigible propositions of their social knowledge were not adequate for the present circumstances. They were removed from the supporting interactional activity that they possessed before the breach occurred.

These refinements had the positive consequence of increasing the bewilderment of the subjects, who became more and more like desocialized schizophrenics, persons completely devoid of any social reality. These refinements produced a negative consequence. They were immoral. Once subjects had experienced the fragility, they could not continue taking the stability of realities for granted. No amount of "cooling out" could restore the subject's faith.

But what is too cruel to impose on others can be tried upon oneself. . . .

## The Permeability of Realities

Because the reflexive use of social knowledge is fragile and interaction dependent, one reality may be altered, and another may be assumed. Cases where a person passes from one reality to another, dramatically different, reality vividly display this permeability feature.

Tobias Schneebaum, a painter who lives periodically in New York, provides an example of a radical shift in realities in his book, *Keep the River on Your Right* (1969). Schneebaum entered the jungles of Peru in 1955 in pursuit of his art. During the trip the book describes, he gradually lost interest in painterly studies. He found himself drawn deeper and deeper into the jungle. Unlike a professional anthropologist, he carried no plans to write about his travels. In fact, the slim volume from which I draw the following discussion was not written until 13 years after his return.

He happened upon the Akaramas, a stone age tribe that had never seen a white man. They accepted him quickly, gave him a new name, "Habe," meaning "ignorant one," and began teaching him to be as they were.

Schneebaum learned to sleep in "bundles" with the other men, piled on top of one another for warmth and comfort. He learned to hunt and fish with stone age tools. He learned the Akaramas' language and their ritual of telling stories of their hunts and hikes, the telling taking longer than the doing. He learned to go without clothing, and to touch casually the genitals of his companions in play.

When one of the men in Schneebaum's compartment is dying of dysentery, crying out at his excretions of blood and pain, the "others laugh and he laughs too" (p. 109). As this man lies among them whimpering and crying in their sleeping pile at night, Schneebaum writes: "Not Michii or Baaldore or Ihuene or Reindude seemed to have him on their minds. It was as if he were not there among us or as if he had already gone to some other forest" (p. 129). When he dies, he is immediately forgotten. Such is the normal perception of death within the Akarama reality. As Schneebaum describes another incident: "There were two pregnant women whom I noticed one day with flatter bellies

and no babies on their backs, but there was no sign of grief, no service . . ." (p. 109).

Gradually, Schneebaum absorbed even these ways and a new sense of time. At one point he left the Akaramas to visit the mission from which he had embarked. He was startled to find that seven months had passed, not the three or four he had supposed. As he was more and more permeated by the stone age reality, he began to feel that his "own world, whatever, wherever it was, no longer was anywhere in existence" (p. 69). As the sense of his old reality disappears, he says, "My fears were not so much for the future . . . but for my knowledge. I was removing my own reflection" (pp. 64–65).

One day, a day like many others, he rises to begin a hunting expedition with his sleeping companions. This day, however, they go much farther than ever before. They paint themselves in a new way and repeat new chants. Finally they reach a strange village. In they swoop, Schneebaum too, shouting their sacred words and killing all the men they can catch, disemboweling and beheading them on the spot. They burn all the huts, kidnap the women and children. They then hike to their own village, without pause, through an entire night. At home, a new dance is begun. The meat of the men they have murdered and brought back with them is cooked. As a new movement of the dance begins, this meat is gleefully eaten. Exhausted at last, they stumble together on the ground. Then the last of the meat is put to ceremonious use:

We sat or lay around the fires, eating, moaning the tones of the chant, swaying forward and back, moving from the hip, forward and back. Calm and silence settled over us, all men. Four got up, one picked a heart from the embers, and they walked into the forest. Small groups of others arose, selected a piece of meat, and disappeared in other directions. We three were alone until Ihuene, Baaldore, and Reindude were in front of us, Reindude cupping in his hand the heart from the being we had carried from so far away, the heart of he who had lived in the hut we had entered to kill. We stretched out flat upon the ground, lined up, our shoulders touching. Michii looked up at the moon and showed it to the heart. He bit into it as if it were an apple, taking a large bite, almost half the heart, and chewed down several times, spit into a hand, separated the meat into six sections and placed some into the mouths of each of us. We chewed and swallowed. He did the same with the other half of the heart. He turned Darinimbiak onto his stomach, lifted his hips so that he crouched on all fours. Darinimbiak growled, Mayaarii-ha! Michii growled, Mayaari-ha!, bent down to lay himself upon Darinimbiak's back and entered him. (pp. 106–107)

Mass murder, destruction of an entire village, theft of all valuable goods, cannibalism, the ritual eating of the heart before publicly displayed homosexual acts—these are some of the acts Schneebaum participated in. He could not have done them his first day in the jungle. But after his gradual adoption of the Akarama reality, they had become natural. It would have been as immoral for him to refuse to join his brothers in the raid and its victory celebration as it would be immoral for him to commit these same acts within a Western community. His reality had changed. The moral facts were different.

Schneebaum's experience suggests that even radically different realities can be penetrated.[6] We would not have this account, however, if the stone age reality had completely obliterated Schneebaum's Western reality. He would still be with the tribe. The more he permeated the Akaramas' reality, the more suspect his old reality became. The more he fell under the spell of the absolutism of his new reality, the more fragile his old reality became. Like the cannibals, Schneebaum says: "My days are days no longer. Time had no thoughts to trouble me, and everything is like nothing and nothing is like everything. For if a day passes, it registers nowhere, and it might be a week, it might be a month. There is no difference" (p. 174).

As the vision of his old reality receded, Schneebaum experienced its fragility. He knew he must leave soon, or there would be no reality to return to. He describes his departure:

A time alone, only a few weeks ago, with the jungle alive and vibrant around me, and Michii and Baaldore gone with all the other men to hunt, I saw within myself too many seeds that would grow a fungus around my brain, encasing it with mold that could penetrate and smooth the convolutions and there I would remain, not he who had travelled and arrived, not the me who had crossed the mountains in a search, but another me living only in ease and pleasure, no longer able to scrawl out words on paper or think beyond a moment. And days later, I took myself up from our hut, and I walked on again alone without a word to any of my friends and family, but left when all again were gone and I walked through my jungle. . . . (p. 182)

The Akaramas would not miss him. They would not even notice his absence. For them, there were no separate beings. Schneebaum felt their reality obliterating "the me who had crossed the mountains in a search." Schneebaum was attached to this "me," and so he left.

In the previous section, I listed three conditions necessary for successful breaches: There can be no place to escape. There can be no time to escape. There can be no one to provide counter evidence. The same conditions are required to move between realities. That is, as Castañeda's (1968, 1971, 1972) work suggests, in order to permeate realities, one must first have the old reality breached. Castañeda has named this necessity the establishment "of a certainty of a minimal possibility," that another reality actually exists (personal communication). Successful breaches must establish that another reality is available for entry. Thus, as Don Juan attempted to make Castañeda a man of knowledge, he first spent years trying to crack Castañeda's absolute faith in the reality of Western rationalism.

Castañeda's work suggests many relations between the fragility and permeability features. It is not my purpose to explore the relations of the five features in this book. But I want to emphasize that such relations can be supposed to exist.

I relied on the "exotic" case of a person passing from a Western to a stone age reality to display the permeability feature of realities. However, any two subsequent interactional encounters could have been used for this purpose. All such passages are of equal theoretic import. Passages between a movie and freeway driving, between a person's reality before and after psychotherapy, between a "straight" acquiring membership in the reality of drug freaks, or before and after becoming a competent religious healer, are all the same. The differences are "merely" methodological, not theoretical. Studying each passage, I would concentrate on how the reflexive, knowledge, interactional, and fragility features affect the shift.

All realities are permeable. Ethnomethodology is a reality. This book is an attempt to breach the reader's present reality by introducing him to the "certainty of a minimal possibility" that another reality exists.

## On the Concept of Reality

Many ethnomethodologists rely on Schutz's concept of reality (e.g., 1962, 1964, 1966). . . . My use of "reality" contrasts with Schutz's view. For Schutz (e.g., 1962, pp. 208ff.), the reality of everyday life is the *one* paramount reality. Schutz says that this paramount reality consists of a number of presuppositions or assumptions, which include the assumption of a tacit, taken for granted world; an assumed practical interest in that world; and an assumption that the world is intersubjective (e.g., 1962, p. 23). Schutz argues that other realities exist, but that they derive from the paramount reality. For example, he discusses the realities of "scientific theorizing" and of "fantasy." These realities appear when some of the basic assumptions of the paramount reality are temporarily suspended. The para-

mount reality of everyday life has an elastic quality for Schutz. After excursions into other realities, we snap back into the everyday.

My view of realities is different. I do not wish to call one or another reality paramount. It is my contention that every reality is equally real. No single reality contains more of the truth than any other. From the perspective of Western everyday life, Western everyday life will appear paramount, just as Schutz maintains. But from the perspective of scientific theorizing or dreaming, or meditating, each of these realities will appear just as paramount. Because every reality exhibits the absolutist tendency I mentioned earlier, there is no way to look from the window of one reality at others without seeing yourself. Schutz seems to be a victim of this absolutist prejudice. As a Western man living his life in the Western daily experience, he assumed that this life was the touchstone of all realities.

My concept of reality, then, has more in common with Wittgenstein (1953) than with Schutz. Wittgenstein (e.g., 1953, pp. 61, 179) recognizes that human life exhibits an empirical multitude of activities. He calls these activities language games. Language games are forever being invented and modified and discarded. The fluidity of language activities do not permit rigorous description. Analysts can discover that at any time a number of language games are associated with one another. This association, too, is not amenable to rigorous description. Instead, language games exhibit "family resemblances." One can recognize certain games going together. But one could no more articulate *the* criteria for this resemblance than one could predict the physical characteristics of some unseen member of a familiar extended family. Wittgenstein (1953, pp. 119, 123) calls a collection of language games bound together by a family resemblance, a *form of life*.[7] Forms of life resemble what I call "realities." Realities are far more aswarm than Schutz's terms "finite" and "province" suggest. Forms of life are always forms of life forming.[8] Realities are always realities becoming.

---

## Notes

1. See Pollner's (1970, 1973) discussions of the reflexive reasoning of the Azande and Polanyi's (1958, pp. 287–294) examination of the same materials. In the Apostolic Church of John Marangue, illness is not bodily malfunction, it is sin. Sin is curable not by medicine, but by confessional healing. When evangelists' attempts to heal church members were not accompanied by recovery, Jules-Rosette (1973, p. 167) reports that church members did not lose their faith in the confessional process. They looked to other "causes" of the "failure." They said things like: Other persons must have been implicated in the sin, and untrue confession must have been given. Once again, contradictions that could potentially challenge a basic faith do not, as the basic faith itself is not questioned.

2. See Gurwitsch (1966) for a more technical discussion of the object constancy assumption. . . .

3. The . . . planet-star example [is] adapted from Pollner (1973). Much of this discussion of reflexivity derives from Pollner's thinking on these matters.

4. Riel (1972) illustrates how talk reflexively constitutes the context it then seems to independently reference. Trying to make a certain point, she reports turning away from an inadequate sentence she had written to explore notes and texts again. Forty-five minutes later she wrote the now-perfect sentence, only to discover it was exactly the same sentence she had rejected before.

5. Cicourel (1968) examines the interactional work that accomplishes external objects in greater detail. He shows that juvenile delinquents and crime rates are constituted by the social activities of law enforcement personnel.

6. For an account of a reality shift in the other direction, from the stone age to industrial Western society, see Kroeber's *Ishi in Two Worlds* (1961). Again the transition was never total, but this was a result of a political decision on the part of the author's husband. As Ishi's official keeper, he wished to keep him primitive for his own and anthropology's benefit.

7. Blum (1970) has previously explored the importance of Wittgenstein's notion of "form of life" for social science.

8. This phrase, like much of this chapter, has been adapted from the unpublished lectures of Pollner. For Pollner's published writings see Zimmerman and Pollner, 1970; and Pollner, 1970, 1973, 1974.

## References

Blum, A. (1970). Theorizing. In J. D. Douglas (Ed.), *Understanding everyday life*. Chicago: Aldine.

Castañeda, C. (1968). *The teachings of Don Juan*. Berkeley: University of California Press.

Castañeda, C. (1971). *A separate reality*. New York: Simon & Schuster.

Castañeda, C. (1972). *A journey to Iztlan*. New York: Simon & Schuster.

Chomsky, N. (1965). *Aspects of the theory of syntax*. Cambridge, MA: MIT Press.

Cicourel, A. V. (1968). *The social organization of juvenile justice*. New York: John Wiley.

Cicourel, A. V. (1973). *Cognitive sociology*. London: Macmillan.

Evans-Pritchard, E. E. (1937). *Witchcraft, oracles and magic among the Azande*. London: Oxford University Press.

Garfinkel, H. (1952). *Perception of the other*. Unpublished Ph.D. dissertation, Harvard University.

Garfinkel, H. (1963). A conception of and experiments with "trust" as a condition of concerted stable actions. In O. J. Harvey (Ed.), *Motivation and social interaction*. New York: Ronald.

Garfinkel, H. (1964). Studies of the routine grounds of everyday activities. *Social Problems, 11*, 225–250 (Chapter 2 in Garfinkel, 1967).

Garfinkel, H. (1967). *Studies in ethnomethodology*. Englewood Cliffs, NJ: Prentice-Hall.

Gasking, D. (1955). Mathematics and the world. In A. Flew (Ed.), *Logic and language*. Garden City, NY: Doubleday.

Gurwitsch, A. (1966). *Studies in phenomenology and psychology*. Evanston, IL: Northwestern University Press.

Jules-Rosette, B. (1973). *Ritual context and social action*. Unpublished Ph.D. dissertation. Harvard University.

Kroeber, T. (1961). *Ishi in two worlds*. Berkeley: University of California Press.

Kuhn, T. S. (1970). *The structure of scientific revolutions*. Chicago: University of Chicago Press.

Polanyi, M. (1958). *Personal knowledge*. Chicago: University of Chicago Press.

Pollner, M. (1970). *On the foundations of mundane reason*. Unpublished Ph.D. dissertation. University of California, Santa Barbara.

Pollner, M. (1973). *The very coinage of your brain: The resolution of reality disjunctures*. Unpublished manuscript.

Pollner, M. (1974). Mundane reasoning. *Philosophy of social sciences, 4*(1), 35–54.

Reich, C. A. (1970). *The greening of America*. New York: Random House.

Riel, M. M. (1972). *The interpretive process*. Paper presented to a seminar led by Paul Filmer, University of California, San Diego.

Roszak, T. (1969). *The making of a counter culture*. Garden City, NY: Doubleday.

Sacks, H., Schegloff, E., & Jefferson, G. (1974). A simplest systematics for the analysis of turn taking in conversation. *Language, 50,* 696–735.

Schneebaum, T. (1969). *Keep the river on your right*. New York: Grove.

Schutz, A. (1962). *Collected papers I: The problem of social reality*. The Hague: Martinus Nijhoff.

Schutz, A. (1964). *Collected papers II: Studies in social theory*. The Hague: Martinus Nijhoff.

Schutz, A. (1966). *Collected papers III: Studies in phenomenological philosophy*. The Hague: Martinus Nijhoff.

Wallace, H. T. (1972). *Culture and social being*. Unpublished master's thesis, University of California, Santa Barbara.

Wieder, D. L. (1970). Meaning by rule. In J. D. Douglas (Ed.), *Understanding everyday life*. Chicago: Aldine.

Wieder, D. L. (1973). *Language and social reality*. The Hague: Mouton.

Wittgenstein, L. (1953). *Philosophical investigations*. London: Basil Blackwell & Mott.

Wittgenstein, L. (1961). *Tractatus logico-philosophicus*. London: Basil Blackwell & Mott. (Original work published in 1921)

Wood, H. (1968). *The labelling process on a mental hospital ward*. Unpublished master's thesis. University of California, Santa Barbara.

Zimmerman, D. H. (1973). Preface. In D. L. Wieder, *Language and social reality*. The Hague: Mouton.

Zimmerman, D. H., & Pollner, M. (1970). The everyday world as a phenomenon. In J. D. Douglas (Ed.), *Understanding everyday life*. Chicago: Aldine.

Zimmerman, D. H., & Wieder, D. L. (n.d.). *The social bases for illegal behavior in the student community: First year report*. San Francisco and Santa Barbara: Scientific Analysis Corporation.

**34**

# A Conception of and Experiments with "Trust" as a Condition of Concerted Stable Actions

## Harold Garfinkel

### Some Preliminary Trials and Findings

Since each of the presuppositions that make up the attitude of daily life assigns an expected feature to the actor's environment, it should be possible to induce experimentally a breach of these expectancies by deliberately modifying scenic events so as to disappoint these attributions. By definition, surprise is possible with respect to each of these expected features. The nastiness of surprise should vary directly with the extent to which the actor complies with the constitutive order of events of everyday life as a scheme for assigning witnessed appearances their status of events in a perceivedly normal environment.

Procedures were used to see if a breach of these presuppositions would produce anomic effects and increase disorganization. These procedures must be thought of as demonstrations rather than as experiments. "Experimenters" were upper division students in the author's courses. Their training consisted of little more than verbal instructions about how to proceed. The demonstrations were done as class assignments and were unsupervised. Students reported their

"A Conception of and Experiments with 'Trust' as a Condition of Concerted Stable Actions" by H. Garfinkel from *Motivation and Social Interaction* (pp. 220–235), edited by O. J. Harvey, 1963. Reprinted by permission of the author.

results in anecdotal fashion with no controls beyond the fact that they were urged to avoid interpretation in favor of writing down what was actually said and done, staying as close as possible to a chronological account.

Because the procedures nevertheless produced massive effects, I feel they are worth reporting. Obviously, however, caution must be exercised in assessing the findings.

### Demonstration 1: Breaching the Congruency of Relevances

This expectancy consists of the following. The person expects, expects that the other person does the same, and expects that as he expects it of the other the other expects the like of him that the differences in their perspectives that originate in their particular individual biographies are irrelevant for the purposes at hand of each and that both have selected and interpreted the actually and potentially common objects in an "empirically identical" manner that is sufficient for the purposes at hand. Thus, for example, in talking about "matters just known in common" persons will discuss them using a course of utterances that are governed by the expectation that the other person *will* understand. The speaker expects that the other person will assign to his remarks the sense intended by the speaker and expects that thereby the other person will permit the speaker the assumption that both know what he is talking about without any requirement of a check-out. Thus the sensible character of the matter that is being discussed is settled by a fiat assignment that each expects to make, and expects the other to make in reciprocal fashion, that as a condition of his right to decide without interference that he knows what he is talking about and that what he is talking about is so, each will have furnished whatever unstated understandings are required. Much therefore that is being talked about is not mentioned, although each expects that the adequate sense of the matter being talked about is settled. The more so is this the case, the more is the exchange one of commonplace remarks among persons who "know" each other.

Students were instructed to engage an acquaintance or friend in an ordinary conversation and, without indicating that what the experimenter was saying was in any way out of the ordinary, to insist that the person clarify the sense of his commonplace remarks. Twenty-three students reported twenty-five instances of such encounters. The following are typical excerpts from their accounts.

*Case 1.* The subject was telling the experimenter, a member of the subject's car pool, about having had a flat tire while going to work the previous day.

(S): "I had a flat tire."
(E): "What do you mean, you had a flat tire?"

She appeared momentarily stunned. Then she answered in a hostile way: "What do you mean? What do you mean? A flat tire is a flat tire. That is what I meant. Nothing special. What a crazy question!"

*Case 2.* (S): "Hi, Ray. How is your girl friend feeling?"

(E): "What do you mean, how is she feeling? Do you mean physical or mental?"
(S): "I mean how is she feeling? What's the matter with you?" (He looked peeved.)

(E): "Nothing. Just explain a little clearer, what do you mean?"
(S): "Skip it. How are your Med School applications coming?"
(E): "What do you mean, 'How are they?'"
(S): "You know what I mean."
(E): "I really don't."
(S): "What's the matter with you? Are you sick?"

*Case 3.* On Friday night my husband and I were watching television. My husband remarked that he was tired. I asked, "How are you tired? Physically, mentally, or just bored?"

(S): "I don't know, I guess physically, mainly."
(E): "You mean that your muscles ache, or your bones?"
(S): "I guess so. Don't be so technical."
(S): (After more watching) "All these old movies have the same kind of old iron bedstead in them."
(E): "What do you mean? Do you mean all old movies, or some of them, or just the ones you have seen?"
(S): "What's the matter with you? You know what I mean."
(E): "I wish you would be more specific."
(S): "You know what I mean! Drop dead!"

*Case 4.* During a conversation (with the male *E's* fiancee) the *E* questioned the meaning of various words used by the subject. For the first minute and a half the subject responded to the questions as if they were legitimate inquiries. Then she responded with "Why are you asking me these questions?" and repeated this two or three times after each question. She became nervous and jittery, her face and hand movements . . . uncontrolled. She appeared bewildered and complained that I was making her nervous and demanded that I "Stop it!" . . . The subject picked up a magazine and covered her face. She put down the magazine and pretended to be engrossed. When asked why she was looking at the magazine, she closed her mouth and refused any further remarks.

*Case 5.* My friend said to me, "Hurry or we will be late." I asked him what did he mean by late and from what point of view did it have reference. There was a look of perplexity and cynicism on his face. "Why are you asking me such silly questions? Surely I don't have to explain such a statement. What is wrong with you today? Why should I have to stop to analyze such a statement. Everyone understands my statements and you should be no exception."

*Case 6.* The victim waved his hand cheerily.

(S): "How are you?"
(E): "How am I in regard to what? My health, my finance, my school work, my peace of mind, my . . ."
(S): (Red in the face and suddenly out of control.) "Look! I was just trying to be polite. Frankly, I don't give a damn how you are."

*Case 7.* My friend and I were talking about a man whose overbearing attitude annoyed us. My friend expressed his feeling.

(S): "I'm sick of him."
(E): Would you explain what is wrong with you that you are sick?"
(S): "Are you kidding me? You know what I mean."
(E): "Please explain your ailment."
(S): (He listened to me with a puzzled look.) "What came over you? We never talk this way, do we?" . . .

*Case 8.* Apparently as a casual afterthought, my husband mentioned Friday night, "Did you remember to drop off my shirts today?"

Taking nothing for granted, I replied, "I remember that you said something about it this morning. What shirts did you mean, and what did you mean by having them 'dropped' off?" He looked puzzled, as though I must have answered some other question than the one asked.

Instead of making the explanation he seemed to be waiting for, I persisted, "I thought your shirts were all in pretty good shape; why not keep them a little longer?" I had the uncomfortable feeling I had overplayed the part.

He no longer looked puzzled, but indignant. He repeated, "A little longer! What do you mean, and what have you done with my shirts?"

I acted indignant too. I asked, "What shirts? You have sport shirts, plain shirts, wool shirts, regular shirts, and dirty shirts. I'm no mind reader. What exactly did you want?"

My husband again looked confused, as though he was trying to justify my behavior. He

seemed simultaneously to be on the defensive and offensive. He assumed a very patient, tolerant air, and said, "Now, let's start all over again. Did you drop off my shirts today?"

I replied, "I heard you before. It's your meaning I wish was more clear. As far as I am concerned dropping off your shirts—whichever shirts you mean—could mean giving them to the Goodwill, leaving them at the cleaners, at the laundromat, or throwing them out. I never know what you mean with those vague statements."

He reflected on what I said, then changed the entire perspective by acting as though we were playing a game, that it was all a joke. He seemed to enjoy the joke. He ruined my approach by assuming the role I thought was mine. He then said, "Well, let's take this step by step with 'yes' or 'no' answers. Did you see the dirty shirts I left on the kitchenette, yes or no?"

I could see no way to complicate his question, so felt forced to answer "Yes." In the same fashion, he asked if I picked up the shirts; if I put them in the car; if I left them at the laundry; and if I did all these things that day, Friday. My answers were "Yes."

The experiment, it seemed to me, had been cut short by his reducing all the parts of his previous question to their simplest terms, which were given to me as if I were a child unable to handle any complex questions, problems, or situations.

### Demonstration 2: Breaching the Interchangeability of Standpoints

In order to breach the presupposed interchangeability of standpoints, students were asked to enter a store, to select a customer, and to treat the customer as a clerk while giving no recognition that the subject was any other person than the experimenter took him to be and without giving any indication that the experimenter's treatment was anything other than perfectly reasonable and legitimate.

*Case 1.* One evening, while shopping at Sears with a friend, I (male) found myself next to a woman shopping at the copper-clad pan section. The store was busy . . . and clerks were hard to find. The woman was just a couple of feet away and my friend was behind me. Pointing to a tea kettle, I asked the woman if she did not think the price was rather high. I asked in a friendly tone. . . . She looked at me and then at the kettle and said "Yes." I then said I was going to take it anyway. She said, "Oh," and started to move sideways away from me. I quickly asked her if she was not going to wrap it for me and take my cash. Still moving slowly away and glancing first at me, then at the kettle, then at the other pans farther away from me, she said the clerk was "over there" pointing off somewhere. In a harsh tone, I asked if she was not going to wait on me. She said, "No, No, I'm not the saleslady. There she is." I said that I knew that the extra help was inexperienced, but there was no reason not to wait on a customer. "Just wait on me. I'll be patient." With that, she flushed with anger and walked rapidly away, looking back once as if to ask if it could really be true.

The following three protocols are the work of a forty-year-old female graduate student in clinical psychology.

*Case 2.* We went to V's book store, noted not so much for its fine merchandise and its wide range of stock as it is in certain circles for the fact that the clerks are male homosexuals. I approached a gentleman who was browsing at a table stacked neatly with books.

*(E):* "I'm in a hurry. Would you get a copy of *Sociopathic Behavior* by Lemert, please?"

*(S):* (Looked *E* up and down, drew himself very straight, slowly laid the book down, stepped back slightly, then leaned forward and in a low voice said) "I'm interested in sociopathic behavior, too. That's why I'm here. I study the fellows here by pretending to be . . . "

*(E):* (Interrupting) "I'm not particularly interested in whether you are or are only pretending to be. Please just get the book I asked for."

*(S):* (Looked shocked. More than surprised, believe me. Stepped around the display table, deliberately placed his hands on the books, leaned forward and shouted) "I don't have such a book. I'm not a clerk! I'm—Well!" (Stalked out of the store.)

*Case 3.* When we entered I. Magnin's there was one woman who was fingering a sweater, the only piece of merchandise to be seen in the shop.

I surmised that the clerk must be in the stockroom.

*(E):* "That is a lovely shade, but I'm looking for one a little lighter. Do you have one in cashmere?"

*(S):* "I really don't know, you see I'm . . .

*(E):* (Interrupting) "Oh, you are new here? I don't mind waiting while you look for what I want."

*(S):* "Indeed I shall not!"

*(E):* "But aren't you here to *serve* customers?"

*(S):* "I'm not! I'm here to . . . "

*(E):* (Interrupts) "This is hardly the place for such an attitude. Now please show me a cashmere sweater a shade or two lighter than this one."

(The clerk entered.)

*(S):* (To clerk) "My dear, this—(pointed her face toward *E*)—*person* insists on being shown a sweater. Please take care of her while I compose myself. I want to be certain this (sweater) will do, and she (pointed her face again at *E*) is so *insistent*." (S carried the sweater with her, walked haughtily to a large upholstered chair, sat in it, brushed her gloved hands free from imaginary dirt, jerked her shoulders, fluffed her suit jacket, and glared at *E*).

*Case 4.* While visiting with a friend in Pasadena, I told him about this being-taken-for-the-clerk experiment. The friend is a Professor Emeritus of Mathematics at the California Institute of Technology and the successful author of many books, some technical, some fictional, and he is most satirical in his contemplations of his fellow man. He begged to be allowed to accompany me and to aid me in the selection of scenes. . . . We went first to have luncheon at the Atheneum, which caters to the students, faculty, and guests of Cal Tech. While we were still in the lobby, my host pointed out a gentleman who was standing in the large drawing room near the entrance to the dining room and said, "Go to it. There's a good subject for you." He stepped aside to watch. I walked toward the man very deliberately and proceeded as follows. (I will use E to designate myself; S, the subject.)

*(E):* "I should like a table on the west side, a quiet spot, if you please. And what is on the menu?"

*(S):* (Turned toward *E* but looked past and in the direction of the foyer) said, "Eh, ah, madam, I'm sure." (looked past *E* again, looked at a pocket watch, replaced it, and looked toward the dining room).

*(E):* "Surely luncheon hours are not over. What do you recommend I order today?"

*(S):* "I don't know. You see, I'm waiting . . ."

*(E):* (Interrupted with) "Please don't keep me standing here while you wait. Kindly show me to a table."

*(S):* "But Madam,—" (started to edge away from door, and back into the lounge in a slightly curving direction around *E*)

*(E):* "My good man—" (At this *S's* face flushed, his eyes rounded and opened wide.)

*(S):* "But—you—I—oh dear!" (He seemed to wilt.)

*(E):* (Took *S's* arm in hand and propelled him toward the dining room door, slightly ahead of herself.)

*(S):* (Walked slowly but stopped just within the room, turned around and for the first time looked directly and very appraisingly at *E*, took out the watch, looked at it, held it to his ear, replaced it, and muttered) "Oh dear."

*(E):* "It will take only a minute for you to show me to a table and take my order. Then you can return to wait for your customers. After all, I am a guest and a customer, too."

*(S):* (Stiffened slightly, walked jerkily toward the nearest empty table, held a chair for *E* to be seated, bowed slightly, muttered "My pleasure," hurried toward the door, stopped, turned, looked back at *E* with a blank facial expression.)

At this point *E's* host walked up to *S*, greeted him, shook hands, and propelled him toward *E's* table. *S* stopped a few steps from the table, looked directly at, then through, *E*, and started to walk back toward the door. Host told him *E* was the young lady whom he had invited to join them at lunch (then introduced me to one of the big names in the physics world, a pillar of the institution!). *S* seated himself reluctantly and perched rigidly on his chair, obviously uncomfortable. *E* smiled, made light and polite inquiries about his work, mentioned various functions attended which had honored him, then complacently remarked that it was a shame *E* had not met him personally before now, so that she should not have mistaken him for the maître-d'. The host

chattered about his long-time friendship with me, while *S* fidgeted and looked again at his pocket watch, wiped his forehead with a table napkin, looked at *E* but avoided meeting her eyes. When the host mentioned that *E* is studying sociology at UCLA, *S* suddenly burst into loud laughter, realized that everyone in the room was looking in the direction of our table, abruptly became quiet, then said to *E* "You mistook me for the maître-d', didn't you?"

*(E):* "Deliberately, sir."

*(S):* "Why deliberately?"

*(E):* "You have just been used as the unsuspecting subject in an experiment."

*(S):* "Diabolic. But clever, I must say (To our host) I haven't been so shaken since ——— denounced my theory ——— of ——— in 19———. And the wild thoughts that ran through my mind! Call the receptionist from the lobby, go to the men's room, turn this woman to the first person that comes along. Damn these early diners, there's nobody coming in at this time. Time is standing still, or my watch has stopped. I will talk to ——— about this, make sure it doesn't happen to 'somebody.' Damn a persistent woman. I'm not her 'good man!' I'm Dr. ———, and not to be pushed around. This can't be happening. If I do take her to that damned table she wants, I can get away from her, and I'll just take it easy until I can. I remember ——— (hereditary psychopath, wife of one of the 'family' of the institution) maybe if I do what *this* one wants she will not make any more trouble than this. I wonder if she is 'off.' She certainly looks normal. Wonder how you can really tell?"

### Demonstration 3: Breaching the Expectancy That a Knowledge of a Relationship of Interaction Is a Commonly Entertained Scheme of Communication

Schutz proposed that from the member's point of view, an event of conduct, like a move in a game, consists of an event-in-a-social-order. Thus, for the member, its recognizably real character is furnished by attending its occurrence with respect to a corpus of socially sanctioned knowledge of the social relationships that the member uses and assumes that others use as the same scheme of expression and interpretation.

It was decided to breach this expectancy by having students treat a situation as something that it "obviously" and "really" was not. Students were instructed to spend from fifteen minutes to an hour in their own homes acting as if they were boarders. They were instructed to conduct themselves in a circumspect and polite fashion: to avoid getting personal; to use formal address; to speak only when they were spoken to.

In nine of forty-nine cases students either refused to do the assignment (five cases) or the try was "unsuccessful" (four cases). Four of the "no try" students said they were afraid to do it; a fifth said she preferred to avoid the risk of exciting her mother who had a heart condition. In two of the "unsuccessful" cases the family treated it as a joke from the beginning and refused, despite the continuing actions of the student experimenter, to change. A third family took the view that something of an undisclosed sort was the matter, but what it might be was of no concern to them. In the fourth family the father and mother remarked that the daughter was being "extra nice" and undoubtedly wanted something that she would shortly reveal.

In the remaining four-fifths of the cases family members were stupefied, vigorously sought to make the strange actions intelligible, and to restore the situation to normal appearances. Reports were filled with accounts of astonishment, bewilderment, shock, anxiety, embarrassment, and anger as well as with charges by various family members that the student was mean, inconsiderate, selfish, nasty, and impolite. Family members demanded explanations: "What's the matter?" "What's gotten into you?" "Did you get fired?" "Are you sick?" "What are you being so superior about?" "Why are you mad?" "Are you out of your mind or are you just stupid?" One student acutely embarrassed his mother in front of her friends by asking if she minded if he had a snack from the refrigerator. "Mind if you have a little snack? You've been eating little snacks around here for years without asking me. What's gotten into you?" One mother, infuriated when her daughter spoke to her only when she was spoken to, began to shriek in angry denunciation of the daughter for her disrespect and insubordination and refused to be calmed by the student's sister. A father berated his daughter for being insufficiently concerned for the welfare of others and for acting like a spoiled child.

Occasionally family members would first treat the student's action as a cue for a joint comedy routine which was soon replaced by irritation and exasperated anger at the student for not knowing "when enough was enough." Family members mocked the "politeness" of the students—"Certainly Mr. Dinerberg!"—or charged the student with acting like a wise guy and generally reproved the "politeness" with sarcasm.

Explanations were sought in terms of understandable and previous motives of the student: the accusation that the student was covering up something important that the family should know; that the student was working too hard in school; that the student was ill; that there had been "another fight" with a fiancee.

Unacknowledged explanations were followed by withdrawal of the offended member, attempted isolation of the culprit, retaliation, and denunciation. "Don't bother with him, he's in one of his moods again." "Pay no attention but just wait until he asks me for something." "You're cutting me, okay. I'll cut you and then some." "Why must you always create friction in our family harmony?" A father followed his son into the bedroom. "Your mother is right. You don't look well and you're not talking sense. You had better get another job that doesn't require such late hours." To this the student replied that he appreciated his consideration, but that he felt fine and only wanted a little privacy. The father responded in high rage, "I don't want any more of *that* out of *you*. And if you can't treat your mother decently, you'd better move out!"

There were no cases in which the situation was not restorable upon the student's explanation. Nevertheless, for the most part, family members were not amused and only rarely did they find the experience instructive, as the student argued that it was supposed to have been. After hearing the explanation, a sister replied coldly on behalf of a family of four, "Please, no more of these experiments. We're not rats you know." Occasionally an explanation was accepted and still it added offense. In several cases students reported that the explanation left them, their families, or both wondering how much of what the student had said was "in character" and how much the student "really meant."

Students found the assignment difficult to complete because of not being treated as if they were in the role that they are attempting to play and of being confronted with situations to which they did not know how a boarder would respond.

There were several entirely unexpected results. (1) Although many students reported extensive rehearsals in imagination, very few of those that did it mentioned anticipatory fears or embarrassment. (2) Although unanticipated and nasty developments frequently occurred, in only one case did a student report serious regrets. (3) Very few students reported heartfelt relief when the hour was over. They were much more likely to report a partial relief. They frequently reported that in response to the anger of others they became angry in return and slipped easily into subjectively recognizable feelings and actions.

### Demonstration 4: Breaching the Grasp of "What Anyone Knows" to Be Correct Grounds of Action of a Real Social World

Among the possibilities that a premedical student could treat as correct grounds for his further inferences and actions about such matters as how a medical school intake inter-

view is conducted or how an applicant's conduct is related to his chances of admission, certain ones (e.g., that deferring to the interviewer's interests is a condition for making a favorable impression) he treats as matters that he is required to know and act upon as a condition of his competence as a premedical candidate. He expects others like him to know and act upon the same things; and he expects that as he expects others to know and act upon them, the others in turn expect the like of him.

A procedure was designed to breach the constitutive expectancies attached to "what-any-competent-premedical-candidate-knows" while satisfying the three conditions under which their breach would presumably produce confusion.

Twenty-eight premedical students of the University of California in Los Angeles were run individually through a three-hour experimental interview. As part of the solicitation of subjects, as well as the beginning of the interview, E identified himself as a representative of an Eastern medical school who was attempting to learn why the medical school intake interview was such a stressful situation. It was hoped that identifying E as a person with medical school ties would minimize the chance that students would "leave the field" once the accent breaching procedure began. How the other two conditions of (a) managing a redefinition in insufficient time and (b) not being able to count on consensual support for an alternative definition of social reality were met will be apparent in the following description.

During the first hour of the interview, the student furnished the facts-of-life about interviews for admission to medical school by answering for the "representative" such questions as "What sources of information about a candidate are available to medical schools?" "What can a medical school learn about a candidate from these sources?" "What kind of a man are the medical schools looking for?" "What should a good candidate do in the interview?" "What should he avoid?" With this much completed, the student was told that the "representative's" research interests had been satisfied. The student was asked if he would care to hear a recording of an actual interview. All students wanted very much to hear the recording.

The recording was a faked one between a "medical school interviewer" and an "applicant." The applicant was depicted as being a boor; his language was ungrammatical and filled with colloquialisms; he was evasive; he contradicted the interviewer; he bragged; he ran down other schools and professions; he insisted on knowing how he had done in the interview and so on.

Detailed assessments by the student of the recorded applicant were obtained immediately after the recording was finished. The following edited assessment is representative:

I didn't like it. I didn't like his attitude. I didn't like anything about him. Everything he said grated the wrong way. I didn't like his smoking. The way he kept saying "Yeah-h!" He didn't show that he realized that the interviewer had his future in his hands. I didn't like the vague way he answered questions. I didn't like the way he pressed at the end of the interview. He was disrespectful. His motives were too obvious. He made a mess of it. He finished with a bang to say the least. . . . His answers to questions were stupid. I felt that the interviewer was telling him that he wasn't going to get in. I didn't like the interview. I felt it was too informal. To a degree it's good if it's natural but . . . the interview is not something to breeze through. It's just not the place for chitchat. He had fairly good grades but . . . he's not interested in things outside of school and didn't say what he did *in* school. Then he didn't *do* very much—outside of this lab. I didn't like the man at all. I never met an applicant like that! "My pal"— Just one of these little chats. I never met anybody *like* that. Wrong-way Corrigan.

The student was then given information from the applicant's "official record." This information was deliberately contrived to contradict the principal points in the student's assessment. For example, if the student said

that the applicant must have come from a lower-class family, he was told that the applicant's father was vice president of a firm that manufactured pneumatic doors for trains and buses. If the applicant had been thought to be ignorant, he was described as having excelled in courses like The Poetry of Milton and Dramas of Shakespeare. If the student said the applicant did not know how to get along with people, then the applicant was pictured as having worked as a voluntary solicitor for Sydenham Hospital in New York City and had raised $32,000 from thirty "big givers." The belief that the applicant was stupid and would not do well in a scientific field was met by citing A grades in organic and physical chemistry and graduate level performance in an undergraduate research course.

The Ss wanted very much to know what "the others" thought of the applicant, and had he been admitted? The "others" had been previously and casually identified by the "representative" as "Dr. Gardner, the medical school interviewer," "six psychiatrically trained members of the admissions committee who heard only the recorded interview," and "other students I talked to."

The S was told that the applicant had been admitted and was living up to the promise that the medical school interviewer and the "six psychiatrists" had found and expressed in the following recommendation of the applicant's characterological fitness.

Dr. Gardner, the medical school interviewer, wrote, "A well-bred, polite young man, poised, affable, and self-confident. Capable of independent thinking. Interests of a rather specialized character. Marked intellectual curiosity. Alert and free of emotional disturbances. Marked maturity of manner and outlook. Meets others easily. Strongly motivated toward a medical career. Definite ideas of what he wants to achieve which are held in good perspective. Unquestioned sincerity and integrity. Expressed himself easily and well. Recommend favorable consideration." The six psychiatric members of the admissions committee agreed in all essentials.

Concerning the views of "other students," S was told that he was, for example, the thirtieth student I had seen; that twenty-eight before him were in entire agreement with the medical school interviewer's assessment; and that the remaining two had been slightly uncertain but at the first bit of information had seen him just as the others had.

Following this, Ss were invited to listen to the record a second time, after which they were asked to assess the applicant again.

*Results.* Twenty-five of the twenty-eight subjects were taken in. The following does not apply to the three who were convinced there was a deception. Two of these are discussed at the conclusion of this section.

Incongruous materials, presented to S in the order indicated, were performance information, and characterological information. Performance information dealt with the applicant's activities, grades, family background, courses, charity work, and the like. Characterological information consisted of character assessments of him by the "medical school interviewers," the "six psychiatrically trained members of the admissions committee," and the "other students."

Subjects managed incongruities of performance data with vigorous attempts to make it factually compatible with their original assessments. For example, when they said that the applicant sounded like a lower-class person, they were told that his father was vice president of a national corporation that manufactured pneumatic doors for trains and buses. Here are some typical replies:

"He should have made the point that he *could* count on money."

"That explains why he said he had to work. Probably his father made him work. That would make a lot of his moans unjustified in the sense that things were really not so bad."

"What does that have to do with values?!"

"You could tell from his answers. You could tell that he was used to having his own way."

"That's something the interviewer knew that *I* didn't know."

"Then he's an out and out liar!"

When Ss said that the applicant was selfish and could not get along with people, they were told that he had worked as a volunteer for Sydenham Hospital and had raised $32,000 from thirty "big givers."

"He seems to be a good salesman. So possibly he's missing his profession. I'd say *definitely* he's missing his profession!"

"They probably contributed because of the charity and not because they were solicited."

"Pretty good. Swell. Did he know them personally?"

"It's very fashionable to work, for example, during the war for Bundles for Britain. So that doesn't—definitely!—show altruistic motives at all. He is a person who is subject to fashion and I'm very critical of that sort of thing.

"He's so forceful he might have shamed them into giving."

"People who are wealthy—his father would naturally see those people—big contributions—they could give a lot of money and not know what they're giving it for."

That he had a straight A average in physical science courses began to draw bewilderment.

"He took quite a variety of courses . . . I'm baffled.—Probably the interview wasn't a very good mirror of his character."

"He did seem to take some odd courses. They seem to be fairly normal. Not normal—but—it doesn't strike me one way or the other."

"Well! I think you can analyze it this way. In psychological terms. See—one possible way—now I may be all *wet* but this is the way I look at *that*. He probably suffered from an inferiority complex and that's an overcompensation for his inferiority complex. His *great* marks—his *good* marks are a compensation for his failure—in social dealings perhaps, I don't know."

"Woops! And only third alternate at Georgia. (Deep sigh) I can see why he'd feel resentment about not being admitted to Phi Bet."

(Long silence) "Well! From what—that leads me to think he's a grind or something like that."

Attempts to resolve the incongruities produced by the character assessment of "Gardner" and "the other six judges" were much less frequent than normalizing attempts with performance information. Open expressions of bewilderment and anxiety interspersed with silent ruminations were characteristic.

(Laugh) "Golly!" (Silence) "I'd think it would be the other way around."—(Very subdued) "Maybe I'm all wro—My orientation is all off. I'm completely baffled."

"Not polite. Self-confident he certainly was. But not polite—I don't know. Either the interviewer was a little crazy or else I am." (Long pause) "That's rather shocking. It makes me have doubts about my own thinking. Perhaps my values in life are wrong. I don't know."

(Whistles) "I—I didn't think he sounded well bred at all. That whole tone of voice!!—I—Perhaps you noticed though, when he said 'You should have said in the first place' before he took it with a smile.—But even so! No, no I can't see that. 'You should have said that before.' Maybe he was being funny though. Exercising a—No! To me it sounded impertinent!"

"Ugh—Well, that certainly puts a different slant on my conception of interviews. Gee—that—confuses me all the more."

"Well—(laugh)—Hhh!—Ugh! Well, maybe he looked like a nice boy. He did—he did get his point across.—Perhaps—seeing the person would make a big difference.—Or perhaps I would never make a good interviewer." (Reflectively and almost inaudibly) "They didn't mention any of the things I mentioned." (HG: Eh?) (Louder) "They didn't mention any of the things I mentioned and so I feel like a complete failure."

Soon after the performance data produced its consternation, an occasional request would be made: "What did the other students make of him?" Only after Gardner's assessment, and the responses to it had been made were the opinions of the "other students" given. In some cases the subject was told "34 out of 35 before you," in others 43 out of 45, 19 out of 20, 51 out of 52. All the numbers were large. For 18 of the 25 students the delivery hardly varied from the following verbatim protocols:

[34 out of 35] I don't know.—I still stick to my original convictions. I—I—Can you tell *me* what—I saw wrong. Maybe—I—I had the wrong idea—the wrong attitude all along. (Can you tell me? I'm interested that there should be such a disparity.) Definitely. —I—think—it would be definitely the other way—I can't make sense of it. I'm completely baffled, believe me. —I—I don't understand how I could have been so wrong. Maybe my ideas—my evaluations of people are—just twisted. I mean maybe I had the wrong—maybe my sense of values—is—off—or—different—from the other 33. But I don't think that's the case—because usually—and in all modesty I say this—I—I can judge people. I mean in class, in organizations I belong to—I usually judge them right. So therefore I don't understand at *all* how I could have been so wrong. I don't think I was under any stress or strain—here—tonight but—I don't understand it.

[43 out of 45] [Laugh] I don't know what to say now. —I'm troubled by my inability to judge the guy better than that. [Subdued] I shall sleep tonight, certainly—[Very subdued] but it certainly bothers me. —Sorry that I didn't—*Well!* One question that arises—I may be wrong—(Can you see how they might have seen him?) No. No, I can't see it, no. —Sure with all that background material, yes, but I don't see how Gardner did it without it. Well, I guess that makes Gardner, Gardner, and me, me. (The other 45 students didn't have the background material.) Yeah, yeah, yeah. I mean I'm not denying it at all. I mean for myself, there's no sense saying—Of course! With their background they would be accepted, especially the second man, good God! —Okay, what else?

[23 out of 25] [Softly] Maybe I'm tired. (HG, "Eh?") [Burst of laughter.] Maybe I didn't get enough sleep last night. —Uhh! —Well—I might not have been looking for the things that the other men were looking for. —I wasn't—Huh! —It puts me at a loss, really.

[10 out of 10] So I'm alone in my judgment. I don't know, sir! I don't know, sir!! —I can't explain it. It's senseless. —I tried to be impartial at the beginning. I admit I was prejudiced immediately.

[51 out of 52] You mean that 51 others stuck to their guns, too? (Stuck to their guns in the sense that they saw him just as the judges saw him.) Uh huh. [Deep sigh] I still don't—Yeah! I see. But just listening I don't think he was a—very good chance. But in light of his other things I feel that the interview was not—showing—the real—him. —Hhh!

[36 out of 37] I would go back on my former opinion but I wouldn't go back too far. I just don't see it. —Why should I have these different standards? Were my opinions more or less in agreement on the first man? (No.) That leads me to think. —That's funny. Unless you got 36 unusual people. I can't understand it. Maybe it's my personality. (Does it make any difference?) It *does* make a difference if I assume they're correct. What I consider is proper, they don't. —It's my attitude—Still in all a man of that sort would alienate me. A wise guy type to be avoided. Of course you can talk like that with other fellows— but in an interview? . . . Now I'm more confused than I was at the beginning of the entire interview. I think I ought to go home and look in the mirror and talk to myself. Do you have any ideas? (Why? Does it disturb you?) Yes it *does* disturb me! It makes me think my abilities to judge people and values are way off from normal. It's not a healthy situation. (What difference does it make?) If I act the way I act it seems to me that I'm just putting my head in the lion's mouth. I did have preconceptions but they're shattered all to hell. It makes me wonder about myself. Why should I have these different standards? It all points to me.

Of the twenty-five *Ss* who were taken in, seven were unable to resolve the incongruity of having been wrong about such an obvious matter and were unable to "see" the alternative. Their suffering was dramatic and unrelieved. Five more resolved it with the view that the medical school had accepted a good man; five others with the view that it had accepted a boor. Although they changed, they nevertheless did not abandon their former views. For them Gardner's view could be

seen "in general," but the grasp lacked convincingness. When attention was drawn to particulars, the general picture would evaporate. These *Ss* were willing to entertain and use the "general" picture, but they suffered whenever indigestible particulars of the same portrait came into view. Subscription to the "general" picture was accompanied by a recitation of characteristics that were not only the opposite of those in the original view but were intensified by superlative adjectives like "supremely" poised, "very" natural, "most" confident, "very" calm. Further, they saw the new features through a new appreciation of the way the medical examiner had been listening. They saw, for example, that the examiner was smiling when the applicant had forgotten to offer him a cigarette.

Three more *Ss* were convinced that there was deception and acted on the conviction through the interview. They showed no disturbance. Two of these showed acute suffering as soon as it appeared that the interview was finished, and they were being dismissed with no acknowledgment of a deception. Three others inadvertently suffered in silence and confounded *E*. Without any indication to *E*, they regarded the interview as an experimental one in which they were being asked to solve some problems and therefore were being asked to do as well as possible and to make no changes in their opinions, for only then would they be contributing to the study. They were difficult for me to understand during the interview because they displayed marked anxiety, yet their remarks were bland and were not addressed to the matters that were provoking it. Finally three more *Ss* contrasted with the others. One of these insisted that the character assessments were semantically ambiguous and because there was insufficient information a "high correlation opinion" was not possible. A second, and the only one in the entire series, found, according to his account, the second portrait as convincing as the original one. When the deception was revealed, he was disturbed that he could have been as convinced as he was. The third one, in the face of everything, showed only slight disturbance of very short duration. However, he alone among the subjects had already been interviewed for medical school, had excellent contacts, despite a grade point average of less than C he estimated his chances of admission as fair, and finally he expressed his preference for a career in the diplomatic service over a career in medicine.

As a final observation, twenty-two of the twenty-eight Ss expressed marked relief—ten of them with explosive expressions—when I disclosed the deception. Unanimously they said that the news of the deception permitted them to return to their former views. Seven Ss had to be convinced that there had been a deception. When the deception was revealed, they asked what they were to believe. Was I telling them that there had been a deception in order to make them feel better? No pains were spared, and whatever truth or lies that had to be told were told in order to establish the truth that there had been a deception.

35

# The Social Construction of Unreality: A Case Study of a Family's Attribution of Competence to a Severely Retarded Child

*Melvin Pollner and Lynn McDonald-Wikler*
*with Commentary by David Reiss*

*Some families develop unusual or extreme versions of reality and sustain them in the face of a torrent of ostensibly discrediting and disconfirming information. Although the psychological dynamics and functions of such shared constructions have been amply considered, little is known about the routine transactions through which these unusual versions of reality are created and maintained. This paper examines the "reality work" of a family that attributed high levels of performance and competence to the severely retarded youngest child. Observation of videotaped interaction between family members and the child revealed practices that presupposed, "documented," and sustained the family's version of the child's competence. The practices are similar to those characteristics of interaction between adults and preverbal children. The implications of this similarity for the analysis of cases of* folie à famille *are discussed.*

In recent years attention has been drawn to the ways in which what group members take to be given, natural, or real is a subtly organized achievement (Berger, 1969; Cicourel, 1973; Garfinkel, 1967). The social world of the group is not a simple reflection of what is "out there" but a continuously developed and sustained construction. The maintenance of a collective construct requires work—information must be selected, edited, and in-

terpreted; anomalies must be explained; heretics from within and critics from without must be discounted, dissuaded, managed, or avoided. As Berger (1969) suggests:

Worlds are socially constructed, socially maintained. Their continuing reality, both objective (as common, taken-for-granted facticity) and subjective (as facticity imposing itself on individual consciousness), depends upon *specific* social processes, namely those processes that ongoingly reconstruct and maintain the particular world in question. (p. 45)

The family is no different. Indeed, in many respects it is an especially intense locus of these constructive processes (Berger & Kellner, 1970). In *The Family's Construction of Reality*, Reiss (1981), for example, proposes

"The Social Construction of Unreality: A Case Study of a Family's Attribution of Competence to a Severely Retarded Child" by M. Pollner and L. McDonald-Wikler, with commentary ("The Social Construction of Reality: The Passion Within Us All") by David Reiss, 1985. *Family Process 24*, pp. 241–254. Reprinted by permission of the author.

that "family paradigms"—the fundamental assumptions a family holds about itself and the world—are realized and conserved through interactional patterns. These patterns create the family's everyday reality and enable members "to experience their own values and assumptions as if they were unquestionable components of outer reality" (p. 228).

The conception of family reality as an interactionally achieved construction may prove especially valuable in exploring the dynamics by which families maintain seemingly extreme, bizarre, or aberrant versions of reality. Although the psychological dynamics and functions of such constructions have received attention (Pulver & Brunt, 1961; Wikler, 1980) and despite numerous case histories in the literature (Gralnick, 1942), relatively little is known about the concrete, detailed activities in which family members use, manage, and "realize" these versions of reality in their day-to-day activities. The constructionist standpoint corrects this imbalance by inviting close examination of the artful, minute, and continuous work through which what might be characterized as "myth," "distortion," or "delusion" from outside the family is rendered a reality for those on the inside.[1]

We have applied this general perspective to a family diagnosed as *folie à famille* and attempted to discern the "reality work"—practices of reasoning, speaking, and acting—through which members documented and maintained their particular world. The family in question was initially encountered at a large psychiatric institute to which the parents had turned in their search for a remedy for 5½-year-old Mary's unusual behavior. Family members stated that Mary was a verbal and intelligent child who malingered and refused to speak in public in order to embarrass the family. Extensive clinical observation and examination revealed Mary to be severely retarded and unable to perform at anywhere near the level of competence claimed by her parents and two older sibs.

Clinical materials collected included video-taped recordings of each family member interacting with the child in the institute. Initial viewings of the tapes suggested that family members' transactions were permeated by subtle, almost artful, practices that could function to create the image of Mary as an intelligent child. Intensive examination of these and other materials yielded a repertoire of such practices, and they constitute a central focus of this report. Although our analysis was driven by the assumption that family members were constructing their reality, our subsequent reflections suggested more complicated possibilities whose dimensions we shall explore in our concluding discussion.

## Case Description

Mary's parents came to a psychiatric institute for an inpatient psychiatric evaluation of their 5½-year-old daughter.[2] Their presenting complaint was that, although at home their child acted normally, she refused to do so in public. They wanted the reason for this peculiar and difficult-to-manage behavior to be identified and then treated. In public, they claimed, she acted retarded. Each of the four family members who lived with Mary agreed with this description:

*Father* (aged 42): She's really a fast child, if anything. Once she even read a note aloud that I had passed over to my wife not intending for Mary to see it.
*Mother* (aged 39): She puts on an act of being retarded in public while acting normally at home.
*Half-Sister* (aged 18): I've had 10-minute long normal conversations with her, but she won't talk in front of most people.
*Brother* (aged 12): 1 don't know why she fakes it; she's like any other 5-year-old.

Prior to coming for the inpatient evaluation, the child had been taken to several reputable outpatient clinics in the general geographical area for work-ups. These had been, according to the parents, frustrating experiences, and they had not received the help they sought. In each case they were essentially told (father's report) that Mary was severely retarded. This was rejected by the parents and instead was regarded by them as an indicator of Mary's capabilities—she had fooled the clinicians. Therefore, they had continued their search for a thorough, long-term evaluation.

Mary was admitted to the children's ward in the Neuropsychiatric Institute, which specialized in evaluation and treatment of retarded children. The admission was made with the clearly stated contingency that the family remain intensively involved with the professional staff throughout her stay. Mary was observed 24 hours a day for eight weeks (except on weekends when she routinely returned home) by a professional nursing staff. The pediatrician and social worker for the ward had their offices on the ward and so had frequent occasions to observe Mary's behavior informally in addition to their formal evaluations. Mary was evaluated by specialists in developmental disabilities from the following disciplines (each using several standardized measures as well as narrative summaries of impressions to reach their conclusions): neurology, psychiatry, pediatrics, psychology, special education, psychiatric nursing, vocational rehabilitation, physical therapy, audiometry, speech pathology, dentistry, social work.

While recognizing the similarity with cases of elective mutism (Rosenberg & Lindblad, 1978), there was no deviation in any of the findings, and there was unanimous agreement on the diagnosis: Mary was severely retarded. She was mildly cerebral palsied; she had petit mal seizures; she was more than three standard deviations below average in height and weight; her language development was below that of a 9-month-old; her receptive language abilities seemed nonexistent, except for intonation; she was not sufficiently maturationally developed to be toilet trained; etc. There was no time at which anyone felt or mentioned in the dis-

cussion of their findings that emotional disturbance or resistance or noncooperation was interfering with the validity of their test results. The evaluation was conclusive in every way; her IQ was set at approximately 20 to 25.

Although by standardized MMPI testing, no psychosis was evident and all members of the family were normal or above in intelligence, the family was diagnosed as delusional. A highly refined testing procedure indicated the mother was disposed to delusions under stress. She was seen as the locus of the family delusion, and the entire family was diagnosed as a case of *folie à famille, imposée.*

In contrast to the professional diagnosis, the family claimed that:

1. Mary is like other children her age; she is normal; she can talk.
2. Mary is often crabby and obstinate; when she's in such moods, she won't cooperate.
3. Mary puts on an act of "being retarded" in public, which the family cannot understand.
4. The professional staff had been fooled by Mary.

Our analysis of the available materials has been instigated by the following questions: How does the family do it? What sorts of skills, practices, and strategies are utilized to create and then "discover" Mary's competence? A number of images and anecdotes had heuristic value for discerning the nature of the family accomplishment. We occasionally thought of a Zen tale, for example, which goes something like this: A Zen master is asked by a novice to draw a perfect circle. The master draws a wretchedly ragged figure. The novice quickly notes that the figure is hardly a "perfect circle." "That is correct," responds the master, "but it is a perfect whatever-it-is." The tale captured for us what we felt was a dominant thrust of the family's practices—they had ways of transforming what others regarded as incompetent performance into exhibits of intelligence and responsiveness. The yield of our analysis has been a set of practices by which family members created Mary's "perfection."

## Family Practices

### Framing

There were several ways in which family members verbally or physically prestructured the environment to maximize the likelihood that *whatever* Mary did could be seen as meaningful, intentional activity. In "framing," Mary's family would establish a definition of the immediate situation and use it as a frame of reference for interpreting and describing any and all of Mary's subsequent behavior. Playing a game with Mary was perhaps the prototype of such framing activity. For example, once the game of "catch" was inaugurated as a definition of "what we are now doing," a variety of game-relevant dimensions for understanding and describing Mary's behavior came into effect. She could be seen as either "catching the ball," "not catching the ball," "dropping the ball," "throwing well," and so forth. The game provided a vocabulary for describing activities that occurred while the frame was in effect. Even activities that seemed to fall outside the frame were describable: Mary's nonresponsiveness might be formulated as "not playing" or "playing very poorly." Framed within the structure of an activity and described with the activity-specific terminology, Mary's behaviors were endowed with an aura of significance and responsiveness. In the exchange in Table 1, for example, Mary's passivity was reformulated into game-relevant terms; the ball tumbling out of Mary's hands was described by Mary's sister as an error; i.e., Mary "dropped" it.

To a certain extent the very structures of discourse provided frames that constituted the possibility of interpreting Mary's behavior as intelligent and responsive. For example, once a question was posed or an invitation proffered, Mary's subsequent behavior

**Table 1**
Framing (Game)

| Verbal Exchange | Movements |
| --- | --- |
| Do you want it? | |
| You gonna catch it for me? Huh? | |
| Come on. | |
| Come on. | |
| Put your hand out. | |
| Come on. | |
| Come on. | Sister puts ball in Mary's hand and Mary doesn't hold onto it. |
| Uh, uh (laughs). | |
| Almost dropped it. | Ball falls. |
| Come on. | Sister throws it to Mary who can't catch it, it drops again. |
| Come on (laughs). | |

might be reviewed for the ways in which whatever she was doing could serve as a response (Schegloff, 1968). Mary, of course, was impervious to the content of such overtures and often to the sheer fact of the overture itself; she never responded to a question or complied with a command behaviorally or verbally. Yet family members often formulated Mary's behaviors following these overtures as deliberately chosen and meaningful courses of activity even if Mary's behavior consisted of the completely unperturbed continuation of what she had been doing prior to the immediate transaction. In one sequence, for example, the mother twice requested "Give Mommy the ball"; when Mary simply continued to stand while holding the ball, the mother said "You don't want to give me the ball," thereby narratively transforming obliviousness into a willful reluctance to give the ball.

In the transaction in Table 2, Mary's involvement with a piling toy was framed by the mother's invitation to build a block

**Table 2**

Framing (Question)

| Verbal Exchange | Movements |
| --- | --- |
| Mo: Let's see, what have we got in here? | Mo pulls out piling toy, sets it on table away; M stands watching. |
| Mo: How about building a block house? | Mo looks up at M, M looks at box. |
| M: Um mmmm. | Mo takes ball out; Mary puts a leg on the table and reaches in box touching the blocks. |
| Mo: O.K.? | Mo takes blocks out and puts them on the table; Mary climbs onto table and reaches for piling toy, begins to pull off a section. After placing box on floor, Mo places hands on toy ball and removes them from the table top and looks at her. M has piece of toy, which Mo removes from her hand. M sits back on her heels, and M drops a toy. Mo reaches for her waist and lifts her down from table onto her lap. |
| M: Ahhhuy aiieo gege. | |
| Mo: Shall we build a house? | |
| Mo: Or are you gonna do that? | |
| M: Uh. | |
| Mo: Let's build a house. Whup! | |

house. Mary's continued fingering of the piling toy was then formulated as a deliberately chosen alternative. The formulation of Mary's activity was itself stated as a question—"Or are you gonna do that?"—with the subsequent result that Mary had been asked a sequence of questions that almost totally exhausted alternative possibilities for activity. In the face of options that covered the range of immediate possibilities—blocks or continued involvement with the piling toy—almost anything Mary did, even if she con-

tinued to do what she had been doing all along, could serve as material for inferring an intelligent choice.

### Postscripting

If framing served prospectively to generate a "space" within which Mary's behaviors might assume meaning, postscripting attempted to generate or discern significance after the fact. In postscripting, family members would in effect track or follow Mary's ongoing behaviors and develop physical or verbal contexts that could render the behaviors intelligent and interactionally responsive.

Perhaps the clearest form of postscripting was expressed in what might be called "commanding the already done," in which family members requested Mary to engage in an activity she had already initiated. That is, family members observed the beginnings of possible actions and then ordered their completion. When done quickly with finesse, the inversion of the temporal sequence was hardly noticeable and the aura of competence enhanced; to the casual eye Mary seems to be following orders.

1. As Mary lay down on the floor, father said, "Mary, you just lie there." She does.
2. As Mary reached up to father with part of a toy in her hand, he said, "Give me that one, too." She gave it to him.
3. As Mary looked at her sister and climbed onto the chair, her sister said, "And you sit down." Mary sat down.

A somewhat more sophisticated form of postscripting entails the interposition of actions into the stream of Mary's behaviors. By discerning a pattern or developmental possibility in Mary's behaviors, the successful postscripter could integrate his or her actions with Mary's so as to achieve the appearance of coordinated interactional activity. Thus, for example, at one point the sister dropped a block while Mary was intently banging a block on the table. As Mary sat down on the floor, the sister bent down from her chair, saying, "Let's find that block."

## Puppeteering

In framing and postscripting, Mary's behaviors were endowed with significance through the artfulness of prebehavior and postbehavior interpretations. In effect, Mary's behaviors were treated as "givens" around which an edifice of meaning was constructed. On some occasions, however, instead of working with whatever Mary happened to do, family members would "create" Mary's behavior. Specifically, Mary would be physically maneuvered through various tasks. Moreover, the maneuvering was accompanied or followed by commentary implying that Mary was performing as an autonomous and responsive agent. We refer to this practice as "puppeteering," and when executed in a masterful way it could succeed in creating the illusion of independence. Indeed, initial viewings of videotaped sequences in Table 3 suggested that Mary could respond to requests and follow instructions. An instruction would be given, the observer would shift visually to view Mary, and Mary could be observed to approximate the behavior that had been requested of her. It was not until later in the analysis, however, that the sequencing of family talk and family touching was seen to be related to the active production of her behavioral response. Mary's movements were often artifacts of the family's physical engineering of her body.

### Semantic Crediting

Mary was responsive to a range of different stimuli, all of which were nonverbal. These were fairly predictable, and they were appropriate for a child with her mental age. [Table 4 contains] a partial list of stimuli Mary responded to, with the corresponding behaviors (from hours of observation on ward and on tape).

These are events that elicited predictable behavioral reactions from Mary, even when embedded in a context that included other stimuli such as talk. Indeed the fact that these

**Table 3**

Puppeteering

| Verbal Exchange | Movements |
| --- | --- |
| **MOTHER AND MARY** | |
| *Mo:* Okay, now. | Mo sitting on floor next to the table, setting up a circle of blocks on table. Mary just slipped to floor. Mo picks M up under her arms to a standing position. With one hand Mother points to the middle of the circle of blocks, *other arm is around and behind M with hand on M's arm; she pushes* M's arm, which has block in it, toward the middle while looking at the table—then looks at M. M's arm moves forward, then stops, and M slips to the floor again. |
| *Put your block in the middle.* | |
| *M:* Ah hayee. | |
| *Mo:* Put your block in— | |
| **SISTER AND MARY** | |
| *Si:* Give me this; give me that. | S grabs the stick and block out of M's hand one at a time, puts her hand briefly on M's hand, then touches the blocks, then touches the truck in pointing gesture. |
| All right; take these, put them in the truck; take the blocks and put them in the truck; *Come on take the* block. | *S puts her hand on M's arm and lifts it over to the block and onto the block;* M holds onto a block briefly. |
| **FATHER AND MARY** | |
| *Fa:* I'm not gonna talk to you unless you get the ball. *Now you go over there and get the ball. Come on Mary.* | Fa sitting on chair, M standing by his knee. Fa moves slightly away from M and puts one hand under his chin. *Fa puts hand on M's shoulder and pushes her toward the* table; lets go of her. |

**Table 4**
Stimuli and Responses

| Stimuli | Responses |
| --- | --- |
| A sudden loud noise: a shout, a knock on the door, a clapping of hands, etc. | Often causes Mary to turn toward the source of the noise, stop what she is doing, look and walk toward the source |
| A sudden movement within her peripheral vision | Often causes Mary to look in that direction, pause |
| A person reaching out to Mary, hand out, palm open, or arms outstretched | Often causes Mary to move toward that person or reach out with her hand |
| A person slapping her or shaking her suddenly | Often causes Mary to pause, orient herself, look at the person, make a face |
| Having an object placed close to her while she's watching | Often causes Mary to look at it, touch it, explore it, pick it up, or put it to her mouth |
| A person walking away | Often Mary will follow |
| Being near a door knob | Often Mary will touch and fiddle with it |

**Table 5**
Semantic Crediting

| Verbal Exchange | Movements |
| --- | --- |
| MOTHER AND MARY | |
| Mo: Come on. (knock on door) | |
| I think somebody wants to get in. Do you wanna open the door? | M looks around and Mo stands up. M reaches for Mo's hand. Mo pulls away and points to the door. |
| Open the door. | M goes to the doorknob and puts both hands on it and twists it. Mo opens the door. |
| Mo: Come on. Get up (whisper). Get up (fierce). Get up (enunciated). | Mo seated by the table, M lying on the floor fiddling with the blocks in her hand. *Mo taps M's foot, then holds out hand close to M.* M lolls on floor, *slowly gets up.* |
| FATHER AND MARY | |
| Fa: You sit in my lap. Come on. | Fa sitting on chair, his hands on his knees, M walking toward him; holds his hands out toward her; she backs off and leans back against a chair. |
| M: Euuuhhn. | |
| Fa: I don't care *whether you* want to; *come on.* | *Fa reaches out with hand, almost touching M,* she raises a leg, then *touches his hand briefly with her own.* He takes hold and picks her up onto lap. |
| SISTER AND MARY | |
| Si: Mary— | Si sitting on chair, M next to her. M drops block out of truck, Si reaches over and picks it up, puts it back in the truck, *slaps M's hand while looking at her face; M looks up at her for a moment.* |
| Hey. | |
| Now listen! | |

triggering items almost invariably occurred in a semantically meaningful configuration created ambiguity as to precisely which features of the environment Mary was reacting to. Insofar as attention was displaced to the utterance accompanying a triggering event or gesture, such as an outstretched arm, it appeared that Mary was able to understand the verbal message, when in fact she was simply responding to a behavioral cue. Table 5 furnishes examples of how these cues might be embedded in or accompanied by a verbal message thereby permitting the inference that Mary's subsequent activity was in response to the meaning of the utterance.

The inference that one would make about Mary's mental acuity would vary dramatically according to which stimulus one considered to be the crucial one: the verbal request or the accompanying cues. The familial claim, of course, was that she understood the words spoken to her and that her competence far exceeded the level of responsiveness involved in merely reaching for an outstretched hand or turning to a loud noise.

### Putting Words in Mary's Mouth

Perhaps the most dramatic, and the most difficult to understand, set of practices were those by which the family created the semblance of Mary's linguistic competence. From the point of hearing of an outside observer-listener, Mary's utterances were interactionally capricious and unintelligible and without promise of any sort of cryptointelligibility. Family members, on the other hand, were insistent that Mary spoke and spoke well, albeit not always and not everywhere. Although it is difficult to specify precisely what family members heard and how they came to hear it, we have located certain interactional styles that seemed to contribute to the image that Mary responded at a timely and appropriate place in a conversational sequence, that she responded intelligently and intelligibly, and that what she said was intersubjectively available. We shall comment on but one aspect of the interactional patterns by which the family sustained the myth of Mary's interactional skill.

Often, when Mary made an utterance, a family member would repeat what Mary said. But, of course, they did not repeat it at all, for they would babble were they to do so. More precisely, then, when family members "repeated," they were actually creating a novel, intelligent utterance and stating it as though they were repeating what they had heard Mary say or imply. While putting words in Mary's mouth, they implicitly claimed that she was putting her words in theirs. Table 6 presents several examples of such "statement by restatement." They were excerpted from a

**Table 6**

Putting Words in Mary's Mouth

1. Mary is wearing a newly bought robe.
*Fa:* Want to see it in the mirror?
*M:* [Gurgling].
*Fa:* She doesn't like it.
*Mo:* You don't like the robe? It fits you.
*M:* [Gurgling].
*Mo:* What did you say about Daddy?
*M:* Mmmmmmm, [gurgle].
*Fa:* She thinks it's too cheap!

2. Encouraging her to talk into the recorder:
*Fa:* OK, you tell me your name and age into that thing, and I'll give you $5 to go out and buy a present that you want to buy yourself.
*M:* [Gurgling].
*Fa:* Your name and age—
*M:* Goo ga [gurgle].
*Fa:* She's bargaining with me for more money!

3. Later:
*Mo:* Time for your pills, Mary.
*M:* Mmmmm.
*Mo:* Time for your pills.
*M:* [Gurgling].
*Mo:* You don't think you need them.
*M:* Mmmmm, ga.
*Mo:* I think you need them.

tape Mary's family made at home and offered as somewhat unsatisfactory (to them) evidence of Mary's competence.

Although we are unable to specify how family members were prompted to "repeat" precisely what they chose to "repeat," we can appreciate one of the possible functions of these procedures for the collective, sense-making enterprise. Specifically, such practices introduced a degree of determinacy and integrity to Mary's talk and allowed family consensus on what Mary has said. In "repeating," or heavily implying the meaning of

Mary's utterance by their response, family members were in fact creating and broadcasting the meaning. If we are not mistaken, such work allowed the family to avoid embarrassing disagreements, to perpetuate the fiction that Mary was speaking intelligibly, and to develop a shared version of precisely what Mary said.

### Explaining in the "Bright" Direction

Although the previously described practices often succeeded in imparting an aura of intelligence and responsiveness to Mary's behaviors, they also provided opportunities for behaviors to be specifically and recognizably inadequate. A parentally inaugurated game of catch, for example, generated the possibility of "missing" or "dropping" the ball over and over and over again. Thus, the practices were not a guarantee of the semblance of competence; they could become methods for displaying incompetence. Indeed, there were a number of occasions on which family members found Mary's behavior remiss, in error, or unresponsive. But such occasions did not result in attributions of incompetence. On the contrary, members could transform these episodes into evidence of Mary's sophistication.

Almost any system of belief is capable of furnishing secondary elaborations that will preserve the sense of the system's validity in the face of seemingly discrediting or subversive evidence. The belief in Mary's competence was protected by a network of such "epicyclical" explanations (Polanyi, 1964; Pollner & Wikler, 1979). Mary's ostensible failures were continuously reinterpreted as successes of sorts or else explained away as the product of normal transient mood shifts or lapses of attention. Thus, for example, instances in which Mary's behavior seemed to defy interpretation as a directly responsive action were treated as the product of Mary's postulated proclivity toward "teasing" and "pretending." Indeed, the fact that psychiatric staff had one version of Mary and her family another was attributed to Mary's fak-

**Table 7**
Explaining in the Bright Direction

| | |
|---|---|
| *Fa:* | Go get the ball, Mary. |
| *M:* | Eigaga. |
| *Fa:* | Come on, Mary, go get the ball. |
| | Come on, come on, go get the ball. |
| | You're not being the least bit cooperative, Mary, you just lie there; okay, you going to sleep? |
| | Come on, get me the ball. |
| | The ball, Mary. |
| *M:* | Ummm. |
| *Fa:* | Hey, I don't care whether you want to or not; do you want to get belted? Go get the ball! Come on. |
| | Come on, Mary. |
| *M:* | Uhnn. |
| *Fa:* | Huh? |
| *M:* | Ewaiuhh. |
| *Fa:* | Mary, you're making it harder on yourself. Come on. |
| | Come on with me, and I'll go over and get the ball with you. |
| | Give me your hand. |
| *M:* | Guheaa. |
| *Fa:* | You're being a bad girl, Mary. |
| *M:* | Agaa. |

ing or malingering. Other failures were explained away by the family as products of orneriness, lack of cooperation, or momentary inattentiveness, as in the interaction between Mary and her father presented in Table 7.

In effect, the belief "Mary is competent" functioned as an "incorrigible assumption" (Gasking, 1965), that is, as an assumption that would not be withdrawn or reevaluated in light of empirical events. Instead, empirical events were interpreted so as to render them compatible with the fundamental claim "Mary is competent." The net effect of such explanatory and descriptive practices was to inhibit the growth of what could have been an enormous catalogue of incompetence. Each instance was explained away in a fashion congenial to the basic belief. Indeed, insofar as "faking" or "cheating" are higher-level activities requiring sophisticated reflections and interpersonal manipulations, there is a sense in which ostensible failures ultimately served to enhance Mary's image among family members.

## Discussion

In a more literal sense than is usually intended, a *folie à famille* makes and lives in its own little world. We have attempted to examine some of the practices through which that world or *nomos* is reproduced and maintained. Although we have succeeded in identifying several practices, questions and issues abound both with respect to the case at hand and *folie à famille* generally.

The first issue is the extent to which the practices discerned were characteristic of the family's routine transactions with Mary. The videotapes were made in a clinic waiting room with several staff members behind a one-way mirror making consequential decisions on the basis of what they observed. It is a difficult task in general and an impossible one in this case, given the absence of materials on routine family relations, to assess the correspondence between performance in clinical and nonclinical settings. It is quite easy on the other hand to imagine ways in which the relation might be problematic, that is, the ways in which family performance in the clinic might have been different from interaction in the home. The very request to interact with Mary under the gaze of others, for example, might have induced a level of self-consciousness and an intensity of effort uncharacteristic of interaction in the home. It is also possible that Mary herself was different in the home. This, of course, was the claim of the family.

Although every piece of clinical information weighed against the competence attributed to Mary by the family, the familiarity of household objects and routines may have contributed to higher levels of displayed competence than observed in the clinic. These are possibilities that defy closure owing to the limits of our materials.

A related issue is the extent to which family members believed or experienced their version of Mary. It is possible if not plausible that family members varied in the depth and nature of their acceptance of the delusional content (Evans & Marskey, 1972). Although again our materials preclude closure, it is of interest to note that family members varied in the adroitness with which they were able to create the aura of Mary's competence for observers—and perhaps for themselves. Mary's mother, for example, by virtue of her active involvement with Mary could achieve a more convincing display of Mary's competence than any other family member. The possibility of various depths and types of commitments to the family delusion means that, although some may have been true believers, others may have had to be continually though implicitly urged to voice the family line and to partake of the appropriate practices. Thus a comprehensive analysis of the "how" of the maintenance of shared delusion would explicate the interactional dynamics by which members are rewarded for honoring the family *doxa* and castigated for heretical tendencies.[3]

A final issue of consequence focuses on the origin of these practices. And although once again we plead limitations of materials, our reflections have taken us to a point suggesting that reformulation of the nature of the practice of delusion may be in order. Initially focused on the "how" of delusion, we did not have well-articulated notions regarding the origin of these practices save for the assumption that they were mobilized or developed in the interest of sustaining a belief that was important in the interpersonal and intrapersonal dynamics of family members. In effect, we regarded the practices and, for that matter, the belief itself as more or less *de novo* creations. As we completed the bulk of our analysis, we noted that the practices we discerned were similar to those many parents seem to employ with their preverbal children. Parent-infant interaction is replete with episodes in which adults playfully treat the child's babbling as an intelligent and complex utterance or manipulate the child through complex sequences of activity while praising the child for the excellence of her performance or describe whatever the child is doing at a particular moment as though it were an intentional project of the child (Bruner, 1983; Lock, 1981; Wertsch, 1978). In the language of our report, interaction between adults and preverbal children is replete with "putting words in the child's mouth," "puppeteering," and "framing."[4]

The similarity between observed family practices and those characteristic of adult/young-child interaction suggests the origins of the former. It may be that family practices are not novel creations but a perseveration of once appropriate practices. Mary's family may have initially interacted with Mary in the fashion that all families interact with infants in the preverbal stage. Somehow those practices persisted despite the fact that Mary was now over five years old and had not acquired the skills and competencies appropriate for her age. Given this possibility, it is not that the family constructs a new world so much as they refuse to relinquish an old one. Accordingly, the question of interest may not be how did the practices originate, but rather how do they endure.

A detailed explication of the processes that might promote the perseveration of "outmoded" practices is beyond the scope of this paper, though some features may be portrayed in a few broad strokes. Consider that families will often have good reason for disattending or otherwise not confronting an actual loss, such as the decline of the position, prestige, or competence of one of its members or the loss of some anticipated state of affairs such as a successful career, happy family life, or healthy child. The psychological and interpersonal costs of addressing such losses may be great. The loss may touch on the foundations of a person's sense of self, other family members' sense of him, family members' relation to one another, and even their relations to others outside the nuclear family. Accordingly, there may be attempts to evade or forestall directly confronting the nature and significance of the loss. There are, of course, a variety of ways to accomplish this. Family members may tacitly agree not to talk about the matter. In other instances, perhaps especially when the loss is not (yet) definitive or clear-cut, the family may persevere in the practices and outlook characteristic of the preloss period—the husband is on the verge of success; we are a happy family; our daughter is a healthy, normal child. Permeated by the sense of catastrophe on the one hand and of hope on the other, these "little tribes in distress" (First, 1975) may continue to do what they have always done.

Depending upon the nature of the threatened loss, old practices may be retained for indefinite lengths of time without confronting directly contradictory or disconfirming information. As the hoped-for reality recedes into the horizon and the dreaded loss becomes actual, however, the retention of old practices means that the family enters a sham world or, more to the point, is left with a sham world (Henry, 1973). Initial participation in sham may have an accelerating effect: A little sham leads to a lot of sham as family members become reluctant and perhaps unable to cease the fiction for fear not only of calling attention to the lost object but also for fear of acknowledging that for the past few minutes, weeks, years, they have been living a fiction. Shamming after all is shameful, particularly with loved ones, and thus participants may find that having taken one step into this world they must take another—and cover their tracks.

## Conclusion

*Folie à deux* (or "shared delusion") is often catalogued among the more exotic pathologies, involving as it does several individuals—the classical number, of course, is two—who share and participate in the same delusional system (Wikler, 1980). Though there may be many differences between these little tribes and other collectivities, the commitment to beliefs whose foundation in reality is problematic is not in itself a distinguishing criterion. As Berger (1969) has noted, all collectivities construct a meaningful order or *nomos*, and every *nomos* is erected in the face of chaos and "irreality." Although it would be naïve and misleading to treat *folie à deux* as nothing but a variant of the *nomos*-building processes characteristic of other groups, there is heuristic value in underscoring the fact that these groups develop meaningful worlds that, like all such symbolic constructs, must be nourished and protected through specific practices of reasoning, speaking, and acting.

In an earlier work, Wikler (1980) explored some of the clinically relevant features of this particular case for family therapists, as an example of the syndrome of *folie à famille*. In this paper, we have examined the practices through which a family, diagnosed as *folie à famille*, sustained its world. Our analysis led us to suggest that some forms of "delusion" may involve not the construction of novel symbolic realms but the buttressing of old ones. Although it is highly unlikely that all forms of *folie à deux* originate through retention of outmoded practice, it is plausible and in keeping with the ubiquitousness of the phenomena (Ferreira, 1963; Gralnick, 1942; Greenberg, 1954; Wikler, 1980) to consider the possibility that, in some instances, shared "delusions" arise not as the consequence of an elected or induced set of practices and beliefs that fly in the face of reality but as a result of reality flying away from an established set of practices and anticipations.[5] Whether this interpretation extends beyond the current case awaits detailed descriptions of the processes by which families create their worlds and respond to the inevitable tremors.

## Notes

1. The social constructionist attitude does not provide privileged exemptions for "expert" or "scientific" constructions of reality. The tacit practices by which clinicians develop, coordinate, use, and defend their versions of reality are as amenable to analysis as those of the families they study. For certain clinical purposes, however, it is necessary to avoid what can turn into an infinitely regressing form of analysis (as when, say, an analysis of the social construction of reality is itself viewed as a construction). Nevertheless, the ceaseless relativism inherent in the constructionist perspective is useful in that it heightens appreciation of the tacit commitments and practices implicated in the development of one's own "authoritative" version of "what really happened."

2. Extensive background and biographical information as well as transcripts of the audiotapes and videotapes used in this report are available in Wikler (1976).

3. The work of Henry (1973) and Goode (1980) provides examples of the kind of "clinical ethnography" necessary to get at family dynamics as they occur in the home setting.

4. In an unpublished paper, David Helm suggests these practices may be characteristic of interaction with any person whose verbal capacity or intelligence is perceived as limited, impaired, or otherwise problematic. A number of colleagues have suggested that similar practices are found in interaction with pets. An unusual development in this regard is a recent critical review of the research on the linguistic ability of primates. Umiker-Sebeok and Sebeok (1980) argue that ostensibly positive evidence may be more an artifact of researchers' procedures and interpretations than a reflection of genuine linguistic competence. Several of the practices identified by the Sebeoks

as the source of artifactual evidence are remarkably similar to the practices described in this report. The Sebeoks note, for example, some of the "no-forfeit" practices through which a primate's signing behaviors, no matter how unusual, are treated as evidence of linguistic ability—anomalous signs are interpreted as jokes, insults, or metaphors. In characterizing the immediate social context of talking primate projects, the Sebeoks all but state the possibility of a *folie à famille*. A team constitutes "a tightly knit social community with a solid core of shared beliefs and goals in opposition to outside visitors, as well as against groups elsewhere which are competing for scarce research resources" (pp. 7–8). The research teams, they indicate, are often led by investigators married to one another (e.g., the Gardners, Premacks, and Rumbaughs), with graduate students and younger colleagues serving as "uncles and aunts" of the subjects.

5. One implication of this portrayal of the path to *folie à famille* is that it is continuous and does not require reference to any qualitatively distinct psychological traits that dispose or propel individuals on their way. This is a problematic assumption, and it may be that there is a crevice between preservation of old practices and "delusion," across which one can leap only if propelled by, say, dependency needs of extreme intensity. It may, however, be worth considering that the point at which the leap occurs is much further away from home base than previously thought and that many families take the path a goodly distance before encountering the schism.

## References

Berger, P. (1969). *The sacred canopy*. Garden City, NY: Doubleday.

Berger, P., & Kellner, H. (1970). Marriage and the construction of reality. In H. P. Dreitzel (Ed.), *Recent sociology* (No. 2). New York: Macmillan.

Bruner, J. (1983). *Child's talk. Learning to use language*. New York and London: Norton.

Cicourel, A. V. (1973). *Cognitive sociology: Language and meaning in social interaction*. Harmondsworth, UK: Penguin.

Evans, P., & Marskey, H. (1972). Shared beliefs of dermal parasitosis: Folie partagée. *Brit. J. Med. Psychol., 45*, 19–26.

Ferreira, J. (1963). Family myth and homeostasis. *Arch. Gen. Psychiat., 9*, 457–463.

First, E. (1975). The new wave in psychiatry. *New York Review of Books, 22*, 8–15.

Garfinkel, H. (1967). *Studies in ethnomethodology*. Englewood Cliffs, NJ: Prentice-Hall.

Gasking, D. (1965). Mathematics and the world. In A. Flew (Ed.), *Logic and language*. Garden City, NY: Doubleday.

Goode, D. (1980). Behavioral sculpting: Parent-child interaction in families with retarded children. In J. Jacobs (Ed.), *Phenomenological approaches to mental retardation*. Springfield, IL: Charles C Thomas.

Gralnick, A. (1942). Folie à deux—The psychosis of association. A review of 103 cases and the entire English literature: With case presentations. *Psychiat. Quart., 16*, 230–263, 491–520.

Greenberg, P. H. (1954). Folie à deux. *Guy's Hospital Reports, 4*, 381–392.

Henry, J. (1973). *Pathways to madness*. New York: Vintage.

Lock, A. J. (Ed.). (1981). *Action, gesture and symbol: The emergence of language*. London: Academic Press.

Polanyi, M. (1964). *Personal knowledge*. New York: Harper & Row.

Pollner, M. (1975). "The very coinage of your brain": The anatomy of reality disjunctures. *Philos. Soc. Sci., 5*, 411–430.

Pollner, M., & Wikler, L. (1979). "Cognitive enterprise" in einem Fall von Folie à Famille. In H. G. Soeffner (Ed.), *Interpretative Verfahren in den Sozial—und Textwissenschaften*. Stuttgart: J. B. Metzler.

Pulver, S. E., & Brunt, M. Y. (1961). Deflection of hostility in folie à deux. *Arch. Gen. Psychiat., 5*, 257–265.

Reiss, D. (1981). *The family's construction of reality*. Cambridge, MA: Harvard University Press.

Rosenberg, J. B., & Lindblad, M. B. (1978). Behavior therapy in a family context. *Fam. Proc., 17*, 77–82.

Schegloff, E. A. (1968). Sequencing in conversational openings. *Am. Anthrop., 70*, 1075–1095.

Umiker-Sebeok, J., & Sebeok, T. A. (1980). Introduction: Questioning apes. In J. Umiker-Sebeok & T. A. Sebeok (Eds.), *Speaking of apes*. New York: Plenum.

Wertsch, J. V. (1978). Adult-child interaction and the roots of metacognition. *Quarterly News-*

*letter of the Institute for Comparative Human Development*, 2, 15–18.

Wikler, L. (1976). *Delusions of competence: A sociobehavioral study of the maintenance of a deviant belief system in a family with a retarded child.* Unpublished doctoral dissertation, University of California, Irvine.

Wikler, L. (1980). Folie à famille: A family therapist's perspective. *Fam. Proc., 19,* 257–268.

# Commentary

# The Social Construction of Reality:
# The Passion Within Us All

## *David Reiss*

This case report by Pollner and McDonald-Wikler is both arresting and poignant. It shares with other beautifully rendered case reports a subtle and complex inner coherence that makes it highly evocative—both intellectually and emotionally. But the interest of this report is much more specific. It deeply etches an image of a family trying to make sense of what most of us would see as a great tragedy. It also shows, in clear detail, the intricate and complex maneuvers the family uses to construct its version of events. One of the great strengths of this report is that, in a short space, and by the use of only one case, it helps evoke a sense of the universality of these processes of reality construction. Indeed, most readers will be quick to recognize similar processes—perhaps less dramatic—in many families they know. Likewise, and here Pollner and McDonald-Wikler are quite explicit in drawing inferences—similar processes may be observed in professional groups (see, for example, their pregnant note 4). If the social construction of reality is universal—if it resides in all groups with a sustained history—what makes this family so unique? Why did it at first attract a long parade of specialists at the Neuropsychiatric In-

stitute; why again did it absorb the meticulous attention of Pollner and McDonald-Wikler; and finally, why have we, as readers, become so riveted to this account? Three features of this family, it seems to me, make it particularly notable. These three features expose some of the ramifications of this family's construction of reality—ramifications that are of central importance to clinician and researcher alike.

First is the *sequestration* of this family. Their construction of reality is, without question, radically different from that of the social context in which they are observed. The Neuropsychiatric Institute had a very different vision, although there must have been a bit of unshakiness to prompt such a long parade of specialists past this family. This family would cotton to none of it. They held to their own construction and (although it is not reported here) must have held themselves, in some measure, aloof. To sustain such a particular or unique view of their youngest child's competence, the family must have had to maintain a highly structured and attenuated tie with their ordinary workaday world, as well as with the care-giving community. Indeed, it is not hard to imagine that most outsiders were viewed with animus and suspicion. Any form of therapeutic alliance with them, any form of "joining," would be an almost impossible dream.

A second feature is the highly structured, almost ritualized *focus and organization around a single individual*. The processes within this family cannot be grasped without the full appreciation that every experiential and transactional detail must take account of the family's vision of Mary. Although the report does not detail it, we may be confident that interactions among others—even when they do not involve Mary—must somehow take the vision of a competent Mary into account. Brother and sister cannot, in some secluded privacy, acknowledge to each other that the whole enterprise is a sham. Even their most intimate moments with each other—and of the mother and father with each other—must be regulated by a common construction of Mary.

Finally, and perhaps most important, the family's vision engages us by the power of its combined *vividness and simplicity*. To be sure, some of the tactics and maneuvers that support this vision are extraordinarily subtle: Pollner and McDonald-Wikler reviewed videotapes many times just to identify, let alone explain, some of them. But the vision itself is disarmingly potent: Mary has a normal intellect but an uncanny knack for fooling outsiders. This view is starkly simple: A small number of postulates ("incorrigible assumptions") are used to explain everything. Paradoxically, the powerful explanatory function of these postulates requires incredible ingenuity, subtlety, and complexity, as the report clearly demonstrates.

These three features that captivate us may give some clue to the underlying mechanisms. Pollner and McDonald-Wikler provide an intriguing start. They note that the family's transactions with Mary may be typical of transactions most families engage in with preverbal children. The family's folly, they speculate, is some grotesque development arrest. The three formal features I have noted give a hint about what might fuel this developmental arrest. Let us briefly reconsider each feature.

*Sequestration.* As several of us have argued, all families engage in some form of idiosyncratic or particular construction of reality (Berger & Kellner, 1964; Reiss, 1981; Kantor & Lehr, 1975; Kantor & Neal, 1985; Strodtbeck, 1958). Indeed, I have suggested that each family can be recognized by a characteristic signature or special construction I have called the "family paradigm." But few families take the burden of construction so exclusively on themselves. Families are embedded in larger social systems: extended families, communities, institutions, and (where they are not hopelessly vitiated) even cultures and religions. It is rare to find a family devoted to such a singular synthetic effort without contextual support (although there may be hidden grandmothers or cults in this clinical picture that are helping to "normalize" this child). One must stand in awe, then, at the extraordinary *creativity, energy, and responsibility* of this family.

*Focus on an Individual.* Again, most families develop particular and, at times, uniquely creative visions of reality, but they are rarely so centered on an individual. When they are, we are most familiar with *degrading* constructions: scapegoating and the attribution of incompetence, illness, or "craziness" to one member. It is much more rare to encounter the elevation or *consecration* of a family member. As clinicians, we are familiar with the dynamics of degradations. See, for example, Eric Bermann's (1973) marvelous depiction of a family that scapegoated a young boy: they saw him as bumbling and incompetent in order to deflect family anxiety from an impending open heart operation for father. Degradation usually involves putting the worst of ourselves into an unfortunate family member. On the other hand, consecration must involve putting the best of ourselves into another; perhaps in this case it was the dreams and aspirations for the future that the family did not dare grasp for themselves when Mary showed signs of a developmental lag. Ironically, perhaps, these dreams became invested in her. But this investment, whatever projective forces are at work, is highly *disciplined*. *All* family members must gear transactions with each other and the outside world to maintain this consecration even if they must subordinate their own interests to do so.

*Vividness and Explanatory Power.* Nothing conveys the full creative and disciplined force of this family better than the remarkable vividness of their shared percept and its power to explain everything. Such a sweeping explanatory power gives the family a sense of meaning, but it also strikes the observer with special force. This family cannot be discounted; they cannot be consigned to the looney bin. It seems to me no accident that the literature has so many descriptions of *folie à deux, folie à trois,* or *folie à famille.* People are shaken, genuinely shaken, by their encounters with such social systems, just as they are shaken by encounters with messianic cults and radical political groups. The power of the explanation to shake us gives us a hint of its force for providing meaning and control to the family. Typically, family constructions are more implicit, more delicately interwoven with broader constructions of a broader social community, and less simplistic. They create meaning through tying together a silken fabric of memories and experiences but do not usually generate a preemptive, fully conscious, explanatory concept.

It seems to me no accident that these very same features—sequestration coupled with extreme creativity, disciplined focus on a single individual, and the force of a vivid, explanatory system—are also features of another form of social group. Griffith and Mullins (1972) summarized a large body of sociological observation of radical scientific groups from the phage workers at Cold

spring Harbor to the Skinnerians at Harvard to the ethnomethodologists at UCLA (one suspects that the authors of this paper are direct lineal descendants of the last of these three).[1] They drew special attention to three features of these groups. First was their sequestration. As they created their own singular vision of reality, they cut themselves off from the everyday workday of their parent disciplines. For example, as these groups developed, they cited each other's work more and more and the rest of the literature less and less. Their work was galvanized around a single individual. Group process required individual subordination to a view attached or identified with one person in particular. The example is clearest with the Skinnerians, but the ethnomethodologists rallied around Garfinkel as did the phage group around Delbruck. Finally, the views had remarkable, perhaps sweeping, explanatory power: relatively simple and stark axioms or principles extended across continents and dealt effectively with objections from those outside the group.

It would trivialize both radical science and the pathos of Mary and her family to draw the parallels here too tightly. I want to emphasize only one point. The constructivist position that Mary's family forces us to take contains within it a critical clinical "stance" (Kantor & Neal, 1985). The principle that reality is what we make it is not an apologia or a curse. That reality is constructed through the actions of social groups is not a degradation of the concept of reality but a consecration of groups. In this case, it generates awe rather than ridicule for Mary's family. As clinicians, we will want in some way to employ the creative energy, discipline, and responsibility inherent in the constructions of this family. By recognizing the dedicated passion with which we create our own reality, we can, without converting them or ourselves, appreciate the zeal of Mary and her family.

But a somber footnote must be added. Mary's family is not a radical scientific group. In the end, their vision will not be sustained by the accolades of an appreciative community of colleagues. Elsewhere (Reiss, 1981) I have presented evidence suggesting that a family's own construction of reality cannot be sustained by the family alone. In the words of Piaget, the constructions of the broader social world are indispensable "ailment" for the family's own constructions. Indeed, the family is sustained by, and contributes to, the constructions of the community in which it lives. The Neuropsychiatric Institute will provide no succor for this construction. Barring membership in a cult that in some way reveres mentally retarded children, this family seems headed for a fall of enormous pain and disorganization. I would amend Pollner and McDonald-Wikler's fundamental question. They ask, "How do they do it?" I ask, "How long can they keep it up?"

## Note

1. I will leave it to the reader's imagination to spot similar parallels with the charismatic groups significant in the history of family therapy. For those who need some prodding for their imagination, see the recent analysis by Kantor and Neal (1985).

## References

Berger, P. L., & Kellner, H. (1964). Marriage and the construction of reality. *Diogenes, 64,* 1–25.

Bermann, E. (1973). *Scapegoat.* Ann Arbor: University of Michigan Press.

Griffith, B. C., & Mullins, H. C. (1972). Coherent social groups in scientific change. *Science, 177,* 959–964.

Kantor, D., & Lehr, W. (1975). *Inside the family.* San Francisco: Jossey-Bass.

Kantor, D., & Neal, J. H. (1985). Integrative shifts for the theory and practice of family systems therapy. *Fam. Proc., 24,* 13–30.

Reiss, D. (1981). *The family's construction of reality.* Cambridge, MA: Harvard University Press.

Strodtbeck, F. L. (1958). Family interaction, values and achievement. In D. C. McClelland, A. L. Baldwin, & U. Bronfenbrenner (Eds.), *Talent and society.* Princeton, NJ: Van Nostrand.

# Self-Fulfilling Prophecies

## *Paul Watzlawick*

A self-fulfilling prophecy is an assumption or prediction that, purely as a result of having been made, causes the expected or predicted event to occur and thus confirms its own "accuracy." For example, if someone assumes, for whatever reason, that he is not respected, he will, because of this assumption, act in such a hostile, overly sensitive, suspicious manner that he brings about that very contempt in others which "proves" again and again his firmly entrenched conviction. This mechanism may be commonplace and well known, but it is based upon a number of facts that are by no means part of our everyday thinking and which have a profound significance for our view of reality.

In our traditional cause-and-effect thinking we usually see event $B$ as the result of a preceding, causal event ($A$)—which in turn has, of course, its own causes, just as the occurrence of $B$ produces its own sequel of events. In the sequence $A \rightarrow B$, $A$ is therefore the cause and $B$ its effect. The causality is *linear* and $B$ follows $A$ in the course of time. Accordingly, in this causality model, $B$ can have no effect on $A$, because this would mean a reversal of the flow of time: The present ($B$)

would have to exert a backward effect on the past ($A$).

Matters stand differently in the following example: In March 1979, when the newspapers in California began to publish sensational pronouncements of an impending, severe gasoline shortage, California motorists stormed the gas stations to fill up their tanks and to keep them as full as possible. This filling up of 12 million gasoline tanks (which up to this time had on the average been 75% empty) depleted the enormous reserves and so brought about the predicted shortage practically overnight. The endeavor to keep the fuel containers as full as possible (instead of getting gas when the tank was almost empty, as had been done before) resulted in endless lines and hours of waiting time at the gas stations, and increased the panic. After the excitement died down, it turned out that the allotment of gasoline to the state of California had hardly been reduced at all.

Here the customary cause-and-effect thinking breaks down. The shortage would never have occurred if the media had not predicted it. In other words, an event that had not yet taken place (i.e., an event in the future) created an effect in the present (the storming of the gas stations), which in turn caused the predicted event to become reality. In this sense it was the future—not the past—that determined the present.

The objection could be raised that all of this is neither astonishing nor unheard of. Are not almost all human decisions and actions largely dependent on the evaluation of their probable effects, advantages, and dangers (or at least should they not be)? Does not the future therefore always play a part in the present? Significant as these questions may be, they do not seem to make much sense here. Whoever tries, usually on the basis of earlier experience, to evaluate the future effect of his decision normally intends the best possible outcome. The specific action tries to take the future into consideration, and subsequently proves to be true or false, correct or incorrect; but it does not have to have any influence whatever on the course of events. However, an action that results from a self-fulfilling prophecy itself produces the requisite conditions for the occurrence of the expected event, and in this sense *creates* a reality which would not have arisen without it, The action that is at first neither true nor false produces a fact, and with it its own "truth."

Here are examples of both perspectives: If someone begins to suffer from headaches, sneezes, and shivers, he will, on the basis of past experience, assume that he is coming down with a cold; and if his diagnosis is correct, he can, with aspirin, hot drinks, and bedrest, favorably influence the (future) course of the illness by these means in the present. By doing so, he has correctly grasped a causal sequence that had at first been totally independent of him, and exerted a partial influence on it.

A fundamentally different sequence results from the practice of collecting taxes in certain countries. Since the revenue agency assumes a priori that no citizen will ever truthfully declare his income, the tax rate is dictated more or less arbitrarily. The revenue offices rely largely on the information of their assessment agents, who take into consideration such vague factors as a person's standard of living, his real estate property, the fur coats of his wife, the make of his car, and so forth. To the income, "ascertained" in this way, there is then added a certain percentage that is supposed to make up for any undeclared income, because—as we said—it is as-

sumed a priori that the taxpayer cheats. This assumption, however, produces the situation in which a truthful declaration of income becomes unacceptable even for an honest taxpayer, and in which dishonesty is practically made a necessity if one wants to escape unfair taxes. Again an assumption believed to be true creates the assumed reality, and again it is irrelevant whether the assumption was originally true or false. And so we see that the difference lies in the fact that, in the example of the head cold, a development that is already taking place in the present is acted upon as best as is possible, and its course is influenced in this way in the present; whereas in the examples of the gasoline shortage and the income tax the course of events is induced by the very measures which are undertaken as a (supposed) reaction to the expected event in question. Therefore what is supposed to be a *reaction* (the effect) turns out to be an action (the cause); the "solution" produces the problem; the prophecy of the event causes the event of the prophecy.

This singular reversal of cause and effect is particularly obvious in interpersonal conflicts, where the phenomenon of the so-called *punctuation* of a sequence of events is invariably present. Making use of an example that has already been employed elsewhere (Watzlawick, Bavelas, & Jackson, 1967, pp. 56–58), we will imagine a married couple struggling with a conflict that they both assume to be basically the other's fault, while their own behavior is seen only as a *reaction* to that of their partner. The woman complains that her husband is withdrawing from her, which he admits, but because he sees his silence or his leaving the room as the only possible reaction to her constant nagging and criticizing. For her this reasoning is a total distortion of the facts: His behavior is the *cause* of her criticism and her anger. Both partners are referring to the same interpersonal reality but assign to it a diametrically opposed causality. The diagram, Figure 1, may illustrate this discrepancy, although it

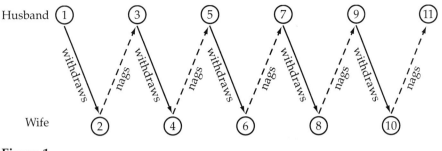

Husband ... Wife

**Figure 1**

postulates—unavoidably but wrongly—a starting point that does not really exist, because the behavior pattern between the two people has been repeating itself for a long time, and the question of who started it has long since become meaningless.

The arrows with the solid lines represent the behavior of the husband ("withdraws"), and the dotted lines that of the wife ("nags"). The husband dissects ("punctuates") the whole of the pattern into the triads 2-3-4, 4-5-6, 6-7-8, and so on, and so sees the interpersonal reality as one in which his wife nags (cause) and he *therefore* withdraws from her (effect). From her point of view, however, it is his cold passivity (cause) that causes her nagging (effect); she criticizes him *because* he withdraws from her, and therefore punctuates the pattern into the triads 1-2-3, 3-4-5, 5-6-7, and so on. With this opposed punctuation, both have literally brought about two contradictory realities and—what is perhaps even more important—two self-fulfilling prophecies. The two modes of behavior, which are seen subjectively as a reaction to the behavior of the partner, cause this very behavior in the other and "therefore" justify one's own behavior.

It goes without saying that self-fulfilling prophecies in an interpersonal context can also be used deliberately and with a specific intent. The dangers of this practice will be discussed later on. As an example here let me only mention the well-known method of former matchmakers in patriarchal societies, who had the thankless task of awakening a mutual interest in two young people, who possibly cared nothing for each other, because their families had decided that for financial reasons, social standing, or other similarly impersonal motives, the two would make a good couple. The matchmaker's usual procedure was to talk with the young man alone and ask him whether he had not noticed how the girl was always secretly watching him. Similarly, he would tell the girl that the boy was constantly looking at her when her head was turned. This prophecy, disguised as a fact, was often quickly fulfilled. Skilled diplomats also know this procedure as a negotiating technique.[1]

Everyday experience teaches us that only few prophecies are self-fulfilling, and the above examples should explain why: Only when a prophecy is believed, that is, only when it is seen as a fact that has, so to speak, already happened in the future, can it have a tangible effect on the present and thereby fulfill itself. Where this element of belief or conviction is absent, this effect will be absent as well. To inquire how the construction or acceptance of such a prophecy comes to be would go far beyond the scope of this essay. (An extensive study of the social, psychological, and physiological effects of self-fulfilling prophecies was published in 1974 by Jones.) Too numerous and various are the factors involved—from the realities one fabricates for oneself during the course of the so-called noncontingent reward experiments (Watzlawick, 1976, pp. 45–54) . . . , to such oddities as the (perhaps unverified, but not improbable) assertion that since Bernadette had a vision of the Virgin Mary in February of 1858, only pilgrims, but not a single inhabitant of Lourdes, found a miraculous cure there.

Of this story one can say, *se non è vero, è ben trovato*,[2] since it helps to build a bridge from our previous, somewhat trivial reflections to manifestations of self-fulfilling prophecies that have a deeper human as well as scientific significance.

The oracle had prophesied that Oedipus would kill his father and marry his mother. Horrified by this prediction, which he undoubtedly believed to be true, Oedipus tries to protect himself from the impending doom, but the precautionary measures themselves lead to the seemingly inescapable fulfillment of the oracle's dictum. As is known, Freud used this myth as a metaphor for the incestuous attraction for the opposite sex inherent in every child, and the consequent fear of retaliation on the part of the parent of the same sex; and he saw in this key constellation, the Oedipus conflict, the fundamental cause of later neurotic developments. In his autobiography the philosopher Karl Popper (1974) refers back to a self-fulfilling prophecy that he had already described two decades earlier and which he called the Oedipus *effect*:

One of the ideas I had discussed in *The Poverty* [*of Historicism*] was the influence of a prediction upon the event predicted. I had called this the "Oedipus effect," because the oracle played a most important role in the sequence of events which led to the fulfillment of its prophecy. (It was also an allusion to the psychoanalysts, who had been strangely blind to this interesting fact, even though Freud himself admitted that the very dreams dreamt by patients were often coloured by the theories of their analysts; Freud called them "obliging dreams.")

Again we have the reversal of cause and effect, past and future; but here it is all the more critical and decisive because psychoanalysis is a theory of human behavior that hinges on the assumption of a linear causality, in which the past determines the present.

And Popper points to the significance of this reversal by explicating further:

For a time I thought that the existence of the Oedipus effect distinguished the social from the natural sciences. But in biology too—even in molecular biology—expectations often play a role in bringing about what has been expected.

Similar quotations, referring to the effect of such "unscientific" factors as simple expectations and assumptions in the sciences, could be collated in abundance—[*The Invented Reality*] is itself intended as such a contribution. In this connection one might recall, for instance, Einstein's remark in a talk with Heisenberg: "It is the theory that determines what we can observe." And in 1958 Heisenberg himself says, "We have to remember that what we observe is not nature in itself, but nature exposed to our method of questioning." And more radical still, the philosopher of science Feyerabend (1978): "Not conservative, but anticipatory suppositions guide research."

Some of the most carefully documented and elegant investigations of self-fulfilling prophecies in the area of human communication are associated with the name of the psychologist Robert Rosenthal of Harvard University. Of particular interest here is his (1968) book with the appropriate title *Pygmalion in the Classroom*, in which he describes the results of his so-called Oak School experiments. They concerned a primary school with 18 women teachers and over 650 students [see Reading 38]. The self-fulfilling prophecy was induced in the members of the faculty at the beginning of a certain school year by giving the students an intelligence test whereby the teachers were told that the test could not only determine intelligence quotients, but could also identify those 20% of the students who would make rapid and above-average intellectual progress in the coming school year. After the intelligence test had been administered, but before the teachers had met their new students for the first time, they received the names (indiscriminately picked from the student list) of those students who supposedly, on the basis of the test, could be expected with certainty to perform unusually well. The difference between these children and the others thus existed solely in the heads of their particular teacher. The same intelligence test was repeated at the end of the school year for all students and showed *real* above-average increases in the intelligence quotients and achievements of these "special" students, and the reports of the faculty proved furthermore that these children distinguished themselves from their fellow students by their behavior, intellectual curiosity, friendliness, and so on.

Saint Augustine thanked God that he was not responsible for his dreams. Nowadays we do not have this comfort. Rosenthal's experiment is only one, although an especially clear example of how deeply and incisively our fellow human beings are affected by our expectations, prejudices, superstitions, and wishful thinking—all purely mental constructions, often without the slightest glimmer of actuality—and how these discoveries erode our comfortable conviction of the surpassing importance of heredity and innate characteristics. For it hardly needs to be expressly emphasized that these constructions can have negative as well as positive effects. We are not only responsible for our dreams, but also for the reality created by our hopes and thoughts.

It would, however, be a mistake to assume that self-fulfilling prophecies are restricted to human beings. Their effects reach deeper, into prehuman stages of development, and are in this sense even more alarming. Even before Rosenthal carried out his Oak School experiment, he reported in a book published in 1966 a similar experiment with rats that was repeated and confirmed by many scholars in the following years. Twelve participants in a laboratory course in experimental psychology were given a lecture on certain studies that purported to prove that good or bad test achievements of rats (for instance, in learning experiments in labyrinth cages) can become innate by selective breeding. Six of the students then received thirty rats whose genetic constitution allegedly made them especially good, intelligent laboratory subjects, while the other six students were assigned thirty rats of whom they were told the opposite, namely, that they were animals whose hereditary factors made them unsuitable for experiments. In fact and truth, the sixty rats were all of the same kind, the one that has always been used for such purposes. All sixty animals were then trained for exactly the same learning experiment. The rats whose trainers believed them to be especially intelligent did not just do better from the very outset, but raised their achievements far above that of the "unintelligent" animals. At the end of the five-day experiment the trainers were asked to evaluate their animals subjectively, in addition to the noted results of the experiments. The students who "knew" that they were working with unintelligent animals expressed themselves accordingly, that is, negatively, in their reports, whereas their colleagues, who had experimented with rats of supposedly above-average talents, rated their charges as friendly, intelligent, ingenious, and the like, and mentioned furthermore that they had often touched the animals, petted them, and even played with them. When we consider the surpassing role rat experiments play in experimental psychology and especially in the psychology of learning, and how often inferences are drawn from them to human behavior, these inferences now seem somewhat questionable.

Rats are known to be very intelligent animals, and the students' reports suggest that in the way they handled their animals, they literally "handed" them their assumptions and expectations. But the results of another research project, reported in 1963 by the research team Cordaro and Ison, suggest that it is not only a matter of such direct influence. In this project the laboratory subjects were earthworms (planaria), who are of great interest for the student of evolution and of behavior alike, in that they are the most primitive form of life possessing the rudiments of a brain. The supposition therefore suggested itself that these worms were capable of training of the simplest kind, as, for instance, a change in direction (to the left or to the right) upon arriving at the crossbeam of a T-shaped groove arrangement. Experiments of this kind began in several American universities in the late fifties. As in the rat experiments, Cordaro and Ison caused the experimenters to believe that they were working with especially intelligent or especially incapable worms, and even here, at this primitive stage of development (which, moreover, left little room for emotional attachment), there grew from the conviction, once it was established, objectively discernible and statistically significant differences in the experimental behavior of the planaria.[3]

For the very reason that these experiments undermine our basic concepts, it is all too easy to shrug them off and return to the comfortable certainty of our accustomed routines. That, for instance, test psychologists ignore these extremely disturbing results and continue to test people and animals with unmitigated tenacity and scientific "objectivity" is only a small example of the determination with which we defend ourselves when our world view is being threatened. The fact that we are responsible to the world in its entirety and to a much higher degree than is dreamed of in our philosophy is for the present almost unthinkable; but it can penetrate our consciousness through a better understanding of the processes of human communication—a study that will encompass many disciplines that heretofore have been either considered as being quite independent of each other or not considered at all. Rosenhan's contribution [see Reading 39] illuminates the alarming possibility that at least some so-called mental illnesses are nothing but constructions, and that the psychiatric institutions actually contribute to the constructions of those realities that are supposed to be treated therein. The chronic problem that still plagues modern psychiatry is that we have only the vaguest and most general concepts for the definition of mental health, while for the diagnosis of abnormal behavior there exist catalogs perfected to the last detail. Freud, for instance, used the concept of the ability to love and work as a basic criterion for mature emotional normalcy (a definition that does not do justice to a Hitler, on the one hand, or to the proverbial eccentricities of men of genius, on the other). The other medical specialties work with definitions of pathology that refer to certain deviations from fairly well-known normal functions of the healthy organism. Quite irrationally, in psychiatry it is just the opposite. Here pathology is considered the known factor, whereas normalcy is seen as difficult to define, if it is definable at all. This opens the floodgates to self-fulfilling diagnoses. There is a great number of very definite patterns of behavior that in the terminology of psychiatry are so tightly associated with certain diagnostic categories (again I refer to Rosenhan) that they virtually function like Pavlovian buzzers, not only in the thinking of the psychiatrist but also in the family environment of the patient. An attempt to show how certain specific forms of behavior take on the meaning of pathological manifestations on the basis of their cultural and societal significance, and how these manifestations in turn become self-fulfilling prophecies, would go beyond the scope of this essay. Of the already quite extensive literature on this topic, *The Manufacture of Madness* by Thomas Szasz (1970) is particularly notable. Suffice it to say that an essential part of the self-fulfilling effect of psychiatric diagnoses is based on our unshakable conviction that everything that has a name must *therefore* actually exist. The materializations and actualizations of psychiatric diagnoses probably originate largely from this conviction.

"Magic" diagnoses, in the actual sense of the word, have of course been known for a very long time. In his classic paper "Voodoo Death," the American physiologist Walter Cannon (1942) described a number of mysterious, sudden, and scientifically difficult to explain deaths that followed curses, evil spells, or the breaking of moral taboos. A Brazilian Indian, cursed by a medicine man, is helpless against his own emotional response to this death sentence and dies within hours. A young African hunter unknowingly kills and eats an inviolably banned wild hen. When he discovers his crime, he is overcome with despair and dies within twenty-four hours. A medicine man in the Australian bush points a bone with magic properties at a man. Believing that nothing can save him, the man sinks into lethargy and prepares to die. He is saved only at the last moment, when other members of the tribe force the witch doctor to remove the spell.

Cannon became convinced that voodoo death exists as a phenomenon,

characteristically noted among aborigines— among human beings so primitive, so superstitious, so ignorant, that they feel themselves bewildered strangers in a hostile world. Instead of knowledge, they have fertile and unrestricted imaginations which fill their environment with all manner of evil spirits capable of affecting their lives disastrously.

At the time when Cannon wrote these lines, hundreds of thousands of human beings who were neither superstitious nor ignorant had every reason to see themselves as bewildered victims of an unimaginably hostile world. From the haunted, shadowy world of the concentration camps Viktor Frankl (1959, pp. 74–75) reports a phenomenon that corresponds to voodoo death:

The prisoner who had lost faith in the future—his future—was doomed. With his loss of belief in the future, he also lost his spiritual hold; he let himself decline and became subject to mental and physical decay. Usually this happened quite suddenly, in the form of a crisis, the symptoms of which were familiar to the experienced camp inmate. We all feared this moment—not for ourselves, which would have been pointless, but for our friends. Usually it began with the prisoner refusing one morning to get dressed and wash or to

go out on the parade grounds. No entreaties, no blows, no threats had any effect. He just lay there.

One of Frankl's fellow prisoners lost his will to live when his own prediction, seen in a dream, did not come true and thereby became a negative self-fulfillment. "I would like to tell you something, Doctor," he said to Frankl,

I have had a strange dream. A voice told me that I could wish for something, that I should only say what I wanted to know, and all my questions would be answered. What do you think I asked? That I would like to know when the war would be over for me. You know what I mean, Doctor— for me! I wanted to know when we, when our camp, would be liberated and our sufferings come to an end. . . . Furtively he whispered to me, "March thirtieth."

But when the day of the prophesied liberation was near and the Allied forces were still far from the camp, things took a fateful turn for Frankl's fellow sufferer, the prisoner F.:

On March twenty-ninth, F. suddenly became ill and ran a high temperature. On March thirtieth, the day his prophecy had told him that the war and suffering would be over for him, he became delirious and lost consciousness. On March thirty-first, he was dead. He had died of typhus.

As a physician, Frankl understood that his friend died because

the expected liberation did not come and he was severely disappointed. This suddenly lowered his body's resistance against the latent typhus infection.

We admire human beings who face death calmly. Dying "decently," in a composed manner, without wrangling with the inevitable, was and is considered in most cultures an expression of wisdom and unusual maturity. All the more surprising and sobering therefore are the results of modern cancer research, which suggest that the mortality rate is higher in those patients who prepare themselves for death in a mature, serene way or who, like the concentration camp prisoner F., fall victim to a negative self-fulfilling prophecy. For those patients, however, who cling to life in a seemingly senseless, irrational, and immature way or who are convinced that they simply "cannot" or "must not" die because they have important work to do or family members to take care of, the prognosis is considerably more favorable. To the American oncologist Carl Simonton (1975), whose name is associated, above all, with the appreciation of the impact of emotional factors, now more and more recognized for their importance in the treatment of cancer, three things are of the utmost significance in this connection: the belief system of the patient, that of the patient's family, and, third, that of the attending physician. That each one of these belief systems can become a self-fulfilling prophecy seems credible in the light of what we have discussed so far. Furthermore, the studies and research reports about the susceptibility of the human immune system to mood swings, suggestions, and visual imagery (O. Simonton & S. Simonton, 1978; Solomon, 1969) are increasing.

How much can and should a physician tell his patients, not only about the gravity of their illnesses, but also about the dangers inherent in the treatment *itself?* At least in certain countries this question is becoming more and more rhetorical. The risk of getting hit with a malpractice suit because a patient has not been informed about his disease and its treatment down to the last technical detail causes many doctors in the United States, for example, to protect themselves in a way that can have serious consequences. The protection consists in asking the patient for a written consent to treatment in which the most catastrophic possible consequences of the illness and of the measures deemed necessary by the doctor are listed in every detail. It is not hard to imagine that this creates a kind of self-fulfilling prophecy that has a paralyzing effect on the confidence and will to recover of

even the most sanguine patient. Who has not read the description of even a seemingly harmless medication and then had the feeling of swallowing poison? How does the layman (or, presumably, even the professional) know that he is not going to be the fourth of the three fatalities reported to date that were inexplicably caused by a medication so far used safely by millions? But *fiat justitia, pereat mundus.*[4]

Since in the patient's eye a doctor is a kind of mediator between life and death, his utterances can easily become self-fulfilling prophecies. The astonishing degree to which this is possible is portrayed in a case reported (but unfortunately not sufficiently documented) by the American psychologist Gordon Allport (1964). What is unusual here is that a misunderstanding shifted the prophecy from death to life:

In a provincial Austrian hospital, a man lay gravely ill—in fact, at death's door. The medical staff had told him frankly that they could not diagnose his disease, but that if they knew the diagnosis they could probably cure him. They told him further that a famous diagnostician was soon to visit the hospital and that perhaps he could spot the trouble.

Within a few days the diagnostician arrived and proceeded to make the rounds. Coming to this man's bed, he merely glanced at the patient, murmured, "Moribundus," and went on.

Some years later, the patient called on the diagnostician and said, "I've been wanting to thank you for your diagnosis. They told me that if you could diagnose me I'd get well, and so the minute you said 'moribundus' I knew I'd recover."

Knowledge of the healing effect of positive predictions is undoubtedly just as ancient as faith in the inescapable consequences of curses and evil spells. Modern use of positive suggestions and autosuggestions ranges from the "I will recover; I feel better every day" of Emile Coué, through numerous forms of hypnotherapeutic interventions (Haley, 1973), to influencing the course of an illness—and not only cancer—by positive imagery. The extent to which such imagery that a (future) event has already taken place can reach into the physical realm is suggested by several studies according to which it is possible to increase a woman's chest measurement by an average of four to five centimeters through the use of certain self-hypnotic techniques (Staib & Logan, 1977; Willard, 1977). I mention these "successes" with all due skepticism and simply as curiosities testifying to the towering importance of the female breast in the North American erotic ethos.

Brief mention should also be made of the modern physiological and endocrinological studies that indicate more and more the possibility of stimulating the functions of the immune system of the human organism by certain experiences and that these functions are by no means completely autonomous (that is, outside conscious control), as was assumed until quite recently. Medical research is likely to make astonishing discoveries in this field in the near future. For instance, it is now known that the organism itself produces a number of morphene-like substances—the so-called endorphins (Beers, 1979)—that are analgesic and whose production is stimulated by certain emotional processes. There is thus a wide-open, unexplored territory in which the phenomenon of self-fulfilling prophecies begins to achieve scientific respectability.

Just as decisive as a doctor's suggestive comments, expectations, and convictions are the measures he takes and the remedies he administers. Of special interest here are placebos[5] (Benson & Epstein, 1975), those chemically inert substances that resemble certain medicines in shape, taste, or color but which have no pharmaceutical effect. We must remember that until about 100 years ago nearly all medications were practically ineffective in the modern sense. They were only slightly more elegant tinctures and powders than the ground toads, the lizard blood, the "sacred oils," or the pulverized horn of the rhinoceros of even earlier times. During my childhood,

people in the rural areas of Austria still believed that a necklace of garlic would protect them from the common cold, to say nothing about the well-known success of magic in the treatment of warts. Even in our time, old "tried and true" remedies or sensational new discoveries (as, for example, Laetrile) are always being unmasked as pharmaceutically ineffective. But that is not to say that they were or are *functionally* ineffective. "One should treat as many patients as possible with the new remedies, as long as these are still working," reads the maxim of a famous physician, attributed to Trousseau, Osler, or Sydenham. Scientific interest in placebos is rapidly increasing. In his contribution to the history of the placebo effect Shapiro (1960) points out that more articles on this topic were published in scientific journals between 1954 and 1957 alone than in the first fifty years of the twentieth century. Most of these reports discuss traditional pharmaceutical effectiveness studies, in which one group of patients receives the new medication while another takes a placebo. The purpose of this well-meaning procedure is to find out whether the course of the illness of the "actually" treated patients is different from that of the placebo group. Only people whose world view is based on classical linear causal thinking (for which there is only an "objective" relationship between cause and effect) react with consternation when they realize that the patients "treated" with placebos often show a quite "inexplicable" improvement in their condition. In other words, the claim of the doctor who administers the placebo that it is an effective, newly developed medicine and the patient's willingness to believe in its effectiveness create a reality in which the assumption actually becomes a fact.

Enough examples. Self-fulfilling prophecies are phenomena that not only shake up our personal conception of reality, but which can also throw doubt on the world view of science. They all share the obviously reality-creating power of a firm belief in the "suchness" of things, a faith that can be a superstition as well as a seemingly strictly scientific theory derived from objective observation. Until recently it has been possible to categorically reject self-fulfilling prophecies as unscientific or to ascribe them to the inadequate reality adaptation of muddleheaded thinkers and romanticists, but we no longer have this convenient escape hatch open to us.

What all this means cannot yet be appraised with any certainty. The discovery that we create our own realities is comparable to the expulsion from the paradise of the presumed suchness of the world, a world in which we can certainly suffer, but for which we need only feel responsible in a very limited way (Watzlawick, 1976).

And here lies the danger. The insights of constructivism may have the highly desirable advantage of allowing for new and more effective forms of therapy (Watzlawick, 1978), but like all remedies, they can also be abused. Advertising and propaganda are two especially repugnant examples: Both try quite deliberately to bring about attitudes, assumptions, prejudices, and the like, whose realization then seems to follow naturally and logically. Thanks to this brainwashing, the world is then seen as "thus" and therefore is "thus." In the novel *1984* (Orwell, 1949) this reality-creating propaganda language is called *Newspeak,* and Orwell explains that it "makes all other modes of thinking impossible." In a recent review of a volume of essays published in London on censorship in the People's Republic of Poland (Strzyzewski, 1977–1978), Daniel Weiss (1980) writes about this magic language:

Compare for example the great number of adjectives, characteristic for Newspeak: Every development is nothing less than "dynamic," every plenary session of the party "historic," the masses always "proletarian workers." A sober communication scientist will find nothing but *redundance* in this inflation of mechanized epithets, drained of meaning. But after listening repeatedly, this automation is felt to have the equality of an incantation: The spoken word is no longer used to carry information, it has become the instrument of magic. (p. 66)

And finally the world simply *is thus*. How it was *made* to be this way was well known to Joseph Goebbels (1933/1976), when he lectured the managers of German radio stations on March 25, 1933:

This is the secret of propaganda: To totally saturate the person, whom the propaganda wants to lay hold of, with the ideas of the propaganda, without him even noticing that he is being saturated. Propaganda has of course a purpose, but this purpose must be disguised with such shrewdness and virtuosity that he who is supposed to be filled with this purpose never even knows what is happening. (p. 120)

In the necessity of disguising the purpose, however, lies the possibility of overcoming it. As we have seen, the invented reality will become "actual" reality only if the invention is believed. Where the element of faith, of blind conviction, is absent, there will be no effect. With the better understanding of self-fulfilling prophecies our ability to transcend them grows. A prophecy that we know to be only a prophecy can no longer fulfill itself. The possibility of choosing differently (of being a heretic) and of disobeying always exists; whether we see it and act on it is, of course, another question. An insight from the seemingly far-removed domain of the mathematical theory of games is of interest here. Wittgenstein (1956) already pointed out in his *Remarks on the Foundations of Mathematics* that certain games can be won with a simple trick. As soon as someone calls our attention to the existence of this trick, we no longer have to continue playing naively (and continue losing). Building on these reflections, the mathematician Howard (1967) formulated his *existential axiom* which maintains that "if a person becomes 'aware' of a theory concerning his behavior, he is no longer bound by it but is free to disobey it" (p. 167). Elsewhere he also says that a conscious decision maker can always choose to disobey any theory predicting his behavior. We may say that he can always "transcend" such a theory. This indeed seems realistic. We suggest that among socio-economic theories, Marxian theory, for example, failed at least partly because certain ruling class members, when they became aware of the theory, saw that it was in their interest to disobey it. (1971)

And almost a hundred years before Howard, Dostoevski's underground man writes in his *Letters from the Underworld* (1913),

As a matter of fact, if ever there shall be discovered a formula which shall exactly express our wills and whims; if ever there shall be discovered a formula which shall make it absolutely clear what those wills depend upon, and what laws they are governed by, and what means of diffusion they possess, and what tendencies they follow under given circumstances; if ever there shall be discovered a formula which shall be mathematical in its precision, well, gentlemen, whenever such a formula shall be found, man will have ceased to have a will of his own—he will have ceased even to exist. Who would care to exercise his willpower according to a table of logarithms? In such a case man would become, not a human being at all, but an organ-handle, or something of the kind. (p. 32)

But even if this kind of mathematical formulization of our lives could ever be achieved, it would in no way comprehend the complexity of our existence. The best theory is powerless in the face of an antitheory; the fulfillment of even the truest prophecy can be thwarted if we know about it beforehand. Dostoevski (1913) saw much more in the nature of man:

Moreover, even if man *were* the keyboard of a piano, and could be convinced that the laws of nature and of mathematics had made him so, he would still decline to change. On the contrary, he would once more, out of sheer ingratitude, attempt the perpetration of something which would enable him to insist upon himself. . . . But if you were to tell me that all this could be set down in tables—I mean the chaos, and the confusion, and the curses, and all the rest of it—so that the possibility of computing everything might remain, and reason continue to rule the roost— well, in that case, I believe, man would *purposely* become a lunatic, in order to become devoid of reason, and therefore able to insist upon himself. I believe this, and I am ready to vouch for this, simply for the reason that every human act arises out of the circumstance that man is forever striving to prove to his own satisfaction that he is a man and not an organ-handle. (p. 37)

However, even the evidence of the underground man is likely to be a self-fulfilling prophecy.

## Notes

1. The following untrue story is a further illustration: In 1974, Secretary of State Kissinger, who is on one of his innumerable mediating missions in Jerusalem, is on his way back to the hotel after a private, late-evening stroll. A young Israeli stops him, introduces himself as an economist out of work, and asks Kissinger to help him find a job through his numerous connections. Kissinger is favorably impressed by the applicant and asks him whether he would like to be the vice-president of the Bank of Israel. The young man thinks of course that Kissinger is making fun of him, but the latter promises quite seriously that he will manage the matter for him. Next day Kissinger calls Baron Rothschild in Paris: "I have a charming young man here, a political economist, talented, going to be the next vice-president of the Bank of Israel. You have to meet him; he would be a jewel of a husband for your daughter." Rothschild growls something that does not sound like total rejection, whereupon Kissinger immediately calls the president of the Bank of Israel: "I have a young financial expert here, brilliant fellow, exactly the stuff to make a vice-president for your bank, and most of all—imagine *that*—he is the future son-in-law of Baron Rothschild's."

2. *Editor's note:* Italian for "If it's not true, it is well written."

3. Here I will briefly mention an interesting sequel to these experiments: For reasons irrelevant to our topic, several researchers (McConnell,

Jacobson, & Humphries, 1961) studied the fascinating theory that at the planaria's primitive stage of development information stored in a worm's ribonucleic acid (RNA) could possibly be directly transferred to other worms. For this purpose they fed untrained animals their already successfully trained fellow worms. Even we laymen can imagine the sensation among experts when the training of the worms provided with such food actually turned out to be much easier and faster. The euphoria lasted for a short while until the experiments, repeated under more rigorous controls, showed themselves to be inconclusive, and serious doubts arose concerning the transferability of intelligence through ground meat. The suspicion suggests itself, but was, as far as I know, never proven, that the original results were due to self-fulfilling prophecies, similar to those whose effects on the worms were already known. (The analogy, however, to the superstition of certain African tribes that eating a lion's heart will confer the lion's courage cannot be dismissed out of hand.)

4. *Editor's note:* Latin for "Let justice be done though the world perish."

5. Latin for "I shall please."

# References

Allport, G. W. (1964). Mental health: A generic attitude. *Journal of Religion and Health, 4,* 7–21.

Beers, R. F. (Ed.). (1979). *Mechanisms of pain and analgesic compounds.* New York: Raven.

Benson, H., & Epstein, M. D. (1975). The placebo effect: A neglected asset in the care of patients. *American Medical Association Journal, 232,* 1225–1227.

Cannon, W. B. (1942). Voodoo death. *American Anthropologist, 44,* 169–181.

Cordaro, L., & Ison, J. R. (1963). Observer bias in classical conditioning of the planaria. *Psychological Reports, 13,* 787–789.

Dostoevski, F. M. (1913). *Letters from the underworld.* New York: Dutton.

Feyerabend, P. K. (1978). *Science in a free society.* London: New Left.

Frankl, V. E. (1959). *From death camp to existentialism.* Boston: Beacon.

Goebbels, J. Quoted in Schneider, W. (1976). *Wörter machen leute. Magie und macht der sprache.* Munich: Piper.

Haley, J. (1973). *Uncommon therapy: The psychiatric techniques of Milton H. Erickson, M.D.* New York: Norton.

Heisenberg, W. (1958). *Physics and philosophy: The revolution in modern science.* New York: Harper & Row.

Howard, N. (1967). The theory of metagames. *General Systems, 2,* 167.

Howard, N. (1971). *Paradoxes of rationality, theory of metagames and political behavior.* Cambridge, MA: MIT Press.

Jones, R. A. (1974). *Self-fulfilling prophecies: Social, psychological and physiological effects of expectancies.* New York: Halsted.

McConnell, J. V., Jacobson, R., & Humphries, B. M. (1961). The effects of ingestion of conditioned planaria on the response level of naive planaria: A pilot study. *Worm Runner's Digest, 3,* 41–45.

Orwell, G. (1949). *1984.* New York: Harcourt, Brace.

Popper, K. R. (1974). *Unended quest.* La Salle, IL: Open Court.

Rosenthal, R. (1966). *Experimenter effects in behavioral research.* New York: Appleton-Century-Crofts.

Rosenthal, R., & Jacobson, L. (1968). *Pygmalion in the classroom: Teacher expectation and pupils' intellectual development.* New York: Holt, Rinehart & Winston.

Shapiro, A. K. (1960). A contribution to a history of the placebo effects. *Behavioral Science, 5,* 109–135.

Simonton, O. C., & Simonton, S. (1975). Belief systems and management of the emotional aspects of malignancy. *Journal of Transpersonal Psychology, 1,* 29–47.

Simonton, O. C., & Simonton, S. (1978). *Getting well again.* Los Angeles: J. P. Tarcher.

Solomon, G. F. (1969). Emotions, stress, the nervous system, and immunity. *Annals of the New York Academy of Sciences, 164,* 335–343.

Staib, A. R., & Logan, D. R. (1977). Hypnotic stimulation of breast growth. *American Journal of Clinical Hypnosis, 19,* 201–208.

Strzyzewski, T. (1977–1978). *Czarna ksiega cenzury PRL* (Black Book of Polish Censorship, 2 vols.). London: "Aneks."

Szasz, T. S. (1970). *The manufacture of madness: A comparative study of the Inquisition and the mental health movement.* New York: Harper & Row.

Watzlawick, P. (1976). *How real is real?* New York: Random House.

Watzlawick, P. (1978). *The language of change: Elements of therapeutic communication.* New York: Basic Books.

Watzlawick, P., Bavelas, J. B., & Jackson, D. D. (1967). *Pragmatics of human communication: A study of interactional patterns, pathologies and paradoxes.* New York: Norton.

Weiss, D. (1980). Sprache und propaganda—Der sonderfall Polen. *Neue Zürcher Zeitung, 39,* 66.

Willard, R. R. (1977). Breast enlargement through visual imagery and hypnosis. *American Journal of Clinical Hypnosis, 19,* 195–200.

Wittgenstein, L. (1956). *Remarks on the foundations of mathematics.* Oxford, UK: Blackwell.

# When Belief Creates Reality: The Self-Fulfilling Impact of First Impressions on Social Interaction

## *Mark Snyder*

For the social psychologist, there may be no processes more complex and intriguing than those by which strangers become friends. How do we form first impressions of those we encounter in our lives? How do we become acquainted with each other? When does an acquaintance become a friend? Why do some relationships develop and withstand the test of time and other equally promising relationships flounder and fall by the wayside? It is to these and similar concerns that my colleagues and I have addressed ourselves in our attempts to chart the unfolding dynamics of social interaction and interpersonal relationships. In doing so,

"When Belief Creates Reality: The Self-Fulfilling Impact of First Impressions on Social Interaction" by M. Snyder from *Experiencing Social Psychology,* edited by A. Pines and C. Maslach (pp. 189–192), 1977. New York: Alfred Knopf. Reprinted by permission of the author.

This research was supported in part by National Science Foundation Grant SOC 75–13872, "Cognition and Behavior: When Belief Creates Reality," to Mark Snyder. For a more detailed description of the background and rationale, procedures and results, implications and consequences of this investigation, see M. Snyder, E. D. Tanke, & E. Berscheid, Social perception and interpersonal behavior: On the self-fulfilling nature of social stereotypes. *Journal of Personality and Social Psychology,* 1977. For related research on behavioral confirmation in social interaction, see M. Snyder & W. B. Swann, Jr., Behavioral confirmation in social interaction: From social perception to social reality. *Journal of Experimental Social Psychology,* 1978.

we chose—not surprisingly—to begin at the beginning. Specifically, we have been studying the ways in which first impressions channel and influence subsequent social interaction and acquaintance processes.

When we first meet others, we cannot help but notice certain highly visible and distinctive characteristics such as their sex, age, race, and bodily appearance. Try as we may to avoid it, our first impressions are often molded and influenced by these pieces of information. Consider the case of physical attractiveness. A widely held stereotype in this culture suggests that attractive people are assumed to possess more socially desirable personalities and are expected to lead better personal, social, and occupational lives than their unattractive counterparts. For example, Dion, Berscheid, and Walster (1972) had men and women judge photographs of either men or women who varied in physical attractiveness. Attractive stimulus persons of either sex were perceived to have virtually every character trait that pretesting had indicated was socially desirable to that participant population: "Physically attractive people, for example, were perceived to be more sexually warm and responsive, sensitive, kind, interesting, strong, poised, modest, sociable, and outgoing than persons of lesser physical attractiveness" (Berscheid & Walster, 1974, p. 169). This powerful stereotype was found for male and female judges and for male and female stimulus persons. In addition, attractive people were predicted to have happier social, professional, and personal lives in store for them than were their less attractive counterparts. (For an excellent and comprehensive review, see Berscheid & Walster, 1974.)

What of the validity of the physical attractiveness stereotype? Are the physically attractive actually more likeable, friendly, sensitive, and confident than the unattractive? Are they more successful socially and professionally? Clearly, the physically attractive are more often and more eagerly sought out for social dates. And well they should be, for the stereotype implies that they should be perceived as more desirable social partners than the physically unattractive. Thus, it should come as little surprise that, among young adults, the physically attractive have more friends of the other sex, engage in more sexual activity, report themselves in love more often, and express less anxiety about dating than unattractive individuals do. But the effect is even more general than this. Even as early as nursery school age, physical attractiveness appears to channel social interaction: The physically attractive are chosen and the unattractive are rejected in sociometric choices.

A differential amount of interaction with the attractive and unattractive clearly helps the stereotype persevere because it limits the chances for learning whether the two types of individuals differ in the traits associated with the stereotype. But the point I wish to focus on here is that the stereotype may also channel interaction so as to confirm itself *behaviorally*. Individuals appear to have different patterns and styles of interaction for those whom they perceive to be physically attractive and for those whom they consider unattractive. These differences in self-presentation and interaction style may, in turn, elicit and nurture behaviors from the target person that are in accord with the stereotype. That is, the physically attractive may actually come to behave in a friendly, likeable, sociable manner, not because they necessarily possess these dispo-

sitions, but because the behavior of others elicits and maintains behaviors taken to be manifestations of such traits.

In our empirical research, we have attempted to demonstrate that stereotypes may create their own social reality by channeling social interaction in ways that cause the stereotyped individual to behave in ways that confirm another person's stereotyped impressions of him or her. In our initial investigation, Elizabeth Decker Tanke, Ellen Berscheid, and I sought to demonstrate the self-fulfilling nature of the physical attractiveness stereotype in a social interaction context designed to mirror as faithfully as possible the spontaneous generation of first impressions in everyday social interaction and the subsequent channeling influences of these impressions on social interaction. In order to do so, pairs of previously unacquainted individuals (designated for our purposes as a *perceiver* and a *target*) interacted in a getting-acquainted situation constructed to allow us to control the information that one member of the dyad (the male perceiver) received about the physical attractiveness of the other individual (the female target). In this way, it was possible to evaluate separately the effects of actual and perceived physical attractiveness on the display of self-presentational and expressive behaviors associated with the stereotype that links beauty and goodness. In order to measure the extent to which the self-presentation of the target individual matched the perceiver's stereotype, naïve observer-judges who were unaware of the actual or perceived physical attractiveness of either participant listened to and evaluated tape recordings of the interaction.

Fifty-one male and fifty-one female undergraduates at the University of Minnesota participated, for extra course credit, in what had been described as a study of the "processes by which people become acquainted with each other." These individuals interacted in male-female dyads in a getting-acquainted situation in which they could hear but not see each other (a telephone conversation). Before initiating the conversation, the male member of each dyad received a Polaroid snapshot of his female interaction partner. These photographs, which had been prepared in advance and assigned at random to dyads, identified the target as either physically attractive (attractive-target condition) or physically unattractive (unattractive-target condition). Each dyad engaged in a ten-minute unstructured telephone conversation that was tape-recorded. Each participant's voice was recorded on a separate channel of the tape.

In order to assess the extent to which the actions of the female targets provided behavioral confirmation of the male perceivers' stereotypes, twelve observer-judges listened to the tape recordings of the getting-acquainted conversations. The observer-judges were unaware of the experimental hypotheses and knew nothing of the actual or perceived physical attractiveness of the individual whom they heard on the tapes. They heard only those tape tracks containing the female participants' voices. Nine other observer-judges listened to and rated only the male perceivers' voices. (For further details of the experimental procedures, see Snyder, Tanke, & Berscheid, 1977.)

In order to chart the process of behavioral confirmation of stereotype-based attributions in these dyadic social interactions, we examined the effects of our manipulation of the target's apparent physical attractiveness on both the male perceivers' initial impressions of their female targets and the females' behavioral self-presentation during their interactions, as measured by the observer-judges' ratings of the tape recordings of their voices.

The male perceivers clearly formed their initial impressions of their female targets on the basis of general stereotypes that associate physical attractiveness with socially desirable personality characteristics. On the basis of measures of first impressions that were collected after the perceivers had been given access to their partners' photographs but be-

fore the initiation of the getting-acquainted conversations, it was clear that (as dictated by the physical attractiveness stereotype) males who anticipated physically attractive partners expected to interact with comparatively cordial, poised, humorous, and socially adept individuals. By contrast, males faced with the prospect of getting acquainted with relatively unattractive partners fashioned images of rather withdrawn, awkward, serious, and socially inept creatures.

Not only did our perceivers fashion their images of their discussion partners on the basis of their stereotyped intuitions about the links between beauty and goodness of character, but the stereotype-based attributions initiated a chain of events that resulted in the behavioral confirmation of these initially erroneous inferences. Analysis of the observer-judges' ratings of the tape recordings of the conversations indicated that female targets who (unbeknown to them) were perceived to be physically attractive (as a consequence of random assignment to the attractive-target experimental condition) actually came to behave in a friendly, likeable, and sociable manner. This behavioral confirmation was discernible even by outside observer-judges who knew nothing of the actual or perceived physical attractiveness of the target individuals. In this demonstration of behavioral confirmation in social interaction, the "beautiful" people became "good" people, not because they necessarily possessed the socially valued dispositions that had been attributed to them, but because the actions of the perceivers, which were based on their stereotyped beliefs, had erroneously confirmed and validated these attributions.

Confident in our demonstration of the self-fulfilling nature of this particular social stereotype, we then attempted to chart the process of behavioral confirmation. Specifically, we searched for evidence of the behavioral implications of the perceivers' stereotypes. Did the male perceivers present themselves differently to the target women whom they assumed to be physically attractive or unattractive? An examination of the observer-judges' ratings of the tapes of only the males' contributions to the conversations provided clear evidence that our perceivers did have different interactional styles with targets of different physical attractiveness.

Men who interacted with women whom they believed to be physically attractive appeared to be more cordial, sexually warm, interesting, independent, sexually permissive, bold, outgoing, humorous, obvious, and socially adept than their counterparts in the unattractive-target condition. Moreover, these same men were seen by the judges to be more attractive, more confident, and more animated in their conversation than their counterparts. They were also considered by the observer-judges to be more comfortable in conversation, to enjoy themselves more, to like their partners more, to take the initiative more often, to use their voices more effectively, to see their women partners as more attractive, and finally, to be seen as more attractive by their partners than men in the unattractive-target condition.

It appears, then, that differences in the expressive self-presentation of sociability by the male perceivers may have been a key factor in the process of bringing out those reciprocal patterns of expression in the target women that constitute behavioral confirmation of the attributions from which the perceivers' self-presentation had been generated. One reason that target women who had been labeled attractive may have reciprocated this sociable self-presentation is that they regarded their partners' images of them as more accurate and their style of interaction to be more typical of the way men generally treated them than women in the unattractive-target condition did. Perhaps, these latter individuals rejected their partners' treatment of them as unrepresentative and defensively adopted more cool and aloof postures to cope with their situations.

Our research points to the powerful but often unnoticed consequences of social stereotypes. In our demonstration, first impressions and expectations that were based on common cultural stereotypes about physical attractiveness channeled the unfolding dynamics of social interaction and acquaintance processes in ways that actually made those stereotyped first impressions come true. In our investigation, pairs of individuals got acquainted with each other in a situation that allowed us to control the information that one member of the dyad (the perceiver) received about the physical attractiveness of the other person (the target). Our perceivers . . . fashioned erroneous images of their specific partners that reflected their general stereotypes about physical attractiveness. Moreover, our perceivers had very different patterns and styles of interaction for those whom they perceived to be physically attractive and to be unattractive. These differences in self-presentation and interaction style, in turn, elicited and nurtured behaviors of the targets that were consistent with the perceived initial stereotypes. Targets who (unbeknown to them) were perceived to be physically attractive actually came to behave in a friendly, likeable, and sociable manner. The perceivers' attributions about their targets based on their stereotyped intuitions about the world had initiated a process that produced behavioral confirmation of those attributions. The initially erroneous impressions of the perceivers had become real. The stereotype had truly functioned as a self-fulfilling prophecy:

The self-fulfilling prophecy is, in the beginning, a *false* definition of the situation evoking a new behavior which makes the originally false conception come *true*. The validity of the self-fulfilling prophecy perpetuates a reign of error. For the prophet will cite the actual course of events as proof that he was right from the very beginning. . . . Such are the perversities of social logic. (Merton 1948, p. 195)

True to Merton's script, our "prophets," in the beginning, created false definitions of their situations. That is, they erroneously labeled their targets as sociable or unsociable persons on the basis of their physical attractiveness. But these mistakes in first impressions quickly became self-erasing mistakes because the perceivers' false definitions evoked new behaviors that made their originally false conceptions come true: They treated their targets as sociable or unsociable persons, and, indeed, these targets came to behave in a sociable or unsociable fashion. Our prophets also cited the actual course of events as proof that they had been right all along. Might not other important and widespread social stereotypes—particularly those concerning sex, race, social class, and ethnicity—also channel social interaction in ways that create their own social reality?

Any self-fulfilling influences of social stereotypes may have compelling and pervasive societal consequences. Social observers have for decades commented on and demonstrated the ways in which stigmatized social groups and outsiders may fall victim to self-fulfilling cultural stereotypes. Consider Scott's (1969) observations about the blind:

When, for example, sighted people continually insist that a blind man is helpless because he is blind, their subsequent treatment of him may pre-clude his own exercising the kinds of skills that would enable him to be independent. It is in this sense that stereotypic beliefs are self-actualized. (p. 9)

All too often, it is the victims who are blamed for their own plight . . . rather than the social expectations that have constrained their behavioral options.

## References

Berscheid, E., & Walster, E. (1974). Physical attractiveness. In L. Berkowitz (Ed.), *Advances in experimental social psychology* (Vol. 7). New York: Academic Press.

Dion, K. K., Berscheid, E., & Walster, E. (1972). What is good is beautiful. *Journal of Personality and Social Psychology, 24,* 285–290.

Merton, R. K. (1948). The self-fulfilling prophecy. *Antioch Review, 8,* 193–210.

Scott, R. A. (1969). *The making of blind men.* New York: Russell Sage.

Snyder, M., Tanke, E. D., & Berscheid, E. (1977). Social perception and interpersonal behavior: On the self-fulfilling nature of social stereotypes. *Journal of Personality and Social Psychology, 35,* 656–666.

# Pygmalion in the Classroom: Teacher Expectation and Pupils' Intellectual Development

## Robert Rosenthal and Lenore Jacobson

There is increasing concern over what can be done to reduce the disparities of education, of intellectual motivation, and of intellectual competence that exist between the social classes and the colors of our school children. With this increasing concern, attention has focused more and more on the role of the classroom teacher, and the possible effects of her or his values, attitudes, and, especially, beliefs and expectations. Many educational theorists have expressed the opinion that the teacher's expectation of her pupils' performance may serve as an educational self-fulfilling prophecy. The teacher gets less because she expects less.

The concept of the self-fulfilling prophecy is an old idea which has found application in clinical psychology, social psychology, sociology, economics, and in everyday life. Most of the evidence for the operation of self-fulfilling prophecies has been correlational. Interpersonal prophecies have been found to agree with the behavior that was prophesied. From this, however, it cannot be said that the prophecy was the cause of its own fulfillment. The accurate prophecy may have been based on a knowledge of the

prior behavior of the person whose behavior was prophesied, so that the prophecy was in a sense "contaminated" by reality. If a physician predicts a patient's improvement, we cannot say whether the doctor is only giving a sophisticated prognosis or whether the patient's improvement is based in part on the optimism engendered by the physician's prediction. If school children who perform poorly are those expected by their teachers to perform poorly, we cannot say whether the teacher's expectation was the "cause" of the pupils' poor performance, or whether the teacher's expectation was simply an accurate prognosis of performance based on her knowledge of past performance. To help answer the question raised, experiments are required in which the expectation is experimentally varied and is uncontaminated by the past behavior of the person whose performance is predicted.

Such experiments have been conducted and they have shown that in behavioral research the experimenter's hypothesis may serve as self-fulfilling prophecy (Rosenthal, 1966). Of special relevance to our topic are those experiments involving allegedly bright and allegedly dull animal subjects. Half the experimenters were led to believe that their rat subjects had been specially bred for excellence of learning ability. The remaining experimenters were led to believe that their rat subjects were genetically inferior. Actually,

"Pygmalion in the Classroom: Teacher Expectation and Pupils' Intellectual Development" by R. Rosenthal and L. Jacobson from *Doing Unto Others* edited by Zick Rubin (pp. 41–47), 1974. Englewood Cliffs, NJ: Prentice-Hall. Reprinted by permission of the authors.

the animals were assigned to their experimenters at random.

Regardless of whether the rat's task was to learn a maze or the appropriate responses in a Skinner box, the results were the same. Rats who were believed by their experimenters to be brighter showed learning which was significantly superior to the learning by rats whose experimenters believed them to be dull. Our best guess, supported by the experimenters' self-reports, is that allegedly well-endowed animals were handled more and handled more gently than the allegedly inferior animals. Such handling differences, along with differences in rapidity of reinforcement in the Skinner box situation, are probably sufficient to account for the differences in learning ability shown by allegedly bright and allegedly dull rats.

If rats showed superior performance when their trainer expected it, then it seemed reasonable to think that children might show superior performance when their teacher expected it. That was the reason for conducting the Oak School Experiment.

## The Oak School Experiment

To all of the children in the Oak School, on the West Coast, the "Harvard Test of Inflected Acquisition" was administered in the spring of 1964. This test was purported to predict academic "blooming" or intellectual growth. The reason for administering the test in the particular school was ostensibly to perform a final check of the validity of the test, a validity which was presented as already well-established. Actually, the "Harvard Test of Inflected Acquisition" was a standardized, relatively nonverbal test of intelligence, Flanagan's Tests of General Ability.

Within each of the six grades of the elementary school, there were three classrooms, one each for children performing at above-average, average, and below-average levels of scholastic achievement. In each of the 18 classrooms of the school, about 20% of the children were designated as academic "spurters." The names of these children were reported to their new teachers in the fall of 1964 as those who, during the academic year ahead, would show unusual intellectual gains. The "fact" of their intellectual potential was established from their scores on the test for "intellectual blooming."

Teachers were cautioned not to discuss the test findings with either their pupils or the children's parents. Actually, the names of the 20% of the children assigned to the "blooming" condition had been selected by means of a table of random numbers. The difference, then, between these children, earmarked for intellectual growth, and the undesignated control group children was in the mind of the teacher.

Four months after the teachers had been given the names of the "special" children, all the children once again took the same form of the nonverbal test of intelligence. Four months after this retest the children took the same test once again. This final retest was at the end of the school year, some eight months after the teachers had been given the expectation for intellectual growth of the special children. These retests were not explained as "retests" to the teachers, but rather as further efforts to predict intellectual growth.

The intelligence test employed, while relatively nonverbal in the sense of requiring no speaking, reading, or writing, was not entirely nonverbal. Actually there were two subtests, one requiring a greater comprehension of English—a kind of picture vocabulary test. The other subtest required less ability to understand any spoken language but more ability to reason abstractly. For shorthand purposes we refer to the former as a "verbal" subtest and to the latter as a "reasoning" subtest. The pretest correlation between these subjects was only +.42, suggesting that the two subtests were measuring somewhat different intellectual abilities.

For the school as a whole, the children of the experimental groups did not show a significantly greater gain in verbal IQ (2 points) than did the control group children. However, in total IQ (4 points) and especially in reasoning IQ (7 points) the experimental children gained more than did the control group children. In 15 of the 17 classrooms in which the reasoning IQ posttest was administered, children of the experimental group gained more than did the control group children. Even after the four-month retest this trend was already in evidence though the effects were smaller.

When we examine the results separately for the six grades we find that it was only in the first and second grades that children gained significantly more in IQ when their teacher expected it of them. In the first grade, children who were expected to gain more IQ gained over 15 points more than did the control group children. In the second grade, children who were expected to gain more IQ gained nearly 10 points more than did the control group children. In the first and second grades combined, 19% of the control group children gained 20 or more IQ points. Two-and-a-half times that many, or 47%, of the experimental group children gained 20 or more IQ points.

When educational theorists have discussed the possible effects of teachers' expectations, they have usually referred to the children at lower levels of scholastic achievement. It was interesting, therefore, to find that in the present study, children of the highest level of achievement showed as great a benefit as did the children of the lowest level of achievement of having their teachers expect intellectual gains.

At the end of the school year of this study, all teachers were asked to describe the classroom behavior of their pupils. Those children from whom intellectual growth was expected were described as having a significantly better chance of becoming successful in the future, as significantly more interesting, curious, and happy. There was a tendency, too, for these children to be seen as more appealing, adjusted, and affectionate and as lower in the need for social approval. In short, the children from whom intellectual growth was expected became more intellectually alive and autonomous—or at least were so perceived by their teachers. These findings were particularly striking among first-grade children; these were the children who had benefited most in IQ gain as a result of their teachers' favorable expectancies.

We have already seen that the children of the experimental group gained more intellectually. It was possible, therefore, that their actual intellectual growth accounted for the teachers' more favorable ratings of these children's behavior and aptitude. But a great many of the control group children also gained in IQ during the course of the year. Perhaps those who gained more intellectually among these undesignated children would also be rated more favorably by their teachers. Such was not the case. In fact, there was a tendency for teachers to rate those control group children who gained most in IQ as *less* well-adjusted, *less* interesting, and *less* affectionate than control group children who made smaller intellectual gains. From these results it would seem that when children who are expected to grow intellectually do so, they may benefit in other ways as well. When children who are not especially expected to develop intellectually do so, they may show accompanying undesirable behavior, or at least are perceived by their teachers as showing such undesirable behavior. It appears that there may be hazards to unpredicted intellectual growth.

A closer analysis of these data, broken down by whether the children were in the high, medium, or low ability tracks or groups, showed that these hazards of unpredicted intellectual growth were due primarily to the children of the low ability group. When these slow track children were in the control group, so that no intellectual gains were expected of them, they were rated less favorably by their teachers if they did show gains in IQ. The greater their IQ gains, the less favorably were they rated, both as to mental health and as to intellectual vitality.

Even when the slow track children were in the experimental group, so that IQ gains were expected of them, they were not rated as favorably relative to their control group peers as were children of the high or medium track, despite the fact that they gained as much in IQ relative to the control group children as did the experimental group children of the high track. It may be difficult for a slow track child, even one whose IQ is rising, to be seen by his teacher as a well-adjusted child, or as a potentially successful child intellectually.

## The Question of Mediation

How did the teachers' expectations come to serve as determinants of gains in intellectual performance? The most plausible hypothesis seemed to be that children for whom unusual intellectual growth had been predicted would be attended to more by their teachers. If teachers were more attentive to the children earmarked for growth, we might expect that teachers were robbing Peter to see Paul grow. With a finite amount of time to spend with each child, if a teacher gave more time to the children of the experimental group, she would have less time to spend with the children of the control group. If the teacher's spending more time with a child led to greater intellectual gains, we could test the "robbing Peter" hypothesis by comparing the gains made by children of the experimental group with gains made by the children of the control group in each class. The robbing Peter hypothesis predicts a negative correlation. The greater the gains made by children of the experimental group (with the implication of more time spent on them) the less should be the gains made by the children of the control group (with the implication of less time spent on them). In fact, however, the correlation was positive, large, and statistically significant (+.57). The greater the gains made by children of whom gain was expected, the greater the gains made in the

same classroom by those children from whom no special gain was expected.

Additional evidence that teachers did not take time from control group children to spend with the experimental group children comes from the teachers' estimates of time spent with each pupil. These estimates showed a slight tendency for teachers to spend *less* time with pupils from whom intellectual gains were expected.

That the children of the experimental group were not favored with a greater investment of time seems less surprising in view of the pattern of their greater intellectual gains. If, for example, teachers had talked to them more, we might have expected greater gains in verbal IQ. But the greater gains were found not in verbal but in reasoning IQ. It may be, of course, that the teachers were inaccurate in their estimates of time spent with each of their pupils. Possibly direct observation of the teacher-pupil interactions would have given different results, but that method was not possible in the present study. But even direct observation might not have revealed a difference in the amounts of teacher time invested in each of the two groups of children. It seems plausible to think that it was not a difference in amount of time spent with the children of the two groups which led to the differences in their rates of intellectual development. It may have been more a matter of the type of interaction which took place between the teachers and their pupils.

By what she said, by how she said it, by her facial expressions, postures, and perhaps by her touch, the teacher may have communicated to the children of the experimental group that she expected improved intellectual performance. Such communications, together with possible changes in teaching techniques, may have helped the child learn by changing his or her self-concept, expectations of his or her own behavior, motivation, as well as cognitive skills. Further research is clearly needed to narrow down the range of possible mechanisms whereby a teacher's expectations become translated into a pupil's intellectual growth. It would be valuable, for example, to have sound films of teachers interacting with their pupils. We might then look for differences in the ways teachers interact with those children from whom they expect more intellectual growth compared to those from whom they expect less. On the basis of films of psychological experimenters interacting with subjects from whom different responses were expected, we know that even in such highly standardized situations, unintentional communications can be subtle and complex (Rosenthal, 1967). How much more subtle and complex may be the communications between children and their teachers in the less highly standardized classroom situation?

## Conclusions

The results of the Oak School experiment provide further evidence that one person's expectations of another's behavior may serve as a self-fulfilling prophecy. When teachers expected that certain children would show greater intellectual development, those children did show greater intellectual development. A number of more recent experiments have provided additional evidence for the operation of teacher expectancy effects, in contexts ranging from the classroom to teaching athletic skills. Although not all of the studies that have been conducted show such effects, a large proportion of them do (Rosenthal, 1971).

It may be that as teacher training institutions acquaint teachers-to-be with the possibility that their expectations of their pupils'

performance may serve as self-fulfilling prophecies, these teacher trainees may be given a new expectancy—that children can learn more than they had believed possible.

Perhaps the most suitable summary of the hypothesis discussed in this paper has already been written. The writer is George Bernard Shaw, the play is *Pygmalion*, and the speaker is Eliza Doolittle:

> You see, really and truly, . . . the difference between a lady and a flower girl is not how she behaves, but how she's treated. I shall always be a flower girl to Professor Higgins, because he . . . treats me as a flower girl, . . . but I know I can be a lady to you, because you always treat me as a lady, and always will.

## Note

An expanded discussion of self-fulfilling prophecies and a full account of the Oak School experiment are presented in R. Rosenthal & L. Jacobson (1968), *Pygmalion in the classroom: Teacher expectation and pupils' intellectual development*, New York: Holt, Rinehart & Winston.

## References

Rosenthal, R. (1966). *Experimenter effects in behavioral research.* New York: Appleton-Century-Crofts.

Rosenthal, R. (1967). Covert communication in the psychological experiment. *Psychological Bulletin, 67,* 356–367.

Rosenthal, R. (1971). Teacher expectation and pupil learning. In R. D. Strom (Ed.), *Teachers and the learning process.* Englewood Cliffs, NJ: Prentice-Hall.

**39**

# On Being Sane in Insane Places

## D. L. Rosenhan

If sanity and insanity exist, how shall we know them?

The question is neither capricious nor itself insane. However much we may be personally convinced that we can tell the normal from the abnormal, the evidence is simply not compelling. It is commonplace, for example, to read about murder trials wherein eminent psychiatrists for the defense are contradicted by equally eminent psychiatrists for the prosecution on the matter of the defendant's sanity. More generally, there are a great deal of conflicting data on the reliability, utility, and meaning of such terms as "sanity," "insanity," "mental illness," and "schizophrenia."[1] Finally, as early as 1934, Benedict suggested that normality and abnormality are not universal.[2] What is viewed as normal in one culture may be seen as quite aberrant in another. Thus, notions of normality and abnormality may not be quite as accurate as people believe they are.

To raise questions regarding normality and abnormality is in no way to question the fact that some behaviors are deviant or odd. Murder is deviant. So, too, are hallucinations. Nor does raising such questions deny the existence of the personal anguish that is often associated with "mental illness." Anxiety and depression exist. Psychological suffering exists. But normality and abnormality, sanity and insanity, and the diagnoses that flow from them may be less substantive than many believe them to be.

At its heart, the question of whether the sane can be distinguished from the insane (and whether degrees of insanity can be distinguished from each other) is a simple matter: do the salient characteristics that lead to diagnoses reside in the patients themselves or in the environments and contexts in which observers find them? From Bleuler, through Kretchmer, through the formulators of the recently revised *Diagnostic and Statistical Manual* of the American Psychiatric Association, the belief has been strong that patients present symptoms, that those symptoms can be categorized, and, implicitly, that the sane are distinguishable from the insane. More recently, however, this belief has been questioned. Based in part on theoretical and anthropological considerations, but also on philosophical, legal, and therapeutic ones, the view has grown that psychological categorization of mental illness is useless at best and downright harmful, misleading, and pejorative at worst. Psychiatric diagnoses, in this view, are in the minds of the observers and are not valid summaries of characteristics displayed by the observed.[3,4,5]

Gains can be made in deciding which of these is more nearly accurate by getting normal people (that is, people who do not have, and have never suffered, symptoms of serious psychiatric disorders) admitted to psychiatric hospitals and then determining whether they were discovered to be sane and, if so, how. If the sanity of such pseudopatients was always detected, there would be prima facie evidence that a sane individual can be distinguished from the insane context in which he is found. Normality (and presumably abnormality) is distinct enough that it can be recognized wherever it occurs, for it is carried within the person. If, on the other hand, the sanity of the pseudopatients were never discovered, serious difficulties would arise for those who support traditional modes of psychiatric diagnosis. Given that the hospital staff was not incompetent, that the pseudopatient had been behaving as sanely as he had been outside of the hospital, and that it had never been previously suggested that he belonged in a psychiatric hospital, such an unlikely outcome would support the view that psychiatric diagnosis betrays little about the patient but much about the environment in which an observer finds him.

This article describes such an experiment. Eight sane people gained secret admission to 12 different hospitals.[6] Their diagnostic experiences constitute the data of the first part of this article; the remainder is devoted to a description of their experiences in psychiatric institutions. Too few psychiatrists and psychologists, even those who have worked in such hospitals, know what the experience is like. They rarely talk about it with former patients, perhaps because they distrust information coming from the previously insane. Those who have worked in psychiatric hospitals are likely to have adapted so thoroughly to the settings that they are insensitive to the impact of that experience. And while there have been occasional reports of researchers who submitted themselves to psychiatric hospitalization,[7] these researchers have commonly remained in the hospitals for short periods of time, often with the knowledge of the hospital staff. It is difficult

to know the extent to which they were treated like patients or like research colleagues. Nevertheless, their reports about the inside of the psychiatric hospital have been valuable. This article extends those efforts.

## Pseudopatients and Their Settings

The eight pseudopatients were a varied group. One was a psychology graduate student in his 20s. The remaining seven were older and "established." Among them were three psychologists, a pediatrician, a psychiatrist, a painter, and a housewife. Three pseudopatients were women, five were men. All of them employed pseudonyms, lest their alleged diagnoses embarrass them later. Those who were in mental health professions alleged another occupation in order to avoid the special attentions that might be accorded by staff, as a matter of courtesy or caution, to ailing colleagues.[8] With the exception of myself (I was the first pseudopatient and my presence was known to the hospital administrator and chief psychologist and, so far as I can tell, to them alone), the presence of pseudopatients and the nature of the research program were not known to the hospital staffs.[9]

The settings were similarly varied. In order to generalize the findings, admission into a variety of hospitals was sought. The twelve hospitals in the sample were located in five different states on the East and West coasts. Some were old and shabby, some were quite new. Some were research-oriented, others not. Some had good staff-patient ratios, others were quite understaffed. Only one was a strictly private hospital. All of the others were supported by state or federal funds or, in one instance, by university funds.

After calling the hospital for an appointment, the pseudopatient arrived at the admissions office complaining that he had been hearing voices. Asked what the voices said, he replied that they were often unclear, but as far as he could tell they said "empty," "hollow," and "thud." The voices were unfamiliar and were of the same sex as the pseudopatient. The choice of these symptoms was occasioned by their apparent similarity to existential symptoms. Such symptoms are alleged to arise from painful concerns about the perceived meaninglessness of one's life. It is as if the hallucinating person were saying, "My life is empty and hollow." The choice of these symptoms was also determined by the *absence* of a single report of existential psychoses in the literature.

Beyond alleging the symptoms and falsifying name, vocation, and employment, no further alterations of person, history, or circumstances were made. The significant events of the pseudopatient's life history were presented as they had actually occurred. Relationships with parents and siblings, with spouse and children, with people at work and in school, consistent with the aforementioned exceptions, were described as they were or had been. Frustrations and upsets were described along with joys and satisfactions. These facts are important to remember. If anything, they strongly biased the subsequent results in favor of detecting sanity, since none of their histories or current behaviors were seriously pathological in any way.

Immediately upon admission to the psychiatric ward, the pseudopatient ceased simulating *any* symptoms of abnormality. In some cases, there was a brief period of mild nervousness and anxiety, since none of the pseudopatients really believed that they would be admitted so easily. Indeed, their shared fear was that they would be immediately exposed as frauds and greatly embarrassed. Moreover, many of them had never visited a psychiatric ward; even those who had, nevertheless had some genuine fears about what might happen to them. Their nervousness, then, was quite appropriate to the novelty of the hospital setting, and it abated rapidly.

Apart from that short-lived nervousness, the pseudopatient behaved on the ward as he "normally" behaved. The pseudopatient spoke to patients and staff as he might ordinarily. Because there is uncommonly little to do on a psychiatric ward, he attempted to engage others in conversation. When asked by staff how he was feeling, he indicated that he was fine, that he no longer experienced symptoms. He responded to instructions from attendants, to calls for medication (which was not swallowed), and to dining-hall instructions. Beyond such activities as were available to him on the admissions ward, he spent his time writing down his observations about the ward, its patients, and the staff. Initially these notes were written "secretly," but as it soon became clear that no one much cared, they were subsequently written on standard tablets of paper in such public places as the dayroom. No secret was made of these activities.

The pseudopatient, very much as a true psychiatric patient, entered a hospital with no foreknowledge of when he would be discharged. Each was told that he would have to get out by his own devices, essentially by convincing the staff that he was sane. The psychological stresses associated with hospitalization were considerable, and all but one of the pseudopatients desired to be discharged almost immediately after being admitted. They were, therefore, motivated not only to behave sanely, but to be paragons of cooperation. That their behavior was in no way disruptive is confirmed by nursing reports, which have been obtained on most of the patients. These reports uniformly indicate that the patients were "friendly," "cooperative," and "exhibited no abnormal indications."

## The Normal Are Not Detectably Sane

Despite their public "show" of sanity, the pseudopatients were never detected. Admitted, except in one case, with a diagnosis of schizophrenia,[10] each was discharged with a diagnosis of schizophrenia "in remission." The label "in remission" should in no way be dismissed as a formality, for at no time during any hospitalization had any question been raised about any pseudopatient's simulation. Nor are there any indications in the hospital records that the pseudopatient's status was suspect. Rather, the evidence is strong that, once labeled schizophrenic, the pseudopatient was stuck with that label. If the pseudopatient was to be discharged, he must naturally be "in remission"; but he was not sane, nor, in the institution's view, had he ever been sane.

The uniform failure to recognize sanity cannot be attributed to the quality of the hospitals, for, although there were considerable variations among them, several are considered excellent. Nor can it be alleged that there was simply not enough time to observe the pseudopatients. Length of hospitalization ranged from 7 to 52 days, with an average of 19 days. The pseudopatients were not, in fact, carefully observed, but this failure clearly speaks more to traditions within psychiatric hospitals than to lack of opportunity.

Finally, it cannot be said that the failure to recognize the pseudopatients' sanity was due to the fact that they were not behaving sanely. While there was clearly some tension present in all of them, their daily visitors could detect no serious behavioral consequences—nor, indeed, could other patients. It was quite common for the patients to "detect" the pseudopatients' sanity. During the first three hospitalizations, when accurate counts were kept, 35 of a total of 118 patients on the admissions ward voiced their suspicions, some vigorously, "You're not crazy. You're a journalist, or a professor [referring to the continual note-taking]. You're checking up on the hospital." While most of the patients were reassured by the pseudopatient's insistence that he had been sick before he came in but was fine now, some continued to believe that the pseudopatient was sane throughout his hospitalization.[11] The fact that the patients often recognized normality when staff did not raises important questions.

Failure to detect sanity during the course of hospitalization may be due to the fact that physicians operate with a strong bias toward what statisticians call the type 2 error.[12] This is to say that physicians are more inclined to call a healthy person sick (a false positive, type 2) than a sick person healthy (a false negative, type 1). The reasons for this are not hard to find: It is clearly more dangerous to misdiagnose illness than health. Better to err on the side of caution, to suspect illness even among the healthy.

But what holds for medicine does not hold equally well for psychiatry. Medical illnesses, while unfortunate, are not commonly pejorative. Psychiatric diagnoses, on the contrary, carry with them personal, legal, and social stigmas.[13] It was therefore important to see whether the tendency toward diagnosing the sane insane could be reversed. The following experiment was arranged at a research and teaching hospital whose staff had heard of these findings but doubted that such an error could occur in their hospital. The staff was informed that at some time during the following three months, one or more pseudopatients would attempt to be admitted into the psychiatric hospital. Each staff member was asked to rate each patient who presented himself at admissions or on the ward according to the likelihood that the patient was a pseudopatient. A 10-point scale was used, with a 1 and 2 reflecting high confidence that the patient was a pseudopatient.

Judgments were obtained on 193 patients who were admitted for psychiatric treatment. All staff who had had sustained contact with or primary responsibility for the patient—attendants, nurses, psychiatrists, physicians, and psychologists—were asked to make judgments. Forty-one patients were alleged, with high confidence, to be pseudopatients by at least one member of the staff. Twenty-three were considered suspect by at least one psychiatrist. Nineteen were suspected by one psychiatrist *and* one other staff member. Actually, no genuine pseudopatient (at least from my group) presented himself during this period.

The experiment is instructive. It indicates that the tendency to designate sane people as insane can be reversed when the stakes (in this case, prestige and diagnostic acumen) are high. But what can be said of the 19 people who were suspected of being "sane" by one psychiatrist and another staff member? Were these people truly "sane," or was it rather the case that in the course of avoiding the type 2 error the staff tended to make more errors of the first sort—calling the crazy "sane"? There is no way of knowing. But one thing is certain: Any diagnostic process that lends itself so readily to massive errors of this sort cannot be a very reliable one.

## The Stickiness of Psychodiagnostic Labels

Beyond the tendency to call the healthy sick—a tendency that accounts better for diagnostic behavior on admission than it does for such behavior after a lengthy period of exposure—the data speak to the massive role of labeling in psychiatric assessment. Having once been labeled schizophrenic, there is nothing the pseudopatient can do to overcome the tag. The tag profoundly colors others' perceptions of him and his behavior.

From one viewpoint, these data are hardly surprising, for it has long been known that elements are given meaning by the context in which they occur. Gestalt psychology made this point vigorously, and Asch[14] demonstrated that there are "central" personality traits (such as "warm" versus "cold") which are so powerful that they markedly color the meaning of other information in forming an impression of a given personality.[15] "Insane," "schizophrenic," "manic-depressive," and "crazy" are probably among the most powerful of such central traits. Once a person is designated abnormal, all of his other behaviors and characteristics are colored by that label. Indeed, that label is so powerful that many of the pseudopatients' normal behav-

iors were overlooked entirely or profoundly misinterpreted. Some examples may clarify this issue.

Earlier I indicated that there were no changes in the pseudopatient's personal history and current status beyond those of name, employment, and, where necessary, vocation. Otherwise, a veridical description of personal history and circumstances was offered. Those circumstances were not psychotic. How were they made consonant with the diagnosis of psychosis? Or were those diagnoses modified in such a way as to bring them into accord with the circumstances of the pseudopatient's life, as described by him?

As far as I can determine, diagnoses were in no way affected by the relative health of the circumstances of a pseudopatient's life. Rather, the reverse occurred: The perception of his circumstances was shaped entirely by the diagnosis. A clear example of such translation is found in the case of a pseudopatient who had had a close relationship with his mother but was rather remote from his father during his early childhood. During adolescence and beyond, however, his father became a close friend, while his relationship with his mother cooled. His present relationship with his wife was characteristically close and warm. Apart from occasional angry exchanges, friction was minimal. The children had rarely been spanked. Surely there is nothing especially pathological about such a history. Indeed, many readers may see a similar pattern in their own experiences, with no markedly deleterious consequences. Observe, however, how such a history was translated in the psychopathological context, this from the case summary prepared after the patient was discharged.

This white 39-year-old male . . . manifests a long history of considerable ambivalence in close relationships, which begins in early childhood. A warm relationship with his mother cools during his adolescence. A distant relationship to his father is described as becoming very intense. Affective stability is absent. His attempts to control emotionality with his wife and children are punctuated by angry outbursts and, in the case of the children, spankings. And while he says that he has several good friends, one senses considerable ambivalence embedded in those relationships also. . . .

The facts of the case were unintentionally distorted by the staff to achieve consistency with a popular theory of the dynamics of a schizophrenic reaction.[16] Nothing of an ambivalent nature had been described in relations with parents, spouse, or friends. To the extent that ambivalence could be inferred, it was probably not greater than is found in all human relationships. It is true the pseudopatient's relationships with his parents changed over time, but in the ordinary context that would hardly be remarkable—indeed, it might very well be expected. Clearly, the meaning ascribed to his verbalizations (that is, ambivalence, affective instability) was determined by the diagnosis: schizophrenia. An entirely different meaning would have been ascribed if it were known that the man was "normal."

All pseudopatients took extensive notes publicly. Under ordinary circumstances, such behavior would have raised questions in the minds of observers, as, in fact, it did among patients. Indeed, it seemed so certain that the notes would elicit suspicion that elaborate precautions were taken to remove them from the ward each day. But the precautions proved needless. The closest any staff member came to questioning those notes occurred when one pseudopatient asked his physician what kind of medication he was receiving and began to write down the response. "You needn't write it," he was told gently. "If you have trouble remembering, just ask me again."

If no questions were asked of the pseudopatients, how was their writing interpreted? Nursing records for three patients indicate that the writing was seen as an aspect of their pathological behavior. "Patient engages in writing behavior" was the daily nursing comment on one of the pseudopatients who was never questioned about his writing. Given that the patient is in the hospital, he must be psychologically disturbed. And given that he is disturbed, continuous writing must be a behavioral manifestation of that disturbance, perhaps a subset of the compulsive behaviors that are sometimes correlated with schizophrenia.

One tacit characteristic of psychiatric diagnosis is that it locates the sources of aberration within the individual and only rarely within the complex of stimuli that surrounds him. Consequently, behaviors that are stimulated by the environment are commonly misattributed to the patient's disorder. For example, one kindly nurse found a pseudopatient pacing the long hospital corridors. "Nervous, Mr. X?" she asked. "No, bored," he said.

The notes kept by pseudopatients are full of patient behaviors that were misinterpreted by well-intentioned staff. Often enough, a patient would go "berserk" because he had, wittingly or unwittingly, been mistreated by, say, an attendant. A nurse coming upon the scene would rarely inquire even cursorily into the environmental stimuli of the patient's behavior. Rather, she assumed that his upset derived from his pathology, not from his present interactions with other staff members. Occasionally, the staff might assume that the patient's family (especially when they had recently visited) or other patients had stimulated the outburst. But never were the staff found to assume that one of themselves or the structure of the hospital had anything to do with a patient's behavior. One psychiatrist pointed to a group of patients who were sitting outside the cafeteria entrance half an hour before lunchtime. To a group of young residents he indicated that such behavior was characteristic of the oral-acquisitive nature of the syndrome. It seemed not to occur to him that there were very few things to anticipate in a psychiatric hospital besides eating.

A psychiatric label has a life and an influence of its own. Once the impression has been formed that the patient is schizophrenic, the expectation is that he will continue to be schizophrenic. When a sufficient amount of time has passed, during which the patient has done nothing bizarre, he is considered to be in remission and available for discharge. But the label endures beyond discharge, with the unconfirmed expectation that he will behave as a schizophrenic again. Such labels, conferred by mental health professionals, are as influential on the patient as they are on his relatives and friends, and it should not surprise anyone that the diagnosis acts on all of them as a self-fulfilling prophecy. Eventually, the patient himself accepts the diagnosis, with all of its surplus meanings and expectations, and behaves accordingly.[17]

The inferences to be made from these matters are quite simple. Much as Zigler and Phillips have demonstrated that there is enormous overlap in the symptoms presented by patients who have been variously diagnosed,[18] so there is enormous overlap in the behaviors of the sane and the insane. The sane are not "sane" all of the time. We lose our tempers "for no good reason." We are occasionally depressed or anxious, again for no good reason. And we may find it difficult to get along with one or another person—again for no reason that we can specify. Similarly, the insane are not always insane. Indeed, it was the impression of the pseudopatients while living with them that they were sane for long periods of time—that the bizarre behaviors upon which their diagnoses were allegedly predicated constituted only a small fraction of their total behavior. If it makes no sense to label ourselves permanently depressed on the basis of an occasional depression, then it takes better evidence than is presently available to label all patients insane or schizophrenic on the basis of bizarre behaviors or cognitions. It seems more useful, as Mischel[19] has pointed out, to limit our discussions to *behaviors*, the stimuli that provoke them, and their correlates.

It is not known why powerful impressions of personality traits, such as "crazy" or "insane," arise. Conceivably, when the origins of and stimuli that give rise to a behavior are remote or unknown, or when the behavior strikes us as immutable, trait labels regarding the *behaver* arise. When, on the other hand, the origins and stimuli are known and available, discourse is limited to the behavior itself. Thus, I may hallucinate because I am sleeping, or I may hallucinate because I have ingested a peculiar drug. These are termed sleep-induced hallucinations, or dreams, and drug-induced hallucinations, respectively. But when the stimuli to my hallucinations are unknown, that is called craziness, or schizophrenia—as if that inference were somehow as illuminating as the others. . . .

## The Consequences of Labeling and Depersonalization

Whenever the ratio of what is known to what needs to be known approaches zero, we tend to invent "knowledge" and assume that we understand more than we actually do. We seem unable to acknowledge that we simply don't know. The needs for diagnosis and remediation of behavioral and emotional problems are enormous. But rather than acknowledge that we are just embarking on understanding, we continue to label patients "schizophrenic," "manic-depressive," and "insane," as if in those words we had captured the essence of understanding. The facts of the matter are that we have known for a long time that diagnoses are often not useful or reliable, but we have nevertheless continued to use them. We now know that we cannot distinguish insanity from sanity. It is depressing to consider how that information will be used.

Not merely depressing, but frightening. How many people, one wonders, are sane but not recognized as such in our psychiatric institutions? How many have been needlessly stripped of their privileges of citizenship, from the right to vote and drive to that of handling their own accounts? How many have feigned insanity in order to avoid the criminal consequences of their behavior, and, conversely, how many would rather stand trial than live interminably in a psychiatric hospital—but are wrongly thought to be mentally ill? How many have been stigmatized by well-intentioned, but nevertheless erroneous, diagnoses? On the last point, recall again that a "type 2 error" in psychiatric diagnosis does not have the same consequences it does in medical diagnosis. A diagnosis of cancer that has been found to be in error is cause for celebration. But psychiatric diagnoses are rarely found to be in error. The label sticks, a mark of inadequacy forever.

## Notes

1. P. Ash (1949), *J. Abnorm. Soc. Psychol.*, 44, 272 (1949); A. T. Beck (1962), *Amer. J. Psychiat.*, 119, 210; A. T. Boisen (1938), *Psychiatry*, 2, 233; N. Kreitman (1961), *J. Ment. Sci.*, 107, 876; N. Kreitman, P. Sainsbury, J. Morrisey, J. Towers, & J. Scrivener (1961), *J. Ment. Sci.*, 107, 887; H. O. Schmitt & C. P. Fonda (1956), *J. Abnorm. Soc. Psychol.*, 52, 262; W. Seeman (1953), *J. Nerv. Ment. Dis.*, 118, 541. For an analysis of these artifacts and summaries of the disputes, see J. Zibin (1967), *Annu. Rev. Psychol.*, 18, 373; L. Phillips & J. G. Draguns (1971), *Annu. Rev. Psychol.*, 22, 447.

2. R. Benedict (1934), *J. Gen. Psychol.*, 10, 59.

3. See in this regard H. Becker (1963), *Outsiders: Studies in the sociology of deviance*, New York: Free Press; B. M. Braginsky, D. D. Braginsky, & K. Ring (1969), *Methods of madness: The mental hospital as a last resort*, New York: Holt, Rinehart & Winston; G. M. Crocetti & P. V. Lemkau (1965), *Amer. Sociol. Rev.*, 30, 577; E. Goffman (1964), *Behavior in public places*, New York: Free Press; R. D. Laing (1960), *The divided self: A study of sanity and madness*, Chicago: Quadrangle; D. L. Phillips (1963), *Amer. Sociol. Rev.*, 20, 963; T. R. Sarbin (1972), *Psychol. Today*, 6, 18; E. Schur (1969), *Amer. J. Sociol.*, 75, 309; T. Szasz (1963a), *Law, liberty and psychiatry*, New York: Macmillan; (1963b), *The myth of mental illness: Foundations of a theory of mental illness*, New York: Hoeber Harper. For a critique of some of these views, see W. R. Gove (1970), *Amer. Sociol. Rev.*, 35, 873.

4. E. Goffman (1961), *Asylums*, Garden City, NY: Doubleday.

5. T. J. Scheff (1966), *Being mentally ill: A sociological theory*, Chicago: Aldine.

6. Data from a ninth pseudopatient are not incorporated in this report because, although his sanity went undetected, he falsified aspects of his personal history, including his marital status and parental relationships. His experimental behaviors therefore were not identical to those of the other pseudopatients.

7. A. Barry (1971), *Bellevue is a state of mind*, New York: Harcourt Brace Jovanovich; I. Belknap (1956), *Human problems of a state mental hospital*, New York: McGraw-Hill; W. Caudill, F. C. Redlich, H. R. Gilmore, & E. B. Brody, *Amer. J. Orthopsychiat.*, 22, 314; A. R. Goldman, R. H. Bohr, & T. A. Steinberg (1970), *Prof. Psychol.*, 1, 427; *Roche Report*, 1 (13 [1971]), 8.

8. Beyond the personal difficulties that the pseudopatient is likely to experience in the hospital, there are legal and social ones that, combined, require considerable attention before entry. For example, once admitted to a psychiatric institution, it is difficult, if not impossible, to be discharged on short notice, state law to the contrary notwithstanding. I was not sensitive to these difficulties at the outset of the project, nor to the personal and situational emergencies that can arise, but later a writ of habeas corpus was prepared for each of the entering pseudopatients and an attorney was kept "on call" during every hospitalization. I am grateful to John Kaplan and Robert Bartels for legal advice and assistance in these matters.

9. However distasteful such concealment is, it was a necessary first step to examining these questions. Without concealment, there would have been no way to know how valid these experiences were; nor was there any way of knowing whether whatever detections occurred were a tribute to the diagnostic acumen of the staff or to the hospital's rumor network. Obviously, since my concerns are general ones that cut across individual hospitals and staffs, I have respected their anonymity and have eliminated clues that might lead to their identification.

10. Interestingly, of the 12 admissions, 11 were diagnosed as schizophrenic and one, with the identical symptomatology, as manic-depressive psychosis. This diagnosis has a more favorable prognosis, and it was given by the only private hospital in our sample. On the relations between social class and psychiatric diagnosis, see A. deB. Hollingshead & F. C. Redlich (1958), *Social class and mental illness: A community study,* New York: John Wiley.

11. It is possible, of course, that patients have quite broad latitudes in diagnosis and therefore are inclined to call many people sane, even those whose behavior is patently aberrant. However, although we have no hard data on this matter, it was our distinct impression that this was not the case. In many instances, patients not only singled us out for attention, but came to imitate our behaviors and styles.

12. T. J. Scheff, *ibid.*

13. J. Cumming & E. Cumming (1965), *Community Ment. Health, 1,* 135; A. Farina & K. Ring (1965), *J. Abnorm. Psychol., 70,* 47; H. E. Freeman & O. G. Simmons (1963), *The mental patient comes home,* New York: John Wiley; W. J. Johannsen (1969), *Ment. Hygiene, 53,* 218; A. S. Linsky (1970), *Soc. Psychiat., 5,* 166.

14. S. E. Asch (1946), *J. Abnorm. Soc. Psychol., 41,* 258; (1952), *Social psychology,* Englewood Cliffs, NJ: Prentice-Hall.

15. See also I. N. Mensch & J. Wishner (1947), *J. Personality, 16,* 188; J. Wishner (1960), *Psychol. Rev., 67,* 96; J. S. Bruner & R. Tagiuri (1954), in G. Lindzey (Ed.), *Handbook of social psychology* (Vol. 2, pp. 634–654), Cambridge, MA: Addison-Wesley; J. S. Bruner, D. Shapiro, & R. Tagiuri (1958), in R. Tagiuri & L. Petrullo (Eds.), *Person perception and interpersonal behavior* (pp. 277–288), Stanford, CA: Stanford University Press.

16. For an example of a similar self-fulfilling prophecy, in this instance dealing with the "central" trait of intelligence, see R. Rosenthal & L. Jacobson (1968), *Pygmalion in the classroom,* New York: Holt, Rinehart & Winston.

17. T. J. Scheff, *ibid.*

18. E. Zigler & L. Phillips (1961), *J. Abnorm. Soc. Psychol., 63,* 69. See also R. K. Freudenberg & J. P. Robertson (1956), *A.M.A. Arch. Neurol. Psychiatr., 76,* 14.

19. W. Mischel (1968), *Personality and assessment,* New York: John Wiley.

# The Discovery of Hyperkinesis: Notes on the Medicalization of Deviant Behavior

## Peter Conrad

## Introduction

The increasing medicalization of deviant behavior and the medical institution's role as an agent of social control has gained considerable notice (Freidson, 1970; Pitts, 1968; Kitterie, 1971; Zola, 1972). By *medicalization* we mean defining behavior as a medical problem or illness and mandating or licensing the medical profession to provide some type of treatment for it. Examples include alcoholism, drug addiction, and treating violence as a genetic or brain disorder. This redefinition is not a new function of the medical institution: Psychiatry and public health have always been concerned with social behavior and have traditionally functioned as agents of social control (Foucault, 1965;

"The Discovery of Hyperkinesis: Notes on the Medicalization of Deviant Behavior" by P. Conrad, 1975. *Social Problems* 23, no. 1 (October), pp. 12–21. Copyright © 1975 by the Society for the Study of Social Problems. Reprinted by permission.

This paper is a revised version of a paper presented at the meetings of the Society for the Study of Social Problems in San Francisco, August 1975. It was partially supported by a National Science Foundation dissertation grant (SOC 74–22043). I would like to thank Drs. Martin Kozloff, James E. Teele, John McKinlay, and the anonymous referees for comments on earlier drafts of this paper.

Szasz, 1970; Rosen, 1972). Increasingly sophisticated medical technology has extended the potential of this type of social control, especially in terms of psychotechnology (Chorover, 1973). This approach includes a variety of medical and quasi-medical treatments or procedures: psychosurgery, psychotropic medications, genetic engineering, antibuse, and methadone.

This paper describes how certain forms of behavior in children have become defined as a medical problem and how medicine has become a major agent for their social control since the discovery of hyperkinesis. By discovery we mean both origin of the diagnosis and treatment for this disorder, and discovery of children who exhibit this behavior. The first section analyzes the discovery of hyperkinesis and why it suddenly became popular in the 1960s. The second section will discuss the medicalization of deviant behavior and its ramifications.

## The Medical Diagnosis of Hyperkinesis

Hyperkinesis is a relatively recent phenomenon as a medical diagnostic category. Only in the past two decades has it been available as a recognized diagnostic category and only in the last decade has it received widespread notice and medical popularity. However, the roots of the diagnosis and treatment of this clinical entity are found earlier.

Hyperkinesis is also known as Minimal Brain Dysfunction, Hyperactive Syndrome, Hyperkinetic Disorder of Childhood, and by several other diagnostic categories. Although the symptoms and the presumed etiology vary, in general the behaviors are quite similar and greatly overlap.[1] Typical symptom patterns for diagnosing the disorder include: extreme excess of motor activity (hyperactivity); very short attention span (the child flits from activity to activity); restlessness; fidgetiness; often wildly oscillating mood swings (he's fine one day, a terror the next); clumsiness; aggressive-like behavior; impulsivity; in school he cannot sit still, cannot comply with rules, has low frustration level; frequently there may be sleeping problems and acquisition of speech may be delayed (Stewart et al., 1966; Stewart, 1970; Wender, 1971). Most of the symptoms for the disorder are deviant behaviors.[2] It is six times as prevalent among boys as among girls. We use the term *hyperkinesis* to represent all the diagnostic categories of this disorder.

### The Discovery of Hyperkinesis

It is useful to divide the analysis into what might be considered *clinical factors* directly related to the diagnosis and treatment of hyperkinesis and *social factors* that set the context for the emergence of the new diagnostic category.

#### Clinical Factors

Bradley (1937) observed that amphetamine drugs had a spectacular effect in altering the behavior of school children who exhibited behavior disorders or learning disabilities. Fifteen of the thirty children he treated actually became more subdued in their behavior. Bradley termed the effect of this medication paradoxical, since he expected that amphetamines would stimulate children as they

stimulated adults. After the medication was discontinued the children's behavior returned to premedication level.

A scattering of reports in the medical literature on the utility of stimulant medications for "childhood behavior disorders" appeared in the next two decades. The next significant contribution was the work of Strauss and his associates (Strauss & Lehtinen, 1947) who found certain behavior (including hyperkinesis behaviors) in postencephaletic children suffering from what they called minimal brain injury (damage). This was the first time these behaviors were attributed to the new organic distinction of minimal brain damage.

This disorder still remained unnamed or else it was called a variety of names (usually just "childhood behavior disorder"). It did not appear as a specific diagnostic category until Laufer, Denhoff, and Solomons (1957) described it as the "hyperkinetic impulse disorder" in 1957. Upon finding "the salient characteristics of the behavior pattern . . . are strikingly similar to those with clear cut organic causation" these researchers described a disorder with no clear-cut history or evidence for organicity (Laufer et al., 1957).

In 1966 a task force sponsored by the U.S. Public Health Service and the National Association for Crippled Children and Adults attempted to clarify the ambiguity and confusion in terminology and symptomology in diagnosing children's behavior and learning disorders. From over three dozen diagnoses, they agreed on the term "minimal brain dysfunction" as an overriding diagnosis that would include hyperkinesis and other disorders (Clements, 1966). Since this time MBD has been the primary formal diagnosis or label.

In the middle 1950s a new drug, Ritalin, was synthesized, that has many qualities of amphetamines without some of their more undesirable side effects. In 1961 this drug was approved by the FDA for use with children. Since this time there has been much research published on the use of Ritalin in the treatment of childhood behavior disorders. This medication became the "treatment of choice" for treating children with hyperkinesis.

Since the early sixties, more research appeared on the etiology, diagnosis, and treatment of hyperkinesis (cf. DeLong, 1972; Grinspoon & Singer, 1973; Cole, 1975)—as much as three-quarters concerned with drug treatment of the disorder. There had been increasing publicity of the disorder in the mass media as well. The *Reader's Guide to Periodical Literature* had no articles on hyperkinesis before 1967, one each in 1968 and 1969, and a total of forty for 1970 through 1974 (a mean of eight per year).

Now hyperkinesis has become the most common child psychiatric problem (Gross & Wilson, 1974, p. 142); special pediatric clinics have been established to treat hyperkinetic children, and substantial federal funds have been invested in etiological and treatment research. Outside the medical profession, teachers have developed a working clinical knowledge of hyperkinesis' symptoms and treatment (cf. Robin & Bosco, 1973); articles appear regularly in mass circulation magazines and newspapers so that parents often come to clinics with knowledge of this diagnosis. Hyperkinesis is no longer the relatively esoteric diagnostic category it may have been twenty years ago; it is now a well-known clinical disorder.

### Social Factors

The social factors affecting the discovery of hyperkinesis can be divided into two areas: (1) The Pharmaceutical Revolution; (2) Government Action.

*1. The Pharmaceutical Revolution.* Since the 1930s the pharmaceutical industry has been synthesizing and manufacturing a large number of psychoactive drugs, contributing to a virtual revolution in drug making and drug taking in America (Silverman & Lee, 1974).

Psychoactive drugs are agents that affect the central nervous system. Benzedrine, Ritalin, and Dexedrine are all synthesized psychoactive stimulants which were indicated for narcolepsy, appetite control (as "diet pills"), mild depression, fatigue, and more recently hyperkinetic children.

Until the early sixties there was little or no promotion and advertisement of any of these medications for use with childhood disorders.[3] Then two major pharmaceutical firms (Smith, Kline, and French, manufacturer of Dexedrine, and CIBA, manufacturer of Ritalin) began to advertise in medical journals and through direct mailing and efforts of the "detail men." Most of this advertising of the pharmaceutical treatment of hyperkinesis was directed to the medical sphere; but some of the promotion was targeted for the educational sector also (Hentoff, 1972). This promotion was probably significant in disseminating information concerning the diagnosis and treatment of this newly discovered disorder.[4] Since 1955 the use of psychoactive medications (especially phenothiazines) for the treatment of persons who are mentally ill, along with the concurrent dramatic decline in inpatient populations, has made psychopharmacology an integral part of treatment for mental disorders. It has also undoubtedly increased the confidence in the medical profession for the pharmaceutical approach to mental and behavioral problems.

*2. Government Action.* Since the publication of the USPHS report on MBD there have been at least two significant governmental reports on treating school children with stimulant medications for behavior disorders. Both of these came as a response to the national publicity created by the *Washington Post* report (1970) that 5 to 10 percent of the 62,000 grammar school children in Omaha, Nebraska were being treated with "behavior modification drugs to improve deportment and increase learning potential" (quoted in Grinspoon & Singer, 1973). Although the figures were later found to be a little exaggerated, it nevertheless spurred a Congressional investigation (U.S. Government Printing Office, 1970) and a conference sponsored by the

Office of Child Development (1971) on the use of stimulant drugs in the treatment of behaviorally disturbed school children.

The Congressional Subcommittee on Privacy chaired by Congressman Cornelius E. Gallagher held hearings on the issue of prescribing drugs for hyperactive school children. In general, the committee showed great concern over the facility in which the medication was prescribed; more specifically that some children at least were receiving drugs from general practitioners whose primary diagnosis was based on teachers' and parents' reports that the child was doing poorly in school. There was also a concern with the absence of follow-up studies on the long-term effects of treatment.

The HEW committee was a rather hastily convened group of professionals (a majority were M.D.s) many of whom already had commitments to drug treatment for children's behavior problems. They recommended that only M.D.s make the diagnosis and prescribe treatment, that the pharmaceutical companies promote the treatment of the disorder only through medical channels, that parents should not be coerced to accept any particular treatment, and that long-term follow-up research should be done. This report served as blue ribbon approval for treating hyperkinesis with psychoactive medications.

## Discussion

We will focus discussion on three issues: How children's deviant behavior became conceptualized as a medical problem; why this occurred when it did; and what are some of the implications of the medicalization of deviant behavior.

How does deviant behavior become conceptualized as a medical problem? We assume that before the discovery of hyperkinesis this type of deviance was seen as disruptive, disobedient, rebellious, antisocial, or deviant behavior. Perhaps the label "emotionally disturbed" was sometimes used, when it was in vogue in the early sixties, and the child was usually managed in the context of the family or the school or in extreme cases, the child guidance clinic. How then did this constellation of deviant behaviors become a medical disorder?

The treatment was available long before the disorder treated was clearly conceptualized. It was twenty years after Bradley's discovery of the "paradoxical effect" of stimulants on certain deviant children that Laufer named the disorder and described its characteristic symptoms. Only in the late fifties were both the diagnostic label and the pharmaceutical treatment available. The pharmaceutical revolution in mental health and the increased interest in child psychiatry provided a favorable background for the dissemination of knowledge about this new disorder. The latter probably made the medical profession more likely to consider behavior problems in children as within their clinical jurisdiction.

There were agents outside the medical profession itself that were significant in "promoting" hyperkinesis as a disorder within the medical framework. These agents might be conceptualized in Becker's terms as "moral entrepreneurs," those who crusade for creation and enforcement of the rules (Becker, 1963).[5] In this case the moral entrepreneurs were the pharmaceutical companies and the Association for Children with Learning Disabilities.

The pharmaceutical companies spent considerable time and money promoting stimulant medications for this new disorder. From the middle 1960s on, medical journals and the free "throwaway" magazines contained elaborate advertising for Ritalin and Dexedrine. These ads explained the utility of treating hyperkinesis and urged the physician to diagnose and treat hyperkinetic children. The ads run from one to six pages. For example, a two-page ad in 1971 stated:

MBD . . . MEDICAL MYTH OR DIAGNOSABLE DISEASE ENTITY? What medical practitioner has not, at one time or another, been called upon to examine an impulsive, excitable hyperkinetic child? A child with difficulty in concentrating. Easily frustrated. Unusually aggressive. A classroom rebel. In the absence of any organic pathology, the conduct of such children was, until a few short years ago, usually dismissed as . . . spunkiness, or evidence of youthful vitality. But it is now evident that in many of these children the hyperkinetic syndrome exists as a distinct medical entity. This syndrome—readily diagnosed through patient histories, neurologic signs, and psychometric testing—has been classified by an expert panel convened by the United States Department of Health, Education and Welfare as Minimal Brain Dysfunction, MBD.

The pharmaceutical firms also supplied sophisticated packets of "diagnostic and treatment" information on hyperkinesis to physicians, paid for professional conferences on the subject, and supported research in the identification and treatment of the disorder. Clearly these corporations had a vested interest in the labeling and treatment of hyperkinesis; CIBA had $13 million profit from Ritalin alone in 1971, which was 15 percent of the total gross profits (Charles, 1971; Hentoff, 1972).

The other moral entrepreneur, less powerful than the pharmaceutical companies, but nevertheless influential, is the Association for Children with Learning Disabilities. Although its focus is not specifically on hyperkinetic children, it does include it in its conception of learning disabilities along with aphasia, reading problems like dyslexia, and perceptual motor problems. Founded in the early 1950s by parents and professionals, it has functioned much as the National Association for Mental Health does for mental illness: promoting conferences, sponsoring legislation, providing social support. One of the main functions has been to disseminate information concerning this relatively new area in education, Learning Disabilities. While the organization does have a more educational than medical perspective, most of the literature indicates that for hyperkinesis members

have adopted the medical model and the medical approach to the problem. They have sensitized teachers and schools to the conception of hyperkinesis as a medical problem.

The medical model of hyperactive behavior has become very well accepted in our society. Physicians find treatment relatively simple and the results sometimes spectacular. Hyperkinesis minimizes parents' guilt by emphasizing "It's not their fault, it's an organic problem" and allows for nonpunitive management or control of deviance. Medication often makes a child less disruptive in the classroom and sometimes aids a child in learning. Children often like their "magic pills" which make their behavior more socially acceptable and they probably benefit from a reduced stigma also. There are, however, some other, perhaps more subtle ramifications of the medicalization of deviant behavior.

### The Medicalization of Deviant Behavior

Pitts has commented that "Medicalization is one of the most effective means of social control and that it is destined to become the main mode of *formal* social control"(1971, p. 391). Kitterie (1971) has termed it "the coming of the therapeutic state."

Medicalization of mental illness dates at least from the seventeenth century (Foucault, 1965; Szasz, 1970). Even slaves who ran away were once considered to be suffering from the disease *drapetomania* (Chorover, 1973). In recent years alcoholism, violence, and drug addiction as well as hyperactive behavior in children have all become defined as medical problems, both in etiology or explanation of the behavior and the means of social control or treatment.

There are many reasons why this medicalization has occurred. Much scientific research, especially in pharmacology and genetics, has become technologically more sophisticated, and found more subtle correlates with human behavior. Sometimes these findings (as in the case of XYY chromosomes and violence) become etiological explanations for deviance. Pharmacological technology that makes new discoveries affecting behavior (e.g., antibuse, methadone, and stimulants) is used as treatment for deviance. In part this application is encouraged by the prestige of the medical profession and its attachment to science. As Freidson notes, the medical profession has first claim to jurisdiction over anything that deals with the functioning of the body and especially anything that can be labeled illness (1970, p. 251). Advances in genetics, pharmacology, and "psychosurgery" also may advance medicine's jurisdiction over deviant behavior.

Second, the application of pharmacological technology is related to the humanitarian trend in the conception and control of deviant behavior. Alcoholism is no longer sin or even moral weakness, it is now a disease. Alcoholics are no longer arrested in many places for "public drunkenness," they are now somehow "treated," even if it is only to be dried out. Hyperactive children are now considered to have an illness rather than to be disruptive, disobedient, overactive problem children. They are not as likely to be the "bad boy" of the classroom; they are children with a medical disorder. Clearly there are some real humanitarian benefits to be gained by such a medical conceptualization of deviant behavior. There is less condemnation of the deviants (they have an illness, it is not their fault) and perhaps less social stigma. In some cases, even the medical treatment itself is more humanitarian social control than the criminal justice system.

There is, however, another side to the medicalization of deviant behavior. The four aspects of this side of the issue include (1) the problem of expert control; (2) medical social control; (3) the individualization of social problems; and (4) the "depoliticization" of deviant behavior.

*1. The Problem of Expert Control.* The medical profession is a profession of experts; they have a monopoly on anything that can be conceptualized as illness. Because of the way the medical profession is organized and the mandate it has from society, decisions related to medical diagnoses and treatment are virtually controlled by medical professionals.

Some conditions that enter the medical domain are not ipso facto medical problems, especially deviant behavior, whether alcoholism, hyperactivity, or drug addiction. By defining a problem as medical it is removed from the public realm where there can be discussion by ordinary people and put on a plane where only medical people can discuss it. As Reynolds states,

The increasing acceptance, especially among the more educated segments of our populace, of technical solutions—solutions administered by disinterested politically and morally neutral experts—results in the withdrawal of more and more areas of human experience from the realm of public discussion. For when drunkenness, juvenile delinquency, sub par performance and extreme political beliefs are seen as symptoms of an underlying illness or biological defect the merits and drawbacks of such behavior or beliefs need not be evaluated. (1973, pp. 220–221)

The public may have their own conceptions of deviant behavior but that of the experts is usually dominant.

*2. Medical Social Control.* Defining deviant behavior as a medical problem allows certain things to be done that could not otherwise be considered; for example, the body may be cut open or psychoactive medications may be given. This treatment can be a form of social control.

In regard to drug treatment Lennard points out: "Psychoactive drugs, especially those legally prescribed, tend to restrain individuals from behavior and experience that are not complementary to the requirements of the dominant value system" (1971, p. 57). These forms of medical social control presume a prior definition of deviance as a medical problem. Psychosurgery on an individual prone to violent outbursts requires a diagnosis that there was something wrong with his brain or nervous system. Similarly, prescribing drugs to restless, overactive, and disruptive school children requires a diagnosis of hyperkinesis. These forms of social control, what Chorover (1973) has called "psychotechnology," are very powerful and often very efficient means of controlling deviance. These relatively new and increasingly popular forms of social control could not be utilized without the medicalization of deviant behavior. As is suggested from the discovery of hospice, if a mechanism of medical social control seems useful, then the deviant behavior it modifies will develop a medical label or diagnosis. No overt malevolence on the part of the medical profession is implied: rather it is part of a complex process, of which the medical profession is only a part. The larger process might be called the individualization of social problems.

*3. The Individualization of Social Problems.* The medicalization of deviant behavior is part of a larger phenomenon that is prevalent in our society, the individualization of social problems. We tend to look for causes and solutions to complex social problems in the individual rather than in the social system. This view resembles Ryan's (1971) notion of "blaming the victim," seeing the causes of the problem in individuals rather than in the society where they live. We then seek to change the "victim" rather than the society. The medical perspective of diagnosing an illness in an individual lends itself to the individualization of social problems. Rather than seeing certain deviant behaviors as symptomatic of problems in the social system, the medical perspective focuses on the individual diagnosing and treating the illness, generally ignoring the social situation.

Hyperkinesis serves as a good example. Both the school and the parents are con-cerned with the child's behavior; the child is very difficult at home and disruptive in school. No punishments or rewards seem consistently to work in modifying the behavior; and both parents and school are at their wit's end. A medical evaluation is suggested. The diagnosis of hyperkinetic behavior leads to prescribing stimulant medications. The child's behavior seems to become more socially acceptable, reducing problems in school and at home.

But there is an alternate perspective. By focusing on the symptoms and defining them as hyperkinesis we ignore the possibility that behavior is not an illness but an adaptation to a social situation. It diverts our attention from the family or school and from seriously entertaining the idea that the "problem" could be in the structure of the social system. And by giving medications we are essentially supporting the existing systems and do not allow this behavior to be a factor of change in the system.

*4. The Depoliticization of Deviant Behavior.* Depoliticization of deviant behavior is a result of both the process of medicalization and individualization of social problems. To our Western world, probably one of the clearest examples of such a depoliticization of deviant behavior occurred when political dissenters in the Soviet Union were declared mentally ill and confined in mental hospitals (cf. Conrad, 1972). This strategy served to neutralize the meaning of political protest and dissent, rendering it the ravings of mad persons.

The medicalization of deviant behavior depoliticizes deviance in the same manner. By defining the overactive, restless and disruptive child as hyperkinetic we ignore the meaning of behavior in the context of the social system. If we focused our analysis on the school system we might see the child's behavior as symptomatic of some "disorder" in the school or classroom situation, rather than symptomatic of an individual neurological disorder.

## Conclusion

I have discussed the social ramifications of the medicalization of deviant behavior, using hyperkinesis as the example. A number of consequences of this medicalization have been outlined, including the depoliticization of deviant behavior, decision-making power of experts, and the role of medicine as an agent of social control. In the last analysis medical social control may be the central issue, as in this role medicine becomes a de facto agent of the status quo. The medical profession may not have entirely sought this role, but its members have been, in general, disturbingly unconcerned and unquestioning in their acceptance of it. With the increasing medical knowledge and technology it is likely that more deviant behavior will be medicalized and medicine's social control function will expand.

## Notes

1. The USPHS report (Clements, 1966) included 38 terms that were used to describe or distinguish the conditions that it labeled Minimal Brain Dysfunction. Although the literature attempts to differentiate MBD, hyperkinesis, hyperactive syndrome, and several other diagnostic labels, it is our belief that in practice they are almost interchangeable.

2. For a fuller discussion of the construction of the diagnosis of hyperkinesis, see Conrad (1976), especially Chapter 6.

3. The American Medical Association's change in policy in accepting more pharmaceutical advertising in the late fifties may have been important. Probably the FDA approval of the use of Ritalin for children in 1961 was more significant. Until 1970, Ritalin was advertised for treatment of "functional behavior problems in children." Since then, because of an FDA order, it has only been promoted for treatment of MBD.

4. The drug industry spends fully 25 percent of its budget on promotion and advertising. See Coleman, Katz, & Menzel (1966) for the role of the detail men and how physicians rely upon them for information.

5. Freidson also notes the medical professional role as moral entrepreneur in this process also: "The profession does treat the illnesses laymen take to it, but it also seeks to discover illness of which the laymen may not even be aware. One of the greatest ambitions of the physician is to discover and describe a 'new' disease or syndrome . . ." (1970, p. 252).

## References

Becker, H. S. (1963). *The outsiders*. New York: Free Press.

Bradley, C. (1937, March). The behavior of children receiving Benzedrine. *American Journal of Psychiatry, 94*, 577–585.

Charles, A. (1971, October). The case of Ritalin. *New Republic, 23*, 17–19.

Chorover, S. L. (1973, October). Big brother and psychotechnology. *Psychology Today*, pp. 43–54.

Clements, S. D. (1966). *Task force I: Minimal brain dysfunction in children* (National Institute of Neurological Diseases and Blindness, Monograph no. 3). Washington, DC: U.S. Department of Health, Education, and Welfare.

Cole, S. (1975, January). Hyperactive children: The use of stimulant drugs evaluated. *American Journal of Orthopsychiatry, 45*, 28–37.

Coleman, J., Katz, E., & Menzel, H. (1966). *Medical innovation*. Indianapolis: Bobbs-Merrill.

Conrad, P. (1972). *Ideological deviance: An analysis of the Soviet use of mental hospitals for political dissenters*. Unpublished manuscript.

Conrad, P. (1976). *Identifying hyperactive children in the medicalization of deviant behavior*. Lexington, MA: D. C. Heath & Co.

DeLong, A. R. (1972, February). What have we learned from psychoactive drugs research with hyperactives? *American Journal of Diseases in Children, 123*, 177–180.

Foucault, M. (1965). *Madness and civilization*. New York: Pantheon.

Freidson, E. (1970). *Profession of medicine*. New York: Harper & Row.

Grinspoon, L., & Singer, S. (1973, November). Amphetamines in the treatment of hyperactive children. *Harvard Educational Review, 43*, 515–555.

Gross, M. B., & Wilson, W. E. (1974). *Minimal brain dysfunction*. New York: Brunner/Mazel.

Hentoff, N. (1972, May). Drug pushing in the schools: The professionals. *Village Voice, 22,* 21–23.

Kitterie, N. (1971). *The right to be different.* Baltimore, MD: Johns Hopkins University Press.

Laufer, M. W., Denhoff, E., & Solomons, G. (1957, January). Hyperkinetic impulse disorder in children's behavior problems. *Psychosomatic Medicine, 19,* 38–49.

Lennard, H. L., & Associates. (1971). *Mystification and drug misuse.* New York: Harper & Row.

Office of Child Development. (1971, January 11–12). *Report of the conference on the use of stimulant drugs in treatment of behaviorally disturbed children.* Washington, DC: Department of Health, Education, and Welfare.

Pitts, J. (1968). Social control: The concept. In D. Sills (Ed.), *International Encyclopedia of the Social Sciences* (Vol. 14). New York: Macmillan.

Reynolds, J. M. (1973). The medical institution. In L. T. Reynolds & J. M. Henslin (Eds.), *American society: A critical analysis* (pp. 198–324). New York: David McKay.

Robin, S. S., & Bosco, J. J. (1973, December). Ritalin for school children: The teachers' perspective. *Journal of School Health, 47,* 624–628.

Rosen, G. (1972). The evolution of social medicine. In H. E. Freeman, S. Levine, & L. Reeder (Eds.), *Handbook of medical sociology* (pp. 30–60). Englewood Cliffs, NJ: Prentice-Hall.

Ryan, W. (1971). *Blaming the victim.* New York: Vintage.

Silverman, M., & Lee, P. R. (1974). *Pills, profits and politics.* Berkeley: University of California Press.

Sroufe, L. A., & Stewart, M. (1973, August). Treating problem children with stimulant drugs. *New England Journal of Medicine, 289,* 407–421.

Stewart, M. A. (1970, April). Hyperactive children. *Scientific American, 222,* 794–798.

Stewart, M. A., Ferris, A., Pitts, N. P., & Craig, A. G. (1966, October). The hyperactive child syndrome. *American Journal of Orthopsychiatry, 36,* 861–867.

Strauss, A. A., & Lehtinen, L. E. (1947). *Psychopathology and education of the brain-injured child* (Vol. 1). New York: Grune & Stratton.

Szasz, T. (1970). *The manufacture of madness.* New York: Harper & Row.

U.S. Government Printing Office. (1970, September 29). *Federal involvement in the use of behavior modification drugs on grammar school children of the right to privacy inquiry: Hearing before a subcommittee of the committee on government operations.* Washington, DC, 91st Congress, 2nd session.

Wender, P. (1971). *Minimal brain dysfunction in children.* New York: John Wiley.

Zola, I. (1972, November). Medicine as an institution of social control. *Sociological Review, 20,* 487–504.

# The Nudist Management of Respectability

*Martin S. Weinberg*

Public nudity is taboo in our society. Yet there is a group who breaches this moral rule. They call themselves "social nudists."

A number of questions may be asked about these people. For example, how can they see their behavior as morally appropriate? Have they constructed their own morality? If so, what characterizes this morality and what are its consequences?[1]

This article will attempt to answer these questions through a study of social interaction in nudist camps. The data come from three sources: two summers of participant observation in nudist camps; 101 interviews with nudists in the Chicago area; and 617 mailed questionnaires completed by nudists in the United States and Canada.[2]

### The Construction of Situated Moral Meanings: The Nudist Morality

The construction of morality in nudist camps is based on the official interpretations that camps provide regarding the moral meanings of public heterosexual nudity. These are (1) that nudity and sexuality are unrelated; (2) that there is nothing shameful about the human body; (3) that nudity promotes a feel-

ing of freedom and natural pleasure; and (4) that nude exposure to the sun promotes physical, mental, and spiritual well-being.

This official perspective is sustained in nudist camps to an extraordinary degree, illustrating the extent to which adult socialization can affect traditional moral meanings. (This is especially true with regard to the first two points of the nudist perspective, which will be our primary concern since these are its "deviant" aspects.) The assumption in the larger society that nudity and sexuality are related, and the resulting emphasis on covering the sexual organs, make the nudist perspective a specifically situated morality. My field work, interview, and questionnaire research show that nudists routinely use a special system of rules to create, sustain, and enforce this situated morality.

### Strategies for Sustaining a Situated Morality

The first strategy used by the nudist camp to anesthetize any relationship between nudity and sexuality[3] involves a system of organizational precautions regarding who can come into the camp. Most camps, for example, regard unmarried people, especially single men, as a threat to the nudist morality. They suspect that singles may indeed see nudity as something sexual. Thus, most camps either exclude unmarried people (especially men), or allow only a small quota of them. Camps that do allow single men may charge them up to 35 percent more than they charge families. (This is intended to discourage single men, but since the cost is still relatively low compared with other resorts, this measure is not very effective. It seems to do little more than create resentment among the singles, and by giving formal organizational backing to the definition that singles are not especially desirable, it may contribute to the segregation of single and married members in nudist camps.)

Certification by the camp owner is another requirement for admission to camp grounds, and three letters of recommendation regarding the applicant's character are sometimes required. These regulations help preclude people whom members regard as a threat to the nudist morality.

[The camp owner] invited us over to see if we were *desirable* people. Then after we did this, he invited us to camp on probation: then they voted us into camp. [Q. Could you tell me what you mean by desirable people?] Well, not people who are inclined to drink, or people who go there for a peep show. Then they don't want you there. They feel you out in conversation. They want people for mental and physical health reasons.

Whom to admit [is the biggest problem of the camp]. [Q][4] Because the world is so full of people whose attitudes on nudity are hopelessly warped. [Q: Has this always been the biggest problem in camp?] Yes. Every time anybody comes, a decision has to be made. [Q] . . . The lady sitting at the gate decides about admittance. The director decides on membership.

A limit is sometimes set on the number of trial visits a nonmember may make to camp. In addition, there is usually a limit on how long a person can remain clothed. This is a strategy to mark guests who may not sincerely accept the nudist perspective.

The second strategy for sustaining the nudist morality involves norms of interpersonal behavior. These norms are as follows:

*No Staring.* This rule controls overt signs of overinvolvement. As the publisher of one nudist magazine said, "They all look up to the heavens and never look below." Such studied inattention is most exaggerated among women, who usually show no recognition that the male is unclothed. Women also recount that they had expected men to look at their nude bodies, only to find, when they finally did get up the courage to undress, that no one seemed to notice. As one woman states: "I got so mad because my husband wanted me to undress in front of other men that I just pulled my clothes right off thinking everyone would look at me." She was amazed (and appeared somewhat disappointed) when no one did.

The following statements illustrate the constraints that result:

[Q: Have you ever observed or heard about anyone staring at someone's body while at camp?] I've heard stories, particularly about men that stare. Since I heard these stories, I tried not to, and have even done away with my sunglasses after someone said, half-joking, that I hide behind sunglasses to stare. Toward the end of the summer I stopped wearing sunglasses. And you know what, it was a child who told me this.

[Q: Would you stare . . . ?] Probably not, 'cause you can get in trouble and get thrown out. If I thought I could stare unobserved I might. They might not throw you out, but it wouldn't do you any good. [Q] The girl might tell others and they might not want to talk to me. . . . [Q] They disapprove by not talking to you, ignoring you, etc.

[Someone who stares] wouldn't belong there. [Q] If he does that he is just going to camp to see the opposite sex. [Q] He is just coming to stare. [Q] You go there to swim and relax.

I try very hard to look at them from the jaw up—even more than you would normally.[5]

*No Sex Talk.* Sex talk, or telling "dirty jokes," is uncommon in camp. The owner of a large camp in the Midwest stated: "It is usually expected that members of a nudist camp will not talk about sex, politics, or religion." Or as one single male explained: "It is taboo to make sexual remarks here." During my field work, it was rare to hear "sexual" joking such as one hears at most other types of re-sort. Interview respondents who mentioned that they had talked about sex qualified this by explaining that such talk was restricted to close friends, was of a "scientific nature," or, if a joke, was a "cute sort."

Asked what they would think of some-one who breached this rule, respondents in-dicated that such behavior would cast doubt on the situated morality of the nudist camp:

One would expect to hear less of that at camp than at other places. [Q] Because you expect that the members are screened in their attitude for nudism—and this isn't one who prefers sexual jokes.

I've never heard anyone swear or tell a dirty joke out there.

No. Not at camp. You're not supposed to. You bend over backwards not to.

They probably don't belong there. They're there to see what they can find to observe. [Q] Well, their mind isn't on being a nudist, but to see so-and-so nude.

*No Body Contact.* Although the extent to which this is enforced varies from camp to camp, there is at least some degree of informal en-forcement in nearly every camp. Nudists mention that they are particularly careful not to brush against anyone or have any body contact for fear of how it might be interpreted:

I stay clear of the opposite sex. They're so sensi-tive, they imagine things.

People don't get too close to you. Even when they talk. They sit close to you, but they don't get close enough to touch you.

We have a minimum of contact. There are more restrictions [at a nudist camp]. [Q] Just a feeling I had. I would openly show my affection more readily someplace else.

And when asked to conceptualize a breach of this rule, the following response is typical:

They are in the wrong place. [Q] That's not part of nudism. [Q] I think they are there for some

sort of sex thrill. They are certainly not there to enjoy the sun.

Also, in photographs taken for nudist magazines, the subjects usually have only limited body contact. One female nudist ex-plained: "We don't want anyone to think we're immoral." Outsiders' interpretations, then, can also constitute a threat.

Associated with the body contact taboo is a prohibition of nude dancing. Nudists cite this as a separate rule. This rule is often talked about by members in a way that indi-cates organizational strain—that is, the rule itself makes evident that a strategy is in op-eration to sustain their situated morality.

This reflects a contradiction in our beliefs. But it's self-protection. One incident and we'd be closed.

*No Alcoholic Beverages in American Camps.* This rule guards against breakdowns in inhi-bition, and even respondents who admitted that they had "snuck a beer" before going to bed went on to say that they fully favor the rule.

Yes. We have [drunk at camp]. We keep a can of beer in the refrigerator since we're out of the main area. We're not young people or carous-ers. . . . I still most generally approve of it as a camp rule and would disapprove of anyone go-ing to extremes. [Q] For common-sense reasons. People who overindulge lose their inhibitions, and there is no denying that the atmosphere of a nudist camp makes one bend over backwards to keep people who are so inclined from going be-yond the bounds of propriety.

Anyone who drinks in camp is jeopardizing their membership and they shouldn't. Anyone who drinks in camp could get reckless. [Q] Well, when guys and girls drink they're a lot bolder—they might get fresh with someone else's girl. That's why it isn't permitted, I guess.

*Rules Regarding Photography.* Photography in a nudist camp is controlled by the camp management. Unless the photographer works for a nudist magazine, his (or her) moral perspective is sometimes suspect. One photographer's remark to a woman that led to his being so typed was, "Do you think you could open your legs a little more?"

Aside from a general restriction on the use of cameras, when cameras are allowed, it is expected that no pictures will be taken without the subject's permission. Members blame the misuse of cameras especially on single men. As one nudist said: "You always see the singles poppin' around out of nowhere snappin' pictures." In general, control is maintained, and any infractions that take place are not blatant or obvious. Overindulgence in picture-taking communicates an overinvolvement in the subjects' nudity and casts doubt on the assumption that nudity and sexuality are unrelated.

Photographers dressed only in cameras and light exposure meters. I don't like them. I think they only go out for pictures. Their motives should be questioned.

Photographers for nudist magazines recognize the signs that strain the situated morality that characterizes nudist camps. As one such photographer commented:

I never let a girl look straight at the camera. It looks too suggestive. I always have her look off to the side.

Similarly, a nudist model showed the writer a pin-up magazine to point out how a model could make a nude picture "sexy"—through the use of various stagings, props, and expressions—and in contrast, how the nudist model eliminates these techniques to make her pictures "natural." Although it may be questionable that a nudist model completely eliminates a sexual perspective for the non-nudist, the model discussed how she attempts to do this.

It depends on the way you look. Your eyes and your smile can make you look sexy. The way they're looking at you. Here, she's on a bed. It wouldn't be sexy if she were on a beach with kids running around. They always have some clothes on too. See how she's "looking" sexy? Like an "Oh, dear!" look. A different look can change the whole picture.

Now here's a decent pose. . . . Outdoors makes it "nature." Here she's giving you "the eye," or is undressing. It's cheesecake. It depends on the expression on her face. Having nature behind it makes it better.

Don't smile like "Come on, honey!" It's that look and the lace thing she has on. . . . Like when you half-close your eyes, like "Oh, baby," a Marilyn Monroe look. Art is when you don't look like you're hiding it halfway.

The element of trust plays a particularly strong role in socializing women to the nudist perspective. Consider this in the following statements made by another model for nudist magazines. She and her husband had been indoctrinated in the nudist ideology by friends. At the time of the interview, however, the couple had not yet been to camp, although they had posed indoors for nudist magazines.

[Three months ago, before I was married] I never knew a man had any pubic hairs. I was shocked when I was married. . . . I wouldn't think of getting undressed in front of my husband. I wouldn't make love with a light on, or in the daytime.

With regard to being a nudist model, this woman commented:

None of the pictures are sexually seductive. [Q] The pose, the look—you can have a pose that's completely nothing, till you get a look that's not too hard to do. [Q: How do you do that?] I've never tried. By putting on a certain air about a person; a picture that couldn't be submitted to a nudist magazine—using———[the nudist photographer's] language. . . . [Q: Will your parents see your pictures in the magazine?] Possibly. I don't really care. . . . My mother might take it all right. But they've been married twenty years and she's never seen my dad undressed.[6]

*No Accentuation of the Body.* Accentuating the body is regarded as incongruent with the nudist morality. Thus, a woman who had shaved her pubic area was labeled "disgusting" by other members. There was a similar reaction to women who sat in a blatantly "unladylike" manner.

I'd think she was inviting remarks. [Q] I don't know. It seems strange to think of it. It's strange you ask it. Out there, they're not unconscious about their posture. Most women there are very circumspect even though in the nude.

For a girl, . . . [sitting with your legs open] is just not feminine or ladylike. The hair doesn't always cover it. [Q] Men get away with so many things. But, it would look dirty for a girl, like she was waiting for something. When I'm in a secluded area I've spread my legs to sun, but I kept an eye open and if anyone came I'd close my legs and sit up a little. It's just not ladylike.

You can lay on your back or side, or with your knees under your chin. But not with your legs spread apart. It would look to other people like you're there for other reasons. [Q: What other reasons?] . . . To stare and get an eyeful . . . not to enjoy the sun and people.

*No Unnatural Attempts at Covering the Body.* "Unnatural attempts" at covering the body are ridiculed since they call into question the assumption that there is no shame in exposing any area of the body. If such behavior occurs early in one's nudist career, however, members usually have more compassion, assuming that the person just has not yet fully assimilated the new morality.

It is how members interpret the behavior, however, rather than the behavior per se, that determines whether covering up is disapproved.

If they're cold or sunburned, it's understandable. If it's because they don't agree with the philosophy, they don't belong there.

I would feel their motives for becoming nudists were not well founded. That they were not true nudists, not idealistic enough.

A third strategy that is sometimes employed to sustain the nudist reality is the use of communal toilets. Not all the camps have communal toilets, but the large camp where I did most of my field work did have such a facility, which was marked, "Little Girls Room and Little Boys Too." Although the stalls had three-quarter-length doors, this combined facility still helped to provide an element of consistency; as the owner said, "If you are not ashamed of any part of your body or any of its natural functions, men and women do not need separate toilets." Thus, even the physical ecology of the nudist camp was designed to be consistent with the nudist morality. For some, however, communal toilets were going too far.

I think they should be separated. For myself it's all right. But there are varied opinions, and for the satisfaction of all, I think they should separate them. There are niceties of life we often like to maintain, and for some people this is embarrassing. . . . [Q] You know, in a bowel movement it always isn't silent.

### The Routinization of Nudity

In the nudist camp, nudity becomes routinized; its attention-provoking quality recedes and nudity becomes a taken-for-granted state of affairs. Thus, when asked questions about staring ("While at camp, have you ever stared at anyone's body? Do you think you would stare at anyone's body?") nudists indicate that nudity generally does not invoke their attention.

Nudists don't care what bodies are like. They're out there for themselves. It's a matter-of-fact thing. After a while you feel like you're sitting with a full suit of clothes on.

To nudists the body becomes so matter-of-fact, whether clothed or unclothed, when you make it an undue point of interest it becomes an abnormal thing.

[Q: What would you think of someone staring?] I would feel bad and let down. [Q] I have it set up on a high standard. I have never seen it happen. . . . [Q] Because it's not done there. It's above that: you don't stare. . . . If I saw it happen, I'd be startled. There's no inclination to do that. Why would they?

There are two types—male and female. I couldn't see why they were staring. I don't understand it.

In fact, these questions about staring elicit from nudists a frame of possibilities in which what is relevant to staring is ordinarily not nudity itself. Rather, what evokes attention is something unusual, something the observer seldom sees and thus is not routinized to.[7]

There was a red-haired man. He had red pubic hair. I had never seen this before. . . . He didn't see me. If anyone did, I would turn the other way.

Well, once l was staring at a pregnant woman. It was the first time I ever saw this. I was curious, her stomach stretched, the shape. . . . I also have stared at extremely obese people, cripples. All this is due to curiosity, just a novel sight. [Q] . . . I was discreet. [Q] I didn't look at them when their eyes were fixed in a direction so they could tell I was.

[Q: While at camp have you ever stared at someone's body?] Yes. [Q] A little girl. She has a birthmark on her back, at the base of her spine.

[Q: Do you think you would ever stare at someone's body while at camp?] No. I don't like that. I think it's silly. . . . What people are is not their fault if they are deformed.

I don't think it would be very nice, very polite. [Q] I can't see anything to stare at whether it's a scar or anything else. [Q] It just isn't done.

I've looked, but not stared. I'm careful about that, because you could get in bad about that. [Q] Get thrown out by the owner. I was curious when I once had a perfect view of a girl's sex organs, because her legs were spread when she was sitting on a chair. I sat in the chair across from her in perfect view of her organs. [Q] For about ten or fifteen minutes. [Q] Nobody noticed. [Q] It's not often you get that opportunity.[8]

[Q: How would you feel if you were alone in a secluded area of camp sunning yourself, and then noticed that other nudists were staring at your body?] I would think I had some mud on me. [Q] . . . I would just ask them why they were staring at me. Probably I was getting sunburn and they wanted to tell me to turn over, or maybe I had a speck of mud on me. [Q] These are the only two reasons I can think of why they were staring.

In the nudist camp, the arousal of attention by nudity is usually regarded as *unnatural*. Thus, staring is unnatural, especially after a period of grace in which to adjust to the new meanings.

If he did it when he was first there, I'd figure he's normal. If he kept it up I'd stay away from him, or suggest to the owner that he be thrown out. [Q] At first it's a new experience, so he might be staring. [Q] He wouldn't know how to react to it. [Q] The first time seeing nudes of the opposite sex. [Q] I'd think if he kept staring, that he's thinking of something, like grabbing someone, running to the bushes, and raping them. [Q] Maybe he's mentally unbalanced.

He just sat there watching the women. You can forgive it the first time, because of curiosity. But not every weekend. [Q] The owner asked him to leave.

These women made comments on some men's shapes. They said, "He has a hairy body or ugly bones," or "Boy his wife must like him because he's hung big." That was embarrassing. . . . I thought they were terrible. [Q] Because I realized they were walking around looking. I can't see that.

### Organizations and the Constitution of Normality

The rules-in-use of an organization *and the reality they sustain* form the basis on which behaviors are interpreted as "unnatural."[9] Overinvolvement in nudity, for example, is interpreted by nudists as unnatural (and not simply immoral). Similarly, erotic stimuli or responses, which breach the nudist morality, are defined as unnatural.

They let one single in. He acted peculiar. . . . He got up and had a big erection. I didn't know what he'd do at night. He might molest a child or anybody. . . . My husband went and told the owner.

I told you about this one on the sundeck with her legs spread. She made no bones about closing up. Maybe it was an error, but I doubt it. It wasn't a normal position. Normally you wouldn't lay like this. It's like standing on your head. She had sufficient time and there were people around.

She sat there with her legs like they were straddling a horse. I don't know how else to describe it. [Q] She was just sitting on the ground. [Q] I think she's a dirty pig. [Q] If you sit that way, everyone don't want to know what she had for breakfast. [Q] It's just the wrong way to sit. You keep your legs together even with clothes on.

[Q: Do you think it is possible for a person to be modest in a nudist camp?] I think so. [Q] If a person acts natural. . . . An immodest person would be an exhibitionist, and you find them in nudism too. . . . Most people's conduct is all right.

When behaviors are constituted as *unnatural*, attempts to understand them are usually suspended, and reciprocity of perspectives is called into question. (The "reciprocity of perspectives" involves the assumption that if one changed places with the other, one would, for all practical purposes, see the world as the other sees it.[10])

[Q: What would you think of a man who had an erection at camp?] Maybe they can't control themselves. [Q] Better watch out for him. [Q] I would tell the camp director to keep an eye on him. And the children would question that. [Q: What would you tell them?] I'd tell them the man is sick or something.

[Q: What would you think of a Peeping Tom—a non-nudist trespasser?] They should be reported and sent out. [Q] I think they shouldn't be there. They're sick. [Q] Mentally. [Q] Because anyone who wants to look at someone else's body, well, is a Peeping Tom, is sick in the first place. He looks at you differently than a normal person would. [Q] With ideas of sex. [A trespasser] . . . is sick. He probably uses this as a source of sexual stimulation.

Such occurrences call into question the taken-for-granted character of nudity in the nudist camp and the situated morality that is officially set forth.

### Inhibiting Breakdowns in the Nudist Morality

Organized nudism promulgates a nonsexual perspective toward nudity, and breakdowns in that perspective are inhibited by (1) con-

trolling erotic actions and (2) controlling erotic reactions. Nudity is partitioned off from other forms of "immodesty" (e.g., verbal immodesty, erotic overtures). In this way, a person can learn more easily to attribute a new meaning to nudity.[11] When behaviors occur that reflect other forms of "immodesty," however, nudists often fear a voiding of the nonsexual meaning that they impose on nudity.

This woman with a sexy walk would shake her hips and try to arouse the men. . . . [Q] These men went to the camp director to complain that the woman had purposely tried to arouse them. The camp director told this woman to leave.

Nudists are sensitive to the possibility of a breakdown in the nudist morality. Thus, they have a low threshold for interpreting acts as "sexual."

Playing badminton, this teenager was hitting the birdie up and down and she said, "What do you think of that?" I said, "Kind of sexy." ———[the president of the camp] said I shouldn't talk like that, but I was only kidding.

Note the following description of "mauling":

I don't like to see a man and a girl mauling each other in the nude before others. . . . [Q: Did you ever see this at camp?] I saw it once. . . . [Q: What do you mean by mauling?] Just, well, I never saw him put his hands on her breasts, but he was running his hands along her arms.

This sensitivity to "sexual" signs also sensitizes nudists to the possibility that certain of their own acts, although not intended as "sexual," might nonetheless be interpreted that way.

Sometimes you're resting and you spread your legs unknowingly. [Q] My husband just told me not to sit that way. [Q] I put my legs together.

Since "immodesty" is defined as an unnatural manner of behavior, such behaviors are easily interpreted as being motivated by "dishonorable" intent. When the individual is thought to be in physical control of the "immodest" behavior and to know the behavior's meaning within the nudist scheme of interpretation, sexual intentions are assigned. Referring to a quotation that was presented earlier, one man said that a woman who was lying with her legs spread may have been doing so unintentionally, "but I doubt it. [Q] It wasn't a normal position. Normally you wouldn't lay like this. It's like standing on your head."

Erotic reactions, as well as erotic actions, are controlled in camp. Thus, even when erotic stimuli come into play, erotic responses may be inhibited.

When lying on the grass already hiding my penis, I got erotic thoughts. And then one realizes it can't happen here. With fear there isn't much erection.

Yes, once I started to have an erection. Once. [Q] A friend told me how he was invited by some young lady to go to bed. [Q] I started to picture the situation and I felt the erection coming on; so I immediately jumped in the pool. It went away.

I was once in the woods alone and ran into a woman. I felt myself getting excited. A secluded spot in the bushes which was an ideal place for procreation. [Q] Nothing happened, though.

When breaches of the nudist morality do occur, other nudists' sense of modesty may inhibit sanctioning. The immediate breach may go unsanctioned. The observers may feign inattention or withdraw from the scene. The occurrence is usually communicated, however, via the grapevine, and it may reach the camp director.

We were shooting a series of pictures and my wife was getting out of her clothes. ——— [the photographer] had an erection but went ahead like nothing was happening. [Q] It was over kind of fast. . . . [Q] Nothing. We tried to avoid the issue. . . . Later we went to see ——— [the camp director] and ——— [the photographer] denied it.

[If a man had an erection] people would probably pretend they didn't see it.

[Q: What do you think of someone this happens to?] They should try to get rid of it fast. It don't look nice. Nudists are prudists. They are more prudish. Because they take their clothes off they are more careful. [Q] They become more prudish than people with clothes. They won't let anything out of the way happen.

As indicated in the remark, "nudists are prudists," nudists may at times become aware of the fragility of their situated moral meanings.

At ——— [camp], this family had a small boy no more than ten years old who had an erection. Mrs. ——— [the owner's wife] saw him and told his parents that they should keep him in check, and tell him what had happened to him and to watch himself. This was silly, for such a little kid who didn't know what happened.

## Deviance and Multiple Realities

There are basic social processes that underlie responses to deviance. Collectivities control thresholds of response to various behaviors, determining the relevance, meaning, and importance of the behavior. In the nudist camp, as pointed out previously, erotic overtures and erotic responses are regarded as unnatural, and reciprocity of perspectives is called into question by such behaviors.

We thought this single was all right, until others clued us in that he had brought girls up to camp. [Then we recalled that] . . . he was kind of weird. The way he'd look at you. He had glassy eyes, like he could see through you.[12]

Such a response to deviance in the nudist camp is a result of effective socialization to the new system of moral meanings. The deviant's behavior, on the other hand, can be construed as reflecting an ineffective socialization to the new system of meanings.

I think it's impossible [to have an erection in a nudist camp]. [Q] In a nudist camp you must have some physical contact and a desire to have one.

He isn't thinking like a nudist. [Q] The body is wholesome, not . . . a sex object. He'd have to do that—think of sex.

Sex isn't supposed to be in your mind, as far as the body. He doesn't belong there. [Q] If you go in thinking about sex, naturally it's going to happen. . . . You're not supposed to think about going to bed with anyone, not even your wife.

As these quotes illustrate, the unnaturalness or deviance of a behavior is ordinarily determined by relating it to an institutionalized scheme of interpretation. Occurrences that are "not understandable" in the reality of one collectivity may, however, be quite understandable in the reality of another collectivity.[13] Thus, what are "deviant" occurrences in nudist camps probably would be regarded by members of the clothed society as natural and understandable rather than unnatural and difficult to understand.

Finally, a group of people may subscribe to different and conflicting interpretive schemes. Thus, the low threshold of nudists to anything "sexual" is a function of their marginality; the fact that they have not completely suspended the moral meanings of the clothed society is what leads them to constitute many events as "sexual" in purpose.

## Notes

1. In my previous papers, I have dealt with other questions that are commonly asked about nudists. How persons become nudists is discussed in my (1966, February) "Becoming a nudist," *Psychiatry, 29*, 15–24. A report on the nudist way of life and social structure can be found in my (1967, Fall) article in *Human Organization, 26*, 91–99.

2. Approximately one hundred camps were represented in the interviews and questionnaires. Interviews were conducted in the homes of nudists during the off season. Arrangements for the interviews were initially made with these nudists during the first summer of participant observation: Selection of respondents was limited to those living within a one-hundred-mile radius of Chicago. The questionnaires were sent to all members of the National Nudist Council. The different

techniques of data collection provided a test of convergent validation.

3. For a discussion of the essence of such relationships, see A. Schutz (1962), *Collected papers: The problem of social reality* (M. Natanson, Ed.), The Hague: Nijhoff, I, pp. 287ff.

4. [Q] is used to signify a neutral probe by the interviewer that follows the course of the last reply, such as "Could you tell me some more about that?" or "How is that?" or "What do you mean?" Other questions by the interviewer are given in full.

5. The King and Queen contest, which takes place at conventions, allows for a patterned evasion of the staring rule. Applicants stand before the crowd in front of the royal platform, and applause is used for selecting the winners. Photography is allowed during the contest, and no one is permitted to enter the contest unless willing to be photographed. The major reason for this is that this is a major camp event, and contest pictures are used in nudist magazines. At the same time, the large number of photographs sometimes taken by lay photographers (that is, not working for the magazines) makes many nudists uncomfortable by calling into question a nonsexual definition of the situation.

6. I was amazed at how many young female nudists described a similar pattern of extreme clothing modesty among their parents and in their own married life. Included in this group was another nudist model, one of the most photographed of nudist models. Perhaps there are some fruitful data here for cognitive-dissonance psychologists.

7. Cf. Schutz (1962), p. 74.

8. For some respondents, the female genitals, because of their hidden character, never become a routinized part of camp nudity; thus their visible exposure does not lose an attention-provoking quality.

9. Compare H. Garfinkel (1963), "A conception of, and experiments with, 'trust' as a condition of concerted stable actions," in O. J. Harvey (Ed.), *Motivation and social interaction*, New York: Ronald.

10. See Schutz (1962), I, p. 11, for his definition of reciprocity of perspectives.

11. This corresponds with the findings of learning-theory psychologists.

12. For a study of the process of doublethink, see J. L. Wilkins (1964), "Doublethink: A study of erasure of the social past," unpublished doctoral dissertation, Northwestern University.

13. Cf. Schutz (1962), I, pp. 229ff.

**42**

# The Persistence of Gender Inequality in Employment Settings

*Cecilia Ridgeway*

Gender hierarchy is a system of social practices that advantages men over women in material resources, power, status, and authority. Oddly, gender hierarchy has persisted in Western societies despite profound changes in the economic arrangements on which it seems, at any given time, to be based. It has continued in one form or another despite major economic transformations such as industrialization, the movement of women into the paid labor force, and, most recently, women's entry into male-dominated occupations. What accounts for gender hierarchy's uncanny ability to reassert itself in new forms when its former economic foundations erode?

Although many factors are involved, one part of the answer lies in the way gender hierarchy in economic and other social arrangements is mediated by interactional processes that are largely taken for granted. Gender processes taking place as people interact during economic and other activities can operate as an "invisible hand" that rewrites gender inequality into new socioeconomic arrangements as they replace the ear-

This reading, "The Persistence of Gender Inequality in Employment Settings," was originally published in 1990 as "Interaction and the Conservation of Gender Equality: Considering Employment," *American Sociological Review, 62*: 218–235. Cecilia Ridgeway has adapted the article specifically for this text.

lier arrangements upon which gender hierarchy was based.)To illustrate this point, I will describe some interactional processes that mediate gender inequality in paid employment and play a role in its persistence. First, however, we should consider how gender and interaction are related.

## Gender and Interaction

Gender is an important part of the organization of interaction. It is striking that people are nearly incapable of interacting with each other if they cannot guess the other's sex. The television program *Saturday Night Live* illustrated this problem in its comedy sequence about "Pat," an androgynous person who wreaks confusion and havoc even in trivial, everyday encounters because the others present cannot place Pat as a man or a woman. The difficulty of dealing with a person whose gender is ambiguous suggests that gender categorization is a basic first step in the cultural rules we use for organizing interaction (West and Zimmerman 1987).

In order to interact with someone, you need some initial idea of "who" you are dealing with. You must classify the person in relation to yourself in socially meaningful ways so that you can draw on cultural knowledge about how "people like this" are likely to behave and how you should act in return. In other words, organizing interaction requires you to categorize the other as well as yourself in socially significant ways. Some of the social rules that you use for categorizing self and other must be so simplified and apparently obvious that they provide an easy means for initially defining "who" self and other are so interaction can begin at all. The cultural rules for classifying people as either male or female provide a quick initial category system—one that everyone takes for granted. Once interaction begins, definitions of self and other that are more complicated and specific to the situation can be introduced.

As research has shown, the cognitive processes by which we perceive others are hierarchically organized (Brewer 1988; Fiske and Neuberg 1990). They begin with an initial, automatic, and usually unconscious classification of the other according to a very small number of primary cultural categories and move on to more detailed typing depending on the circumstances. The evidence shows that gender is one of these primary categories in Western societies so that we automatically and unconsciously gender-categorize any specific other to whom we must relate.

In institutional settings, such as workplaces, there are often clear social scripts that define who self and other are and frame interaction (e.g., supervisor and worker). Yet gender categorization continues in these settings because the actual process of enacting a social script with a concrete other evokes habitual person perception and with it, the cultural rules that define gender as something that must be known to make sense of others. Research shows that when institutional roles become salient in the process of perceiving someone, those roles become nested within the prior understanding of that person as a man or woman and take on slightly different meanings as a result (Brewer 1988). We may be able to imagine an ungendered institutional script whereby "the student talks to the teacher" but we cannot interact with any actual students or teachers without first clas-

sifying them as male or female. The gender categorization of self and others, even in institutionally scripted settings, is a fundamental, unnoticed process that involves gender in the activities and institutional roles that people enact together.

Gender categorization in work-related encounters sets the stage for two interactional processes that contribute to and help preserve gender inequality in paid employment. Gender categorization cues gender status beliefs that can unconsciously shape people's assumptions about how competent women in the situation are compared to similar men. Gender categorization also unconsciously biases whom people compare themselves to. Comparisons, in turn, affect the rewards to which people feel entitled and the wages for which they will settle.

## Gender Status Processes

Gender status beliefs are widely held cultural beliefs that posit one gender as generally superior and diffusely more competent than the other. Such beliefs are well established in Western societies. Gender categorization in interaction makes gender status beliefs implicitly accessible to shape actors' perceptions of one another.

In interaction, people are never just males or females without simultaneously being many other social identities (e.g., young or old, of a given ethnic group, a worker or a student). The impact of gender status beliefs (and other cultural assumptions about men and women) on people's perceptions and behaviors in a given situation depends on the relevance of gender to the situation compared to other identities that are also salient. In work settings, work-related identities are likely to be in the foreground of peoples' perceptions and shape behavior most powerfully. Gender often acts as a *background identity* that flavors the performance of those work identities. Research shows, however, that even when other identities are the strongest determinant of behavior, gender status beliefs are still sufficiently salient to measurably affect people's expectations and behavior under two conditions: in mixed gender settings and when gender is relevant to the purposes or context of the setting (e.g., a women's caucus group) (Berger et al., 1977; Deaux and Major 1987). This means that gender status beliefs are effectively salient in many but not all work-related interactions.

When gender status beliefs are effectively salient like this in a work setting, they have three types of effects on goal-oriented interaction that affect employment inequality. First, they cause both men and women to unconsciously expect slightly greater competence from qualified men than from similarly qualified women. These implicit expectations tend to become self-fulfilling, shaping men's and women's assertiveness and confidence in the situation, their judgments of each other's ability, their actual performances, and their influence in the setting (see Ridgeway 1993 for details).

Second, gender status beliefs, when salient, cause people to expect and feel entitled to rewards that are commensurate with their relative status and expected competence in the setting. Thus, if gender status beliefs cause people in a work setting to assume the men are more important and competent than women, both men and women in the situation will also presume that men are entitled to higher levels of rewards such as pay or "perks." Consequently, when gender status is salient, men may react negatively if they are placed on the same reward level as a similarly qualified woman. They may experience this situation as an implicit status threat.

Third, because gender status beliefs advantage men, men in interaction are less likely to notice, and more likely to discount if they do notice, information about self or other that might diminish or eliminate the effects of gender status beliefs on expectations for competence or rewards. This effect of gender status beliefs is due to the way

people's interests in a situation unconsciously bias what they perceive. The effect makes it more difficult for women in the interaction to introduce information that would alter the lower expectations held for them. For example, there is a tendency in meetings for persons to attribute interesting or new ideas to a male speaker, even if a woman was the first to raise the point. Men who are "rewarded" for having expressed the good idea do not seem to notice that a woman may have mentioned the idea first. If the woman were to try to claim credit for the idea, and thereby lay claim to her competence, it is likely that she would be regarded as being pushy or out of line.

### Gender-Biased Comparisons and Rewards

In addition to cueing gender status beliefs, gender categorization of self and other in workplace relations affects who people compare themselves to when they evaluate their own rewards or outcomes on the job. In general, people search out information about people whom they see as similar to them in order to evaluate whether they are receiving the rewards to which they are entitled. Automatic gender categorization causes people to unconsciously compare their own rewards more closely to those of the same gender than to those of opposite gender. If pay, perks, or other rewards are distributed unequally among men and women on the job, then the tendency to compare with same-gender others will cause men to form higher estimates of what the "going rate" is for people with their qualifications. Women, gathering more comparisons from other women, form lower estimates of the going rate for the same qualifications. Not recognizing that their estimates of what others earn on the job have been biased by their tendency to compare with same-gender others, women form lower expectations for the pay and rewards to which they are entitled than do similar men. Such reward expectations become self-fulfilling because they affect people's willingness to settle for a given level of pay or to press for more (see Major 1989 for research on this process).

## Gender Inequality in Employment

Gender inequality in employment is something of a puzzle. Theoretically, competitive market forces should wipe out gender discrimination because employers who prefer men and pay higher wages to get them will be driven out of business by smarter employers who hire cheaper but equally qualified women for the same jobs. Yet gender inequality in wages and gender segregation in occupations (i.e., the tendency for men and women to work in different occupations) have stubbornly persisted and improved only slowly over decades. England (1992) argues that gender inequality persists despite the flattening effect of market forces because it is continually being created anew, even if is worn down slightly over time. A consideration of how interaction drives gender categorization in work contexts and brings in gender status and comparison processes can help explain why the work world is so relentlessly gendered. It can also help explain why such gendering persists despite ongoing economic and organizational change.

Most work-related interaction takes place in organizational contexts with established job structures and institutional rules that heavily constrain what happens. Under business-as-usual conditions, gender status and comparison-reward processes occurring in these interactions are just part of the means by which existing gender-biased job structures and practices are enacted and sustained. Interactional gender processes, however, become important in themselves, rather than merely the agents of organizational structures and rules, at the interstices of organizations and under conditions that force change on an organization. In these transition zones where organizational structures are less clearly defined, gender categorization, status, and comparison processes play a part in shaping the interaction through which actors create new organizational rules and structural forms and map gender hierarchy into them as they do so.

Occupational arrangements and wage outcomes are mediated by interaction in many ways, whether it be face-to-face, computer-mediated (e.g., email), or indirect interaction through exchanges on paper. Workers learn about jobs and evaluate them through contact with others. Employers hire workers through direct (e.g., interviews) or indirect interaction (e.g., reviewing resumes and references). On the job, performance, evaluations, task assignments, and promotions involve interactions among people in complex ways. All these mediating interactions through which the world of work is conducted are potential sites where interactional mechanisms can map gender hierarchy into the occupational patterns and wages that result.

## The Sex Labeling of Workers and Jobs

Gender inequality in employment begins with the gender labeling of workers. This point seems so obvious and natural that we don't bother to explain it. Yet why should all workers be either male workers or female workers and not just workers? Why is gender a primary descriptor of workers at all? The answer lies in the way interaction evokes gender categorization, infusing gender in to the hiring processes as it mediates employers' recruitment and placement of workers. Because interaction triggers gender categorization, employers can never interview or read the resume of a gender-neutral worker. Similarly, workers cannot interact with a gender-unclassified co-worker, boss, subordinate, or client.

The taken-for-granted, unconscious gender labeling of workers begins a process that also leads to the labeling of jobs themselves as men's or women's jobs. As the economy changes and develops, jobs that have been traditionally labeled as men's or women's jobs may fade in importance and new jobs, such as computer programmer, are continually created. Theoretically, these new occupations could be gender neutral. Yet, in an example of the force of gender in the organization of work, most of these new occupations are themselves quickly labeled as either men's or women's occupations. The persistent gender labeling of new jobs continually renews the gender-segregated nature of our occupational structure.

Gender categorization in workplace interaction plays a role in the continual gender labeling of jobs by priming workers and employers alike to infuse stereotypic assumptions about gender into the institutional scripts by which a job is enacted and represented to others. Employers often begin the process by implicitly or explicitly seeking workers of a particular gender on the basis of assumptions about labor costs that are themselves suffused by the effect of gender status beliefs. Employees of one gender come to predominate in the job. Since gender categorization in interaction primes people's cultural beliefs about gender even in segregated contexts, workers and employees may use gender-stereotypic terms to justify the activities in a gender-segregated job even when those activities originally seemed gender irrelevant. Thus, electronic assembly comes to be represented as a woman's job requiring *women's* "attention to detail and manual dexterity." Selling securities becomes a *man's* job requiring masculine "aggressiveness."

As the stories and social scripts that represent a job in the media and elsewhere come to be gendered as masculine or feminine, the differential status attached to men and women spreads to the job as well. Research shows that a job or task, when labeled feminine, is viewed by both job evaluators and those in the job themselves as requiring less ability and effort and as worth less compensation than the identical job or task is when labeled masculine. Other research shows that

the gender composition of a job alone has a significant impact on what it pays, as does the association of the job with stereotypically feminine tasks such as nurturance (see Ridgeway 1997 for more details). Continual gender categorization in workplace interactions reinforces the tendency to apply gender labels to activities and perpetuates gender-based evaluations of jobs and activities.

## Men and Women as Interested Actors in the Workplace

The interests of those in more powerful positions in employment organizations (e.g., bosses), who are more often men, are represented more forcefully than the interests of those who are in less powerful positions (e.g., secretaries). When gender status is salient in workplace interactions it creates a number of apparently gender-interested behaviors on the part of men, whether as employers, workers, or customers. The men themselves as well as observers of both genders will tend to see men in a situation as a bit more competent and deserving of rewards than similarly qualified women. They may miss or discount information in the situation that undermines these perceptions and perceive an implicit status threat when equivalent men and women are put on the same reward level.

All these effects usually occur as a modification or biasing of behavior during the enactment of an occupational or institutional identity that is more salient in the situation than the background identity of gender. A man acting in his role as an electrical engineer or union representative, for instance, may slightly bias his treatment of other men over women, usually in an implicit way that he himself does not recognize. Only occasionally will gender be so salient in the situation that men act self-consciously to preserve their interests as men. Yet the repeated background activation of gender status over many workplace interactions, biasing behavior in subtle or more substantial degrees, produces the effect of men acting in their gender interests, even when many men feel no special loyalty to their gender.

What about women in the workplace? Don't they pursue their interests as well? Yes, but the effect of gender status beliefs in interaction handicaps their efforts. It is in women's interests to introduce into a situation added information about their skills and accomplishments that undermines status-based assumptions about their competence compared to men and the rewards that they deserve. It is often difficult to introduce such information, however, precisely because gender is usually a background identity in workplace interactions. The participants do not explicitly think of gender as part of "what is going on here." The implicitness of gender in workplace interaction complicates the task of recognizing when bias is occurring and introducing countervailing information in the real time of actual interaction. The process is difficult as well because men's own status interests tend to make them more cognitively resistant to such information.

As a result, women on the job may periodically sense that something prejudicial is happening to them, but be frustrated in their efforts to act effectively against it. They will be vulnerable to "role encapsulation" whereby others define them in their work identities in implicitly gendered terms (e.g., "too nice" or "passive") that limit their effectiveness as actors in their own interests.

### Employers' Preferences for Male Workers

Reskin and Roos (1990) argue that employers show general preferences for hiring male workers, especially for "good," well-paying jobs. There are exceptions, of course, as when employers actually prefer female workers for jobs like nursery school teacher that involve tasks that are stereotypically associated with women. For other jobs, however, Reskin and Roos suggest that employers' preferences for

male workers is a key factor that maintains gender inequality in wages and access to jobs with status and authority. While competitive market forces work against such preferences, they are nevertheless maintained by institutional rules and practices that embody them and by the implicit effects of gender status on workplace relations.

When an employer's automatic gender categorization of a potential employee cues gender status beliefs, these beliefs affect the employer's judgment of the worker's potential productivity. Expectations about competence based on gender status make the male worker appear "better" than an equally qualified woman. Also, an equally competent job or test performance by the two appears to the employer to be more indicative of ability and skill in the man than in the woman (see Ridgeway 1997 for a description of this research). On the surface merit is the basis of judgment. Yet the workers' gender is connected with merit by the way employers' evaluations of workers involve interactions that are unconsciously shaped by gender status beliefs. The result is what is called "error discrimination" where two workers who would perform equally are judged to be different and paid accordingly.

Gender status beliefs operating in the workplace can contribute to this process because they bias employers' expectations for workers' performances and these expectations tend to be self-fulfilling. This tendency often produces employer experiences with male and female workers that confirm the employers' initial judgments about them. A competent performance by a woman worker appears less competent coming from her than from her male co-worker. Also, and more insidious, the pressure of an employer's low expectations for them can actually interfere with some women workers' performances. Some male workers, on the other hand, may feel buoyed by their employer's confidence in them and perform even better than they otherwise might have. Thus, the effect of an employer's status-based expectations on some men and some women can create "real" differences in the average performance and productivity of groups of similar male and female workers. When interactional gender categorization makes gender salient in the hiring process, the employer's experience of these average differences also becomes salient. The employer may react by preferring male workers across the board (statistical discrimination). This form of discrimination is especially powerful in maintaining gender inequality in the workplace because it is more resistant to the equalizing effects of market forces than are other types of discrimination (England 1992).

### Why Do Women Workers Accept Lower Wages?

An employer's ability to attract and retain women workers for lower wages is also critical for maintaining gender inequality in employment. Why do women settle for less than similarly qualified men? Here, too, gender processes in interaction play a role by shaping different senses of entitlement on the part of similarly qualified men and women.

Although many women work in predominantly female jobs (e.g., nurses, secretaries, or elementary school teachers), their work performance is often evaluated through direct or indirect interaction with male supervisors, clients, or customers. Also, their work may have become typed a stereotypically female task. In any of these situations, gender categorization during interaction will activate status beliefs affecting women workers' own performance and expectations for rewards as well as their employer's and fellow workers' expectations for them. In fact, the evidence shows that women underestimate the quality of their performances in comparison with men. This makes them susceptible to arguments that they deserve less pay.

Gender categorization in work relations also unconsciously biases women's choices of whom to seek out in order to compare the pay they are receiving and evaluate whether it is fair. As we saw, women's tendency to compare their pay more closely with other women than similar men can cause them to underestimate the going rate for work by people with given qualifications. Such underestimates of possible pay rates is a second factor that causes women to peg the compensation they deserve at lower rates than do men.

If women workers inadvertently underestimate the rewards they are entitled to, employers can more easily force them to settle for lower wages (Major 1989). If corresponding gender status and biased comparison processes cause male workers to overestimate what they deserve, then employers find it harder to force lower wages on them. Out of such processes, women inadvertently accept lower wages than men. Women's unintentional acceptance of lower pay helps sustain gender hierarchy in employment over time by moderating women's resistance to pay differences.

### Women's Entrance into Male Occupations

In recent decades, women have entered male occupations in large numbers. Yet wage inequality and the gender segregation of jobs has not declined as much as one might expect. As Reskin and Roos point out (1990), the problem is that as women enter a male occupation in number, men often flee it so that it "turns over" to become a women's occupation. This has happened to the job of bank teller over the past couple of decades. Sometimes, when women enter a male occupation, instead of men leaving the occupation altogether, the occupation becomes reorganized so that some specialties within it are predominantly female while others are predominantly male. Thus, as women have entered medicine in recent years, pediatrics has become a women's specialty while neurosurgery has remained overwhelmingly male. Again, wage inequality and gender segregation of jobs are preserved despite women's entrance into the formerly male profession of medicine.

While many processes are behind these transformations of occupations, once again, gender processes during interaction are involved. Given employer preferences for male workers, women often gain access to men's occupations when the demand for workers in that occupation outstrips the pool of interested male workers available at an acceptable wage. As the shortage of male workers brings women into the job, gender-based status interests become increasingly salient in the workplace and may create tensions. Gender status beliefs activated by the mixed-sex context cause women's presence to subtly devalue the status and reward-worthiness of the job in the eyes of both workers and employers. Male workers may react to this perceived threat to their status and rewards by hostility towards women in the job. More men may begin to leave the job.

As women become more numerous in the job, supervisors' gender status beliefs and women workers' lower sense of entitlement exert self-fulfilling effects on women's pay and other rewards and these effects increasingly spread to the job itself. This situation makes it easier for employers to introduce organizational and technological changes to the job that further reduce the status and rewards that it offers. Although this scenario is not inevitable, when it occurs, it often results in the job becoming a women's job with lowered status and pay. Or the job may resegregate by specialty with lower pay and status for the female specialties.

Such transitions in occupations maintain gender hierarchy over a change in the technological and organizational structure of jobs. In the many interactions through which these transitions occur, activated gender status processes and biased reward comparisons create a complex mix of discrimination, status-based competitions of interests, differences in entitlement, and differential perceptions of alternatives. The result is a system of interdependent gender effects that are every-

where and nowhere because they develop through multiple workplace interactions, often in taken-for-granted ways. Their aggregate result is the preservation of wage inequality and the gender segregation of jobs.

## Conclusion

Adding an interactional perspective to labor market and organizational explanations for inequality in employment helps explain why gender is such a major force in the organization of work. Hiring, job searches, placement, performance evaluation, task assignment, promotion, and dealing with customers, clients, bosses, co-workers, and subordinates all involve direct or indirect (e.g., via resumes) interaction. Interaction with a concrete other evokes primary cultural rules for making sense of self and of other, pushing actors to gender-categorize one another in each of these interactions. Gender categorization pumps gender into the interactions through which the world of work is enacted. It cues gender status beliefs and biases the choice of comparison others. The process is insidious because gender is usually an implicit background identity that acts in combination with more salient work identities and tinges their performance with gendered expectations.

In highly structured organizational work contexts, gender processes in interaction become part of the processes through which more formal structures that embody bias, such as job ladders and evaluation systems, are enacted. Gender processes in interaction contribute to the gender labeling of jobs, to the devaluation of women's jobs, to forms of gender discrimination by employers, to the construction of men as gender-interested actors, to the control of women's interest, to differences between men's and women's pay expectations, and to the processes by which women's entrance into male occupations sometimes leads to feminization of the job or resegregation by specialty.

In less bureaucratically organized work

contexts, such as those at organizational interstices, in start-up companies, in newly forming professions, or in some types of works (e.g., screen writers), interpersonal processes come to the fore and are sufficient in themselves to create gender inequality in wages and gender typing of work. As they do so, interactional processes conserve gender inequality despite significant, ongoing changes in the organization of work and the economy, writing inequality into new work structures and practices as they develop.

If this inequality is to be reduced, it is vital to understand that gender inequality is maintained by structural processes and interactional processes acting together. Change will require intervention at both the structural and interactional level through policies such as affirmative action that change the interpersonal configuration of actors and, potentially, create stereotype disconfirming experiences for all.

While much has been learned about gender inequality in employment, the study of gender-based interactional processes may help to answer some of the stubborn questions that persist. These questions include the reasons why new jobs that develop as occupations change continue to acquire connotations as men's or women's jobs, how employer's apparent preferences for male workers persist even under competitive market pressures, why women's work is devalued, whether and how people act in their gender interests in employment matters, and why women accept lower wages than men for similar work.

## References

Berger, Joseph, M. Hamit Fisek, Robert Z. Norman, and Morris Zelditch, Jr. 1977. *Status Characteristics and Social Interaction.* New York: Elsevier.

Brewer, Marilynn. 1988. "A Dual Process Model of Impression Formation." Pp. 1–36 in *Advances in Social Cognition*, Vol. 1, edited by Thomas Srull and Robert Wyer. Hillsdale, NJ: Earlbaum.

Deaux, Kay, and Brenda Major. 1987. "Putting Gender Into Context: An Interactive Model of Gender-Related Behavior." *Psychological Review* 94: 369–389.

England, Paula. 1992. *Comparable Worth: Theories and Evidence.* New York: Aldine.

Fiske, Susan, and Steven Neuberg. 1990. "A Continuum of Impression Formation, From Category-Based to Individuating Processes: Influences of Information and Motivation on Attention and Interpretation." Pp. 1–73 in *Advances in Experimental Social Psychology*, edited by Mark Zanna. New York: Academic Press.

Major, Brenda. 1989. "Gender differences in Comparisons and Entitlement: Implications for Comparable Worth." *Journal of Social Issues* 45: 99–115.

Reskin, Barbara, and Patricia Roos. 1990. *Job Queues, Gender Queues: Explaining Women's Inroads into Male Occupations.* Philadelphia: Temple University Press.

Ridgeway, Cecilia L. 1993. "Gender, Status, and the Social Psychology of Expectations." Pp. 175–198 in *Theory on Gender/Feminism on Theory*, edited by Paula England. New York: Aldine.

———. 1997. "Interaction and the Conservation of Gender Inequality: Considering Employment." *American Sociological Review* 62: 218–235.

West, Candance and Don Zimmerman. 1987. "Doing Gender." *Gender and Society* 1: 125–151.

**43**

# Practices of Truth-Finding in a Court of Law: The Case of Revised Stories

*Kim Lane Scheppele*

## Silences, First Accounts, and Revised Stories

Rape victims, battered women, victims of sexual harassment and incest survivors have a lot in common. They are all victims of sexualized violence and many have similar responses. Many women do not report the violence against them to authorities and many do not talk about the events with anyone at the time (Scheppele, 1987: 1096–1097; Pollack, 1990; Mango, 1991). Those who do talk about it at the time often present first accounts that try to make things normal again and to smooth out social relations, by minimizing the harm of the abuse, by engaging in self-blame, by telling stories that offer alternative explanations of events so that the full consequences of the abuse do not have to be dealt with at the time and by disguising the horribleness of the abuse through descriptive distortions of events (Walker, 1979; Scheppele and Bart, 1983; Herman, 1992). Later, however, often through working in therapy, or becoming overtly feminist, or getting enough emotional distance on the events to begin to deal with them, the women revise

"Practices of Truth-Finding in a Court of Law: The Case of Revised Stories" by K. L. Scheppele, from *Constructing the Social* (pp. 84–100), edited by T. Sarbin and J. Kitsuse, 1994. London: Sage Publications. Copyright © 1994 by Sage Publications, Inc. Reprinted by permission of Sage Publications Ltd.

their stories (Herman, 1992). Women who were silent begin to speak out for the first time. Women who denied at the time that anything abusive happened, or who took the blame themselves if they admitted that something had happened, begin to tell stories of injury and harm. These later *revised stories*, replacing either silence or an alternative version of events, present problems in the law. They present problems because one of the implicit rules juries and judges use for finding stories to be true is that the stories stay the same over time. Stories told at the time of the abuse are believed much more than revised stories told later.

### Anita Hill v. Clarence Thomas

We can see the strength of this bias toward first versions in the highly publicized second round of confirmation hearings on the Supreme Court nomination of Clarence Thomas, in which Anita Hill presented evidence that Thomas had sexually harassed her. Though the members of the Senate Judiciary Committee holding the hearings repeatedly emphasized that the proceedings were not a trial, legalistic conceptions of "burden of proof" and "presumption of innocence" were used throughout the three days of marathon sessions. But there the legal formality ended. Evidence was introduced without witnesses to support it; insinuations were made about Anita Hill's motivation and credibility that had no basis in evidence at all; questioning was limited by the unwillingness of then-Judge Thomas to answer questions outside the scope that he deemed fit for inquiry; witnesses who had relevant evidence to introduce were kept dangling and ultimately not asked for the information they had as part of the hearings. Whatever the Senate hearings might have been designed to accomplish, they were not well designed to work out what had happened and they proceeded at variance with the sorts of rules of evidence that would be used in a trial. But the hearings do reveal some popular biases in the evaluation of evidence, particularly where women are making claims that they have been the target of abuse.

Those defending Clarence Thomas repeatedly emphasized that Anita Hill had changed her story. And there were many versions of events presented during the course of the hearings. Once her allegations became public, Anita Hill had three opportunities to narrate what had happened: once to the FBI agents who arrived at her house one evening after work to interview her; once to the Senate Committee staffers who were trying to work out what she would say if called as a witness; once as the whole world watched her testimony live on television before the Senate Judiciary Committee. In each of these stories, new details emerged that had not been present in the earlier versions, though none of the new details conflicted with earlier more general versions. In addition to these versions, all of which were recorded in permanent form, four friends and colleagues of Hill's testified from memory to versions of the harassment story that Hill had told them either at the time that it occurred (witnesses Ellen Wells, Susan Hoerchner, and John Carr) or when she was applying for jobs and had to explain why she had left the Equal Employment Opportunity Commission (EEOC) where she worked with Clarence Thomas (witness John Paul).

On the other side, Clarence Thomas denied Hill's allegation and substituted in part his own narrative of what had happened—that he had always treated his whole staff professionally, cordially and without the interjection of personal distractions. Witnesses supporting Thomas presented alternative narrative contexts for Anita Hill's charges of sexual harassment, ranging from Hill's alleged grandiosity and ambition (witness J. C. Alvarez) to her status as a "scorned woman" (witness Phyllis Berry) to her alleged flights of fantasy (witness John Doggett). Other witnesses for Thomas expressed incredulity that he could do the acts alleged (witnesses Nancy Fitch and Diane Holt). Three versions from Hill's own accounting, a blanket denial from Thomas and many other versions from various witnesses left the Senate Judiciary Committee with a lot to pick apart. And much of the strategy of those who won by getting Thomas through the confirmation process and onto the Supreme Court depended on presenting Anita Hill's story to the committee as a revised account. Clarence Thomas deployed this strategy as much as any of the Senators working to defend him. In response to a question, Thomas answered:

The facts keep changing, Senator. When the FBI visited me, the statements to this committee and the questions were one thing. The FBI's subsequent questions were another thing, and the statements today as I received summaries of them were another thing. It is not my fault that the facts changed. What I have said to you is categorical; that any allegations that I engaged in any conduct involving sexual activity, pornographic movies, attempted to date her, any allegations, I deny. It is not true. So, the facts can change, but my denial does not. (Federal Informations Systems Corporation [FISC], October 11, 1991, LEXIS: 78)

Thomas clearly was trying to use the idea that statements that remain the same over time appear more reliable than statements that appear to change. He was asserting that his categorical denials were more true than Hill's "changing" facts precisely because his denials had never been subject to revision.

Senator Arlen Specter's cross-examination of Anita Hill spent much time on pointing out the differences between Hill's accounts to the FBI and her public testimony, in an attempt to discredit her credibility (FISC, October 11, 1991, LEXIS: 25–28). Later, Specter pressed Hill on why she did not keep contemporaneous notes, knowing that such records would be admissible in court as particularly strong evidence of her perceptions at the time of events (FISC, October 11, 1991, LEXIS: 45–46). The notes Hill had before her were written out in preparation for the hearings, Specter ascertained, clearly implying that such notes could have been fabricated for the event. Throughout Specter's cross-examination, Hill's public testimony was presented as a *revised* version of events—revised, and therefore unreliable.

The Hill–Thomas hearings were not a judicial forum. But the tactics used in an attempt to discredit Hill's testimony borrow both from the courtroom and from daily life. Stories that are revised over time—elaborated, altered in tone, emerging in public out of a silence that went before—are presented as suspect *precisely because* they are revised. Though closer examination of the statements that Hill made to the FBI, to the Senate Committee and to her friends revealed that they varied only in the specificity of their allegations and not in their basic shape, the specter that her story had been revised continued to haunt the hearings. And Clarence Thomas was confirmed.

### Reed v. Shepard

When we look at actual courtroom proceedings, we can see how the alleged revision of stories is mobilized to discredit the later accounts. This strategy is particularly common in sexual harassment cases. In *Reed* v. *Shepard*, 939 F. 2d 484 (1991), JoAnn Reed worked as a "civilian jailer" in the Vandenburgh County (Indiana) Sheriff's Department, beginning in mid-1979. The civilian jailer program employed people to take care of prisoners—guarding, feeding, transporting, and processing them—as less costly substitutes for the more expensive deputy sheriffs who had formerly performed those jobs. In 1984, Reed was fired, without a hearing, for alleged misconduct in her job. In response to a charge brought under Section 1983 of the U.S. Code that she had been denied due process, the district court and the appeals court found that she was not entitled, as an at-will employee, to have a hearing before her employment was terminated and that the allegations of misconduct were serious enough to justify her termination in any event. But she had sued on multiple counts, and in the others, she charged that her employer had engaged in sexual discrimination and that she had been sexually harassed on the job in violation of Title VII of the Civil Rights Act. The story she told about sexual harassment was clearly a revised story.

According to the trial judge (quoted by the Court of Appeals):

Plaintiff contends that she was handcuffed to the drunk tank and sally port doors, that she was subjected to suggestive remarks . . . , that conversations often centered around oral sex, that she was physically hit and punched in the kidneys, that her head was grabbed and forcefully placed in members' laps, and that she was the subject of lewd jokes and remarks. She testified that she had chairs pulled out from under her, a cattle prod with an electrical shock was placed between her legs, and that they frequently tickled her. She was placed in a laundry basket, handcuffed inside an elevator, handcuffed to the toilet and her face pushed into the water, and maced. Perhaps others. (Unpublished opinion of Judge Gene E. Brooks, dated May 25, 1990, quoted at 939 F. 2d 486).

"The record confirms these and a number of other bizarre activities in the jail office," the appeals court added. "By any objective standard, the behavior of the male deputies and jailers toward Reed revealed at trial was, to say the least, repulsive" (939 F. 2d 486).

Why, then, did the court go on to conclude that, however offensive the conduct of her male co-workers was, it was *not* sexual harassment? Because, the court found, the conduct was apparently not repulsive to Reed *at the time:*[1]

Reed not only experienced this depravity with amazing resilience, but she also relished reciprocating in kind. At one point during her job tenure Reed was actually put on probation for her use of offensive language at the jail. At the same time, she was instructed to suspend the exhibitionistic habit she had of not wearing a bra on days she wore only a T-shirt to work. She also participated in suggestive gift-giving by presenting a softball warmer to a male co-worker designed to resemble a scrotum and by giving another a G-string. Reed enjoyed exhibiting to the male officers the abdominal scars she received from her hysterectomy which necessarily involved showing her private area. Many witnesses testified that Reed revelled in the sexual horseplay, instigated a lot of it, and had "one of the foulest mouths" in the department. In other words, the trial revealed that there was plenty of degrading humor and behavior to go around. (939 F. 2d 486–487)

The court emphasized that this reprehensible conduct did not happen to other women working in the jail, but only to Reed. Three women working there testified that they had not been further harassed after they asked the men to stop doing these sorts of things to them. But apparently, Reed never told the men to stop. Why? Reed testified at trial:

Because it was real important to me to be accepted. It was important for me to be a police officer and if that was the only way that I could be accepted, I would just put up with it and kept [sic] my mouth shut. I had supervisors that would participate in this and you had a chain of command to go through in order to file a complaint. One thing you don't do as a police officer, you don't snitch out [sic] another police officer. You could get hurt. (Quoted at 939 F. 2d 492. [Sic]s in the original.)

Reed's case involves a complicated reconstruction. She was not presented as having narrated the events in question any particular way at all at the time that they happened. Her "initial story" was constructed from the observations of her co-workers, inferring from her actions what her story must have been. As a result, the story that she presented in court appeared to be a revised story against the backdrop of this inferred narrative. And the Seventh Circuit Court of Appeals found that she was complicit in her treatment, barring recovery for sexual harassment.

Quoting from the Supreme Court's decision in *Meritor Savings Bank* v. *Vinson* (477 U.S. 57 [1986]), the Seventh Circuit panel indicated that harassment must be so severe or pervasive as "to alter the conditions of [the victim's] employment and create an abusive working environment" (quoted at 939 F. 2d 491), if a claim is to succeed. But to show that this conduct was "in fact" harassing, the victim of such treatment had to indicate *at the time* that she did not welcome the behavior in question. In this instance, Reed's claim could not succeed because she had not indicated while these events were occurring that this treatment was unwelcome. In other words, contemporaneous evidence is required to establish any claim of sexual harassment, and this requirement is hard-wired into the doctrine. Judge Manion quoted the trial judge approvingly that the plaintiff had been treated this way "because of her personality rather than her sex" and that the "defendants cannot be held liable for conditions created by [Reed's] own action and conduct" (939 F. 2d 492). Her failure to object at the time to this behavior and her attempt to deal with it by trying to act like "one of the boys" not only defeated her ability to make a claim, but justified the conclusion that she had brought this treatment on herself and was therefore the person who was primarily responsible.

But the record sustains another story, one not narrated by her co-workers who were witnesses at the trial. The record documents that Reed was physically beaten, that she was punched in the kidneys, that she had an electric cattle prod shoved between her legs, that she was forceably restrained by being handcuffed on numerous occasions, that her head was shoved into a toilet, that she was repeatedly tickled and that she was maced. That was on top of the extensive and personalized verbal abuse to which she was subjected. The court could have concluded that this evidence supported another account, one that did not erase the violence against Reed by constructing her as a consenting woman, but one that did present her at a minimum as the coerced victim of physical abuse.[2] Although Reed did not explicitly object at the time, the violence to which her co-workers subjected her would be considered felonies anywhere other than in a "friendly" setting.

The court failed to see her claim, I believe, because her sexual harassment complaint was delayed. Her complaint did not emerge for the first time until after she had been fired. The story she told in court was inconsistent with her co-workers' interpretations presented as if those interpretations were contemporaneous accounts. And the court, believing her co-workers' account as an initial story, discounted Reed's story as revised, assuming she had enjoyed the abuse at the time as her co-workers testified. When stories appear to have been revised, judges and juries use that very fact as evidence that the later story is false even when the victim did not grasp the chance to tell the first story herself.

### State v. Frost

But not all revised stories are discounted by courts. Sometimes a victim's story of sexualized abuse can survive the usual screening rules. In recent years, this has sometimes happened when testimony of expert witnesses has been used to demonstrate that the victims of sexualized violence suffer from a form of post-traumatic stress disorder and therefore have *first* reactions that are not to be trusted. The professional undermining of initial stories allows the revised stories to be believed. *State v. Frost*, 242 N.J. Super. 601 (1990) provides one example of a case where expert testimony was successful in getting a revised story believed by a jury, and later by judges on appeal.

Early one April morning in 1986, L.S. was still sleeping when her former boyfriend, Gregory Frost, tapped on her shoulder. He had broken into her house. As she started to wake up, he started to yell at her. He hit her. Their baby began to cry, so L.S. picked up the child and ran to the front door to escape. Before she was able to open the door, Frost caught up with her and cut her arm deeply with a razor-edged box cutter.

Knowing how out-of-control he could be, L.S. tried to talk with him eventually suggesting that they have sex because "that would calm him down." After they had sex, they went to the place where L.S.'s mother worked to get her car keys to go to the hospital to have the wound treated. L.S. asked her mother not to call the police. At the hospital, L.S. said she had cut her arm on the refrigerator. Her arm needed 4 sutures underneath the skin and 11 stitches to close the skin. But the story she told at the time was that she had cut herself accidentally, that she was in good hands with Frost to take care of her, and that she was okay.

After L.S. was treated, she, Frost and the baby went to L.S.'s home to get money, then went to a park where they drank beer and talked together. Eventually they went back to L.S.'s home again. L.S. was supposed to pick her mother up at work, but never did so. When L.S.'s mother arrived angry at having to find another ride home, she and L.S. got into such a huge fight that neighbors called the police. When the police arrived, they saw Frost running from the apartment wearing no shoes, socks, or shirt. They recognized him as the person against whom a restraining order had been issued and arrested him. They charged him with contempt of court (for violating the restraining order) as well as burglary (for breaking into the house), assault (for stabbing L.S.), and various weapons charges (for possession of the razor). Notably, he was not charged with rape. He was convicted on all counts.

At the trial, Frost had claimed that L.S. had consented to spend the day with him, which he thought should cast doubt on any claim that he had broken in and attacked her that morning. But the prosecution introduced evidence that indicated that the relationship between Frost and L.S. had been plagued by Frost's frequent outbursts of violence against L.S. She estimated that he had hit her at least once per month during the time they had been romantically involved, starting on the second day that they knew each other. Police testified that she had called them to the house at least nine times to stop his violence. After suffering through three and a half years of battering, L.S. had left Frost to go to live with her mother. She got a restraining order to keep Frost away from her and the baby. Eventually Frost was sent to prison for theft from another person. L.S. had been responsible for his arrest in that case and, on the day he broke into her house and cut her with the razor, he had just been let out of prison. His first act as a free man was coming to get her.

Prosecutors also introduced expert testimony to the effect that L.S. was suffering from battered woman's syndrome, an identifiable medical condition that was characterized by the court as follows:

The battered woman places herself in the role of a victim. She blames herself, thereby becoming even more vulnerable to the point where she almost expects it. She is reluctant to tell anybody about what occurs, usually for a variety of reasons. She may be embarrassed, the man might keep her isolated from others, she may hope the situation will change, or she may fear it will get worse if she reports anything. Most significantly, the battered woman cannot just walk away from the situation. She is emotionally dependent on her "man" and is often involved in a love–hate relationship. (242 N.J. Super. 611)

The effect of the historical and the expert testimony was to provide a context within which a jury could believe that all the things L.S. said on the day of the attack were motivated by fear and therefore could be considered unusually suspect. Such a fear-induced account could be overridden by a revised story later. Without this framing, however, a jury might reasonably conclude (as Frost tried to argue) that she was now trying to get Frost in trouble because they had had a falling out after a pleasant day. After all, L.S. presented repeated and consistent explanations on the day in question about how she was okay, how she had just cut herself on the refrigerator, how no one should call the police because she was fine. But the specific violent history of the relationship between Frost and L.S. as well as the use of expert testimony convinced the jury that Frost had committed these acts and that L.S. had not consented. On appeal, the admissibility of the expert testimony so crucial to the prosecution's case was upheld.

Expert testimony can be very helpful to women in situations like this. But it comes at a price. Such testimony is effective with a jury because it gives them an explanation for a victim's conduct at the time in question by saying she is suffering from a form of mental illness. The victim stayed with her batterer because she was suffering from stress and shock. The victim may have *thought* things were going to get better, she may have *thought* he loved her, she may have *thought* that she wanted to be with him, but she was wrong, deluded, and not a good judge of these things. As a result, whatever she may have *thought* happened on the day in question is also to be judged suspiciously. But making revised stories credible is very hard to do without an expert.

In this case, L.S. apparently wanted Frost convicted for these crimes. But she also visited him 11 times while he was awaiting trial back in prison.

## The Problem of Truth in Law

So, how do judges and juries know when they have found the truth? It is an astonishing accomplishment that courts as well as ordinary individuals manage to operate on a daily basis as if the bases of factual judgments were clear and solid. While the idea of truth has been a contested subject among philosophers for as long as philosophy has existed, the idea of truth in daily life seems to generate much less debate. When asked to find "the facts" of a case, judges and juries do not puzzle over the meaning of that instruction. Why? The simple answer is that judges and juries, spectators and litigants, ordinary folks in the dailiness of life and specialists in the creation of knowledge, know truth when they see it. Within our own system of truth-finding, some cases may be easier and other cases are harder, but the idea of truth itself is rarely in doubt. If the truth is unclear in a particular instance, default rules are employed to settle matters provisionally so that whatever needs to happen next can happen without delay. In law, for example, default rules about the "burden of proof" or rules requiring proof "beyond a reasonable doubt" resolve uncertain cases in definite ways.

The structure of American courts relies on the widespread facility of ordinary citizens in reasonably workable practices of truth-finding. The jury system is premised on the idea that citizens, selected to serve on juries, can listen to the presentation of evidence and work out "what happened" independent of any specialized knowledge of the law (Scheppele, 1990). Lawyers and trial judges generally receive no special training in the evaluation of evidence or in strategies for discerning truth and so they too must draw on socially situated, unremarkable methods for determining "what happened." It is generally assumed that anyone who is not connected with the parties to the case and who does not have a special interest in the outcome of the case can figure out what to believe from evidence presented in a trial without specialized instruction. This is done because in the business of the evaluation of evidence, almost everyone is enough of an expert to be entrusted with finding facts.

But as we have seen with the examples detailed above, truth-finding is a socially situated practice. We all have a set of interpretive conventions, practices of truth-finding, that tell us when a particular story seems more credible than another, when one witness appears to be telling the truth and another seems to be lying. Most of us engage in the evaluation and construction of truth on a routine basis, finding the activity generally nonproblematic and straightforward. Never mind that we are often dead wrong in doing this, regardless of our experience and professional training (Bennett and Feldman, 1981; Ekman and O'Sullivan, 1991). Most of the time, we are successful enough (or blind enough to the consequences of our inaccuracies) not to reevaluate our practices. Whenever our failures call attention to our inadequacies in this regard, we engage in a patch-up effort to work out what went wrong in the particular case but rarely reevaluate our entire scheme for evaluating the evidence that daily life presents us. And when we have to deal with the law, whether as professionals who do this all the time, as jurors or litigants who are called upon to do this on rare occasions, or even as observers or scholars of the judicial process, we bring our interpretive conventions with us.

So, what do people operating in the legal process see when they are presented with evidence? What interpretive conventions do people invoke when called upon to figure out "the facts" of cases?

The attribution of truth by judges and juries depends on properties of the stories witnesses tell (Bennett and Feldman, 1981; Jackson, 1988; Papke, 1991). Judges and juries decide whether a witness is telling the truth by evaluating how the story is constructed rather than by judging what it says. Some of the properties that matter in this judgment include internal consistency, narrative coherence, the reliance on "hard" or physical evidence and perhaps most importantly as we have seen, the stability of tellings of the story over time.

## Narratives All the Way Down

Clifford Geertz is one teller of a tale that reports a cosmology in which the world rests on the back of an elephant, which stands on the back of a turtle. When asked what the turtle stands on, an informant answered, "Ah, Sahib, after that, it is turtles all the way down" (Geertz, 1973: 29). This is not exactly a comforting answer if one wants to believe that there is some stable bedrock somewhere. But (as with the elephant and its turtles) in stories, it is narrative all the way down (Bruner, 1990, 1991; Sarbin, 1986; Carr, 1986). Narratives become their own best evidence.

Why is this? Judges and juries cannot do what a correspondence theory of language would have them do; they cannot hold up testimony against events in the world to see which versions "match" better. They cannot do this most obviously because events are long over before cases come to trial and the "reality" in question is not around to hold any descriptions up against. (The idea of holding descriptions "up against" the world is metaphorical, and could not be done literally anyway. Some procedures would have to be devised for working out when a description corresponded to reality. Those procedures, then, not the "matching," would be doing all the work.)

But even if the descriptions were being constructed simultaneously with events or the events in question were preserved somehow (as happened with the videotape in the trial of the Los Angeles police accused of beating Rodney King), judges and jurors could not work out which single description best "matched" the world. The whole idea of matching descriptions against the world is misleading because it assumes that there is only one perspective, only one point of view, only one ideology, no room for multiple readings, no potential for disagreement—in short, no problem with understanding how accounts as socially situated cultural products relate to evidence of the world. But particular "true" stories and particular descriptive statements are always selected from among a set of arguably accurate versions of reality—it is just that other descriptions in the set give very different impressions about what is going on. The vexing question is not just whether the descriptions are accurate in some way, though it is crucially important to screen out lies, but rather how it is that some particular description rather than some other comes to be forwarded as the authoritative version of events (Goodman, 1978). This raises questions of power and ideology, of the "situatedness" of the descriptions that pass for truth and the social agendas they support (Haraway, 1991).

In law, these questions are not explicitly raised as problems. Questions about multiple versions of reality are largely ignored in the subject of evidence, where what is of greatest concern are limits to the sorts of statements that might be taken as accurate. Rules of evidence screen out *types* of information that are thought to be misleading, merely prejudicial, nonprobative, or just plain unreliable. But the rules of evidence themselves are at best probabilistic judgments about categories of information and their likelihood in being false or irrelevant. It is not clear that rules of evidence actually accomplish their purpose of aiding in truth-finding, especially in light of the fact that most of us frequently use legally excludable evidence in making judgments outside of courtroom settings without apparently being wrong much of the time. Rules of evidence proceed on the assumption that individual bits of information can be screened out as unreliable, misleading or untruthful and that any "reasonable" assemblage of what is left counts as truth.

Rules of evidence provide no guidance about what to do once particular bits of information are admitted as evidence. In practice, judges and juries do the best they can to evaluate evidence the only way they can—through assessing the way the stories hang together with what else they know about the world and through spotting key characteristics in the stories that they hear, characteristics they believe are signs of truth.

Given the dependence of legal conventions of truth-finding on ordinary conventions of truth-finding, it is worth asking just what these ordinary conventions are for several reasons. First, the outcomes of individual cases are highly dependent on what is found to be "the truth" in that instance, so the integrity and reliability of the judicial process depends on these factual determinations. How they are made and what conventions they invoke should be made explicit if law is to be justifiable to those who are subject to it (Macedo, 1991: 38–77). Second, interpretations of fact and interpretations of law are not easily separable activities in the process of legal reasoning (Scheppele, 1990), and so any theory of judging needs to include some account of the interpretive conventions used in the construction of facts to represent the process adequately (Scheppele, 1989). Third, law often pretends to be above politics, prejudice, and partiality by virtue of the principled nature of its practices in judging. Insofar as a large part of that practice depends on unexamined and possibly prejudicial conventions for assessing the facts on which judicial judgment depends, the practice of judging can hardly be said to be above these "contaminating" influences. So, we should explore these influences before relying on the assumption that law manages to sanitize bias through its appeal to principle.

In addition to these worries about legal legitimacy in the abstract, there is a more immediate practical issue involved in working out *whose* conventions of truth-finding are to be invoked, where there is more than one set of conventions operating in the social settings that a given legal system embraces. If we have learned anything in recent years about the operation of social practices, it is that they are usually specific to time, place, social location, and embodiment in the lives of particular people. Saying that "we" have a set of conventions for truth-finding is al-

ready to beg the questions of who is in the "we" and whether "we" share these practices at all (Scheppele, 1989: 2077–2079). So, working out how information is constituted as fact (or, at the risk of creating an unwieldy neologism, how information is "enfacted") requires both looking at the way conventions of practice are historically, socially, culturally situated in the lives of particular people and asking whose truth is being found when jurors and judges find it. But when we look more closely, we see that the whole metaphor of "finding" rather than "constructing" the truth relies on the assumption that truth is "out there" to be located rather than constituted through the operation of social practices. This way of talking about truth shows how the "facticity" of a truth-claim must be presented as if it is compelled by the external-ness of its referent rather than compelled or allowed by the agreement on conventions of description.

## Evaluating Revised Stories

With these theoretical considerations in mind, we can now return to the specific problem of revised stories. If people generally believe that the first versions of stories are true and that later versions must be suspect unless there is some special reason to distrust the earlier version, what must their picture of truth look like?

The image people must have is of a precarious and fragile truth that decays over time, or is subject to the continual risk of subsequent distortion. As a result, information gathered before these inevitable processes of decay and distortion erode too much truth is considered to be especially important in figuring out "what happened." If accounts seem to change over time, it must be because something other than the initial, accurate perception of reality is being incorporated into the story.

But the distinction people make between initial stories and revised stories obscures an important feature they both share. They are both narratives, and as such they both represent strategies for organizing and making sense of evidence (Carr, 1986; Sarbin, 1986; Bruner, 1990). Neither story represents "perception without conception." We should not fall into the trap of thinking that the first versions of stories are raw material, processed by the mind without interpretation, and that revised stories take this raw material and shape it through interpretive processes absent in the first construction. As Wittgenstein showed in the duck–rabbit demonstration, "seeing" is often "seeing as" (Wittgenstein, 1976: 194). We do not first see things "as they are" and then interpret them. We see with the interpretive frameworks we bring to events as much as we see with our eyes. The woman who sees her abusive husband as revealing his love through his violence is not seeing some deeper, uninterpreted truth that is *then* interpreted through consciousness-raising. She is interpreting her husband's actions as much as a feminist observer or her husband's defense lawyer would. The difference is that she uses an interpretive framework the others would not use. In distinguishing between initial stories and revised stories, we might be tempted to contrast pure and untainted perception with contaminated and altered accounts. But all narratives are constructions and all descriptions are socially situated, making use of concepts and categories that are made available through the cultural location one occupies.

Nevertheless, we learn to describe as *true* the impressions we have at first because they appear to involve no conscious alteration, even though there may be a physical basis for other reports of those perceptions. Nelson Goodman reports that most of us on viewing a round table from the side still describe it as round, even though our eyes are perceiving the shape as oval because of the angle of vision (Goodman, 1978). Clearly, there is a large element of construction, however rapid and implicit, even in the most apparently uncontroversial descriptions.

What this all amounts to is that first accounts appear to be *simply true* as if perception were somehow free of organizing concepts and categories that are themselves social products. First versions are the "obvious" way to describe what has happened, while revised versions seem to involve conscious hard work to "make sense" of what has happened and are therefore more obviously contestable. The accounts we take to be "simply true" feel as though they are "straight" read-outs of unbiased perception. The accounts we arrive at by revising our stories to "make sense" of things seem to pull away from those initial perceptions and are distrusted as a result.

This is a general problem in the believability of narratives and it looks like a neutral rule. But it falls particularly hard on women. We know from experience, social science research, and observation of the legal process that women who are the victims of sexualized violence often need to take time to understand what has happened to them because women have learned both to put up with sexual violence as a feature of daily life and to blame themselves for it as a first-pass explanation (Scheppele and Bart, 1983; Scheppele, 1987). Courts' exclusion of revised stories works disproportionately against women because women are disproportionately the victims of a socialization that masks the immediate recognition of sexualized abuse *as* abuse. Overcoming the first reactions takes time—but it is precisely the delay such realization requires that courts generally suspect as evidence of lying. The first stories we tell are not constructed in the absence of frameworks that help us to make sense of what has happened; they are simply constructed with our most uncritical frameworks, frameworks that may or may not be the ones we would think best to invoke upon further reflection.

Women's initial reactions in sexually abusive situations may lead others, particularly the men with whom they interact and those who judge women's reactions in court, to conclude that women enjoy the abuse and are encouraging the conduct. In a study of rape victims in Chicago that I worked on a decade ago, I was surprised to find how many women reported that they attempted to fight off their attackers by crying, by telling the rapists their life stories and by apparently agreeing to sex in order to lower the violence level in the assault (Scheppele and Bart, 1983). Several of the women in our sample of nearly one hundred each said that she began to tell the rapist (often a stranger) intimate details of her life in the attempt to get him to see her as a human being. If he saw her as a person, she thought, then he could not do this to her. Many women reported crying and bargaining rather than punching and screaming. Talking, crying, and bargaining very rarely worked, but women thought of these strategies as aggressive attempts to defend themselves while the rapists no doubt interpreted these reactions as a lack of meaningful resistance. In the absence of bruises and scratches that come with a physical struggle, these women often had great difficulty proving their nonconsent in court. As a surprising number of first reactions revealed in this study of sexual assault victims, women are afraid to stop being polite, even when they are being attacked. This may be because women have been found to be concerned with maintaining relationships, keeping them from breaking apart (Gilligan, 1982).

In cases of sexual harassment, what victims seem to want most is for the conduct to stop. They do not want to leave their jobs, file formal grievances, or rip up their lives to avoid what was not their fault to begin with (Pollack, 1990). Women often do not report sexual harassment, hoping it will go away (Mango, 1991). By the time they decide to fight it, it is too late. The initial story that they were consenting, or at least not objecting, has already stuck.

If we have a legal system that uses rules of evidence and principles for judging truth that are hostile to revised stories, then women will continue to be victims in court. But the few revised stories that *are* currently accepted by courts are not an unqualified good thing in empowering women. The revised stories that courts currently accept are generally the versions urged by expert testimony, not just by the woman herself. The presence of experts may remove a woman's individuality and unique voice by substituting a politically correct average experience that all women are supposed to share for the detailed, potentially idiosyncratic experiences each of us has. What a woman gains in feminist insight as a result, she may lose in distinctiveness. The use of expert testimony allows a woman to win a case against a man by having a "qualified person" testify that she was suffering from trauma or delusion and so was not in her right mind when she blamed herself, acted like nothing had happened from numbness, tried to show her deluded love for the person who injured her or changed her story. What she *really* meant (only the expert can say) was something else.

Not all revised stories should be believed. Nor should all first drafts of accounts. Strategies of belief need to be more complicated than that to do justice to the variety of knowledges present in any given society. Understanding how the stories are socially constituted as believable in the first place is one important step in that process.

## Notes

I would like to thank Jane Bennett, Jerome Bruner, Sally Burns, Fernando Coronil, Peggy Davis, Louisa Bertch Green, John Kitsuse, Rick Lempert, Jack Meiland, Ted Sarbin, David Scobey, Peter Seidman, Richard Sherwin, Julie Skurski, and particularly Roger Rouse as well as seminar participants at New York Law School and New York University Law School for making more comments than I could possibly take into account in revising this paper. The first account of these ideas was presented at the annual meetings of the American Political Science Association in August 1991, and readers will have to judge for themselves whether to believe the revised version.

1. I should explain something important about this case to put discussion of this opinion in context. Reed had been charged with trafficking marijuana to some of the inmates in the prison and with encouraging two female inmates to assault and beat another inmate with whom they shared a cell. There was apparently substantial evidence to sustain these charges, including a confession, though the evidence does not appear in the appeals court report and the confession was later retracted. The court clearly seemed to believe that Reed was not a terribly sympathetic character in general, and this undoubtedly affected their treatment of her sexual harassment claims. But the principles of law the three-judge panel unanimously confirmed and the evidence they used to illustrate such principles have implications for the consideration of sexual harassment claims more generally. I focus on the court's treatment of the sexual harassment claims in isolation, then, because the reasoning presumably applies even to more sympathetic victims.

2. In *Meritor* itself, the Supreme Court found that the appearance of voluntary participation by the victim did not defeat a successful harassment claim. The behavior that Michele Vinson complained of in *Meritor* was so obviously harassment in the view of the unanimous Supreme Court that her failure to object directly to her boss (who had forced her into a sexual relationship with him) did not bar her subsequent claim.

## References

Bennett, W. L., and Feldman, M. (1981) *Reconstructing Reality in the Courtroom*. New Brunswick, NJ: Rutgers University Press.

Bruner, J. B. (1990) *Acts of Meaning*. Cambridge, MA: Harvard University Press.

Bruner, J. B. (1991) The narrative construction of reality, *Critical Inquiry*, 18: 1–21.

Carr, D. (1986) *Time, Narrative and History*. Bloomington, IN: Indiana University Press.

Ekman, P., and O'Sullivan, M. ( 1991 ) Who can catch a liar? *American Psychologist*, 46: 913–920.

Federal Information Systems Corporation (1991) Transcripts of the Hearings on the Nomination of Clarence Thomas. Available through LEXIS.

Geertz, C. (1973) Thick description: Toward an interpretive theory of culture, in C. Geertz (ed.), *The Interpretation of Cultures*. New York: Basic Books.

Gilligan, C. (1982) *In a Different Voice*. Cambridge, MA: Harvard University Press.

Goodman, N. (1978) *Ways of Worldmaking*. Indianapolis: Hackett.

Haraway, D. (1991) Situated knowledges: The science question in feminism and the privilege of partial perspective, in D. Haraway, *Simians. Cyborgs and Women: The Reinvention of Nature*. New York: Routledge.

Herman, J. L. (1992) *Trauma and Recovery: The Aftermath of Violence—From Domestic Abuse to Political Terror*. New York: Basic Books.

Jackson, B. S. (1988) *Law, Fact and Narrative Coherence*. Liverpool, UK: Deborah Charles Publications.

Macedo, S. (1991) *Liberal Virtues: Citizenship, Virtue and Community in Liberal Constitutionalism*. Oxford, UK: Oxford University Press.

Mango, K. (1991) Students v. professors: Combatting sexual harassment under Title IX of the Education Amendments of 1982, *Connecticut Law Review*, 23: 355–407.

Papke, D. R. (1991) *Narrative and Legal Discourse: A Reader in Storytelling and the Law*. Liverpool, UK: Deborah Charles Publications.

Pollack, W. (1990) Sexual harassment: Women's experiences vs. legal definitions, *Harvard Women's Law Journal*, 13: 35–75.

Sarbin, T. R. (1986) The narrative as a root metaphor for psychology, in T. R. Sarbin (ed.), *Narrative Psychology: The Storied Nature of Human Conduct*. New York: Praeger.

Scheppele, K. L. (1987) The revision of rape law, *Chicago Law Review*, 54: 1095–1116.

Scheppele, K. L. (1989) Telling stories, *Michigan Law Review*, 87: 2073–2098.

Scheppele, K. L. (1990) Facing facts in legal interpretation, *Representations*, 30: 42–77.

Scheppele, K. L., and Bart, P. B. (1983) Through women's eyes: Defining danger in the wake of sexual assault, *Journal of Social Issues*, 39: 63–80.

Walker, L. (1979) *The Battered Woman*. New York: Harper & Row.

Wittgenstein, L. (1976) *Philosophical Investigations*, third edition. Translated by G. E. M. Anscombe. New York: Macmillan.

# PART V

# Ambiguity, Complexity, and Conflict

*Advocating the mere tolerance of difference . . . is the grossest reformism. Difference must be not merely tolerated, but seen as a fund of necessary polarities between which our creativity can spark like a dialectic. Only then does the necessity for interdependence become unthreatening.*

(Audre Lorde, "The Master's Tools . . . ")

*These conflicts which break forth are not between the ideal and reality, but between two different ideals, that of yesterday and that of today, that which has the authority of tradition and that which has the hope of the future.*

(Émile Durkheim, *The Cultural Logic of Collective Representations*)

*What I claim is to live to the full contradiction of my time.*

(Roland Barthes, *Mythologies*)

# Boundaries and Contradictions

I recall wondering as a child whether the people on television continued their activities when the set was turned off. What did they do when I was not around to operate the box they lived in? Why was it that whenever I wanted to invite one of the TV people to my birthday party, the adults in my life said the TV people couldn't come because they lived somewhere else? If they lived somewhere else, why were they always in my living room? And when some of the TV people frightened me, my parents always said not to worry because the TV people weren't real. How confusing it was to figure out what separated me and the adults I knew from the TV people!

Erving Goffman, in one of his characteristically astute observations, notes that children must be taught not to call to people through walls. The reason for this, he suggests, is that children don't recognize the wall as a boundary between themselves and other people whom they know to be on the other side of the wall. Once people become aware of "walls," however, whether they are tangible or are mental constructs, they can have a profound influence on how reality is perceived.

## Boundaries

Two people huddled closely together in a public place, such as a coffee house, have an invisible wall around them. The wall is constructed from body language and gestures that we have learned to interpret as "intimacy." The action prescription that accompanies this knowledge is that it is impolite to "intrude" on someone's "walls" of intimacy. Goffman wrote an entire book, *Behavior in Public Places*, based on his observations of the manner in which persons who occupy the same physical space are able to construct unseen walls that delineate degrees of closeness and belonging. Walls also exist in the form of categorical boundaries about who we think we are or are not. Similarly, interactional routines consist of behavioral boundaries that denote what is within and without the realm of general acceptance in the situation, the group, or the culture.

Try this thought experiment. If you go to the bathroom in a public place in which there are two rooms, each with a single toilet, and the

*Note:* All personal reflections in this essay refer to Jodi O'Brien's experiences.

only difference is the signs that say Men and Women, would you use the other bathroom if the one marked for your gender was occupied? I recently went to a public bathroom and found a couple of women waiting in line for the one marked Women. The Men's was free. "Why don't we use that one?" one of the waiting women suggested. "We can keep a lookout for each other." Keep a lookout? For what? I wondered—The gender police? What would happen if the women suddenly climbed over the wall and used the Men's toilet? In this case the gender wall was invisible, but real to the extent that these women shared some mild anxiety about "getting caught" using the "wrong" bathroom.

The walls or boundaries that delineate experience and environment into "islands of meaning" are social accomplishments. When people define something, they trace boundaries around it; they wall it off and define what it is *not* in order to highlight and solidify what it *is*. Eviatar Zerubavel, a sociologist, has written a compelling book on the topic, *The Fine Line: Making Distinctions in Everyday Life* (see also his essay in Part II). Zerubavel points out that the term *define* is derived from the Latin expression for boundary, *finis*. He tells this story:

> There is a joke about a man whose house stood right on the Russian-Polish border. When it was finally decided that it was actually in Poland, he cried out: "Hooray. Now I don't have to go through those terrible Russian winters anymore." (p. 28)

Zerubavel concludes the following:

> Such reification of the purely conventional is the result of our tendency to regard the merely social as natural. Despite the fact that they are virtually mental, most gaps—as well as the quantum leaps necessary for crossing them—are among the seemingly inevitable institutionalized "social facts" that constitute our social reality. (pp. 28–29)

Thus, the signs Men and Women signify more than the location of toilets. They reflect deeply etched mental lines representing gender, one of the most basic boundaries of difference in our culture. In contemplating whether or not to use the bathroom of the "other," we are contemplating crossing over into another territory entirely.

Another illustration of a social boundary that we tend to regard as natural is the Four Corners, a popular tourist destination for travelers in the southwestern United States. In this location, four states—Utah, Colorado, New Mexico, and Arizona—all meet at a common boundary. Thousands of tourists flock to the site and engage in the contortions necessary to claim that their bodies are in four states at once. They buy souvenirs and take pictures and home videos. Is there something special about this small patch of land? If you have visited the Four Corners site, you know that it is off the beaten path and, with the exception that it's the conjunction of the four states, it's relatively unremarkable terrain. However, the conception of being in one "state" or another is a powerful reference point for the visitors. Nothing about the physical land suggests that the states should be demarcated as they are currently, but our mental maps have a firmly etched knowledge of these social boundaries.

I lived in Switzerland in my youth. This small country is home to peoples representing at least four distinct ethnic cultures—French, German, Italian, and Romanian. The first three countries border Switzerland. In crossing from one region to another, a matter of only a few kilometers in some cases, I was always struck by the ethnic distinctness of the towns. By literally walking across an imaginary line separating a German from an Italian village, I could travel between two completely different worlds. The Swiss are as obsessively tidy as the stereotypes emphasize. Cars are parked neatly within carefully painted lines, and people speak in hushed tones, queue up patiently, and always deposit their litter in one of the many handy trash cans— which are always sparkling clean. Just across the border, the Italians sing and chatter merrily as they jostle one another. Traffic rules are a fiction, and motorists park in any unoccupied space that is close to their destination and often simply stop to chat with passersby.

Near my home, in Zurich, was a complicated five-way intersection. In the middle stood an enclosed podium from which a single traffic cop directed traffic—except during lunchtime. At exactly noon every working day, the traffic cop would climb down from the podium and go home for lunch. No matter that this was the time many drivers were also driving home for the noon meal. For the traffic cop, it was time to go home. It didn't seem to make much of a difference whether the traffic cop was there, however. The Swiss took turns at the intersection with the same clocklike precision that prevailed when the traffic cop was present.

To this point in the book, we have developed a theory of social psychology suggesting that the way humans make sense of and carve up our realities is social. We have provided detailed information regarding the cognitive processes of "making meaning" and the interactional processes through which meaning is communicated, negotiated, and solidified. We have described these processes at the personal, interpersonal, and cultural levels. By now, you know that realities are socially constructed and that organized systems of thought and rules for behavior differ from group to group. This picture is a useful representation of social reality, but it is too simple. Although we have noted that boundaries are socially drawn and that different people and communities draw them differently, the impression left by much of the literature we have covered to this point is that these worlds exist as distinctly as do the worlds of the Swiss and the Italians. It may seem that negotiation proceeds, once it is routinized, as smoothly as the Swiss navigating the busy intersection at Kreuzplatz during lunchtime. However, social reality is often more complicated than this picture suggests.

## Contradictions

When different identities and cultural realities are mapped onto each other, it is evident that boundaries clash. Identities and cultures are not islands. They cannot be turned on and off like the people on TV. Different realms and territories overlap, and when they do, seemingly distinct selves and routines come crashing together. In the very process of trying to define who we are, as individuals and as groups, we encounter contradictions. We trespass across boundaries that we hold dear. We transgress against our own systems of meaning.

Boundaries depict differences in the beliefs, interests, and relative power *among* individuals and *among* groups. Trespasses and transgressions make evident the contradictions *within* ourselves and our groups. Émile Durkheim, one of the founders of sociology, wrote that in the act of defining deviance, a culture (or individual) defines and reinforces its own moral boundaries. George Herbert Mead's theory of the self is grounded in the notion of an ongoing internal conversation regarding struggle between the experiences and desires of the "I" and the moral boundaries drawn by the "me." The "self" is not one or the other, it is a manifestation of the conversation between the socialized "me" and conflicting desires and ideals that occur through ongoing social encounters. Karl Marx represents society as an ongoing struggle between those who control the means of production and those who do not. Society is not the victor of one or another of these struggling groups, it is an expression of the continuous conflict between them. Social institutions and practices reflect the contradictions between the haves and have nots.

In this final part of the book, we develop the thesis that contradictions and transgressions make people continually aware of what the boundaries are. Wrestling these contradictions is the dynamic force of self and society. The wrestling process reveals and shapes who and what we are.

# Contradictions and Conflict in Self-Production

The orderly precision of Swiss society belies the fact that foreigners, or even errant locals, often transgress codes of conduct. Many a hapless visitor has thoughtlessly dropped litter to the ground, only to have an observant Swiss pick it up and return it to its "owner" with the polite inquiry, "Did you lose this?" Parking the family car was always a traumatic event for my mother because, inevitably, just as she was about to exit the car, a vigilant local would tap on the window and describe to her the way in which she had misparked. This "helper" would then redirect her into the appropriate angle.

If you imagine this process of social correction as an internal conversation, you will have a picture of Mead's "generalized other" telling the "me" what to do. Both Mead and Sigmund Freud recognized that a person often engages in activities that conflict with or contradict expected routines of behavior. To the extent that the person has been socialized by the codes and expectations of the group, he or she will experience a voice, somewhat like the Swiss tapping the litterer on the shoulder, reminding the transgressor of what is expected. Thus, to a large extent, *intrapersonal* conflict as it is discussed by Mead and Freud emphasizes the conflict between the unsocialized will—individual passions, urges, and so forth—and the internalized voices of significant groups. This picture of cultural imprinting is a bit like that of a free-spirited animal that wants to belong to the herd but resists being fenced into a pasture.

In this discussion, we focus on yet another type of intrapersonal conflict. Certainly, much self-development occurs through channeling desires and urges into expected social forms, by learning to give these feelings and drives names and to harness them accordingly. However, socialized adults are likely to encounter many circumstances in which more than one set of "generalized other" voices compete for the reins. In those cases the person is not struggling with the conflict between "unsocialized" drives and social expectations but rather with the clamorings and demands of distinct and contradictory voices representing different states of being, distinct commitments, and diverse "generalized others."

Consider this passage from *Living with Contradiction: A Married Feminist*, written by Angela Barron McBride in 1973:

> I am a married feminist. What does that mean? Am I part of a new breed of women, or someone about to burst because of the contradictions in my person? There are weeks and months when I'm not sure which description best fits me, but such tensions are the essence of being a married feminist.

I am a woman who feels pulled in two directions—between traditional values and conventions on one hand, and a commitment to feminist ideology on the other. A woman who finds custom appealing and comforting, yet despises the patriarchal patterns that make women second-class citizens. I am a woman who wants a loving, long-term relationship with a man, but bitterly resents being considered only someone's other *half*. A woman who values family life, but deplores the sterile, functional view of man as the head of the family and woman as its heart. . . . A wife who wants to belong to one man, yet not be his private property.

The apparent contradictions felt by a married feminist are legion. I've listened to fashion plates sing the hedonistic pleasures of not being a mother, and felt like putting them over my knees and spanking them for their selfishness. I've heard gingham types say all they ever wanted out of life was to be a wife and a mother, and felt choked by their smugness. I bristle when people spit out the word "feminist" as if it were a communicable disease: I protest when others sneer at marriage as if it were an outdated misery. . . . Press the button and I can feel guilty about anything. I feel guilty that I never seem to have the time to make an assortment of Christmas cookies from scratch, *and* I feel guilty about feeling guilty about that. (pp. 1–3)

Note the teeter-totter between two roles, two selves—both of which have considerable cachet with different groups but are defined in opposition to each other. McBride's conversation with herself is a veritable ricochet from one wall to another. In searching for her own sense of self, she wrestles with her generalized notions of what these possible selves represent. For middle-class white women in the sixties and seventies, the cacophony of voices about who and what they should be was loud and, in many ways, contentious.

And consider the content of these generalized voices today. Are people still inclined to represent the extremes in women's identities as "gingham types" and "radical feminists"? To some extent these contradictions have been bridged, and the boundaries are now less sharply etched into the consciousness of young women (and men). This result stems from the attempts by the women of McBride's generation to establish some balance on the teeter-totter.

The search for new names for one's self is often prompted by the attempt to reconcile contradictions. The process can be much more complex than simply choosing one option or the other. Often the individual does not have a choice. Although contradiction and conflict may lead to change, the form of the change is always informed by the existing boundaries.

## Vocabulary, Social Position, and Self

In recent decades many scholars have focused their attention on understanding the ways in which social position affects persons differently. It's obvious, for instance, that a wealthy person has a different perspective on her options when she is shopping than someone with a low-paying hourly job and a family to feed. But do these economic differences affect the self-image of each person and if so, how? Certainly both persons have the potential to have high self-esteem and a positive self-image, but it is also true that each is likely to have vastly different day-to-day experiences. It is these experiences that combine to become the focus of the internal dialogue that make up a sense of self. In this way, social position can have profound effects on self-development. Regardless of what one thinks of oneself, certain features or characteristics denoting social status "mark" the interactional milieu in certain predictable ways. These "marked" interactions affect one's sense of self.

To continue the example, someone who is wealthy is likely to be treated with respect whenever she shops. Overall a day of shopping is likely to be a positive experience for her and the appraisals she receives from others will likely reflect her own sense of high self-worth. Conversely, there is a tendency among store clerks to treat persons who look poor as potential thieves. Thus, regardless of her own sense of personal integrity, a person "marked" as poor frequently encounters rude stares and attitudes of suspicion when she is shopping. Whereas the wealthy person takes her high self-worth for granted and has this reaffirmed through interaction, the poor person may have to continually remind herself that she really is a decent and valuable human being, despite interactional information in which she is treated as if she may not be honest.

Many concepts have been developed to describe this process of differentiation in interaction. We will review a few of them here with the aim of providing a working vocabulary. Then we turn our focus to the ways in which these processes of interactional differentiation influence self-image.

Some of the terms you may have encountered to refer to a person's social position are hegemonic position, hierarchical status, center/margin, subject/object, and marked/unmarked. We make sense of the various terms this way: Although there are many different, often-competing stories and perspectives that make up a culture, there are usually some stories or perspectives that are more acceptable and dominant than others. The dominant perspective is referred to as the *hegemonic* position. Whether they agree with it or not, most persons aware of the hegemonic position and its legitimacy is usually taken for granted. It is the position that is seen as "most normal" and "most desirable." In the contemporary United States, some of the hegemonic positions include "rationality," "heterosexuality," "middle-class," "Protestant," "male," and "white."

Some scholars refer to this hegemonic cluster as "the *center*." Recall the discussion in Part II and you will recognize the center as the default perspective. Those who do not have these centrist characteristics (e.g., are not white) are considered "other" or "marginal." Some scholars study various hegemonies and look at the consequences for persons who are in marginal positions in the hegemony. Another way of saying this is persons who are low in a particular social hierarchy as defined by the hegemonic position. For instance, it can be said that economic status is a significant or hegemonic status in this society. There is a social hierarchy that exists according to economic status. Middle-class is the dominant or taken-for-granted position in this hierarchy (not necessarily the "best" position, but the one that is assumed to be "normal"). Persons who are poor are seen as low in the hierarchy and marginal.

For the purpose of understanding how these positions operate in interaction, we find the terms "marked/unmarked" and "subject/object" useful. When a person has characteristics that are consistent with the default position in a social hierarchy then the status of the person is said to be "unmarked." The default position is *unmarked* because, cognitively, it is what people expect to see, all else being equal. A person's status is said to be "marked" if it is distinct from the expected norm. Thus, as we noted in Part II, when we refer to a "basketball player," we are inclined to think of a male basketball player. If we are talking about a basketball player who is female we tend to mark this by saying, "the woman basketball player." Similarly, when white people mention someone who is not white, race is one of the first characteristics mentioned ("I was just talking to that black guy over there"). Alternately, when referencing a white person, mention is seldom made of race ("I was just talking to that guy over there"). The latter sentence is racially unmarked and thus reflects a cultural hegemony wherein white is considered "normal."

"Subject" refers to the person who is in an active role; "object" refers to the person upon whom the subject is acting. At least this is probably the definition you were taught in English grammar. In interaction routines however, presumably all persons are subjects. They are all interacting. In any given moment, it can be said that a particular person who is projecting a definition of the situation is the subject and the persons to whom they are directing their actions are, in Goffman's terms, the audience (which is a more active position than "object"). In the vocabulary of symbolic interaction, persons are *subjects* to the extent that they are able to actively project their own contextual sense of self into the interactional dynamics. Someone is an *object* if he or she is seen by others only in terms of some marked social characteristic. If you came to talk with me about how much you want to go to law school and I respond by asking you how it was for you to be the only Chicana in your class, I would be responding to you as an *ethnic object* and denying you your self-presentation as a serious student interested in law. Or imagine I responded by stating that I'm sure you would do well because Asians are so smart. In this instance, I am treating you as an ethnic object and also imposing a particular ethnic stereotype on you. In both cases, I put you in a position in which (1) I am not granting you the specific subjective position that you are presenting and (2) you have to adjust the interaction to respond to having been put into a categorical box that may or may not have anything to do with what you are trying to talk with me about.

The paradox of subject/object is that to some extent we are always objectifying others when we interact with them. As you have learned by now, we put others into categorical boxes (label them) in order to locate their role, and our own, in the interaction. A problem arises however when we interact with someone only in terms of stereotypical categories; when we do not give them the opportunity to project their own subjectivity. *Persons who can be identified by marginal, marked statuses are more likely to be treated as objects and less likely to be perceived as subjects*. A way to think about this is how free are you to write your own narrative in a given interaction? As we have seen, power determines who can do and say what in many interactions. To what extent does a highly marked status give you even less power in an interaction? Or, conversely, when do you find yourself treating someone else in terms of a social category (as an object) rather than as a subject?

We turn now to a discussion of some of the ways in which marked/unmarked statuses shape perception, interaction, and self-image. Keep in mind that the significant analytical point is the varying degrees to which persons in interaction have control over the roles and images they are able to present to others. We will look at just a few manifestations of this process: privilege and entitlement, marked positions and awareness, subjective freedom, stigmatized identities, authenticity, and interactional mirrors. Each of these processes reflects tensions and contradictions that occur as persons attempt to "realize" themselves in interaction with others.

## Privilege and Entitlement

A noteworthy feature of hegemonic or unmarked positions is that those who occupy them are often unaware of their own relative subject freedom in interaction. They are more likely to pass through their everyday interactions without much friction. Their actions usually go unchallenged or don't need to be accounted for. They are generally given more space to express themselves, and their definition of the situation is likely to be accepted as the basis for the working consensus. For such people, the relationship between who they would like to be, who they think they are, and who they think they should be is likely to be isomorphic and noncontradictory. This unified and clearly delineated self-image is reflected back to them and reaffirmed in myriad small ways, especially through the ease with which they conduct their everyday interactions. This is not to say that such persons may not occupy contradictory roles—they simply have more control to make sure that these roles don't come clashing together.

Consider a small example: It is sometimes misassumed by middle-class people who live in suburbs that working-class people living in urban areas are more likely to engage in extramarital sex. In fact, the rates of extramarital sexual encounters may be the same across both classes, but middle-class people often have more resources for compartmentalizing their contradictory activities. Single-family homes ensure more privacy than do apartments with shared entries and thin walls. If you have money and credit cards, you can lead a duplicitous life farther away from prying eyes than if you do not have these resources. In short, it may be easier for a person with material wealth to move between one reality and another without experiencing too much social contradiction.

In *Carte Blanche,* a painting by Henri Magritte, a group of horseback riders is engaged in a fox hunt. In the foreground is a woman in fine riding clothes atop a handsome stallion. She sits astride her horse with ease and grace looking as if she hadn't a care in the world. In the background are several riders, less well clad, who are hunched low in the saddle, earnestly navigating their way around the trees of the forest through which they are riding. The woman, who represents privilege, is unaware of the trees because her horse is simply passing through them. What are obstacles for others don't exist for her. This is "carte blanche." The implication is that her life is like a blank check—relatively speaking, she can do as she pleases because her social position eclipses obstacles that others must navigate.

One interactional consequence of this privilege is a sense of social entitlement. In a powerful essay about growing up as "poor white trash," author Dorothy Allison writes:

[My people] were the *they* everyone talks about . . . the ones who are destroyed or dismissed to make the "real" people, the important people, feel safer. Why are you so afraid? My lovers and friends have asked me the many times I suddenly seemed a stranger, someone who would not speak to them, would not do the things they believed I should do, simple things like applying for a job, or a grant, or some award they were sure I could acquire easily. Entitlement, I have told them, is a matter of feeling like we rather than they. You think you have a right to things, a place in the world, and it is so intrinsically a part of you that you cannot imagine people like me, people who seem to live in your world, who don't have it. I have explained what I know over and over, in every way that I can, but I have never been able to make clear the degree of my fear, the extent to which I feel myself denied: I was born poor in a world that despises the poor. (p.14)

Entitlement in this sense can be defined as a taken-for-granted expectation that one has a *right* to pursue certain goals and to participate in various interactions. The person who feels entitled does not worry about being seen as an imposter or about being rejected or dismissed. Consider what sorts of internal conversations a person is likely to have if he or she feels entitled to participate in most realms of social life versus someone who would like to participate but is not sure if he or she has a right to do so. To what extent does this sense of entitlement provide someone with a script for pursuing such things as advice from professors, asking for letters of recommendation for graduate school, and so forth? A sense of entitlement is enhanced through repeated interactions in which a person is affirmed for her or his efforts. The more affirmed one feels, the more he or she will pursue new and risky opportunities that may lead to even greater social advantages. Relatedly, a person who feels entitled to certain things is more likely to get upset if things don't go as he or she planned.

## Marked Positions and Social Awareness

For those who occupy marginal, marked statuses, the simplest interaction may pose a contradiction between how they would like to see themselves and how others see them. A lack of role support combined with the necessity of pushing harder to project a definition of the situation can have profound effects on someone's sense of self. Social psychologists have studied the relationship between self-esteem and people's tendency to attribute successes and failures to external or internal factors. For instance, if you perform well on an exam and attribute this outcome to your own intelligence and the fact that you studied, you have made an internal attribution—the result is a consequence of something you did. If, on the other hand, you perform poorly and say that it was because the exam was too hard, you have made an external attribution—the outcome is due to factors beyond yourself.

A second attributional dimension is the extent to which you perceive the cause to be stable and within your control. For instance, if you perform poorly on an exam but attribute your performance to lack of study, you have made an internal attribution and concluded that the circumstances are potentially within your control: "I could pass that exam, I just need to study harder." If, however, you attribute your grade to the instructor's dislike of you, you have concluded that your evaluation is based on external factors beyond your control. Social psychologists are inclined to agree that external attributions lead to feelings of helplessness—the individual feels that nothing he or she can do will alter the outcome.

In a class exercise, I asked students to write a description of an occasion in which they were uncertain about whether some outcome in their lives was due to personal (internal) factors or social (external) factors. Most of the students were middle class, but some interesting differences in their responses did appear. Without hesitation, the women in the class and the students of color bent their heads and wrote intensely for several minutes. What surprised me was the response of many of the white men. They chewed on their pencils, looked puzzled, and asked me to repeat the question.

When students read their responses, several of the women told of instances in which they had not gotten jobs or had not been allowed to participate in certain activities. They were unsure whether the outcome was because they were female or because they didn't have the right skills. Students of color had thought of similar instances. One Chinese-American male told of winning an essay contest in his first year of college. Subsequently he was invited to a national forum to read the essay. When he arrived he noted that all the other "winners" were also students of color. He was unable to decide whether he had won because he wrote a terrific essay or because of his ethnicity. Many of the Hispanic- and Asian-American students related similar experiences. All of them were familiar with the day-to-day uncertainty about whether to attribute events in their lives to personal or social factors. For them, everyday self-awareness includes an ongoing conversation about whether their experiences are a result being "marked" racially, ethnically, in terms of gender biases, or a result of personal skill and talent. One consequence of this ongoing deliberation is a feeling of walking along volatile boundary lines and never being certain if one is inside or outside.

The white men, meanwhile, looked increasingly ill at ease during this classroom activity. One by one, they read papers that began, "I'm not sure what the question is . . . " or "I'm not sure what you're getting at here . . . " In subsequent reflective essays, however, many of these young men noted that they had gained a much greater recognition of how complicated self-awareness and self-evaluation are for people who cannot be certain whether or not an outcome in their lives is due to something within their control or because they are marked as particular objects. The white male students also began to take note of the many additional boundaries, such as social class and society's expectations for them (for instance, financial productivity, heterosexuality, and masculinity), that circumscribe who and what they think they can be.

Whatever a person's status, greater self-awareness occurs as a result of recognizing the complex interplay among the positions that constitute social boundaries. Like other social routines that become ossified, and even naturalized over time, these positions are likely to be taken for granted by some and not by others. The less able a person is to take them for granted, the more likely he or she is to be aware of the boundaries—and the conflicts and contradictions— within all social systems. One outcome of dealing with contradiction is an ability to comprehend more complex theories of social life.

## Subjective Freedom

Subjective freedom can be described as how much freedom one has to successfully convey a definition of the situation. If others in the interactional setting see the person only in terms of a particular stereotypical status—as an object—then the person cannot expect to be seen on her or his own terms. For instance, in education re- search it has been demonstrated that students respond very differ- ently to the same material depending on whether it is taught by a white man or a woman of color. The white man, who occupies the unmarked or expected position for the role of a college professor, is usually seen as "in control," "apolitical," "fair," and "informative" when he teaches material such as that being discussed in this essay. A woman of color teaching exactly the same thing is often evaluated by students as being "too political," "too biased," "lacking author- ity," and "uninformed." Not only do perceptions differ dramatically, in this case the man has more subjective freedom than the woman. A woman who is aware of these stereotypical reactions among students can develop strategies to counter this tendency, but in doing so, she has to shape the interaction in response to stereotypical perceptions. She is not as free to "be herself" in the same way that the man is. In presenting her subjective position (in this case as a teacher), she must navigate around the ways in which others mark her only as an object of her race and gender.

Recall Reading 22 by Brent Staples in Part III. As a black man liv- ing in a society that stereotypes the black male as a villain, Staples is not as free as his white male counterpart to walk the streets without harassment or worries that he will stir fear in others. His own subjec- tive understanding of himself is complicated by the racial stereotypes that others impose on him in interaction. He has to work harder to get himself seen in the ways that he would like to be seen.

As we noted above, persons who occupy highly marked positions are usually aware of the contradictions between how they see themselves and how others see them. The dilemma is complicated further by the fact that these marked positions are also a part of someone's subjectivity. A professor who is also a woman of color does not necessarily want to be treated *as if* she were white. This "colorblind" attitude reinforces the hegemony that white is the default and desired position. The challenge in developing *multicultural consciousness* is to overcome mindless stereotypes so that persons do not have to navigate their way out of boxes that objectify them in order to present their own subjectivity.

Ironically, as Ellen Langer notes in Part II (Reading 14), dismantling stereotypes requires a *more* discriminating attitude. This does not mean discrimination in the sense of stereotyping, but discrimination as a form of discernment and awareness. Langer admonishes us to pay attention to details that otherwise go unnoticed because they may not fit the object stereotype that we hold of the person whom we have encountered. An employer who is mindfully discerning, for instance, will force herself to get over the fact that the job interviewee is in a wheelchair and focus instead on features such as the person's seemingly high intelligence and expert experience. At the same time, she will be aware that the person is in fact in a wheelchair and that this is obviously of some consequence for him. The ways in which it is of consequence should be the subject's own story to tell, however. The more he perceives that he is being treated genuinely as a subject, rather than as a "handicapped" object, the more free he will be to present his own complex rendering of self.

## Stigmatized Identities

Some statuses are not only highly marked, but are marked in ways that are stigmatizing for the individual and for those associated with the individual. This stigmatization can have significant consequences for interaction and self-image. Consider a person who responds with the following profile to the Who Am I? question:

- daughter
- granddaughter
- graduate student
- white
- middle class
- computer geek

- cat lover
- girlfriend
- feminist
- music lover

Are you formulating an image of this person? Can you tell something about the important things and people in her life from this list (e.g., parents, grandparents, cats, school, etc.)? This is her own subjective rendering of herself. All of these self-referential characteristics are features that she would be probably be able to bring up in conversation with others and not expect conflict to occur (except maybe in terms of types of computers or favorite bands, but this would only reaffirm her commitment to these aspects of "self"). In other words, there doesn't appear to be a lot of role conflict in this initial list. Suppose however that she added "lesbian" to the list. Is this something that she can tell her grandmother about? Obviously that depends on the particular grandmother and the relationship between the two of them. Regardless, we can assume that this particular aspect of self may exist in conflict with some of the other relationships that she may value. Even if her parents are accepting of her lesbian status in their interactions with their daughter, they may find themselves in conflict when they encounter old friends who ask if their daughter is married yet. Do they "come out" as the parents of a lesbian or deflect the question in a way that will preserve their unmarked status?

Add one more item to the list—"erotic dancer." Now what happens to your own mental image of this person? Are you doing a bit of mental scrambling to make all the characteristics fit? For many people, once they are aware of this particular status, all other aspects of the person fade to the background. A stigmatized identity has a tendency to become a "master identity." Everything else about the person takes a backseat to, or is evaluated in terms of, the master identity. Stigmatized master identities also reflect archetypal social beliefs, such as the belief that someone can be a mother or an erotic dancer, but not both simultaneously. Someone might ask, for instance, How can you be a feminist and also be a stripper? Or how can you be a graduate student and do that kind of work? These sorts of questions reflect entrenched social expectations about which social roles go together and which do not. There is a tendency to assume that a person with a stigmatized role is nothing other than that particular role.

A person who engages in activities that are considered stigmatized has to do a great deal of interactional work to manage information. In this case, how free do you think the person is to share with classmates, teachers, family, and friends the fact that she dances nude for a living? Even when she does mention it, how likely is it that they will accept her definition of this particular subject position, rather than impose their own?

This example illustrates a highly marked, problematic aspect of self (stigma) that has consequences in interaction with others. It also illustrates the fact that all of us have multiple, contradictory, shifting selves. We are many things both to ourselves and to one another. We enact various selves contextually. We may push out one aspect of self in one setting (erotic dancing) and another in another setting (participation in a seminar on the feminist implications of sex work). We may keep certain features hidden (lesbian) in order to preserve a valued relationship (with a grandmother). "Stigma" is an interactional feature. An aspect of self is stigmatized only to the extent that persons define it as beyond the boundaries of expected or acceptable practices. Yet stigma can have very real consequences in shaping how persons make sense of the contradictions they perceive in their own self image and how they grapple with these contradictions in interaction with others.

Many stigmatized identities exist in the form of highly marked stereotypes (handicapped, homeless, ex-convict, hooker, drug addict, mental patient, welfare recipient, etc.). But any aspect of self about which someone feels extreme shame or embarrassment has the potential to operate as a stigmatized identity. If you are ashamed of being gay or lesbian, of being from a working-class background, of being a single parent, of your religious background, and so forth, then you may feel impelled to try to hide this aspect of yourself from others. Many social psychologists suggest that "shame" about an aspect of self-identity develops when a person internalizes social scripts that convey certain statuses as marked and undesirable. The person's own internal gaze or mirror is a reflection of social images whereby the identity is defined as loathsome. As a consequence of looking at this internal image, the person develops a sense of self-loathing. Persons who engage in behaviors that are stigmatized may or may not feel shame or embarrassment themselves. The extent to which they are able to deflect the shame directed at them by others depends on what sort of larger repertoire of self-understanding they have, their history of interactions with significant others, and their position in various social hierarchies.

For instance, when I am traveling in certain areas I can expect to be called names or even spat at by persons who perceive me to be a lesbian. At times I feel unsafe in certain areas. However, for the most part I have the freedom to avoid these situations, and to the extent that I do have to deal with bigotry, I have a well-developed set of responses. My self-image as a lesbian (a non-stigmatized identity for me) is shaped by the fact that I am a tenured professor in a respectable university. I am aware that one part of who I am—my sexual identity—is socially stigmatized, but I view that part as normal and unremarkable. In interaction, I project a definition that invites others to treat me accordingly. And for the most part, they do. Students and colleagues may privately despise me for this part of who I am, but I don't provide any opportunity for them to project this definition onto my interaction. My ability to achieve this interactional destigmatization is based on much critical reflection about how I want to incorporate this aspect of myself into my everyday interactions; many positive experiences in which my own self-view has been affirmed by people who matter to me; and, perhaps most importantly, the fact that I have a great deal of power in the particular hierarchy in which I spend most my time—a college campus.

All of us experience some degree of tension and contradiction (such as shame and guilt) in the various behaviors that we consider to be aspects of our core self. The way in which we work through these contradictions shapes our developing sense of self. Our resources for wrestling with these contradictions reflects personal interactional history and the repertoire of stories we have for ourselves.

### Interactional Mirrors

One of the features of a hegemonic or central position is that persons who occupy these positions can be relatively certain of encountering others like them wherever they go. One outcome of this is that the person's reality is likely to be reflected back by others and thereby continually reaffirmed. In contrast, persons who occupy marginal positions and who interact primarily with persons who hold mainstream positions may often feel isolated and conflicted about how to interpret their own experiences. As the poet Adrienne Rich puts it, "It's like looking into a mirror and seeing nothing."

Being able to interact with others whose experiences and struggles match your own is not simply a privilege, it is an occasion to (re)affirm the reality of your own impressions and feelings. Many of us transgress boundaries every day because we are "outsiders." The vertigo of these experiences can be overcome, to some extent, if we are able to interact with others who share our conflicting circumstances and contradictory experiences. Conversations with these others provide us with new names and meanings that help us bridge the contradictions. This opportunity to associate and redefine reality is one of the reasons why special interest groups and clubs are important for people who share marginalized, marked, or stigmatized statuses. These groups provide interactional mirrors that reflect the complexities of crossing through contradictory states of being. In encounters with others who experience similar contradictions and tensions, people broaden their repertoire, learn new scripts for acting, and have an opportunity to express more subjective freedom.

In this country, suicide is the leading cause of death among gay, lesbian, and transgendered youths aged 15–24 (Herdt & Roxer, 1993). These young people often experience their sexual or gender feelings as being completely outside the boundaries of the self-images that have been inculcated by significant others, such as parents, family, friends, teachers, and church and community leaders. Without positive imagery and role models for how to incorporate their differences into the rest of their self-image, these young people may suffer the contradictions deeply. Irreconcilable feelings of helplessness can lead to extreme despair. The opportunity to encounter people whose self-image reconciles the identities of "homosexual" and "productive, accepted member of society" can turn these young people away from the brink of suicide.

Similarly, women and students of color benefit from programs designed specifically for them to interact with others who share similar points of view. For these alternative perspectives to be interactionally supported and to gain the stature of commonly understood realities, they must sometimes be enacted separately from mainstream culture. Renato Rosaldo, an anthropologist who has participated actively in the development of such programs at Stanford University calls the programs "safe houses":

> Why do institutions need safe houses? Safe houses can foster self-esteem and promote a sense of belonging in often alien institutions. Safe houses are places where diverse groups—under the banners of ethnic studies, feminist studies, or gay and lesbian studies—talk together and become more articulate about their intellectual projects. When they enter the mainstream seminars such students speak with clarity and force about their distinctive projects, concerns, and perspectives. The class is richer and more complex, if perhaps less comfortable, for its broadened range of perspectives. (p. xi)

Rosaldo is delineating the interactional steps whereby persons have an opportunity to express their subjectivity without having to navigate the imposition of stereotypes and prejudices. In the kind of interactional setting that he describes, persons develop a clearer and more articulate sense of who they are *in all their complexity*. When they bring this complexity into mainstream interactions, it can have the effect of altering the stereotypical routine.

It is important to note that status as an insider or an outsider is situational and may change with circumstance. In *Falling from Grace*, Katherine Newman describes the experiences of men in middle and upper managerial positions who have lost their jobs. For most of these men, selfhood pivots around their ability, as holders of privileged positions, to move with ease through a world in which they wield considerable control. When they lose their jobs, they lose access to a tremendous amount of interactional privilege (such as control over space and conversation) that is the basis for their maintaining a positive self-image. Many of these men are unaccustomed to contradictory self-images and, as a result, are ill prepared for the quick downward spiral that they experience when they fall outside the lines of their primary reference group. Lacking alternative points of reference and feeling ashamed of having been "downsized," these men are at high risk for suicide. Support groups for men like these do not simply provide a way to get through the hard times—they are interactional situations in which the men learn to project and juggle a new self-image, one that is quite different from the self they have been accustomed to being.

## Authenticity

The preceding discussion reveals a picture of the social self as multiple, shifting, and contradictory. How we see ourselves and the selves we present to others shifts from context to context and can be contradictory within a given situation. We are more committed to some aspects of self than others. We may be inclined to hide or deflect certain significant identities in some situations. These observations lead to the question, Who are you really? The question of "authenticity" is something that concerns many scholars as well as individuals. Our answer to the question comes in the form of a paradox: We all live contradictory lives, but we tend to act *as if* our lives were not filled with ambiguity and contradiction. One cultural expectation that many of us share is the *norm of consistency*. Is consistency the same thing as authenticity? For many people it is. We believe someone is "authentic" when we observe them behaving consistently across different settings and circumstances ("She must be genuinely kind, because she is kind even when someone is mean to her"). It is possible that persons strive to make their behavior consistent because others expect us to behave consistently. Over the course of time, with repeated interactions and affirmation, we may develop self-routines that are so consistent that we believe them to be authentic expressions of self. Furthermore, to the extent that others strive to show us consistency and to hide the inconsistencies, we may come to believe that people are, indeed, consistent or authentic.

In a related way, we may strive to hide aspects of self that might strike others as contradictory according to pre-existing social scripts about what sorts of behaviors go together ("He can't possibly be gay and also be a minister"). In doing so, we reaffirm these social scripts and fail to express the fact that selves are indeed multiple and contradictory.

From our perspective as symbolic interactionists who recognize the existence of multiple, shifting, contradicting self-expressions, our answer to the question "Who are you really?" is this: We are really the *way* in which we work through the contradictions that characterize our day-to-day interactions. We are the *process of wrestling contradictions* that is reflected in internal conversation and external expression. Two people can have a similar profile of self-referential identities and characteristics but very different self-images and interactional responses. Consider again the woman described in the "Who am I?" question above. She might keep her more stigmatized statuses (lesbian, erotic dancer) closeted from others whom she suspects will not be able to handle the "contradictions" these statuses imply, or she might reveal all and express an attitude of "I have a right to be *all* these various selves, even if it confuses you." How she views her own selves and how she chooses to portray them to others—in all their complexity and ambiguity—reveals the process of who she really is.

In this way, we conclude that selves are always in a state of becoming, this becoming is shaped through the processes of interaction and revealed through the internal dialogues in which we observe, comment on, feel, and try to make sense of our own complexity.

## Readings

Each of the readings in the first section of Part V portrays an internal dialogue between the various selves of the subjects. The first reading, written in 1903, is by a man who has come to be known as one of the greatest U.S. theorists of race, W. E. B. Du Bois. The title, "Double-Consciousness and the Veil," conveys his notion that many black Americans have a double-consciousness, or "two souls," because they are separated from normative representations of "real" Americans by the wall of race. His use of the term *veil* to denote this wall is a powerful image. The image of a veil suggests being able to see through the boundary but not being able to completely touch the desired self-image of belonging in the United States. For Du Bois, this conflict results in a "double-sightedness" and, at the same time, an inability to find reflections that mirror back the black American's experience of who he or she is.

"Stephen Cruz" is excerpted from Studs Terkel's book of interviews, *American Dreams: Lost and Found*. In this first-hand account,

Stephen Cruz wrestles the contradictions of his understanding of himself as a Chicano who has worked hard to earn his piece of the "American" pie. He feels indebted to those who fought for the civil rights that he thinks are partly responsible for his own success. But simultaneously he experiences a growing gap between himself, a "man of wealth," and his fellow Chicanos. His conflict is whether to relax and enjoy his accomplishments or to use his success to help "his people."

In Reading 46, "Growing Up with Privilege and Prejudice," Karen Russell reflects on how her life was influenced by the privileges associated with a father who was a famous basketball player and the prejudices she encountered because of being black in Boston. In brief Readings 47 and 48, authors Stoll and Avicolli consider how gender expectations shaped their experiences and self-understanding in their youth.

Jeffrey Weeks—in Reading 49, "Sexual Identification Is a Strange Thing"—writes from the position of a gay, Anglo male. He observes the complexities and contradictions of a culture that does not recognize sexual attraction to members of the same sex as a legitimate form of sexual expression. He asks, Why does anyone have to stake out a sexual identity in this culture? How has sexuality become an aspect of self-definition rather than an "activity"? Weeks further notes that many of the "names" available to gay Brits and Americans are at odds with other aspects of self. For example, can someone identify openly as homosexual and simultaneously be a devout Christian? The search for sexual identity among those who find themselves transgressing one of the most deeply etched boundaries of U.S. society brings into focus several intersecting contradictions regarding the taken-for-granted connections among love, companionship, reproduction, household economies, spirituality, goodness, and morality that constitute the institution of "heterosexuality."

In an intriguing switch, Mary Crawford writes in Reading 50—"Identity, 'Passing,' and Subversion"—about what it is like to be a heterosexual woman within a reference group that does not take heterosexuality for granted. This piece is taken from a book titled *Heterosexuality,* in which women who consider themselves feminists and contemporary scholars in the social sciences and humanities were asked to reflect on their sexual identity. Several of the women wrote that, in a context where heterosexuality is often equated with oppression, identifying as a heterosexual can promote intense interpersonal conflict. As some of the women remark, being asked to write for this forum was a bit like being asked to "come out of the closet as a straight woman."

In Reading 51, "Her Son/Daughter," author and performance artist Kate Bornstein describes the experiences of attending her mother's funeral and encountering old acquaintances who remember her only as her mother's son.

In each of these readings, note the ways in which the authors' conversations with themselves (and the reader) reflect their own perceptions of social expectations. How do they grapple with these expectations and the contradictions that they imply in each case?

As you read through these selections, keep in mind some of the general principles that we have laid out in this book. All humans use language-based systems to create conceptual meaning. This process creates definitional boundaries. All people compartmentalize. Different individuals encounter these boundaries differently. The process of self-understanding is a continual interplay between personal experience and attempts to fit experience into existing conceptual categories and representations. All of us struggle to make sense of ourselves, to find ways of self-expression, and to be heard and understood. The self undergoes constant revision as it encounters friction, contradiction, and conflict among the various boundaries that give the self meaning.

## Conflict and Change in Cultural Production

Cultural production, like self-production, is a dialectical process of definition. Within groups and societies, people struggle over what significant symbols mean and who has the authority to project public definitions. The struggle over frames of meaning organize people's lives.

In this struggle to create definitions, cultural institutions are a resource—a source of privilege for some and an obstacle for others. Various institutions—family, government, religion, and the economy, for example—can wield great influence in the creation or maintenance of socially shared definitions. This influence may be unintended, or it may be consciously directed toward supporting a particular status quo. Again, however, power is an issue. Not everyone is equally able to participate in the construction of meaning. Some people's beliefs and interests are given more legitimacy than others.

As we discussed in Part IV, hegemonic practices of inequality persist because people play out the scripts expected of them—even when they may be privately opposed to these practices. People participate in practices of domination and inequality for a variety of reasons: They may not realize the extent to which they contribute to the maintenance of particular definitions of the situation (hence the popular bumper-sticker "Question authority"). Or, as is often the case, they may not have the resources necessary to break the chains of the existing reality. This complicity in oppression is what Marx refers to when he says that the "tradition of the dead generations weighs like a *nightmare* on the brain of the living" [italics added]. Prevailing realities suggest certain lines of action and forestall others. The possibility for change is in the conception of alternative lines of interaction. Alexis de Tocqueville once observed: "A grievance can be endured so long as it seems beyond redress, but it becomes intolerable once the possibility of removing it crosses people's minds." To be realized, however even the most eloquent theories must be acted out. Change must be performed on the social stage.

We conclude the book with a set of readings that challenge some of the taken-for-granted assumptions and practices of conventional realities. In Reading 52, "Maid in the U.S.A.: A Personal Narrative on the Development of a Research Problem," sociologist Mary Romero describes the invisibility and stigma attached to domestic work. She tells how she became aware of some of the indignities domestic workers experience and how they struggle to maintain their pride. In response to these insights, she designed a research project to explore the experiences of Chicana domestic workers. This research is Romero's attempt to make the invisible visible.

In Reading 53, "Talking Back," bell hooks considers what happens when an oppressed actor does not engage in expected forms of deference. Oppression is a construction that requires the cooperation of many social actors, both those that are doing the oppressing and those who are being oppressed. According to hooks, we choose to either join in the construction of oppression or to withdraw our support. She points out that we can all actively work to breach realities that work against our interests. We can talk back.

Jewelle Gomez echoes this theme in her essay "Because Silence Is Costly" (Reading 54). She elaborates on the significance of speaking out and telling the stories that people may not want to hear. It is only through the public telling of these stories that new stories can be formed and lived.

An essay written by Gloria Anzaldúa is Reading 55, "*La Conciencia de la Mestiza*/Toward a New Consciousness." Anzaldúa's thesis is that those who walk the boundaries and live the contradictions are aware of both the advantages and limitations of existing cultural institutions. Individuals and groups at the margins of, or between, cultural institutions are not likely to take these institutional forms for granted. They are more likely to be aware of other possibilities and may offer a richer, more complex frame for the future. As you read this piece, consider what it means to live in a country that promotes "freedom and justice" for all. The benefit of a multiple, complex national consciousness is the vigorous debate it generates. Cultural pluralism legislated through democracy is the organizing principle of this freedom.

We conclude with the poem "Ceremony" by Leslie Marmon Silko. This poem is about the stories we use to organize and give meaning to our collective lives. One of the paradoxes of human social life is that cultural stories both constrain us and make our lives meaningful.

In conclusion, we emphasize that contradiction is not necessarily a bad thing. To the extent that each of us recognizes and learns to wrestle the contradictions that are an inevitable part of social existence, we each add increasingly complex lines of definition to our sense of who and what we can be. We increase our social muscle and expand our repertoire of possibilities.

The 19th-century poet Rainer Maria Rilke—who himself lived on the cultural boundaries of Bohemia, Austria, and Germany—expresses repeatedly throughout his poetry that the courageous and moral life consists of people learning to span bridges across contradictions:

> As once the winged energy of delight
> carried you over childhood's dark abysses,
> now beyond your own life build the great
> arc of unimagined bridges. . . .
> Take your practiced powers and stretch them out
> until they span the chasm between two
> contradictions. . . . For the god
> wants to know himself in you. (p. 261)

Elsewhere Rilke likens the process of identifying and grappling with contradiction to wrestling an angel. His reference to "the god" can be read as an association between the human ability to generate new meaning (the generative power of language to produce social form) and the creative powers of gods. Spinning imaginative bridges that span existing, contradictory social forms is a first step toward creating new forms of self and society.

## References

Allison, D. (1994). *Skin: Talking about Sex, Class and Literature*. Ithaca, NY: Firebrand Books.

Goffman, E. (1963). *Behavior in public places*. New York: Free Press.

Herdt, G., & Roxer, A. (1993). *Children of horizons*. Boston: Beacon.

McBride, A. B. (1973). *Living with contradictions: A married feminist*. New York: Harper Collins.

McIntosh, P. (1992). "White privilege and male privilege." In M. L. Anderson & P. H. Collins (Eds.), *Race, Class, and Gender: An Anthology*. Belmont, CA: Wadsworth.

Newman, K. (1988). *Falling from grace*. New York: Free Press.

Rilke, R. M. (1989). *The selected poetry of Rainer Maria Rilke* (S. Mitchell, Trans.). New York: Vintage.

Rosaldo, Renato. 1993. *Culture and truth: The remaking of social analysis*. Boston: Beacon Press.

Zerubavel, E. (1991). *The fine line: Making distinctions in everyday life*. Chicago: University of Chicago Press.

# Double-Consciousness and the Veil

*W. E. B. Du Bois*

O water, voice of my heart, crying in the
    sand,
All night long crying with a mournful cry,
As I lie and listen, and cannot understand
The voice of my heart in my side or the
    voice of the sea,
O water, crying for rest, is it I, is it I?
All night long the water is crying to me.

Unresting water, there shall never be rest
Till the last moon droop and the last tide
    fail,
And the fire of the end begin to burn in the
    west;
And the heart shall be weary and wonder
    and cry like the sea,
All life long crying without avail,
As the water all night long is crying to me.
              —Arthur Symons

Between me and the other world there is ever
an unasked question: unasked by some
through feelings of delicacy; by others
through the difficulty of rightly framing it.
All, nevertheless, flutter round it. They approach me in a half-hesitant sort of way, eye
me curiously or compassionately, and then,
instead of saying directly, How does it feel to
be a problem? they say, I know an excellent
colored man in my town; or, I fought at
Mechanicsville; or, Do not these Southern

"Double-Consciousness and the Veil" from *The Souls of
Black Folk* by W. E. B. Du Bois, 1903. New York: Bantam.

outrages make your blood boil? At these I
smile, or am interested, or reduce the boiling
to a simmer, as the occasion may require. To
the real question, How does it feel to be a
problem? I answer seldom a word.

And yet, being a problem is a strange experience—peculiar even for one who has
never been anything else, save perhaps in ba-
byhood and in Europe. It is in the early days
of rollicking boyhood that the revelation first
bursts upon one, all in a day, as it were. I remember well when the shadow swept across
me. I was a little thing, away up in the hills of
New England, where the dark Housatonic
winds between Hoosac and Taghkanic to the
sea. In a wee wooden schoolhouse, something put it into the boys' and girls' heads to
buy gorgeous visiting-cards—ten cents a
package—and exchange. The exchange was
merry, till one girl, a tall newcomer, refused
my card—refused it peremptorily, with a
glance. Then it dawned upon me with a certain suddenness that I was different from the
others; or like, mayhap, in heart and life and
longing, but shut out from their world by a
vast veil. I had thereafter no desire to tear
down that veil, to creep through; I held all
beyond it in common contempt, and lived
above it in a region of blue sky and great
wandering shadows. That sky was bluest
when I could beat my mates at examination-
time, or beat them at a foot-race, or even beat
their stringy heads. Alas, with the years all
this fine contempt began to fade, for the

words I longed for, and all their dazzling opportunities, were theirs, not mine. But they should not keep these prizes, I said; some, all, I would wrest from them. Just how I would do it I could never decide: by reading law, by healing the sick, by telling the wonderful tales that swam in my head—some way. With other black boys the strife was not so fiercely sunny: their youth shrunk into tasteless sycophancy, or into silent hatred of the pale world about them and mocking distrust of everything white; or wasted itself in a bitter cry: Why did God make me an outcast and a stranger in mine own house? The shades of the prison-house closed round about us all: walls strait and stubborn to the whitest, but relentlessly narrow, tall, and unscalable to sons of night who must plod darkly on in resignation, or beat unavailing palms against the stone, or steadily, half hopelessly, watch the streak of blue above.

After the Egyptian and Indian, the Greek and Roman, the Teuton and Mongolian, the Negro is a sort of seventh son, born with a veil, and gifted with second-sight in this American world—a world which yields him no true self-consciousness, but only lets him see himself through the revelation of the other world. It is a peculiar sensation, this double-consciousness, this sense of always looking at one's self through the eyes of others, of measuring one's soul by the tape of a world that looks on in amused contempt and pity. One ever feels his twoness—an American, a Negro; two souls, two thoughts, two unreconciled strivings; two warring ideals in one dark body, whose dogged strength alone keeps it from being torn asunder.

The history of the American Negro is the history of this strife—this longing to attain self-conscious manhood, to merge his double self into a better and truer self. In this merging he wishes neither of the older selves to be lost. He would not Africanize America, for America has too much to teach the world and Africa. He would not bleach his Negro soul in a flood of white Americanism, for he knows that Negro blood has a message for the

world. He simply wishes to make it possible for a man to be both a Negro and an American, without being cursed and spit upon by his fellows, without having the doors of Opportunity closed roughly in his face.

This, then, is the end of his striving: to be a co-worker in the kingdom of culture, to escape both death and isolation, to husband and use his best powers and his latent genius. These powers of body and mind have in the past been strangely wasted, dispersed, or forgotten. The shadow of a mighty Negro past flits through the tale of Ethiopia the Shadowy and of Egypt the Sphinx. Through history, the powers of single black men flash here and there like falling stars, and die sometimes before the world has rightly gauged their brightness. Here in America, in the few days since Emancipation, the black man's turning hither and thither in hesitant and doubtful striving has often made his very strength to lose effectiveness, to seem like absence of power, like weakness. And yet it is not weakness—it is the contradiction of double aims. The double-aimed struggle of the black artisan—on the one hand to escape white contempt for a nation of mere hewers of wood and drawers of water, and on the other hand to plough and nail and dig for a poverty-stricken horde—could only result in making him a poor craftsman, for he had but half a heart in either cause. By the poverty and ignorance of his people, the Negro minister or doctor was tempted toward quackery and demagogy; and by the criticism of the other world, toward ideals that made him ashamed of his lowly tasks. The would-be black *savant* was confronted by the paradox that the knowledge his people needed was a twice-told tale to his white neighbors, while the knowledge which would teach the white world was Greek to his own flesh and blood. The innate love of harmony and beauty that set the ruder souls of his people a-dancing and a-singing raised but confusion and doubt in the soul of the black artist; for the beauty revealed to him was the soul-beauty of a race which his larger audience despised, and he could not articulate the message of another people. This waste of double aims, this seeking to satisfy two unreconciled ideals, has wrought sad havoc with the courage and faith and deeds of ten thousand thousand people—has sent them often wooing false gods and invoking false means of salvation, and at times has even seemed about to make them ashamed of themselves.

Away back in the days of bondage they thought to see in one divine event the end of all doubt and disappointment; few men ever worshipped Freedom with half such unquestioning faith as did the American Negro for two centuries. To him, so far as he thought and dreamed, slavery was indeed the sum of all villainies, the cause of all sorrow, the root of all prejudice; Emancipation was the key to a promised land of sweeter beauty than ever stretched before the eyes of wearied Israelites. In song and exhortation swelled one refrain—Liberty; in his tears and curses the God he implored had Freedom in his right hand. At last it came—suddenly, fearfully, like a dream. With one wild carnival of blood and passion came the message in his own plaintive cadences—

Shout, O children!
Shout, you're free!
For God has bought your liberty!

Years have passed away since then—ten, twenty, forty; forty years of national life, forty years of renewal and development, and yet the swarthy spectre sits in its accustomed seat at the Nation's feast. In vain do we cry to this our vastest social problem—

Take any shape but that, and my firm nerves
Shall never tremble!

The Nation has not yet found peace from its sins; the freedman has not yet found in freedom his promised land. Whatever of good may have come in these years of change, the shadow of a deep disappointment rests upon the Negro people—a disappointment all the more bitter because the unattained ideal was unbounded save by the simple ignorance of a lowly people.

The first decade was merely a prolongation of the vain search for freedom, the boon that seemed ever barely to elude their grasp—like a tantalizing will-o'-the-wisp, maddening and misleading the headless host. The holocaust of war, the terrors of the Ku-Klux Klan, the lies of carpetbaggers, the disorganization of industry, and the contradictory advice of friends and foes, left the bewildered serf with no new watchword beyond the old cry for freedom. As the time flew, however, he began to grasp a new idea. The ideal of liberty demanded for its attainment powerful means, and these the Fifteenth Amendment gave him. The ballot, which before he had looked upon as a visible sign of freedom, he now regarded as the chief means of gaining and perfecting the liberty with which war had partially endowed him. And why not? Had not votes made war and emancipated millions? Had not votes enfranchised the freedmen? Was anything impossible to a power that had done all this? A million black men started with renewed zeal to vote themselves into the kingdom. So the decade flew away, the revolution of 1876 came, and left the half-free serf weary, wondering, but still inspired. Slowly but steadily, in the following years, a new vision began gradually to replace the dream of political power—a powerful movement, the rise of another ideal to guide the unguided, another pillar of fire by night after a clouded day. It was the ideal of "book-learning"; the curiosity, born of compulsory ignorance, to know and test the power of the cabalistic letters of the white man, the longing to know. Here at last seemed to have been discovered the mountain path to Canaan; longer than the highway of Emancipation and law, steep and rugged, but straight, leading to heights high enough to overlook life.

Up the new path the advance guard toiled, slowly, heavily, doggedly; only those who have watched and guided the faltering feet, the misty minds, the dull understandings, of the dark pupils of these schools know how faithfully, how piteously, this people strove to learn. It was weary work. The cold statistician wrote down the inches of progress here and there, noted also where here and there a foot had slipped or someone had fallen. To the tired climbers, the horizon was ever dark, the mists were often cold, the Canaan was always dim and far away. If, however, the vistas disclosed as yet no goal, no resting-place, little but flattery and criticism, the journey at least gave leisure for reflection and self-examination; it changed the child of Emancipation to the youth with dawning self-consciousness, self-realization, self-respect. In those sombre forests of his striving his own soul rose before him, and he saw himself—darkly as through a veil; and yet he saw in himself some faint revelation of his power, of his mission. He began to have a dim feeling that, to attain his place in the world, he must be himself, and not another. For the first time he sought to analyze the burden he bore upon his back, that dead-weight of social degradation partially masked behind a half-named Negro problem. He felt his poverty; without a cent, without a home, without land, tools, or savings, he had entered into competition with rich, landed, skilled neighbors. To be a poor man is hard, but to be a poor race in a land of dollars is the very bottom of hardships. He felt the weight of his ignorance— not simply of letters, but of life, of business, of the humanities; the accumulated sloth and shirking and awkwardness of decades and centuries shackled his hands and feet. Nor was his burden all poverty and ignorance. The red stain of bastardy, which two centuries of systematic legal defilement of Negro women had stamped upon his race, meant not only the loss of ancient African chastity, but also the hereditary weight of a mass of corruption from white adulterers, threatening almost the obliteration of the Negro home.

A people thus handicapped ought not to be asked to race with the world, but rather allowed to give all its time and thought to its own social problems. But alas! while sociologists gleefully count his bastards and his prostitutes, the very soul of the toiling, sweating black man is darkened by the shadow of a vast despair. Men call the shadow prejudice, and learnedly explain it as the natural defence of culture against barbarism, learning against ignorance, purity against crime, the "higher" against the "lower" races. To which the Negro cries Amen! and swears that to so much of this strange prejudice as is founded on just homage to civilization, culture, righteousness, and progress, he humbly bows and meekly does obeisance. But before that nameless prejudice that leaps beyond all this he stands helpless, dismayed, and well-nigh speechless; before that personal disrespect and mockery, the ridicule and systematic humiliation, the distortion of fact and wanton license of fancy, the cynical ignoring of the better and the boisterous welcoming of the worse, the all-pervading desire to inculcate disdain for everything black, from Toussaint to the devil—before this there rises a sickening despair that would disarm and discourage any nation save that black host to whom "discouragement" is an unwritten word.

But the facing of so vast a prejudice could not but bring the inevitable self-questioning, self-disparagment, and lowering of ideals which ever accompany repression and breed in an atmosphere of contempt and hate. Whisperings and portents came borne upon the four winds: Lo! we are diseased and dying, cried the dark hosts; we cannot write, our voting is vain; what need of education, since we must always cook and serve? And the Nation echoed and enforced this self-criticism, saying: Be content to be servants, and nothing more; what need of higher culture for half-men? Away with the black man's ballot, by force or fraud—and behold the suicide of a race! Nevertheless, out of the evil came something of good—the more careful adjustment of education to real life, the clearer perception of the Negroes' social responsibilities, and the sobering realization of the meaning of progress.

So dawned the time of *Sturm und Drang:* storm and stress today rocks our little boat on the mad waters of the world-sea; there is within and without the sound of conflict, the burning of body and rending of soul; inspiration strives with doubt, and faith with vain questionings. The bright ideals of the past—physical freedom, political power, the training of brains and the training of hands—all these in turn have waxed and waned, until even the last grows dim and overcast. Are they all wrong—all false? No, not that, but each alone was oversimple and incomplete—the dreams of a credulous race-childhood, or the fond imaginings of the other world which does not know and does not want to know our power. To be really true, all these ideals must be melted and welded into one. The training of the schools we need today more than ever—the training of deft hands, quick eyes and ears, and above all the broader, deeper, higher culture of gifted minds and pure hearts. The power of the ballot we need in sheer self-defense—else what shall save us from a second slavery? Freedom, too, the long-sought, we still seek—the freedom of life and limb, the freedom to work and think, the freedom to love and aspire. Work, culture, liberty—all these we need, not singly but together, not successively but together, each growing and aiding each, and all striving toward that vaster ideal that swims before the Negro people, the ideal of human brotherhood, gained through the unifying ideal of Race; the ideal of fostering and developing the traits and talents of the Negro, not in opposition to or contempt for other races, but rather in large conformity to the greater ideals of the American Republic, in order that some day on American soil two world-races may give each to each those characteristics both so sadly lack. We the darker ones come even now not altogether empty-handed: There are today no truer exponents of the pure human spirit of the Declaration of Independence than the American Negroes; there is no true American music but the wild sweet melodies of the Negro slave; the American fairy tales and folklore are Indian and African; and, all in all, we black men seem the sole oasis of simple faith and reverence in a dusty desert of dollars and smartness. Will America be poorer if she replace her brutal dyspeptic blundering with light-hearted but determined Negro humility? or her coarse and cruel wit with loving jovial good-humor? or her vulgar music with the soul of the Sorrow Songs?

Merely a concrete test of the underlying principles of the great republic is the Negro Problem, and the spiritual striving of the freedmen's sons is the travail of souls whose burden is almost beyond the measure of their strength, but who bear it in the name of an historic race, in the name of this the land of their fathers' fathers, and in the name of human opportunity.

45

# Stephen Cruz

## *Studs Terkel*

He is thirty-nine.

"The family came in stages from Mexico. Your grandparents usually came first, did a little work, found little roots, put together a few bucks, and brought the family in, one at a time. Those were the days when controls at the border didn't exist as they do now."

You just tried very hard to be whatever it is the system wanted of you. I was a good student and, as small as I was, a pretty good athlete. I was well liked, I thought. We were fairly affluent, but we lived down where all the trashy whites were. It was the only housing we could get. As kids, we never understood why. We did everything right. We didn't have those Mexican accents, we were never on welfare. Dad wouldn't be on welfare to save his soul. He woulda died first. He worked during the depression. He carries that pride with him, even today.

Of the five children, I'm the only one who really got into the business world. We learned quickly that you have to look for opportunities and add things up very quickly. I was in liberal arts, but as soon as *Sputnik*[1] went up, well, golly, hell, we knew where the bucks were. I went right over to the registrar's office and signed up for engineer-

ing. I got my degree in '62. If you had a master's in business as well, they were just paying all kinds of bucks. So that's what I did. Sure enough, the market was super. I had fourteen job offers. I could have had a hundred if I wanted to look around.

I never once associated these offers with my being a minority. I was aware of the Civil Rights Act of 1964, but I was still self-confident enough to feel they wanted me because of my abilities. Looking back, the reason I got more offers than the other guys was because of the government edict. And I thought it was because I was so goddamned brilliant. (Laughs.) In 1962, I didn't get as many offers as those who were less qualified. You have a tendency to blame the job market. You just don't want to face the issue of discrimination.

I went to work with Procter & Gamble. After about two years, they told me I was one of the best supervisors they ever had and they were gonna promote me. Okay, I went into personnel. Again, I thought it was because I was such a brilliant guy. Now I started getting wise to the ways of the American Dream. My office was glass-enclosed, while all the other offices were enclosed so you couldn't see into them. I was the visible man.

They made sure I interviewed most of the people that came in. I just didn't really think there was anything wrong until we got a new plant manager, a southerner. I received instructions from him on how I should interview blacks. Just check and see if they smell, okay? That was the beginning of my training program. I started asking: Why weren't we hiring more minorities? I realized I was the only one in a management position.

I guess as a Mexican I was more acceptable because I wasn't really black. I was a good compromise. I was visibly good. I hired a black secretary, which was *verboten*. When I came back from my vacation, she was gone. My boss fired her while I was away. I asked why and never got a good reason.

Until then, I never questioned the American Dream. I was convinced if you worked hard, you could make it. I never considered myself different. That was the trouble. We had been discriminated against a lot, but I never associated it with society. I considered it an individual matter. Bad people, my mother used to say. In '68 I began to question.

I was doing fine. My very first year out of college, I was making twelve thousand dollars. I left Procter & Gamble because I really saw no opportunity. They were content to leave me visible, but my thoughts were not really solicited. I may have overreacted a bit, with the plant manager's attitude, but I felt there's no way a Mexican could get ahead here.

I went to work for Blue Cross. It's 1969. The Great Society[2] is in full swing. Those who never thought of being minorities before are being turned on. Consciousness raising is going on. Black programs are popping up in universities. Cultural identity and all that. But what about the one issue in this country: economics? There were very few management jobs for minorities, especially blacks.

The stereotypes popped up again. If you're Oriental, you're real good in mathematics. If you're Mexican, you're a happy guy to have around, pleasant but emotional. Mexicans are either sleeping or laughing all the time. Life is just one big happy kind of event. *Mañana*. Good to have as part of the management team, as long as you weren't allowed to make decisions.

I was thinking there were two possibilities why minorities were not making it in business. One was deep, ingrained racism. But there was still the possibility that they were simply a bunch of bad managers who just couldn't cut it. You see, until now I believed everything I was taught about the dream: The American businessman is omnipotent and fair. If we could show these turkeys there's money to be made in hiring minorities, these businessmen—good managers, good decision makers—would respond. I naïvely thought American businessmen gave a damn about society, that given a choice they would do the right thing. I had that faith.

I was hungry for learning about decision-making criteria. I was still too far away from top management to see exactly how they were working. I needed to learn more. Hey, just learn more and you'll make it. That part of the dream hadn't left me yet. I was still clinging to the notion of work your ass off, learn more than anybody else, and you'll get in that sphere.

During my fifth year at Blue Cross, I discovered another flaw in the American Dream. Minorities are as bad to other minorities as whites are to minorities. The strongest weapon the white manager had is the old divide and conquer routine. My mistake was thinking we were all at the same level of consciousness.

I had attempted to bring together some blacks with the other minorities. There weren't too many of them anyway. The Orientals never really got involved. The blacks misunderstood what I was presenting, perhaps I said it badly. They were on the cultural kick: A manager should be crucified for saying "Negro" instead of "black." I said as long as the Negro or the black gets the job, it doesn't mean a damn what he's called. We got into a huge hassle. Management, of course, merely smiled. The whole struggle fell flat on its face. It crumpled from divisiveness. So I learned another lesson. People have their own agenda. It doesn't matter what group you're with, there is a tendency to put the other guy down regardless.

The American Dream began to look so damn complicated, I began to think: Hell, if I wanted, I could just back away and reap the harvest myself. By this time, I'm up to twenty-five thousand dollars a year. It's beginning to look good, and a lot of people are beginning to look good. And they're saying: "Hey, the American Dream, you got it. Why don't you lay off?" I wasn't falling in line.

My bosses were telling me I had all the "ingredients" for top management. All that was required was to "get to know our business." This term comes up all the time. If I could just warn all minorities and women whenever you hear "get to know our business," they're really saying "fall in line." Stay within that fence, and glory can be yours. I left Blue Cross disillusioned. They offered me a director's job at thirty thousand dollars before I quit.

All I had to do was behave myself. I had the "ingredients" of being a good Chicano, the equivalent of the good nigger. I was smart. I could articulate well. People didn't know by my speech patterns that I was of Mexican heritage. Some tell me I don't look Mexican, that I have a certain amount of Italian, Lebanese, or who knows. (Laughs.)

One could easily say: "Hey, what's your bitch? The American Dream has treated you beautifully. So just knock it off and quit this crap you're spreading around." It was a real problem. Every time I turned around, America seemed to be treating me very well.

Hell, I even thought of dropping out, the hell with it. Maybe get a job in a factory. But what happened? Offers kept coming in. I just said to myself: God, isn't this silly? You might as well take the bucks and continue looking for the answer. So I did that. But each time I took the money, the conflict in me got more intense, not less.

Wow, I'm up to thirty-five thousand a year. This is a savings and loan business. I have faith in the executive director. He was the kind of guy I was looking for in top management: understanding, humane, also looking for the formula. Until he was up for consideration as executive v.p. of the entire organization. All of a sudden everything changed. It wasn't until I saw this guy flip-flop that I realized how powerful vested interests are. Suddenly he's saying: "Don't rock the boat. Keep a low profile. Get in line." Another disappointment.

Subsequently, I went to work for a consulting firm. I said to myself: Okay, I've got to get close to the executive mind. I need to know how they work. Wow, a consulting firm.

Consulting firms are saving a lot of American businessmen. They're doing it in ways that defy the whole notion of capitalism. They're not allowing these businesses to fail. Lockheed was successful in getting U.S. funding guarantees because of the efforts of consulting firms working on their behalf, helping them look better. In this kind of work, you don't find minorities. You've got to be a proven success in business before you get there.

The American Dream, I see now, is governed not by education, opportunity, and hard work, but by power and fear. The higher up in the organization you go, the more you have to lose. The dream is *not losing*. This is the notion pervading America today: Don't lose.

When I left the consulting business, I was making fifty thousand dollars a year. My last performance appraisal was: You can go a long way in this business, you can be a partner, but you gotta know our business. It came up again. At this point, I was incapable of being disillusioned any more. How easy it is to be swallowed up by the same set of values that governs the top guy. I was becoming that way. I was becoming concerned about losing that fifty grand or so a year. So I asked other minorities who had it made. I'd go up and ask 'em: "Look, do you owe anything to others?" The answer was: "We owe nothing to anybody." They drew from the civil rights movement but felt no debt. They've quickly forgotten how it happened. It's like I was when I first got out of college. Hey, it's really me, I'm great. I'm great. I'm as angry with these guys as I am with the top guys.

Right now, it's confused. I've had fifteen years in the business world as "a success." Many Anglos would be envious of my progress. Fifty thousand dollars a year puts you in the one or two top percent of all Americans. Plus my wife making another thirty thousand. We had lots of money. When I gave it up, my cohorts looked at me not just as strange, but as something of a traitor. "You're screwing it up for all of us. You're part of our union, we're the elite, we should govern. What the hell are you doing?" So now I'm looked at suspiciously by my peer group as well.

I'm teaching at the University of Wisconsin at Platteville. It's nice. My colleagues tell me what's on their minds. I got a farm next-door to Platteville. With farm prices being what they are (laughs), it's a losing proposition. But with university work and what money we've saved, we're gonna be all right.

The American Dream is getting more elusive. The dream is being governed by a few people's notion of what the dream is. Sometimes I feel it's a small group of financiers that gets together once a year and decides all the world's issues.

It's getting so big. The small-business venture is not there any more. Business has become too big to influence. It can't be changed internally. A counterpower is needed.

**Notes**

1. *Sputnik:* Satellite launched by the Soviet Union in 1957; this launch signaled the beginning of the "space race" between the United States and the USSR.

2. *The Great Society:* President Lyndon B. Johnson's term for the American society he hoped to establish through social reforms, including an antipoverty program.

46

# Growing Up with Privilege and Prejudice

*Karen K. Russell*

To our children . . . in the hope that they will grow up as we could not . . . equal . . . and understanding.
—William Felton Russell, William Frances McSweeny

In 1966, my father and his co-author dedicated his first autobiography, *Go Up for Glory*. Today, in 1987, having just received my Doctor of Laws degree, I wonder if I can fulfill the dreams of my parents' generation. They struggled for integration, they marched for peace, they "sat in" for equality. I doubt they were naïve enough to think they had changed the world, but I know they hoped my generation would be able to approach life differently. In fact, we have been able to do things my parents never thought possible. But that is not enough.

I am a child of privilege. In so many ways, I have been given every opportunity— good grade schools, college years at Georgetown, the encouragement to pursue my ambitions. I have just graduated from Harvard Law School. My future looks promising. Some people, no doubt, will attribute any successes I have to the fact that I am a black woman. I am a child of privilege, and I am angry.

In *The Book of Laughter and Forgetting*, Milan Kundera writes: "The struggle of man against power is the struggle of memory against forgetting." It seems that we have not come very far in that struggle in this country. We have entered the post–civil rights, post-feminist era, both movements I owe so much to. Meanwhile, my parents' dreams are still around us, still unrealized.

It is perhaps somewhat ironic that I came back for my postgraduate work to Boston, a city my father once described as the most racist in America. My father is Bill Russell, center for the Boston Celtics dynasty that won 11 championships in 13 years. Recently, I asked him if it was difficult to send me to school here. When he first went to Boston in 1956, the Celtics' only black player, fans and sportswriters subjected him to the worst kind of unbridled bigotry. When he retired from the National Basketball Association in 1969, he moved to the West Coast where he has remained.

I found his response to my question surprising. "I played for the Celtics, period," he said. "I did not play for Boston. I was able to separate the Celtics institution from the city and the fans. When I sent you to Harvard, I expected you to be able to do the same. I wanted you to have the best possible education and to be able to make the best contacts. I knew you'd encounter racism and sexism, and maybe, in some ways that's a good thing. If you were too sheltered, I'm afraid you'd be too naïve. If you were too sheltered, you might not be motivated to help others who do not have your advantages."

Looking back on my tenure at Harvard, I guess he was right; the last three years have opened my eyes, but law school was only part of it. I became much more aware of disparities in wealth, gender, status. The race issue had always been with me, but it hadn't occurred to me that my generation would still be saddled with so many other limitations.

Actually, people of my generation have a new breed of racism (and sexism and classism) to contend with. The new racism is more subtle, and in some ways more difficult to confront. Open bigotry is out, but there have been a number of overtly racist incidents recently, at Howard Beach in New York, for example, and on college campuses throughout the country. What provokes these incidents? The new racism seems to be partially submerged, coming out into the open when sparked by a sudden confrontation. Then there is the sort of comment Al Campanis, then a Los Angeles Dodgers vice president, made recently on the ABC News program "Nightline," that blacks "may not have some of the necessities" required to achieve leadership positions in baseball. Campanis continued that lacking necessities could be demonstrated in other areas: Blacks are not good swimmers, he said, "because they don't have the buoyancy." (I've already ordered my "I'm Black and I'm Buoyant" bumper sticker.)

The Campanis incident is more than your garden-variety, knee-jerk racism. I sincerely doubt that Campanis meant any harm to come from his remarks; in fact, he probably doesn't think of himself as a racist. But does it matter? How am I supposed to react to well-meaning, good, liberal white people who say things like, "You know, Karen, I don't understand what all the fuss is about. You're one of my good friends, and I never think of you as black." Implicit in such a remark is "I think of you as white," or perhaps just, "I don't think of your race at all." Racial

neutrality is a wonderful concept, but we are a long way from achieving it. In the meantime, I would hope that people wouldn't have to negate my race in order to accept me.

Last year, I worked as a summer law associate, and one day a white lawyer called me into her office. She told me, laughing, that her secretary, a young black woman, had said that I spoke "more white than white people." It made me sad; that young woman had internalized all of society's negative black people to the point that she thought of a person with clear diction as one of "them."

I am reminded of the time during college that I was looking through the classifieds for an apartment. I called a woman to discuss the details of a rental. I needed directions to the apartment, and she asked me where I lived. I told her I lived in Georgetown, to which she replied, "Can you believe the way the blacks have overrun Georgetown?" I didn't really know how to respond. I said, "Well, actually, I can believe that Georgetown is filled with blacks because I happen to be black." There was a silence on the other end. Finally, the woman tried to explain that she hadn't meant any harm. She was incredibly embarrassed, and, yes, you guessed it, she said, "Some of my best friends are. . . ." I hung up before she could finish.

I was afraid to come back to Boston. My first memory of the place is of a day spent in Marblehead, walking along the ocean shore with a white friend of my parents. I must have been 3 or 4 years old. A white man walking past us looked at me and said, "You little nigger." I am told that I smiled up at him as he went on: "They should send all you black baboons back to Africa." It was only when I turned to look at Kay that I realized something was wrong.

We lived in a predominantly Irish Catholic neighborhood in Reading, Mass. For a long time, we were the only black family there. It was weird to be the only black kid at school, aside from my two older brothers. I knew we were different from the other children. Notwithstanding that, I loved school. In 1968, in the first grade, we held mock Presidential elections, and the teacher kept a tally on the blackboard as she counted ballots. There were 20 votes for Hubert H. Humphrey, four or five votes for Richard M. Nixon, and one vote Dick Gregory. No one else in the classroom had heard of Gregory. I was mortified. But I had just done what the other kids had done: I had voted like my parents.

I think my brothers and I may have been spared some of the effects of racism because my father was a celebrity. But I know that his position also made us a bit paranoid. Sometimes it was hard to tell why other kids liked us, or hated us, for that matter. Was it because we had a famous father? Was it because we were black? We had one of those "fun" houses—lots of food, lots of toys, and, the coup de grace, a swimming pool. I was proud to have friends over. They were awed by my father's trophy case. Actually, so were we.

One night we came home from a three-day weekend and found we had been robbed. Our house was in a shambles, and "NIGGA" was spray-painted on the walls. The burglars had poured beer on the pool table and ripped up the felt. They had broken into my father's trophy case and smashed most of the trophies. I was petrified and shocked at the mess; everyone was upset. The police came, and after a while, they left. It was then that my parents pulled back their bedcovers to discover that the burglars had defecated in their bed.

Every time the Celtics went out on the road, vandals would come a tip over our garbage cans. My father went to the police station to complain. The police told him that raccoons were responsible, so he asked where he could apply for a gun permit. The raccoons never came back.

The only time we were *really* scared was after my father wrote an article about racism in professional basketball for *The Saturday Evening Post*. He earned the nickname Felton X. We received threatening letters, and my parents notified the Federal Bureau of Investigation. What I find most telling about this episode is that years later, after Congress had passed the Freedom of Information Act, my father requested his F. B. I. File and found that he was repeatedly referred to therein as "an arrogant Negro who won't sign autographs for white children."

My father has never given autographs, because he thinks they are impersonal. He would rather shake a person's hand or look that person in the eye and say, "Pleased to meet you." His attitude has provoked racist responses, and these have tended to obscure the very basic issue of the right to privacy. Any professional athlete, and certainly any black professional athlete, is supposed to feel grateful to others for the fame he or she has achieved. The thoughtless interruptions, the insistence by fans that they be recognized and personally thanked for their support, never let up. I'll never forget the day I left for college at Georgetown. I had never been away from either parent for more than two weeks, and now I was moving 3,000 miles away. I was crying so hard that I actually cried my contact lens out. And I was hugging my dad—it was a real Hallmark moment. A man came up, oblivious to the gathering, and said to him, "You're Wilt Chamberlain, aren't you?" We all turned to look at him as though he were crazy. He asked for an autograph. My father declined.

I always admired the way my father dealt with these intrusions. He never compromised his values. It would have been easier to acquiesce to the fans—or to a sponsor who offered him a lower fee than they would a white person for endorsing a product. But he would not. I struggle to emulate him.

I went to college with Patrick Ewing, whose playing style has been compared to my father's. Patrick came to Georgetown from the public high school in Cambridge, just a few blocks from the Harvard campus. I have a lot of sympathy for him. When he played in college, people in the stands—presumably educated people—held up signs that said "Patrick Ewing Can't Read Dis."

When my father first played for the Celtics, the fans called him "chocolate boy," "coon," "nigger," —you name it, he was called it. Almost three decades later, Patrick Ewing was facing the same sort of treatment, and I was, in a way, reliving my father's experience in watching it happen. I never talked to Patrick about it because I respected his privacy. From being in public with my father, I knew how difficult it was to be someone like Patrick. Aside from everything else, when you're over 6 feet, 9 inches tall—as both of them are—it's hard to be inconspicuous. Your presence seems to make other people uncomfortable, and everyone seems to feel further compelled to speak to you. Still, I hoped that Patrick knew he wasn't alone.

Several weeks ago, I heard on the news about a racial incident in Taunton, a town not far from Cambridge. It concerned two girls, high-school students and best friends. One was black, the other white. When the school yearbook arrived, it was discovered that the caption under the photograph of the white girl included the words "Nigger Lover." On the news, the school principal said that the incident was just an isolated "prank," not a racist act.

I remember a day in my own high school when a guy who was really popular walked by me in the hall and hissed "nigger" under his breath. I told one of my close friends, and she insisted that I must have misunderstood him, that he must have said "bigger." I felt betrayed.

I feel awful for those girls in Taunton. Adolescents can be really cruel. Adults may have the same thoughts, but they are not as likely to say them to your face. Not that the latter is necessarily an improvement. I could always pinpoint the source of bigotry in my high school, but the new bigot is much harder to detect. Our society has taken to the presumption that racism—and sexism—no longer exist, and that any confrontations are the work of a few "bad actors." Given this myth, the person who complains about

genuine harassment can expect to be seen as the source of conflict.

In Taunton, they crossed out the epithet in every copy of the yearbook. It would apparently have been too expensive to recall the edition. Too expensive for whom? . . .

My friends, from Harvard and elsewhere, reflect my fragmented background. I could never invite them all to the same party and survive. Nor can I meet them all on the same ground. At the law school, I made friends with fellow anti-apartheid protesters and members of a loose-knit group of leftists known as the counterhegemonic front. I have other friends whose politics I strongly disagree with. I have sometimes been drawn to the children of famous or wealthy parents because of an immediate sense of commonality; we know how to protect one another. One of my best friends is Chris Kennedy, son of Ethel and the late Robert F. Kennedy. We never use last names when introducing each other, because we resent people who only remember our last names. . . .

How will I deal with racism in my life? I have no brilliant solution. On a personal level, I will ask people to explain a particular comment or joke. When I have trouble hailing a cab in New York, as frequently happens—cabbies "don't want to go to Harlem" —I will copy down the medallion numbers and file complaints if necessary. On the larger level, I will work with others to confront the dilemma of the widening gap between the black middle class and the black lower class, a gap that must be closed if my generation is to advance the cause of racial equality.

Like many middle-class children who grew up accustomed to a comfortable life style, I will also have to work to balance the desire for economic prosperity with the desire to realize more idealistic goals.

If I ever do find a man and get married (after all those magazine and newspaper articles, I realize I have a better chance of becoming a member of the Politburo!), will we want to raise our kids in a black environment? Sometimes I really regret that I didn't go to an all-black college. When I was in high school on Mercer Island, I didn't go out on dates. A good friend was nice enough to escort me to my senior prom. I don't know if I want my kids excluded like that. If it hadn't been my race, it might have been something else; I guess a lot of people were miserable in high school. Yet, I have to wonder what it would be like to be the norm.

I am concerned about tokenism. If I am successful, I do not want to be used as a weapon to defeat the claims of blacks who did not have my opportunities. I do not want someone to say of me: "See, she made it. We live in a world of equal opportunity. If you don't make it, it's your own fault."

I also worry about the fallout from this article. One day during college, I was walking down the street when a photographer asked if he could take my picture for the Style section of *The Washington Post*. The photograph appeared with a caption that said that I worked at a modeling agency, which I did—as a booking agent. Two things happened. I got asked out on some dates, which I didn't mind. And I received a letter that, accompanied by detailed anatomical description, said I was "a nigger bitch who has no business displaying your ugly body." What kind of letters and comments can I expect to receive as a result of this article? Although I am speaking as an individual, I run the risk of being depersonalized, even dehumanized, by others.

Daddy told me that he never listened to the boos because he never listened to the cheers. He did it for himself. I guess I have to, too.

# A Player

*Kate Stoll*

There I was, PF Flyers laced, ready to race out the back door and straddle my new glistening gold 1971 Schwinn with the high chrome sissy bar, baseball glove dangling from the handlebars. I was anticipating a great game today and the clock was keeping me from it, ticking off the last five minutes of the half hour way too slowly. Though it was summer and the day had begun hours earlier, I wasn't allowed out of the house to commit juvenile havoc in the neighborhood until 8:30 A.M. This rule was put into effect because I had a habit of bolting out of the house at 7:00 A.M. and waking up all my friends' parents by banging on their doors, looking for someone to play with. My three older siblings never had this rule, lacking as they did any sense of adventure or fun.

I lived on the middle of the three blocks that constituted Arlington Avenue. No one worth any playing value lived at the north end of the street, on either side. The only fun lay to the south. Running out my back door as the minute hand reached six, I hopped on my bike, yelled bye to my mom, and pedaled standing up to Glenn's house, three doors south, my first stop on the potential-playmate route.

Glenn was eleven, a year older than I, and, some said, the better athlete. Rather than being a cause of jealousy between us, though, our mutual athleticism bound us, made us best friends. In the summer I would spend the night at his house twice a week and we would stay up until the morning hours, playing with our Hot Wheels, sorting our baseball cards, or watching television. It didn't matter to his parents that we left the house at 7:00 A.M. Glenn rarely spent the night at my house: We had to turn the television off when the news came on, and the lights out soon after. Sometimes, I didn't want to spend the night at my house, either.

Glenn, who knew about my 8:30 rule, was usually at his back door waiting for me, but not today. I rapped on the aluminum door three times with my knuckles. That woke the south and the north ends of the street, not to mention Glenn's teenage sister, who came to the door blinking dazedly and yawning, retainer in mouth, and declared, "Glenn is at work with Dad."

I decided to quietly move out of her sight. If I was lucky, she might think my waking her was a dream.

Now I had to go knocking on the Hickmans' door all by myself. Shoot, I had already woken Glenn's sister—why not go for broke? The Hickmans' house had six kids to wake up.

I hopped onto my bike and sped out of Glenn's driveway, popping a wheelie at the first tar mark in the road and holding it twenty-five feet, until the next tar mark, breaking my record from the day before. Narrowly dodging stereophonic honks, I darted through the intersection and turned sharply into the Hickmans' driveway. No signs of activity.

I came to an abrupt stop with a short, sharp squeal that left little rubber. An all-star skid. Mr. Hickman would have lost more hair if he saw any trace of my tire tracks on his long clean driveway. As it was, the squeal probably gave him back spasms as he lay in bed.

I opened the gate to the Hickman's backyard slowly and deliberately. I had learned not to knock immediately, but instead would peer through the screen door into the kitchen to see if anyone was awake before arousing the entire household. Today, my peering was rewarded: Doug was scooping the last spoonful of Cap'n Crunch into his open mouth. All right! Someone to play catch with.

A skinny boy with bright red hair, freckles, and eyes big and white, Doug smiled as he glimpsed me through the door. Despite being two years younger than I, he was fun most of the time, full of energy and usually full of himself. He tried desperately to keep up with Glenn and me, always willing to do anything we asked of him. He enjoyed hanging out with us more than he did his own birthday. We slammed the gate shut and sped off on our bikes.

The next stop on the baseball tour was a quick ride: Brian and Steve Stuart, who were three and four years younger than I, lived next door to Doug and were just getting onto their bikes, baseball gloves and bats in hand. Success: I had now collected enough baseball players for a game, using criteria little less rigorous than a scout for the Chicago Cubs might use.

A game of hardball down at Lincoln Elementary School was what I had dreamt of the night before. Quickly, we pedaled to the field for a game of two on two. Pushing down our kickstands and setting our bikes on the warm blacktop, we stood looking over the cement playing field. This was the short field, where we usually played when the Stuarts were playing, because they were younger. Here I could hit the ball over the fence many times, whereas in the long field, I could hit, maybe, two or three a day. This is where Glenn had me beat. He could always pop the ball over the fence and into the street on either field.

Ten home runs later, with a win for Steve and me, we stopped and went to wet our whistles with Pepsis from the fire barn. Just a dime for sixteen whole chugable ounces of sweet carbonation.

The pop machine was located inside the fire barn, next to the recreation area for the firemen. To our pride, we knew some of them by name. Sometimes they would watch us play ball from across the street and impersonate Jack Brickhouse, the television announcer for the Cubs. Other times they would be off saving cats or putting out fires, leaving the fire barn vacant. Then it was our duty to protect the large red brick structure while they were out.

The sun was pushing up the mercury today. I downed two pops. After a few burps from the gang, we cruised to our respective homes to eat. After my bologna sandwich, I went back to Glenn's house, where he was now waiting for me. Hopping onto the back of my bike, he held on dearly to my sissy bar, for he knew I was Evel Knievel on a Schwinn. We soared over the curb and off to the second half of our double-header.

Spotting Pete Jensen in his backyard, we stopped to recruit him. The Stuart boys couldn't play with us in the afternoon, so Pete would round out our team.

A year younger than I, Pete was a nice boy with a great laugh. He was playing with his older sister Ruth, with whom I was also friends. She was Glenn's age. Glenn and I cruised up their driveway, and pretty soon Julie from across the street came over. Glenn asked Pete if he wanted to play ball with us and Doug. Before Pete could answer, Ruth shouted, "I want to play too."

"No!" Glenn barked. Usually no one messed with him.

Knowing he had Glenn's support, Pete talked back to his sister. "You can't play with us."

"We can play every bit as good as you guys can," said Julie, glaring into my eyes.

They could, too. I spoke up: "If Ruth and Julie don't play, neither do I."

Glenn and Pete looked stunned. The girls looked at me happily. Knowing he couldn't disagree with me, Glenn suggested that we play pickle instead. Pickle it was. The girls decided they didn't want to play after all. Glenn turned his smirk in my direction as he claimed his small victory over the girls and me.

After a few rounds of pickle, Glenn and Pete took off their shirts and suggested we get a drink at Doug's while we rustled him up to play more baseball. Taking off my sweaty Cubs shirt and tucking a wad of it in my back pocket, I sprinted over the sidewalk and into Doug's yard, neck and neck with Glenn, who touched the Hickmans' gate barely ahead of me. He happily chided me for not being as fast as he was. I just smiled at my friend as he opened the gate for me. Pete came in a distant third, laughing, and shut the gate behind him.

While Doug finished his lunch, we drank from his hose and rested before the next game. Sweat trickled down my sides and back as, baseball cap soaked with sweat and dusted with dirt, I stretched out in the shade of the Hickmans' oak tree and drifted off into a fantasy while the guys talked about the upcoming game. There I was: standing in the on-deck circle at Wrigley Field, waiting in my pinstripes for my turn at bat behind Ernie Banks. I *was* a professional baseball player. Then *bang!* Just as I was hitting in the winning run, the Hickmans' screen door slammed, jolting me out of my fantasy.

I looked up to see a stern Mrs. Hickman, hands on hips, taking a good look at us three bare-chested youngsters. She hesitated for a long time, collecting her thoughts. What was she going to say? Were we in trouble? Was I in trouble for waking Mr. Hickman? Suddenly her sharp voice rang out: "Laura, put your shirt back on. You are not a boy. What would your mother say? Girls don't play baseball."

I was stunned. Not a boy! Who said I was? I was just a hot and thirsty baseball player taking a break between innings. I had to act different because I was a girl? I thought I was just a kid, having a good time with friends and dreaming about playing in the big leagues.

The rest of the day was ruined for me. Too embarrassed to play with the boys anymore, I sadly pedaled home and changed into a clean red t-shirt, contemplating my existence as a girl. From the moment Mrs. Hickman stopped shouting at me, I knew things were going to be a lot different than I had ever imagined.

48

# He Defies You Still: The Memoirs of a Sissy

*Tommi Avicolli*

You're just a faggot
No history faces you this morning
A faggot's dreams are scarlet
Bad blood bled from words that scarred[1]

### Scene One

A homeroom in a Catholic high school in South Philadelphia. The boy sits quietly in the first aisle, third desk, reading a book. He does not look up, not even for a moment. He is hoping no one will remember he is sitting there. He wishes he were invisible. The teacher is not yet in the classroom so the other boys are talking and laughing loudly.

Suddenly, a voice from beside him:

"Hey, you're a faggot, ain't you?"

The boy does not answer. He goes on reading his book, or rather pretending he is reading his book. It is impossible to actually read the book now.

"Hey, I'm talking to you!"

The boy still does not look up. He is so scared his heart is thumping madly; it feels like it is leaping out of his chest and into his throat. But he can't look up.

"Faggot, I'm talking to you!"

To look up is to meet the eyes of the tormentor.

Suddenly, a sharpened pencil point is thrust into the boy's arm. He jolts, shaking off the pencil, aware that there is blood seeping from the wound.

"What did you do that for?" he asks timidly.

"Cause I hate faggots," the other boy says, laughing. Some other boys begin to laugh, too. A symphony of laughter. The boy feels as if he's going to cry. But he must not cry. Must not cry. So he holds back the tears and tries to read the book again. He must read the book. Read the book.

When the teacher arrives a few minutes later, the class quiets down. The boy does not tell the teacher what has happened. He spits on the wound to clean it, dabbing it with a tissue until the bleeding stops. For weeks he fears some dreadful infection from the lead in the pencil point.

### Scene Two

The boy is walking home from school. A group of boys (two, maybe three, he is not certain) grab him from behind, drag him into an alley and beat him up. When he gets home, he races up to his room, refusing dinner ("I don't feel well," he tells his mother through the locked door) and spends the

"He Defies You Still: The Memoirs of a Sissy" from *Radical Teacher,* 24, 1985, pp. 4–5. Reprinted by permission.

night alone in the dark wishing he would die. . . .

These are not fictitious accounts—I *was* that boy. Having been branded a sissy by neighborhood children because I preferred jump rope to baseball and dolls to playing soldiers, I was often taunted with "hey sissy" or "hey faggot" or "yoo hoo honey" (in a mocking voice) when I left the house.

To avoid harassment, I spent many summers alone in my room. I went out on rainy days when the street was empty.

I came to like being alone. I didn't need anyone, I told myself over and over again. I was an island. Contact with others meant pain. Alone, I was protected. I began writing poems, then short stories. There was no reason to go outside anymore. I had a world of my own.

In the schoolyard today
they'll single you out
Their laughter will leave your ears ringing
like the church bells
which once awed you. . . .[2]

School was one of the more painful experiences of my youth. The neighborhood bullies could be avoided. The taunts of the children living in those endless repetitive row houses could be evaded by staying in my room. But school was something I had to face day after day for some two hundred mornings a year.

I had few friends in school. I was a pariah. Some kids would talk to me, but few wanted to be known as my close friend. Afraid of labels. If I was a sissy, then he had to be a sissy, too. I was condemned to loneliness.

Fortunately, a new boy moved into our neighborhood and befriended me; he wasn't afraid of the labels. He protected me when the other guys threatened to beat me up. He walked me home from school; he broke through the terrible loneliness. We were in third or fourth grade at the time.

We spent a summer or two together. Then his parents sent him to camp and I was once again confined to my room.

**Scene Three**

High school lunchroom. The boy sits at a table near the back of the room. Without warning, his lunch bag is grabbed and tossed to another table. Someone opens it and confiscates a package of Tastykakes; another boy takes the sandwich. The empty bag is tossed back to the boy who stares dumbfounded. He should be used to this; it has happened before.

Someone screams, "faggot," laughing. There is always laughter. It does not annoy him anymore.

There is no teacher nearby. There is never a teacher around. And what would he say if there were? Could he report the crime? He would be jumped after school if he did. Besides, it would be his word against theirs. Teachers never noticed anything. They never heard the taunts. Never heard the word "faggot." They were the great deaf mutes, pillars of indifference; a sissy's pain was not relevant to history and geography and God made me to love, honor, and obey him, amen.

**Scene Four**

High school Religion class. Someone has a copy of *Playboy*. Father N. is not in the room yet; he's late, as usual. Someone taps the boy roughly on the shoulder. He turns. A finger points to the centerfold model, pink fleshy body, thin and sleek. Almost painted. Not real. The other asks, mocking voice, "Hey, does she turn you on? Look at those tits!"

The boy smiles, nodding meekly; turns away.

The other jabs him harder on the shoulder, "Hey, whatsamatter, don't you like girls?"

Laughter. Thousands of mouths; unbearable din of laughter. In the Arena: thumbs down. Don't spare the queer.

"Wanna suck my dick? Huh? That turn you on, faggot!"

The laughter seems to go on forever . . .

Behind you, the sound of their laughter
echoes a million times
in a soundless place
They watch you walk/sit/stand/
   breathe. . . .[3]

What did being a sissy really mean? It was a
way of walking (from the hips rather than
the shoulders); it was a way of talking (often
with a lisp or in a high-pitched voice); it was
a way of relating to others (gently, not wanting to fight, or hurt anyone's feelings). It was
being intelligent ("an egghead" they called it
sometimes); getting good grades. It means
not being interested in sports, not playing
football in the street after school; not discussing teams and scores and playoffs. And it involved not showing fervent interest in girls,
not talking about scoring with tits or *Playboy*
centerfolds. Not concealing naked women in
your history book; or porno books in your
locker.

On the other hand, anyone could be a
"faggot." It was a catch-all. If you did something that didn't conform to what was the acceptable behavior of the group, then you
risked being called a faggot. If you didn't get
along with the "in" crowd, you were a faggot. It was the most commonly used put-
down. It kept guys in line. They became angry when somebody called them a faggot.
More fights started over someone calling
someone else a faggot than anything else.
The word had power. It toppled the male
ego, shattered his delicate facade, violated
the image he projected. He was tough. Without feeling. Faggot cut through all this. It
made him vulnerable. Feminine. And feminine was the worst thing he could possibly
be. Girls were fine for fucking, but no boy in
his right mind wanted to be like them. A boy
was the opposite of a girl. He was not feminine. He was not feeling. He was not weak.

Just look at the gym teacher who growled
like a dog; or the priest with the black belt
who threw the kids against the wall in rage
when they didn't know their Latin. They
were men, they got respect.

But not the physics teacher who preached
pacifism during lectures on the nature of
atoms. Everybody knew what he was—and
why he believed in the anti-war movement.

My parents only knew that the neighborhood kids called me names. They begged me
to act more like the other boys. My brothers
were ashamed of me. They never said it, but I
knew. Just as I knew that my parents were
embarrassed by my behavior.

At times, they tried to get me to act differently. Once my father lectured me on how to
walk right. I'm still not clear on what that
means. Not from the hips, I guess, don't
"swish" like faggots do.

A nun in elementary school told my
mother at Open House that there was "something wrong with me." I had draped my
sweater over my shoulders like a girl, she
said. I was a smart kid, but I should know
better than to wear my sweater like a girl!

My mother stood there, mute. I wanted
her to say something, to chastise the nun; to
defend me. But how could she? This was a
nun talking—representative of Jesus, protector of all that was good and decent.

An uncle once told me I should start "acting like a boy" instead of like a girl. Everybody seemed ashamed of me. And I guess I
was ashamed of myself, too. It was hard not
to be.


**Scene Five**

*Priest:* Do you like girls, Mark?
*Mark:* Uh-huh.
*Priest:* I mean *really* like them?
*Mark:* Yeah—they're okay.
*Priest:* There's a role they play in your salvation.
   Do you understand it, Mark?
*Mark:* Yeah.
*Priest:* You've got to like girls. Even if you should
   decide to enter the seminary, it's important to
   keep in mind God's plan for a man and a
   woman. . . .[4]

Catholicism of course condemned homosexuality. Effeminacy was tolerated as long

as the effeminate person did not admit to being gay. Thus, priests could be effeminate because they weren't gay.

As a sissy, I could count on no support from the church. A male's sole purpose in life was to father children—souls for the church to save. The only hope a homosexual had of attaining salvation was by remaining totally celibate. Don't even think of touching another boy. To think of a sin was a sin. And to sin was to put a mark upon the soul. Sin—if it was a serious offense against God—led to hell. There was no way around it. If you sinned, you were doomed.

Realizing I was gay was not an easy task. Although I knew I was attracted to boys by the time I was about eleven, I didn't connect this attraction to homosexuality. I was not queer. Not I. I was merely appreciating a boy's good looks, his fine features, his proportions. It didn't seem to matter that I didn't appreciate a girl's looks in the same way. There was no twitching in my thighs when I gazed upon a beautiful girl. But I wasn't queer.

I resisted that label—queer—for the longest time. Even when everything pointed to it, I refused to see it. I was certainly not queer. Not I.

We sat through endless English classes, and history courses about the wars between men who were not allowed to love each other. No gay history was ever taught. No history faces you this morning. You're just a faggot. Homosexuals had never contributed to the human race. God destroyed the queers in Sodom and Gomorrah.

We learned about Michelangelo, Oscar Wilde, Gertrude Stein—but never that they were queer. They were not queer. Walt Whitman, the "father of American poetry," was not queer. No one was queer. I was alone, totally unique. One of a kind. Were there others like me somewhere? Another planet, perhaps?

In school, they never talked of the queers. They did not exist. The only hint we got of this other species was in religion class. And even then it was clouded in mystery—never spelled out. It was sin. Like masturbation. Like looking at *Playboy* and getting a hard-on. A sin.

Once a progressive priest in senior year religion class actually mentioned homosexuals—he said the word—but was into Erich Fromm, into homosexuals as pathetic and sick. Fixated at some early stage; penis, anal, whatever. Only heterosexuals passed on to the nirvana of sexual development.

No other images from the halls of the Catholic high school except those the other boys knew: swishy faggot sucking cock in an alley somewhere, grabbing asses in the bathroom. Never mentioning how much straight boys craved blow jobs, it was part of the secret.

It was all a secret. You were not supposed to talk about the queers. Whisper maybe. Laugh about them, yes. But don't be open, honest; don't try to understand. Don't cite their accomplishments. No history faces you this morning. You're just a faggot    faggot no history    just a faggot

## Epilogue

The boy marching down the Parkway. Hundreds of queers. Signs proclaiming gay pride. Speakers. Tables with literature from gay groups. A miracle, he is thinking. Tears are coming loose now. Someone hugs him.

You could not control
the sissy in me
nor could you exorcise him
nor electrocute him
You declared him illegal illegitimate
insane and immature
But he defies you still.[5]

## Notes

1. From the poem "Faggot" by Tommi Avicolli, published in *GPU News*, Sept. 1979.
2. *Ibid.*

3. *Ibid.*

4. From the play *Judgment of the Roaches* by Tommi Avicolli, produced in Philadelphia at the Gay Community Center, the Painted Bride Arts Center and the University of Pennsylvania; aired over WXPN-FM, in four parts; and presented at the Lesbian/Gay Conference in Norfolk, VA, July, 1980.

5. From the poem "Sissy Poem," [by Tommy Avicolli], published in *Magic Doesn't Live Here Anymore* (Philadelphia: Spruce Street Press, 1976).

# Sexual Identification Is a Strange Thing

*Jeffrey Weeks*

One difficulty is that not all homosexually inclined people want to identify their minority status—or even see themselves as homosexual. Sexologists, at least since Kinsey, have pointed out that there is no necessary connection between sexual behavior and sexual identity. According to Kinsey's best-known statistic, some 37 percent of men had homosexual experiences to orgasm. But perhaps less than 4 percent were exclusively homosexual—and even they did not necessarily express a homosexual identity, a concept of which, in any case, Kinsey disapproved.

Sexual identification is a strange thing. There are some people who identify as gay and participate in the gay community but do not experience or wish for homosexual activity. And there are homosexually active people who do not identify as gay. Many black homosexuals, for example, prefer to identify primarily as "black" rather than "gay" and align themselves with black rather than gay political positions. Obviously, as Barry Dank has argued, "the development of

a homosexual identity is dependent on the meanings that the actor attaches to the concepts of homosexual and homosexuality." These processes in turn depend on the person's environment and wider community. Many people, it has been argued, "drift" into identity, battered by contingency rather than guided by will. Four characteristic stages have been identified by Plummer: "sensitization," when the individual becomes aware of the possibility of being different; "signification," when he or she attributes a developing meaning to these differences; "subculturalization," the stage of recognizing oneself through involvement with others; and "stabilization," the stage of full acceptance of one's feelings and way of life. There is no automatic progression through these stages; each transition is dependent as much on chance as on decision; and there is no necessary acceptance of a final destiny, in an explicit identity. Some choices are forced on individuals, whether through stigmatization and public obloquy or through political necessity. But the point that needs underlining is that *identity* is a choice. It is not *dictated* by internal imperatives.

The implication of this is that "desire" is one thing, while subject position, that is, identification with a particular social position and organizing sense of self, is another. This means that labels such as "gay" and "lesbian" increasingly become *political* choices, and in that process the sexual connotations can all but disappear. This is clearest in recent debates about a lesbian identity. Among gay men the issue has fundamentally concerned sex, validating a denied sexuality. In debates on lesbianism, on the other hand, there have been heated exchanges about the necessary connection of a lesbian identity to sexual practices. Conventional wisdom and, even more stringently, sexological expertise, have defined lesbianism as a sexual category. But increasingly it has been proposed by feminists as primarily a political definition, in which sexuality plays a problematic role. As Lillian Faderman puts it, "Women who identify themselves as lesbians generally do not view lesbianism as a sexual phenomenon first and foremost." It is instead a relationship in which two women's strongest emotions and affection are directed towards one another. It becomes a synonym for sisterhood, solidarity, and affection, and as such a fundamental attribute of feminism.

Recent lesbian-feminist writers have understandably largely rejected the social-science and sexological definitions of lesbianism. Traditionally female homosexuality has been seen almost exclusively in terms derived from the experience or study of males. Male homosexuality has invariably been more closely observed and researched than lesbianism, partly because of its greater public salience, partly because it challenged the dominant definitions of male sexuality, and partly because female sexuality has usually been studied only insofar as it was responsive to male sexuality, and lesbianism was hardly understandable in those terms. More recently, ethnographies of female homosexuality have tended to adopt research techniques honed in investigation of male behavior, concentrating, for example, on "coming out," contact patterns, sexual expression, and duration of relationships. The impact of this has been to conceptualize lesbianism, like male homosexuality, as a specific minority experience little different in its implications from male patterns. This has been criticized in turn by some lesbian feminists as inevitably having the effect of establishing male homosexuality as the norm, while ignoring the implications of lesbianism for feminism.

The most powerful exponent of a "political lesbianism" position has been Adrienne Rich. In her influential essay "Compulsory Heterosexuality and Lesbian Existence," she argues that a distinction has to be made between the "lesbian continuum" and "lesbian existence." The latter is equivalent to a lesbian identity but its character is not defined by sexual practice. It is the sense of self of women bonded primarily to women who are sexually and emotionally independent of men. In turn this is the expression of the "lesbian continuum," the range through women's lives of woman-identified experience. Such experiences go beyond the possibility of genital sex, to embrace many forms of primary intensity, including the sharing of inner life, the bonding against male tyranny, practical and political support, marriage resistance, female support networks and communities. Such possibilities of bonding between women are denied by "compulsory heterosexuality." Rich speaks of "the rendering invisible of the lesbian possibility, an engulfed continent which rises fragmentedly to view from time to time only to become submerged again." "Compulsory heterosexuality" is the key mechanism of control of women, ensuring in its tyranny definition the perpetuation of male domination. Lesbianism is the point of resistance to this heterosexual dominance, its central antagonistic force.

Lesbianism is thus about the realization of the male-free potential of women, and in drawing on this essence, male definitions are cast aside. Rich sharply dissociates lesbianism from male homosexuality because of the latter's presumed relationship, *inter alia*, to pederasty, anonymous sex, and ageism. Lesbianism, on the other hand, she argues, is a profoundly *female* experience, like motherhood, and she looks forward to a powerful new female eroticism.

Against the passion and conviction of Rich's position three fundamental criticisms have been made. In the first place it is based on a romantic naturalization of female bonds. It is not always clear whether Rich sees the "lesbian continuum" as a powerful solidarity that is there but constantly suppressed, or as a potentiality that could be realized in a mythical future, but in either case it stretches towards an essentialism about femininity which can distort the complexities of the construction of women, and obscure the necessary politics. As Cora Kaplan has noted, in Rich's scenario, "female heterosexuality is socially constructed and female homosexuality is natural. . . . Political lesbianism becomes more than a strategic position for feminism, it is a return to nature." Nature is now benign, female and affectionate, sensual and creative, revolutionary and transcendent—and lesbian. But all the problems in naturalistic explanations of sex still come to the fore: its untheorized and untheorizable claims to truth, its transhistorical pretensions, and its strong moralism: this is how you must behave because nature tells us so. The result is a narrowing in political focus, and this is the second major objection. The view that attributes all women's oppression to "compulsory heterosexuality" suggests that somehow women are always socially controlled by men. Women are, in consequence, inevitably presented as perpetual sufferers and victims, beyond the possibility of resistance.

Finally, the political lesbian position tends to deny the specifics of lesbian sexuality. Lesbian activists such as Pat Califia have suggested that there is a history of a specific lesbian eroticism which has been historically denied, and which has produced its own forms of struggle and institutionalization. According to Ann Ferguson, Rich's view:

undermines the important historical development of an explicit identity connected to genital sexuality. My own view is that the development of such an identity, and with it the development of a sexuality valued and accepted in a community of peers, extended women's life options and degree of independence from men.

For such feminists, the elevation of female sexuality in general into a semimystical bonding, where bodily contact and genital pleasure are secondary or even nonexistent, denies the possibilities of female eroticism, including the real potentiality of lesbianism.

This is not the place to enter a full discussion of these differing positions. The point that requires emphasizing here is that like the gay male identity, the lesbian identity has a political as well as a social and personal implication. That means that there need be no necessary relationship between sexual practice and sexual identity. On the other hand the existence of a specific identity testifies to the historic denial of a particular form of female desire—and the struggle necessary to affirm it. As with the homosexual male, the lesbian identity—whatever its "true" meaning—is historically contingent but seemingly inevitable; potentially limiting—but apparently politically essential.

Identity is not a destiny but a choice. But in a culture where homosexual desires, female or male, are still execrated and denied, the adoption of lesbian or gay identities inevitably constitutes a *political* choice. These identities are not expressions of secret essences. They are self-creations, but they are creations on ground not freely chosen but laid out by history. So homosexual identities illustrate the play of constraint and opportunity, necessity and freedom, power and pleasure. Sexual identities seem necessary in the contemporary world as starting-points for a politics around sexuality. But the form they take is not predetermined. In the end, therefore, they are not so much about who we really are, what our sex dictates. They are about what we want to be and could be. But this means they are also about the morality of acts and the quality of relations. We live in a world of proliferating "sexual identities" as specific desires (pedophile, sadomasochistic, bisexual) become the focus either for minute subdivisions of well-established notions (gayness or lesbianism) or spin off into wholly new ones. Can we therefore say that all identities are of equal value, and that minute subdivisions of desire, however apparently bizarre and esoteric, deserve social recognition on the basis of the right to erotic difference and sexual identity?

Such questions have led to the development of what may be termed a "relationship paradigm" as opposed to the traditional "identity paradigm" as a way of thinking through some of the conceptual—and political—issues. If, as many advocates of gay politics have suggested, identity is a constraint, a limitation on the flux of possibilities and the exploration of desires, if it is only an historical acquisition, then surely its assertion should be historically junked or at least modified. The difficulty is to find a replacement that would equally satisfactorily provide a basis for personal coherence and social recognition. One possibility is to celebrate the flux, to indulge in a glorification of the "polysexualities" to which, on a radical reading of the Freudian tradition, we are all heirs. The unfortunate difficulty with this is that most individuals do not feel "polymorphously perverse." On the contrary they feel their sexual desires are fairly narrowly organized, whatever use they make of those desires in real life. Moreover, a social identity is no less real for being historically formed. Sexual identities are no longer arbitrary divisions of the field of possibilities; they are encoded in a complex web of social practices—legal, pedagogic, medical, moral, and personal. They cannot be willed away.

The aim of the "relationship paradigm," in contrast, is not to ignore questions of identity but to displace them, by stressing instead the need to examine relationships. If this is done we can look again both at our sexual history and our sexual presence. Historically, we need no longer look for the controversial emergence of identities. Instead we can see the complicated net of relationships through which sexuality is always expressed, changing over time. Looked at from a contemporary point of view, we see not the culmination of a process of identity development but the formation of new types of relationships, validating hitherto execrated sexualities, in complex communities of interest around sex.

This is a very tempting position to adopt. In particular it potentially allows sexual thinking to move away from a "morality of acts," where all debate is about the merits of this form of sexuality as opposed to that, to an "ethics of choice," where the question becomes one of the quality of involvement and the freedom of relationships. This puts the whole debate on quite a new footing, allowing questions of power, diversity and sexual pluralism to be brought in.

The difficulty with the "relationship paradigm" is that it is offered as an alternative to questions of identity. This is a false antinomy. Identities are always "relational" in the general sense that they only exist in relation to other potential identities. More crucially, identities must always be about relationships: to ourselves, precarious unities of conflicting desires and social commitments, "composed of heterogeneous fragments of fossilized cultures," and to others, who address us and call upon our recognition in diverse ways and through whom our sense of self is always negotiated. A sense of identity is essential for the establishment of relationships. As Foucault has argued, "sex is not a fatality, it's a possibility for creative life." For a variety of historical reasons that possibility is mediated through a recognition of identity. Identity may well be a historical fiction, a controlling myth, a limiting burden. But it is at the same time a necessary means of weaving our way through a hazard-strewn world and a complex web of social relations. Without it, it seems, the possibilities of sexual choice are not increased but diminished.

**50**

# Identity, "Passing" and Subversion

## *Mary Crawford*

I remember the first time I was accused of being a heterosexual (bourgeois heterosexual at that). It was 1971, and I had just joined my first CR [consciousness raising] group. My "natural" sexual and emotional attachment to men was thoroughly attacked and disparaged by the Marxist lesbian feminists I had naively joined in the name of sisterhood. I began to wish I'd stayed in the closet.

The early 1970s were a pivotal time for my identity. Around me, friends were coming out as lesbians. Important feminist theorists were espousing separatism. Women were naming sexism, exploring the conditions of our lives, and making connections with each other. During those years I changed my thinking about women and gender relations in massive ways—yet, here I am, in 1992, still living with a man. Still living with the *same* man.

One thing that feminism has taught me is to question oppositional categories. "Heterosexuals" can't exist without the corresponding category of "homosexuals." The opposition of the two categories allows either to be used as an instrument of social control. It also obscures the many dimensions along which an individual might choose to place herself as a sexual, sensual, and social being.

It is clear that women do not always mean the same things when they say "I am a heterosexual" (or bisexual or lesbian) (Golden, 1987; Shuster, 1987). Sexual identity is much too fluid, and behavior much too variable, to be so neatly categorized. (This is not to say that everyone *experiences* sexual identity in terms of fluidity and possibilities—cf. Kitzinger, 1987.) Although I was asked to write this comment as a "heterosexual feminist," I certainly do not ascribe unitary meaning to the notion of being a heterosexual.

A quandary for me, as a feminist, is how to acknowledge the instability of the categories and the possibility of oppression through categorization, while also acknowledging the right of women to name themselves as they see fit. For the moment, I resolve this dilemma by respecting women who identify as lesbian, bisexual, or heterosexual but resisting a sexual label for myself. Naming can be an affirmative act of self-definition; labeling and categorization are acts of those in power directed at those with less power.

Moreover, none of the labels seems adequate for who I am. There are many women whom I love for their bodies, their minds, their quirks, their brilliant individualities and their ways of being in the world. I recognize my sexual attraction to particular women, and to particular men other than my life partner, though I choose not to act on it. As a rule, I prefer the companionship of women, though I make exceptions for a few gentle men. I also experience rage at what some men have done to women. The label "heterosexual" as usually applied doesn't really encompass these complexities of love, respect, anger, and sensuality. Rather, I think of myself as a woman-identified person who, because of a decision to enter into a long-term affectional and sexual relationship with a man, is situated in a largely heterosexual social context.

## On Passing

What are the costs and benefits of living in ways that others recognize as heterosexual? Although I do not accept the situation as morally right, I inevitably enjoy what my lesbian friends call heterosexual privilege—braided, in my case, with class and color privilege. Mundane life is *easier* for me. No one discounts my feminist analysis of social problems by calling me a man-hater. (They use other arguments instead!) No one hassles me at my child's school, at the doctor's office, or at work. No one tells me I'm an unfit mother. Because I am legally married, my job provides health care benefits for my partner and family (an urgent necessity in the USA where health care is a privilege of the wealthy). Wills and mortgages, taxes and auto insurance, retirement pensions and school enrollment for the children—all the ways that individuals ordinarily interface with social structures—are designed to fit people like me and my partner.

Although we reject the notion of ownership in relationships, my partner and I live in a context that views women as properly the property of men. It is easy and comfortable to travel or go out socially with my partner. Waiters see us, clerks wait on us, while street harassers ignore us to focus on the woman who is alone or with another woman. Well-dressed white men and the women who "accompany" them get respect! Even when we are not together, his presence in my social network cushions me—for example, from the miseries of trying to live on a single wage or two "women's" wages. On the other hand, the heterosexual cushion can be an illusion. In the first draft of this paragraph I wrote that my partner's presence in my life "cushions me from (some) sexual harassment at work." (I had wanted to make the point that men who do not hesitate to violate a woman's personhood with sexual harassment sometimes balk at violating another *man's* "property rights" and thus choose to harass single more than married women.) Both my partner and my friend wrote indignantly on the margins. She: "You've been harassed!" He: "No, it didn't did it?!" My parenthetical "some" had been my covert acknowledgment that male protection had failed me; my assertion of invulnerability had glossed my wishful thinking that *he* who loves me could/should have protected me.

## On Subverting Heterosexism

Being taken for a standard-issue heterosexual bestows a credibility that can be used to subvert heterosexism. I always begin my psychology of women course with dialogue (Unger and Crawford, 1992; Crawford et al., 1992). I interview students, and they interview me, about why we have chosen to teach/learn in this course, what skills and interests we bring to it, and what personal background we feel is relevant to working together. Invariably the students ask whether I am married. I know that this question is at least partly a code for the "L word." I never respond directly. Instead, I ask them, What do you believe you would know about me if you knew my marital status? What does this fact tell you about who I am, how I might teach, what I believe? Is it more relevant in this class than if I were teaching, say, experimental methods? Is marital status a relevant dimension for evaluating your male professors? After we follow this discussion along its (always fascinating) byways, I ask them what they would "know" about me if I were to state that I am a lesbian. In refusing to label myself, and in helping my students articulate their stereotypes of lesbians, straight women, and heterosexual marriage as the normative human condition, I speak from a position of heterosexual privilege that grants me safety in my classroom—yet I use that position to subvert their comfortable assumptions. Paradoxically, I use heterosexual privilege to subvert heterosexism.

As for my feminist politics, I cannot personally accept theories that treat men as an homogeneous class, espouse separatism, or emphasize fundamental personality differences between males and females. Such theories look too simplistic and oppositional to me. Being situated in a heterosexual social network means that there are boys and men I spend a great deal of time with and know intimately. I continue to believe in their possibilities as lovers, life partners, and friends. At the same time, as a feminist and a woman-identified woman, I work to eliminate patriarchal inequities of status and power.

## References

Crawford, M., Unger, R., and Stark, A. (1992) Instructor's Manual to accompany *Women and Gender: A Feminist Psychology*. New York: McGraw-Hill.

Golden, C. (1987) "Diversity and Variability in Women's Sexual Identities," in Boston Lesbian Psychologies Collective (eds.), *Lesbian Psychologies*, pp. 18–34. Urbana: University of Illinois Press.

Kitzinger, C. (1987) *The Social Construction of Lesbianism*. London: Sage.

Shuster, R. (1987) "Sexuality as a Continuum: The Bisexual Identity," in Boston Lesbian Psychologies Collective (eds.), *Lesbian Psychologies*, pp. 56–71. Urbana: University of Illinois Press.

Unger, R. K., and Crawford, M. (1992) *Women and Gender: A Feminist Psychology*. New York: McGraw-Hill; Philadelphia, PA: Temple University Press.

# Her Son/Daughter

## Kate Bornstein

"Who are you?" asks the third blue-haired lady, peering up at me through the thick lenses of her rhinestone cat glasses. Only it comes out in one word: "Hoowahyoo?" I'm wearing black; we all are. It's my mother's funeral service, after all, and the little old ladies are taking inventory of the mourners. Me, I have to take inventory of my own identities whenever someone asks me who I am, and the answer that tumbles out of my mouth is rarely predictable. But this is my mother's funeral, and I am devastated, and to honor the memory of my mom, I'm telling each of them the who of me I know they can deal with.

"I'm Kate Bornstein," I answer her in this quiet-quiet voice of mine, "Mildred's daughter."

"Daughter?!" She shoots back incredulously the same question each of her predecessors had asked, because everyone knew my mother had two sons.

"Mildred never mentioned she had a daughter." The eyes behind those glasses are dissecting my face, looking for family resemblances. When I was a boy, I looked exactly like my father. Everyone used to say so. Then, when I went through what people would call my sex change, they would say, "You know, you look just like your mother."

"Her Son/Daughter" from *The New York Times Sunday Magazine,* January 17, 1991, p. 3. Copyright © The New York Times Company. Reprinted by permission.

Except I'm tall. Nearly six feet of me in mourning the passing of my mother, and I'm confronting this brigade of matrons whose job seems to be to protect my mother from unwanted visitors on this morning of her funeral on the Jersey Shore.

"You're her daughter? So who's your father? It's not Paul, am I right?" Now there would be a piece of gossip these women could gnaw on over their next mah-jongg game. "Mildred had another child," they'd say after calling two bams. "A daughter no less! And Paul, God rest his soul, he never knew."

My mother was raised in a nearly orthodox Jewish household. She lived her life measuring her self-worth by the presence of the men in her life. Her father, a successful merchant, died a year before I was born. Her husband, a successful doctor, died a year before I told her that one of her two sons was about to become a dyke. She preferred the word "lesbian." "My son, the lesbian," she would tell her close friends.

My mother was there the night the rabbi asked me who I was. I was a senior in college, a real hippie: beard, beads, and suede knee-high moccasins with fringe hanging down past my calves. I was home for some holiday or other, and my parents wanted to show off their son who was going to Brown. I had always enjoyed Friday night services. To this day I don't remember what about the rabbi's sermon outraged me, but there I was, jumping to my feet in the middle of the sermon, arguing some point of social justice.

My father was grinning. (He had never been bar mitzvahed, having kicked his rabbi in the shins the first day of Hebrew school.) My mother had her hand over her mouth to keep from laughing. She was never very fond of our rabbi, not since the time he refused to make a house call to console my mother the night my grandfather died. So there we were, the rabbi and the hippie, arguing rabbinical law and social responsibility. He finally dismissed me with a nod. I dismissed him with a chuckle, and the service continued. On the way out of the synagogue, we had to file by the rabbi, who was shaking everyone's hand.

"Albert," he said to me, peering up through what would later be known as John Lennon glasses. "Hoowahyoo? You've got the beard, so now you're Jesus Christ?"

I've done my time as an evangelist. Twleve years in the Church of Scientology, and later, when I had escaped Hubbard's minions, four or five years as a reluctant poster child for the world's fledgeling transgender movement.

My mother never heard the blue-haired ladies ask "Hoowahyoo?" of the tall-tall woman with mascara running down her cheeks. She never heard a producer from the Rikki Lake show ask me, "Who are you?" when I told her I wasn't a man or a woman. My mother never heard the Philadelphia society matron ask me the same question when I tried to attend her private women-only Alchoholics Anonymous group.

My mother only once asked me, "Who are you?" It was about a week before she died. "Hoowahyoo, Albert?" she asked anxiously, mixing up names and pronouns in the huge dose of morphine. "Who are you?"

I told her the truth: I was her baby, I always would be. I told her I was her little boy, and the daughter she never had. I told her I loved her.

"Ha!" she exclaimed, satisfied with my proffered selection of whos. "That's good. I didn't want to lose any of you, ever."

# Maid in the U.S.A.: A Personal Narrative on the Development of a Research Problem

*Mary Romero*

When I was growing up many of the women whom I knew worked cleaning other people's houses. Domestic service was part of my taken-for-granted reality. Later, when I had my own place, I considered housework something you did before company came over. My first thought that domestic service and housework might be a serious research interest came as a result of a chance encounter with live-in domestics along the U.S.–Mexican border. Before beginning a teaching position at the University of Texas in El Paso, I stayed with a colleague while apartment hunting. My colleague had a live-in domestic to assist with housecleaning and cooking. Asking around, I learned that live-in maids were common in El Paso, even among apartment and condominium dwellers. The hiring of maids from Mexico was so common that locals referred to Monday as the border patrol's day off because the agents ignored the women crossing the border to return to their employers' homes after their weekend off. The practice of hiring undocumented Mexican women as domestics, many of whom were no older than fifteen,

seemed strange to me. It was this strangeness that raised the topic of domestic service as a question and made problematic what had previously been taken for granted.

I must admit that I was shocked at my colleague's treatment of the sixteen-year-old domestic whom I will call Juanita. Only recently hired, Juanita was still adjusting to her new environment. She was extremely shy, and her timidity was made even worse by constant flirting from her employer. As far as I could see, every attempt Juanita made to converse was met with teasing so that the conversation could never evolve into a serious discussion. Her employer's sexist, paternalistic banter effectively silenced the domestic, kept her constantly on guard, and made it impossible for her to feel comfortable at work. For instance, when she informed the employer of a leaky faucet, he shot her a look of disdain, making it clear that she was overstepping her boundaries. I observed other encounters that clearly served to remind Juanita of her subservient place in her employer's home.

Although Juanita was of the same age as my colleague's oldest daughter and but a few years older than his two sons, she was treated differently from the other teenagers in the house. She was expected to share her bedroom with the ironing board, sewing machine, and other spare-room types of objects.[1]

More importantly, she was assumed to have different wants and needs. I witnessed the following revealing exchange. Juanita was poor. She had not brought toiletries with her from Mexico. Since she had not yet been paid, she had to depend on her employer for necessities. Yet instead of offering her a small advance in her pay so she could purchase the items herself and giving her a ride to the nearby supermarket to select her own toiletries, the employer handled Juanita's request for toothbrush, toothpaste, shampoo, soap, and the like in the following manner. In the presence of all the family and the house guest, he made a list of the things she needed. Much teasing and joking accompanied the encounter. The employer shopped for her and purchased only generic brand items, which were a far cry from the brand-name products that filled the bathroom of his sixteen-year-old daughter. Juanita looked at the toothpaste, shampoo, and soap with confusion; she may never have seen generic products before, but she obviously knew that a distinction had been made.

One evening I walked into the kitchen as the employer's young sons were shouting orders at Juanita. They pointed to the dirty dishes on the table and pans in the sink and yelled "WASH!" "CLEAN!" Juanita stood frozen next to the kitchen door, angry and humiliated. Aware of possible repercussions for Juanita if I reprimanded my colleague's sons, I responded awkwardly by reallocating chores to everyone present. I announced that I would wash the dishes and the boys would clear the table. Juanita washed and dried dishes alongside me, and together we finished cleaning the kitchen. My colleague returned from his meeting to find us in the kitchen washing the last pan. The look on his face was more than enough to tell me that he was shocked to find his houseguest—and future colleague—washing dishes with the maid. His embarrassment at my behavior confirmed my suspicion that I had violated the normative expectations of class behavior within the home. He attempted to break the tension with a flirtatious and sexist remark to Juanita which served to excuse her from the kitchen and from any further discussion.

The conversation that followed revealed how my colleague chose to interpret my behavior. Immediately after Juanita's departure from the kitchen, he initiated a discussion about "Chicano radicals" and the Chicano movement. Although he was a foreign-born Latino, he expressed sympathy for *la causa*. Recalling the one Chicano graduate student he had known to obtain a Ph.D. in sociology, he gave several accounts of how the student's political behavior had disrupted the normal flow of university activity. Lowering his voice to a confidential whisper, he confessed to understanding why Marxist theory has become so popular among Chicano students. The tone of his comments and the examples that he chose made me realize that my "outrageous" behavior was explained, and thus excused, on the basis of my being one of those "Chicano radicals." He interpreted my washing dishes with his maid as a symbolic act; that is, I was affiliated with *los de abajo*.

My behavior had been comfortably defined without addressing the specific issue of maids. My colleague then further subsumed the topic under the rubric of "the servant problem" along the border. (His reaction was not unlike the attitude employers have displayed toward domestic service in the United States for the last hundred years.)[2] He began by providing me with chapter and verse about how he had aided Mexican women from Juarez by helping them cross the border and employing them in his home. He took further credit for introducing them to the appliances found in an American middle-class home. He shared several funny accounts about teaching country women from Mexico to use the vacuum cleaner, electric mixer, and microwave (remember the maid scene in the movie *El Norte*?) and implicitly blamed them for their inability to work comfortably around modern conveniences. For this "on-the-job training" and introduction to

American culture, he complained, his generosity and goodwill had been rewarded by a high turnover rate. As his account continued, he assured me that most maids were simply working until they found a husband. In his experience they worked for a few months or less and then did not return to work on Monday morning after their first weekend off. Of course it never dawned on him that they may simply have found a job with better working conditions.

The following day, Juanita and I were alone in the house. As I mustered up my best Spanish, we shared information about our homes and families. After a few minutes of laughter about my simple sentence structure, Juanita lowered her head and in a sad, quiet voice told me how isolated and lonely she felt in this middle-class suburb literally within sight of Juarez. Her feelings were not the consequence of the work or of frustrations with modem appliances, nor did she complain about the absence of Mexican people in the neighborhood; her isolation and loneliness were in response to the norms and values surrounding domestic service. She described the situation quite clearly in expressing puzzlement over the social interactions she had with her employer's family: Why didn't her employer's children talk to her or include her in any of their activities when she wasn't working? Her reaction was not unlike that of Lillian Pettengill, who wrote about her two-year experience as a domestic in Philadelphia households at the turn of the century: "I feel my isolation alone in a big house full of people."[3]

Earlier in the day, Juanita had unsuccessfully tried to initiate a conversation with the sixteen-year-old daughter while she cleaned her room. She was of the same age as the daughter (who at that moment was in bed reading and watching TV because of menstrual cramps—a luxury the maid was not able to claim). She was rebuffed and ignored and felt that she became visible only when an order was given. Unable to live with this social isolation, she had already made up her mind not to return after her day off in Juarez. I observed the total impossibility of communication. The employer would never know why she left, and Juanita would not know that she would be considered simply another ungrateful Mexican whom he had tried to help.

After I returned to Denver, I thought a lot about the situations of Juanita and the other young undocumented Mexican women living in country club areas along the border. They worked long days in the intimacy of American middle-class homes but were starved for respect and positive social interaction. Curiously, the employers did not treat the domestics as "one of the family," nor did they consider themselves employers. Hiring a domestic was likely to be presented within the context of charity and good works; it was considered a matter of helping "these Mexican women" rather than recognized as a work issue.

I was bothered by my encounter along the border, not simply for the obvious humanitarian reasons, but because I too had once worked as a domestic, just as my mother, sister, relatives, and neighbors had. As a teenager, I cleaned houses with my mother on weekends and vacations. My own working experience as a domestic was limited because I had always been accompanied by my mother or sister instead of working alone. Since I was a day worker, my time in the employer's home was limited and I was able to return to my family and community each day. In Juanita's situation as a live-in domestic, there was no distinction between the time on and off work. I wondered whether domestic service had similarly affected my mother, sister, and neighbors. Had they too worked beyond the agreed upon time? Did they have difficulty managing relationships with employers? I never worked alone and was spared the direct negotiations with employers. Instead, I cooperated with my mother or sister in completing the housecleaning as efficiently and quickly as possible.

I could not recall being yelled at by employers or their children, but I did remember anger, resentment, and the humiliation I had felt at kneeling to scrub other people's toilets while they gave step-by-step cleaning instructions. I remember feeling uncomfortable around employers' children who never acknowledged my presence except to question where I had placed their belongings after I had picked them up off the floor to vacuum. After all, my experience was foreign to them; at the age of fourteen I worked as a domestic while they ran off to swimming, tennis, and piano lessons. Unlike Juanita, I preferred to remain invisible as I moved around the employer's house cleaning. Much later, I learned that the invisibility of workers in domestic service is a common characteristic of the occupation. Ruth Schwartz Cowan has commented on the historical aspect of invisibility:

The history of domestic service in the United States is a vast, unresolved puzzle, because the social role "servant" so frequently carries with it the unspoken adjective *invisible*. In diaries and letters, the "invisible" servant becomes visible only when she departs employment ("Mary left today"). In statistical series, she appears only when she is employed full-time, on a live-in basis; or when she is willing to confess the nature of her employment to a census taker, and (especially since the Second World War) there have frequently been good reasons for such confessions to go unmade.[4]

Although I remained invisible to most of the employers' family members, the mothers, curiously enough, seldom let me move around the house invisibly, dusting the woodwork and vacuuming carpets. Instead, I was subjected to constant supervision and condescending observations about "what a good little girl I was, helping my mother clean house." After I had moved and cleaned behind a hide-a-bed and lazy-boy chair, vacuumed three floors including two sets of stairs, and carried the vacuum cleaner up and downstairs twice because "little Johnny"

was napping when I was cleaning the bedrooms—I certainly didn't feel like a "little girl helping mother." I felt like a domestic worker!

There were employers who attempted to draw parallels between my adolescent experience and their teenagers' behavior: They'd point to the messy bedrooms and claim, "Well, you're a teenager, you understand clothes, books, papers, and records on the floor." Even at fourteen, I knew that being sloppy and not picking up after yourself was a privilege. I had two brothers and three sisters. I didn't have my own bedroom but shared a room with my sisters. Not one of us would think of leaving our panties on the floor for the others to pick up. I didn't bother to set such employers straight but continued to clean in silence, knowing that at the end of day I would get cash and confident that I would soon be old enough to work elsewhere.

Many years later, while attending graduate school, I returned to domestic service as an "off-the-record" means to supplement my income. Graduate fellowships and teaching assistantships locked me into a fixed income that frequently was not enough to cover my expenses. So once again I worked alongside my mother for seven hours as we cleaned two houses. I earned about fifty dollars for the day. Housecleaning is strenuous work, and I returned home exhausted from climbing up and down stairs, bending over, rubbing, and scrubbing.

Returning to domestic service as a graduate student was awkward. I tried to reduce the status inconsistency in my life by electing to work only in houses from which families were absent during the day. If someone appeared while I worked, I ignored their presence as they did mine. Since working arrangements had been previously negotiated by my mother, I had limited face-to-face interactions with employers. Most of the employers knew I was a graduate student, and fortunately, most seemed reluctant to ask me too many questions. Our mutual silence served as a way to deal with the status inconsistency of a housewife with a B.A. hiring [a doctoral student] to clean her house.

I came to El Paso with all of these experiences unquestioned in my memory. My presuppositions about domestic service were called into question only after observing the more obviously exploitative situation in the border town. I saw how vulnerable undocumented women employed as live-in domestics are and what little recourse they have to improve their situation, short of finding another job. Experiencing Juanita's shame and disgust at my colleague's sons' behavior brought back a flood of memories that eventually influenced me to study the paid housework that I had once taken for granted. I began to wonder professionally about the Chicanas employed as domestics that I had known throughout my own life: How vulnerable were they to exploitation, racism, and sexism? Did their day work status and U.S. citizenship provide protection against degradation and humiliation? How did Chicanas go about establishing a labor arrangement within a society that marked them as racial and cultural inferiors? How did they deal with racial slurs and sexist remarks within their employers' homes? How did Chicanas attempt to negotiate social interactions and informal labor arrangements with employers and their families?

## The Research Process

Intending to compare my findings with the research on U.S. minority women employed as domestics, I chose to limit my study to Chicanas, that is, women of Mexican descent born and raised in the United States. Although many women born in Mexico and living in the United States consider themselves Chicanas, my sample did not include women born outside the United States. My major concern in making this distinction was to avoid bringing into the analysis immigra-

tion issues that increase the vulnerability of the women employed as domestics. I wanted to keep conditions as constant as possible to make comparisons with the experiences Judith Rollins, Bonnie Thornton Dill, and Soraya Moore Coley report among African American women and with Evelyn Glenn's study of Japanese American women.[6] In order to duplicate similar residential and citizenship characteristics of these studies, I restricted my sample to Chicanas living in Denver whose families had migrated from rural areas of New Mexico and Colorado. All of the women interviewed were U.S. citizens and lived in Denver most of their adult lives.

I began the project by soliciting the cooperation of current and former domestics from my own family. I relied on domestics to provide entree into informal networks. These networks turned out to be particularly crucial in gaining access to an occupation that is so much a part of the underground economy. My mother, sister, and sister-in-law agreed to be interviewed and to provide names of relatives, friends, and neighbors. I also identified Chicana domestics in the community with the assistance of outreach workers employed by local churches and social service agencies. The snowball sampling was achieved by asking each interviewee to recommend other Chicana domestics as potential interviewees.

The women were extremely cautious about offering the names of friends and relatives. In most cases, they contacted the person first and only then gave me the name and telephone number. This actually turned out to be quite helpful. Potential interviewees had already heard about my study from someone who had been interviewed. They had a general idea of the questions I was going to ask and in some cases a little background information about who I was. However, on three occasions, I called women to ask for an interview and was confronted with resistance and shame. The women expressed embarrassment at being identified by their work—as a "housekeeper" or "cleaning lady." I responded by sharing my research interests in the occupation and in the relationship between work and family. I also shared my previous experience as a domestic.[7] One woman argued with me for twenty minutes about conducting research on an occupation that was low status, suggesting instead that I study Chicana lawyers or doctors, that is, "another occupation that presents our people in a more positive light." Another woman denied ever having worked as a domestic even though several women, including her sister-in-law, had given me her name as someone currently employed as a domestic.

The stigma of domestic service was a problem during the interviews as well. From the outset, it was very important for each woman to establish herself as someone more than a private household worker. Conducting nonstructured, free-flowing, and open-ended interviews allowed the women to establish multiple identities, particularly diffuse family and community roles.

The interviews were conducted in the women's homes, usually while sitting in the living room or at the dining room table with the radio or television on in the background. Although family members peeked in, for the most part there were few interruptions other than an occasional telephone call. From time to time, the women called to their husbands in the other room to ask the name of a street where they had once lived or the year the oldest son had been born in order to figure out when they had left and returned to work. The average interview lasted two hours, but I often stayed to visit and chat long after the interview was over. They told me about their church activities and plans to remodel the house and asked me for my opinion on current Chicano politics. Some spread out blankets, tablecloths, and pillow covers to exhibit their needlework. They showed me pictures of their children and grandchildren, giving me a walking tour of living rooms and bedrooms where wedding and high school portraits hung. As each one was identified, I learned more about their lives.

I conducted twenty-five open ended interviews with Chicanas living and working in the greater Denver metropolitan area. The most visible Chicano communities in Denver are in the low-income neighborhood located in the downtown area or in one of two working-class neighborhoods in the northern and western areas of the city. I interviewed women from each of these communities. I asked them to discuss their overall work histories, with particular emphasis on their experiences as domestics. I probed for detailed information on domestic work, including strategies for finding employers, definitions of appropriate and inappropriate tasks, the negotiation of working conditions, ways of doing housework efficiently, and the pros and cons of domestic service. The accounts included descriptions of the domestics' relationships with white middle-class mistresses and revealed Chicanas' attitudes toward their employers' lifestyles.

All of the interviewees' families of orientation were from northern New Mexico or southern Colorado, where many of them had lived and worked on small farms. Some of the women had arrived in Denver as children with their parents, others as young brides, and still others as single women to join siblings and cousins in Denver's barrios. Several women recalled annual migrations to northern Colorado to pick sugar beets, prior to their permanent relocation to Denver. In some cases, the women's entire families of orientation had migrated to Denver; in others, parents and siblings had either remained behind or migrated to other cities. Many older women had migrated with their husbands after World War II, and several younger women interviewed had arrived at the same time, as children. Women who had migrated as single adults typically had done so in the last ten or fifteen years. Now they were married and permanently living in Denver. . . .

## Profile of Chicana Household Workers

Only the vaguest statistical data on Chicana private household workers are available; for the most part these workers remain a doubly hidden population. The reasons are themselves instructive. Domestic workers tend to be invisible because paid domestic work has not been one of the occupations recorded in social science surveys, and the U.S. Census Bureau uses a single code lumping together all private household workers, including launderers, cooks, housekeepers, child-care workers, cleaners, and servants. Even when statistics on domestics can be teased out of the census and labor data bases, they are marred by the common practice of under-reporting work in the informal sector. Unlike some of the private household workers in the East, Chicana domestics are not unionized and remain outside the "counted" labor force. Many private household workers are not included in the statistics collected by the Department of Labor. The "job" involves an informal labor arrangement made between two people, and in many cases payment is simply a cash transaction that is never recorded with the Internal Revenue Service (IRS).

Governmental undercounting of Chicanos and Mexican immigrants in the United States further adds to the problem of determining the number of Chicanas and Mexicanas employed as private household workers. For many, domestic service is part of the underground economy, and employing undocumented workers is reported neither to the IRS nor to the Immigration and Naturalization Service (INS), thus making another source of statistical information unreliable. Chicanos continue to be an undercounted and obscure population. Problems with the categorization of domestics have been still further complicated by changing identifiers for the Mexican American population: Mexican, Spanish-speaking, Hispanic, Spanish-surnamed, and the like make it impossible to segment out the Chicano population.

The twenty-five Chicanas whom I interviewed included welfare recipients as well as working-class women, ranging in age from twenty-nine to sixty-eight. Thirteen of the twenty-five women were between twenty-nine and forty-five years old. The remaining twelve were over fifty-two years old. All the women had children and the older women also had grandchildren. The smallest family consisted of one child, and the largest family had seven children. The average was three children. All but one of the women had been married. Five of the women were single heads of households, two of them were divorced and the other three were single, separated, or widowed. The married women were currently living with husbands employed in blue collar positions, such as construction and factory work. At the time of the interview, the women who were single heads of households were financially supporting no more than two children.

Educational backgrounds ranged from no schooling to completion of high school. Six women had completed high school, and seven had no high school experience, including one who had never attended school at all. The remaining twelve had at least a sixth grade education. Although the least educated were the older women, eight of the women under forty-two had not completed high school. The youngest woman with less than an eighth grade education was fifty-three years old. The twelve women over fifty averaged eight years of schooling. Three of the high school graduates were in their early thirties, two were in their early forties, and one was fifty-seven years old. Although one woman preferred to be interviewed in Spanish, all the women spoke English.

Work experience as a private household worker ranged from five months to thirty years. Women fifty years and older had worked in the occupation from eight to thirty years, while four of the women between the ages of thirty-three and thirty-nine had worked as domestics for twelve years. Half of the women had worked for more than ten years as private household workers. Only three women had worked as domestics prior to marriage; each of these women had worked in live-in situations in rural areas in Colorado. Several years later, after marriage and children, they returned as day workers. All the other women, however, had turned to nonresidential day work in response to a financial crisis; in the majority of cases, it was their first job after marriage and having children. Some of the women remained domestics throughout their lives, but others moved in and out of domestic work. Women who returned to domestic service after having other types of jobs usually did so following a period of unemployment.

The work histories revealed that domestic service was only one of several low-paying, low-status jobs the women had held during their lives. They had been hired as waitresses, laundresses, janitors, farmworkers, nurses aides, fast-food servers, cooks, dishwashers, receptionists, school aides, cashiers, babysitters, salesclerks, factory workers, and various types of line workers in poultry farms and car washes. Almost half of the women had worked as janitors in hospitals and office buildings or as hotel maids. About one-fourth of the women had held semiskilled and skilled positions such as beauticians, typists, and medical-record clerks. Six of the women had worked only as domestics.

## Paid and Unpaid Domestic Work

In describing their daily routine activities, these Chicanas drew my attention to the interrelationship between paid and unpaid housework. As working women, Chicana private household workers face the "double day" or "second shift," but in their case both days consisted of the same types of tasks. Paid housework done for an employer was qualitatively different from housework done for their own families.

In the interviews, Chicanas described many complexities of domestic service. They explained how they used informal networks to find new employers for themselves and for relatives and friends. As they elaborated on the advantages and disadvantages of particular work arrangements and their reasons for refusing certain household tasks, I soon realized that these women not only knew a great deal about cleaning and maintaining homes, but they understood the influence of social relationships on household tasks. Analysis of the extensive planning and negotiation involved in the informal and underground arrangements of domestic service highlighted the significance of the social relationships surrounding housework.

Their work histories included detailed explanations of beginning, returning to, and continuing in domestic service. In the discussions, I began to understand the paradox of domestic service: On the one hand, cleaning houses is degrading and embarrassing; on the other, domestic service can be higher paying, more autonomous, and less dehumanizing than other low-status, low-skilled occupations. Previous jobs in the beet fields, fast-food restaurants, car washes, and turkey farms did not offer annual raises, vacations or sick leave. Furthermore, these jobs forced employees to work long hours and to keep rigid time schedules, and they frequently occurred outside or in an unsafe work environment. Unlike the other options available, domestic service did have the potential for offering flexible work schedules and autonomy. In most cases, domestic service also paid much more. Although annual raises, vacation, and social security were not the norm for most Chicanas in domestic service, there remained the possibility that such benefits could be negotiated with employers. Furthermore, as former farmworkers, laundresses, and line workers, the women found freedom in domestic work from exposure to dangerous pesticides, poor ventilation, and other health risks. This paradox foreshadowed a critical theoretical issue, the importance of understanding the social process that constructs domestic service as a low-status occupation.

Stigma as a perceived occupational hazard of domestic service emerged during the initial contact and throughout most of the interviews. The stigma attached to domestic service punctuated the interviews. I knew that many women hid their paid household labor from the government, but I did not realize that this secrecy encompassed neighbors, friends, and even extended family members. Several women gave accounts that revealed their families' efforts to conceal their employment as domestics. Children frequently stated that their mothers "just did housework," which was ambiguous enough to define them as full-time homemakers and not necessarily as domestics.

Faced with limited job opportunities, Chicanas selected domestic service and actively sought to make the most of the situation. In comparison with other jobs they had held, domestic service usually paid more and offered greater flexibility in arranging the length of the work-day and work-week. Although other jobs did not carry the stigma of servitude, workers were under constant supervision, and the work was similarly low status. Therefore, the women who chose domestic service over other low-paying, low-status jobs based their selection on the occupation that offered some possibility of control. Their challenge was to structure the work so as to reap the most benefits: pay, work hours, labor, and autonomy. Throughout the interviews, the women emphasized job flexibility as the major advantage of domestic service over previous jobs. Nonrigid work schedules allowed time to do their own housework and fulfill family obligations, such as caring for sick children or attending school functions. By stressing the benefits gained by doing day work, Chicanas diffused the low status in their work identities and emphasized their family and community identities. The ways in which they arranged both work and family revealed coping strategies used to deal with the stigma, and this drew me to analyze housework as a form of labor having both paid and unpaid manifestations.

The conventional social science separation of work and family is an analytical construct and is not found in the lived reality of Chicana domestics. Invariably the interviewees mixed and intertwined discussions of work and family. Moreover, the actual and practical relationships between work and family were explicit in their descriptions of daily activities: The reasons for seeking employment included the family's financial situation and the desire to raise its standard of living; earning extra money for the household was viewed as an extension of these women's roles as mothers and wives; arranging day work involved planning work hours around the children's school attendance, dentist and doctor appointments, and community and church activities; in some cases, young mothers even took their preschool-age children with them to work. The worlds of paid and unpaid housework were not disconnected in the lives of these women.

Attending to the importance of the relationship between paid and unpaid domestic work led me to ponder new questions about the dynamics of buying and selling household labor. How does housework differ when it is paid work? How does the housewife role change when part of her work is allocated to another woman? What is the range of employer-employee relationship in domestic service today? And is there a difference in the type of relationships developed by employed and unemployed women buying household labor?

The importance of attending to both paid and unpaid housework in researching domestic service became more apparent as I began presenting my research to academic audiences. When I read papers on the informal labor market or on family and community networks used to find work, some of my colleagues responded as women who employed domestics. Frequently question-and-answer sessions turned into a defense of such practices as hiring undocumented workers, not filing income taxes, or gift-giving in lieu of raises and benefits. Although I was aware that as working women, many academics employed someone to clean their houses, I was not prepared for scholars and feminists to respond to my scholarly work as housewives or employers. I was also surprised to discover that many of the maternalistic practices traditionally found in domestic service were common practices in their homes. The recurring responses made me realize that my feminist colleagues had never considered their relationships with the "cleaning woman" on the same plane as those with secretaries, waitresses, or janitors; that is, they thought of the former more or less in terms of the mistress-maid relationship. When, through my research, I pointed out the contradiction, many still had difficulty thinking of their homes—the haven from the cruel academic world—as someone's workplace. Their overwhelming feelings of discomfort, guilt and resentment, which sometimes came out as hostility, alerted me to the fact that something more was going on.

Although written over a decade ago, Margaret Mead's depiction of the middle-class woman's dilemma still seems to capture the contradictory feelings and attitudes that I hear among feminists today.

Traveling around the country, I meet a great many young wives and mothers who are struggling with the problem that seems to have no solution—how to hold down two full-time jobs at once. . . . As I listen I realize how many of them—guiltily but wistfully—yearn for the bygone days of servants. . . . They are guilty because they don't quite approve of anyone's working as a servant in someone else's home.[8]

In a society that espouses egalitarian values, we can expect yearnings "for the bygone days of servants" to be experienced as a contradiction. A century ago, Jane Addams discussed the awkward feelings and apprehensiveness academic women feel:

I should consider myself an unpardonable snob if, because a woman did my cooking, I should not hold myself ready to have her for my best friend, to drive, to read, to attend receptions with her, but that friendship might or might not come about, according to her nature and mine, just as it might or might not come about between me and my college colleague. On the other hand, I would consider myself very stupid if merely because a woman cooked my food and lived in my house I should insist upon having a friendship with her, whether her nature and mine responded to it or not. It would be folly to force the companionship of myself or my family upon her when doubtless she would vastly prefer the companionship of her own friends and her own family.[9]

In her book on black domestics and white employers in the South, Susan Tucker addresses the deeper psychological and class factors involved in hiring servants.

Most studies of domestic work maintain that the prime motivation for hiring a servant is the enhancement of the employer's image as a superior being. Yet, many women certainly must feel some discomfort, even when paying a decent wage, about the possibility of such a motivation. . . . There are many conflicting principles and traditions surrounding the employment of a socially and economically disadvantaged woman who goes daily into a wealthy home. One might feel discomfort if one were aware of any number of different types of ideas-feminist, egalitarian, religious.[10]

Domestic service must be studied because it raises a challenge to any feminist notion of "sisterhood." A growing number of employed middle- and upper-middle class women escape the double-day syndrome by hiring a poor women of color to do housework and child care. David Katzman underscored the class contradiction:

Middle-class women, the employers, gained freedom from family roles and household chores and assumed or confirmed social status by the employment of a servant. . . . The greater liberty of these middle-class women, however, was achieved at the expense of working-class women, who, forced to work, assumed the tasks beneath, distasteful to, or too demanding for the family members.[11]

Housework is ascribed on the basis of gender, and it is further divided along class lines and, in most cases, by race and ethnicity. Domestic service accentuates the contradiction of race and class in feminism, with privileged women of one class using the labor of another woman to escape aspects of sexism. . . .

## Notes

1. The conditions I observed in El Paso were not much different from those described by D. Thompson in her 1960 article, " Are Women Bad Employers of Other Women?" *Ladies Home Journal:* "Quarters for domestic help are usually ill placed for quiet. Almost invariably they open from pantry or kitchen, so that if a member of the family goes to get a snack at night he wakes up the occupant. And the live-in maid has nowhere to receive a caller except in the kitchen or one of those tiny rooms." "As a general rule anything was good enough for a maid's room. It became a catchall for furniture discarded from other parts of the house. One room was a cubicle too small for a regular-sized bed." Cited in Linda Martin and Kerry Segrave. *The Servant Problem: Domestic Workers in North America*, p. 25.

2. David Katzman addresses the "servant problem" in his historical study of domestic service, *Seven Days a Week, Women and Domestic Service in Industrializing America.* Defined by middle-class housewives, the problem includes both the shortage of servants available and the competency of women willing to enter domestic service. Employers' attitudes about domestics have been well documented in women's magazines. Katzman described the topic as "the bread and butter of women's magazines between the Civil War and World War I"; moreover, Linda Martin and Kerry Segrave, *The Servant Problem*, illustrate the continuing presence of articles on the servant problem in women's magazines today.

3. Lillian Pettengill's account *Toilers of the Home: The Record of a College Woman's Experience as a Domestic Servant* is based on two years of employment in Philadelphia households.

4. Ruth Schwartz Cowan, *More Work for Mother: The Ironies of Household Technology from the Open Hearth to the Microwave*, p. 228.

5. Earning money as domestic workers to pay college expenses not covered by scholarships is not that uncommon among other women of color in the United States. Trudier Harris interviewed several African American women public school and university college teachers about their college day experiences in domestic service. *From Mammies to Militants: Domestics in Black American Literature*, pp. 5–6.

6. Judith Rollins, *Between Women: Domestics and Their Employers*; Bonnie Thornton Dill, "Across the Boundaries of Race and Class: An Exploration of the Relationship Between Work and Family among Black Female Domestic Servants;" idemo, "'Making Your Job Good Yourself': Domestic Service and the Construction of Personal Dignity." In *Women and the Politics of Empowerment* eds. Ann Bookman and Sandra Morgen; Soraya Moore Coley, "'And Still I Rise'" An Exploratory Study of Contemporary Black Private Household Workers;" Evelyn Nakano Glenn, *Issei, Nisei, War Brides: Three Generations of Japanese American Women in Domestic Service.*

7. In some cases, it was important to let women know that my own background had involved paid housework and that my mother and sister were currently employed full-time as private household workers. Sharing this information conveyed that my life had similarities to theirs and that I respected them. This sharing of information is similar to the concept of "reciprocity." R. Wax, "Reciprocity in Field Work," in *Human Organization Research: Field Relationships and Techniques*, eds. R. N. Adams and J. J. Preiss, 90–98.

8. Margaret Mead, "Household Help," p. 42.

9. Jane Addams, "A Belated Industry," p. 545.

10. Susan Tucker, *Telling Memories among Southern Women: Domestic Workers and Their Employers in the Segregated South*, p. 231.

11. Katzman, *Seven Days a Week*, p. 269–70.

## References

Addams, Jane. 1896. "A Belated Industry," American Journal of Sociology 1:536–50.

Coley, Soraya Moore. 1981. "'And Still I Rise': An Exploratory Study of Contemporary Black Private Household Workers:" Ph.D. diss., Bryn Mawr College.

Cowan, Ruth Schwartz. 1983. *More Work for Mother: The Ironies of Household Technology from the Open Hearth to the Microwave*. New York: Basic.

Dill, Bonnie Thornton. 1979. "Across the Boundaries of Race and Class: An Exploration of the Relationship between Work and Family among Black Female Domestic Servants," Ph.D. diss., New York University.

———. 1988. "'Making Your Job Good Yourself'. Domestic Service and the Construction of Personal Dignity," In *Women and the Politics of Empowerment*, edited by Ann Bookman and Sandra Morgen, 33–52. Philadelphia: Temple University Press.

Glenn, Evelyn Nakano, 1981. "Occupational Ghettoization: Japanese American Women and Domestic Service, 1905–1970:" *Ethnicity 7* (4):352–86.

Harris, Trudier. 1982. *From Mammies to Militants: Domestics in Black American Literature*. Philadelphia: Temple University Press.

Katzman, David. 1981. *Seven Days a Week. Women and Domestic Service in Industrializing America*. Chicago: University of Illinois Press.

Martin. Linda, and Kerry Segrave. 1985. *The Servant Problem: Domestic Workers in North America*. Jefferson, N.C.: McFarland.

Mead, Margaret. 1976. "Household Help," *Redbook Magazine*, October, 42, 45, 47.

Pettengill, Lillian. 1903. *Toilers of the Home: The Record of a College Woman's Experience as a Domestic Servant*. New York: Doubleday.

Rollins, Judith. 1985. *Between Women: Domestics and Their Employers*. Philadelphia: Temple University Press.

Tucker, Susan. 1988. *Telling Memories among Southern Women: Domestic Workers and Their Employers in the Segregated South*. Baton Rouge: Louisiana State University Press.

Wax, R. 1960. "Reciprocity in Field Work." In *Human Organization Research: Field Relationships and Techniques*, edited by R. N. Adams and J. J. Preiss, 90–98. New York: Dorsey.

53

# Talking Back

*bell hooks*

In the world of the southern black community I grew up in, "back talk" and "talking back" meant speaking as an equal to an authority figure. It meant daring to disagree and sometimes it just meant having an opinion. In the "old school," children were meant to be seen and not heard. My great-grandparents, grandparents, and parents were all from the old school. To make yourself heard if you were a child was to invite punishment, the back-hand lick, the slap across the face that would catch you unaware, or the feel of switches stinging your arms and legs.

To speak then when one was not spoken to was a courageous act—an act of risking and daring. And yet it was hard not to speak in warm rooms where heated discussions began at the crack of dawn, women's voices filling the air, giving orders, making threats, fussing. Black men may have excelled in the art of poetic preaching in the male-dominated church, but in the church of the home where the everyday rules of how to live and how to act were established it was black women who preached. There, black women spoke in a language so rich, so poetic, that it felt to me like being shut off from life, smothered to death if one was not allowed to participate.

It was in that world of woman talk (the men were often silent, often absent) that was born in me the craving to speak, to have a voice, and not just any voice but one that could be identified as belonging to me. To make my voice, I had to speak, to hear myself talk—and talk I did—darting in and out of grown folk's conversations and dialogues, answering questions that were not directed at me, endlessly asking questions, making speeches. Needless to say, the punishments for these acts of speech seemed endless. They were intended to silence me—the child—and more particularly the girl child. Had I been a boy they might have encouraged me to speak believing that I might someday be called to preach. There was no "calling" for talking girls, no legitimized rewarded speech. The punishments I received for "talking back" were intended to suppress all possibility that I would create my own speech. That speech was to be suppressed so the "right speech of womanhood" would emerge.

Within feminist circles, silence is often seen as the sexist "right speech of womanhood"—the sign of woman's submission to patriarchal authority. This emphasis on woman's silence may be an accurate remembering of what has taken place in the households of women from WASP backgrounds in the United States, but in black communities (and diverse ethnic communities) women have not been silent. Their voices can be heard. Certainly for black women, our struggle has not been to emerge from silence into speech but to change the nature and direction of our speech, to make a speech that compels listeners, one that is heard.

Our speech, "the right speech of womanhood," was often the soliloquy, the talking into thin air, the talking to ears that do not hear you—the talk that is simply not listened to. Unlike the black male preacher whose speech was to be heard, who was to be listened to, whose words were to be remembered, the voices of black women—giving orders, making threats, fussing—could be tuned out, could become a kind of background music, audible but not acknowledged as significant speech. Dialogue—the sharing of speech and recognition—took place not between mother and child or mother and male authority figure but among black women. I can remember watching fascinated as our mother talked with her mother, sisters, and women friends. The intimacy and intensity of their speech—the satisfaction they received from talking to one another, the pleasure, the joy. It was in this world of woman speech, loud talk, angry words, women with tongues quick and sharp, tender sweet tongues, touching our world with their words, that I made speech my birthright—and the right to voice, to authorship, a privilege I would not be denied. It was in that world and because of it that I came to dream of writing, to write.

Writing was a way to capture speech, to hold onto it, keep it close. And so I wrote down bits and pieces of conversations, confessing in cheap diaries that soon fell apart from too much handling, expressing the intensity of my sorrow, the anguish of speech—for I was always saying the wrong thing, asking the wrong questions. I could not confine my speech to the necessary corners and concerns of life. I hid these writings under my bed, in pillow stuffings, among faded underwear. When my sisters found and read them, they ridiculed and mocked me—poking fun. I felt violated, ashamed, as if the secret parts of my self had been exposed, brought into the open, and hung like newly clean laundry, out in the air for everyone to see. The fear of exposure, the fear that one's deepest emotions and innermost thoughts would be dismissed as mere nonsense, felt by so many young girls keeping diaries, holding and hiding speech, seems to me now one of the barriers that women have needed and still need to destroy so that we are no longer pushed into secrecy or silence.

Despite my feelings of violation, of exposure, I continued to speak and write, choosing my hiding places well, learning to destroy work when no safe place could be found. I was never taught absolute silence, I was taught that it was important to speak but to talk a talk that was in itself a silence. Taught to speak and yet beware of the betrayal of too much heard speech, I experienced intense confusion and deep anxiety in my efforts to speak and write. Reciting poems at Sunday afternoon church service might be rewarded. Writing a poem (when one's time could be "better" spent sweeping, ironing, learning to cook) was luxurious activity, indulged in at the expense of others. Questioning authority, raising issues that were not deemed appropriate subjects brought pain, punishments—like telling mama I wanted to die before her because I could not live without her—that was crazy talk, crazy speech, the kind that would lead you to end up in a mental institution. "Little girl," I would be told, "if you don't stop all this crazy talk and crazy acting you are going to end up right out there at Western State."

Madness, not just physical abuse, was the punishment for too much talk if you were female. Yet even as this fear of madness haunted me, hanging over my writing like a monstrous shadow, I could not stop the words, making thought, writing speech. For this terrible madness which I feared, which I was sure was the destiny of daring women born to intense speech (after all, the authorities emphasized this point daily), was not as threatening as imposed silence, as suppressed speech.

Safety and sanity were to be sacrificed if I was to experience defiant speech. Though I risked them both, deep-seated fears and anxieties characterized my childhood days. I would speak but I would not ride a bike, play hardball, or hold the gray kitten. Writing about the ways we are hurt by negative traumas in our growing-up years, psychoanalyst Alice Miller makes the point in *For Your Own Good* that it is not clear why childhood wounds become for some folk an opportunity to grow, to move forward rather than backward in the process of self-realization. Certainly, when I reflect on the trials of my growing-up years, the many punishments, I can see now that in resistance I learned to be vigilant in the nourishment of my spirit, to be tough, to courageously protect that spirit from forces that would break it.

While punishing me, my parents often spoke about the necessity of breaking my spirit. Now when I ponder the silences, the voices that are not heard, the voices of those wounded and/or oppressed individuals who do not speak or write, I contemplate the acts of persecution, torture—the terrorism that breaks spirits, that makes creativity impossible. I write these words to bear witness to the primacy of resistance struggle in any situation of domination (even within family life); to the strength and power that emerges from sustained resistance and the profound conviction that these forces can be healing, can protect us from dehumanization and despair.

These early trials, wherein I learned to stand my ground, to keep my spirit intact, came vividly to mind after I published *Ain't I a Woman* and the book was sharply and harshly criticized. While I had expected a climate of critical dialogue, I was not expecting a critical avalanche that had the power in its intensity to crush spirit, to push one into silence. Since that time I have heard stories about black women, about women of color, who write and publish (even when the work is quite successful), having nervous breakdowns, being made mad because they cannot bear the harsh responses of family, friends, and unknown critics, or becoming silent, unproductive. Surely, the absence of a humane critical response has tremendous impact on the writer from any oppressed, colonized group who endeavors to speak. For us, true speaking is not solely an expression of creative power; it is an act of resistance, a political gesture that challenges the politics of domination that would render us nameless and voiceless. As such it is a courageous act—as such, it represents a threat. To those who wield oppressive power, that which is threatening must necessarily be wiped out, annihilated, silenced.

Recently, efforts by black women writers to call attention to our work serve to highlight both our presence and absence. Whenever I peruse women's bookstores I am struck not by the rapidly growing body of feminist writing by black women but by the paucity of available published material. Those of us who write and are published remain few in number. The context of silence is varied and multi-dimensional. Most obvious are the ways racism, sexism, and class exploitation act as agents to suppress and silence. Less obvious are the inner struggles, the efforts made to gain the necessary confidence to write, to rewrite, to fully develop craft and skill—and the extent to which such efforts fail.

Although I have wanted writing to be my life-work since childhood, it has been difficult for me to claim "writer" as part of that which identifies and shapes my everyday reality. Even after publishing books, I would often speak of wanting to be a writer as though these works did not exist. And though I would be told, "you are a writer," I was not yet ready to fully affirm this truth. Part of myself was still held captive by domineering forces of history, of familial life that had charted a map of silence, of right speech. I had not completely let go of the fear of saying the wrong thing, of being punished. Somewhere in the deep recesses of my mind, I believed I could avoid both responsibility and punishment if I did not declare myself a writer.

One of the many reasons I chose to write using the pseudonym bell hooks, a family name (mother to Sarah Oldham, grand-mother to Rosa Bell Oldham, great-grand-mother to me), was to construct a writer-identity that would challenge and subdue all impulses leading me away from speech into silence. I was a young girl buying bubble gum at the corner store when I first really heard the full name bell hooks: I had just "talked back" to a grown person. Even now I can recall the surprised look, the mocking tones that informed me I must be kin to bell hooks—a sharp-tongued woman, a woman who spoke her mind, a woman who was not afraid to talk back. I claimed this legacy of defiance, of will, of courage, affirming my link to female ancestors who were bold and daring in their speech. Unlike my bold and daring mother and grandmother, who were not supportive of talking back, even though they were assertive and powerful in their speech, bell hooks as I discovered, claimed, and invented her, was my ally, my support.

The initial act of talking back outside the home was empowering. It was the first of many acts of defiant speech that would make it possible for me to emerge as an indepen-dent thinker and writer. In retrospect, "talk-ing back" became for me a rite of initiation, testing my courage, strengthening my com-mitment, preparing me for the days ahead—the days when writing, rejection notices, periods of silence, publication, ongoing de-velopment seem impossible but necessary.

Moving from silence into speech is for the oppressed, the colonized, the exploited, and those who stand and struggle side by side a gesture of defiance that heals, that makes new life and new growth possible. It is that act of speech, of "talking back," that is no mere gesture of empty words, that is the ex-pression of moving from object to subject—the liberated voice.

**54**

# Because Silence Is Costly

## *Jewelle Gomez*

I have come to believe over and over again that what is most important to me must be spoken, made verbal and shared, even at the risk of having it bruised or misunderstood. That the speaking profits me; beyond any other effect.
—Audre Lorde, "The Transformation of Silence into Language and Action," in *Sister Outsider*

To speak of who we are as African-Americans has traditionally been a sign of triumph over adverse conditions. It was the telling of how we rose "up from slavery" into freedom and independence. It was a tale told in the early narratives of former slaves collected while other Black women and men were still held in bondage in this country. And in letters, magazine articles, and autobiographies written by African-Americans during the past two centuries. This tale of survival was and still is told around the kitchen tables of Black Americans in banter, jokes, in song and legend. And, most exquisitely, it is written in the fiction the Black women and men have been creating almost as long as we have been sharing our oral histories.

To speak of who we are as Black lesbians and gays is equally as urgent and as triumphant a story, one whose telling has been somewhat more guarded. To say you are a

lesbian or gay man to your family, friends, or co-workers is made difficult by a number of factors that have raised coming out (that process of speaking who we are) from a simple declaration into an important rite of passage. The psychological, social, and biblical misinformation dominating heterosexual assessment of lesbian/gay life makes coming out a nightmare for many of us, regardless of ethnicity. My own was unusually rewarding: My family responded as thinking, loving people, not as heterosexuals gripped by fear. The only pain was in the years before I was actually able to speak the words aloud. But other reactions vary—threats (and actual) institutionalization, physical violence, ostracizing one's partner, rejection from the family. And because of a presumption of heterosexuality in this society, coming out is a process which must be repeated over and over again.

In the telling of our lives as African-Americans, being lesbian or gay was not something to "speak on." It did not fit the social picture of normality African-Americans wished to project in order to combat racist stereotypes. Nor did it suit the political strategies outlined by church and civil rights leaders for liberation.

Nevertheless, an individual's need to come out of the closet and name her/himself sexually is not only part of a political strategy but is, more fundamentally, at the core of accepting adulthood and validating one's own experience. Coming out is not merely announcing a personal choice to the world, it is a step in accepting your identity. For Black lesbians/gays it means saying both *I am gay* and also declaring *I am still Black.*

The coming-out story has acted as a major unifying thread in a lesbian/gay community that is as diverse as the United States itself. At any women's bar, or lesbian caucus, or lesbian and gay film festival, the participants represent a cross section of America, embracing divergent class, political, and ethnic identities. This diversity, which has been an important part of the strength of the Movement, also makes it difficult to maintain coalitions. A reinterpretation of the traditional coming-of-age story, the coming-out story has been the one bond that touches all. Everyone, whether already out or deeply closeted, is able to discuss the experience of sharing their life choice. It becomes a linguistic currency that allows all lesbians and gays at least one place in which they can identify with each other. As such, it also places Black lesbians and gays in conflict with Black culture where it is considered a risk to the entire community to say such things aloud.

The coming-out story occupies an important place in African-American letters for several reasons. First, its genesis in a political movement, as well as its frequent practice by nonwriters and professional writers alike, are significant literary factors, much as they were when slave narratives were being collected, or during the Black Arts movement of the 1960s. Second, and perhaps most interesting, is the close relationship the coming-out story has to the pure oral tradition of African-Americans and the slave narratives of the nineteenth and early-twentieth centuries. It preserves the natural speech patterns of the one who is telling the story, and is usually a tale of triumph over repressive conditions in which the narrator emerges with a stronger, more positive identity. The emphasis in coming-out stories is, as is often true in autobiographies and slave narratives, on the importance of the story itself rather than the literary form in which the story is conveyed.

It captures the irony, wit, and wisdom frequently exhibited in traditional African-American storytelling. And it is through the interview or oral narrative that the stories of those who do not consider themselves writers are best recorded, giving a truer reflection of the breadth of the Black lesbian and gay community.

The Black coming-out story continues to evolve in a variety of forms. The overriding theme and focus of these stories is a reconciliation of gay lifestyles with Black identity, a regaining of a sense of wholeness within oneself and with one's Black community. But any move toward this reconciliation must always confront the peculiar position the Black community has historically held regarding sex. In her article, "The Failure to Transform: Homophobia in the Black Community," Cheryl Clarke points out:

We have expended much energy trying to debunk the racist mythology which says our [Black] sexuality is depraved. Unfortunately, many of us have overcompensated and assimilated the Puritan value that sex is procreation, occurs only between men and women, and is only valid within the confines of heterosexual marriage.[1]

The growth of the women's movement, following on the energy of the Civil Rights movement in the 1960s and in tandem with the Anti-War movement of the seventies, provided a crucial opportunity for Black women to explore their lives, history, and art. Despite the repressive attitude toward public discussion of sex and gender in this country, such movements inevitably led to the exploration of sexuality and heterosexual roles for both women and men. Before "outing" became a political tool and a way to sell magazines, activists extolled the virtues of coming out as a serious political and personal action. But outing was always a tactic favored in some quarters.

Such was the case with civil-rights leader Bayard Rustin as he organized the historic 1963 March on Washington. Speaking in a newspaper interview in 1987, Rustin recalled:

Then Strom Thurmond stood in the Senate speaking for three-quarters of an hour on the fact that Bayard Rustin was a homosexual, a draft dodger, and a communist. Newspapers all over the country came out with the front-page story. Mr. [A. Philip] Randolph waited for the phone to ring. And it did indeed ring.[2]

Rustin indicates in that article and others that his sexual orientation was always known among the political leaders with whom he worked, including Mr. Randolph, Martin Luther King, Jr., and Roy Wilkins. In 1960 Rustin had agreed to step down as an adviser to Dr. King when it was suggested that his participation might jeopardize any effort King led. Rustin was nevertheless charged with organizing the 1963 march. He indicates that the accusations of homosexuality were lost, a response Thurmond could not have anticipated, among those of draft evasion (Rustin, a Quaker, had spent three years in prison as a conscientious objector) and communism (he had been a socialist). Although Rustin received support from both Randolph and King, his public presence diminished greatly after the Strom Thurmond attack. Before his death in 1987, Rustin worked quietly with the A. Philip Randolph Educational Fund and contributed his support to gay organizations such as Men of All Colors Together and the National Coalition of Black Lesbians and Gays. His sentiments on coming out were unequivocal. "Every Gay who is in the closet is ultimately a threat to the freedom of Gays. . . . Remaining in the closet is the other side of prejudice against Gays."[3]

On the other hand, for renowned blues singer Alberta Hunter, the idea of coming out publicly as a lesbian was unthinkable. The distinct difference between her feelings and those of Bayard Rustin may, in part, be explained by their age difference (she was probably more than ten years his senior). But upbringing was certainly an important factor.

The strongest impulses that Hunter, also a songwriter, with material recorded by singers such as Bessie Smith, appears to have followed throughout her life and career were establishing financial security and promoting an air of personal propriety. A friend, Harry Watkins, recalls that Hunter "even had Confederate Dollars. That's how much she saved money!"[4] And Hunter certainly learned strict lessons at home about modesty. She recalls that when growing up in Memphis she was not allowed to go barefoot even inside her house. Her sense of privacy, which was certainly a by-product of such upbringing was reinforced by some of her friends. Watkins, being interviewed for Hunter's biography after her death, when questioned about her long-lasting affair with Lottie Tyler, refused to comment. "He rolled his eyes and sang a few lines of 'T Ain't Nobody's Business If I Do'."[5]

Despite her growing popularity in the United States and Europe, Hunter guarded her personal relationships with women with a tenacity most others, like comedian Jackie "Moms" Mabley, refused to bother with. A ladylike presence was imperative to the persona Hunter created on the stage and to her own sense of self. In her biography, she expresses her reluctance to sing on the infamous Beale Street in New Orleans. This attitude helped to isolate Hunter within the context of her relationships from a community of women who were less closeted than she. According to her biographers, "Alberta was a lesbian . . . but did everything to conceal this preference all her life. In her mind lesbianism tarnished the image of propriety and respectability she struggled so hard to achieve."[6] No doubt the perceived threat of losing her audience was a major factor in her concern about exposure. Ironically, by the time Hunter made her triumphant comeback in the 1970s, her lesbianism was legend and drew an entirely new audience of young women who came to see a part of lesbianism history, sitting side by side with those who remembered her from her earlier career.

. . . in the open fact of our loving
with not only our enemies' hands

raised against us
means a gradual sacrifice
of all that is simple
dreams . . .
—Audre Lorde[7]

One of the first Black lesbians to freely identify herself as such is Anita Cornwell, who published fiction and articles in *The Ladder*, the lesbian journal originally produced by the Daughters of Bilitis. The publication amazingly survived the McCarthy era. Episodes in Cornwell's coming-out story are collected in her book, *Black Lesbian in White America*. The six chapters written in the third person relate Cornwell's initially secret relationship with her first woman lover, Zelmar, who seems to straddle both the lesbian and straight worlds. At the start, Cornwell's only connection with women in a lesbian context is her relationship with Zelmar, but she is aware of the gap already opening between her and her past life:

Emotionally, she [Anita] was still trapped within the wall she had erected around herself long ago when she was unable to fully cope with her environment in any other fashion. . . . Although her friends were probably unaware of it, Anita was slowly edging away from them. Since the Gay world was unknown to her, however, she was moving into limbo.[8]

While the relationship with Zelmar opens Cornwell to other relationships with women, it is not until much later that she locates a women's community which gives her a certainty of identity and the promise of a fulfilling life as a lesbian.

When Cornwell began writing this material (1972), Ann Allen Shockley's novel, *Loving Her*, the first explicit and sympathetic book about a Black lesbian, was still two years in the future. In that light, Cornwell remains the first visible Black lesbian activist, and her work is designed as a documentation—much as the slave narratives recorded in the early twentieth century were.

Another coming-out story that is also essentially a documentation is that of Mabel Hampton, which appeared in the *Lesbian Herstory Archives Newsletter*. It is a transcribed oral presentation, including a question-and-answer segment done by Hampton, who was born in 1902. Its charm lies in its immediacy and Hampton's sparkling personality. The beginning is a long narrative describing her running away from home at an early age and being raised in Jersey City, New Jersey. It blossoms, though, when Hampton describes her life as a dancer, and meeting Lillian, who was to become her life partner for over forty years:

In 1932 I was on Lexington Avenue waiting for the streetcar. There were streetcars in those days and a girl says "Are you going . . ." She was just my height. She said, "Are you going uptown?" I said "Yes." She said "You gonna catch the car?" I said "I'm gonna catch the streetcar." So she says "All right I'm going to too." I looked her up and down and said to myself, goodness gracious, this is a good-looking chick. I said, I wonder if she's in my life, because you see I had danced on the stage and knew all the answers.[9]

The final part of the story is in the form of questions and answers in which specific inquiries are made about nightspots the women who were "in the life" (lesbians) visited and other elements of Hampton's social life. When asked how old she was when she came out, Hampton responds: "Well, I must have come out when I was eight years old. To tell the truth I never was in so I must have been out."[10]

The oral form captures Hampton's turn of phrase, sense of humor, and playfulness, and with it more of the essence of the Harlem Renaissance and the Depression eras. It also gives insight into the postwar period when Hampton had retired from the stage and worked as a cleaning woman in New York City. Her particularly inclusive manner of narrating, capturing colloquialisms of the period and providing physical details, gives her story a very broad perspective.

Leave my eyes    alone
why should I make
believe this place entirely
is white
and I am nothing . . .
—June Jordan[11]

In 1979, the same year I came out to my mother and grandmother in a Times Square movie theater, *Essence* magazine published a coming-out story of Chirlane McCray:

When I decided to write this article, I said, "I'm writing this for my gay sisters . . ." As I wrote and relived the pain, I realized that the fears, which I had assumed to be gone, were still within me. . . . I worry that no employer will hire me again, that my free-lance writing assignments will dwindle, that my gay friends who are still in the closet will disassociate themselves from me. I fear, in sum, that the monster of conformity will rear its angry head and devour me.[12]

Her father's response, "You're Black and you're a woman . . . I don't see why you want to be involved in something like this,"[13] echoes a common attitude among some in the Black community. The fallacy that homosexuality is "white" has been used frequently to try to shame Black gays into "recanting."

Neither of McCray's parents was wholly approving, but she was not met with hatred or reprisals. This reaction certainly played a part in enabling her to publish her coming-out story under her own name in a national magazine. Her purpose—to offer an example to those living in isolation—could not have been better fulfilled than by writing in a glossy fashion magazine marketed to the mainstream population of Black women, many of whom might never have the courage to look for a lesbian community.

*Essence* had, in an earlier (June 1978) issue, published an interview with Lea Hopkins, who was identified as the first Black *Playboy* bunny, from Kansas City, Missouri. At the time of the interview Hopkins was no longer working as a bunny or a model, but was active in the Missouri lesbian political community. The interview was, unlike a coming-out story, a glossy magazine profile. It avoided any lengthy discussion of emotional or political issues. Although the piece was not sensationalistic, the focus was on Lea Hopkins as a startling phenomenon rather than on the impact of her personal journey. Her lesbianism could well have been skydiving, yak farming, or any hobby Blacks don't "usually" do. McCray's first-person account assumes the social and political importance of her information and disallows any shock value her discussion might have.

In 1991, *Essence* magazine published another coming-out story, this one written by *Essence* editor Linda Villarosa and her mother, Clara Villarosa, a bookseller.[14] Using alternating narratives between daughter and mother, each expresses their expectations and disappointments with the roles they've been assigned. With the emphasis this time on the mother's coming to terms with her daughter's orientation, it is almost Clara Villarosa's coming-out story as much as it is Linda's. The article acknowledges that coming out is a growing-up process, and that in order for it to work both the lesbian or gay child and her/his parents and friends must share in the experience. The Villarosa coming-out story more clearly places the lesbian experience within the context of a Black family. Both daughter and mother explored what the process was of coming to terms with their identities (lesbian and mother of a lesbian) more easily within that realm, a perspective offered by few coming-out stories. It is a coming out made possible only by the hundreds of others that came before it. . . .

The 1980s saw the publication of the first full-length coming-out stories by Black writers, Audre Lorde's *Zami: A New Spelling of My Name* (1982) and Larry Duplechan's *Blackbird* (1986), in which a broader range of issues are addressed.[15] Each offers that important perspective of speaking from both inside and outside a Black community in a distinctive voice. The stories occur in different time periods and different parts of the United States, but each testifies in a similar way to the endurance of Black consciousness and the ability to integrate the many aspects of one's personality and create a whole person. . . .

In view of the difficulty the Black community has had with the imagery assigned to our sexuality, as well as its ambivalence about the role of those with nontraditional (i.e., not white middle-class perceptions of) sexual lives, it is significant that Lorde chooses to treat the sexual aspects of her narrative openly. She refuses to equivocate in her coming-out story, never attempting to either ignore her Blackness or to indicate that she is a lesbian in spite of it. She also is able to acknowledge and describe her political perspective on race, gender, and sexuality without relinguishing the specifics of her sexuality as a Black woman and as a lesbian. Lorde's open exploration of the sexual nature of her life is an important departure from the majority of writing by African-Americans, either fictional or autobiographical. *Zami* offers one of the first honest glimpses of Black lesbian sexuality in American literature devoid of a need to place blame or locate causality.

Lorde's celebration of the sexuality essential to her life, and significant in lesbian and gay life generally, is an exciting step in African-American literature. For many years, and certainly in the recent past shadowed by AIDS, gays have often downplayed the role of sexuality in an effort to deflect criticism. In addition, antipornography activists, representing in many cases more repressive elements of feminism, have attempted to set standards for the appropriate and inappropriate depiction of sexuality. This has cast a pall over some members of the creative community who might consider exploring sex in their literary fiction or autobiographical material. Lorde's work is a coming out not only as a Black lesbian but also as a sexual being whose goal is the successful integration of all of these elements of her life.

In an article entitled "The Historical Text as Literary Artifact," Hayden White says, ". . . histories gain part of their explanatory effect by their success in making stories out of mere chronicles . . ."[16] Lorde strives to pull her story out of the realm of "mere chronicle" by defining it as a "biomythography." She opens up the autobiography to include the political and historical perspectives she feels are crucial to the telling of her story as a Black lesbian. It also allows Lorde, the poet, to use the lyrical imagery that marks her other writing, imbuing her coming-out story with a mythical quality. Lorde's abilities as a poet and essayist provide her story with the best elements of direct oral history as well as those of historical fiction. With her good ear for dialogue, she captures the powerful turns of phrase which give events immediacy. She also utilizes the dramatic tension that enhances all storytelling, whether traditional or fictional. *Zami* is the most fully realized coming-out story that the gay and Black communities have. It offers a vision of what it means to be *other*, explores the overlapping issues faced by both groups, and makes clear the bonds that will forever bind anyone who is a member of both the gay and Black communities.

The appearance of two full-length works, Lorde's biomythography and Duplechan's fiction, signifies a shift in the perceived value of the coming-out story and its place in the literary canon of African-Americans. Until recently, most coming-out stories were like those of Hampton or Vernon: short pieces reproduced in anthologies. The presumption is that these longer works will appeal not only to those struggling with their own coming-out stories but also to a broad audience interested in history and autobiography and African-Americans.

Anthropologist John Langston Gwaltney, in preparing his book of twentieth-century narratives, *Drylongso,* found that "In black culture there is a durable, general tolerance, which is amazingly free of condescension. for the individual's right to follow the truth wherever it leads."[17] The important accomplishment of the books by Audre Lorde and Larry Duplechan is their success in following the truths of a Black lesbian/gay experience, and their unflinching portrayal of the Black community's varied response, even when it is shameful. Neither book sacrifices the exciting patterns of Black speech, the nuances of Black life in white America, the exploration of the African-American ambivalence about sexual imagery, or the complexity of gender relations in the Black community. Yet both maintain their integrity as gay stories. As narratives, these books do what the Black coming-out story is intended to do: integrate racial and sexual identities in a way that creates a fully realized whole with potential for a positive impact.

In an article on the autobiographical writings of African-American women, Frances Smith Foster quotes historian Roy Harvey Pierce:

"When we come to try to understand our literature in our history and our history in our literature, . . . *we have to* be ready to see new forms, new modes, new styles emerging and to realize how all that is new results from a particular confrontation of [one] culture made by a particular [person] at a particular time."[18]

In coming-out stories it is first the revitalization of traditional forms—storytelling and narratives—that is most significant. Then it is the emergence of a new form—biomythography—which contributes to our understanding of our literature and our history. The validity of these forms in African-American culture reasserts itself in the new and the old voices which essentially tell stories of triumph from Black gays and lesbians.

Despite the effort of those in the Black community who have forsaken the tradition of "durable tolerance" that Gwaltney identified, banishing Black gays and lesbians from their homes or their literary forums, the coming-out story reaffirms the legitimacy of the role Black gays and lesbians continue to play in the Black community whether they are openly gay or not.

Many writers and editors in the fast-emerging commercial lesbian and gay community have exalted the development of lesbian/gay writing by saying it is no longer "just" coming-out stories. In some ways this is true. Lesbian and gay stories have many forms and always will. From Monique Wittig to Isabel Miller to Nikki Baker, from John Rechy to John Preston to Melvin Dixon to Assotto Saint, the stories take us many places besides out of the closet.

But the coming-out story may prove to be the most energetic and engaging aspect of the autobiographical form which is itself experiencing a resurgence in popularity. Bio-mythography is certainly an exciting genre for creative writers who wish to record their African-American sojourn within the language and emotional scope they've lived it. The blend of history, biography, and poetic spirit seems most suitable for Lorde's need to express both a strong political perspective as well as a highly charged personal account—a need that is familiar to many African-Americans who believe that "what is most important . . . must be spoken. . . ."

*Black/Out*,[19] the magazine published by the National Coalition of Black Lesbians and Gays, carried four stark words on the cover of one of its issues. They answered the question of why, in spite of fear, Black lesbians and gay men continue to write and speak their coming-out stories. The four simple words are the answer to the why of slave narratives and oral histories handed down to each generation. They tell us why coming-out stories find their niche so comfortably among the stories of all our forebears: Because silence is costly.

## Notes

1. Cheryl Clarke, "The Failure to Transform: Homophobia in the Black Community," in *Home Girls: A Black Feminist Anthology,* ed. Barbara Smith (Albany, NY: Kitchen Table: Women of Color Press, 1983) p. 199.

2. Bayard Rustin, interviewed in the *Village Voice,* June 30, 1987, p. 28.

3. Bayard Rustin, interviewed in *Black/Out*, Vol. I, Nos. 3-4, p. 18.

4. Frank C. Taylor with Gerald Cook, *Alberta Hunter: A Celebration in Blues* (New York: McGraw-Hill, 1987) p. 72.

5. *Ibid.*, p. 7.

6. *Ibid.*, p. 43.

7. Audre Lorde, "Outlines," in *Our Dead Behind Us* (New York: W. W. Norton, 1986) p. 14.

8. Anita Cornwell, "Fleeing the Myths of Motherhood" in *Black Lesbian in White America* (Tallahassee, FL: Naiad Press, 1983) p. 53.

9. Mabel Hampton, "Coming-Out Story," *Lesbian Herstory Archives Newsletter*, No. 7, (1981) p. 32.

10. *Ibid.*, p. 33.

11. June Jordan, "And Who Are You?" in *Things I Do in the Dark* (Boston: Beacon Press, 1981) p. 98.

12. Chirlane McCray, "I Am a Lesbian," *Essence*, September 1979, p. 91.

13. *Ibid.*, p. 161.

14. Linda Villarosa and Clara Villarosa, *Essence*, May 1991, pp. 82, 126.

15. Audre Lorde, *Zami: A New Spelling of My Name* (Watertown, MA: Persephone Press, 1982). Larry Duplechan, Blackbird (New York: St. Martin's Press, 1986).

16. Hayden White, "The Historical Text as Literary Artifact," in *Critical Theory Since 1965*, ed. Hazard Adams and Leroy Searles (Tallahassee: Florida State University Press, 1985) p. 397.

17. John Langston Gwaltney, *Drylongso* (New York: Random House, 1980) p. xxvii.

18. Roy Harvey Pierce, *Historicism Once More* (Princeton, NJ: Princeton University Press, 1969) p. 59. Quoted by Frances Smith Foster, "Adding Color and Contour to Early American Self-Portraits," in *Conjuring*, ed. Marjorie Pryse and Hortense J. Spillers (Bloomington: Indiana Univerity Press, 1985) p. 25.

19. Cover caption, *Black/Out*, Vol. 1, Nos. 3–4, 1987.

**55**

# La Conciencia de la Mestiza[1]/
# Towards a New Consciousness

## Gloria Anzaldúa

*Por la mujer de mi raza
hablará el espíritu.*[2]

Jose Vasconcelos, Mexican philosopher, envisaged *una raza mestiza, una mezcla de razas afines, una raza de color—la primera raza síntesis del globo.*[3] He called it a cosmic race, *la raza cósmica*, a fifth race embracing the four major races of the world.[4] Opposite to the theory of the pure Aryan,[5] and to the policy of racial purity that white America practices, his theory is one of inclusivity. At the confluence of two or more genetic streams, with chromosomes constantly "crossing over," this mixture of races, rather than resulting in an inferior being, provides hybrid progeny, a mutable, more malleable species with a rich gene pool. From this racial, ideological, cultural, and biological cross-pollination, an "alien" consciousness is presently in the making—a new *mestiza* consciousness, *una conciencia de mujer.*[6] It is a consciousness of the Borderlands.

*Una lucha de fronteras/*
**A Struggle of Borders**

Because I, a *mestiza*,
continually walk out of one culture
and into another,
because I am in all cultures at the same time,
*alma entre dos mundos, tres, cuatro,
me zumba la cabeza con lo contradictorio.
Estoy norteada por todas las voces que me
    hablan
simultáneamente.*[7]

The ambivalence from the clash of voices results in mental and emotional states of perplexity. Internal strife results in insecurity and indecisiveness. The mestiza's dual or multiple personality is plagued by psychic restlessness.

In a constant state of mental nepantilism, an Aztec word meaning torn between ways, *la mestiza* is a product of the transfer of the cultural and spiritual values of one group to another. Being tricultural, monolingual, bilingual, or multilingual, speaking a patois,[8] and in a state of perpetual transition, the *mestiza* faces the dilemma of the mixed breed: Which collectivity does the daughter of a dark-skinned mother listen to?

*El choque de un alma atrapado entre el mundo del espíritu y el mundo de la técnica a veces la deja entullada.*[9] Cradled in one culture, sandwiched between two cultures, straddling all three cultures and their value systems, *la mestiza* undergoes a struggle of flesh, a struggle of borders, an inner war. Like all people, we perceive the version of reality that our culture communicates. Like others having or living in more than one culture, we get multiple, often opposing messages. The coming together of two self-consistent but habitually incompatible frames of reference[10] causes *un choque,* a cultural collision.

Within us and within *la cultura chicana,*[11] commonly held beliefs of the white culture attack commonly held beliefs of the Mexican culture, and both attack commonly held beliefs of the indigenous culture. Subconsciously, we see an attack on ourselves and our beliefs as a threat and we attempt to block with a counterstance.

But it is not enough to stand on the opposite river bank, shouting questions, challenging patriarchal, white conventions. A counterstance locks one into a duel of oppressor and oppressed; locked in mortal combat, like the cop and the criminal, both are reduced to a common denominator of violence. The counterstance refutes the dominant culture's views and beliefs, and, for this, it is proudly defiant. All reaction is limited by, and dependent on, what it is reacting against. Because the counterstance stems from a problem with authority—outer as well as inner—it's a step towards liberation from cultural domination. But it is not a way of life. At some point, on our way to a new consciousness, we will have to leave the opposite bank, the split between the two mortal combatants somehow healed so that we are on both shores at once and, at once, see through serpent and eagle eyes.[12] Or perhaps we will decide to disengage from the dominant culture, write it off altogether as a lost cause, and cross the border into a wholly new and separate territory. Or we might go another route. The possibilities are numerous once we decide to act and not react.

## A Tolerance for Ambiguity

These numerous possibilities leave *la mestiza* floundering in uncharted seas. In perceiving conflicting information and points of view, she is subjected to a swamping of her psychological borders. She has discovered that she can't hold concepts or ideas in rigid boundaries. The borders and walls that are supposed to keep the undesirable ideas out are entrenched habits and patterns of behavior; these habits and patterns are the enemy within. Rigidity means death. Only by remaining flexible is she able to stretch the psyche[13] horizontally and vertically. *La mestiza* constantly has to shift out of habitual formations; from convergent thinking, analytical reasoning that tends to use rationality to move toward a single goal (a Western mode), to divergent thinking,[14] characterized by movement away from set patterns and goals and toward a more whole perspective, one that includes rather than excludes.

The new *mestiza* copes by developing a tolerance for contradictions, a tolerance for ambiguity. She learns to be an Indian in Mexican culture, to be Mexican from an Anglo point of view. She learns to juggle cultures. She has a plural personality, she operates in a pluralistic mode—nothing is thrust out, the good the bad and the ugly, nothing rejected, nothing abandoned. Not only does she sustain contradictions, she turns the ambivalence into something else.

She can be jarred out of ambivalence by an intense, and often painful, emotional event which inverts or resolves the ambivalence. I'm not sure exactly how. The work takes place underground—subconsciously. It is work that the soul performs. That focal point or fulcrum, that juncture where the *mestiza* stands, is where phenomena tend to collide. It is where the possibility of uniting all that is separate occurs. This assembly is not one where severed or separated pieces merely come together. Nor is it a balancing of opposing powers. In attempting to work out a synthesis, the self has added a third element which is greater than the sum of its severed parts. That third element is a new consciousness—a *mestiza* consciousness—and though it is a source of intense pain, its energy comes from continual creative motion that keeps breaking down the unitary aspect of each new paradigm.

*En unas pocas centurias*,[15] the future will belong to the *mestiza*. Because the future depends on the breaking down of the paradigms, it depends on the straddling of two or more cultures. By creating a new mythos—that is, a change in the way we perceive reality, the way we see ourselves, and the ways we behave—*la mestiza* creates a new consciousness.

The work of *mestiza* consciousness is to break down the subject-object duality that keeps her a prisoner and to show in the flesh and through the images in her work how duality is transcended. The answer to the problem between the white race and the colored, between males and females, lies in healing the split that originates in the very foundation of our lives, our culture, our languages, our thoughts. A massive uprooting of dualistic thinking in the individual and collective consciousness is the beginning of a long struggle, but one that could, in our best hopes, bring us to the end of rape, of violence, of war. . . .

### *El camino de la mestiza*
### The Mestiza Way

Caught between the sudden contraction, the breath sucked in and the endless space, the brown woman stands still, looks at the sky. She decides to go down, digging her way along the roots of trees. Sifting through the bones, she shakes them to see if there is any marrow in them. Then, touching the dirt to her forehead, to her tongue, she takes a few bones, leaves the rest in their burial place.

She goes through her backpack, keeps her journal and address book, throws away the Muni-BART metromaps.[16] The coins are heavy and they go next, then the greenbacks flutter through the air. She keeps her knife, can opener, and eyebrow pencil. She puts bones, pieces of bark, *hierbas*,[17] eagle feather, snakeskin, tape recorder, the rattle and drum in her pack and she sets out to become the complete *tolteca*.[18]

Her first step is to take inventory. *Despojando, desgranando, quitando paja*.[19] Just what did she inherit from her ancestors? This weight on her back—which is the baggage from the Indian mother, which the baggage from the Spanish father, which the baggage from the Anglo?

*Pero es difícil*[20] differentiating between *lo heredado, lo adquirido, lo impuesto*.[21] She puts history through a sieve, winnows out the lies, looks at the forces that we as a race, as women, have been a part of. *Luego bota lo que no vale, los desmientos, los desencuentros, el embrutecimiento. Aguarda el juicio, hondo y enraizado, de la gente antigua*.[22] This step is a conscious rupture with all oppressive traditions of all cultures and religions. She communicates that rupture, documents the struggle. She reinterprets history and, using new symbols, she shapes new myths. She adopts new perspectives toward the darkskinned, women, and queers. She strengthens her tolerance (and intolerance) for ambiguity. She is willing to share, to make herself vulnerable to foreign ways of seeing and thinking. She surrenders all notions of safety, of the familiar. Deconstruct, construct. She becomes a *nahual*,[23] able to transform herself into a tree, a coyote, into another person. She learns to transform the small "I" into the total Self. *Se hace moldeadora de su alma. Según la concepción que tiene de sí misma, así será*.[24]

### *Que no se nos olvide los hombres*[25]

*"Tú no sirves pa' nada*[26]—
you're good for nothing.
*Eres pura vieja*."[27]

"You're nothing but a woman" means you are defective. Its opposite is to be *un ma-*

cho. The modern meaning of the word "machismo," as well as the concept, is actually an Anglo invention. For men like my father, being "macho" meant being strong enough to protect and support my mother and us, yet being able to show love. Today's macho has doubts about his ability to feed and protect his family. His "machismo" is an adaptation to oppression and poverty and low self-esteem. It is the result of hierarchical male dominance. The Anglo, feeling inadequate and inferior and powerless, displaces or transfers these feelings to the Chicano by shaming him. In the Gringo[28] world, the Chicano suffers from excessive humility and self-effacement, shame of self and self-deprecation. Around Latinos he suffers from a sense of language inadequacy and its accompanying discomfort; with Native Americans he suffers from a racial amnesia which ignores our common blood, and from guilt because the Spanish part of him took their land and oppressed them. He has an excessive compensatory hubris[29] when around Mexicans from the other side. It overlays a deep sense of racial shame.

The loss of a sense of dignity and respect in the macho breeds a false machismo which leads him to put down women and even to brutalize them. Coexisting with his sexist behavior is a love for the mother which takes precedence over that of all others. Devoted son, macho pig. To wash down the shame of his acts, of his very being, and to handle the brute in the mirror, he takes to the bottle, the snort, the needle, and the fist.

Though we "understand" the root causes of male hatred and fear, and the subsequent wounding of women, we do not excuse, we do not condone, and we will no longer put up with it. From the men of our race, we demand the admission/acknowledgment/disclosure/testimony that they wound us, violate us, are afraid of us and of our power. We need them to say they will begin to eliminate their hurtful put-down ways. But more than the words, we demand acts. We say to them: We will develop equal power with you and those who have shamed us.

It is imperative that *mestizas* support each other in changing the sexist elements in the Mexican-Indian culture. As long as woman is put down, the Indian and the Black in all of us is put down. The struggle of the *mestiza* is above all a feminist one. As long as *los hombres* think they have to *chingar mujeres*[30] and each other to be men, as long as men are taught that they are superior and therefore culturally favored over *la mujer,*[31] as long as to be a *vieja*[32] is a thing of derision, there can be no real healing of our psyches. We're halfway there—we have such love of the Mother, the good mother. The first step is to unlearn the *puta/virgen*[33] dichotomy and to see *Coatlapopeuh-Coatlicue* in the Mother, *Guadalupe*.[34]

Tenderness, a sign of vulnerability, is so feared that it is showered on women with verbal abuse and blows. Men, even more than women, are fettered to gender roles. Women at least have had the guts to break out of bondage. Only gay men have had the courage to expose themselves to the woman inside them and to challenge the current masculinity. I've encountered a few scattered and isolated gentle straight men, the beginnings of a new breed, but they are confused, and entangled with sexist behaviors that they have not been able to eradicate. We need a new masculinity and the new man needs a movement.

Lumping the males who deviate from the general norm with man, the oppressor, is a gross injustice. *Asombra pensar que nos hemos quedado en ese pozo oscuro donde el mundo encierra a las lesbianas. Asombra pensar que hemos, como femenistas y lesbianas, cerrado nuestros corazónes a los hombres, a nuestros hermanos los jotos, desheredados y marginales como nosotros.*[35] Being the supreme crossers of cultures, homosexuals have strong bonds with the queer white, Black, Asian, Native American, Latino, and with the queer in Italy, Australia, and the rest of the planet. We come from all colors, all classes, all races, all time periods. Our role is to link people with each other—the Blacks with Jews with Indians with Asians with whites with extraterrestrials. It is to transfer ideas and information from one culture to another. Colored homosexuals have more knowledge of other cultures; have always been at the forefront (although sometimes in the closet) of all liberation struggles in this country; have suffered more injustices and have survived them despite all odds. Chicanos need to acknowledge the political and artistic contributions of their queer. People, listen to what your *jotería*[36] is saying.

The *mestizo* and the queer exist at this time and point on the evolutionary continuum for a purpose. We are a blending that proves that all blood is intricately woven together, and that we are spawned out of similar souls.

### Somos una gente[37]

*Hay tantísimas fronteras*
*que dividen a la gente*
*pero por cada frontera*
*existe también un puente.*[38]
—Gina Valdés[39]

### Divided Loyalties

Many women and men of color do not want to have any dealings with white people. It takes too much time and energy to explain to the downwardly mobile, white middle-class women that it's okay for us to want to own "possessions," never having had any nice furniture on our dirt floors or "luxuries" like washing machines. Many feel that whites should help their own people rid themselves of race hatred and fear first. I, for one, choose to use some of my energy to serve as mediator. I think we need to allow whites to be our allies. Through our literature art, *corridos*,[40] and folktales we must share our history with them so when they set up committees to help Big Mountain Navajos[41] or the Chicano farm-

workers or *los Nicaragüenses*[42] they won't turn people away because of their racial fears and ignorances. They will come to see that they are not helping us but following our lead.

Individually, but also as a racial entity, we need to voice our needs. We need to say to white society: We need you to accept the fact that Chicanos are different, to acknowledge your rejection and negation of us. We need you to own the fact that you looked upon us as less than human, that you stole our lands, our personhood, our self-respect. We need you to make public restitution: to say that, to compensate for your own sense of defectiveness, you strive for power over us, you erase our history and our experience because it makes you feel guilty—you'd rather forget your brutish acts. To say you've split yourself from minority groups, that you disown us, that your dual consciousness splits off parts of yourself, transferring the "negative" parts onto us. (Where there is persecution of minorities, there is shadow projection. Where there is violence and war, there is repression of shadow.) To say that you are afraid of us, that to put distance between us, you wear the mask of contempt. Admit that Mexico is your double, that she exists in the shadow of this country, that we are irrevocably tied to her. Gringo, accept the doppelganger[43] in your psyche. By taking back your collective shadow the intracultural split will heal. And finally, tell us what you need from us.

### By Your True Faces We Will Know You

I am visible—see this Indian face—yet I am invisible. I both blind them with my beak nose and am their blind spot. But I exist, we exist. They'd like to think I have melted in the pot. But I haven't, we haven't.

The dominant white culture is killing us slowly with its ignorance. By taking away our self-determination, it has made us weak and empty. As a people we have resisted and we have taken expedient positions, but we have never been allowed to develop unencumbered—we have never been allowed to be fully ourselves. The whites in power want us people of color to barricade ourselves behind our separate tribal walls so they can pick us off one at a time with their hidden weapons; so they can whitewash and distort history. Ignorance splits people, creates prejudices. A misinformed people is a subjugated people.

Before the Chicano and the undocumented worker and the Mexican from the other side can come together, before the Chicano can have unity with Native Americans and other groups, we need to know the history of their struggle and they need to know ours. Our mothers, our sisters and brothers, the guys who hang out on street corners, the children in the playgrounds, each of us must know our Indian lineage, our Afro-*mestisaje*,[44] our history of resistance.

To the immigrant *mexicano* and the recent arrivals we must teach our history. The 80 million *mexicanos* and the Latinos from Central and South America must know of our struggles. Each one of us must know basic facts about Nicaragua, Chile, and the rest of Latin America. The Latinoist movement (Chicanos, Puerto Ricans, Cubans, and other Spanish-speaking people working together to combat racial discrimination in the market place) is good but it is not enough. Other than a common culture we will have nothing to hold us together. We need to meet on a broader communal ground.

The struggle is inner: Chicano, *indio*,[45] American Indian, *mojado*,[46] *mexicano*, immigrant Latino, Anglo in power, working class Anglo, Black, Asian—our psyches resemble the bordertowns and are populated by the same people. The struggle has always been inner, and is played out in the outer terrains. Awareness of our situation must come before inner changes, which in turn come before changes in society. Nothing happens in the "real" world unless it first happens in the images in our heads.

## Notes

1. *La conciencia de la mestiza: mestiza* consciousness; consciousness of the *mestiza* (a woman of mixed racial heritage).

2. This is my own "take off" on Jose Vasconcelos' idea. Jose Vasconcelos, *La Raza Cósmica: Misión de la Raza Ibero-Americana* (México: Aguilar S.A. de Ediciones, 1961). [Author's note] *Por la mujer de mi raza . . .* : the spirit shall speak through the women of my race.

3. *Una raza mestiza . . .* : a multiracial race, a mixture of kindred races, a race of color, the first synthetic race of the world.

4. Vasconcelos. [Author's note]

5. *The theory of the pure Aryan*: the myth espoused by Adolf Hitler and others of the racial superiority of white northern Europeans.

6. *Una conciencia de mujer*: a female consciousness.

7. *Alma entre dos mundos . . .* : a soul caught between two, three, four worlds. My head aches with contradictions. I'm led north by all the voices that speak to me simultaneously.

8. *Patois*: nonstandard dialect.

9. *El choque de una alma atrapado . . .* : The struggle of a soul trapped between the world of the spirit and the world of technology sometimes leaves it paralyzed.

10. Arthur Koestler termed this "bisociation." Albert Rothenberg, *The Creative Process in Art, Science, and Other Fields* (Chicago, IL: University of Chicago Press, 1979), 12. [Author's note]

11. *La cultura chicana*: chicana culture. Elsewhere in *Borderlands*, Anzaldúa writes, "La Cultura chicana identifies with the mother (Indian) rather than with the father (Spanish). Our faith is rooted in indigenous attributes, images, symbols, magic, and myth" (Chapter 3).

12. *See through serpent and eagle eyes*: "The eagle symbolizes the spirit (as the sun, the father); the serpent symbolizes the soul (as the earth, the mother). Together, they symbolize the struggle between the spiritual/celestial/male and the underworld/earth/feminine" (*Borderlands*, Chapter 1).

13. *The psyche*: the soul or self.

14. In part, I derive my definitions for "convergent" and "divergent" thinking from Rothenberg, 12–13. [Author's note]

15. *En unas pocas centurias*: in a few centuries.

16. *Muni-BART metromaps*: maps of bus and rail transportation in the San Francisco Bay area.

17. *Hierbas:* herbs.

18. Gina Valdés, *Puentes y Fronteras: Coplas Chicanas* (Los Angeles, CA: Castle Lithograph, 1982), 2. [Authors' note] *tolteca:* The Toltec empire predates the Aztec in ancient Mexico. Anzaldúa associates the Toltecs with more woman-centered culture and religion than those of the warlike, patriarchal Aztecs.

19. *Despojando, desgranando, quitando paja:* stripping, removing the grain or the straw.

20. *Pero es difícil:* But it is difficult.

21. *Lo heredado, lo adquirido, lo impuesto:* the inherited, the acquired, the imposed.

22. *Luego bota lo que no vale . . . :* Then she discards whatever is useless, falsehoods and brutality. She waits for the deep, probing common sense of the ancient people.

23. *Nahual:* sorceress.

24. *Se hace moldeadora . . . :* She is able to mold her soul. Whatever image she has of herself, so she will be.

25. *Que no se nos olvide los hombres:* Let us not forget men.

26. *Tú no sirves pa' nada:* You're good for nothing.

27. *Eres pura vieja:* You're nothing but a woman.

28. *Gringo:* Anglo.

29. *Hubris:* exaggerated pride or self-confidence.

30. *Chingar mujeres:* fuck women.

31. *La mujer:* the woman.

32. *Vieja:* old woman.

33. *Puta/virgen:* whore/virgin.

34. *Coatlapopeuh-Coatlicue in the Mother, Guadalupe:* a reference to the dual identity (Indian/pagan and Spanish/Christian) of the Virgin of Guadalupe. Anzaldúa argues that "after the conquest, the Spaniards and their Church . . . desexed Guadalupe, taking Coatlalopeuh, the serpent/sexuality, out of her" (*Borderlands,* Chapter 3).

35. *Asombra pensar que nos hemos quedado, . . . :* It's astonishing to think that we have stayed in that dark well where the world locks up lesbians. It's astonishing to think that as feminist lesbians, we have closed our hearts to men, to our gay brothers, as disinherited and alienated as we are.

36. *Jotería:* gayness.

37. *Somas una gente:* We are one people.

38. *Hay tantísimas fronteras . . . :* There are so many borders/dividing people/but through each border there/passes a bridge.

39. Richard Wilhelm, *The I Ching or Book of Changes,* trans. Cary F. Baynes (Princeton, NJ: Princeton University Press, 1950), 98. [Author's note]

40. *Corridos:* ballads or narrative folk songs of Mexico.

41. *Big Mountain Navajos:* Big Mountain is an area in New Mexico at the center of a Navajo and Hopi dispute over land rights and treaty conditions.

42. *Los Nicaragüenses:* The Nicaraguans.

43. *Doppelganger:* a double.

44. *Afro-mestisaje:* mixed-blood Latino people of African descent.

45. *Indio:* Indian (of Mexico/Central America).

46. *Mojado:* wetback.

56

# Ceremony

*Leslie Marmon Silko*

I will tell you something about stories,
[he said]
They aren't just for entertainment.
Don't be fooled.
They are all we have, you see,
all we have to fight off
illness and death.

You don't have anything
if you don't have the stories.

Their evil is mighty
but it can't stand up to our stories.
So they try to destroy the stories
let the stories be confused or forgotten.
They would like that
They would be happy
Because we would be defenseless then.

He rubbed his belly.
I keep them here
[he said]
Here, put your hand on it
See, it is moving.
There is life here
for the people.

# Epilogue

*The mind that has conceived a plan of living must never lose sight of the chaos against which that pattern was conceived.*
(Ralph Ellison, *Invisible Man*)

*God can be shaped. God is Change.*
(Octavia Butler, *Parable of the Sower*)

In the book *The Sword and the Stone,* by T. H. White, a wise old badger tells his young apprentice, Wart, how all the creatures of the earth came to be as they are. According to the badger, God assembled a multitude of fledgling embryos before him on the sixth day of creation and explained that He was going to hand out gifts. The embryos could each choose two or three gifts. These gifts would serve as a set of tools that would mark the creature's unique existence on earth. The embryos chattered excitedly among themselves about the possible combinations of tools each might ask for. When the time came, each embryo stepped forward and requested its gifts from God. Some asked for arms that were diggers or garden forks, some chose to use their arms as flying machines, others asked for bodies like boats and arms that were oars. One of the lizards decided to swap its entire body for blotting paper. Still others asked to be able to use their mouths as drills or offensive weapons. Finally it was the turn of the embryo called "human." This small, naked creature approached God and stammered shyly, "I have considered your generous offer, and I thank you for it, but I choose to stay as I am."

"Well chosen," thundered God. "In deciding to retain your embryonic form you will have use of all the gifts that mark the being of each of the other creatures. You will exist always as potential: the potential to take up and put down the tools of the other creatures, the potential to create uniforms and tools of your own design and to wear and discard them as you see fit. You have chosen wisely, human. We wish you well in your earthly journey."

An important lesson of symbolic interactionism is that humans exist as embryonic potential. We are capable of creating, taking on, and casting off various identities and cultural institutions. Our potential is limited only by our imagination and our ability to assemble the materials necessary to realize our visions.

As social beings, the ability to create shared meaning is the distinctive mark of our species. However, the history of Western consciousness suggests a somewhat paradoxical acceptance of this ability. We are eager to embrace our creative potential but at the same time reluctant to recognize our own authority as social creators and the responsibility that this implies. As conclusion to this text, we offer a few thoughts on this conundrum, which has come to be known more commonly as the "postmodern crisis of meaning."

## Symbolic Interaction and the "Postmodern Crisis of Meaning"

How do you determine what is true and right and good? This is the question with which we opened this book. The intellectual tradition known as "postmodernism" arose as a critique of the "modernist" ideals that there is a single universal truth, or reality, and that this truth is revealed in the patterns of nature and can be discovered using the methods of science. Modernist reasoning applied to questions of justice suggest that, within this "natural order," some ways of being are better than others according to "natural law" (e.g., heterosexuality is "more natural" than homosexuality; poor people are poor because they are intellectually inferior). Postmodernist scholars dismantled this line of reasoning by demonstrating that, in human societies, there is no single truth; no simple, non-contradictory reality; and no single version of justice and authority. In contrast to modernist notions of a *universal, univocal* truth, postmodern theories set out to demonstrate that social reality is *contextual, multivocal,* and *complex.*

The postmodernist approach, called *critical theory,* employs a method known as *deconstructionism.* Postmodern scholars use critical theory to demonstrate that dominant (hegemonic) forms of social order are not "natural," but actually represent the perspective and values of a privileged few. They demonstrate this by "deconstructing" the taken-for-granted assumptions underlying modern Western thought. The goal of deconstructionism is to demonstrate that the ideas of the dominant group are in fact self-fulfilling realities and not instances of a natural order that inevitably controls all of us. Exponents of critical theory have demonstrated that many social institutions reflect the interests and values of groups who control the means of cultural and economic production. Critical inquiry also led to the conclusion that many of the aims and "findings" of science have reflected the interests of upper-middle-class Anglo-European men. Critical theorists have tried to show that the science practiced by this class is not, in fact, based on natural law, as its proponents have claimed, but rather on a socially constructed reality that serves to maintain the privileged position of this small group.

A critique that some scholars have made against postmodern theories is that the perspective results in a "crisis of meaning." Any and all cultural institutions can be disassembled to point out the prejudices and taken-for-granted assumptions embedded in a group's beliefs and values. In general, the practice of deconstructionism is a sound one. It instructs us to dig beyond the obvious to uncover the philosophies and interests that perpetuate our social institutions. These nonobvious special interests often lead to unintended and undesirable personal and social consequences. Thus, it is useful to be *critically* aware of the assumptions underlying our own ideals. Many observers have noted, however, that this line of reasoning leads to cynicism and cultural disaffection. Deconstructionism becomes a sort of cultural wrecking ball for tearing down all that a group holds meaningful and leaving nothing in its place except the rubble of dismantled values. To the extent that this is so, some critics have gone so far as to call postmodern or critical theory an immoral practice.

Symbolic interactionism as a form of intellectual inquiry predates postmodernism. The two traditions do share the premise that realities are multiple, shifting, contradictory, and situationally specific. However, whereas critical theorists have focused on deconstructing cultural beliefs and practices, symbolic interactionists have focused on studying *how* people learn and sustain certain culturally specific practices and beliefs through everyday patterns of interaction. Similar to postmodernism, SI too has been criticized as perpetuating cynicism and social dissolution. If you really follow the logic of the symbolic interactionist perspective, you will note that it implies (1) interactions are always fraught with misunderstandings, miscues, misinformation, and possibly even attempts to mislead and manipulate, and (2) meaning is *always negotiated*: It is always in flux and always reflects the interactional context and the relationship between persons in the interaction. In concert with the postmodern dictum, SI states there is no universal meaning or "truth."

Therefore, students of these perspectives sometimes conclude that it is not worthwhile to participate in social life because, ultimately, there is no *real* meaning. The conclusion they draw is that nothing really matters. The dilemma, as they represent it to themselves, is whether to participate in social relations that are, by definition of critical insight, always in flux.

We recognize that this may be a very real dilemma for persons who are newly aware of the complex, contradictory, and shifting aspects of social relations. However, the crisis, as we see it, is not so much a crisis of meaning that has been brought about by symbolic interactionist studies and critical inquiries, but a crisis that arises because people who learn these perspectives remain stuck in modernist mindset: the lingering premise in modernist thought that there *should be* a stable and transcendent truth. The real postmodern dilemma, as we have come to see it, is not that there is no universal meaning, but that persons fail to comprehend the significance of their own expressive and creative potential.

## Meaning, Stability, Authority, and Authenticity

Some of the vestiges of the modernist mindset include the beliefs that something is meaningful only if it is stable and if its authority transcends the persons who "created" it. Thus, if the implications of SI listed above are correct, meaning is unstable (always negotiated and in flux) and there is no ultimate authority. Furthermore (taking the logic of deconstruction to its extreme), why should we even bother to produce this text? If we actually believe what we are saying, then the underlying premise is that nothing, not even the tenets of the theory that we have tried to lay out here, are "real." So why bother? What seems to bother people about the implications of this perspective is that meaning is not stable, there is no ultimate authority outside of situational human relations, and, if people's selves are shifting, where is the authenticity?

## Stability and "Outcomes"

Imagine using a similar logic if you intended to build a sandcastle on the beach. It will only be washed away by the tides or eroded by the wind. It's fragile and temporary, so why bother? *Why* do people build sandcastles? Certainly not so that they will endure, but rather for the sheer pleasure of doing so. The experience lingers long after the sand form has crumbled away. Why do people form friendships, get married, or invest time and energy in pursuing a vocation (such as graduate school or the ministry), even though they may have doubts about its "permanence"? Presumably these activities are more stable than the sandcastle, but is this so because they are "naturally" more stable, or because we care enough to remain continually engaged in their ongoing creation?

Modernist assessments of meaning and value are rooted in notions of "outcomes." What is the likely *outcome* of your education? Will you be able to get a good job? Make more money? Is the outcome worth the effort and the cost involved? Presumably education is a stable, predictable course of action toward a desired end. The meaning and worth of the education are assessed in terms of this end. If someone were to demonstrate for you that the link between education, occupation, and income was a social construction, would that make it any less real in the consequences? And what about other aspects of your education, such as the *process* of learning? Does this have any meaning and value in itself? A cynic who explored the connections between education and business in a capitalist world might conclude that higher education was nothing more than a means to train workers for docile servitude. This critical theory may have some truth to it, but it doesn't necessarily have to lead *you* to conclude that *your* education has to turn out that way *for you*. Through critical awareness and mindful engagement, you have the potential to turn the *process* of your experience in higher education into a meaningful activity.

Another lesson of the symbolic interactionist perspective is that *there are stable, predictable patterns of behavior and systems of belief.* A central focus of this perspective is to demonstrate the existence of these patterns and to show the ways in which ordinary people create and re-create them. Just because these patterns are the result of human activity does not make them any less meaningful. The pertinent question is whether people are *mindfully engaged* in these practices or *mindlessly* rattling around in old routines and beliefs that may have lost their meaning.

## Authority and Authenticity

Another vestige of modernism is the notion that, no matter how relative truth and meaning appear to be, there is a real truth in the authority of nature or God. Postmodern thought has done away with both God and nature as sources of authority that exist independently of human relations. This "crisis of authority" seems to be the crux of the problem. A central implication of social constructionism is that humans are the sole authors of the shared cultural meaning that makes their existence worthwhile. Somehow this notion disappoints many people. They would rather trade in their creative, observable embryonic potential for an unseen, elusive form of natural order. The latter presumably offers more security. It also frees people from assuming responsibility for the existence and perpetuation of embarrassing or undesirable social institutions. If these institutions can be attributed to forces beyond our control, then we do not have to participate in changing them. But to embrace this logic is to allow the ghost of a philosophy of natural order to haunt the possibilities of purposefully constructed realities. This logic also implies that, because cultural forms are human creations, they are somehow less worthwhile than if they were the result of an extrahuman force. This is a rather odd and hasty dismissal of human potential as a creative entity. It implies that our own constructions are not worth anything simply because we have the ability to deconstruct them as well.

Consider the Great Wall of China, a remarkable feat of human coordination and labor. Are you any less amazed by its existence when you pause to ponder the reasons for its construction or the fact that it could also be disassembled, stone by stone, by the same human hands that initially constructed it? Why are we so reluctant to experience a similar awe and wonderment when we contemplate human culture, which is also the product of a highly complex and intricate set of coordinated human actions?

A new way to think of this is to consider the idea that *we are the gods*. We create and re-create our own systems of meaning and ideals. The fact that we are the creators doesn't make these beliefs and practices any less real. In fact, our ability to analyze, critique, and *change* our practices for the common good is a mark of our creative potential. Again, the pertinent point is the extent to which persons are mindfully engaged in the process of social relations. When you are engaged and critically aware of the role you play in various systems of meaning, then you are also able to take responsibility for your actions and to participate in ongoing discussions about what is "right" and "good." Authority, morality, and authenticity are *embedded* in these social relations. The actual process of involvement can be seen as an enactment of morality and authenticity.

We like to think that most people who were given a choice between (1) living a life in mindless ignorance of the social processes that shape who and what we are and (2) becoming mindfully and critically aware of these processes would choose mindful awareness. This process of becoming aware can itself be an act of meaningful engagement. At the same time, it can also be painful. Kahlil Gibran once wrote that pain is the experience of breaking the shell that encapsulates understanding. The implication is that, in the process of stretching one's intelligence and understanding, there will always be the pain of breaking old habits and relinquishing old ways of knowing. Meaningful living is mindful living, and this can be a risky enterprise.

## Mindful (Re)Construction

If, as we have suggested, social realities are fragile and require maintenance, then it is reasonable to conclude that our active participation is required to keep personal and social routines meaningful. Of course, it is possible to maintain many cultural institutions through mindless, unexamined participation in taken-for-granted routines. To the extent that we each do so, we perpetuate realities that have little meaning for us and fail to consider ways we might actively and meaningfully produce alternative realities. But learning about alternative realities teaches ways to grapple with complexity and provides an the awareness of other possible scripts. Through critical reflection and analysis, we learn to discern taken-for-granted beliefs and practices; through engaged, mindful participation, we contribute to the ongoing creation of a mindful existence. In conclusion, we consider two pitfalls to avoid in the pursuit of a mindful, meaningful existence: ossification and entropy.

### Ossification

We have discussed the tendency for human routines and ideas to harden, or "ossify," into habits and entrenched systems of belief (see the introductory essay in Part IV). We have also discussed some of the reasons why (desire for predictability, cognitive efficiency, mindlessness) this occurs in human relations. Ossified social practices (a.k.a. "social institutions") are not necessarily bad. The problems arise when we forget the purpose of the initial routine or practice and/or fail to remain mindful about the fact that these are socially created routines. What may have served as a useful basis for achieving some particular end becomes an ideology and an end in itself. We may persist in maintaining these ossified constructions simply because they have become permanent, hardened features of our social landscape. But at the same time, we may be contributing to the maintenance of our own prisons.

People usually know when to tear down a building that has ceased to serve any useful function and may even be a source of danger. However, we sometimes rattle around in social institutions that are cracked and crumbling simply because we fail to realize that it is within our power to step beyond the confines of these structures and build others. The point is not that all old social institutions should be torn down; it is that we should be mindful of the purpose of the social institutions that our actions (or inactions) help to perpetuate. Unfortunately, such purposes become increasingly difficult to recognize—and change becomes more difficult—the more hardened, or ossified, the institution becomes.

Consider the social institution prevalent in U.S. universities of giving exams. In our seminar for graduate students on how to teach, we ask these prospective college teachers to provide us with a rationale for giving exams. At first this seems like a simple task, but the seminar participants usually end up struggling once they begin to think about it. The practice of giving exams has become such an ossified element of the educational landscape that many instructors engage in the practice mindlessly. They really don't know why they do it. If exams are written and administered with a particular purpose, such as providing feedback for the student and the instructor or as an incentive to organize chunks of information, then teachers are participating in the mindful maintenance of this social institution. But to give exams simply because "that's what's always been done" is to perpetuate a potentially meaningless social routine.

Once the purpose for a particular social routine is isolated, it is possible to devise potentially more useful routes to achieve it. For example, a sometimes-unfortunate outcome of the exam procedure is the unnecessary rank-ordering of students. If the purpose of exams is to motivate students to organize and articulate their knowledge, then it may be possible to create an alternative exercise that more directly serves the intended purpose and avoids the pitfalls. It is possible, however, that the purpose of exams is indeed to rank-order persons—perhaps to facilitate their entrance into a stratified institution, such as the labor market. In that case, instructors should be mindfully aware that their examination procedures serve to perpetuate social stratification, and that they are performing a gate-keeping role for other social institutions.

The point is to understand how one's participation in particular cultural routines perpetuates the existence of social institutions. Here, in the exploration of ossified structures, is where the tools of deconstruction serve a useful end. Such explorations need not lead to the conclusion that the entire structure should be dismantled, however. Mindful construction instructs us to ask what purpose the social ritual serves and whether we want to participate in that purpose.

Two points are worth underscoring here. First, social institutions are created and maintained through the active participation of individuals. To the extent that we are aware of our reasons for participating in various cultural productions, we can be said to be mindfully engaged in the construction of reality. If, however, we are simply participating in patterns that "have always been," then we risk being social robots living in the brittle houses constructed by previous generations for their own purposes. Second, change does not occur simply by tearing down these structures. A meaningful existence requires that we construct other institutions in place of those that have been torn down.

## Entropy

If any pattern in nature seems to play itself out in human relations, it is entropy—the natural process that results in decay. According to the laws of thermodynamics, coherent molecular systems require constant input of energy to maintain their structure. If this energy is diverted, the system (whether molecule, leaf, or earlobe) will erode or fall apart into increasingly random elements. This tendency toward randomness is entropy. Similarly, the meaning and purpose of many of our social routines are constantly threatened with erosion unless participants infuse these routines with mindful energy.

As we have pointed out, a great deal of mindful intellectual energy has been devoted to deconstructing ossified social realities. But often this activity produces isolated individuals cut adrift from any meaningful social activity—in other words, cynics. The path toward cynicism is exacerbated by the process of entropy. If we do not invest energy in those social productions that matter, they will cease to exist as meaningful systems.

What about some of the meaningful activities or relationships in your life that you may take for granted? Do you have a spouse or family member whom you love but "don't have enough time for"? Consider the trap that people set when they depend on ossified routines to provide a sense of meaning and purpose while neglecting to contribute adequate energy to the maintenance of the routine. Imagine an attorney who decides to commit her services to the struggle to allow gays access to military service. After mindful consideration, she has decided to devote her time and talent to fighting what she perceives to be an injustice. In effect, she has chosen to participate in tearing down one social system, the heterosexual military, and to contribute to its replacement with an alternative reality, one suggesting that combat and sexuality are separate systems. Now imagine this same woman explaining to her spouse and children that she does not have time to celebrate birthdays and anniversaries because she is busy fighting for an important social cause. She is often absent from family meals and other everyday rituals as well. One day she awakens to the discovery that she is no longer a meaningful element of her family.

This example illustrates the simple but profound point that if we do not actively participate in the production of those realities that we wish to maintain as the foundation of our lives, they will be eroded by the forces of entropy. Love and family involvement require ongoing, active participation in the ritual interactions that maintain these institutions. We can't take for granted even seemingly well-established social institutions such as "the family." These social institutions do not endure without active maintenance.

## Mindful Engagement

Together ossification and entropy suggest that, left to themselves, our social institutions will harden into brittle and nonserviceable cultural forms that bind us even while they cease to hold much meaning for us. This is not a pleasant outcome. Yet it has been predicted by many of the classical sociological thinkers. Max Weber, for example, referred to the stultifying process of the "Iron Cage." Karl Marx warned that individuals who were denied meaningful forms of social activity would suffer alienation and cynicism. Émile Durkheim proposed that groups would not be able to regulate the behavior of members if the groups failed to produce meaningful social rituals; members would suffer from a sense of purposelessness and lack of regulation known as *anomie*. The challenge for students of sociology is to understand these processes so they can be guided more purposefully.

The messages are (1) be choosy about the realities that you intend to produce or reproduce and (2) recognize that the production of any reality requires your participation. To the extent that you participate mindfully, your life will take on increased meaning and purpose.

Trudy the bag lady, introduced in Reading 4 by Jane Wagner, is a true hero from the perspective of the mindful construction of reality.

She has scrutinized the social institutions in which she dwells and found them to be unacceptable. Rather than turn away in despair, she has created a rich, lively alternative reality for herself. Now, as she describes it, her days are "jam-packed and fun-filled." Trudy is both a product of the general social realities that form this society and a commentator on them. We find her commentary compelling because it is both informed and hopeful. She is neither a social robot nor a cynic. She has taken responsible control for the construction of her own reality, and she invests in this production with enthusiasm and vigor. She is an intriguing character in that, although she is a street person, we do not feel pity for her. We may in fact feel a bit envious of her insightful, energetic reality, mad though it may appear by conventional standards. Trudy is bursting with potential.

Our own realities can be similarly produced, whether by doing something as simple as participating wholeheartedly in small daily rituals with those you love or as revolutionary as "talking back to outrage" in the form of large-scale collective protest. The message we find useful is that it takes insight, courage, and responsibility to engage in the mindful production of reality. This is the basis of a meaningful existence.

# Name Index

Page references followed by *n* indicate notes.

# Subject Index

Page references followed by *n* indicate notes.

Stimulus-response relationship, 39
Stories
    coming-out, 558–564
    cultural, 362–364
    importance of, 573
    revised, 470–481
Storytelling, 325–328
Strip clubs, 279–287
    defining reality in, 279–280
    enforcing the rules in, 284–286
    maintaining reality in, 281–286
    precarious situations in, 281
    setting the mood in, 281–284
Subjective freedom, 497–498
Subjectivity, 26, 27, 40
Subjects, 492–493
Suicide, 502, 503
Superstitions, 40, 352–353
Swiss society, 487, 489
*Sword and the Stone, The* (White), 577
Symbolic interactionism, 35, 44–47
    behaviorism and, 46–47
    constructivism and, 48–51
    humanness and, 9–11
    importance of symbols in, 89–96
    interpretation and, 50–51, 64–65
    postmodern crisis of meaning
        and, 577–579
    reality and, 11–12
    shared meanings and, 63–84
    social patterns and, 58–59
    utilitarianism and, 45–46
Symbolic meaning
    language and, 69–82, 172–173
    naming process and, 66–69
Symbolic reference, 110, 111
Symbolic system, 87, 95
Symbols, 12
    assigning meaning with, 66–68
    color-based, 172–173
    human nature and, 87–88
    individuals and, 92–95
    social interaction and, 89–90
    society and, 90–91
Syntax, 72

# T

Tact, 197, 232
Talk
    reflexivity of, 368, 379n
    sex, in nudist camps, 453–454
    *See also* Conversation; Speech

Talking back, 554–557
*Te of Piglet, The* (Hoff), 3
Teachers
    effects of expectations of, 356,
        414–415, 429–433
    madams as, 247–253
*Teachings of Don Juan, The*
    (Castañeda), 371
Theater metaphor, 193
Theatersports, 199
Theatrical performance. *See* Perfor-
    mance
Thought
    abstract, 77–78
    conceptual, 77–78, 124
    culture and, 79–82
    deliberation and, 93
    language and, 71–74, 75–76, 79–
        82, 92–93, 111–112
    neurological impairment of, 111–
        112
    social action and, 290–291
Time, transcendence of, 93–94
*Time* magazine, 173, 176
Tokenism, 523
*Tom Sawyer* (Twain), 191–192
Tomboys, 524–527
Topographical memory, 122
Trainers, personal, 255–263
Training relationships
    defining parameters for, 255–257
    negotiating boundaries in, 257–
        258
    power dynamics in, 258–260
    sexualizing, 260–262
Transcendence
    of one's own person, 94
    of time and space, 93–94
Transitivity, 42
Transsexuals, 332, 334, 336, 338–339,
    341–342, 343–344, 540–541
Tribes, 175–176
Trudy (bag lady), 14, 29–34, 67, 585–
    586
Trust, 356–357
Truth
    agreement as basis of, 27–28
    determining in courts of law, 361,
        470–481
    dictionary definitions of, 25
    metaphors and, 133–134

Turn-outs, 247–253
Twenty statements test, 52
Type 2 error, 437, 441

# U

Unconscious desires, 41
Unreality, 393–405
Utilitarianism, 37–39, 54
    symbolic interactionism and, 45–
        46
Utopian society, 41

# V

*Vindication of the Rights of Women*
    (Wollstonecraft), 137–138
Violence
    cultural justifications for, 10–11
    fear of black men and, 244–246
Visions, 349–350
Visual memories, 122
Vividness, 408, 409
Voodoo death, 416–417

# W

Wages
    domestic servants and, 549–550
    gender inequalities and, 467
*Walden Two* (Skinner), 41
War metaphor, 124–125, 132–133
*Washington Post*, 523
Weather predictions, 352
Wernicke's aphasia, 107
Women. *See* Gender issues
*Women and Language News*, 170
Words, 69–70
    *See also* Language
*Words and Women* (Miller and Swift),
    160, 170
Work issues. *See* Employment;
    Occupations
Working consensus, 195, 231
    negotiating, 198–201
*World as Representation and Will, The*
    (Schopenhauer), 120

# Z

*Zami: A New Spelling of My Name*
    (Lorde), 562, 563